The Peasants of Ottobeuren, 1487–1726
A Rural Society in Early Modern Europe

The Peasants of Ottobeuren offers a new perspective on one of the enduring problems of early modern European history: the possibilities for economic growth and social change in rural society. As such it is the most detailed reconstruction of its kind to date, and one of the first to analyze the structure of land and credit markets, the character of rural commerce, and the internal economy of the peasant family.

Based on the voluminous records of the Swabian Benedictine monastery of Ottobeuren, the book underscores the limitations of the traditional narrative of a sixteenth-century boom which foundered on the productive rigidities of the peasant economy and then degenerated into social crisis in the seventeenth century. Population growth did strain resources at Ottobeuren, but the peasantry continued to produce a sizable agricultural surplus. More importantly, peasants reacted to demographic pressure by deepening their involvement in land and credit markets, and more widely and aggressively marketing the fruits of their labor. Marriage and inheritance underwent a similar process of commercialization which made heavy demands on the peasantry, but which also produced a degree of social stability remarkably resilient to the devastations of war, plague, and famine.

GOVIND P. SREENIVASAN is Associate Professor of History, Brandeis University, Waltham, Massachusetts.

Past and Present Publications

General Editors: LYNDAL ROPER, *University of Oxford*, and
CHRIS WICKHAM, *University of Birmingham*

Past and Present Publications comprise books similar in character to the articles in the journal *Past and Present*. Whether the volumes in the series are collections of essays – some previously published, others new studies – or monographs, they encompass a wide variety of scholarly and original works primarily concerned with social, economic and cultural changes, and their causes and consequences. They will appeal to both specialists and non-specialists and will endeavour to communicate the results of historical and allied research in the most readable and lively form.

For a list of titles in Past and Present Publications, see end of book.

The Peasants of Ottobeuren, 1487–1726

A Rural Society in Early Modern Europe

GOVIND P. SREENIVASAN

CAMBRIDGE
UNIVERSITY PRESS

CAMBRIDGE UNIVERSITY PRESS
Cambridge, New York, Melbourne, Madrid, Cape Town, Singapore, São Paulo

Cambridge University Press
The Edinburgh Building, Cambridge CB2 8RU, UK

Published in the United States of America by Cambridge University Press, New York

www.cambridge.org
Information on this title: www.cambridge.org/9780521834704

First published 2004
This digitally printed version 2007

A catalogue record for this publication is available from the British Library

Library of Congress Cataloguing in Publication data
Sreenivasan, Govind P.
The Peasants of Ottobeuren, 1487–1726: a rural society in early modern Europe /
Govind P. Sreenivasan.
p. cm. – (Past and present publications)
Includes bibliographical references and index.
ISBN 0 521 83470 8 (hb)
1. Peasantry – Germany – Ottobeuren – History. 2. Ottobeuren (Germany) – Rural
conditions. I. Title.
HD1536.G3S74   2004
305.5′633′094337 – dc22   2003047254

ISBN 978-0-521-83470-4 hardback
ISBN 978-0-521-04458-5 paperback

To my father, S. Ranga Sreenivasan,
and to the memory of my mother,
Claire de Reineck Sreenivasan

Contents

Figures

Maps

Tables

Acknowledgements

This book has occupied fifteen years of my life. It has been a good run. My interest in the peasants of early modern Europe was first kindled at McGill University by Pierre H. Boulle and Michael Perceval-Maxwell and the doctoral dissertation on which this book is based was generously supervised by Steven Ozment of Harvard University. The work could not have been undertaken without the assistance of the Archiv des Bistums Augsburg and the Stadtarchiv Memmingen; I was unfortunately unable to consult the holdings of the Klosterarchiv Ottobeuren due to its closure for renovations. I owe a particular debt of gratitude to Archivdirektor Reinhard H. Seitz and the staff of the Staatsarchiv Augsburg, who put up with my virtually permanent residence in the reading room in 1991–2 and thereafter patiently bore my incessant requests for microfilm. Financial support for the research was provided by the German Academic Exchange Service (DAAD), the Mrs. Giles Whiting Foundation, the Cornell Peace Studies Foundation, the National Endowment for the Humanities, and Brandeis University.

Along the way, Lawrence Duggan, Hermann Rebel, David Sabean, and Tom Scott offered invaluable advice and encouragement, and had Lyndal Roper not taken an interest in my project, it might never have gone to print. I also want to thank my dear friend Karl Dietrich for sustaining me in countless ways over the years, and my students at Brandeis University for insisting that the study of peasants be enlivened by stories. Milena Penta and Robert Dees kindly provided last-minute data on details I hadn't had time to check.

Above all, I am grateful to my family. My parents nurtured my interest in history from the very beginning, and my brothers and sisters have kept me sane. My children, Sujata and Vineet, have endured bedtime stories overpopulated with peasants and have cheerfully accepted a suspicious number of medieval-themed toys. Finally, I must apologize to my wife, Allison Dussias, for the want of words to thank her enough. She is the only person outside the Press who has read the entirety of the manuscript, and it owes more to her unfailing support, thoughtful criticism, and personal inspiration than she herself knows.

Newton, Massachusetts

Note on weights, measures, and currencies

During the sixteenth century, the most common unit of currency in the account books of the monastery was the *Pfund Heller*. The *Pfund*, or pound, was divided as follows:

1 pound (£) = 20 shillings (ß) = 240 pennies (d.)

By the early seventeenth century, the pound had been replaced in the accounts by the *Rheinische Gulden*:

1 *gulden* = 1.75 pounds

and

1 *gulden* (fl.) = 15 *batzen* = 60 *kreuzer* (kr.) = 480 *heller* (h.)

Arable and wooded land was measured in *jauchert*, while meadow and garden land was measured in *tagwerk*.

1 Ottobeuren *jauchert* = 1 Ottobeuren *tagwerk* = 0.4224 hectares[1]

Grain was measured in *malter*, usually the *malter* of the nearby city of Memmingen. For the so-called "heavy grains," i.e. wheat, rye, and *kern* (husked spelt):

1 *malter* = 8 *viertel* = 32 *metzen*

For the "light grains," i.e., oats and *vesen* (unhusked spelt):

1 *malter* = 17 *viertel* = 68 *metzen*

For barley:

1 *malter* = 12 *viertel* = 48 *metzen*

Also:

1 Memmingen *malter* = 2.1867 hectolitres[2]

---

[1] Wilhelm Lochbrunner, "1550–1880: Ländliche Neuordnung durch Vereinödung," *Berichte aus der Flurbereinigung* 51 (1984), p. 40. The *jauchert* and *tagwerk* were traditional measures of surface area in Swabia; they varied in size from territory to territory.
[2] Thomas Wolf, *Reichsstädte in Kriegszeiten* (Memmingen, 1991), p. 172

HESSE

Frankfurt a.M.

Würzburg   Bamberg

FRANCONIA

Nürnberg

Speyer   Heidelberg   Rothenburg o.d.T.

HOHENLOHE

Schwäbisch Hall

Stuttgart   Nördlingen

Strassburg   WÜRTTEMBERG

Ulm   Augsburg

LANDS OF THE MONASTERY
OF OTTOBEUREN
Rottweil   Babenhausen   BAVARIA

Mindelheim
Landsberg
Memmingen

UPPER SWABIA   Kaufbeuren

Leutkirch

Kempten

Lindau   ALLGÄU

0   20   40   60   80   100 km

Map 1 Southern Germany, c. 1620

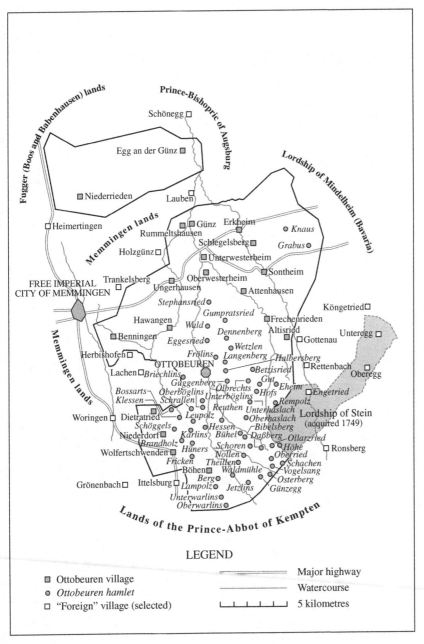

Fugger (Boos and Babenhausen) lands

Prince-Bishopric of Augsburg

Lordship of Mindelheim (Bavaria)

Schönegg □

Egg an der Günz □

□ Niederrieden   Lauben □

□ Heimertingen   Memmingen lands   □□ Günz   Erkheim
                        Rummeltshausen   ● Knaus
                          Schlegelsberg □   Grabus ●
            Holzgünz □
                          □ Unterwesterheim
                                            □ Sontheim
FREE IMPERIAL   Trankelsberg   ■ Oberwesterheim
CITY OF MEMMINGEN   □   Ungerhausen   Königetried □
                          ■ Attenhausen
                    Stephansried ●
                      Gumpratsried ●   Königetried □
        Hawangen   Wald ●   □ Frechenrieden
              ■   Dennenberg Altisried   Unteregg □
        ■ Benningen   Eggesried ● ●   □ Gottenau
     Herbishofen □   ● Wetzlen
                    Frölins ● Langenberg Halbersberg
                OTTOBEUREN   ●   □ Rettenbach
      Lachen □ Briechlins   ● Betzisried   Oberegg
              Guggenberg ●─●   Gut
        Bossarts   Oberböglins Ölbrechts ● ● Eheim
        Klessen   Schrallen Unterböglins ● Hofs □ Engetried
     Woringen □ Dietratried Reuthen Unterhaslach   Rempolz
              Schöggels ● Leupolz ● Oberhaslach Lordship of Stein
      Niederdorf □   Karlins ● Hessen ● Bibelsberg (acquired 1749)
            Brandholz   Bühel ● Daßberg Ollarzried
      Wolfertschwenden □ Hüners Schoren ●─● ● Höhe   □ Ronsberg
              Fricken   Nollen ● Oberried
          □ Böhen ● Theillen ●   Schachen
                    Berg ● Waldmühle ● Vogelsang
      Grönenbach □ Ittelsburg □ Lampolz ● Jetzlins Osterberg
              Unterwarlins ●   Günzegg
              Oberwarlins ●

Lands of the Prince-Abbot of Kempten

LEGEND

□ Ottobeuren village
● Ottobeuren hamlet
□ "Foreign" village (selected)

━━━━━ Major highway
───── Watercourse
⊢─┴─┴─┴─┴─┤ 5 kilometres

Map 2 The lands of the monastery of Ottobeuren, 1620

Introduction

The specter haunting the historiography of early modern Europe is the specter of transition. To be sure, the relatively recent[1] designation of the period c. 1450–c. 1750 as an era unto itself represented multiple intellectual currents, in the first instance a rising interest in social and economic (as opposed to religious and political) questions. At the same time, however, the definition of these centuries as the decisive and traumatic passage from a medieval to a modern world generated a literature pervaded by themes of crisis and revolution (agricultural, commercial, financial, military, scientific, etc.), culminating in a breakthrough variously defined as the beginnings of industrialization, the end of the economic *ancien régime*, or the transition from feudalism to capitalism.[2] Of course, it was always recognized that economic growth was hardly a universal experience in early modern Europe, but this was accounted for by labeling some parts of the continent (the Mediterranean in general and Spain in particular) as examples of failed transitions and others (northwest Europe in general and England and the Netherlands in particular) as successes. Outcomes were bound to vary, it was

---

[1] The first English-language textbook to frame sixteenth- and seventeenth-century European history in these terms was George Norman Clark's *Early Modern Europe from about 1450 to about 1720* (London, 1957). This periodization gained broad acceptance during the following decade, reflected by the inauguration (1970) of the "Cambridge Studies in Early Modern History." The conception of an early modern period is much older in English historical linguistics, and dates back to the 1930s at least.

[2] The literature on the crisis is huge. The concept originated in Eric Hobsbawm's "The General Crisis of the European Economy in the Seventeenth Century," *Past and Present* 5 (1954), pp. 33–56 and 6 (1954), pp. 44–65. This article and others it inspired are collected in Trevor Ashton, ed. *Crisis in Europe 1560–1660* (London, 1965); subsequent echoes in Geoffrey Parker and L. M. Smith, eds. *The General Crisis of the Seventeenth Century* (London, 1978). Jan de Vries, *The Economy of Europe in an Age of Crisis 1600–1750* (Cambridge, 1976) has been very influential. See also Immanuel Wallerstein, *The Modern World-System*, Vol. I: *Capitalist Agriculture and the Origins of the European World-Economy in the Sixteenth Century* (San Diego, 1974) and Vol. II: *Mercantilism and the Consolidation of the European World-Economy 1600–1750* (New York, 1980); Peter Kriedte, *Peasants, Landlords and Merchant Capitalists*, trans. V. R. Berghahn (Cambridge, 1983). A more recent contribution is Sheilagh C. Ogilvie, "Germany and the Seventeenth Century Crisis," *Historical Journal* 35, 2 (1992), pp. 417–41.

felt, in such a wide-ranging struggle between the forces of growth and change and traditional social and economic limits.

Over time, the transitional narrative of early modern social history has lost much of its initial coherence. First and foremost, fifty years of research have forced historians to acknowledge that the performance of the early modern European economy as a whole was sluggish at best.[3] The special status claimed for these centuries has also been eroded from without, as a consensus emerges over the decidedly modest pace of economic growth during the early Industrial Revolution,[4] while the turbulence of the later Middle Ages is now reframed as an episode of such "creative" destruction that there was virtually nothing left to be accomplished during the subsequent early modern era.[5] Nevertheless, historians have been extremely hostile to the one attempt to face this conundrum squarely: Emmanuel LeRoy Ladurie's famous 1974 pronouncement that the quintessential feature of early modern European society was its "immobility," that is, its inability to escape the limits to economic growth imposed by the technological backwardness of agriculture.[6] Increasingly uncomfortable with an earlier insouciance in judging success and failure, scholars have in recent years preferred to reconceptualize early modern economic stagnation and depression as "readjustment,"[7] while monographic investigations increasingly stress the adaptability, hard work, and above all the agency of all peasants and commoners.[8] As the sixteenth and seventeenth centuries become an age in which everybody wins and all must have prizes while no fundamental social change occurs, textbooks have been at pains either to minimize differential economic performance and its

[3] For a recent overview, see Jan Luiten van Zanden, "Early Modern Economic Growth: A Survey of the European Economy, 1500–1800" in Maarten Prak, ed., *Early Modern Capitalism: Economic and Social Change in Europe, 1500–1800* (London, 2001), pp. 69–87.

[4] N. F. R. Crafts, "British Economic Growth, 1700–1831: A Review of the Evidence," *Economic History Review* 36, 2 (1983), pp. 177–99; Jeffrey G. Williamson, "Why was British Growth so Slow during the Industrial Revolution?" *Journal of Economic History* 44, 3 (1984), pp. 687–712.

[5] See the seminal work of Stephan Epstein, in particular his *Freedom and Growth: The Rise of States and Markets in Europe, 1300–1750* (London, 2000). Note his conclusion (p. 69) that "the late medieval crisis . . . may have marked the most decisive step in the continent's long trajectory to capitalism and world hegemony." L. R. Poos, *A Rural Society after the Black Death: Essex, 1350–1525* (Cambridge, 1991) makes a different (but compelling) case against a sharp break between the later Middle Ages and the early modern period.

[6] Emmanuel LeRoy Ladurie, "History that Stands Still," [orig. pub. 1974] in *The Mind and Method of the Historian*, trans. Siân and Ben Reynolds (Chicago, 1981), pp. 11–27.

[7] See the essays collected in I. A. A. Thompson and Bartolomé Yun Casalilla, eds., *The Castilian Crisis of the Seventeenth Century: New Perspectives on the Economic and Social History of Seventeenth-Century Spain* (Cambridge, 1994), especially chapters 3–4.

[8] See, for example, Jürgen Schlumbohm, *Lebensläufe, Familien, Höfe: die Bauern und Heuerleute des Osnabrückischen Kirchspiels Belm in proto-industrieller Zeit, 1650–1860* (Göttingen, 1994) and Liana Vardi, *The Land and the Loom: Peasants and Profit in Northern France, 1680–1800* (Durham, 1993).

causes, or even to eschew explanatory characterization altogether.[9] Originally conceived as a fundamental hinge in European social history, the early modern period is now threatened with reduction to an arbitrary chronological convenience.[10]

The irony of this conceptual implosion is that the early modern period is gaining increased significance from the broader perspective of world history just as it loses its cachet within European history. That medieval Europe was no wealthier (and probably poorer) than the Islamic and East Asian worlds has long been known.[11] It is now also becoming clear that the standard indices originally developed to gauge the economic performance of early modern Europe – life expectancy, urbanization levels, agricultural productivity, and so on – reveal no significant European lead over much of Asia before 1800.[12] Yet unless one wishes to write off to historical accident the undeniable gulf in material prosperity which emerged between the West and "the Rest" during the nineteenth century,[13] three crucial implications follow. First, the long-term causes of European economic primacy are to be sought in the early modern period. They are also to be sought within European society, since, for all the suffering it inflicted on the non-Western world, European colonialism never generated profits on a large enough scale to explain the Industrial Revolution.[14] Second, whatever differentiated Western Europe as a whole from the non-Western world ultimately mattered more than regional variation within Western Europe.[15] Finally, any discussion of the economic origins of the rise of the West will have to go beyond the question of technologies of production. Technical innovation did become

[9] See, for example, Peter Musgrave, *The Early Modern European Economy* (Basingstoke, 1999) and Robert S. DuPlessis, *Transitions to Capitalism in Early Modern Europe* (Cambridge, 1997).

[10] William J. Bouwsma, "The Renaissance and the Drama of Western History," *American Historical Review* 84, 1 (1979), pp. 1–15 is a stimulating analysis of the similar fate befalling the concept of the Renaissance, itself a victim of the invention of the early modern period.

[11] The most important work in this kind of comparative history has been done by Angus Maddison. See in particular his *The World Economy: A Millennial Perspective* (Paris, 2001), *Chinese Economic Performance in the Long Run* (Paris, 1998) and *Dynamic Forces in Capitalist Development: A Long-Run Comparative View* (Oxford, 1991). See also Paul Bairoch, *Economics and World History: Myths and Paradoxes* (New York, 1993).

[12] Roy Bin Wong, *China Transformed: Historical Change and the Limits of European Experience* (Ithaca, 1997).

[13] As in Kenneth Pomeranz, *The Great Divergence: Europe, China, and the Making of the Modern World Economy* (Princeton, 2000). For an insightful critique of some of the excesses of anti-Eurocentrism, see Ricardo Duchesne, "Between Sinocentrism and Eurocentrism: Debating Andre Gunder Frank's *Re-Orient: Global Economy in the Asian Age*," *Science and Society* 65, 4 (Winter) (2001–2), pp. 428–63.

[14] Patrick O'Brien, "European Economic Development: The Contribution of the Periphery," *Economic History Review* 35, 1 (1982). See also his "The Foundations of European Industrialization: From the Perspective of the World," *Journal of Historical Sociology* 4, 3 (1991), pp. 288–317.

[15] Philip C. C. Huang, *The Peasant Economy and Social Change in North China* (Stanford, CA, 1985), pp. 9–10.

the hallmark of European economic superiority, but the origins of that superiority in an era of technological stagnation suggest that a history of innovation depends on a prior history of incentives and institutions.[16]

In my own view, the question of early modern social transition has been encumbered by an unfortunate fixation on the technology of production, which was in no small part derived from post-war models of Third World economic development. The problem started with the perfectly correct observation that industrial societies have more efficient technologies of production than pre-industrial societies, allowing the former to produce necessary goods (above all food) in far greater amounts and with far fewer workers than the latter. Industrial societies thereby free a great many people to produce luxuries, offer services, and do all of the other things that make the industrialized world an allegedly better place to live. Indeed, industrial societies have a lot more *people*, period, than pre-industrial societies.

Now, in the particular context of early modern Europe, two empirically irrefutable observations played a key role in ushering in the preoccupation with productive technology. First, Europe was in these centuries an over-whelmingly rural society operating at (by modern standards) a rather modest level of technical efficiency (especially in agriculture). Second, early modern Europe seems to have experienced considerable difficulties in sustaining the people that it did have. From the last decades of the sixteenth century onwards, historians have documented soaring increases in food prices, slumps in long-distance trade and industrial production, the multiplication of plagues and famines, and demographic stagnation or even decline in region after region all over the continent. It was thus an easy step to conclude that a biological ceiling was imposed by these technological shortcomings, a ceiling lifted only with the advent of modern science and technology during the Enlightenment. Having reached this at least initially plausible (and far from preposterous) conclusion, historians then began hunting – all too often in vain, as it turned out[17] – for the surge in productivity and production that allowed early modern Europe to escape the constraints of the biological ceiling.

The unexamined assumption of this Malthusian vision of early modern social history (associated in particular with a group of French scholars known as the

---

[16] Which is not to say that every specific invention was directly produced by its institutional context or that context can explain the timing of what have been called "macroinventions." Joel Mokyr, *The Lever of Riches: Technological Creativity and Economic Progress* (New York, 1990). Also N. F. R. Crafts, "Macroinventions, Economic Growth, and 'Industrial Revolution' in Britain and France," *Economic History Review* 48, 3 (1995), pp. 591–8; David S. Landes, "Some Further Thoughts on Accident in History: A Reply to Professor Crafts," *Economic History Review* 48, 3 (1995), pp. 599–60.

[17] Michel Morineau, *Les faux-semblants d'un démarrage économique: agriculture et démographie en France au XVIIIe siècle* (Paris, 1971) is a classic investigation.

Annales school)[18] is that the technological capacity for increased production itself called into being the necessary institutions and practices to distribute surpluses and allow for economic specialization and development. This assumption, if I may be forgiven the metaphor, puts the cart before the horse. The argument here is that secure and transferable property rights, dense market networks, and the widespread use of money and credit were essential prerequisites for any dramatic gains in agricultural production.[19] Furthermore, I would contend, the pervasion of both the individual peasant household and rural society as a whole by market relations amounted to a genuine social and even cultural transformation, independent of the subsequent realization of increased productivity.[20]

It will of course be objected that nobody really believes in the original Malthusian model any more, and furthermore that there is no reason to revive an outdated Marxist preoccupation with the transition between various historical modes of production. Surely the prudent course would be to content ourselves with the position that the early modern economy was never completely stationary, but grew very slowly in the very long term with so much regional variation that any analytical generalizations are hazardous. Prudent, yes, but deeply disingenuous as well.

In the first place, such an approach refuses honest engagement with the mass of accumulated evidence that something began to go seriously wrong with the early modern European economy at the end of the sixteenth century. Even in the case of England, the most credible early modern success story, fourteenth-century levels of population and agricultural productivity would not be exceeded until after 1750.[21] In the same way, recent efforts to rehabilitate the agrarian economy of early modern France have produced an overall picture strikingly similar to LeRoy Ladurie's conclusion that "For [all] the apparent movement, things had really stayed much the same."[22] If the fate of all grand historical

---

[18] For overviews of the work of this school, see Peter Burke, *The French Historical Revolution: The Annales School, 1929–89* (Stanford, CA, 1990) and Philippe Carrard, *Poetics of the New History: French Historical Discourse from Braudel to Chartier* (Baltimore, 1992).

[19] This is not to deny the often reciprocal relation between institutions and technical change, but when all qualifications have been made I still incline towards the logical priority of the former. See in this regard Mark Overton, *Agricultural Revolution in England: The Transformation of the Agrarian Economy 1500–1850* (Cambridge, 1996), esp. pp. 146–7, 203–7.

[20] On this subject the work of Jan de Vries is indispensable, in particular his "The Industrial Revolution and the Industrious Revolution," *Journal of Economic History* 54, 2 (1994), pp. 249–70 and "Between Purchasing Power and the World of Goods: Understanding the Household Economy in Early Modern Europe" in John Brewer and Roy Porter, eds., *Consumption and the World of Goods* (London, 1993), pp. 85–132.

[21] Bruce M. S. Campbell and Mark Overton, "A New Perspective on Medieval and Early Modern Agriculture: Six Centuries of Norfolk Farming *c.* 1250–*c.* 1850," *Past and Present* 141 (1993), pp. 38–105.

[22] LeRoy Ladurie, "History that Stands Still," p. 21. Philip T. Hoffman, *Growth in a Traditional Society: The French Countryside, 1450–1815* (Princeton, 1996) is an impressive

theories is either falsification or banality, it is surely the latter which has befallen the *Annales* school. Much more seriously, by retaining the traditional analytic categories while disputing the numbers, the gradualist continuity narrative per-petuates an older expectation of where to look for meaningful social change and thereby impedes appreciation of those significant developments which did occur, but outside the realm of output statistics.

I therefore offer this book as an effort to reconcile the impressive empirical basis of the Malthusian scenario with its inherently implausible implication that most of Europe experienced no significant social change in the two centuries after 1560. This is, in other words, an effort to redeem the old question of the transition from feudalism to capitalism,[23] and the key to that redemption is to reconsider the terms originally used to frame the project of social transition. Recent work in development economics is highly suggestive here, as it is an open secret that the traditional neoclassical economic model is powerless to explain the gross disparities of material well-being which persist in the world today. In a world of frictionless exchange, inefficient practices and groups should rapidly be weeded out and replaced by more efficient competitors. That this has not, in fact, taken place underscores the problems of co-ordination and inclusion in human societies, problems heavily influenced by the structure of property rights and exchange practices.[24]

The essential precondition for realizing the potential of innovative productive technologies is a reliable, dense and broadly based network of socio-economic exchanges. Hindrances to such a network can be social, economic, or cultural, and the shift from a fragmented to a networked society is likely to be a com-plicated, drawn-out, but very significant process. Furthermore, I would argue, one of the most helpful ways to follow these changes concretely is to look at the inscription of human activity in time and space. That the time–space con-stitution of human activity is no mere backdrop, but rather an essential part of what those activities are is hardly an idea original to myself, and has become a commonplace in recent theoretical sociology (associated in particular with the

critique of the *Annales* vision, but its conclusion that growth averaged one half percent per annum, was confined to selected regions, and was vulnerable to erasure in times of crisis qualifies but hardly shatters the argument advanced by Morineau in 1971. Recent quanti-tative analysis of French demographic and price data confirms a close correlation between grain prices and mortality during the seventeenth century. See David R. Weir, "Life under Pressure: France and England 1670–1870," *Journal of Economic History* 44, 1 (1984), pp. 27–48.

23 The modern discussion began with the debate (1950–2) in *Science and Society*; the relevant articles are collected in Paul Sweezy, Maurice Dobb, Kohachiro Takahashi, et al., *The Transition from Feudalism to Capitalism* (London, 1978). See also R. J. Holton, *The Transition from Feudalism to Capitalism* (Basingstoke, 1985).

24 I must here acknowledge a considerable theoretical debt to the work of Douglass C. North, in particular his *Structure and Change in Economic History* (New York, 1981) and *Institutions, Institutional Change and Economic Performance* (Cambridge, 1990).

work of Anthony Giddens).[25] On the other hand, the extension of this insight to historical research has almost exclusively focused on the industrial era and on the transformation of experience by technological, rather than institutional, change.[26] For the early modern period, the latter was the more important vector and receives correspondingly more attention here.

The argument that superficial continuities of form can conceal dramatic shifts in underlying mechanisms also governed the choice of the region for investigation: the lands of the Benedictine monastery of Ottobeuren, located in the countryside of Upper Swabia amid the political confetti of the German southwest. No serious scholar would advance Germany, and least of all its agrarian sector, as an economic "leader" in early modern Europe, and German industrialization was late by West European standards.[27] In world historical perspective, however, the rapidity with which the late nineteenth-century German economy – and German agriculture, too[28] – caught up with England and the Low Countries seems rather more significant than Germany's late start. Bavaria clearly had rather more in common with Belgium than it ever did with Bengal, and I find the long-term convergence in the social history of Western Europe a rather more compelling concern than the narrower question "Why was England first?"[29] And yet, although research on the early modern German peasantry has accelerated dramatically in recent years,[30] it is the political relations between subject and overlord which have commanded most attention. Material life looms rather larger in this account of a region – usually known as the Allgäu – which never industrialized, and which in modern Germany is notable primarily for its

[25] See his *Central Problems in Social Theory: Action, Structure and Contradiction in Social Analysis* (Berkeley, CA, 1979); *A Contemporary Critique of Historical Materialism*, Vol. I: *Power, Property and the State* (Berkeley, CA, 1981); *The Constitution of Society: Outline of the Theory of Structuration* (Cambridge, 1984). Also suggestive is Henri Lefebvre, *The Production of Space*, trans. Donald Nicholson-Smith (Oxford, 1991).

[26] E. P. Thompson, "Time, Work-Discipline, and Industrial Capitalism," *Past and Present*, 38 (1967), pp. 56–97 and Wolfgang Schivelbusch, *The Railway Journey: The Industrialization of Time and Space in the 19th Century* (Berkeley, CA, 1986) have been enormously influential in different ways. See also Stephen Kern, *The Culture of Time and Space 1880–1918* (Cambridge, MA, 1983).

[27] Hubert Kiesewetter, "Zur Dynamik der regionalen Industrialisierung in Deutschland im 19. Jahrhundert: Lehren für die Europäische Union?" *Jahrbuch für Wirtschaftsgeschichte* 1 (1992), pp 79–112 and Richard Tilly, "German Industrialization and Gerschenkronian Backwardness," *Rivista di Storia Economica* 6, 2 (1989), pp. 139–64.

[28] Patrick K. O'Brien and Leandro Prados de la Escosura, "Agricultural Productivity and European Industrialization, 1890–1980," *Economic History Review* 45, 3 (1992), pp. 514–36.

[29] Moreover, given the current relative economic strengths of Britain and Germany, one might feel justified in suggesting that at least in the long run, first is not necessarily best. In this regard see P. K. O'Brien, "Path Dependency, or Why Britain Became an Industrialized and Urbanized Economy Long Before France," *Economic History Review* 49, 2 (1996), pp. 213–49.

[30] The best recent introductions are the relevant volumes of the *Enzyklopädie Deutscher Geschichte*, in particular André Holenstein, *Bauern zwischen Bauernkrieg und Dreißigjährigem Krieg* (Munich, 1996) and Werner Trossbach, *Bauern 1648–1806* (Munich, 1993).

impenetrable dialect and conservative politics. Usually overlooked in the contemporary perception of the Allgäu is its unusually resilient agrarian economy[31] and its unusual agrarian history: during the early modern period the Allgäu became the bread-basket for the industrialization of neighboring Switzerland. The peasants of Ottobeuren clearly figured something out. This is their story.

---

[31] In an economic climate where German farmers are increasingly dependent on supplementary by-employment, the region boasts one of the highest proportions of full-time farms in the country. Geoff A. Wilson and Olivia J. Wilson, *German Agriculture in Transition: Society, Politics and Environment in a Changing Europe* (Basingstoke, 2001), pp. 31–5.

1. Right and might (c. 1480–c. 1560)

History does not record when Anna Maier was born; neither does it record when she died.[1] It does pay rather closer attention to her older brother Johann, who entered the world perhaps two years before his sister in November of 1486, and predeceased her by at least twenty-five years in February of 1543. Both siblings grew up in the Upper Swabian village of Egg, in what is now part of the German province of Bavaria, and was then the lordship of the Benedictine monastery of Ottobeuren. Johann left Egg at the age of eight to be schooled by his uncle Martin Maier, a priest in the city of Rottenburg. The boy went on to study philosophy, law, and theology at the universities of Heidelberg, Cologne and Freiburg, changed his name to Johann Eck, and rose to fame (and notoriety) as the theologian who locked horns with Martin Luther at the Leipzig disputations of 1519.[2] As for Anna, whose story this is, she remained in Egg and inherited the family farm.

The *Hof*, as a large farm like this was called, had originally been held by Anna's grandfather. It came to her father, Michael Maier, in 1483,[3] and sometime around the year 1515 passed to her husband, Thoma Schaupp.[4] It was

---

[1] Anna is not among the four children listed with her parents in Staatsarchiv Augsburg [hereinafter StAA], Kloster Literalien [hereinafter KL] Ottobeuren 601-I, "Leibeigenbuch 1486/7," f. 21r. The original dating of this MS. to *c.* 1450–80 is incorrect. Through a close comparison with the monastery's charters, I have found that the register must have been drawn up sometime between November 1486 and May 1487. This redating has been accepted by the Staatsarchiv Augsburg (personal communication 13 July 1998).

[2] Theodor Wiedmann, *Dr. Johann Eck, Professor der Theologie an der Universität Ingolstadt* (Regensburg, 1865), pp. 425–31 remains the most detailed treatment of Johann Eck's family. For a more recent, though in this regard derivative work, see Max Ziegelbauer, *Johannes Eck: Mann der Kirche im Zeitalter der Glaubensspaltung* (St. Ottilien, 1987), pp. 3–11. Neither of these discusses Eck's family on the basis of manuscript sources.

[3] StAA, Kloster Urkunden [hereinafter KU] Ottobeuren 414 [1 Nov. 1483].

[4] Thoma Schaupp's charter of admission has not survived. There is, however, a record of Michael Maier's retirement from farming and the associated maintenance agreement between him and Schaupp in StAA, KU Ottobeuren 973 [16 Aug. 1524]. By this time Schaupp already held the *Hof*. Note that since Anna was not born before 1488, she is unlikely to have married earlier than 1513.

9

the largest *Hof* in Egg, measuring some 110 *jauchert* or 46.5 hectares,[5] and it instantly made Anna's household one of the richest in the village.[6] With wealth came social status: Anna's father served as village *Amman*, or mayor, until his death in 1525, and the office would subsequently be handed along with the *Hof* to Anna's husband.[7] Retaining that position of wealth and prominence, on the other hand, turned out to be more of a struggle.

Thoma Schaupp died during the later 1520s, whereupon Anna took to husband a certain Simon Bürklin. Simon's death in 1533 again left Anna a widow, but she soon remarried, this time to Jerg Wagner.[8] Quite apart from the attendant emotional strain, these repeated losses imposed serious fiscal pressure on Anna's household. In law, the *Hof* was never owned outright by any of those who farmed it. Instead, formal ownership remained with the monastery, which leased the *Hof* to each new (male) tenant for the term of his life. As a woman, Anna could not lease the *Hof* by herself, and thus could not remain a widow if she wanted to stay on the property. It did not matter that Anna had been born on the *Hof*; each remarriage required a new lease to the "new" tenant. And at each new grant, the monastery exacted a hefty transfer fee, known as *Erdschatz*. Three *Erdschatz* payments within twenty-five years was a great deal of money, especially since Anna had so many children – a 1548 census lists her with eight[9] – to care for.

The repeated *Erdschatz* charges seem to have been a source of considerable anger to Anna's family. Her brother Johann Eck, now far away in Ingolstadt, took time from his polemics against the Reformation to write several letters to the Ottobeuren monk and humanist Nikolaus Ellenbog, sometimes asking for Ellenbog's intercession with the Abbot on behalf of Eck's relatives,[10] and

---

[5] The size and size rank of the *Hof* are documented in StAA, KL Ottobeuren 102, "Steuerbuch 1620," ff. 272r–294v. The *Maierhof* is the first property listed. The earliest (1575) measurement of the *Hof*'s surface area is recorded in StAA, KL Ottobeuren 27, "Erdschatzbuch 1576–1603" (*sic*), f. 228r.

[6] For Thoma Schaupp's wealth see StAA, KL Ottobeuren 541, Heft 2 "Generalrechnung 1529." This document has been mislabeled; it is in fact a tax register drawn up in 1525. The returns from Egg are on ff. 26r–29r; Thoma Schaupp is assessed 8.5 *gulden* on f. 28v.

[7] For Michael Maier's service as *Amman* see Ziegelbauer, *Johannes Eck*, p. 3. For the wealth and service as *Amman* of Anna's third husband, Jerg Wagner, see StAA, KL Ottobeuren 64, "Steuerregister 1546," f. 17r.

[8] Simon Bürklin is mentioned as holding the Egg *Maierhof* in 1530. StAA, KL Ottobeuren 4, "Rotulus Probationum Tomus IV," Document 309C, ff. 1131r–1137r (*Urfehdebrief* of Caspar Maÿr of Egg [4 Apr. 1530]). The 'Rotulus Probationum' is an enormous multi-volume compilation of document copies drawn up in 1616 in connection with a lawsuit. Jerg Wagner's 1533 admission to the *Maierhof* is recorded in StAA KL Ottobeuren 27, f. 225r.

[9] StAA, KL Ottobeuren 600, "Leibeigenbuch 1548," f. 188r.

[10] Nikolaus Ellenbog, *Briefwechsel*, edited by Andreas Bigelmair and Friedrich Zoepfl, *Corpus Catholicorum* 19/21 (Münster in Westfalen, 1938), VI/28, pp. 320–1; Johann Eck to Nikolaus Ellenbog, 23 Apr. 1533. Eck wrote "Caeterum sororem meam commendo tibi et conventui," but promptly warned "faciatis, quod aequum est, ne provocetis Eckium ad ea, a quibus semper pro honore monasterii abstinuit."

sometimes raging that "in dealing with my relatives your Abbot has always not only greatly humiliated them but also despised them."[11] One way or another, Anna and her third husband managed not only to stay solvent, but even to prosper,[12] and Jerg Wagner remained the tenant of both her family's ancestral *Hof* and the village inn in Egg for thirty-two years.

Matters took a turn for the worse when Wagner died in 1565.[13] Concerned that the properties should remain inside the kin group, the family enlisted the help of Anna's half-brother, Simon Thaddeus Eck, who was also the chancellor of the Duke of Bavaria. Simon Thaddeus approached Abbot Caspar Kindelmann and asked that Anna's son Sebastian Wagner, already married and with children,[14] be admitted to both holdings.[15] The Abbot agreed, and Sebastian's admission duly took place on 2 July, but the terms of the lease had been modified in several significant respects. First, although Sebastian was granted tenure of the *Hof* for the term of his life, his lease on the inn was only for one year at a time. Second, although the grain rent for the properties remained unchanged at 10 *malter*, the cash rent was increased by 2 *gulden*. Finally, the *Erdschatz*, or entry fine for the admissions, was set at 200 *gulden*.

The family was furious. Chancellor Eck dispatched a blistering letter to the Abbot, protesting the "high and unheard of" level of the *Erdschatz*, which he feared would ultimately drive his nephew into bankruptcy and oblige him to give up the property. Eck pointed out that "this *Hof* has now been received for the fourth time for a life term by my sister's family . . . and the three [previous] times hardly more than half as much was taken as what has now been [taken] by Your Grace." After a devastating fire, Eck added, Anna's family had put more than a thousand *gulden* as well as enormous "work and effort, also hard sweat" into rebuilding the *Hof*, improving it greatly. His sister's heirs, Eck declared,

---

[11] Eck to Ellenbog, 8 Sep. 1534 in Ellenbog, *Briefwechsel*, VI/67, pp. 335–6. "Moleste semper tuli ac peracerbe . . . abbatem tuum multis illicibus ad amicitiam mei pertractum illam semper fortiter abiecisse non modo, verum etiam comtempsisse . . ." Eck took all of this as a personal affront, and went on to claim "quod enim contra sororium meum tam acriter egit, omnia eo videbantur tendere, ut contemptui mei parerent, et hoc quidem absque ullo meo demerito." In an earlier letter Eck had likened the Abbot of Ottobeuren to Phalaris, the Greek tyrant of Agrigentum (*c.* 570–554 BC) who burned his victims in a bull of bronze. Eck to Ellenbog, 21 Dec. 1532 in ibid., VI/25, pp. 318–18.

[12] Jerg Wagner had no debts to the monastery in 1543: StAA, KL Ottobeuren 409, "Bauding-buch 1543," ff. 12r–14v. The 1544 rent roll also records no rent arrears, although Wagner was slightly behind in a tithe payment. StAA, KL Ottobeuren 29, "Gültbuch 1544," ff. 146r–147r. He ranked third of 77 households (i.e. in the top 5.2 percent) by taxable wealth in 1546. StAA, KL Ottobeuren 64, ff. 17r–21r.

[13] StAA, KL Ottobeuren 27, f. 227r.

[14] Sebastian married a certain Ursula Maier in 1561. See the retrospective record of their marriage in StAA, KL Ottobeuren 903, "Briefprotokolle 1603–7," f. 103r (*Freibrief* of their son Sebastian junior [28 July 1604]). The couple are recorded with two children in StAA, KL Ottobeuren 25, ehemaliger Münchner Bestand [hereinafter Mü.B.], "Leibeigenbuch 1564," f. 194.

[15] The documents relating to this case are all contained in StAA, Kloster Akten [hereinafter KA] Ottobeuren 86, "Besitz- und Bestandverhältnisse zu Egg 1566–1622."

deserved the grace and favor of the Abbot, and he was incensed "that . . . the rightful heirs [sic!] should be expelled from their ancient paternal home and [that] the same [home] thereafter should be given to other selfish people, who secretly by means of money and other evil practices expel their neighbors from house and home."[16]

Abbot Caspar was unmoved by this missive and conceded nothing. He felt he had been generous, and that Eck ought more properly to have sent him a letter of thanks. The year-to-year lease for the inn was a long-standing tradition. Regarding the money invested by Anna's family in the burned-out *Hof*, the Abbot declared that "the damage and building costs were nowhere near as high as you imagine, [and] as for all of the wood [for the reconstruction], he [Anna's husband, Jerg Wagner] received the same gratis and at no cost from us and from our village community, not to mention the fifty *gulden* in rebuilding assistance also given to him by us." As for the claim

that your grandparents and in-laws made good use of this *Hof*, they did nothing more than what they were required to do according to the lease and charter of admission, for the land and fields are of such a nature that if cared for as they should be, they require no improvement. It may well be that it [i.e. the land] was well cared for [literally "helped"] by yourself and your deceased brother[-in-law], and that they [i.e. Anna's family] also thereby derived great wealth. Whether, however, the said [wealth] was applied to the improvement of the property or to [a] costly and excessive lifestyle, this should become clear upon a thorough investigation of the matter.

The Abbot claimed that the *Hof* annually yielded more than 150 *malter* of grain and 30 to 40 *gulden* worth of hay. It could easily bear an *Erdschatz* payment of even 400 *gulden*. That Eck's relatives had farmed the *Hof* for so long in no way entitled them to be spared an increase in the entry fine. On the contrary, "for experience has repeatedly shown, that where a . . . life-term property remains for too long with one kin-group [*geschlecht*] without any increase in the rent and entry fine, the tenant may ultimately claim [to hold] the said life-term property as a heritable property [*Erblehen*]."[17]

This, clearly, was the heart of the matter, for the monastery could already look back on more than a century of dispute with its subjects over purported heritability of the large, life-term *Höfe*. Thus, what Simon Thaddeus saw as a threatened dispossession of his nephew was for the Abbot an essential safeguard against being dispossessed himself.

Though never formally acknowledged, a *modus vivendi* was worked out in the end. The monastery retained formal ownership and the right to set entry fines

---

[16] Ibid., Simon Eck to the Abbot of Ottobeuren [17 July 1565]. Eck was right about the size of the entry fine; the *Erdschatz* register records no fines this high before 1565. StAA, KL Ottobeuren 27.

[17] StAA, KA Ottobeuren 86, undated draft of the Abbot's response to Simon Eck.

at will, while in practice the *Hof* would continue to be handed down within the same family. Anna's son Sebastian held the property until his premature death in 1575. After the manner of Anna herself, who is last mentioned in 1568,[18] Sebastian's widow, Ursula Maier, quickly remarried, to one Michael Schütz.[19] And although the *Hof* was again saddled with an *Erdschatz* payment of 200 *gulden*, Abbot Caspar's assessment of its carrying capacity seems to have been correct: Schütz, his wife, and then later his second wife[20] would farm it successfully for more than fifty years.[21]

Just as the *Hof* had supported the affluence and status of Anna and her children, so it would do for her grandchildren. Michael Wagner become a provost and archdeacon of Garsch in Bavaria. Johann Wagner studied at the University of Ingolstadt and rose to the position of senior judge in Bamberg and *Kastner* of Neu-Ötting. Jerg Wagner was educated in the Ottobeuren monastery school and became a ducal advocate in Landshut.[22] Catharina Wagner married the innkeeper of nearby Unterwesterheim, became a respected member of village society and served as godmother to at least thirty-one children.[23] Altogether, Anna's grandchildren received inheritances from the *Hof* totalling well over a thousand *gulden*.[24]

What is the value of Anna Maier's story? It adds detail to the family history of a minor Reformation figure. It also provides dramatic, albeit anecdotal evidence on the possibilities of peasant social mobility during the fifteenth and sixteenth

---

[18] She is described as still alive in a letter from Chancellor Eck to the Bishop of Augsburg, dated 9 April 1568 in StAA, KA Ottobeuren 86. Eck was at this date still trying to enlist help against the Abbot of Ottobeuren, complaining that the Abbot should have had proper regard for (among other things) the fact that "my dear deceased brother Doctor Johann Eck worked so truly for the Christian church."

[19] The remarriage is documented in the inheritance arrangements Schütz concluded with his stepchildren in 1583 and 1584. See the sources cited below at note 22.

[20] Schütz's second marriage is documented in StAA, KL Ottobeuren 903, ff. 268r–269r, Heirats-brief [19 Nov. 1606]. The fee he paid for this exogamous marriage (i.e. his wife was not an Ottobeuren serf) is recorded in StAA, KL Ottobeuren 583, "Verhörgefälle 1581–1632," Heft 24 (1607–8).

[21] Transfer of tenancy and *Erdschatz* payment dated 29 July 1575 in StAA, KL Ottobeuren 27, f. 228r. Michael Schütz is listed as tenant of the *Hof* in both StAA KL Ottobeuren 39, "Gültbuch 1606," f. 39r and StAA, KL Ottobeuren 225, "Kornrechnungen 1621/2," f. 102r (this account also includes a rent roll).

[22] StAA, KL Ottobeuren 901, "Amtsprotokolle 1583–4," ff. 31v (*Schuldbrief* [14 June 1583]) and 146r–v (*Schuldbrief* [4 Dec. 1584]).

[23] According to StAA, KL Ottobeuren 27, f. 187v, Jacob Amman was admitted to the inn on 6 June 1593. The marriage probably took place in that year. It is in any case documented in StAA, KL Ottobeuren 903, f. 271v (*Quittung* [29 Nov. 1606]), whereby Jacob Amman, husband of Catharina Wagner, confirms the receipt of 50 *gulden* from Michael Schütz of Egg "in Abschlag seiner Schuldtsuma sein dreÿen Stiefsohn." For Catharina's prominence as a godmother between 1595 and 1625, see the Westerheim parish register [hereinafter West PR], Vol. I, pp. 3–66. She died in February of 1633 (ibid., Vol. I, p. 123).

[24] See the final accounting in StAA, KL Ottobeuren 903, ff. 240r–241r (two *Schuldbriefe* [16 June 1606]).

centuries. The real significance of the foregoing account, however, is the way in which it must be told, and indeed the fact that it can be told at all.

From the middle of the fifteenth century, the Ottobeuren peasantry intrudes into the historical record in ever larger numbers. Not as an amorphous subject population, but as individuals, with names and deeds and life stories. Moreover, they appear to us not from the narratives of monastic chroniclers or the illustrations of illuminated manuscripts, but from property records. Every single document used to reconstruct the lives of Anna Maier and her kin – whether a tenancy charter, a letter of appeal to the Bishop of Augsburg, an *Erdschatz* register, or a notarial protocol – was drawn up in connection with property.

The fact that it is property which, somewhat abruptly, offers a window on to the lives of late medieval Swabian peasants needs more than a passing acknowledgment. It behooves us to ask why the window appears, and why just then? Property also mattered at least as much to Anna's family then as it does to the historian now. The *Hof* in Egg was the foundation of who the Maiers were and what they ultimately made of themselves. And as far as can be told from the irate correspondence of two family members, they needed no reminding of this.

Finally, it must also be emphasized that the "window" of property records is deceptively clear. Much more is known of the Maier family than of their poorer, less propertied neighbors. Even within the family, some members are much more prominent in the records than others. Indeed, the irony of Maier family history is that, although Anna was the genealogical linchpin of the various personal dramas bound up with the fate of the *Hof*, she never appears on stage herself. She received no charters, she appears in no rent rolls or tax books, and she is never even mentioned by name in her brothers' epistolary tirades. Were it not for the Ottobeuren law that children derived their legal status from their mothers (as a result of which the monastery's serf registers kept track of both genders), and the Upper Swabian custom that women retained their surnames at marriage, she would have been invisible in the midst of her own story (Eck's biographers didn't even know her name). To tell the history of the Ottobeuren peasantry, we may be obliged to begin with property. Due regard must, however, be given not just to the fact and origin of the property relation, but also to the way in which the relation was used and contested, and to those whom the relation excluded.

Peasant property rights emerged at Ottobeuren at the end of the Middle Ages as part of a transformation of the monastery's land tenure system. The term "system" is in fact rather misleading, for in contrast to much better-organized ecclesiastical territories elsewhere in the German southwest, Ottobeuren landlordship at the beginning of the fourteenth century was decidedly unsystematic.[25] The monastery lands were granted out in large chunks

---

[25] There is a brief overview in Josef Heider, "Grundherrschaft und Landeshoheit der Abtei Ottobeuren: Nachwirkungen im 19. und 20. Jahrhundert," *Studien und Mitteilungen zur Geschichte des Benediktiner-Ordens und seiner Zweige* 73, 2–4 (1962), pp. 63–95, at pp. 63–7.

to lower nobiliar vassals known as *ministeriales*, who in turn leased out land-holdings to the peasants as they saw fit.[26] The *ministeriales* seem to have been responsible for collecting rents from the peasants and then turning over some proportion to the monastery, but the monks never exercised much oversight over the process. The mediated character of the relation between the monastery and its subjects means that the (few) surviving documents from this period tell us very little about the mechanics of land tenure. It does seem clear that this was not a system based on written rules or documents (which is itself not insignificant). It was – at least superficially – a rather cheap system that required very little in the way of an administrative apparatus. It was also, however, a system with serious problems.

The *ministeriales* were a quarrelsome and intractable lot, rather like the monks themselves, only more so. As vassals, they were in the habit of hiving off sections of the monastery's lands into their own private possession, and spoliating the monastery's remaining properties. The "system" offered no formal rights or guarantees to the hapless peasantry, whose relations with their aggressive immediate overlords can only be imagined. Even an abbot who insisted too forcefully on the rights and prerogatives of the monastery could be subject to violent reprisals. This was spectacularly demonstrated in the early fifteenth century, when Abbot Eggo's refusal to pay extra monies to one Friedrich of Ellerbach led to his assassination in 1416.[27] Indeed, the main reason the monks began assiduously collecting papal and imperial privileges in the twelfth century (and equally assiduously forging privileges from the eighth, ninth and tenth centuries) was to protect the monastery's possessions from the depredations of its own vassals.[28]

Paradoxically, however, a much more serious danger was that, in the long run, the lineages of the *ministeriales* tended either to bankrupt themselves, or to die out altogether. This opened the door for other competitors – above all the burghers and municipal institutions of the nearby free imperial city of Memmingen – to buy up the lands of the *ministeriales*, and thereby honeycomb the Ottobeuren lands with a rival and more durable source of power and authority. During the fourteenth and especially the fifteenth century, therefore, the monks were forced to buy back lands both from their own

---

[26] The multi-layered structure of land tenure in this period can be glimpsed from charters in which a ministerial sells to a second party land which is described as a fief (*Lehen*) of the monastery of Ottobeuren, and which is at the same time worked by a named peasant tenant. Hermann Hoffmann, ed. *Die Urkunden des Reichsstiftes Ottobeuren 764–1460* (Augsburg, 1991), charters nos. 109–10 [23 June 1365], no. 133 [24 July 1384], no. 159 [16 Oct. 1401], no. 175 [9 Oct. 1408], no. 178 [23 Apr. 1409], no. 212 [24 July 1416] and no. 253 [2 Dec. 1429].

[27] Franz Ludwig Baumann, *Geschichte des Allgäus* (4 vols. Kempten, 1883–94; repr. Aalen, 1971–3), II, pp. 39, 387–8.

[28] Hans-Martin Schwarzmaier, *Königtum, Adel und Klöster im Gebiet zwischen oberer Iller und Lech* (Augsburg, 1961), pp. 118–48.

ministeriales and from a series of land-hungry Memmingen burghers.[29] At the same time, the monastery was also finally obliged to replace the old vassalage system with a formal administration of its own, so as to exercise closer supervision of its lands. Sensible as this response was, however, it was bound to be expensive.

To make matters worse, the need for increased revenue came at a time when the monastery's grip on its primary source of income, i.e. the peasantry, had weakened dramatically. The short-term cause of this problem was an exhausting struggle between the monastery and its spiritual overlord, the Bishop of Augsburg. Simply stated, the Bishop wanted to reform the monastery and the moral lives of the monks who lived there. The effort was resisted for a variety of reasons, some more edifying than others. On the one hand, the free-living monks resented the strictures which the reformers sought to impose on their lives. On the other hand, they (correctly) saw the reform program as part of a larger effort by the Bishop to reduce the monastery's autonomy and subject it to his own lordship.

The Augsburg reform efforts touched off a protracted conflict which began in 1408 and continued for fully a hundred years (the more fundamental dispute over the monastery's legal status lasted much longer, and culminated in a 1626 accord which entrenched Ottobeuren's status as a free imperial monastery). A complicated tangle of events[30] led to the occupation of the monastery lands and deposition of the Abbot by the Bishop's troops in 1460. The Abbot's successor proved equally resistant to reform, and nine years later he suffered a similar fate. In 1471 a papal commissioner ruled that the original Ottobeuren monks were completely incorrigible, and recommended that they be dispersed and replaced wholesale with more reform-minded members of the Benedictine order from Augsburg and Elchingen. The Ottobeuren monks promptly fled the monastery and elected a rival Abbot. In 1486 the disgruntled exiles and their anti-Abbot returned and mounted an unsuccessful assault on the monastery. The dispute was finally ended with the election of the reform-minded Abbot Leonhard Widenmann in 1508. Ottobeuren became a model Benedictine house, and its sixteenth-century Abbots were themselves often asked to conduct visitations to reform other religious houses.

The subject population was quick to exploit the power vacuum generated by the squabbling of rival masters. The peasantry intervened repeatedly in the struggle between Abbot and Bishop, assembling in defence of "their" monks against would-be reformers from Nuremberg in 1447, and refusing

---

[29] Peter Blickle, "Leibherrschaft als Instrument der Territorialpolitik im Allgäu: Grundlagen der Landeshoheit der Klöster Kempten und Ottobeuren" in Heinz Haushofer and Willi A. Boelcke, eds., *Wege und Forschungen der Agrargeschichte: Festschrift zum 65. Geburtstag von Günther Franz* (Frankfurt a.M., 1967), pp. 51–66, esp. p. 62.

[30] This compressed narrative is based on Baumann, *Geschichte des Allgäus*, Vol. II, pp. 389–95.

to pay taxes to Augsburg in 1464. Indeed, the schism itself was ultimately decided by the peasantry when they refused to recognize the anti-Abbot in 1486.

Debilitating as all of this infighting was, it paled by comparison with the havoc wreaked by the epidemics of the fourteenth century. Like most south German ecclesiastical[31] and secular[32] lordships, the monastery of Ottobeuren suffered grievous financial wounds after its subject population was decimated by the plague. Farms lay abandoned and rent receipts collapsed. By the 1370s the monastery was heavily in debt, and in 1380 it was forced to sell the entire village of Günz along with the tithes in Günz and Rummeltshausen for £1,100 to the Memmingen burgher Hans Merz.[33] In 1420 Abbot Johann Schedler wrote to Pope Martin V that the monastery had become so impoverished that its income, which had once supported forty monks, was now only large enough to support the Abbot and four others.[34]

As the monastery floundered in debt, its subject population became correspondingly more restive. In a climate of acute labor shortages, the bargaining position of the peasants had become much stronger, and they exploited this advantage to the fullest. In 1353 the Ottobeuren peasantry secured a privilege from Emperor Charles IV forbidding the Abbot from burdening his subjects with onerous taxes and confining the monastery's death duty claim to the best head of livestock and best garment of a deceased serf. The privilege was reconfirmed by a series of emperors in 1414, 1439, 1488, and 1498.[35] In 1406 the peasants began a rent strike[36] which was only settled two years later through the intervention of the Bishop of Augsburg. The Abbot was required to grant the peasants rent reductions when their crops were damaged by war, wind, hail, or pests, and to accept the annual grain rent payments in the quality grown that year. Any peasant who felt that his rent was excessive could now appeal to the Bishop of Augsburg, whose servants had the power to investigate and regulate the matter.[37] Finally, in 1434 the peasants forced the monastery to agree to a codification of their inheritance rights. Not only were children to have the right to inherit property from both mother and father, but brothers were also to inherit from brothers and sisters from sisters. Only if the deceased had neither lineal

---

[31] The fundamental study is still Gero Kirchner, "Probleme der spätmittelalterlichen Klostergrundherrschaft in Bayern: Landflucht und bäuerliches Erbrecht," *Zeitschrift für Bayerische Landesgeschichte* 19, 1 (1956), pp. 1–94.

[32] Werner Rösener, "Grundherrschaft des Hochadels in Südwestdeutschland im Spätmittelalter" in Hans Patz, ed., *Die Grundherrschaft im späten Mittelalter* (Sigmaringen, 1983), Vol. II, pp. 87–176.

[33] Hoffmann, ed. *Urkunden*, no. 130 [4 July 1380].   [34] Ibid., no. 219 [30 Jan. 1420].

[35] The originals of these privileges are no longer extant, but they have all been copied into StAA, KU 1354 [4 Feb. 1550].

[36] Alfred Weitnauer, *Allgäuer Chronik* (4 vols., Kempten, 1969–84), Vol. III, pp. 230–1.

[37] Hoffmann, ed. *Urkunden*, no. 174 [31 July 1408].

nor collateral heirs was the property to go to the monastery. Death duties were now restricted to the best head of livestock alone.[38]

The most spectacular self-assertion by the subjects of the monastery was their participation in the German Peasants' War of 1525. The Ottobeuren lands lay in the heartland of the revolt, and after renouncing their allegiance to the Abbot in February of 1525, the peasants soon joined the mass uprising which swept across most of southwestern and central Germany. The celebrated Twelve Articles, demanding (among other things) a reduction of rents and entry fines, control of the tithe, and the outright abolition of serfdom, were printed in the neighboring city of Memmingen. The monastery itself was stormed and plundered by its own subjects, and the Abbot was restored only by the armed might of the Swabian League in July.

Many Ottobeuren peasants did not even bother to agitate or negotiate for better conditions, but simply left the monastery lands altogether, either for tenancies in other territories, presumably under better conditions, or for nearby cities. Some also contrived to acquire the intermediate status of *Pfahlbürger*, i.e. a peasant who had acquired the citizenship (and protection) of a city but still continued to live on the land. The monastery was quite alarmed at these developments and sought to prevent the problem of "land flight" in various ways. The Abbots secured privileges of their own from the Emperor, forbidding the subjects of the monastery from emigrating to cities and forbidding the cities from receiving them. In 1356 the Golden Bull of Emperor Charles IV abolished the status of *Pfahlbürger* outright, and a similar decree was issued by Emperor Sigismund in 1431.[39] From those of its subjects who had unsuccessfully attempted to flee, the monastery extracted oaths that they would not try again and bonds from their relatives to ensure compliance. Thus on 30 November 1388, Cuncz der Lang of Wolfertschwenden and his wife, Katherin die Kolhúndin, swore to remain within the monastery lands, not to carry off their children, and to take on no citizenship "in either deed or appearance" without the permission of the monastery. The couple also furnished nine guarantors, each of whom was liable for a fine of ten pounds if either of the couple broke the oath.[40]

Despite occasional resort to coercive measures like these, the Abbots eventually realized that the only effective means of bringing abandoned holdings back into cultivation and of improving the output of existing ones was to make concessions to their subjects. The *ad hoc* and chaotic relations of vassalage were recognized as both an encumbrance on the peasantry and an impediment to the proper supervision of the lordship's resources. Under the prodding of the

---

[38] Ibid., no. 268 [31 Jan. 1434].
[39] Ibid., nos. 70 [19 Dec. 1334], 99 [10 Jan. 1356], and 258 [25 Mar. 1431].
[40] Ibid., no. 141. Similarly nos. 187 [24 Feb. 1412] and 215 [15 Mar. 1418].

Bishop of Augsburg, the monastery therefore began to put peasant land tenure on a different and much more secure footing.

The largest and choicest properties at Ottobeuren (*Höfe*, singular *Hof*) were held under a form of life-term tenure called *Gotteshausrecht*, or "monastery right." The origin of these *Höfe* is obscure. In other south German lordships, the *Höfe* can be shown to have descended from the very large demesnes of the Carolingian era. Smaller, dependent holdings known as *Huben* or *Güter* were attached to the demesne, which was administered by a powerful official known as a *villicus* or *Maier*. During the high Middle Ages, the demesnes were broken up into several large *Höfe*, the biggest of which was often known as the *Maierhof*.[41] A similar process may well have taken place at Ottobeuren. Most of the villages had a *Maierhof*, and as late as the sixteenth century, we find small tenancies owing payments to the *Maierhof*.[42] Unfortunately, the minimal administrative apparatus of the thirteenth and fourteenth centuries has left us very little direct evidence with which to work.

During the last third of the fifteenth century, and especially from the 1480s, the monastery began issuing formal, sealed charters of tenancy (*Lehensreverse*) to the holders of the *Gotteshausrecht Höfe*. These charters explicitly itemized the tenant's obligations to the monastery, and certified his lifelong right to the *Hof* as long as these obligations were met. At this time the monks also began compiling a series of rent rolls (*Gültbücher*) which listed – and, significantly, fixed – the rent payment owed from each *Hof*. All of this was part of a general expansion of the monastery's documentary apparatus (see Figure 1.1),[43] which swelled dramatically as the century came to an end.

The formalization of the tenant's rights and obligations was only part of the transformation of tenurial relations at Ottobeuren. Equally important was the creation of new and more favorable terms of tenure altogether. In 1459, for example, Abbot Johann Kraus granted a large *Hof* in the village of Haldenwang to one Alexander Grus both for Grus' own lifetime and thereafter to his children for their lifetimes.[44] Still more generous than the extended lease was the granting of a heritable tenure, or *Erblehenrecht*, which invested the tenant and all of his heirs with a right to the property. As long as each new tenant paid his rent and

---

[41] Werner Rösener, *Grundherrschaft im Wandel: Untersuchungen zur Entwicklung geistlicher Grundherrschaften im südwestdeutschen Raum vom 9. bis 14. Jahrhundert* (Göttingen, 1991), pp. 467–89.

[42] E.g. StAA, KU Ottobeuren 1191 [4 Nov. 1538].

[43] Figure 1.1 is only an approximate indication of documentary activity, since it includes charters received by the monastery from others, and excludes charters issued by the monastery of which no Ottobeuren copy was kept. It also omits the accounts and rent rolls maintained in increasing numbers from the 1520s.

[44] Hoffmann, ed. *Urkunden*, no. 373 [27 Apr. 1459]. Similarly StAA, KU Ottobeuren 262a [4 June 1462], Oberböglins, and KU Ottobeuren 263 [26 July 1462], Schlegelsberg.

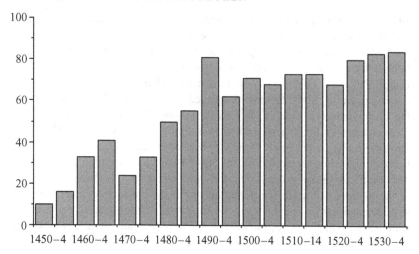

Figure 1.1 Charters of the monastery of Ottobeuren in five-year intervals, 1450/4–1535/9
Source: StAA, KU Ottobeuren 220–1213

an entry fine (*Lehengeld*) fixed at one fortieth of the value of the property at investiture, inheritance was guaranteed in perpetuity.[45]

The earliest documented grant of a heritable tenure in the monastery lands occurred in 1379 when Abbot Johann von Hocherer converted the tenure of Ralf der Zehender's *Hof* in Dietratried from *Gotteshausrecht* to *Erblehenrecht*.[46] Similar conversions are documented for the mills in Engetried (1407) and Benningen (1415),[47] but the real surge in *Erblehenrecht* grants did not come until the abbacy of Johann Schedler, who reigned from 1416 to 1443. Of Abbot Johann the later monastic chroniclers would write that "no abbot granted out more of the monastery's lands in heritable tenure and none before him made as much progress with [the monastery's] finances as this Abbot Johann."[48] In 1417 he granted out holdings in Oberried and Dassberg, and in 1418 lands in Hüners and Lietzheim. In the 1420s and 1430s lands were converted to *Erblehenrecht* in the hamlets of Bossarts, Bibelsberg, Warlins, Kräpflins, Schoren, and Leupolz. Still further grants were made in the hamlets Rempolz, Hofs, Reuthen, and Berg. After the 1440s there were also several conversions to *Erblehenrecht* in the villages, particularly in Böhen, Wolfertschwenden, and Niederdorf. In

---

[45] There is a useful discussion of *Erblehenrecht* in Karl Siegfried Bader, *Rechtsformen und Schichten der Liegenschaftsnutzung im mittelalterlichen Dorf* (Vienna, Cologne and Graz, 1973), pp. 16–53. The norm of one fortieth (2.5 percent) is taken from the mass of *Erblehen* charters copied into StAA, KL Ottobeuren 18.

[46] Hoffmann, ed. *Urkunden*, no. 129 [18 May 1379].

[47] Ibid., nos. 171 [10 Sep. 1407] and 207 [28 Sep. 1415].

[48] Maurus Feyerabend, *Des ehemaligen Reichsstiftes Ottenbeuren, Benediktiner Ordens in Schwaben, sämmtliche Jahrbücher* (4 vols., Ottobeuren, 1813–16), Vol. II, p. 621.

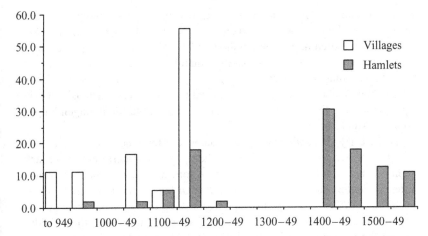

Figure 1.2 Distribution (percent) of Ottobeuren settlements by earliest documentary reference
Sources: StAA, KL Ottobeuren 18, 64 and 541 (2), Ralf Heimrath, "Ortsnamen und Siedlungsgeschichte seit dem 6. Jahrhundert" in Aegidius Kolb, ed., *Landkreis Unterallgäu* (2 vols., Mindelheim, 1987), Vol. I, pp. 72–84

1463 the Bishop of Augsburg authorized the monastery to convert its remaining *Gotteshausrecht* farms to *Erblehenrecht*,[49] and the Abbots would continue to make new grants into the early decades of the sixteenth century.[50]

In the long run, the concessions made by the monastery redounded to its benefit. The peasants were not only prepared to pay ready money for the conversion of life term to heritable tenure, they were also willing to clear new land in exchange for the grant of *Erblehenrecht*. The fifteenth century thus saw a dramatic expansion of cultivation, as peasants moved out of the old villages and established new settlements in the still-forested southern region of the monastery lands (see Figure 1.2). The novelty of these clearances is underscored not only by the virtual universality of *Erblehenrecht* in the region, but also by a striking difference in the form of settlement. Whereas the inhabitants of the older settlements in the north of the Ottobeuren lands lived in large nucleated villages, those who carried out the fifteenth-century clearances to the south settled into small, scattered hamlets, which were grouped for administrative purposes into a half-dozen or so headmanships, or *Hauptmannschaften*.

This expansion of rent- and tithe-paying land and the more diligent cultivation of the old settled land soon restored the monastery's financial health.

---

[49] StAA, KU Ottobeuren 265 [14 Jan. 1463]. The monastery did not, of course, convert *all* of its *Gotteshausrecht* farms.
[50] Feyerabend, *Ottenbeuren Jahrbücher*, Vol. II, pp. 621–2 (conversions in the years 1417–18), 627–8 (in 1424–40), and 715 (in 1480). Also ibid., Vol. III, pp. 113–14 (in 1534). A great many *Erblehenrecht* charters have been copied into StAA, KL Ottobeuren 18.

By the second quarter of the fifteenth century, the monks were able to begin repurchasing alienated lands and acquiring new ones. Between 1427 and 1448, the monks acquired more than ten thousand *gulden* worth of properties in the settlements surrounding the monastery,[51] thereby eliminating most other landlords in the villages of Dietratried, Egg, Frechenrieden, and Niederrieden. In 1468 Abbot Wilhelm von Lustenau capped the monastery's acquisition drive by repurchasing the alienated village of Günz from the Memmingen burgher Jodokus Ampfelbronn.

By the early sixteenth century, the outcome of these developments at Ottobeuren was the combination of entrenched peasant property and inheritance rights with a decidedly moderate form of lordship. Rents remained fixed at fifteenth-century levels not only for *Erblehen* land,[52] but also for the *Gotteshausrecht Höfe*[53] which yielded the lion's share of the monastery's groundrents (*Gülten*). The ability of peasants to pass on their lands to their children had been greatly enhanced by the spread of *Erblehenrecht*, and by the imperial privileges restricting the monastery's claims to the property of its subjects.

Peasant rights to the sprawling *Gotteshausrecht Höfe* were in theory much inferior. The grant of land under *Gotteshausrecht* was for the full term of the tenant's life, but no longer. The tenant's children had no legal claim to the land after his death. In addition, the statutes of the monastery insisted that

> every year as soon as My Gracious Lord or His Grace's delegate shall arrive at the *Bauding* [annual assembly of the peasantry], from that hour on in keeping with ancient usage, tradition, custom, and habit each and every *Hof*, *Hube* and *Gut* which is held from his grace . . . according to *Gotteshausrecht* is free, discharged and released to His Grace [and] each and every one who holds such a *Hof*, *Hube* and *Gut* shall with trembling hands [*mit wagendter handen*] again receive it from My Gracious Lord until the next *Bauding*.[54]

The object of this ceremony was to make it clear that the land remained the property of the monastery and not that of the tenant. The practice proved inadequate to dissuade peasant claims of hereditability, however, and the monastery began inserting additional clauses in the leases to strengthen its position. Thus when Jerg Hering was admitted to a small property in Altisried in 1569, the *Erdschatz* register stipulated that "if Hering the current tenant has a son who is suitable to serve the monastery, My Gracious Lord consents also to support the

---

[51] Hoffmann, ed. *Urkunden*, nos. 248, 253, 260, 264, 267, 277, 284, 285, 300, 303, 313, 316, 326, 334.

[52] E.g. "Bölers Gut" in the village of Sontheim was leased at an annual grain rent of 2 *malter* in 1464. In 1544 the rent was the same. StAA, KL Ottobeuren 18, ff. 275v–276r; KL Ottobeuren 29, f. 70v. See also StAA, KU Ottobeuren 678 [25 July 1503].

[53] E.g. the *Maierhof* in Attenhausen was leased at an annual grain rent of 15 *malter* in 1483. The property was divided in 1512, but the combined rent of the two halves in 1544 was still 15 *malter*. StAA, KU Ottobeuren 406, 803, 804 and 1026. KL Ottobeuren 29, f. 65r.

[54] StAA, KL Ottobeuren 4, Document 289X, f. 372r (*c*. 1551).

Table 1.1 *Transmission patterns for* Gotteshausrecht Höfe *at Ottobeuren, 1480–1549ᵃ*

	Kin transfers	Non-kin transfers	Total	% kin transfers
1480–9	4	14	18	22.2
1490–9	15	17	32	46.9
1500–9	15	15	30	50.0
1510–19	25	16	41	61.0
1520–9	12	17	29	41.4
1530–9	16	18	34	47.1
1540–9	14	20	34	41.2

Note: ᵃ Transfers by peasants to the monastery have been excluded as these were invariably a prelude to the property being regranted to a third party. The number of these transfers was in any case insignificant before 1525.
Source: StAA, KU Ottobeuren

said [son], but only voluntarily, and the *Erdschatz* payment is forgiven to him [i.e. Hering] but only in exchange for his service, and no [right of] succession shall result either to his wife or child."

Stern as these conditions may seem, they do not accurately reflect actual practice. Jerg Hering was in fact succeeded on the *Gotteshausrecht* holdings by his son in 1593,[55] and in general, *Gotteshausrecht* holdings passed so often in practice from father to son or son-in-law that they might as well have been hereditable in law (see Table 1.1). Of course, no tenant took even *de facto* heritability of these *Höfe* for granted, and notarial evidence indicates that contingency plans were made in case the heir was not admitted to the land. Be that as it may, the 1565 dispute between the Abbot and the Wagner family discussed at the beginning of this chapter shows how strongly the peasants felt about their right even to *Gotteshausrecht* land. The inheritance arrangements of remarrying widows are even more revealing in this regard. That a son might be contractually required not even to ask the Abbot for the tenancy of a *Gotteshausrecht Hof* (so that it might instead pass to his stepfather) offers powerful testimony of the practical strength of peasant property rights.[56]

The reality of these rights has here been emphasized because the tendency of most discussions of fifteenth- and sixteenth-century Germany has been to stress the arbitrary and exploitative nature of lordship. In so far as peasants labored and the monastery took part of the fruits away from them, exploitation

---

55 StAA, KL Ottobeuren 27, ff. 117v–118r.
56 Cf. StAA, KU Ottobeuren 443 [6 Mar. 1487]. A Bauer gives up the *Hof* for which he has not been paying the rent and asks that it be granted to his son Hans; it is. For the contractual stipulation that a son not ask to be admitted to the family's *Gotteshausrecht Hof*, see KL Ottobeuren 901, ff. 91v–92r [5 Mar. 1584] and 102r–v [30 Apr. 1584].

continued at least until the secularization of the monastery in 1803 (and arguably until late in the nineteenth century, when the peasants finally bought out the rights that the Bavarian state had conveniently assumed from the monastery it had secularized). Nevertheless, the clear outcome of the struggles of the fifteenth century was that the monks learned that they had no choice but to keep exploitation within limits. Above all, property relations at Ottobeuren came to be governed by a rule of law to which the monastery itself was subject.

Of course these laws favored the monastery in a contest with any individual peasant. The monastery's vastly superior powers of collecting and preserving information gave it an unrivaled ability to exploit the technicalities of the land law. Thus in February of 1549, when four recent heirs to *Erblehen* holdings in the hamlet of Vogelsang neglected to seek formal admission to their *Höfe*, the secretary of the monastery was able to declare them to have forfeited their tenures.[57] In the same way, Jerg Hörter and his six sons found themselves overmatched in 1519 when they insisted that their modest holding in Egg was a freehold property and thus bore no obligation of rent payment. Abbot Leonhard disagreed.

> Since they can show us *nothing besides their mere words* to prove this [claim], we contend that this property, since it has [in fact] been yielding us and our monastery a permanent annual rent of seven *viertel* of rye, eleven shillings, one hen and two pullets, belongs to us and our monastery, and is to be leased under *Gotteshausrecht* like other holdings of this sort.[58]

The Hörters' claim was rejected.

Despite the unevenness of these contests, however, the monastery did not go on to steamroll the peasantry. In the first place, even when peasants did lose these legal battles (and they most certainly did not always lose),[59] the resulting deterioration of their property rights was minor. The four tenants from Vogelsang received their forfeited lands back under a kind of tenure known as *Freilehenrecht*. An entry fine now had to be paid both at the investiture of a new tenant and at the investiture of a new abbot, but the prized heritability of the land was preserved.[60] As for Jerg Hörter and his sons, Abbot Leonhard

---

[57] StAA, KL Ottobeuren 16, "Lehenbuch 1547/83," ff. 31r–v [1 and 2 Feb. 1549].

[58] StAA, KL Ottobeuren 18, ff. 321r–v. Emphasis mine. The original charter is StAA, KU Ottobeuren 907 [14 Nov. 1519].

[59] See the 1541 dispute between the monastery and Hans Moser and Veit Köberlin of Egg over the *Erblehen* status they claimed for their meadows in StAA, KL Ottobeuren 18, ff. 327v–329v. The Abbot conceded that "since we have found credible references in our rent rolls and also in the old charters of sale that the said meadow was granted out in heritable tenure by our predecessors, we [too] have newly granted and given out the four *tagwerk* of meadow as an *Erblehen* and according to *Erblehenrecht*."

[60] StAA, KL Ottobeuren 16, ff. 31r–v. The heritability of *Freilehen* land is attested by the multiple entries in the *Lehenbuch* to tenants paying entry fines for land which they are explicitly declared to have inherited. See e.g. ibid., ff. 102v (1547), 91v (1553), 58r (1555), 63r (1566), 82v (1567), and 77v–78r (1582).

proved ultimately willing to compromise. The land ended up being declared neither freehold nor *Gotteshausrecht* but *Freilehen*. The Abbot seems to have been prepared even to forgo the rent payment,[61] and Hörter remained on the land for almost thirty years.[62]

Most of the time, in fact, the monastery was markedly lenient with forgetful or defaulting tenants. In 1497, for example, the monastery seized the holding of one Adam Rentzlin of Niederrieden "because of much outstanding and bygone rent and interest." The Abbot was persuaded, however, to regrant the property to Rentzlin's son-in-law, Hans Teuffel.[63] The peasants of Böhen secured similarly generous terms from the monastery after a forfeiture in 1485. In 1463 the Abbot had granted out a series of properties known as the Schlauen, the Mößer, and the Schwendi to the village community. The villagers were to clear the land, divide it into shares, and attach each share to a specific holding in the village. The shares were then to remain "never again at any time changed, mortgaged or sold, but that each and every one shall be used [under the understanding that it shall] belong in the said village and in the said holdings and always remain there."[64] Twelve years later the properties were confiscated by the angry Abbot after it was revealed that some of the villagers had dared "to separate their allotted shares . . . from their holdings in the village of Böhen." In the end, however, there was little that the Abbot could do but regrant the land to the villagers with the admonition that all clauses of the original arrangement were to be observed. In addition, if in the future a member of the village community wished to sell both his share of the cleared land and his holding in the village, the sale price was to be determined by a group of four men, two of whom were to be appointed by the Abbot and two by the village community.[65] The monastery listened sympathetically to Mathias Knebel of Böhen who "says that he bought his [*Freilehen*] land twelve years ago [but] didn't realize that he was obliged to be formally invested,"[66] and actually went so far as to fine one Barthlome

---

[61] There is no entry for the property in Egg in the 1544 rent roll. StAA, KL Ottobeuren 29, ff. 90r–101v.

[62] He ranks in the bottom 42.9 percent of Egg taxpayers in the 1546 tax register. StAA, KL Ottobeuren 64, ff. 17r–21r.

[63] StAA, KL Ottobeuren 18, ff. 300r–302v [27 June 1497]. Similarly the fate of Jäck Döpprich of Benningen, who was obliged by non-payment of rent to surrender his *Hof* back to the monastery. Döpprich requested that the land be regranted to his son Hans, and it was. StAA, KU Ottobeuren 443 [6 Mar. 1487].

[64] StAA, KU Ottobeuren 266 [2 May 1463]. There is a copy in StAA, KL Ottobeuren 18, ff. 228r–229r.

[65] Ibid., ff. 229v–230v. The orginal charter is StAA, KU Ottobeuren 433 [6 Oct. 1485]. See also Hoffmann, ed. *Urkunden*, no. 374 [23 June 1459], the arbitration of a dispute between the Memmingen burgher Jacob Ratz and the monastery of Ottobeuren. The Abbot had impounded Ratz's holding for non-payment of rent, but was persuaded to regrant it to him.

[66] StAA, KL Ottobeuren 16, f. 94v [8 May 1579]. Knebel was admitted to the land. See also StAA, KU Ottobeuren 1444 [15 May 1553], the *Lehensrevers* of Hans Kopp of Sontheim, who forfeited his *Hof* "through a misunderstanding" and was readmitted to it.

Schmidt of Egg in 1575 for not presenting himself for readmission to *Erblehen* which he had forfeited![67]

Furthermore, when the monastery did choose to take a hard line, it was often able to prevail only at cost of considerable effort, regardless of the strength of its case. In 1537, for example, a court was covened in the market town of Ottobeuren to try the title of one Pantelion Frech of Altisried to two *tagwerk* of meadow in the neighboring village of Frechenrieden. Although he was not an heir to the property, Frech had seized control of the meadow after the death of the previous tenant, Othmar Sÿngÿbel, and had then refused to apply for formal admission. The monastery accordingly resolved to eject him. On 5 July, the original 1478 *Erblehen* charter was read out in court, whereupon the Abbot's attorney, Johann Kötterlin, argued that Frech had violated several of the charter's provisions and had therefore forfeited the land.

Frech himself made no answer to these charges. In fact, he didn't even bother to show up in court. The *Amman* of Böhen, who had been appointed as judge, then asked whether Frech had been told to appear at the trial. The bailiff got up and duly swore that

> On the previous Saturday, in the presence of the sheriff of Frechenrieden, he informed Pantelion Frech of this court date. Pantelion replied to him, the witness, that he could not make this date because he would not yet be back in the lordship by then. The witness then told him that he [Pantelion] could easily return to the lordship [in time for the court date]. Whereupon Pantelion retorted that he was within his rights, and that whoever had something to dispute with him could seek him out by himself. He [Pantelion] would neither come to nor appear at this court date.

Incensed by this testimony, Kötterlin argued that Pantelion's insolence was by itself grounds enough for forfeiture, but the presiding judge was unwilling to be so hasty. He ruled that the defendant should be given another chance to explain himself, and set a new court date for two days later. Again Frech did not show up, and again the Abbot's attorney demanded a declaration of forfeiture. But still the *Amman* of Böhen was concerned whether Pantelion Frech had been fairly informed of the new court date. The bailiff was sworn in for a second time, and testified that

> he, the witness, took with him the *Amman* and one of the members of the village council [*Vierer*] to Altisried, and looked for Pantelion Frech in his house, but they did not find him. They then looked for him where his wife was, in one of her freehold meadows, and [since he was not there either, they] announced to her that her husband was to appear before the tenurial court on this current day at seven o'clock in the morning.

---

[67] StAA, KL Ottobeuren 587-I, Heft 7 "Strafregister 1575/6."

By now even the judge's patience was exhausted. The meadow was declared forfeit, whereupon the monastery granted it out as an *Erblehen* to a new tenant.[68] The significance of this episode is not the substance of the legal dispute; Pantelion Frech very likely knew that he had no defensible claim to the land, which explains his refusal to plead his case in court. Much more important is the fact that even when it had the law on its side, the monastery was bound by rules of procedure which effectively precluded arbitrary dispossession.[69] The spectacle of the Abbot's attorney *requesting* a peasant court to declare property to be forfeit belies any suspicion that the land law was merely a tool of feudal oppression. The peasant judges may have been appointed to their positions by their overlord, but this did not make them his catspaws. If they were unconvinced by the Abbot's agents, they would not rule in their favor.[70]

The foregoing discussion of the thicket of legal constraints on the monastery's power over its subjects and their property brings us to a second general feature of peasant–overlord relations in the fifteenth and sixteenth centuries: even when the Abbot had the law completely on his side, this often failed to translate into effective powers of coercion. That weakness should have obtained during the turbulence and insolvency of the fourteenth century is perhaps unsurprising. That it should also have been manifest at the point of maximum lordly strength – the aftermath of the Swabian League's victory in the Peasants' War of 1525 – is a telling illustration of the realities of power in the countryside.

According to the terms of capitulation drawn up in 1525, the Swabian League was entitled to levy a reparations tax of 6 *gulden* per hearth on every town and village in the pacified area.[71] As the League had been the decisive force in suppressing the revolt, this tax had absolute priority over all others. Local lords wanting to impose their own reparations taxes on the peasants – and almost all of them did – were enjoined from so doing until the claims of the League had been satisfied. Individual tax payments were adjusted to the wealth of the

---

[68] StAA, KL Ottobeuren 2, Document 185, ff. 338r–344r. The original ruling of the Böhen *Lehengericht* is preserved in StAA, KU Ottobeuren 1174 [7 July 1537]. The *Erblehen* charter has been copied both in the court proceedings themselves and in StAA, KL Ottobeuren 18, ff. 262r–263r. The latter also records the 1537 forfeiture and the subsequent regrant to a certain Jerg Oschwald.

[69] See in this regard the ruling of the Niederrieden village court that the Abbot was required to wait more than six weeks before being permitted to reclaim a *Gotteshausrecht* property whose tenant had been formally declared to be in arrears of rent. StAA, KU Ottobeuren 562 [14 Jan. 1493]. A widow who went completely bankrupt a few years later was allowed to retain her garments, bed, and bedclothes. StAA, KU Ottobeuren 576 [15 Apr. 1496] (Ruling by Peter Stehelin, *Amman* of Ottobeuren on the lands of the widow Margaret Märck of Betzisried).

[70] StAA, KL Ottobeuren 4, Document 308M, ff. 1081r–1083r (*Urfehdebrief* of Mang Möslin of Niederrieden [24 Sep. 1538]). Möslin had been asked to sentence an accused criminal, and sarcastically retorted that "I will be glad to pronounce sentence as soon as the *Vogt* of Ottobeuren can show me the truth of his charge."

[71] This was a not inconsiderable sum; 6 *gulden* would buy enough grain to feed three adults for an entire year.

household; a total sum was levied on the village and then apportioned among the households by the village community. Two categories of people were exempted from the tax: widows, orphans, and the poor on one hand, and those who could prove that they had not taken part in the revolt on the other.

Since the local lords could not be relied upon in the matter, the Swabian League resolved to collect the reparations on its own. This was initially conducted on an *ad hoc* basis, but by May of 1525 (and thus before the pacification of the Ottobeuren lands in July) the Swabian League had assembled a formidable bureaucratic apparatus to wring the money from the peasantry. The pacified areas were divided into districts, each of which was assigned to a team of collection agents. The agents then dispatched horsemen into the district to record the number of hearths in each village and to enforce payment of the tax. In addition, special security forces totaling 800 cavalry were stationed in Ulm, Heilbronn, Bamberg, Kaufbeuren, and Kempten. These squadrons roamed the countryside, maintaining quiescence through a combination of brutality and intimidation. This took place with the full approval of the League, which regarded the dark reputation of the mercenaries as an ideal deterrent to further rebellion. It goes without saying that it also expedited payment of the reparations.[72]

The Ottobeuren lands were part of a tax district administered from the city of Memmingen. As was the case throughout Upper Swabia and the Allgäu, the collection effort in this district was pressed remorselessly. Barring detailed proof to the contrary, all peasants were considered guilty of rebellion and therefore liable for the tax. Local authorities often sought to shield their subjects with the argument that the peasants had only unwillingly joined the rebels, but the League paid little attention to such objections. Appeals for exemption due to poverty met with a similar lack of sympathy. Although widows, orphans, and the destitute were officially exempted from the tax, the League issued so few actual remissions that it is impossible to avoid the conclusion that many of the poor were none the less forced to pay.[73]

Multiple taxation was another common abuse. The League was supposed to issue receipts for the sums collected, but its agents frequently neglected to do so, often deliberately (the League's mercenaries were in the habit of collecting "unofficial" reparations while on the march). Those unfortunates who could not prove that they had already paid were routinely compelled to do so again. In other cases the League amended the original assessments with

---

[72] Thomas F. Sea, "Schwäbischer Bund und Bauernkrieg: Bestrafung und Pazifikation" in Hans-Ulrich Wehler, ed., *Der Deutsche Bauernkrieg 1524–1526* (Gottingen, 1975), pp. 129–67, at pp. 133, 151–6; Baumann, *Allgäu*, Vol. III, pp. 133–5.

[73] Sea found that in the area around Augsburg, only 313 [= 11.3 percent] of 2,774 assessed hearths were exempted from the reparations tax. Moreover, of these 313 exemptions, "only 73 [= 2.6 percent of the total] can be definitely identified as exemptions due to extreme poverty." Thomas F. Sea, "The Economic Impact of the German Peasants' War: The Question of Reparations," *Sixteenth Century Journal* 8, 3 (1977), pp. 75–97, at pp. 83–4, 87.

predictable results. Ottobeuren's district was saddled with an initial obligation of 25,000 *gulden*. Most of this sum had been collected by March of 1526,[74] but a battered register now in the Staatsarchiv Augsburg indicates that the League imposed a further round of taxes on the monastery villages the following summer.[75] In many cases the peasants just did not have the money, but this was hardly an obstacle to the rapacity of the tax collectors. Penniless peasants were simply forced to borrow the money, with the result that payments arising from the reparations taxes were still being made for years after the war had ended.[76] At Ottobeuren indirect evidence indicates that payments continued at least into 1532.[77] The subjects of the Prince-Abbot of Kempten were still making payments in 1548, long after the Swabian League itself had ceased to exist.[78]

All in all it was a striking if distasteful achievement. In a region of extremely fragmented political sovereignty the Swabian League succeeded in creating a supra-territorial taxation machine that squeezed one-quarter of a million *gulden* from the devastated villages of the German southwest.[79] The League's example was followed by countless local lords – the Abbot of Ottobeuren among them – who imposed their own taxes on the peasants the instant the League's claims had been satisfied. Yet, despite the apparent success of the taxation effort, there were definite limits to the power that any authority could exercise in the villages. In the first place, fiscal extraction on this scale was possible only in the very short run. The aforementioned evidence of peasant indebtedness makes it clear that these collections could never have been sustained. As it was, the collection

---

[74] The precise figure was 24,768 fl. 36 kr. Sea, "Economic Impact," pp. 92–4.

[75] StAA, KL Ottobeuren 159, ff. 10r–14v. "Raÿß gelt Anno 1526 von deß pauren kriegs wegen." The document is bound with a muster roll from 1499 and a second war tax list from 1532. The assessments for the market town of Ottobeuren and the villages of Benningen and Niederrieden are missing from the 1526 list. Since almost all of the assessments in the (complete) 1532 list bear a relation between 0.53 and 0.59:1 to those of 1526, however, the missing earlier assessments can be interpolated on the basis of the mean 1532/1526 coefficient (0.556). The total second assessment for 1526 can thus be estimated at 425 fl. Note also that although all of the money initially levied in the Memmingen area had been collected by March of 1526, the accounts of the Swabian League for January 1527 list a (new) outstanding sum of 1,570 fl. Sea, "Economic Impact," pp. 92–4.

[76] Ibid., pp. 83–7. In the Augsburg area, at least 40 percent of the total assessment of 14,993 fl. was financed by debt.

[77] StAA, KL Ottobeuren 159. "Raÿß gelt Anno 1532 deß turrgen kriegs wegen." Part of this war tax granted to Charles V in 1532 was later revoked, with the result that some of the money already collected was to be returned to the peasants. In recording these repayments, the scribe who drew up the tax register repeatedly entered a credit against outstanding payments from the reparations levied in 1526 instead of actually handing back the money to the peasants. See also the letter from Charles V to the Abbot of Ottobeuren [28 Dec. 1533] ordering him to issue receipts to the peasantry for monies paid to the Swabian League. StAA, KL Ottobeuren 2, "Rotulus Probationum," Vol. II, Document 181, ff. 328v–329v.

[78] Baumann, *Allgäu*, Vol. III, p. 135. See also Sea, "Schwäbischer Bund," p. 162.

[79] The total initially levied in 1526 comes to 247,941 fl. 48 kr. Of this 93 percent had been collected by June of 1527. Sea, "Economic Impact," p. 86.

still had to be carried out at swordpoint. Moreover, the primary post-war goal had been the creation of a politically docile subject population, and this was not so easily accomplished.

The point is not that the authority of a sixteenth-century lord was precarious but rather that it was exceedingly superficial. Although his power could be focused in particular instances to collect a tax or punish a malefactor, it was never a continuous presence in the villages and was rarely successful in shaping the actual behavior of his subjects. The reason for this impotence is perfectly straightforward: an adequate coercive apparatus simply did not exist. The military muscle deployed by the Swabian League in 1525–7 was a temporary force, and even as such was beyond the capacity of most individual lordships. At Ottobeuren, for example, the monks could only count on their *Vogt*, a single local noble who arranged for peasant compliance with the monastery's decrees when the moral authority of the Abbot was insufficiently persuasive. Beyond the *Vogt*, the monastery was dependent upon the admonitions of the parish priest, a clutch of scribes and administrators, and a dozen poorly paid *Pittel*, or sheriffs, to maintain order among thousands of stubborn, well-armed, and litigious peasants. For almost all of his subjects the Abbot's authority was thus an episodic and often reactive intrusion into their lives. The Abbot could try to keep a lid on unrest in the villages, but the boil itself he was powerless to prevent.

With the dispersal of the insurgent bands in July of 1525, the monastery took up the task of punishing the defeated rebels. Executions played no role in this process, for not only did the monks concede the legitimacy of some peasant grievances,[80] but the financial exigencies of the monastic community ultimately outweighed any desire for vindictiveness among its members. Similar patterns obtained throughout the region; there was a scattered handful of executions,[81] but, as one perceptive noble put it, "If all of the peasants are killed, where shall we get other peasants to make provision for us?"[82] At Ottobeuren the situation was further simplified by the fact that many of the rebels not slain in battle (and there had been a few casualties in a confused clash on the banks of the river

---

[80] Thus the Ottobeuren monk and humanist Nikolaus Ellenbog (1481–1543) in his tract *De servis et servitute corporali*: "for many years [the lords] had inflicted no small injustice upon their subjects, and the yoke which they placed on them was heavy beyond all measure. Thus did God allow that the servants rose up against the masters so that those who had done evil [now] also felt evil, those who had resorted to violence also suffered violence [and] those who had oppressed the poor were themselves oppressed, so that they were judged by the same standards with which they had judged." See Friedrich Zoepfl, "Der Humanist Nikolaus Ellenbog zur Frage der bäuerlichen Leibeigenschaft," *Historisches Jahrbuch* 58, 1/2 (1938), pp. 129–35, at p. 134.

[81] Baumann, *Allgäu*, Vol. III, p. 138. See also Sea, "Schwäbischer Bund," pp. 133–4, 148–51.

[82] A. W. Ward, G. W. Prothero, and Stanley Leathes, eds. *The Cambridge Modern History*, Vol. II: *The Reformation* (Cambridge, 1903), p. 191.

Leubas when the Swabian League moved into the Ottobeuren lands)[83] hastily relocated to the comparative safety of the Swiss cantons.[84] A separation of the sheep from the goats was none the less deemed necessary. After a general reparations tax had been levied on all of the inhabitants (in direct violation of the prerogatives of the Swabian League),[85] a register was drawn up of "all those who are to be singled out from the general settlement."[86] These alleged instigators and leaders of the revolt were either fined or ordered to perform labor services for the monastery. In a few cases the fines were set at crippling levels of 50, 60, and even 100 *gulden*, but by the standards of the day most of the punishments were rather mild: a fine of 10 to 12 *gulden*, ten days of field work, or the obligation to cart a specified quantity of grain, nails, or stone. Indeed, some of the punishments were trivial. Jerg Lang and Hans Maier of Unterwolfertschwenden, for example, were merely fined a single *gulden* each.

A fuller picture of the lenience of the post-war settlement is provided by a series of documents known as *Urfehdebriefe*. A holdover from the medieval institution of the *Fehde*, or feud, an *Urfehdebrief* was the formal renunciation of the right of vengeance on the part of a convicted criminal. It is perhaps most helpfully likened to the modern notion of a plea bargain. An *Urfehdebrief* typically begins with a confession of misdeeds and an acknowledgment that serious punishment was deserved. But in exchange for a more lenient sentence, the criminal forswore both formal vengeance and the right to appeal his sentence

---

[83] The tax register drawn up by the monastery in the fall of 1525 (StAA, KL Ottobeuren 541, Heft 2, "Generalrechnung 1529 [*sic*]") lists the names of the householders in each village and the tax imposed upon them. Next to many of these names has been inserted "shot dead at the Leubas," "stabbed at the Leubas," "remained at the Leubas," and so on.

[84] Baumann, *Allgäu*, Vol. III, pp. 138–9. See also the letter dated 17 Dec. 1526 from a collection of Ottobeuren exiles asking permission to return to their homes in StAA, KL Ottobeuren 2, Document 174, ff. 307v–309v.

[85] It has long been incorrectly asserted (e.g. Baumann, *Allgäu*, Vol. III, p. 135) that the Abbot of Ottobeuren never imposed any reparations taxes on his peasants, and Sea has gone so far as to argue (although this may be the result of a mistranslation) that the Abbot paid the peasants' Swabian League taxes out of his own pocket! (Sea, "Schwäbischer Bund," p. 161). The confusion is understandable, since the facts were erroneously reported in an otherwise reliable monastic chronicle in 1814, and a crucial document now in the Staatsarchiv Augsburg was miscatalogued in 1899 and has therefore gone unnoticed. The document in question is StAA, KL Ottobeuren 541, Heft 2. The MS. has been labeled "Generalrechnung 1529," but careful examination shows it to be a tax register. The title page is missing from the MS. (this must have contributed to the cataloguing error), but has been preserved in an abbreviated copy in StAA, KL Ottobeuren 4, Document 290A, ff. 419v–426v. The title reads "In this register is written how and at which amounts the market town of Ottobeuren [and] all [of the] villages and parishioners have been reconciled with my gracious lord of Ottobeuren regarding the damages inflicted. Actum Monday after St. Mang's Day [i.e. 11 Sep.], Anno XXV."

[86] This register survives as an abbreviated copy in the *Rotulus Probationum*. StAA, KL Ottobeuren 4, Document 290B, ff. 426v–432v. The scribe notes that "this register has not been [copied] word for word, but only the names of those punished and the *specificationes* of the punishments [have] briefly [been] *bona fide* extracted."

to higher courts. The criminal also vowed on pain of severe chastisement to obey his lord in the future and never to commit such an offense again.[87]

Considerable numbers of *Urfehdebriefe* were issued at Ottobeuren after the Peasants' War. These charters reveal that the monastery pursued a deliberate policy of rehabilitating the ex-rebels. Although some of the *Urfehdebriefe* were issued to peasants captured and imprisoned by Ottobeuren's *Vogt*, just as many were issued to fugitives who voluntarily turned themselves in to prison after the Abbot promised to spare their lives.[88] Moreover, no offense was so heinous as to rule out the possibility of pardon. *Urfehdebriefe* were issued to looters of the monastery, to Lutheran agitators, and to officers in the insurgent armies.[89] The offer of amnesty was even extended to the notorious "miller of Sontheim," a chief instigator of the revolt and attack on the monastery.[90] The various fines and prohibitions imposed in the *Urfehdebriefe* are not easily reconciled with modern notions of clemency. There is also ample evidence to show that the pardoned rebels bitterly resented the disabilities imposed on them by the monastery. Still, it is important to keep in mind the horror with which sixteenth-century authorities beheld any insurrection by the lower orders. Given the hideous punishments then routinely meted out to even petty criminals, the monks themselves must have felt they were acting with exemplary restraint.

Although there never was another mass revolt at Ottobeuren, this did not mean that the peasantry had finally been cowed into submission. Religious dissent survived by going underground. Thus, when an Anabaptist was apprehended in nearby Erkheim in 1530, the ensuing interrogation revealed that the sect had secret members in at least two Ottobeuren villages.[91] Crypto-Protestantism

---

[87] Scholars have paid very little attention either to the *Urfehde* as an institution or to the documents it generated. A helpful introduction may be found in Andrea Boockmann, "Urfehde und ewige Gefangenschaft im mittelalterlichen Göttingen," *Studien zur Geschichte der Stadt Göttingen* Band 13 (Göttingen, 1980). See also G. Steinwascher, "Die Osnabrücker Urfehdeurkunden," *Osnabrücker Mitteilungen* 89 (1983), pp. 25–59.

[88] Thus, for example, the *Urfehdebrief* of Jacob Ornenberg of Ottobeuren, who turned himself in "of [my] own free will at the pleasure and displeasure [of the Abbot] but my life guaranteed." StAA, KL Ottobeuren 4, Document 291F, ff. 467v–470r [3 Feb. 1526]. Similarly the *Urfehdebrief* of Martin Müller, joiner of Ottobeuren. Ibid., Document 291G, ff. 470r–472v [23 Feb. 1526].

[89] Ibid., Documents 291J, ff. 477r–481r (*Urfehdebrief* of Adam Mayr of Ottobeuren [25 Aug. 1526]), 291O, ff. 491r–493r (*Urfehdebrief* of Hans Konlin of Ottobeuren [3 Feb. 1527]), 293A, ff. 552r–555v (*Urfehdebrief* of Martin Aberöll of Stephansried [9 Feb. 1526]), and 293J, ff. 634r–636r (*Urfehdebrief* of Balthas Traber of Ollarzried [2 Nov. 1525]).

[90] This man has an object of particular vilification in the older monastic chronicles, and this reputation has passed down via Feyerabend into Baumann. In fact, it turns out that he was not even a miller (his surname was "Müller"), and that after intervention by Anna von Freundsberg he was grudgingly allowed by the Abbot to return to his home village. See Feyerabend, *Ottenbeuren Jahrbücher*, Vol. III, pp. 69–70 and Baumann, *Allgäu*, Vol. III, p. 141. The letter of intervention from Anna von Freundsberg has been preserved in StAA, KL Ottobeuren 2, Document 176, ff. 310r–v [14 Feb. 1528].

[91] StAA, KL Ottobeuren 4, Documents 304P, ff. 920r–922r and 308H, ff. 1069v–1072r (*Urfehdebriefe* of Hanns Sumer of Sontheim and Gallus Schmidt of Niederrieden [both 19 May 1530]).

was punished harshly in the monastery lands, and Anabaptists in particular were subjected to incarceration, exile, and the revocation of their land leases.[92] Nevertheless, as late as 1547, more than twenty years after the end of the Peasants' War, the monastery was shocked to discover in the village of Sontheim a "secret clandestine hidden conventicle" of peasants who gathered to listen to heretical sermons. Significantly, the conventicle included leaders of the revolt of 1525. Its activities were also abetted by the reformist sympathies of the local parish priest. The Abbot regarded the very existence of the conventicle as treason pure and simple, and all participants were clapped into prison. The conventicle was dissolved and the priest was banished.[93]

Political opposition among the peasantry was still longer lived. In 1561 a certain Barthlome Schückh – again of Sontheim – was arrested for his "wicked, unseemly and rebellious plots, advice and deeds, [both] secretly and publicly uttered and committed." A specification of these misdeeds is not recorded in his *Urfehdebrief*, but we do know that he was ordered on pain of fines and imprisonment henceforth to avoid all secret gatherings and meetings and was forbidden to come to the officially sanctioned meetings of the *Gemeinde*.[94] The implication is transparent, and the Abbot was to struggle mightily to stamp out shadowy, unofficial village assemblies. His efforts do not, however, seem to have been crowned with success. Although the fragmentary criminal court papers do not reveal what was discussed or achieved at these illicit gatherings, they do record the arrest of dozens of people at a time in the hamlet of Ollarzried (1582)[95] and in the villages of Hawangen (1578),[96] Böhen (1586),[97] Benningen (1597),[98] and Günz (1602).[99]

---

[92] StAA, KU Ottobeuren 1449 [3 Nov. 1553]. Mathias Schwegelin of Böhen loses his lands for having become an Anabaptist. He had been admitted to one *Hof* in 1541 and a second in 1551. In 1546 he ranked in the top 13.5 percent of Böhen taxpayers. StAA, KL Ottobeuren 27, ff. 56r and 90r; KL Ottobeuren 64, ff. 21v–23v.

[93] StAA, KL Ottobeuren 4, Documents 304V–X, ff. 940v–949r (*Urfehdebriefe* of Georg Gerhardt and Paul Wagner of Sontheim, Hans Menneler alias Nestelin and Hans Hölzlin of Sontheim, and Barthlome Bärtlin "now preacher in Wöringen," respectively dated 26, 29, and 16 August 1547). Hans Menneler alias Nestelin not only had participated in the Peasants' War, he had been elected "to the inner Council of Four" of the rebels. Ibid., Document 304M, ff. 909v–913r (*Urfehdebrief* of Hans Menneler alias Nestelin [9 Sep. 1527]).

[94] Ibid., Document 304F, ff. 890v–894v (*Urfehdebrief* of Barthlome Schückh of Sontheim [3 May 1561]). Note that in that same week at least twelve other men were arrested for similar offenses in Sontheim. Ibid., Document 304G, ff. 895r–897r (*Urfehdebrief* of Hans, Jörg, and Heus Stedele, Hans Schneider, Ambrosi Widenmann, Hans Meichelböckh, Martin Schmidt, Augustin Lamp, Blesy Rewel, Jacob Walther, and Hans Grabusser [30 April 1561]). These eleven confessed that "we showed and proved ourselves to be rebellious and in other ways obstinate and disobedient to the authorities." Also ibid., Document 304H, ff. 897r–901r (*Urfehdebrief* of Christa Hörman of Sontheim [3 May 1561]). His offense was word-for-word the same as Barthlome Schückh's.

[95] StAA, KL Ottobeuren 587-I. "Straf- und Frevelregister 1546–1592/3," Heft 12 (1582/3).

[96] Ibid., Heft 9 (1578/9).   [97] Ibid., Heft 14 (1586/7).

[98] StAA, KL Ottobeuren 587-II. "Straf- und Frevelregister 1593–1615," Heft 19 (1597/8).

[99] Ibid., Heft 22 (1602/3).

But opposition to the lordship of the monastery was not always so furtive. Open and even brazen defiance of authority was already apparent in the immediate aftermath of the Peasants' War. The Swabian League's reparations tax, for example, encountered instant resistance from the Ottobeuren peasantry. Often this went no further than public insolence, as in the case of one Niederrieden peasant's remark: "I would gladly pay the reparations tax if only the Peasants' War would continue."[100] Other cases were more serious. Claus Guggeisen of Niederrieden made speeches against the tax. He proposed that the village wait and see if others would join the opposition before handing out any money and cursed those of his neighbors who went ahead and paid.[101]

Worse was yet to come. Although upon release from prison the rebels had all sworn new oaths of fealty to the Abbot, many of them went straight back to political agitation. Jerg Schalckh of Frechenrieden reswore his oath, but then turned around and declared, "Had I not [just] sworn [fealty] to my lord, I would never do it again! He is not my lord and I will not have him for my lord!"[102] His neighbor Martin Schorer stood up in front of the officially appointed village council and burst into a series of slogans including "The lesser shall take the place of the greater" and – perhaps less subversively but certainly more pungently – "I shit upon you."[103] Hans Hewel attacked a passing nobleman and attempted to stab and strangle him, all the while howling "I will never swear loyalty to any lord for the rest of my life."[104] Most voluble of all was a certain Ulrich Blenck from the perennial troublespot of Sontheim who

> outrageously and with great impudence and in order that the village should turn false and obstinate and be moved to disobedience did rebuke my gracious lord of Ottobeuren that he [the Abbot] was no spiritual lord and in his dealings worthy of no honor or dignity and in the same way [did rebuke] His Grace the said *Obervogt* and all the other officials and servants in the monastery that they were tyrants and worthy of no honor and did also say I could never gain justice from them and from [the village officials] of Sontheim, who are also villains, the Turk is a juster lord and once I am released [from prison] I will keep no oath [made there].[105]

---

[100] StAA, KL Ottobeuren 4, Document 308E, ff. 1063r–1065v (*Urfehdebrief* of Jörg Deckhler of Niederrieden [14 June 1526]).

[101] Ibid., Document 308D, ff. 1061r–1063r (*Urfehdebrief* of Claus Guggeisen of Niederrieden [25 June 1526]).

[102] Ibid., Document 301B, ff. 810r–813r (*Urfehdebrief* of Jerg Schalckh of Frechenrieden [24 Apr. 1526]).

[103] Ibid., Document 301C, ff. 813r–816r (*Urfehdebrief* of Martin Schorer of Frechenrieden [24 Apr. 1526]).

[104] Ibid., Document 293C, ff. 614r–616r (*Urfehdebrief* of Hans Hewel of Hohenheim [15 Mar. 1526]).

[105] Ibid., Document 304O, ff. 914v–920r (*Urfehdebrief* of Ulrich Blenck of Sontheim [3 Nov. 1529]).

The Abbot's "pacified" subjects, he must ruefully have realized, were as stubborn and refractory as ever.

But if there were limitations on how far the monks could coerce the peasants, there were also limitations on how far the peasants could, or even wanted to, weaken their overlord. The enhanced property rights secured over the course of the fifteenth century now gave the peasants a considerable investment in the lordship of the monastery as the most effective guarantor of those rights. The tenant, it must be emphasized, sought security not only against the fiscal claims of his overlord, but also against the encroachments of his neighbors. Thus in *Erblehen* charters, the monastery routinely promised not only to leave the rent unchanged, but also to warrant the tenant's rights against rival claimants.

Major confrontations between the monastery and its subjects therefore almost always took the form of negotiation. Violent rebellion was rare. Moreover, by the early 1500s, a century's experience of blustering and haggling had established a familiar and reliable formula for peasant negotiation with the monastery. Grievances which the monastery refused to redress were regularly appealed to a higher authority, usually the Holy Roman Emperor. The Emperor would then commission some prominent authority – the Abbot of Weingarten, Truchsess Georg von Waldburg, the Bishop of Augsburg, etc. – as a mediator. Mediation invariably forced the monastery to disgorge at least some concessions, while preserving its essential prerogatives intact.

Occasionally there are indications that the negotiating process was aborted, as in 1499 when the monastery effectively bought off two of its subjects who had filed suit in the *Reichskammergericht* in order to gain imperial confirmation of a charter of freedom.[106] Most of the time, however, overlord and subjects kept to a time-honored script which minimized hostility and embarrassment on both sides. Thus, when Leonhard Widenmann was elected Abbot in 1508, the monastery's subjects were enjoined to swear an oath to remain "true, responsible, liable to service, obedient and servant-like [*Pothmeßig*], to advance His Grace's and [the] cloister's benefit and godliness and to warn [them] of [any] danger . . . and to seek or accept no other defender or protector besides His Grace."[107] The peasants tactfully replied that they would "gladly" accept the new abbot as their lord and swear loyalty to him, "But they [still] had a grievance with His Grace and his cloister regarding wood [use rights], as His Grace knew, and added that they hoped that His Grace would therefore come to an agreement with them about this."[108] The Abbot took the hint – the peasants had already brought the matter before the Holy Roman Emperor – and promptly

---

[106] Copy of the agreement in StAA, KL Ottobeuren 2, Document 139, ff. 226r–228r.
[107] Ibid., Document 149, f. 243r.   [108] Ibid., f. 243v.

concluded an agreement guaranteeing his subjects access to wood for fuel and building.[109]

Of course, the veneer of civility was not always maintained, and the monastery did from time to time simply arrest peasants it suspected of sedition. In 1530, for example, Gregori Epplin of Ollarzried was obliged to confess that in violation of [my oath] I did keep and bear with me a spear and did also a few days ago in the market town of Ottobeuren on the street when ordered by Anthoni Zettler, the bailiff of the Bishop of Augsburg, to pay the head tax, for wicked reasons and out of insolence outrageously declare "I will give you nothing! Instead I will first await the decision of the Diet in Augsburg [although] I doubt I will be satisfied with it in this and other matters." Now were this outrageous talk, which did not become me at all and whereby my [true] intentions may be recognized, to have reached the Common Man, nothing less than another uprising and rebellion like the one which already happened could have resulted.[110]

In this case, however, the monastery seems to have lost its nerve. It had been only five years since the Peasants' War, and Epplin's status as an ex-rebel doubtless made the monks particularly jittery. All the same, the fact that Epplin's offense consisted in refusing to pay taxes pending a ruling by the Imperial Diet underscores the adherence of most peasants to established legal channels of protest. A similar legalism was evinced by six men arrested five years later in Sontheim, who confessed that

in the space of just a few days we did of our own undertaking [and] without the knowledge and permission of our lord two or three times call together and hold a meeting of the village community [Gemeinde] of Sontheim, and did draw up among ourselves a number of pretended articles against our gracious lord and did thus form a conspiracy.[111]

Here again, the "conspiracy" to which these men were obliged to confess bore all the hallmarks – a convocation of the village community, the drafting of articles of complaint, etc. – of time-honored[112] methods of articulating grievances. There is no indication that violence was attempted or even contemplated. In the end, the monastery itself recognized the limited nature of the Sontheimers' challenge; all of the "ringleaders" were released from prison on Urfehde oaths.

---

[109] Ibid., Document 150, ff. 244r–247r. The peasants were divided into four wealth classes. The members of the richest class were to receive 7 claffter of firewood per annum, the members of the next class 4, the next class 3, and then the poorest class 2 claffter of firewood per annum.

[110] Ibid., Document 293K, ff. 636r–640v (Urfehdebrief of Gregori Epplin of Ollarzried [7 Nov. 1530]).

[111] Ibid., Document 304R, ff. 924r–928v (Urfehdebrief of Hans Stelzlin, Thoma Schussman, Bartolme Dreysser, Clas Mayer, Hans Vögelin the Blacksmith, and Hans Widenmann [all 12 Apr. 1535]).

[112] See StAA, KU Ottobeuren 1397 [11 Apr. 1551]. Abbot Caspar grants the peasantry of the hamlet of Günzegg the right of assembly.

Now, to emphasize the negotiated and legalistic nature of these confrontations between the peasants and their overlord is not to pretend that they were amicable, or that concessions were cheerfully made. In all of these instances, the relationship of the two sides was clearly adversarial. At the same time, the great German Peasants' War has cast so long a shadow over the historiography of this era that violent uprising has come to be seen as the most authentic expression of peasant attitudes to lordship. Some historians go so far as to view 1525 as the final consummation of a "crisis of feudalism," when the internal contradictions of lordship in all its forms precipitated "an effort to overcome the crisis . . . through a revolutionary transformation of socio-political relations."[113] I find this apocalyptic vision implausible.

In the first place, the structure of late medieval Swabian lordship proved to be rather more durable than some historians would like, remaining unchanged in its essentials from the close of the fifteenth century to the Napoleonic era. Moreover, and as has been seen, in 1525 the Ottobeuren peasantry were not a people with their backs to the wall. Far from reeling under the assault of a seigneurial reaction, they had been paring back the claims of the monastery and consolidating their own property rights for more than a century.

Indeed, at least at Ottobeuren, the Peasants' War itself began as a traditional form of landlord–tenant bargaining. After some initial tensions between the monastery and the burghers of the market town of Ottobeuren in September of 1524,[114] open discontent erupted in February of 1525 when the villages of Sontheim and Attenhausen refused to swear loyalty to the Abbot. Joined by the residents of the market town and other of the monastery's subjects, the peasants called for a meeting on 20 February to discuss their grievances among themselves.[115] The response of the monastery to these events is highly significant. The Abbot was clearly worried; the monastic chroniclers concede

---

[113] Peter Blickle, *The Revolution of 1525*, trans. Thomas A. Brady Jr. and H. C. Erik Midelfort (Baltimore, 1981), p. 187. The same conclusion (word for word) in the third edition (1993), p. 289.

[114] Franz Ludwig Baumann, ed. *Akten zur Geschichte des deutschen Bauernkriegs aus Oberschwaben* (Freiburg im Breisgau, 1877), no. 58b, p. 35. The actual substance of the dispute is not reported, but a charter issued by Emperor Charles V on 4 November 1524 suggests that it again concerned the autonomy of the market town, centering on the appointment procedures for the *Amman* and *Vierer*. The election procedure underwent a slight modification: instead of the Abbot choosing the *Amman* from two candidates proposed by the *Gemeinde*, the *Gemeinde* was now to choose from two candidates proposed by the Abbot (see Peter Blickle, *Memmingen; Historischer Atlas von Bayern* [1967], Vol. IV, Munich, p. 63. There is a copy of the new agreement in StAA, KL Ottobeuren 2, ff. 304r–305r). It is unclear whether this development represented a victory for the monastery. The Abbot himself was clearly unhappy with the outcome, for in 1536 he complained to the Emperor that the current election procedure allowed for too much meddling by the townspeople, and that the language of the agreement was marred by the "most grievous deficiencies." StAA, KL Ottobeuren 2, Document 183, ff. 331v–333r.

[115] Baumann, *Akten zur Geschichte des deutschen Bauernkriegs*, no. 58b, p. 36.

that he sent to the cities of Ulm and Kempten to buy a few weapons.[116] It is none the less clear from other sources that the Abbot was also willing, indeed eager, to negotiate, and promised his subjects that "what[ever] other peasants [should] receive from dukes, lords, cities or prelates, that they should also receive from him, and [he] was willing to concede this immediately."[117]

Mediated by the *Bürgermeister* and City Council of Memmingen, the negotiations seem to have lasted at least into the beginning of March.[118] Shortly thereafter, however, matters took a turn for the worse, and on 30 March[119] the monastery was stormed and plundered by its own subjects; "not a single foreigner was there," a neighboring chronicler noted.[120] The monastery complex was plundered from end to end. The windows were smashed, the monastery's cattle were driven off, the church was desecrated, and then every scrap of paper the peasants could find was delivered up to the flames.[121] On 8 April the revolt culminated in a posse of spear-toting peasants breaking into the nearby

---

[116] "Abt Leonhard beschickte von Kempten 60 Pf. Pulver, welche damals 7 fl. 44 kr. kosteten, und von Ulm für fünf Gulden Helleparten und Speise. Eine gewiß nicht allzufeindlich gemeinte Rüstung." Feyerabend, *Ottenbeuren Jahrbücher*, Vol. III, p. 33.

[117] The full text of the Memmingen Ratsprotokoll, dated 18 February 1525 is: "Ferner die pfarleut zu Ottobewrn und ander haben auch beschwerung gegen dem abt, derhalb ain tag auf montag [20 Feb.] die bawrschaft under inen zelbs zusamen bei Yttenbewrn uff der Lindaw zusamen zu komen und der andern bawrschaft maynung zu vernemen [angesetzt]. Der Abt het den tag gern gewend, aber das nit erheben mugen. Es hab inen auch der abt zugesagt, was ander bawrn bei fursten, herrn, stetten oder prelaten erlangen, das sollen sy bei ime auch erlangt haben, und wel ihen dasseb yetz schon zugeben haben. Solhs alles hab dem abt nit mugen helfen." Baumann, *Akten zur Geschichte des deutschen Bauernkriegs,* no. 58b, p. 38.

[118] Suggested by the following entry in the Memmingen Ratsprotokolle, dated 1 March 1525: "Den von Yttenbewrn ist die Antwurt geben, ain rat hab bißher trewlich zu in gesetzt, geraten und geholfen als gute nachpawrn, das wel man noch thun und in beholfen und beraten sein, sovil sy inen schuldig seien zu thun und pillich ist, wa sy auch not als gut nachpawrn etwas darin handlen kinden, das erpeut sich ain rat von ainer gantzen gemaind wegen gutwillig." On 15 March the Ratsprotokoll notes that "Den bawrn von Yttenbewrn ist verzigen, den Helfer hinaußzulaßen." Ibid., pp. 39, 41.

[119] The sack is often misdated to 2 April, probably based on the report that day of the incident to the council of the Swabian League by its commander Ulrich Artzt. Wilhelm Vogt, ed. "Die Correspondenz des schwäbischen Bundeshauptmannes Ulrich Artzt von Augsburg aus den Jahren 1524–1527," *Zeitschrift des Historischen Vereins für Schwaben und Neuburg* [henceforth *ZVSN*] 7 (1880), no. 170, pp. 234–6. It is clear, however, from the account in the Irsee monk P. Marcus Furter's "Historia Belli Rusticorum" ("nam diebus ante actis [31 Mar.] ipse Johannes Melder fui in monsterio ottenburano, quod simili modo eorum subdti capitavere") that Ottobeuren was stormed no later than 30 March. Franz Ludwig Baumann, ed., *Quellen zur Geschichte des Bauernkriegs in Oberschwaben* (Tübingen, 1876), p. 329. Artzt must (unsurprisingly) have learned about the incident a few days after it took place.

[120] "Item das clostern Ottobeuren ward eingenomen von den aygnen pauren, kain fremder dabey, das zerrussen sy jämerlich, hielteß in, ach geplindert." Remarks of Nicolaus Thoman, chaplain of the St. Leonharduskapelle in Weissenhorn in his "Weissenhorner Historie." Baumann, *Quellen zur Geschichte des Bauernkriegs in Oberschwaben*, p. 93.

[121] StAA, KL Ottobeuren 4, Documents 291D–G, ff. 461r–472v (*Urfehdebriefe* of Jacob Kimerlin, Jacob Unglert, Jacob Ornenberg, and Martin Müller all of Ottobeuren [21 Oct. 1525, 3 and 26 Feb. 1526]).

Franciscan convent of Maria Garten in search of the Abbot himself. As their quarry had already taken the rather sensible precaution of decamping, however, the angry pursuants were reduced to the fruitless exercise of poking through the haystacks of the surrounding countryside.[122]

Traumatic as this eruption of violence undoubtedly was (and monastic chroniclers would continue to dwell on it for hundreds of years to come), I find it more significant that the peasants had resumed negotiations with the Abbot in less than a week.[123] In other words, before the Treaty of Weingarten (which dissolved the Upper Swabian peasant armies) on 17 April, and long before the armed forces of the Swabian League actually moved into the Ottobeuren lands in early July,[124] the monastery peasants had returned to the traditional form in which the revolt had begun. At least at Ottobeuren, therefore, the Peasants' War does not seem to have aimed at a fundamental transformation of socio-political relations. Instead, the "Revolution of 1525" looks much more like another episode in the time-honored process of negotiation for advantage between the peasants and their overlord, except that this time the process spun briefly out of control.

But if the Peasants' War at Ottobeuren was conventional in both its origins and most of its course, why did it ever take a radical turn at all? This is in fact an old problem, for it has long been recognized that in many regions the rebellion began with a "moderate" phase, followed by a "radical" phase. Some historians have suggested that the peasants were radicalized by the intransigence of their overlords. The more common understanding, however, is that the resort to "Godly Law," i.e. the appeal to the Bible as a test of the legitimacy of the social order, impelled the peasantry to take more drastic action than was possible on the basis of the traditional invocation of custom, or "Old Law."

There is much truth in both of these readings. On the one hand, there is unambiguous evidence that the largest peasant mobilization in the Ottobeuren lands was sparked by the news that the army of the Swabian League was advancing upon them. On the other hand, the activities of crypto-Protestant radicals, above all the parish priest of the village of Sontheim, also played a decisive role in the assault on the monastery. Nevertheless, it is worth pointing out that both of the foregoing visions are conversion narratives, i.e. they also assume that the peasants spoke with a single voice which subsequently changed its tune. This is in many ways an odd assumption, for it has long been known that even at

---

[122] Feyerabend, *Ottenbeuren Jahrbücher*, Vol. III, pp. 53–4.

[123] The peasants met to discuss negotiations on 14 April (ibid., pp. 55–6) and dispatched a letter to the Abbot the following day. Baumann, *Akten zur Geschichte des deutschen Bauernkriegs*, no. 225, p. 238.

[124] The military commander of the League's army, Truchsess Georg von Waldburg, was ordered to restore the Abbot of Ottobeuren (and punish his subjects, "welche sich für ander ungeschickt gehalten haben") only on 4 July 1525. Vogt, ed. "Die Correspondenz des schwäbischen Bundeshauptmannes Ulrich Artzt," *ZVSN* 9 (1882), p. 42 (no. 566).

the high tide of the revolt serious differences of opinion separated the peasant bands within Upper Swabia.

As early as the first week of March 1525, wrangling over the redaction of the peasant army's Field Ordinance revealed the Lake Constance and Allgäu bands to have been much more defensive-minded than the Baltringen band. Indeed, differences were so strong that the Lake Constance and Allgäu bands ultimately did not go to the aid of the Baltringen band when the Swabian League moved against it in April. The scale of this disunity was also known to the League itself, and is much commented upon in the suriviving correspondence between the League and its generals.

Crucially, this dissension seems at times to have had a social dimension. In the Habsburg lands Archduke Ferdinand I went so far as openly to seek the separation of the "notables" among the rebels from the "common rabble." In the same way, Heinz Dopsch has pointed out that during the uprisings in Salzburg in 1525/6, the propertied tenant farmers (*Bauern*) continued to negotiate with the Archbishop while the rural proletariat "who had nothing to lose, joined the revolt en masse." A similar pattern obtained at Ottobeuren: those who sacked the monastery in March were not the same people, and in particular not the same kind of people, who reopened negotiations with the Abbot in April.

By all accounts the Peasants' War began at Ottobeuren in the market town of the same name, and was initially led by the wealthy burgher Hans Konlin, who was elected "highest leader and special councilor and ruler" of the rebels. In the monastery lands as a whole, those who instigated and led the revolt were also overwhelmingly (79.4 percent) drawn from the ranks of the *Bauern*, or *Hof*-tenants.[125] The sack of the monastery, on the other hand, was headed by someone from the opposite end of the social spectrum: a poor *Seldner*, or cottager, and former mercenary from the village of Sontheim who made himself military commander of the revolt's radical phase. This second man is not named in Feyerabend's narrative,[126] but he was almost certainly one Hans Nestelin of Sontheim, to whom the rebels in nearby Kamlach appealed for military assistance,[127] and who later confessed to having been elected

---

[125] See the discussion in my "The Social Origins of the German Peasants' War in Upper Swabia," *Past and Present* 171 (2001), pp. 30–65. The monastery records name ninety-seven instigators and leaders of the revolt. Of these, seventy-seven were *Bauern*, fourteen were *Seldner*, and the remaining six cannot be classified with certainty. Austrian and Salzburg evidence at p. 57.

[126] The man is described by Feyerabend as a *Söldner*, which can mean either "cottager" or "mercenary" (cf. Feyerabend, *Ottenbeuren Jahrbücher*, Vol. III, p. 61 for an instance where *Söldner* unequivocally means "cottager"). The latter reading does gain support from the man's assumption of military leadership, but the two possibilities are hardly mutually exclusive. Not only were mercenaries disproportionately recruited from the humbler ranks of rural society, but Feyerabend's own source, the "Chronologia Ottoburana" of Gallus Sandholzer (*c.* 1600) explicitly describes the man as "a poor *Söldner* from Sontheim" ("ain armer söldner von Sontheim"). StAA, KL Ottobeuren 8 (Mü.B), ff. 717–18.

[127] Pfister Hans zu Kamlach to Hans Nestele, Hauptmann zu Sontheim *c.* 13 April 1525. Vegt, ed. "Correspondenz des schwäbischen Bundeshauptmannes Ulrich Artzt," *ZVSN* 7 (1880), no. 206, p. 269.

to the rebel "inner council of four."[128] He is listed in the 1525 tax roll as a *Seldner*.[129]

Nestelin was by no means the only member of the "radical poor." It is admittedly difficult to divide the rebels of 1525 into "traditionalists" and "radicals." Much of the pillaging was clearly motivated by purely material motives. The Ottobeuren humanist Nikolaus Ellenbog liked to recount the story of a peasant who stole a world map from the monastery; his wife then washed the map off so she could use the linen it was painted on.[130] This said, several of the surviving *Urfehdebriefe* detail actions redolent of a militant opposition to the lordship of the monastery. Although the number of these documents is not large, it is striking that two-thirds of the identifiable "radicals" were the craftsmen and *Seldner* (smallholders) who were underrepresented among the uprising's instigators (see Table 1.2).

Furthermore, there are clear indications that the radical phase of the revolt at Ottobeuren ran against the wishes of the rural elite. Leonhard Hagg, a prosperous tenant farmer (*Bauer*) and the *Amman* of the village of Sontheim, opposed both the revolt and the activities of the crypto-Protestant parish priest, Leonhard Gantner.[131] The April 14 meeting at which it was agreed to resume negotiations with the Abbot was attended by Conrad Steuer, the *Amman* of Altisried, Hans Scheuffelin, the *Amman* of Frechenrieden, and Thoma Schußman of Sontheim – all of them major landholders – and approved by the wealthy Hans Konlin.[132] And all of this at a time when the military commanders of the Winzer and Allgäu bands were appealing to the rebels at Ottobeuren to join in an attack on the Swabian League.[133]

The foregoing sociology of the Peasants' War brings us to a third fundamental feature of Ottobeuren rural society in the later Middle Ages: its subdivision into sharply differentiated and at times antagonistic subsets. If the extension and consolidation of peasant property rights reshaped the relation between overlord and subject, the markedly uneven distribution of those rights among the peasants had equally momentous consequences for the internal sociability of the rural community. By the eve of 1525, the tenurial developments of the previous two

---

[128] "zu einem innigen Rath der Vierer." StAA, KL Ottobeuren 4, Document 304M, ff. 909v–913r, *Urfehdebrief* (copy) of Hans Minneler genannt Nestelin [9 Sep. 1527]. The original charter may be found in StAA, KU Ottobeuren, Neuburger Urkundensammlung G179.

[129] StAA, KL Ottobeuren 541 (2), ff. 36r–41r.

[130] Ellenbog, *Briefwechsel*, 329 [18 May 1534].

[131] StAA, KL Ottobeuren 541 (2), f. 40v; Feyerabend, *Ottenbeuren Jahrbücher*, Vol. III, p. 62.

[132] StAA, KL Ottobeuren 541 (2) ff. 31v, 40r. As will be seen, an *Amman* was by definition a *Bauer*. Feyerabend, *Ottenbeuren Jahrbücher*, Vol. III, p. 55. Feyerabend's account is taken from Sandholzer's "Chronologia Ottoburana," the relevant extract of which is printed in Baumann, *Akten zur Geschichte des deutschen Bauernkriegs*, no. 225a, p. 238.

[133] Martin Purssjäger, commander of the Winzer band, and the commanders of the Allgäu band to the commanders of the Ottobeuren band 13 April 1525: "szo ist main und derselben mainung und beger, das ir wollendt zu uns gen Suntheym rucken und ziehn da werdn wir … unßer faind haimsuchen." Vogt, ed. "Die Correspondenz des schwäbischen Bundeshauptmannes Ulrich Artzt," *ZVSN* 7 (1880), no. 206, p. 269.

Table 1.2 *Social status of Ottobeuren "radicals," 1525*

Name and village	Doc. (StAA, KL Ottob. 4)	Declared offense	Class (from KL 541 [2])
Peter Räwel (Ottobeuren)	291H; 473r–477r	Brought a "heretical priest" to Ottobeuren, received the sacrament in both kinds from him; abolished the singing of the Salve Regina	Tailor
Hans Hewel (Hohenheim)	293C; 614r–616r	Attacked passing nobleman; attempted to kill him, shouted "I will never swear loyalty to any lord for the rest of my life"	Bauer
Balthas Traber (Ollarzried)	293J; 634r–636r	Preached "misleading heretical materials, called Lutheran"	Seldner
Johann Ruoff (Schoren)	293L; 640v–642v	Declared that nothing should be given to lords or creditors	Seldner[a]
Caspar Maier (Niederdorf)	297A; 738r–741r	Shouted "I want to help strangle the monks" and helped search for them	Tailor, Seldner
Balthas Weidle (Wolfertschwenden)	298A; 751v–753r	Forced the parish priest to say mass in German	Bauer
Jerg Unglert Sr. (Wolfertschwenden)	298B; 753v–758v	Declared "What good is that heap of stones, the monastery? It should be burned"	Bauer
Jerg Schalckh (Frechenrieden)	301B; 810r–813r	Declared "The Abbot of Ottobeuren is not my lord . . . I will not have him for my lord"	Seldner
Gori Schütz (Attenhausen)	303A; 835v–838v	Wanted "to establish the Gospel . . . according to my own understanding"	Seldner

Note: [a] Johann Ruoff is not actually listed in the 1525 tax roll, but since Schoren was a tiny hamlet of only five households, all of them *Bauern*, we can be virtually certain that he was not a *Bauer*. StAA, KL Ottobeuren 541 (2), f. 56v. Note that Ruoff's *Urfehdebrief* is dated 15 September 1525, only one week after the tax roll itself was compiled (7 September 1525), so there is no reason to believe he was absent at the time of assessment.

centuries had endowed the propertied with an interest in both the landholding regime and lordship in general which the rural poor did not share.

To be sure, the gap between rich and poor did not originate in the fifteenth century. Explicit references to cottage-cum-garden parcels, or *Selden*, appear at Ottobeuren as early as 1332 and in other Swabian lordships as early as 1236. More general evidence for the existence of smallholdings is older still and can be found in monastic charters of foundations such as Steinheim near Dillingen (1135/40) and Annhausen am Brenz (1143).[134] As far back as the historical

[134] Grees, *Ländliche Unterschichten*, pp. 10–23, 84–95.

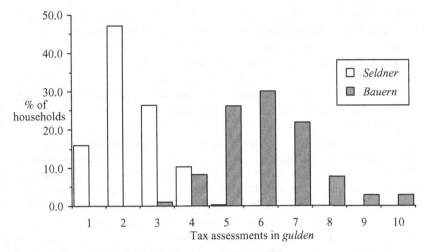

Figure 1.3 Wealth distribution in nine Ottobeuren villages, 1525
Note: The nine villages in question were Dietratried, Frechenrieden, Hawangen, Niederrieden, Ober- and Unterwesterheim, Oberwolfertschwenden, Schlegelsberg, and Sontheim. The *Halbbauern* have been counted as *Bauern*.
Source: StAA, KL Ottobeuren 541 (2)

record extends, therefore, the Swabian peasantry was a heterogeneous amalgam of rich and poor. Moreover, the scramble for tenants in the wake of the Black Death meant that the material conditions of the poor almost certainly improved during the century and a half which followed. All the same, the reality of rural poverty persisted none the less, and with the increasing juridification of social relations in the fifteenth century, the differences between rich and poor were formalized into glaring prominence in almost every facet of late medieval life on which documentation has survived.

The aftermath of the Peasants' War is in this respect as revealing an occasion as the uprising itself. For example, the reparations tax imposed by Abbot Leonhard upon his reinstatement was based on a fixed average amount to be collected per household, with each settlement left to apportion the burden among its members according to their wealth. Analysis of the tax register generated by this process produces three interesting results. First, the rural population was explicitly divided in the manuscript – apparently by the decision of the various *Gemeinden* – into two distinct groups: *Bauern* and *Seldner* (plus an occasional *Halbbauer*). Second, the two groups were sharply separated in terms of wealth (see Figure 1.3). Third, the decidedly poorer *Seldner* already made up 62.7 percent of the households. The compensatory labor services imposed at the same time also recognized the dichotomy: the *Seldner* were to provide a day's work with their hands while the *Bauern* owed a day's work with a team of draught animals. The *Bauer/Seldner* boundary was thus the Swabian expression of that fundamental articulation of the West European peasantry: the distinction between those villagers who were substantial enough to operate a plough and team and those who were not.[135]

In and of itself the *Bauer/Seldner* divide is of course unremarkable, and the picture of a countryside dominated by a class of prosperous tenant farmers is by now a historiographical commonplace. It is less well appreciated, however, that the rural elite's disproportionate share of economic resources went hand in hand with a stranglehold on the institutional expression of the rural community, i.e. the offices of the *Gemeinde*. The rural *Gemeinde* is something of a sacred cow in the literature on the German peasantry; it has apparently become impossible to discuss landlord–tenant relations without solemnly proclaiming "the bearer of resistance was the *Gemeinde*." It is less often asked precisely *who* we mean by the *Gemeinde*. In theory most Swabian rural *Gemeinden* were composed of all the adult males in the village. The "community" thus did include both *Bauern* and *Seldner*, although women and day laborers were excluded. In terms of the actual exercise of authority, however, the *Gemeinde* at Ottobeuren consisted of a decidedly small group of people holding two kinds of offices: first, the *Amman*, or mayor, and second, the *Vierer*, or members of the "council of four." In formal documents the *Amman* and *Vierer* regularly spoke "in the name of the entire *Gemeinde*." With these five men we might also group the two churchwardens, who among other things oversaw the lending of parish funds (at 5 percent interest) to those in need of liquid capital.

At Ottobeuren, both the *Amman*[136] and the *Vierer*[137] were appointed by the Abbot himself. The only exception to this rule was the market town of Ottobeuren, where the Abbot chose between two candidates proposed by the *Gemeinde*.[138] What kind of people were appointed to these offices? The rich. A complete list of the Ottobeuren *Ammänner* is available for the year 1564.[139] *Every single one of them* was a current or recently retired *Hof* tenant.[140] Indeed, the link to property holding was so explicit that an *Amman* was often invested

---

[135] Further clarification is provided by a c. 1551 ordinance requiring every *Hof* to be equipped with a plough and a wagon. StAA, KL Ottobeuren 4, Document 289X, ff. 368v–369r; "Bauding Buch Anno 1551 – Concerning the parish and inhabitants of Ottobeuren: Item the following articles govern all those who hold and work properties under *Gotteshausrecht*." Identical provisions for those holding properties under this form of tenure in the nucleated villages are detailed on ff. 372r–v.

[136] StAA, KL Ottobeuren 4, "Rotulus Probationum," Document 303A, ff. 835v–838v (1525).

[137] This is clear from StAA, KU Ottobeuren 433 [6 Oct. 1485].

[138] Blickle, *Memmingen: Historischer Atlas von Bayern*, p. 63.

[139] The document in question is StAA, KL Ottobeuren (Mü.B) 25, "Leibeigenbuch 1564," which has been edited as Richard Dertsch, ed. "Das Einwohnerbuch des Ottobeurer Klosterstaats vom Jahre 1564," *Allgäuer Heimatbücher* 50 [*Alte Allgäuer Geschlechter* 34] (1955).

[140] Names of *Ammänner* checked against StAA, KL Ottobeuren 30, "Gültbuch 1567" and KL Ottobeuren 27, "Erdschatzbuch 1576–1603." Note that Hans Bürklin, the *Amman* of Ober-westerheim, held his *Hof* from the Heilig-Geist Spital in Memmingen, rather than from the monastery of Ottobeuren. StAA, KL Ottobeuren 744b.

with his office and *Hof* at the same time.[141] Although the monastery controlled appointment, the office sometimes passed from father to son.[142] The social origins of the *Vierer* were no different. Although they are less often identified in the surviving records, twenty different *Vierer* from five different villages can be identified in the Ottobeuren notarial protocols for the year 1583/4;[143] fully 95 percent of them were *Hof* tenants or (in the market town of Ottobeuren) among the wealthiest burghers in the town. Even the position of churchwarden, which was an explicitly elected office,[144] was dominated by the same elite. Some twenty-two churchwardens can be identified from the period 1580–4; 91 percent of them were *Hof* tenants or wealthy townsmen.[145]

The monopolization of community offices by the rich does not mean that the *Gemeinde* was merely a vehicle for their own self-interest. It does mean, however, that the efforts to expand the autonomy and competence of the *Gemeinde* (widely regarded as one of the driving impulses of 1525) lay primarily in the interests of the rural elite.[146] And even if the *Gemeinde* could not be "run" in the naked or exclusive interest of the *Vollbauern*, it certainly could be – and was – run disproportionately in their favor.

The classic instance of this practice was the administration of village common lands. Most Swabian communities allotted "shares" of the common land use rights in proportion to the size of a peasant's landholding.[147] A *Bauer* was

---

[141] Thus, for example, the following passage in StAA, KL Ottobeuren 27, f. 211r: "Anno [15]39 ist Jergen Knab der Maÿerhoff zue Niderrieden sambt dem Aman ampt daselbst verlihen worden mit dem andern Anhang, ob er sich im Ambt ettwaß dem Gotzhaus widerwerttig halten oder denselben nach deß Gotzhaus Nutz nitt threwlich außwarten wurde, daß alsßdan mein gnediger Herr Mach hab, ime ab dem Maÿerhoff sambt dem Ambt widerumb zupiette[n]."

[142] For example, when Balthas Brög, the *Amman* of Attenhausen in 1548, died, his widow, Ursula Negelin, married Blesi Maierrog, who was admitted both to Brög's *Hof* and to the office of *Amman*. Upon Maierrog's death in 1568, property and office passed to his stepson Paul Brög (Balthas' son), who remained *Amman* until his death in 1593. StAA, KL Ottobeuren 600, "Leibeigenbuch 1548," f. 237v; KL Ottobeuren 27, ff. 125v, 128v, 133r. See also KL 30, ff. 69r–73r and KL 31, "Gültbuch 1584," f. 7r.

[143] *Vierer* named in StAA, KL Ottobeuren 901, "Amtsprotokolle 1583–4," ff. 25r (Benningen), 49r (Ottobeuren), 53v (Böhen), 67v–68r (Frechenrieden), and 92v (Niederrieden). Identifications from StAA, KL Ottobeuren 27, KL Ottobeuren 31, and KL Ottobeuren 676a, "Steuerregister der Markt Ottobeuren 1585." The townsmen were in the richest 14 percent of taxpayers.

[144] See the names of those "zu hailgen pfleger erwelt" in StAA, KL Ottobeuren 701, "Einkommen der Pfarrei Sontheim 1527–36."

[145] Churchwardens named in StAA, KL Ottobeuren 901, ff. 45r (Sontheim), 60v–61r (Böhen), 62r (Dietratried), 122v (Ollarzried), 137r–v (Ottobeuren), and KL Ottobeuren 918, "Amtsprotokolle 1576–80," ff. 12r (Niederdorf), 15v–16r (Altisried), 20r (Niederrieden), 46v–47r (Benningen), 58v–59r (Egg), and 69v (Schlegelsberg). Identifications as in note 141, also StAA, KA Ottobeuren 344, "Höfe und deren Verkauf zu Sontheim" and KL 491-I (3), "Leibhennenbuch 1587." The townsmen were in the richest 7 percent of taxpayers.

[146] As argued by David Warren Sabean, *Landbesitz und Gesellschaft am vorabend des Bauernkriegs: eine Studie der sozialen Verhältnisse im südlichen Oberschwaben in den Jahren vor 1525* (Stuttgart, 1972), p. 102.

[147] That this was also the case at Ottobeuren is clear from StAA, KL Ottobeuren 27, f. 94r. On 27 March 1581 Jerg Schmidt of Böhen was admitted to a *Hof* from which the monastery had separated 6 *tagwerk* of meadow and leased them to the village innkeeper, "darbey auch

entitled to maintain more livestock on the common meadow than a *Seldner*. He was allowed to take more wood from the common forest[148] and was allotted a larger parcel of the common meadow when it was temporarily divided up and converted to arable land. The sixteenth century saw the beginning of a protracted struggle over this institutionalized inequity, as the *Seldner* – who felt the inferiority of their rights rather keenly – agitated for equal access to the common lands as a mechanism to counterbalance the growing disparity of wealth in the villages.[149]

At Ottobeuren, the best example of this kind of bias comes from the village of Böhen. When faced with the monastery's demand for reparations taxes in the aftermath of 1525, the *Gemeinde* decided that there were fourteen *Seldner* householders in the village liable for payment. Eleven years later, however, by which point the number of *Seldner* had increased to about twenty-five,[150] the *Gemeinde* decided that it was rather differently constituted. In 1536 the Böhen *Gemeinde* contracted an agreement with the monastery to clear and convert to meadow a wooded area near the village. The "larger part" of the cleared land was then to be assigned to the large farms held by the *Bauern*. The "smaller part" was to go to the village *Seldner*, who were declared to be only nine in number and were also required in exchange to surrender their collective rights to all but two *jauchert* of a pair of wooded areas known as the Bannholz and the Schweinwald.[151]

These manifest biases in the day-to-day operations of the Ottobeuren *Gemeinde* were equally evident in its conflicts with its overlord. Clashes between the monastery and its subjects can be documented as far back as the end of the thirteenth century, and by the 1460s the peasants were able to co-ordinate resistance in all of the monastery villages through the institution of the village mayorships.[152] Nevertheless, the demands of these rural "communities" – many of which later reappeared in the Twelve Articles, the manifesto of the Peasants' War of 1525 – often disproportionately reflect the interests of village oligarchs.

---

abgerödt, das Schmid denn uffschlag mit seinem viehe, nichtsdestoweniger wie von alters hero *one abgang* haben, niessen und gebrauchen soll" (emphasis mine).

[148] See note 109.

[149] Hermann Grees, *Ländliche Unterschichten und Ländliche Siedlung in Ostschwaben*, Tübinger Geographische Studien, Heft 58 [Sonderband 8] (1975), pp. 27–41. Similarly Hans-Hermann Garlepp, *Der Bauernkrieg von 1525 um Biberach a.d. Riß* (Frankfurt a.M., 1987), pp. 113–17.

[150] Interpolating between the counts of twenty-nine households in 1525 (KL 541 [2], ff. 68r–69v) and forty households in 1546 (KL 64, ff. 21v–23v). The number of *Bauern* remained unchanged between these two dates. See also StAA, KL Ottobeuren 29, ff. 55v–57v.

[151] StAA, KL Ottobeuren 18, "Lehenbuch 1550," ff. 225r–226r. This volume is actually a *Kopialbuch*, or collection of document copies, recording land tenure charters (*Lehensreverse*) from the period 1300–1551.

[152] See the charter dated 19 October 1464 whereby the assembled *Ammänner* of all of the Ottobeuren villages refuse to pay taxes to the Bishop of Augsburg in StAA, KL Ottobeuren 2, ff. 151r–154r.

Table 1.3 *Mean tax payment (kreuzer) in five Ottobeuren villages, 1546–8*

Village	Ottobeuren serfs		Serfs of other lords		Freemen	
	N	kr.	N	kr.	N	kr.
Attenhausen	40	31.6	2	20.0	9	12.2
Frechenrieden	44	31.9	6	9.0	7	24.4
Sontheim	48	35.7	8	18.6	26	14.5
Günz	13	48.6	4	85.5	8	12.6
Egg	29	65.9	9	30.3	16	17.9
Total	174	39.8	29	29.6	66	15.8

Source: StAA, KL Ottobeuren 64, 600

Since 1299, the most common source of friction at Ottobeuren (as elsewhere in Upper Swabia) was the death duties collected by the monastery from its serfs.[153] The basic objection of the peasantry was that these death duties defeated inheritance. The actual material impact of these death duties will be discussed in chapter 3, but for the time being I would like to focus on the question of precisely *who* was liable for these payments. The primary mechanism for enserfment at Ottobeuren was admission to one of the large *Höfe*. The monastery insisted that only its own serfs were eligible for *Hof* tenancy.[154] The passage from freedom to serfdom thus often also represented formal ascent into the rural oligarchy. Of course, serfdom (like freedom) was also a heritable status, and by the sixteenth century most of the inhabitants of the monastery lands were serfs either of Ottobeuren itself (56.6 percent) or of other lords (20.1 percent). Nevertheless, the imprint on rural society of the original connection between serfdom and *Hof*-tenancy was so strong that Ottobeuren serfs were on average much wealthier than either serfs of other lords or the free (see Table 1.3).

But the privileged status of the Ottobeuren serfs was more than a mere statistical happenstance; it was explicitly reinforced in negotiations between the peasants and their overlord. In 1518, for example, the "entire *Gemeinde*" of Egg concluded an agreement with the monastery over wood usage rights in a nearby forest. The agreement allowed those who leased *Gotteshausrecht Höfe* from the monastery to take wood for building at no cost, but obliged those who held other kinds of property to pay for the same right.[155] Three years later a subsequent agreement introduced a sliding scale of payments for the non-*Hof* tenants, but the basic disparity remained in force.[156]

---

[153] Hoffmann, *Urkunden*, charter no. 52 [6 Mar. 1299].
[154] See for example StAA, KU Ottobeuren 429, *Lehensrevers* [8 Apr. 1485]: Johann Hayden admitted to the smithy in Hawangen; he promises to remain a serf of the monastery.
[155] StAA, KL Ottobeuren 2, "Rotulus Probationum," Document 160, ff. 281r–282r.
[156] Ibid., Document 167, ff. 296r–298v. Those who hauled their wood out with four horses (i.e. the more prosperous peasants) were to pay 2 *kreuzer* for their wood, while those who had only one or two horses to haul their wood were to pay 1 *kreuzer*.

The disparity was also resented. In July of 1521, an Imperial Commission headed by the Abbot of Weingarten and the Truchsess of Waldburg arbitrated a dispute between the Abbot of Ottobeuren and his subjects, "especially those who are affiliated through serfdom to other lords." These serfs of other lords complained that the Abbot barred them from access not only to *Gotteshausrecht* farms, but also to *Erblehen* land. The Abbot cheerfully admitted his refusal to allow those "who were neither born nor raised in his lordship" to buy or rent land "without special conditions," but insisted that he was fully within his rights to do so. In the end, the Commission did extract from the Abbot a promise to treat all of his subjects equally in this respect, "irrespective of whether they are his serfs [or not]."[157] Nevertheless, it is clear that this promise was never really honored. The monastery's registers do record the admission of non-Ottobeuren serfs to *Gotteshausrecht* land in the 1530s and 1540s, but only on condition – the same "special conditions" the Abbot adverted to in 1521 – that they become Ottobeuren serfs.[158]

The other major bone of contention at Ottobeuren was the *Gülten*, or grain rents, collected by the monastery from peasant landholdings. Disputes over these rents flared up in 1408[159] and would later underlie the eighth of the Twelve Articles of 1525. Here again, the grievance was primarily the concern of the rural elite, because the monastery collected grain rents almost exclusively from lands held under *Gotteshausrecht*,[160] almost all of which lands were the large *Höfe* farmed by the *Bauern*. Of course, not everyone who held land under *Gotteshausrecht* was rich, and the rich were not all *Hof* tenants, but the close overlap between the two groups is unmistakable (see Figure 1.4).

Did all these inequities mean that *Bauern* and *Seldner* were constantly at each other's throats? No. Each group needed the other too much to allow for that kind of infighting. Since the *Seldner* almost by definition could not maintain their own draught teams, they needed the help of the *Bauer* to plough their small plots of arable land and to cart produce and other goods. In a similar fashion, it was not possible for the *Bauer* families to meet the labor requirements of working

---

[157] The original charter is apparently no longer extant; there is a copy in StAA, KL 2, "Rotulus Probationum," Document 166, ff. 292v–295r [5 July 1521].

[158] E.g. the grant of a *Hof* in Niederrieden to one Peter Schmidt in 1541: "he shall, however, give himself to the monastery in [*lit.* with] serfdom, otherwise the grant is void." StAA, KL Ottobeuren 27, f. 212r. Even for an Ottobeuren serf, admission to a *Hof* might take place "with the condition, that he, when he marries, shall take a [wife] who is [either] a serf of the monastery, or [who] shall become one without cost to the monastery" (1542) or on condition that the serf's wife and six children "as well as those which they [may] later have" become serfs of the monastery (1538). Ibid., ff. 125r, 81r.

[159] Hoffman, *Urkunden*, no. 174 [31 July 1408].

[160] Comparison of the monastery's rent rolls with its tax registers makes this clear. The pattern is most obvious in the more detailed records of the early seventeenth century, e.g. StAA, KL Ottobeuren 225 ("Gültbuch 1621/2") and KL 102 ("Steuerbuch 1620"), but is already clear in their mid-sixteenth-century counterparts.

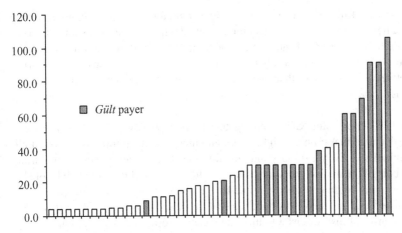

Figure 1.4 Tax payments (kr.) of Böhen households, 1546
Sources: StAA, KL Ottobeuren 29, ff. 68r–69v and KL Ottobeuren 64, ff. 21v–23v

the large *Höfe*, particularly with respect to seasonal and highly labor-intensive tasks such as meadow mowing, grain harvesting, etc. Accordingly, it became a common Swabian pattern for *Bauern* and *Seldner* to hire each other for tasks that they could not or found it difficult to perform for themselves.

Although the existence of these labor-exchange arrangements may seem self-explanatory (and therefore undeserving of further comment), we would do well not to trivialize this aspect of *Bauer–Seldner* relations. Village ordinances often elevated these labor exchanges to the status of formal obligations, such that *Bauern* might be legally prohibited from putting their horses out to pasture before the fields of the *Seldner* had been ploughed. In other villages the local ordinances listed all the services which *Bauern* and *Seldner* were obliged to perform for each other and fixed the wage rates for each. Clearly, then, the reciprocal exchange of labor services across the divide between rich and poor was a central feature of Swabian village life.[161]

But even if relations between *Bauern* and *Seldner* were marked by a significant degree of co-operation, it would be misleading to describe the two groups as mutually interdependent. There is a tautological sense in which the *Seldner* were in much more pressing need of the services and employment opportunities provided by the *Bauern* than vice versa; this kind of dependence is, after all, what poverty has always entailed. And although the inevitable emotional consequences of a position of greater vulnerability – frustration, rage, and no doubt a great deal of envy – only rarely finds voice in the surviving records, it can but have left an indelible mark on social relations in the villages. When Georg

---

[161] Grees, *Ländliche Unterschichten*, pp. 42–8.

Schorer of Buchenbrunnen's chronically bad relations with his neighbors came to a head in 1582, he stationed himself outside their houses and shouted, "You should only work hard and [still] come to nothing! I will make you as poor as I am!"[162] The outburst is a sobering reminder of the harsher side of the disparity between rich and poor that even the most communitarian way of life could not erase.

In 1329 Pope John XXII promulgated the bull *Quia Vir Reprobus*, in which he declared that property rights were an inherent and natural possession of all humankind. Even a solitary individual in the state of nature, simply by virtue of being human, had property rights over those material goods which he or she used. This argument was contested by members of the Franciscan Order, who insisted that property was purely a feature of social life, and in particular of human legal institutions. On this latter view, property was constituted not by the use or possession of an object, but by the owner's ability either to convey his or her right to someone else, or above all to exclude others from the use of the good in question.[163] As philosophy, the papal position has much to commend it, first and foremost its decisive contribution to the first Western theory of inherent universal human rights. As history, however, it obscures much of what was important about the new landholding regime established at Ottobeuren by the beginning of the sixteenth century.

John XXII's conception of property as a relation of person to thing does illuminate part of the significance of the tenurial developments discussed in this chapter. The prospect of more reliably or more exclusively profiting from the fruits of their labors provided the subjects of the monastery with a powerful incentive for greater productivity. Yet important as this perspective is, it suffers from the exclusive preoccupation with the decision-making of the atomized individual producer. By contrast, the Franciscan construction of property as a relationship *between people* with respect to the things allows us to focus on the distinctions and exclusions which necessarily accompanied the formalization of property rights at Ottobeuren. More clearly to specify what a *Bauer* had was also more sharply to demarcate what a *Seldner* did not have. Disparities of property rights segmented rural society into distinct communities of differential general privilege. And property, as shall presently be seen, was only the beginning of these divisions.

---

[162] StAA, KL Ottobeuren 4, Document 291NN, ff. 538r–548v (*Urfehdebrief* of Georg Schorer of Buchenbrunnen [28 Apr. 1584]). Schorer was not a subject of the monastery but hailed from the nearby lands of Jacob Fugger, lord of Kirchberg, Weissenhorn, and Babenhausen. A fugitive from the law, he was arrested at Ottobeuren by the monastery's *Vogt* at Jacob Fugger's request.

[163] Richard Tuck, *Natural Rights Theories: Their Origin and Development* (Cambridge, 1979), pp. 20–4.

2. The discrete society (c. 1480–c. 1560)

Leonhard Hagg of Sontheim was a short-tempered man. Given prevailing peasant notions of honor and personal justice, it might be unfair to call his reactions to life's disappointments those of a bad-tempered man, but a short-tempered man he certainly was. The disappointments themselves were real enough. Leonhard's grandfather had emigrated to Sontheim from Gundelfingen in 1521, acquiring a large *Hof* and fishing rights in the river that ran through the village.[1] He rose to become one of the richest men in Sontheim, and as village *Amman* distinguished himself (in the monastery's eyes, at least) by opposing rebellion during the Peasants' War of 1525.[2] With his death in the 1530s,[3] however, decline rapidly set in. It was not so much that the family lost its wealth, but rather that precious little of it – only the fishing rights – came to Leonhard's own family. By Leonhard's boyhood in the mid-1540s, his own father, Johann, had plummeted into the poorer half of Sontheim's households, struggling to pay the rent for the fishwater while Leonhard's grandmother retained both the *Hof* and her place among the Sontheim oligarchs.[4] Leonhard's father didn't give up, and in 1550 he managed to secure the lucrative lease to the Sontheim inn.[5] Leonhard was able to marry, and by the time of his father's death in 1563, the heir apparent to the inn already had several children.[6] But it was not to be. The Abbot transferred

---

[1] StAA, KU Ottobeuren 923 [7 Jan. 1521]. The *Hof* measured 63 *jauchert*. KL Ottobeuren 27, f. 146r [13 Feb. 1592].

[2] Leonhard Hagg senior's 1525 tax payment put him in the top 5 percent of the village households. StAA, KL Ottobeuren 541 (2), ff. 36r–41r. For his activities during the uprising, see Chapter 1, pp. 40–1.

[3] StAA, KL Ottobeuren 4, Document 304Q, ff. 922r–924r [17 Nov. 1531] and Document 3045, 928v–934r [30 Feb. 1539].

[4] StAA, KL Ottobeuren 64, ff. 50r–52v, KL Ottobeuren 409, f. 23r; KL Ottobeuren 29, f. 72v. For a widow to be a *Hof*-tenant was a most unusual (and invariably temporary) arrangement; see below, pp. 54–5.

[5] StAA, KL Ottobeuren 27, f. 140r.

[6] StAA, KL Ottobeuren (Mü.B) 25, f. 106. Leonhard's *Urfehdebriefe* suggest that his father died in 1563.

the lease of the inn to a cousin, who, as it happens, had previously snapped up Grandfather Hagg's *Hof*.[7] Leonhard lost his temper. "The inn rightfully belongs to and should have been leased to me!" he shouted as the churchwarden vainly tried to calm him down. "I'll shit in the Abbot's cape and on his bald head!" He lost his temper again when the hospital of Memmingen canceled his lease on a meadow for non-payment of rent. Leonhard threatened both the new tenant and the *Pfleger*, or administrator of the hospital, vowing that he would kill "at least one of them, and where one arquebus wouldn't do would buy two." We don't even know why he lost his temper with Augustin Lamp, although Lamp was himself hardly a model of Christian forbearance, having the previous year been found guilty of murder.[8] Leonhard missed Lamp with his gaff hook; Lamp's horse wasn't so lucky and was seriously wounded.

The affair with his dead brother's son Hans began at least in the same way: there was a dispute, and Leonhard insulted his nephew. Here the pattern changes, for Hans was as proud as the next man and refused to let the insult pass. Instead of replying either in kind or with his fists, however, Hans resolved to take his uncle to court. This struck a nerve, for Leonhard regarded potential intervention by the authorities as unwelcome in the extreme. Accordingly, he confronted Hans in the village and remonstrated with him to leave the matter alone. The nephew proved obdurate, and Leonhard's temper again got the better of him. He struck Hans with the flat of a machete and knocked him to the ground. This, understandably, only deepened the nephew's resolve to seek legal redress. Hans picked himself up and headed for the market town of Ottobeuren. Leonhard went barreling after him on horseback. He overtook Hans just outside the village of Attenhausen and rode him into the ground. His fury still unabated, Leonhard leapt from his horse and proceeded to pummel his nephew's prostrate body. A shocked passerby who called out for peace was told to hold his tongue or he would suffer the same fate.[9]

Reluctant as we may be to dignify Leonhard's brutality through reference to an underlying principle, there was clearly more at work in this last act of violence than a short temper alone. For Leonhard,[10] as for most of the Abbot's subjects, the distinction between kin and non-kin was a boundary of enormous moral

---

[7] StAA, KL Ottobeuren 30, ff. 73r–77r.

[8] StAA, KL Ottobeuren 4, Document 304AA, ff. 956r–963r [7 Mar. 1566]. Lamp had been paroled on an *Urfehde* oath.

[9] StAA, KL Ottobeuren 4, Documents 304J and 304BB, ff. 901r–906r [8 Feb. 1563] and ff. 963v–969r [3 Mar. 1567].

[10] Leonhard's story has a fairly happy ending. He regained the fishing rights, married one Elisabeth Stroheubler after the death of his first wife, Margareta, and lived on in the village into his late fifties or early sixties. At Leonhard's death in 1593, his son Enderas was admitted not only to the fishing rights, but to a large *Hof* of his own. StAA, KL Ottobeuren 27, f. 157r; KL Ottobeuren 102, ff. 333v–334r.

significance. Such was the respect accorded to the ties of blood and marriage that contact was maintained with relatives as far away as the Rhineland.[11] For a relation actually to invite interference by the authorities in the matters of kin was therefore to subvert the most basic social category of village life.[12]

If an insider's betrayal of the integrity of the kin group could bring down (or in Leonhard's case intensify) the wrath of other members, an outsider's affront was even more likely to provoke retribution. Allegiance to the kin group produced a sense of collective honor such that vengeance was often sworn on behalf of aggrieved relatives. Thus when Jacob Müller's three sons were arrested in 1566, he declared that he would revenge himself on the "bodies and properties" of those responsible.[13] Gallus Jung of Sontheim was still more explicit. After his wife was fined for an infraction in 1559, the enraged Gallus "did with many threatening words let it be known that [he] would kill and strike dead those who were responsible for [his] wife's fine."[14]

Not surprisingly, the peasants also felt that loyalty to the kin group transcended obligations to any external authority. Simon Bürklin of Egg was apprehended by the village *Pittel*, or sheriff, in 1532. The *Pittel* was attempting to transfer him to prison in the market town of Ottobeuren, when he was spotted by Bürklin's brother Peter. Howling "Thief! Villain! Traitor!" Peter called together a collection of relatives and friends who then mounted a mass attack on the unfortunate *Pittel*.[15] This resistance to outside interference actually had a quasi-legal status. Attacking the *Pittel* was of course illegal, but the monastery's ordinances none the less extended a certain amount of deference to the kin of an offender. Let us consider the following passage from the "Bauding Buch Anno 1551":

> Item when my gracious lord, or His Grace's *Vogt* and officials send out a bailiff to catch and apprehend a [criminal], all those [who live] at the place sent to shall do nothing illegal or unpeaceful against the said bailiff either with words or deeds, actions or intentions, and whosoever shall be called upon to assist the said bailiff, be he *Amman*, *Vierer* or *Hauptmann*, judge or court official, shall do so without [any] objection, *unless he who is called upon to help is by blood a member of the family or lineage of the person who is to be arrested*, [in which case] he shall stand [aside] quietly and not interfere in the matter, and whosoever shall do so in any way, [whether] greatly or

---

[11] StAA, KL Ottobeuren 4, Document 293Q, ff. 656r–659v [20 Oct. 1558].
[12] In this regard see also the case of Adam Maier of Rempolz, who was arrested for illegal financial dealings with Jews. He suspected his brother Ulrich of involvement with his arrest and seems to have threatened him on that account. After release from prison Adam was required to swear an *Urfehde* oath not only to the authorities but also to his brother. Ibid., Document 293F, ff. 621r–627v [20 May 1549].
[13] Ibid., Document 295J, ff. 729v–735v [26 Oct. 1566].
[14] Ibid., Document 304D, ff. 885v–888v [20 Mar. 1559].
[15] Ibid., Document 309D, ff. 1137–1142r [1 Apr. 1532].

slightly, he shall whether man or woman be punished for his actions on his body and property.[16]

The monastery harbored few illusions about where the primary loyalty of its subjects lay.

It may seem perverse to center a discussion of kinship around the violence generated by the imperative of group loyalty. Kinship has a host of different meanings, and is in any case more commonly analyzed by historians and anthropologists as a way of regulating access to property and marriage partners.[17] On this view, the habit of distinguishing kin from non-kin is best understood in terms of its social function. My interest at this point, however, is more basic. I wish to focus on the habit of drawing distinctions itself.

All societies, of course, draw at least some distinctions between the kinds of their members. What is noteworthy at Ottobeuren is the pervasiveness, rigor, and especially the public nature of the boundaries between categories of people, even within the intimate world of the village. Moreover, the import of these demarcations was not merely their outcome, i.e. that they powerfully influenced an individual's rights, obligations, opportunities, and dangers (although this was certainly also the case). The compartmentalization of kinds of people made peasant life what it was; it was a constitutive feature of sixteenth-century rural society.[18]

The boundary between men and women was perhaps the most fundamental distinction of persons. Enemies could perhaps become friends, outsiders could with the right connections change their place of residence, and non-kin could marry into a lineage, but the disabilities placed on women were permanent. Women could not hold any community office. Each village did have an official midwife, but this was not a position which carried any political authority and was in any case subordinate to the village *Amman*.[19] Women could not be tenants of *Erblehen* or *Gotteshausrecht* land. On rare occasions women were admitted to *Gotteshausrecht* farms, but this was invariably an interim solution prompted by the premature death of a husband or father. As soon as the designated male heir

---

[16] Ibid., Document 289X, ff. 380v–381r.

[17] There is a helpful overview in David Warren Sabean, *Kinship in Neckarhausen, 1700–1870* (1998), pp. 2–36. Sabean himself argues that "perhaps it is best to take a less preprogrammed view and regard kinship as an 'idiom' through which a great many relations are conceptualized and a great many transactions are negotiated" (p. 6).

[18] Similar disscussions of the centrality of boundary in German rural life may be found in Hermann Heidrich, "Grenzübergänge. Das Haus in der Volkskultur der frühen Neuzeit" in Richard van Dülmen, ed., *Kultur der einfachen Leute: Bayerisches Volksleben vom 16. bis zum 19. Jahrhundert* (Munich, 1983), pp. 17–41 and John Theibault, *German Villages in Crisis: Rural Life in Hesse-Kassel and the Thirty Years' War, 1580–1720* (Atlantic Highlands, NJ, 1995), pp. 45–66.

[19] StAA, KL Ottobeuren 587-I, Heft 12 (1582/3). Barthlome Lonnettnen and Hans Kharrer of Benningen fined £2 for having resorted to "foreign" midwives "behind the back of the *Amman* and *Vierer*."

reached the age of majority, the *Hof* was transferred to him.[20] Women could own freehold properties, but only under the supervision of two adult male guardians. In this respect women were thus equated with children.

The restriction of a woman's property rights exposed her to considerable danger if her husband was a wastrel, or, in the language of the time, a "bad householder." Michael Blank of Ottobeuren, for example, was a poor man who ranked in the bottom third of the town's taxpayers. He exacerbated his circumstances by sitting in the tavern "from one midnight to the next" and ultimately plunged his wife and children into hunger and destitution.[21] Christa Rapp of Wolfertschwenden was another self-confessed drunkard and waster of his own property, flaws for which he attempted to compensate by repeatedly enlisting as a soldier and then deserting as soon as he received his first wages.[22] The monastery did attempt to intervene in cases like these, and regularly extracted promises from husbands that they would henceforth stay out of taverns or "keep better company."[23] The efficacy of these efforts was undercut, however, by the continued subordination of women to their husbands. Releasing a neglectful husband or father from prison only on condition that he agree to reform may have alleviated the public scandal, but as long as his wife could not assume control of the household, the threat to the family's well-being remained.

The economic vulnerability of women was compounded by their exposure to male violence. This is an unpleasant subject, but the physical abuse of women by men was so persistent a feature of rural life that it cannot be ignored. This does not mean that all or even most women were subjected to violence. We must be sensitive to the nature of the surviving evidence on the character of the early modern family, which for Ottobeuren consists almost exclusively of court records. The Abbot did not issue congratulatory charters to couples who lived together in harmony for thirty years.[24] He did, on the other hand, prosecute husbands who beat their wives, in consequence of which we are much

---

[20] Thus, for example, in Hawangen Johann Sauter's *Hof* passed in 1543 to his widow, Elisabeth Weissenhorn, and upon her death in 1554 to their son Johann Sauter junior (who must then have been quite young as he lived until 1601). In Dietratried Anthoni Lang's *Hof* was entrusted at his death in 1552 to a daughter, Catharina, who retained it only until a son, Stoffel, was able to take over the property in 1556. Similarly, the widow of Ulrich Hegel of Attenhausen was admitted to her deceased husband's *Hof* in 1534, but shortly thereafter the *Hof* passed to her son Alexander. StAA, KL Ottobeuren 27, ff. 14r [3 Sep. 1543], 15v [6 Aug. 1554], 33v [9 Mar. 1601], 65r [6 Mar. 1552], 65v [20 Feb. 1556], 125r [undated 1534 and 2 Aug. 1538].

[21] StAA, KL Ottobeuren 64, ff. 44r–46v, KL Ottobeuren 4, ff. 529r–v [13 Mar. 1550].

[22] Ibid., Document 298F, ff. 767v–768v [22 Feb. 1557].

[23] Ibid., Document 308O, ff. 1085r–1086v [8 June 1564].

[24] The nearest equivalent that I have been able to find is the burial record of one Georg Depperich, a weaver of Hawangen, who was buried on 10 July 1704. Depperich is described as "tentor Hawangensi, vivens cum una uxore Anna Hiemerin in matrimonio pacifice et exemplariter 45 anni, aetatis suae 64 annorû circiter." Hawangen Parth register [hereinafter HawPR], Vol. II, f. 31.

better informed about the unhappier than the happier side of domestic life at Ottobeuren.

Moreover, it is highly significant that all of the surviving evidence on domestic violence comes from the records of its punishment in the courts. At least as far as the monastic authorities were concerned, the physical abuse of a wife was not merely disapproved of but stigmatized as a crime. Of course, the domestic ideal envisioned by the Abbot would not satisfy contemporary notions of marital equality. Wives were expected to defer to and obey their husbands, and the courts would also prosecute women for such offenses to femininity as "riding around the fields like men" (i.e. astride the horse instead of side-saddle).[25] Nevertheless, even on an unsympathetic interpretation, it cannot be denied that the monastery upheld the principle that although a wife was subordinate to her husband, she was to be treated with honor and respect.

Indeed, so concerned was the Abbot for domestic harmony among the peasantry that he often took up the role of marriage counselor to his own subjects. In 1535, for example, the Abbot called in a certain Christoff Aberöll of Stephansried, who had mistreated his wife and driven her out of the house. After determining that the man had no real grounds for complaint against his wife "other than that she is from her mouth somewhat sharp with words," the Abbot patiently advised him to let his wife come home and henceforth to live with her honorably and to treat her properly as befit a pious husband. This, the Abbot added, would doubtless please God the Almighty and make Aberöll and his wife praiseworthy and honorable in the world. If in the future Aberöll had legitimate reasons for not living with his wife, the Abbot continued, he should take up the matter with the episcopal consistory in Augsburg. Aberöll's own tongue turned out to be as sharp as his wife's, and he retorted that even if he had no formal complaints against her, "if my wife comes into our house through the front door I shall leave her and our children by the back door and stay no longer with them together." The Abbot was not amused and clapped Aberöll into the dungeon until he changed his tune.[26]

Despite the monastery's good intentions, however, there was in practice little that it could do to control the domestic behavior of errant men. Ten years after his exchange with the Abbot, Christoff Aberöll was back in court, this time because

> I did some time ago take into service a dissolute woman, who also has a still-living husband and . . . with her I committed the sin of unchastity and impregnated her . . . and through my harsh conduct, unseemly strokes and blows, [I] caused my good wife to leave me, our children and her marital home and flee into lamentable destitution.[27]

[25] StAA, KL Ottobeuren 587-I, Heft 14 (1586/7), Egg.
[26] StAA, KL Ottobeuren 4, Document 293B, ff. 555v–561v [27 July 1535].
[27] Ibid., Document 293C, ff. 561v–569v [20 Apr. 1545].

There followed the usual stint in prison, another vow to reform, and a promise by his relatives to pay a staggering fine of 200 *gulden* if Christoff ever broke his oath . . . and within four years Christoff was again in trouble for (among other infractions) not having put away a certain Margaretha Schwärzler.[28]

Christoff was not alone in his behavior. The Ottobeuren court records are littered with cases in which wives were chased out of the house, beaten, threatened with death, and even attacked with weapons by their husbands. At times it is clear that heavy drinking lay behind this violence; at times it seems that we have simply encountered a monster. To judge by the following confession from 1569, Marx Fünckh of Attenhausen fell into the latter category:

[I confess that] I did for a long time treat my spouse and housewife most abusively and dishonorably and did drag her around and beat her to such an excessive and unseemly degree that the neighbors and even my own friends and relatives bewailed [the situation] and were repeatedly [and] properly moved to take pity on and endure with her, and also I did not only at the time when she was with child stamp on her most monstrously with my feet and pitilessly cover her with many blows, but even [when she was] in childbed and after [the delivery did] treat her so injuriously in violation of [both] divine and natural law that both she and the child repeatedly feared for and were in great danger to their lives and limbs.[29]

Difficult though it may be to make sense of individual cases, there were two general features of rural life which undoubtedly contributed to the abuse of women. The first, quite simply, was the almost universal conviction among men that women were an essentially different and inferior sort of being. This justified a woman's subjection to her husband's authority and thereby to his chastisement. When men were prosecuted for domestic violence, it is often clear that the offense was that the husband "did beat his wife excessively" or "did often [and] in a senseless manner beat his wife most cruelly," rather than that he beat her at all.

Even the rare case of a husband who refused to beat his wife at all turns out to be less encouraging than it first appears. In September of 1541, a wood turner by the name of Thomas Gross was arraigned for slandering the wife of one Veit Motz of Ottobeuren. Gross had told Motz that his wife had "a wicked, lying snout" and demanded that Motz punish her "so that she stop telling lies" about him. Motz's reply, according to the witness Gertrauta Lachenmaier, was that "he had nothing for which to punish her, for she was older than he. He had a pious, honorable wife from whom he had honorable children." Noble as this declaration may seem, the more detailed account of a second witness casts Motz's refusal in a different and decidedly less edifying light:

---

[28] Ibid., Document 293D, ff. 569v–576r [26 Oct. 1549].
[29] Ibid., Document 303M, ff. 869v–872r [12 Nov. 1569].

Simon Dietz, burgher of Ottobeuren, testifies . . . that the turner went to Veit Motz and told him he had something to discuss with him. "Talk to your wife so that she leaves me . . . unslandered, and punish her as well. If you do not punish her so that she leaves me unslandered, I will punish her myself." To this Veit Motz said that he, the turner, should punish her. The turner [then] said to Veit, "What did you promise and vow [at your wedding]? Can you not chastise your [own] wife?" Whereupon Veit went home and brought his wife before his, the witness's, door. There the turner said to Veit Motz's wife, "Catherine, why do you harm me by slandering me thus? You have a wicked snout, and should leave me alone!" At this the witness [intervened and] sent her [back] home, for he feared that further discord would ensue.[30]

Veit Motz may have been unwilling to punish his wife himself, but he not only lacked the courage to shield her from the abuse of others, he was weak-willed enough to expose her to it directly.

The second general constituent of violence against women was a habit of predatory male sexuality. Here again, the construction of gender differences as qualitative otherness of being allowed for the view of men as subjects and women as objects. Thus, where a woman would feel constrained to go to court to defend her name from even the suspicion of unchaste behavior, only a man would boast openly of the extent and identities of his conquests.[31] It has already been seen in the case of Christoff Aberöll how a husband's abuse of his wife accompanied his acquisition of another sexual partner. This pattern is evident in several of the court cases, and added the tribulation of public humiliation and ridicule to the wife's physical mistreatment.[32] On occasion the adultery does seem to have been entered into by mutual agreement,[33] but the frequency with which the man's second partner turns out to be a subordinate, typically a servant or even a stepdaughter, underscores the more commonly exploitative nature of these liaisons.

It is in fact perfectly clear that a great many of these male sexual adventures were crimes of violence. Thus Jerg Schmidt and Caspar Maier of Unterwolfertschwenden confessed in 1530 that they

in neglect of our respectable [sic] and married status . . . did criminally, willfully, and with utter violence attempt to commit the works of impurity with [one] Margareta. When, however, she would not comply, and we were

---

[30] StAA, KL Ottobeuren 900, ff. 3v–6r [15 Sep. 1541], on f. 4r.

[31] StAA, KL Ottobeuren 4, Document 294G, ff. 699r–703r [18 Aug. 1555].

[32] StAA, KL Ottobeuren 4, Document 293E, ff. 602v–605v [17 Nov. 1569]; Documents 305A, ff. 975r–977r and 305C, ff. 979r–980v [both 18 Oct. 1527]. The last document explicitly refers to the fact that an adulterer's wife and children "were as a result gravely insulted and mistreated, and deprived of honor and respect."

[33] Ibid., Document 293E, ff. 782v–785r [24 July 1545].

unable to realize our willfullness and desire to do these secret things, with shoves, blows and kicks we did grievously beat her almost to death . . .[34] Or Hanns Helzlin of Böhen, who in 1555 admitted that he "repeatedly with unchaste demeanor did desire of my stepdaughter, that she should surrender her will to me for the purpose of unchastity, and I did a few days ago force myself upon her and would not yield in my desire. Through the help of the Almighty, however, she [was able] to escape from me unstained."[35] Or Michael Kempter of Ottobeuren, who was prosecuted in 1582 because he "knocked down a maid who was in service in [the village of] Benningen, attempted to force her, and tore her belt and keys from her body. Master Thomas Dochtermann [then] came to save her. Kempter chased him around the field with a drawn blade; the maid in the mean time did [manage to] escape."[36] Violence of this sort could crop up even in the context of a marriage proposal. Gallus Schmidt of Niederrieden was determined to marry Ursula Knab, the widow of Hans Dreier. Not satisfied with threatening the lives and property of her other suitors, Schmidt actually broke into the widow's house one night in 1541 "and addressed her with criminal, unseemly words [and] threats."[37]

It will not do to dismiss this violence against and sexual exploitation of women as the aberrant acts of a few deviants. In the first place, the court records demonstrate that several of those prosecuted were repeat offenders, such as Martin Bröll of Niederrieden, who in 1547 and again in 1548 was found to be maintaining a concubine in his home "in addition to his wife." Still more compulsive was the *Bauer*'s son Paul Heffelin of Sontheim, who after impregnating his own maid in 1569 went on to commit adultery with at least two other maids in 1577 and 1578. Second, there is evidence that women were at times victimized by entire groups of men. Thus in 1577 the *Amman* of Hawangen and four other men in the village were fined for sleeping with the wife of the drifter Jacob Fröschlin. Still more shocking was the prosecution in that same year of nine men in the village of Sontheim, who had all been having sexual relations with the maid of the local miller. The offenders included the wealthy miller himself, two of his sons (by one of whom the unfortunate woman was now pregnant), the poor baker Johann Wagner, the aforementioned Paul Heffelin, and the widowed *Bauer* Johann Aberöll, who "slept with her but was unable to do anything."[38]

Cases like this may seem to approach a kind of rural prostitution, but the context was worlds apart from the urban brothel, where prostitutes enjoyed

---

[34] Ibid., Document 297C, ff. 744r–749r [30 Dec. 1530].
[35] StAA, KL Ottobeuren 4, Document 299F, ff. 785r–788r [28 Jan. 1555].
[36] StAA, KL Ottobeuren 587-I, Heft 12 (1582/3), Ottobeuren Markt und Pfarr.
[37] StAA, KL Ottobeuren 4, Document 308P, ff. 1086v–1091v [24 Mar. 1541].
[38] Ibid., Document 308R, ff. 1095r–1100v [25 Feb. 1547] and Document 308V, ff. 1107r–1111r [28 Feb. 1548]; KL Ottobeuren 587-I, Heft 5 (1569/70), Sontheim; Heft 8 (1577/8), Sontheim and Hawangen; Heft 9 (1578/9), Sontheim.

a measure of institutional protection and qualified public acceptance.[39] The debauched rural maid was a ruined woman. She could not remain in the village and ply her trade. If the monastery was willing to force her seducers to pay her some child support, it nevertheless refused to tolerate her presence in its territories. Thus in 1593 we find Johann Hering of Hawangen being fined £26 5 ß for committing adultery with and impregnating the maid of the miller of Eggenthal, and Michael Rauch of Benningen fined £1 for sheltering her.[40]

That women were so often victimized is of course not to say that they all suffered passively. Some battered wives simply packed up and went back to their families; others appealed to the episcopal consistory in Augsburg for separation from their husbands. The occasional woman also returned force with force; when Jacob Schuster of Westerheim hit the local tavernkeeper's wife in the face, "she defended herself, seized him by the beard [and] well and bravely struck him down."[41] Even women who (as far as we can tell) were not abused by their spouses sometimes found rather unusual solutions to dissatisfaction with their marriages. In 1545 the village of Böhen saw the prosecution of an adulterous liaison between Agnesa Rot and one of her husband's relatives. It turned out that Agnesa had not only been carrying on the relationship for nine years, she had "deceitfully and with ill-tempered, burdensome words convinced [her] husband to allow the said person to come to [her] openly [both] day and night, just as [she] in the same way came and went to the said person's house by [both] day and night." The monastery jailed Agnesa for her adultery and her husband for his inability to control his wife.[42] Finally, and most ominously, the peasant women seem to have known of a recipe for what can only be termed a black widow potion: an aphrodisiac used to draw the affections of a man but then subsequently kill him off. The modern mind is inclined to scoff at the existence, not to mention the efficacy, of these concoctions, but the prosecution of an actual death in the village of Egg in November of 1548 leaves open the possibility that some women found unobtrusive but none the less permanent solutions to disabilities attendant upon their subordinate status.[43]

---

[39] Lyndal Roper, *The Holy Household: Women and Morals in Reformation Augsburg* (Oxford, 1989), pp. 89–102.

[40] StAA, KL Ottobeuren 587-II, Heft 17 (1593/4), Benningen and Hawangen.

[41] Note also that a women paid only half of a man's fine for the same offense. Karl Bosl, ed. *Dokumente zur Geschichte von Staat und Gesellschaft in Bayern. Abteilung II: Franken und Schwaben vom Frühmittelalter bis 1800*, Vol. IV: *Schwaben von 1268 bis 1803*, edited by Peter Blickle and Renate Blickle (Munich, 1979), Document 94. 1540 IX 11. Strafordnung von Abt Leonhard von Ottobeuren, p. 357. StAA, KL Ottobeuren 587-II, Heft 28 (1615), f. 33r.

[42] StAA, KL Ottobeuren 4, Document 299E, ff. 782v–785r [24 July 1545], similarly ibid., Document 293C, ff. 596v–599v [7 Sep. 1549], for the prosecution of Anna Klein of Guggenberg, who committed adultery with Caspar Vögelin, "for which [offense] my husband then left me unpunished."

[43] Ibid., Documents 291EE and 309H, ff. 525r–526v and 1150r–1154r [5 Nov. 1548].

The fault line separating men from women was taken so much for granted by so many people that it has rarely occasioned comment in the documentary record. Differences between different kinds of men, by contrast, were more obvious to contemporaries. Oddly enough, one of the most helpful introductions to the social tectonics of this sort is the concept of judicial impartiality. Each Ottobeuren village had its own court presided over by judges elected by the villagers and the *Amman*, or mayor, who cast the deciding vote in the event the judges could not reach a majority decision (capital cases were decided at a special court in the market town of Ottobeuren). Upon election each *Amman* and judge swore an oath to uphold (among other things) a standard of impartiality constructed around the principle that the law should be blind to social distinctions which suffused peasant life. The wording of this oath provides a convenient summary of the categories in terms of which the boundaries of alterity were drawn:

> You the *Amman* and you the judges, each and every one [of you] shall swear and promise to God and the saints . . . to consider the motions brought forward by [both of] the parties and anyone else with equal attentiveness; and in all legal matters brought before you regarding which you are asked to rule, to give to the best of your understanding the same justice to the poor as to the rich, to the rich as to the poor, to the visitor as to the native, to the native as to the visitor . . . and every one of you [shall swear] never to take account of the pangs of love, friendship, enmity, kinship, wardship, favor, fear, gifts of money or monetary equivalents . . .[44]

The previous chapter has shown how the wealth attendant upon *Hof* tenancy split the Ottobeuren peasantry into two distinct and often antagonistic subsets. We have also just seen the depth of the divide between kin and non-kin, and between men and women. We now turn to the remaining two main kinds of social boundaries to which sixteenth-century law accorded particular recognition: those separating friend from enemy, and native from foreigner.

When the Ottobeuren judge's oath referred to enmity (*Feindschaft*), it meant a state of antagonism much sharper than mere dislike or resentment, and connoted a positive desire to do harm to an adversary. And the Abbot's subjects did in fact do rather a lot of harm to each other. The tools lay ready to hand.

Like most minor German potentates, the Abbot of Ottobeuren had no means of defending his dominions other than a mobilization of his subjects into a general militia, and external security was no minor concern. The monastery lands suffered occupation by the Bishop of Augsburg in 1460, by the Schmalkaldic League in 1552, the marauding of deserters and demobilized soldiers from the Turkish wars in the 1590s, and then a second occupation by the Bishop of

---

[44] Ibid., Document 289 X, f. 365r: "Bauding Buch Anno 1551 – Oath of an *Amman* and a Judge."

Augsburg in 1612.[45] Despite his fears of peasant rebellion, then, the Abbot felt compelled by other security concerns not only to permit but even to require that every householder provide himself with a weapon, and if possible with a suit of armor.[46] The peasants needed little encouragement. By the early seventeenth century the Ottobeuren militia numbered 743 musketeers, 364 cavalry, and 346 armored soldiers – over fourteen hundred armed men in all.[47]

This arsenal did not just collect dust in the attic. But although the militia was occasionally mobilized in response to an external threat, the peasants made much more frequent use of the weapons against each other. Violent episodes involving swords, axes, gaff hooks, and pig spears cover the pages of the monastery's judicial records. Most of this violence was on a fairly small scale, involving no more than two or three miscreants. At times, however, these incidents escalated far beyond mere brawls, as in a 1530 incident from the village of Egg. Armed groups including ex-rebels from the Peasants' War clashed in a virtual battle, in the course of which the local blacksmith was shot dead with an arquebus.[48]

It is not possible to estimate the rate of violent crime at Ottobeuren. The surviving documentation has several gaps, and even with a continuous set of records it is unlikely that the number of prosecutions accurately reflects the actual incidence of crime (murder would be a possible exception). But even without the benefit of the quantitative representation in which the modern mind takes so much comfort, the circumstances of violent crime at Ottobeuren alone belie the image of an Arcadian rural society. The sheer brutality of so many of the offenses is simply shocking. Heinrich Knopf and Kreitz Wölflin emerged from a scuffle each with "a hole smashed in the head."[49] The wife of Christian Sitt gashed a hole in another woman's face with a spindle.[50] Michael Gerardt beat another man "blue-white."[51] Gori Hartman pulled a knife on Mathias Wurm who replied with an ax-blow to the face.[52]

Equally revealing is the fact that no one in the village was safe from the threat or reality of assault. Although most recorded violence at Ottobeuren was committed by and against adult men, both wandering beggars, servants, and women on the one hand, and mayors and sheriffs on the other also figure regularly as victims of physical abuse. That the weak should have been victimized is perhaps to be expected in almost any society. That the danger should also

---

[45] Baumann, *Allgäu*, Vol. II, pp. 389–91 and Vol. III, pp. 153–8, 428. Also StAA, KL Ottobeuren 4, Document 289T, ff. 347r–350v: "Mandat wider die gartierenden Knechten" [16 Sep. 1597].

[46] Ibid., Document 289X, f. 384r.

[47] StAA, KL Ottobeuren 159a. These numbers from the 1621 muster roll.

[48] StAA, KL Ottobeuren 4, Document 309C, ff. 1131r–1137r [4 Apr. 1530].

[49] StAA, KL Ottobeuren 587-I, Heft 10 (1579/80), Ottobeuren Markt und Pfarr.

[50] StAA, KL Ottobeuren 587-II, Heft 19 (1597/8), Benningen.

[51] Ibid., Sontheim und Schlegelsberg.

[52] StAA, KL Ottobeuren 587-I, Heft 7 (1575/6), Frechenrieden.

have extended to those in positions of power and authority is a more telling indication of the pervasiveness of violence among the Ottobeuren peasantry.

Primary responsibility for the enforcement of the law at Ottobeuren rested on the shoulders of the *Pittel*, or sheriff. Provided with a house and an annual grain salary by the monastery, the *Pittel* was assigned the task of admonishing the villagers to abide by the monastery's ordinances and to arrest those who refused to comply.[53] Both of these duties could be hazardous. In 1505 the *Pittel* of Böhen instructed a certain Hans Lachenmaier to pipe off some dammed-up water and was subjected to an armed assault for his trouble.[54] Making an actual arrest could provoke an even more dramatic response, as was seen above in the 1532 case of Simon Bürklin of Egg. And even if a *Pittel* did manage to secure someone behind bars, there was always the possibility that the prisoner would either break out himself, or be the object of a rescue attempt by friends and kinsmen.[55]

Some of this open contempt for the authority of the *Pittel* may have stemmed from the fact that the post was usually held by men drawn from the poorer segment of the village population. By contrast the office of *Amman*, as was seen in the previous chapter, was a prestigious position monopolized by the wealthiest householders in the village. The *Amman* sat on the village court and presided with the *Vierer* ("council of four") over the meetings of the *Gemeinde*. He served as the principal intermediary between the monastery and the village community, and was in a sense the most important person in the village. Just as in the case of the *Pittel*, however, the office of *Amman* carried a series of definite risks.

Naturally, every public official had to expect a certain amount of harassment, and we ought not to assign much significance to incidents where the *Amman* was publicly insulted[56] or suffered a few knocks when breaking up a fist fight.[57] Cold-blooded plots to murder the *Amman* were another matter altogether. In 1526 an unnamed fugitive from justice disclosed to Hans Schussman his intention to burn down the house of the *Amman* of Sontheim. Schussman not only provided the man with both food and shelter, but also calmly offered the following advice: "don't do that; [the house] won't burn down without causing [other] damage. He rides each day to the charcoal burners; you can easily shoot

[53] StAA, KU Ottobeuren 563 [9 Feb. 1495] and 690 [23 May 1504].
[54] StAA, KL Ottobeuren 4, Document 299A, ff. 772v–775v [19 May 1505].
[55] Ibid., Document 293D, ff. 616v–619r (*Urfehdebrief* of Jos Hölzlin junior of Hohenheim [15 June 1532]). Hölzlin was imprisoned for an unspecified offense and then broke out of jail at night. See also ibid., Document 308W, ff. 1111r–1115v (*Urfehdebrief* of Hans Knab of Niederrieden 20 Jan. 1551). Knab wounded the *Pittel* in an attempt to free from custody a certain Merckh Miller, who had been condemned to death by breaking on the wheel
[56] StAA, KL Ottobeuren 4, Document 305B, ff. 977r–979r (*Urfehdebrief* of Simon Hess of Oberwesterheim [9 Sep. 1527]); KL Ottobeuren 587-I, Heft 3 (1566/7), Schoren.
[57] StAA, KL Ottobeuren 587-I, Heft 5 (1569/70), Wolfertschwenden

him dead there." This particular *Amman* seems to have been widely unpopular, for when the plot was foiled and Schussman was arrested, the entire village community appealed (successfully) to the Abbot for clemency![58] But even if Schussman was an unusual case, he was not the only hothead in the village. Thirteen years later another Sontheim *Amman* was ambushed and almost killed by a villager armed with a pig spear.[59]

But enough of this tableau of crimes and misfortunes, at least for the moment. How is the endemic violence at Ottobeuren to be explained? We ought perhaps to begin with the more basic question of whether formal interpretation is really necessary. After all, in the majority of cases the violence can be accounted for by reference to explosive tempers and the inherent volatility of a population under arms. But simple irascibility is an inadequate explanation for the widespread scorn for the offices of the law and *a fortiori* for the aforementioned attempts on the life of the *Amman*. These latter incidents were premeditated acts of vengeance, and this brings us to the institution of the feud.

The feud was a time-honored tradition in Upper Swabia, and although it had fallen from favor among the territorial lords by the middle of the sixteenth century, the same cannot be said of their subjects. This is not to suggest that the medieval tradition of nailing a formal declaration of enmity (*Feindbrief*) to the door of the parish church was the usual prelude to an outbreak of violence.[60] Be that as it may, it remains true that the essential characteristic of the feud – the resolution of conflicts by private justice instead of through the courts – was a constant theme at Ottobeuren, and was seen as a more serious threat to the social order than simple violence itself. In 1548, for example, Simon Kopp of Attenhausen was arrested on two separate charges. He had on behalf of a third party affixed a *Feindbrief* to the door of the village blacksmith, and had stabbed a certain Peter Stehelin with a pig spear. For the first offense, which was considered a "violation of the Imperial Peace, the Golden Bull [of 1356] and the public common law," he was fined £15 15 ß, but for the second offense he was fined only £10.[61]

Does it matter that peasant violence so often took the form of a feud? I submit that it does. Distinctive of the feud is a formalized separation of people into the

---

[58] StAA, KL Ottobeuren 4, Document 304L, ff. 906r–909r (*Urfehdebrief* of Hans Schussman of Sontheim [14 June 1526]).

[59] Ibid., Document 304S, ff. 928v–934r [18 Feb. 1539].

[60] E.g. ibid., Document 309B, ff. 1127v–1131r (*Urfehdebrief* of Hans Rot genannt Bayer of Nider-galtingen in Bavaria [30 Oct. 1486]). Rot confessed that he "under cover of night and fog did deliver threatening letters to Contz Schöffler of Egg regarding some pretended claim . . . [and also] affixed them to the door of the church . . ."

[61] Ibid., Document 303G, ff. 851v–855r [30 July 1548]. Also StAA, KL Ottobeuren 587-I, Heft 2 (1548), Attenhausen and Ottobeuren Markt und Pfarr. Kopp had just been permitted to return to Ottobeuren after fleeing to escape prosecution for other crimes. See KU Ottobeuren 1296/2 9 Feb. 1547.

antithetical groupings of friends and enemies. This is the same compartmentalizing habit of mind which has been seen to characterize conceptions of both kinship and gender roles at Ottobeuren. It shares with these distinctions, and also with the *Bauer/Seldner* divide, a deeply ingrained tendency to segment the world into rival corporations of insiders and outsiders.

Due to the laconic nature of the surviving records, it is often difficult to discern the motives (if any) behind peasant violence. There are, however, three indications that a thirst for private justice underlay much of that violence. Most obvious is the observation that so much of the evidence about criminality at Ottobeuren has come down to us in the form of *Urfehdebriefe*, the plea-bargain arrangement previously encountered in the aftermath of the Peasants' War. The simple range of offenders at whose punishment an oath of *non*-retaliation was demanded – from petty thieves and wife beaters to witches and political rebels – illustrated the monks' appreciation for the deep roots of the feud in peasant society. In this regard it is also worth noting that it had not been all that long since the monastery itself had engaged in feuds. In 1482 the Ritter von Hohenheim proclaimed a feud with the monastery and was then promptly waylaid and killed by a commando of peasants dispatched by the Abbot for just that purpose.[62]

A more direct piece of evidence for peasant feuding is the frequency with which the threat of vengeance was issued. The use of the *Feindbrief* continued through the sixteenth century, although there was no longer anything to match a spectacular incident in 1495 when a disgruntled serf of the Graf von Montfort proclaimed a feud with the Abbot, his servants, and the entire population of the monastery lands![63] Threats of vengeance did not need to be written to be credible, however. There are plenty of cases where the authorities were concerned enough to arrest a peasant simply because he had threatened to strangle a rival[64] or burn down the house of a neighbor,[65] and some peasants were even bold enough to issue death threats to the *Vogt* himself for having imprisoned them.[66] Crucially, it is clear that private vengeance was often seen as an alternative to the justice offered by the courts. Thus, when Michael Burger of Benningen lost a legal ruling against his brother-in-law and another friend, he declined to appeal the ruling. Instead, Burger threatened his opponents in a "violent and murderous manner" and publicly announced his intention to revenge himself by burning down a number of houses in the village of Benningen.[67]

A final indication of the connection between peasant violence and the feud is a brief phrase which crops up again and again in the *Urfehdebriefe* of those

[62] Feyerabend, *Ottenbeuren Jahrbücher*, Vol. II, pp. 716–17.   [63] Ibid., pp. 745–7.
[64] StAA, KL Ottobeuren 4, Document 303L, ff. 866r–869v [28 July 1569].
[65] Ibid., Document 306D, ff. 1010v–1013v [20 Nov. 1554].
[66] Ibid., Document 291DD, ff. 523r–525r [4 Sep. 1545] and Document 305E, ff. 984r–990r [2 Aug. 1548].
[67] Ibid., Document 295B, ff. 708r–711v [23 Sep. 1556].

prosecuted for violence: the offense had been committed *über gemachten Frid* or in violation of a pre-existing formalized accord. The monastery attempted to head off potential conflicts and defuse existing ones by mediating peace agreements between the feuding parties and their respective families. These *Verträge* (literally "contracts") were particularly important where someone had been killed, and in murder cases the accord usually required the guilty party to pay compensation to the victim's kinfolk in addition to the (heavy) fine levied by the monastery.[68]

As may be expected, it was not always easy to arrive at a settlement. When Erhardt Steidlin of Sontheim was killed in a fight in 1566, the Abbot worried that "all sorts of lamentable escalations, discord, unrest, hatred, and ultimately the ruin of His Grace's subjects could arise and follow." To forestall this possibility, the friends, heirs, and kin of both the deceased and his killers were called together to work out an accord. Initial hopes for a peaceful resolution were dashed, however, when Steidlin's nephew Jerg Schückh leapt to his feet and

> did not only rebuke the perpetrators as thieves, scoundrels and murderers, but [did] also . . . most grievously attack and insult my gracious lord [and] also His Grace's *Vogt*, servants and officials as beggar- and scoundrel-lords and did in addition unjustly . . . accuse them that with respect to the matter of the aforesaid murder they had made a dishonorable [and] worthless scoundrel's accord.[69]

The hot-tempered nephew was hauled off and imprisoned (the Abbot was himself sensitive about his honor); we do not know if an accord was ever reached.

Even when mediation was initially successful, however, there was always the possibility that the thirst for vengeance would later return. This can be illustrated with a few examples from the village of Niederrieden. In 1525 Enderas Schmidt and Michael Reder were arrested and convicted for the killing of Jörg Maier. The Ottobeuren *Vogt* and the monastery secretary mediated an accord between Maier's family and the killers, but peace remained elusive. When Schmidt and Reder ran into the brother and relatives of the deceased outside the market town of Ottobeuren, a fracas ensued and the intervention of the *Vogt* was required.[70]

---

[68] E.g. StAA, KL Ottobeuren 587-I, Heft 8 (1577/8). Jerg Eggler of Ungerhausen killed Martin Lorre of Ungerhausen in the village of Hawangen. Eggler paid 23 fl. to Lorre's relatives and 64 fl. to the monastery. Other evidence of this custom of payments to the relatives of the deceased is contained in ibid., Heft 3 (1566/7) (a peasant from Wolfertschwenden and a man from Grönenbach agree to pay 55 fl. to the family of a murdered Grönenbach man) and Heft 15 (1590/1) (the *Amman* of Arlesried and a man from Mussenhausen agree to pay 129.4 fl. to the family of a murdered man from Günz). Note that when the *Maier* of Niederrieden's son killed a vagabond in 1597, the son was fined 8 fl., but there is no record of any payment to the vagabond's family. KL 587-II, Heft 19 (1597/8).

[69] StAA, KL Ottobeuren 4, Document 304AA, ff. 956r–963v [7 Mar. 1566].

[70] Ibid., Document 308B, ff. 1054r–1059r (*Urfehdebrief* of Enderas Schmidt of Niederrieden and Michael Reder of Heimertingen [13 Jan. 1525]).

Gallus Schmidt's oath to uphold an accord with his neighbor Michael Maier and Maier's relatives did not prevent him from attacking Maier's son in the nearby village of Heimertingen in 1528.[71] Equally ineffective was the accord between Jeronimus Kessler the younger and a certain Melchior Fesema; in 1535 young Kessler stabbed Fesema in the back.[72]

The original impulse to these feuds may often have been relatively minor: border disputes, unpaid debts, and so on. Nevertheless, the probability that an initial squabble would escalate into violence was greatly increased by a sensitive sense of honor shared by lord and peasant alike. Thus Michael Gerardt (the same one who beat another man "blue-white") flew into a rage and had to be restrained from pulling a knife when a neighbor presumed to dance with Gerardt's wife at a village gathering.[73] In a similar vein we have in the previous chapter seen how Ulrich Blenck's 1529 tirade against the Abbot and his servants as tyrants and villains also contained the revealing denunciation that they were "worthy of no honor."

The most explicit indications of the importance of personal honor in rural life are the provisions of the Penal Ordinance of Abbot Leonhard Widenmann issued in 1540. The ordinance has two striking features. One is the precision in the grading of offenses to honor. Simple insults "which however do not touch or damage his [the aggrieved party's] honor or reputation" were punishable by a fine of 5 shillings. Calling someone a liar resulted in a fine of 10 shillings, whereas to do so in a defamatory manner such as "you lie like a scoundrel" increased the fine to 60 shillings. Most severely punished were those "who defame, abuse and denounce another as a thief, rogue, murderer, scoundrel, traitor, arsonist or similar defamatory words which affect and diminish honor, reputation and standing." This last offense was punishable by the staggering fine of 200 shillings.[74]

The second significant feature of the 1540 ordinance is that it formally codifies the position that affronts to honor should be considered more serious offenses than simple physical violence. Thus simple brawling (fine of 10 shillings), drawing blood (30 shillings) and even breaking another's limbs or crippling him (100 shillings) were all punished much less severely than a serious attack on someone's personal honor.[75]

---

[71] Ibid., Document 308G, ff. 1067v–1069v (*Urfehdebrief* of Gallus Schmidt of Niederrieden [4 Nov. 1528]). Schmidt was forbidden to bear weapons as part of this *Urfehde* agreement, but was arrested for doing so just two years later. Ibid., Document 308J, ff. 1072r–1076r (*Urfehdebrief* of Gallus Schmidt of Niederrieden [12 Feb. 1530]).

[72] Ibid., Document 308K, ff. 1076r–1078r (*Urfehdebrief* of Jeronimus Kessler junior alias Schmidt of Niederrieden [1 Feb. 1535]).

[73] StAA, KL Ottobeuren 587-I, Heft 10 (1579/80), Sontheim und Schlegelsberg.

[74] Bosl, ed. *Dokumente*, Vol. IV, Document 94. 1540 IX 11. Strafordnung von Abt Leonhard von Ottobeuren, p. 354.

[75] Ibid., pp. 354–6.

The premium the peasant placed on personal honor should not be carica-
tured as simple touchiness. If we are to understand the centrality of boundary
at sixteenth-century Ottobeuren, we must first appreciate that the social radius
of rural life was extremely intimate. This is not to say that no one ever traveled
or left the home village, but rather that face-to-face relations in the local community had an overriding importance. The centrality of honor is a reflection
of this fact. Since word of mouth was the prime source of information among
the peasantry, everything from commercial and employment opportunities to
a person's chances on the marriage market was strongly influenced by reputation. A man with a name for not paying his debts, a servant suspected of
pilfering, a woman rumored to be unchaste, all of these stood to lose a great
deal in the intimate world of the village. For just this reason, false accusations
of this kind were treated as criminal offenses and the accusers were punished
accordingly.[76]

If wealth, kinship, gender, and enmity all fragmented the peasant's world
into sets of insiders and outsiders, a similar effect was produced by residence.
When the judge's oath distinguished between natives and foreigners, the latter
term was understood to include all of those who did not live in the monastery
lands. It was thus entirely possible for someone to live within sight of a nearby
village where he would none the less be considered a foreigner. In practice,
the people mentioned as "foreigners" in the monastery records fell into two
general categories. The first were simply people who lived elsewhere who
happened to be traveling through the monastery lands. The second were people
without fixed residences, a drifting assortment of pedlars, beggars, vagrants, and
runaways.

The attitude of the Ottobeuren peasantry to these various sorts of outsiders
is best described as ambivalent. On the one hand, as the Abbot himself noted
in 1549, "there are few small and humble villages like the ones in this region
where one may when necessary more readily receive shelter and hospitality
than here."[77] This hospitality was a rather durable tradition. In 1551 alarm over
the growing numbers of transients on the roads prompted an official prohibition on giving shelter to "wandering laborers, vagrants and beggars" outside of
public inns.[78] The proclamation was widely ignored. The criminal court papers

---

[76] StAA, KL Ottobeuren 587-I, Heft 14 (1586/7), Frechenrieden: "Heÿß Wurm Blacksmith
accosted Hanns Heffelin with hot words regarding a debt that had been paid long ago – [fined]
5 shillings"; Hawangen: "Hans Schmidt accused his maid of having stolen four *batzen* from his
mother; this was found to be untrue – [fined] 1 pound"; StAA, KL Ottobeuren 587-II, Heft 17
(1593/4), Westerheim: "Conrad Gufer accused a woman from Kamlach that he had previously
had dishonorable doings with her; he later retracted this and settled with her – [fined] 3 pounds
14 shillings 8 *heller*."

[77] StAA, KL Ottobeuren 4, Document 289X, f. 392r: "Ordinance and Commandment regarding
Innkeepers, Butchers and Bakers proclaimed Anno 1549."

[78] Ibid., Document 289X, f. 398r–v: "Swabian Circle Decision and thence derived Mandate concerning Wanderers, Demobilized Soldiers, Beggars and Gypsies" [31 May 1551].

regularly record the fines of villagers who in violation of the law had sheltered beggars, demobilized soldiers, and vagrants. In some cases the kindness extended to strangers is rather moving. Hans Kramer of Betzisried took in a sick beggar woman in the winter of 1575, and despite the danger to his family – some of whom contracted her illness – kept her in his house until the following spring.[79]

At the same time, strangers and especially vagrants were often regarded with profound suspicion. Nobody knew or could know what sort of person a wanderer was. Strangers were by definition preceded by no reputation. They belonged nowhere; they had no community. And thus it happened that in the very 1549 ordinance where the Abbot recounted the Swabian tradition of hospitality, he also noted that

> It has with the greatest of complaints and lamentations been daily brought to our attention by many [both] rich and poor, noble and other foreign non-resident persons . . . who due to the onset of the night or to other needs or reasons sought and required shelter [here] that they were not only not admitted by those who maintain public inns . . . and other establishments but were also with unseemly and offensive replies refused and driven from one [establishment] to another.[80]

To suggest that foreigners at Ottobeuren were regularly met with both hospitality and abuse may seem paradoxical, but both attitudes were clearly in evidence. How else to explain the following 1579 entry from the criminal court papers: "Caspar Heuss of Westerheim sheltered a vagrant in violation of the prohibition; Heuss and his brother's wife did [also] beat the vagrant with their fists – fined 1 £ 5 ß"?[81]

Of course, if exposure to blows and insults was the only consequence of the suspicion with which foreigners were beheld, they were being treated in more or less the same way the peasants behaved towards each other. Regrettably, the dangers of being a foreigner were much more serious than the foregoing would suggest, and are most glaringly obvious in the fate of those unfortunates who fell foul of the law. This can be seen in the following tale of two thieves. In 1573 an Ottobeuren serf by the name of Lorenz Frewlin was arrested in Benningen for a string of robberies. He had been stealing grain, meat, and other goods as well as having raided his neighbors' beehives and haystacks by night. After appeals by his brother and brothers-in-law for mercy, Frewlin received a pardon. He was released from prison but ordered to leave the monastery lands. His wife, who had helped him in his thievery, was also exiled.[82] The sentence seems rather harsh, unless one considers how much worse it could have been. Three years

---

[79] StAA, KL Ottobeuren 587-I, Heft 7 (1575/6), Ottobeuren Markt und Pfarr.
[80] StAA, KL Ottobeuren 4, Document 289X, ff. 391r–v.
[81] StAA, KL Ottobeuren 587-I, Heft 10 (1579/80), Westerheim.
[82] StAA, KL Ottobeuren 4, Document 295F, ff. 720v–724v [17 Feb. 1573].

earlier two foreigners had fallen under suspicion of stealing fish and chickens in the village of Günz. Both men, Leonhardt Amman of Hiltenfingen and Thoma Cramer of Eberhausen, were arrested and interrogated, and when their answers proved inconsistent they were subjected to torture. This last procedure rapidly produced confessions, whereupon both men were sentenced to death. Amman was to be broken on the wheel and then hung up on a gibbet. Cramer was to be burned alive. As in the case of Lorenz Frewlin, there were appeals for mercy, this time from the parish priests of the monastery lands. The court relented. The men had their sentences commuted to decapitation, although Amman's corpse was still to be strung from the gibbet and Cramer's remains were still to be burned.[83]

In all fairness, it must be conceded that these two cases are drawn from different classes of documents. The pardon of Lorenz Frewlin and his wife is taken from a series of *Urfehdebriefe*, which by definition detail a commuted sentence. The execution of the two foreigners, by contrast, is related in the proceedings of the *Peinliche Halsgericht*, or court for capital crimes, whose final decision was almost invariably a death sentence. Still, this difference of provenance does not do away with the suggestion of judicial bias against foreigners. It turns out that in the documents preserved in the *Rotulus Probationum*, foreigners made up only 5.1 percent of the defendants in cases resolved by *Urfehdebriefe*, but fully 52.9 percent of the defendants in the cases decided by the *Peinliche Halsgericht*.[84] Again, it could be objected that foreigners were more likely to commit those crimes such as theft which most often resulted in a death sentence. And it is true that in most of the theft cases decided by the *Peinliche Halsgericht* (seven of nine cases, or 77.8 percent), the defendant was a foreigner. Nevertheless, in so far as the sixteenth-century *Urfehdebriefe* record repeated pardons for native thieves[85] and none at all for their foreign counterparts, there remain good reasons to believe that a foreigner arrested at Ottobeuren was likely to be judged more harshly than a local offender.

In a sense this is hardly surprising. The clemency embodied in an *Urfehde* agreement was granted not simply because it was requested, but more importantly because the future good behavior of the defendant could be guaranteed

---

[83] StAA, KL Ottobeuren 4, Document 292A, ff. 1048r–1049v [20 June 1570].

[84] Foreigners appeared in 13 of 256 *Urfehdebrief* cases but 9 of 17 *Peinliche Halsgericht* cases. Another intimation of judicial prejudice is provided by the "Tower-Register" kept by Adam von Stein, the Ottobeuren *Obervogt* for the years 1582–1601. This document, which has survived only as an incomplete copy in ibid., Document 311, ff. 1173r–1178r, records the names, offenses, and punishments of those arrested for various reasons by the *Obervogt*. Foreigners account for six of seven (85.7 percent) death sentences; of those arrested one of eight (12.5 percent) natives but six of nineteen (31.6 percent) foreigners were executed.

[85] E.g. StAA, KL Ottobeuren 4, Documents 291BB, ff. 517v–521r (*Urfehdebrief* of Hanns Hiebeler genant König of Ottobeuren [6 Aug. 1545]) 294A, ff. 677r–679r (*Urfehdebrief* of Kilian Linckh of Hawangen [15 May 1529]; and 305F, ff. 990r–996r (*Urfehdebrief* of Jacob Schiess of Oberwesterheim [11 Dec. 1554]).

by those close to him. In the case of Lorenz Frewlin, his relatives bound themselves either personally to hunt him down and bring him to jail within a month or to pay the Abbot a fine of 15 fl. (=£26 5 ß) if he ever broke his *Urfehde* oath. Without guarantors like these, the convicted foreigner at Ottobeuren was in a very bleak position. The *Amman* and townspeople who staffed the *Peinliche Halsgericht* had nothing but the word of an unknown convicted felon to move them to clemency. If a traveler could secure intervention from his overlord or from the public authorities in his home town, he might well be spared,[86] but this remedy was clearly unavailable to the genuinely transient. For the vagrants and beggars, the masterless men and women of the highways, the rootlessness which normally drew suspicion at the least all too often sealed their fate when they were brought before the vengeful rural tribunal.

In light of the foregoing, it is hardly surprising that the offices of the law should have been so concerned to keep justice blind to the internal divisions of rural society. It is also significant that, at least with respect to the treatment of foreigners, the effort was almost certainly a failure. But the rural world was also divided along other residential fault lines to which the judge's oath makes no reference: settlement form. According to a serf roll drawn up in 1564, only 63.8 percent (4,999) of the Abbot's eight thousand-odd subjects lived in the nucleated villages commonly regarded as definitive of the world of the peasantry. Fully 27.2 percent (2,129) lived in *Weiler*, or scattered hamlets which were systematically differentiated from the villages in the monastery's records. The remaining 8.9 percent (699) lived in the central market town, or *Markt*, of Ottobeuren.[87]

Did these distinctions matter? They did. We have already seen how the *Weiler* grew out of a very different settlement process from the one which produced the villages, as a result of which the hamlets displayed strikingly different patterns of land tenure from their more densely populated counterparts. Hamlet and village were also marked by equally prominent differences of political organization. Each village maintained an impressive collection of local officialdom including an *Amman* (mayor), two *Hauptleute* ('headmen'), four *Vierer* (the 'council of four'), the *Pittel* (Sheriff), and the judges who together with the *Amman* staffed the *Dorfgericht*, or village court.[88] In addition, the

---

[86] For a late example see ibid., Document 304CC, ff. 969r–972r (*Urfehdebrief* of Georg Sylvanus of Bamberg [9 May 1611]). A self-proclaimed traveling soldier ("although I could show no evidence or *Passbort* of my service"), Sylvanus stole 4 *gulden* from an old man with whom he was sharing a room at the Sontheim inn. In consideration of his youth, promises of improvement, and especially a "commendation" from a Bamberg court official, Sylvanus was spared a flogging and stint in the pillory, and was instead banished from the Ottobeuren lands for the rest of his life.

[87] Dertsch, "Das Einwohnerbuch des Ottobeurer Klosterstaats 1564," pp. III–V.

[88] Blickle, *Memmingen*, p. 247.

villagers annually elected two *Heiligenpfleger*, or churchwardens, to oversee the financial administration of the parish church. The political organization of the hamlets was rudimentary by contrast. The monastery clustered the hamlets into groups of eight to twelve and then placed each *Hauptmannschaft*, as these agglomerations were called, under the administration of a *Hauptmann*, or headman. The *Hauptmann* aside, there do not seem to have been any other local officials in the hamlets; legal matters were referred to the *Gerichte* of either the village of Böhen or the market town of Ottobeuren.

Now, this difference between the villages and the hamlets may in no small part be explained by the modest administrative requirements of a lower population density. The significance of the institutional contrast is not, however, thereby to be dismissed. We have already seen how often peasant protest grew out of or at least represented a subversion of officially sanctioned political patterns such as the meeting of the *Gemeinde* and the deliberations of the village court. It is also worth emphasizing that the inveterate tradition of dissent in the village of Sontheim and the long-running conflict between the Abbot and the village of Egg over wood rights had no counterpart in the small and scattered settlements in the south of the monastery lands. The suggestion is obvious: the relative political quiescence of the hamlets was at least in part a consequence of their institutional underdevelopment.

In a third, and jealously guarded category of its own was the market town, or *Markt* of Ottobeuren. The *Markt* had a pre-eminent rank among the settlements of the Abbot's dominions. The *Markt*'s court had jurisdiction over all capital cases in the monastery lands and by 1457 its *Amman* possessed the dignity of affixing his own seal to official documents.[89] Above all, and as the name would suggest, the *Markt* had the special right to hold a weekly market every Thursday and two annual markets on St. Urban's Day (25 May) and on St. Mauritius' Day (22 September). This status, which was conferred by the Emperor Maximillian in 1498, was not just a privilege but an exclusive (and therefore lucrative) right to hold markets. All buying and selling in the monastery lands was required by law to take place in and be overseen by the officials of the *Markt*, which thus became the commercial hub of the Ottobeuren *Klosterstaat*.

Now, we should be careful not to overdraw the difference between the *Markt* and the nucleated villages. The *Markt* Ottobeuren was really rather small. In 1564 it numbered a mere 699 inhabitants, making it not much larger than the villages of Sontheim (population 549) and Hawangen (population 618), and actually smaller than the village of Benningen (population 794).[90] And while it is true that the occupational structure of the *Markt* was dominated by trade and craft work, it is clear that a great many of the town's inhabitants were also at least

---

[89] Ibid., pp. 62–3.
[90] Dertsch, "Das Einwohnerbuch des Ottobeurer Klosterstaats 1564," pp. III–V.

partially engaged in occupations such as crop raising[91] and animal husbandry.[92] In the eyes of someone from a true city like Memmingen, the *Markt* Ottobeuren must have seemed like nothing so much as a glorified peasant village with pretensions.[93]

But despite the partially agrarian character of the *Markt* Ottobeuren, the town dwellers (or at least the more prosperous among them) had a very strong sense of their distinctiveness from the inhabitants of the surrounding countryside. This distinctiveness found concrete expression in the institution of *Bürgerrecht*, or citizenship. By the beginning of our period, the inhabitants of the *Markt* were already divided into those who held *Bürgerrecht* and those who did not.[94] Only the citizens were eligible for public office, and they alone had use rights to the common lands. It is not clear what proportion of the inhabitants of the *Markt* enjoyed the *Bürgerrecht*, although it is certain that the non-citizens were concentrated among the poorest segment of the town population.[95]

The value placed on these citizenship rights is most readily apparent in the rise of restrictive legislation governing *Bürgerrecht* in the later sixteenth century. Over the course of the sixteenth century, the growth of population in the Swabian countryside prompted many peasants to leave their crowded native villages and hamlets in search of a better life elsewhere. Like many territorial lords, the Abbot of Ottobeuren was greatly concerned by the stream of migrants into his dominions, and moved to restrict immigration "so that the monastery's

---

[91] A 1544 rent roll lists twenty-two persons in the *Markt* Ottobeuren renting arable and meadow parcels from the monastery. StAA, KL Ottobeuren 29, ff. 1v–4v, "Gültbuch 1544." This represents between a sixth and a seventh of the households [StAA, KL Ottobeuren 64, ff. 44r–46v] and the 1548 serfbook lists 132 households [StAA, KL Ottobeuren 600, ff. 8r–30r]). In so far as the Gültbuch 1544 records only that small minority of properties in the *Markt* held under *Gotteshausrecht*, the overall proportion of town dwellers cultivating some kind of land must have been much higher.

[92] The small tithe registers of Ottobeuren parish show that at least sixty-five households in the *Markt* produced calves in 1564. This represents 38 percent of all households, a figure which is an underestimate in so far as not all those who kept cows raised calves every year. StAA, KL Ottobeuren 688-I, "Rechnungen der Pfarrei Ottobeuren," Heft 2 (1564), ff. 1r–7r. Compare with Hefte 1, ff. 23v–28v (1563), 3, ff. 1r–6v (1565), and 4, ff. 25v–30v (1566). Household total from KL Ottobeuren 25 (Mü.B.), pp. 1–18.

[93] See for example the letter dated 7 August 1600 from the *Bürgermeister* and *Rat* of Memmingen to Kaiser Rudolph dismissing the *Markt* Ottobeuren because it "maintains no market or inspection ordinances regarding buying and selling or goods and victuals . . . and also does not have the people to institute the necessary ordinances and is not even located on the highway but in fact lies out of the way *in solitudine*." StadtA MM A. Reichsstadt [bisher Stadtarchiv] 40/1.

[94] The antiquity of the *Bürgerrecht* at Ottobeuren is unclear. The title "burgher of Ottobeuren" is documented at least as far back as the early fifteenth century. Hoffmann, ed., *Urkunden*, no. 179 [26 Apr. 1409].

[95] This does not conversely mean that all *Bürger* were rich. A certain Michael Blank was a *Bürger* of Ottobeuren in 1550 (StAA, KL Ottobeuren 4, Document 291HH, ff. 529r–v. (*Urfehdebrief* of Michael Blank of Ottobeuren [13 Mar. 1550]). According to the 1546 tax register (StAA, KL Ottobeuren 64, ff. 44r–46v), only 20.6 percent of the taxpayers in the *Markt* had a lower tax assessment than he.

districts, market town, villages and hamlets do not become overpopulated with large numbers of foreign and alien persons, and [so that] those who were born and raised inside [the monastery lands] are not bought out, outnumbered and burdened by such foreigners."[96]

The problem was particularly acute in the *Markt* Ottobeuren, where in the two generations after the Peasants' War the number of households rose by some 70 percent.[97] The influx of country dwellers provoked deep resentment among the more established inhabitants, who felt that their rights and privileges as citizens of the *Markt* were being diluted by the admission of too many undesirable outsiders to the community. The Abbot was sympathetic to these concerns and in the 1570s promulgated a series of decrees culminating in an elaborate *Heiratsordnung*, or marriage ordinance, issued in 1576.

The 1576 ordinance was drawn up in consultation with the *Amman* and *Vierer* (council of four) of the *Markt*.[98] Its stated goal was the prevention of two social evils: clandestine marriage, which will be discussed in chapter 5, and the burdensome excess of "foreigners" in the *Markt* Ottobeuren. With respect to the latter, the ordinance focuses on the regulation of marriages between *Bürger* of the *Markt* and "outsiders," since simple unauthorized immigration by foreigners had itself already been repeatedly forbidden by the monastery.[99] The basic fear of the citizenry was that poor outsiders might gain entrance into their community of privilege through marriage. Accordingly, the 1576 ordinance provided that if a woman married someone from outside the *Markt* and had neither a house of her own nor a credible expectation of acquiring one, she forfeited her *Bürgerrecht* and was obliged to move out of the *Markt* to live with her husband. If, on the other hand, a woman did own or expected to inherit a house, her foreign husband would be allowed to move into the *Markt* to live with her after providing, first, documentation of the value of his property and, second, a specification of whether it was in the form of cash or goods. Even then, however, the husband had to have property worth at least 40 *gulden* above the value of his clothing and personal effects, or he would not be allowed to live in the town.

---

[96] StAA, KL Ottobeuren 4, Document 289K, f. 321r: "Mandat der underthanen, hindersäßen, und leibaignen leithen des Gottshauß heürat betreffendt 1571."

[97] The tax register for 1525 does not have a complete listing for the market town of Ottobeuren, but suggests a total of 100 households. In 1546 there were 141 households in the *Markt* (StAA, KL Ottobeuren 64, ff. 44r–46v) and in 1564 there were 171 (Dertsch, "Das Einwohnerbuch des Ottobeurer Klosterstaats 1564," pp. 3–10).

[98] StAA, KL Ottobeuren 4, Document 289N, ff. 327r–331r: "Heiratsordnung" [18 Aug. 1576].

[99] Ibid., Documents 289G, ff. 308v–311r ("Gebott und Statut der auslendischen leibaignen, so sich in des gottshauß Ottenbeüren gerichten einzuedringen understehen") [4 Sep. 1561] and 289H, ff. 311r–314v (same title as previous ordinance) [10 Dec. 1567]. See the prosecution of Hans Gonser of Babenhausen, a would-be emigrant to the *Markt*, who was fined £7 "because he moved into the lordship of his own accord [and] without [official] permission." StAA, KL Ottobeuren 587-I, Heft 11 (1580/81).

The ordinance does not have explicit provisions for the expulsion to their wives' homes of poor male *Bürger* who married foreigners, but this does not seem to have reflected an intention to allow more freedom of choice to men in marriage (there were, of course, many other areas of the law such as property holding in which men were indeed allowed a great deal more independence than women). Rather, since the authorities who drew up the ordinance assumed that patrilocality was the normal social pattern,[100] they probably did not consider the case of a man who moved to live with his wife common enough to be worthy of formal regulation. Whatever the case may be, the 1576 ordinance clearly states that whether or not male *Bürger* had their own houses, their prospective foreign spouses were to be subjected to the same 40 *gulden* property requirement if they wanted to move into the *Markt* with their husbands.

It is instructive to note precisely how the 1576 ordinance defines outsiders. Here the text speaks best for itself:

The aforesaid articles are to be understood to apply not only to foreigners born outside the monastery lands, but also to all subjects of the monastery who do not have *Bürgerrecht* here [in the *Markt*], but were born and raised in other districts of the monastery lands outside of the *Markt*, such that these other subjects of the monastery, whether they are men or women, if they do not have property worth 40 *gulden*, are ineligible for *Bürgerrecht*, and in this case it shall be dealt with them as with other foreigners.[101]

The good burghers of Ottobeuren thus exemplify the trait that Mack Walker saw as characteristic of German home town dwellers – the desire to protect their community against all outsiders, foreigners and peasants alike.[102]

Although the classification of individuals on the basis of their residence meant that the compartmentalization of persons came to entail the compartmentalization of space, the latter practice was not merely derivative of the former. The physical space of the monastery lands was as consciously segmented into bounded, autonomous subunits of differential privilege as were the people who inhabited it. It may seem unremarkable that Abbot Leonhard's 1540 Penal Code doubled the fine for any offense if it were committed inside a church. It must

---

[100] Thus for example in an earlier ordinance ". . . since according to the common law, a woman is to move to live with the man to whom she is bound in marriage . . ." StAA, KL Ottobeuren 4, Document 289K, ff. 317r–320v "Ordnung der gemain Gottsleithen heißlich einlaßen betreffendt auf widerrueffen gestellt 1570."

[101] StAA, KL Ottobeuren 4, Document 289N, f. 330r [18 Aug. 1576].

[102] Mack Walker, *German Home Towns: Community, State and General Estate 1648–1871* (Ithaca and London, 1971), pp. 30–1. Walker cites the following eighteenth-century legal maxim as an expression of the home town's animosity towards the peasantry: "No shit-hens fly over the town wall." I do not myself share Walker's view that the farm village had *no* interest in excluding outsiders, although it is certainly true that the town was markedly more protective of its membership than the village.

be emphasized, however, that the same doubling applied to offenses committed inside mills, smithies, and inns.[103] In other words, those places deemed essential to the material sustenance of rural society were singled out for the same special status accorded to those essential to its spiritual sustenance.

The moral geography of the Ottobeuren lands is thrown into still sharper relief by the aftermath of the Peasants' War. It has been seen that the Abbot was ultimately willing to readmit to the fold even the most unruly of his wayward subjects, but he also needed to ensure that the events of 1525 would never be repeated. Accordingly, upon release from prison the ex-rebels were saddled with a series of prohibitions, which were imposed either for life or until lifted by the monastery. Some of these disabilities were straightforwardly political, such as ineligibility of the pardoned rebels for election as judge, Amman, or Vierer or the abrogation of their rights to bear weapons.

More strikingly spatial was the social quarantine which the monastery sought to impose on the ex-rebels. They were forbidden to attend the meetings of the Gemeinde, and with the exception of attendance at mass they were further prohibited from visiting "taverns, public festivals . . . common bathhouses or any other occasion or place or general gathering of the people" (in extreme cases the pardoned rebel might also be forbidden to leave his home village without the foreknowledge and consent of the Vogt).[104] The monks knew that these public places were nodes of sociability where individual grievances readily coalesced into collective protest. By ridding these spaces of those subjects whose loyalty was deemed suspect, the monks hoped to fragment any subversive tendencies among the peasantry and thereby minimize the risk of further uprisings.

But political dissent was far from the only offense punished by these kinds of spatial restrictions. Throughout the sixteenth century, the monastery would impose similar bans on leaving the monastery lands (at all) or even one's home village (for more than a day) on a whole range of offenders, including those guilty of assault, wood theft, adultery and incest, fraud, or even threats and insults.[105] Repeat offenders might even be required to promise "if two or three [people] are standing together in the village, not to stand or come near them."[106]

---

[103] Bosl, ed. Dokumente, Part 2, Vol. IV, Document 94. Strafordnung 1540, § 12, p. 355.

[104] StAA, KL Ottobeuren 4, Documents 291 P–R, ff. 493r–499r (Urfehdebriefe of Hanns Syber, Benedict Dietz, and Hanns Dietz all of Ottobeuren [all 3 Feb. 1527]).

[105] Ibid., respectively Documents 301L, ff. 828r–830r (Urfehdebrief of Ulrich Böckh of Frechenrieden [17 Aug. 1559]); 293W, ff. 668r–671r (Urfehdebrief of Hans Besch of Untermotz [9 Sep. 1557]); 300F, ff. 805r–808r (Urfehdebrief of Simon Enderas genannt Stromair of Hüners [21 Aug. 1559]); 307C, ff. 1029r–1032v (Urfehdebrief of Veit Hiltprandt of Günz [18 Jan. 1530]); 30AA, ff. 956r–963v (Urfehdebrief of Jörg Schlückh of Sontheim [7 Mar. 1566]).

[106] Ibid., Document 308J, ff. 1072r–1076v (Urfehdebrief of Gall Schmidt of Niederrieden for assault with weapons [12 Feb. 1530]). For his earlier violent offense of unspecified nature see Document 308G, ff. 1067v–1069v (Urfehdebrief of Gall Schmidt of Niederrieden [4 Nov. 1528]).

There were in fact two different kinds of quarantines. Some offenders the monastery thought best to hold within certain spatial limits, others it preferred to keep without. Thus Hans Sauter of Attenhausen, convicted of slander in 1531, was given two weeks to leave the lordship of the monastery and was forbidden ever to return without special permission. Waldburga Schuechstein and her cousin and guardian, Christoff Claus of Frechenrieden, were banished on similar notice and conditions when found guilty of incest in 1559, but Georg Nueber of Oberwesterheim was given only three days to leave in 1548 after threatening to haul the *Vogt* from his saddle and kill him.[107]

Banishments of this sort were often accompanied by demarcations of extraordinary detail. In 1462, for example, Johann Städelin of Sontheim was required not only to leave the monastery lands proper, but also to stay out of the area "within one half-mile distance in a circle around the said monastery [lands]." Enderas Schmidt of Niederrieden was saddled with a two-mile exclusion zone in 1544, while ten years later Jacob Schiess and his wife, Hillaria Wieland, were ordered to stay at least twelve miles away. Georg Schorer of Buchenbronnen was not only ordered to keep fully twenty miles away from the Abbot's borders, he was also obliged to promise not to spend two nights in the same place until he had reached the prescribed distance.[108] Unsatisfied with this level of specificity, the monastery also mapped out "amnesty corridors" within the various exclusion zones in an effort to mitigate the severity of banishment. The cleric Bartholme Bärtlin, exiled from his parish of Sontheim in 1547 for covert Protestant preaching, was forbidden ever again to live in the monastery lands, but he was allowed the right to traverse them as long as he promised to stay only in public inns and then not to talk to the subjects of the monastery "without honest and honorable cause."[109]

Perhaps the best example of the persistently spatial focus of Ottobeuren criminal law is provided by the career of Adam Mayr of Rempolz. In 1549 Adam's fiscal mismanagement (he was deeply indebted to a series of Jewish moneylenders) and his "criminal, rebellious and insulting public threats of violence against the monastery and its subjects" earned him a prohibition on leaving the Ottobeuren lands. Two years later, with the help of his wife, Adam added a series of thefts to his record. He was again arrested, but this time he was interrogated, tortured, and sentenced to death on the gallows. Upon a request for mercy by relatives, the monastery agreed to commute Adam's sentence, but it insisted that he and his wife and family leave the Ottobeuren lands and

---

107 Ibid., respectively Document 303D, ff. 842v–845r [21 Nov. 1531]); Document 301K, ff. 826v–828r [17 Aug. 1559]; Document 305E, ff. 984r–990r [2 Aug. 1548].
108 Ibid., respectively Document 304B, ff. 876v–882v [6 July 1462]; Document 308Q, ff. 1091v–1095r [9 May 1544]; Document 305F, ff. 990r–996r [11 Dec. 1554]; Document 291NN, ff. 538r–548r [28 Apr. 1584].
109 Ibid., Document 304X, ff. 946r–949r [16 Aug. 1547].

remain at least twelve miles away for the rest of their lives. As for Adam's four young children, the Abbot ruled that "as soon as they leave his household [*Unterhaltung*], they shall be allowed to travel through the monastery's lands and to use the common highways [through them], in order to seek their fortunes, but they shall in no way, unless specifically permitted by the Abbot, be allowed to establish permanent residence in the monastery lands."[110]

Still more carefully protected than the privileged public places was the peasant's house. The law punished any offense committed against someone inside his or her own house with a fourfold fine.[111] Rural culture accorded similar respect to the house, and angry peasants habitually challenged their enemies to come out into the street and fight, rather than violate the integrity of the house.[112] Efforts by the monastery to regulate peasant dwellings with regard to fire safety[113] were also regarded as an affront to the autonomy of the house. In 1586, four peasants in the hamlet of Waldmühle went so far as to assemble an illegal meeting of the *Gemeinde* in order to prevent house inspection by the headman, *Vierer*, and *Pittel*.[114]

The walls of the house were a barrier not just from the outside in, but also from the inside out. Just as the monastery sought to prevent political criminals from entering public spaces, it also sought to prevent other criminals from leaving private ones. Elsa Steler of Niederrieden was arrested for witchcraft after multiple denunciations in 1561. She must have been a woman of uncommon strength and courage, for despite physical infirmity, she withstood torture without confessing to anything. Impressed by her fortitude and moved by the pleas of her husband and relatives (though not completely convinced of her innocence), the *Vogt* released her from prison, but under a telling set of conditions. Elsa was obliged to promise that

---

[110] Ibid., Document 293F, ff. 621r–627v [20 May 1549] and Document 293G, ff. 627v–632r [10 Oct. 1551].

[111] Bosl, ed. *Dokumente*, Part 2, Vol. IV, Document 94. Strafordnung 1540, § 13, pp. 355–6.

[112] StAA, KL Ottobeuren 4, Document 300B, ff. 794r–797r (*Urfehdebrief* of Michael and Hans Kessler of Berg [10 June 1555]); Document 301D, ff. 816r–818r (*Urfehdebrief* of Jörg Biechler of Frechenrieden [22 June 1529]); Document 307H, ff. 1043r–1044v (*Urfehdebrief* of Jörg Zöberlin of Schweighausen [27 Mar. 1556]); Document 308L, ff. 1078r–1081r (*Urfehdebrief* of Andreas Schmidt of Niederrieden [4 Aug. 1533]).

[113] Ibid., Document 298X, ff. 381v–382r: "Bauding Buch Anno 1551". These regulations required every house to be equipped with fire hooks and ladders, and also ordered village officials to conduct regular house and hearth inspections to ensure compliance.

[114] StAA, KL Ottobeuren 587-I (14) 1586/7, Böhen: Leonhard Lang, Jacob Schindelin, Jerg Geromüller and Johann Martin "haben in der Waldtmille ein Gemaindt gehalten, den Pittel, hauptman, und vier die feuer statten nit besuchen wellen lassen." Note in the same register for the village of Niederrieden: "Martin Maÿr hatt als ain Gerichtsman, der sollich suchen verschweygen soll, den Miller gewarndt, man werde ime die Mille besuchen – [fined] £4 heller." Hanns Eegartter of the same village was also fined £4 for forewarning the miller of the impending inspection. The two village mills themselves were found wanting and their owners were fined £4. Note also in this register the fining of ten residents of the village of Wolfertschwenden £1 each for having unsafe hearths.

henceforth, and for the rest of my life, unless I receive permission from the said lord *Vogt*, or his successor or from the lordship [i.e. the monastery], I will not leave the house in which I now live or into which I may in the future move. [I will] not go out for any reason, but will peacefully and inoffensively remain within, unless it should happen that I must leave because of fire, which God forbid, and otherwise not, and [I will] also not cause or move any company to come to [visit] me.[115]

Although similar kinds of disabilites would also be imposed on adulteresses and suspected (female) poisoners,[116] I can find no example of a man being punished in the same way. This disparity of punishment is thus yet another example of the instinctively patriarchal bent of law at Ottobeuren. At the same time the *form* which punishment took – circumscription of the offender's daily life – must be recognized as an expression of an equally fundamental instinct: the ideal of a discrete living space, within which the household enclosed its own evils, and from which it defended itself from the evils of the outside world.

This ideal of the autonomous household, separate and independent from the others around it, found its most socially consequential expression in the inheritance customs of the peasantry. Although Upper Swabia has traditionally been regarded as a region of impartible inheritance, this was manifestly not the case in the fifteenth and sixteenth centuries. The monks certainly supported the residential distinctness of individual households. As in other Swabian lordships,[117] it was in fact an offense at sixteenth-century Ottobeuren for married children to remain in the same house as their parents without special permission.[118] With

---

[115] StAA, KL Ottobeuren 4, Document 308Y, ff. 1118r–1124v (*Urfehdebrief* of Elsa Steler and her husband Peter Mair of Niederrieden [26 Sep. 1561]). As was the case with most Upper Swabian monasteries, there seem to have been very few witchcraft trials at Ottobeuren (for the general pattern see Wolfgang Behringer, *Witchcraft Persecutions in Bavaria: Popular Magic, Religious Zealotry and Reason of State in Early Modern Europe*, trans. J. C. Grayson and David Lederer, (Cambridge, 1997), p. 152). Elsa's qualified acquittal is the only sixteenth-century trial that I have found, and it is suggestive that women accused of poisoning at Ottobeuren were not automatically charged with witchcraft (see note 116). The peasantry themselves certainly believed in witches. In 1602, Hans Sommer of Hawangen and his wife accused Hans' aunt of being a witch ("Unholdin"), and Hans beat the unfortunate woman very severely ("gar ubl"). The monastery, by contrast, was uninterested in prosecuting the aunt, although it did fine Hans £2 for his brutality. StAA, KL Ottobeuren 587-II, Heft 22 "Strafregister 1602/3."

[116] StAA, KL Ottobeuren 4, Document 299E, ff. 782v–785r (*Urfehdebrief* of Agnesa Rot of Böhen [24 July 1545]); Document 308S, ff. 1100v–1104v (*Urfehdebrief* of Agatha Schweiggart and her husband Jörg Rewel of Niederrieden [23 Nov. 1548]).

[117] The 1528 village ordinance of nearby Volkratshofen explicitly forbade married children from staying longer than one year with their parents, Blickle, *Memmingen*, p. 247 n. 497.

[118] StAA, KL Ottobeuren 587-I, Heft 1 (1546): "Lang Hans" of Benningen fined £1 5 ß for allowing his son-in-law to move in with him without permission. Similarly KL Ottobeuren 587-II, Heft 25 (1604/5): Jerg Nueber of Westerheim's daughter "is always at her father's [house]; she is ordered to leave because of her husband who was from Attenhausen – [fined] 10 ß." See also ibid., Heft 17 (1593/4) where Christian Sitt of Benningen is fined 10 ß because he "has repeatedly taken in his stepson and his [i.e. the stepson's] wife, despite prohibition." It is possible that in

regard to peasant landholding, on the other hand, the monastery was concerned to preserve the integrity of rent-producing units. Once the peasantry gained firmer title to the land, however, it was harder to prevent them from doing what they wanted with it. And what a great many of the Abbot's subjects wanted to do with the land was divide it.

The strength of this fissile impulse was often remarkable. The hamlet of Schachen, for example, consisted of a single large *Hof* which was acquired by Johann Biler in 1524. Biler saw three of his children grow to adulthood, and in 1542 he ceded half of the land to his son-in-law, Jos Epplin, while promising to give the other half later to his son, Johann the younger. The second daughter was given an interest in her sister's share. Equitable and decisive though it may seem, the partition was still not enough to content Jos Epplin's prickly sense of independence, and he was soon embroiled in a series of quarrels with his father-in-law. The two men seem to have found a great deal to argue about, but it is striking how many of the disputes were over the specificity and integrity of the boundaries between the two farms. How were the costs of maintaining the water pipes to be shared? Was Johann senior entitled to drive a cart through his son-in-law's property? To whom did the two cherry trees along the village street belong? Exactly how should the garden be divided between the households? In the end the dispute consumed both of them. By 1546 Johann senior was dead, while money problems had forced Jos Epplin to undergo the humiliation of selling back his share of the land to his mother-in-law.[119]

In the face of peasant insistence, the monastery was ultimately willing to set aside its misgivings about subdivision, as long as its landlordly rights and perquisites remained unaffected. In the hamlet of Stephansried, for example, the Aberöll family was granted a property in *Erblehenrecht* in 1457. In 1479 they petitioned the monastery for permission to divide the property among themselves, and were allowed to do so provided "that they the tenants none the less shall and will hold the property according to the [terms of the 1457] *Erblehen* charter, and also [provided] that this subdivision occasion no prejudice to or diminution of the majesty, freedom, prerogatives, annuities, revenues, tithes, and rents of the monastery and overlord, as if this subdivision had not been permitted."[120]

During the fifteenth century, the conversion to and creation of *Erblehen* tenures often went hand in hand with authorization to subdivide. Thus in 1427, two isolated holdings known as Bernhalden and Kräpflins were granted in heritable tenure to one Johann der Menknecht and his heirs "that they should

this last case the stepson had been banished for a criminal offense, but there is no suggestion of this in the MS., and the term "despite prohibition" (*uber verbott*) is ambiguous.

[119] StAA, KU Ottobeuren 969 [6 June 1524], 1240 [12 Feb. 1542], 1289 [14 June 1546], 1293 [25 Nov. 1546], and 1355 [3 Mar. 1550].

[120] StAA, KL Ottobeuren 18, ff. 33r–34r.

keep them tilled and build [upon] them as many houses and barns as they desire, always, however, without any damages to the overlord."[121] Alternatively a single landholding might be granted out in heritable tenure to a group of people on the understanding that they might subdivide it. A 1466 charter granting a wood and field to Peter Hartmann, Hans Maier, and Hans Dreier in the village of Böhen declares that "the tenants shall make no changes to the *Erblehen* [property]; they may, however, divide the property among themselves, and make four parts out of it, or keep the land together undivided, as they wish."[122] Sometimes the monastery would even divide up its own properties itself. Thus in 1462, Abbot Wilhelm von Lustenau converted the tenure of a *Gotteshausrecht* holding known as the "Geyßell" in the hamlet of Leupolz to *Erblehenrecht*, and granted it to Jos Schweygger, Connrat Khlockher, and Hanns Lautterweinn. The tenants received shares of one half, one quarter, and one quarter of the "Geyßell" respectively.[123]

By the sixteenth century, there was less forested land available for clearance and therefore somewhat fewer new *Erblehen* holdings were created. This did not, however, put a stop to the subdivision of existing ones. In the hamlet of Wolfarts, the widow Ursula Winneberger began the subdivision of her deceased husband's *Hof* by ceding one quarter of the land to her son-in-law, Veit Zedtler, in 1504.[124] In 1524 we find five siblings who have inherited "half of seven parts of the holding in Motzen."[125] A charter issued in 1534 describes a tenant as holding "one quarter of the entire [hamlet of] Karlass, which has been divided into five parts."[126] In the hamlet of Bibelsberg, the huge *Maierhof*, intact at least since 1421, was split among three members of the Aberöll family in 1540.[127]

The long-term implications of this pattern are obvious: fragmentation of the heritable tenancies. In 1443 the hamlet of Langenberg consisted of only two such holdings, farmed by the widow Anna Blenckh and her children. By 1544, however, the two holdings had been subdivided into seven and by 1551 into nine smaller holdings.[128] A similar process unfolded in the hamlet of Hohenheim, which is first mentioned in the Ottobeuren charters in 1403. A single large *Hof* was divided into halves in 1441, into quarters by 1480, and by 1544 into nine

---

[121] Ibid., ff. 234v–235r. Similarly the grant in (Warlins and Lampolz) in 1430, where the charter declares that the tenants "may also build additional houses upon it [the *Hof*], [but only if this is done] without [causing] loss to the monastery." Ibid., ff. 254r–v.

[122] Ibid., ff. 221r–222v.

[123] Ibid., ff. 150r–151v. Similarly the grant of the Felsenberg near Dietratried in equal shares to five tenants in 1463. Ibid., ff. 197r–198r.

[124] StAA, KU Ottobeuren 684 [27 Mar. 1504].

[125] StAA, KU Ottobeuren 970 [13 June 1524].

[126] StAA, KU Ottobeuren 1120 [9 Jan. 1534].

[127] StAA, KL Ottobeuren 18, ff. 117r–119v.

[128] Ibid., ff. 44r–45r; KL Ottobeuren 29, ff. 8v–10r.

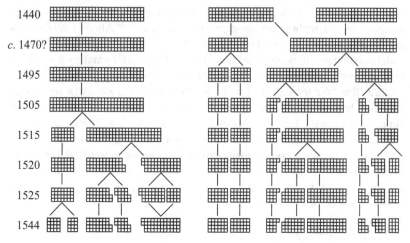

Figure 2.1 Subdivision of the *Höfe* in the Hamlet of Reuthen, 1440–1544

Note: The squares represent proportional shares of the total rent payment, which was calibrated to the surface of the holdings. Reconstruction is helped by the fact that the scribe of the 1544 rent roll preserved a record of the hamlet's original structure by grouping the fragmented holdings as subdivisions of the original three *Höfe*. See StAA, KL Ottobeuren 29, ff. 19v–21v.

Sources: StAA, KU Ottobeuren 501–1256; KL Ottobeuren 18, 29, 64, 541 (2) and 600

small tenancies.[129] Still more dramatic was the fragmentation of the hamlet of Reuthen (see Figure 2.1). In 1440 Abbot Johann Schedler granted the hamlet's original three large *Höfe* in *Erblehenrecht* to Jacob Öxlin, Hans Maier, and Conrad Maier. The annual *Gült* for each *Hof* was to be five, six, and six *viertel* of oats, respectively, for a total of seventeen. In 1544, the total rent obligation recorded in the monastery's rent roll was virtually the same: seventeen and a quarter *viertel* of oats. Over the course of the intervening 104 years, however, the three large *Höfe* had been cut up into thirteen smaller tenancies.

Since a grant in *Erblehenrecht* invested not only the tenant, but also his heirs with a right to the property, it may seem unsurprising that heritable tenancies were so often subdivided. A grant in *Gotteshausrecht*, by contrast, was a right limited to a single person for the term of his own life only. Not only did *Gotteshausrecht* charters routinely contain explicit prohibitions on partitioning the land,[130] but the monastery's ordinances even prescribed a list of farm equipment and supplies (a wagon, a plough, two bales of hay, twenty-four *viertel* of oats, and all of the straw and manure) which a departing tenant was forbidden

---

[129] Hoffmann, ed. *Urkunden*, no. 161 [28 May 1403]. StAA, KL Ottobeuren 18, ff. 62v–68r; KL Ottobeuren 29, ff. 13v–14v.
[130] See for example StAA, KU Ottobeuren 419 [6 Feb. 1484]. Note thas this *Hof* was none the less partitioned thirteen years later. KU Ottobeuren 596 [1 Dec. 1497]. See also Figure 2.2.

to remove from the *Hof*.[131] Nevertheless, sternness of language was mitigated by flexibility of practice. And as was the case with *de facto* heritability, *Gotteshausrecht* farms proved no less susceptible to partition than their *Erblehenrecht* counterparts.

Evidence for the partibility of life-term *Höfe* is of two sorts. The first is the simple description of these properties in the monastery's charters and *Erdschatzbücher*, or entry fine registers. These descriptions provide unambiguous evidence that even the *Gotteshausrecht* holdings must have undergone subdivisions at some point in the past. There is no other way to explain the repeated use of the term "half-*Hof*" to describe *Gotteshausrecht* properties in the villages of Sontheim (1521, 1549), Hawangen (1536, 1537, 1541), Attenhausen (1542), Schlegelsberg (1550), Dietratried (1554), Böhen (1558), and Oberwesterheim (1561). In the village of Böhen there are even references to quarter-*Höfe* (1526, 1542) and eighth-*Höfe* (1543).[132]

The monastery's rent rolls provide further indirect evidence of the subdivision of the *Gotteshausrecht* properties. On a number of occasions the roll records the names of two tenants for a single *Hof* and then two separate rent payments, one for each tenant. The obvious implication is that although the *Hof* is considered by the monastery to be a single fiscal unit, it has for the purposes of land use effectively been divided into two.[133] Thus for example the rent roll for 1544 lists a *Hof* in Untermoosbach held by Barthlome Weissenhorn and Lienhart Bürklin. The total grain rent was 6.5 *malter*, half of which was paid by each tenant. The same pattern may be found for a single *Hof* in Böhen jointly held by Barthlome Hegel and Hans Höltzlin: a total rent of 3.71 *malter* of which 2.47 *malter* was paid by Hegel and the remaining 1.24 *malter* by Höltzlin.[134]

The mass of sixteenth-century references to subdivided *Gotteshausrecht* holdings do not by themselves establish that partition was then still current, but there is abundant evidence from other charters that this was in fact the case. A large *Hof* in Oberwesterheim was split between Alexander Maier and his brother Johann in 1511.[135] The Attenhausen *Maierhof* was subdivided in

---

131 StAA, KL Ottobeuren 4, Document 289X (*c.* 1551), ff. 368r–369v (regulations for the hamlets of Ottobeuren parish) and ff. 372r–373v (regulations for the villages). If the new tenant objected to the quality of the wagon left behind, he was to be compensated with a full cartload of manure.

132 StAA, KU Ottobeuren 923, 986, 1164, 1170, 1333, and 1365; StAA, KL Ottobeuren 27, ff. 13v, 65v, 85v, 89v, 91r, 125r, and 179r. The monastery's ordinance (*c.* 1551) regulating the stocking of *Gotteshausrecht* holdings explicitly recognizes a difference between "full" and "half" *Höfe*. StAA, KL Ottobeuren 4, Document 289X, ff. 368v–369v.

133 The 1544 rent roll also documents this pattern for *Erblehenrecht* properties, e.g., in Unter- and Oberwolfertschwenden. StAA, KL Ottobeuren 29, ff. 43r, 46r.

134 Ibid., ff. 31r, 55v.

135 StAA, KU Ottobeuren 796 [8 Nov. 1511]. See also KU Ottobeuren 863 [6 Oct. 1516], in which Alexander's *Hof* passes to the man his widow later married.

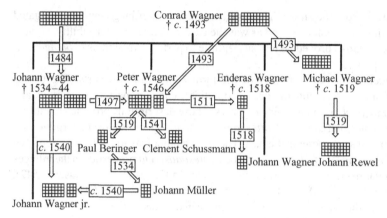

Johann Wagner jr.

Figure 2.2 Subdivision of the *Höfe* of the Wagner family of Sontheim, 1484–1541. Death dates are denoted by †.
Sources: StAA, KU Ottobeuren 419–1233; KL Ottobeuren 27, 29, 64, 541 (2), 600 and 601-I

1512,[136] as was the *Hof* of Adam Schick.[137] The brothers Thoma and Johann Dreier of Dietratried each received half of a *Hof* after their stepfather gave up his own tenancy in 1513.[138] After the death of Hans Brew of Benningen, his land was divided between his brother Michael and his widow, Ursula Blödler, in 1513. An additional piece was split off from Michael's share in 1518; the remnant passed to his son in 1533.[139] In some cases, charters have survived in sufficient numbers to permit the documentation of multi-generational partition, as in the case of the Wagner family of Sontheim (see Figure 2.2).

Explicit divisions of *Gotteshausrecht* holdings are also recorded in the *Erdschatzbücher*. In the village of Sontheim, for example, Jerg Schick's *Hof* was divided between his nephews Barthlome and Jerg Schick in 1546.[140] Jacob Weissenhorn's *Hof* in the village of Hawangen was split into two halves, which passed separately to his two sons-in-law in 1559 and 1560.[141] Some divisions even took place without the pressure of kin. Thus in the hamlet of Guggenberg, a *Hof* was split among three apparently unrelated people in 1571.[142]

---

[136] StAA, KU Ottobeuren 803 and 804 [both 1 Mar. 1512]. Caspar Maier had been admitted to the entire *Maierhof* on 3 February, 1483. KU Ottobeuren 406.

[137] StAA, KU Ottobeuren 802 and 805 [both 1 Mar. 1512]. Adam Schick had been admitted to the entire *Hof* on 15 March 1498. KU Ottobeuren 604.

[138] StAA, KU Ottobeuren 816–17 [12 Feb. 1513].

[139] StAA, KU Ottobeuren 822 and 823 [14 Oct. 1513], KU 876 [8 Jan. 1518], and KU 1107 [14 Jan. 1533].

[140] The original *Hof* is described in the 1544 rent roll at StAA, KL Ottobeuren 29, f. 70v; the transfer is recorded in StAA, KL Ottobeuren 27, ff. 139v–140r. Note that the 1567 roll still treats the separated halves as a single rent-paying unit with two tenants. StAA, KL Ottobeuren 30, ff. 73r–v.

[141] StAA, KL Ottobeuren 29, f. 29v; KL Ottobeuren 27, f. 16r. These two holdings were also classed as a single unit in 1567. StAA, KL Ottobeuren 30, f. 31r.

[142] StAA, KL Ottobeuren 27, f. 9r.

Uneven documentary survival makes it difficult to assess the long-term pattern of partibility of the *Gotteshausrecht Höfe* (as was possible in the case of the hamlet of Reuthen). For the short term, a partial balance sheet can be drawn up for the village of Attenhausen, where the 1544 rent roll lists twenty-one *Hof* complexes. At least nine of these descended from the partition of four larger *Höfe* between 1504 and 1533. Other subdivisions may well have taken place in this interval, but ambiguities of the evidence make it difficult to pronounce with certainty.[143]

As significant as the frequency of these partitions is the circumstances under which they took place: in opposition to the wishes of the monastery. The conveyances of the Kopp family of Attenhausen[144] are a good example of this pattern (see Figure 2.3). Enderas Kopp, who is first mentioned in 1473,[145] was the tenant of a very large *Gotteshausrecht Hof* measuring some 113 *jauchert* (46.8 hectares), including a valuable sawmill.[146] In 1504 he asked to convey all but 10 *jauchert* and the sawmill to his nephew Peter Kopp. The monastery was leery about the proposal, and agreed only after extracting separate sealed oaths from Enderas and his son Veit that the separated lands would be reunited with the sawmill and retained remnant at Enderas' death.[147] Not only was the agreement never honored, but the monastery found itself obliged to assent to a second partition in 1511, when Peter split off half of his *Hof* and gave it to his son Galli. So completely had the 1504 agreement been abandoned that the monastery agreed to allow Galli to build a new house on his half of the land, and even to provide the building materials itself. Two days later Galli's cousin Veit was quietly invested with the sawmill.[148]

The fragmentation which characterized spaces of production at Ottobeuren was an equally prominent feature of spaces of circulation. That is to say, marketplaces and exchange circuits were marked by an encapsulation and

---

[143] For example, the *Hof* of Caspar Hegel first appears in the Ottobeuren records in 1536, when it passed to him from one Conrad Sauter. The land had quite possibly been split off from the large *Hof* to which a certain Ulrich Hegel (Caspar's father?) was admitted in 1512. When Ulrich Hegel died in 1534, his (unnamed) widow was given temporary custody of at least some of his land, which then passed to a son, Alexander, in 1538. Ulrich's widow may have married Conrad Sauter, but there is no way to be sure. StAA, KU Ottobeuren 802 [1 Mar. 1512], 1142 [11 Jan. 1536], and 1188 [2 Aug. 1538]. See also the less detailed entries of KL Ottobeuren 27, f. 125r. A more complex problem is presented by the career of Hans Schmidt, who accumulated at least four separate holdings, including the Attenhausen smithy, between 1490 and 1498. He conveyed one to an apparently unrelated man in 1498, and then divided the rest between his son and son-in-law in 1501. Given the disparate origin of Schmidt's properties, it seems misleading to class the "subdivision" of his lands in 1501 as an example of partible inheritance. KU Ottobeuren 481 [26 Jan. 1490], 519 [7 Feb. 1492], 600 and 602 [both 29 Jan. 1498], 611 [9 Aug. 1498], 640 and 641 [both 21 Apr. 1501].

[144] StAA, KL Ottobeuren 601-II, ff. 12r–v; KL Ottobeuren 600, ff. 235v, 237r, and 238r.

[145] StAA, KU Ottobeuren 339 [10 Nov. 1473].

[146] This estimate is based on measurements of the remnants made between 1569 and 1572. StAA, KL Ottobeuren 27, ff. 128v–129v.

[147] StAA, KU Ottobeuren 681–2 [18 Mar. 1504].

[148] StAA, KU Ottobeuren 787 and 788 [28 and 30 May 1511].

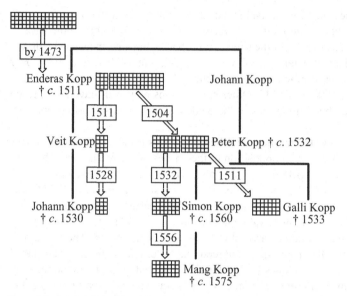

Figure 2.3 Subdivision of the *Höfe* of the Kopp family of Attenhausen, 1473–1556. Death dates are denoted by †.
Sources: StAA, KU Ottobeuren 339–1112; KL Ottobeuren 25 (Mü.B.), 27, 29, 64, 541 (2), 600 and 601-I

rivalry strongly reminiscent of the subcommunities of wealth, gender, kinship, enmity, and residence into which the Ottobeuren peasantry was divided. This description may seem odd to the modern mind, which regards commerce as an inherently integrative process (hence the tendency to think in terms of 'the' market). As shall be seen, however, sixteenth-century markets did not function in this way, and in large part because almost no one wanted them to.

It was not for lack of marketplaces that the sixteenth-century economy was so internally disconnected. Indeed, the most striking feature of the economic geography of the region at the close of the Middle Ages was the creation of new markets all over the countryside. In neighboring Bavaria, the establishment of rural markets had tapered off after the High Middle Ages, with few foundations post-dating the year 1300.[149] In Upper Swabia, by contrast, the late fifteenth century saw a surge of foundations (including Pfaffenhofen in 1479, Legau, Martinszell, Unterthingen, and Buchenberg in 1485, Kirchheim in 1490, Oberstdorf in 1495, and Ottobeuren itself in 1488, privileges expanded

---

[149] Wilhelm Liebhart, "Zur spätmittelalterlichen, landesherrlichen Marktgründungspolitik in Ober- und Niederbayern" in Pankraz Fried, ed., *Bayerische Landesgeschichte an der Universität Augsburg 1975–1977* (Sigmaringen, 1979), pp. 151–2.

in 1498), with the result that the countryside was much more thickly strewn with markets than the Wittelsbach dominions to the east.[150] Of course, the multiplication of markets is not an unambiguous sign of commercial quickening, since new foundations also reflected political and territorial considerations. At the same time, it would be wrong to attribute the overall pattern entirely to the machinations of statecraft. The rural market network in southern Germany persisted in the form it had reached by 1500 almost without alteration for another three hundred and fifty years.[151] Had the late medieval foundations been attempts to plant markets in a commercial desert, they would have withered away *en masse*, as a few of them actually did.[152]

The dense urban network of the German southwest further intensified the prominence of markets in rural life. At Ottobeuren the monastery lands were ringed by cities on all sides, first and foremost Memmingen immediately to the west, but also Isny and Kempten to the south, Mindelheim and Augsburg to the east and northeast, and Ulm to the far north. Commerce was the lifeblood of these cities, and their merchants traded all over Europe. The Völins of Memmingen, for example, maintained factors as far afield as Saragossa, Antwerp, Vienna, and Venice. For the trade in luxury items, the role of the city was often no more than that of a conduit. Thus ginger and pepper might be purchased in Genoa, hauled over the Alps to Memmingen, and then shipped down the Rhine to Cologne, occasioning barely a ripple in the Ottobeuren villages. The bulk of Memmingen's trade, however, was in more modest articles produced in the immediately surrounding region.[153] And as buyers and sellers of grain, salt, cattle, and textiles, the merchants of Memmingen exercised a profound influence on the economic life of the monastery lands.

During the closing decades of the fifteenth century and the opening decades of the sixteenth, the commercial ties between Memmingen and its rural hinterland strengthened considerably. The bond had always been close. The Abbot of Ottobeuren was a citizen of the city and maintained a house there for the sale of rent-derived agricultural products. Both the currency and the weights and measures of the city were in standardized use throughout the Abbot's dominions.

---

[150] See the map of medieval and early modern market towns in Max Spindler, *Bayerischer Geschichtsatlas* (Munich, 1969), pp. 22–3. Based on 1844 boundaries, Upper Bavaria had one market town for every 228 square kilometers, whereas Bavarian Swabia had one for every 131 square kilometers. Areas taken from the *Statistisches Jahrbuch für das Königreich Bayern*, Band XII (Munich, 1913), p. 1.

[151] Roman Maurer, "Entwicklung und Funktionswandel der Märkte in Altbayern seit 1800," *Miscellanea Bavarica Monacensia* 30 (1971), p. 9.

[152] The same point has been made by Tom Scott for the Upper Rhine, which saw a similar multiplication of rural markets at this time. Tom Scott, "Economic Conflict and Co-operation on the Upper Rhine 1450–1600" in E. J. Kouri and Tom Scott, eds., *Politics and Society in Reformation Europe* (New York, 1987), pp. 210–31, at pp. 220–223.

[153] Raimund Eirich, *Memmingens Wirtschaft und Patriziat von 1347 bis 1551* (Weissenhorn, 1971), pp. 106–12, 146–50.

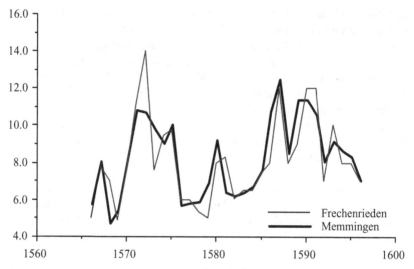

Figure 2.4 Rye prices in Memmingen and Frechenrieden in *Pfunde* per *malter*, 1566–96
Sources: StadtA MM D Folioband 99, D 102/1a-1b; StAA, KL Ottobeuren 654

In the 1490s Memmingen went to considerable efforts to improve the roads connecting it to its hinterland, and both the city fathers (1491) and the Abbot (1498) acquired toll privileges in order to profit from the swelling flow of trade through the region. This commercial surge was primarily driven by local exchange, as is indicated by the expansion in the 1520s of the Memmingen weekly market, which was dominated by buyers and sellers from the immediate region, and the concomitant decline in the 1530s of the annual market, whose patrons came from further afield.[154]

The later sixteenth century provides a still more vivid example of the commercial intertwining of the Abbot's dominions and the city. Every year the churchwardens in the monastery villages drew up an account of the receipts and disbursements of the parish church. A certain proportion of the income was derived in grain, which was sold and the cash value then entered into the account. These *Heiligenrechnungen*, as the accounts are known, thus provide an invaluable record of rural grain prices which may fruitfully be compared with equivalent Memmingen prices. A fairly complete run of these accounts is available for a number of villages during the years 1566–96. The close synchrony of prices between town and country is illustrated in Figure 2.4.

At least on the surface, then, the comforting presence of familiar categories – money prices and markets – imparts a respectably modern appearance to

---

[154] Rolf Kiessling, *Die Stadt und ihr Land – Umlandpolitik, Bürgerbesitz und Wirtschaftsgefüge in Ostschwaben vom 14. bis ins 16. Jahrhundert* (Cologne and Vienna, 1989), pp. 430–43.

sixteenth-century rural exchange. If we dig a little deeper, however, two kinds of anomalies begin to emerge. First, buying and selling turn out to have had a highly unusual shape at Ottobeuren, by which is meant that monetary exchange was altogether differently constituted in time and space than superficial resemblances to a modern market would lead us to believe. Second, money itself had a different role to that which it has in a modern economy.

Let us begin with the spatial dimension of market exchange. We have seen that the impulse for exchange among the peasantry was served by a dense network of rural markets, a network fortified by the overarching commercial penumbra of the city of Memmingen. Intuitively, it seems that this commercial landscape should result in a single homogeneous market. Traders would quickly capitalize on any opportunity to buy low in one locality and sell high in another, with the result that internal price discrepancies would rapidly be levelled. Indeed, for those who take a supply and demand approach to price formation, the very existence of a market is defined in terms of this homogeneity. In the words of Marshall's classic 1890 formulation, "Economists understand by the term *market* the whole of any region in which buyers and sellers are in such free intercourse with one another that the prices of the same goods tend to equality easily and quickly."[155] This does not mean that prices throughout an economy are everywhere the same. But in a small marketing region such as the Ottobeuren villages, where close proximity made for negligible differences in transport costs, prices should be uniform. And yet they were not.

Price differentials in the sixteenth century were surprisingly high, even between neighboring villages. In 1569, for example, the price of a *malter* of rye in the village of Hawangen was 2.4 *gulden*. Next door in Frechenrieden the price was 2.8 *gulden*. In Günz the *malter* of rye sold for 2.86 *gulden*, and in Niederdorf for 4.0 *gulden*. In other words, in four neighboring villages all within walking distance of each other, the price of the same measure of the same grain varied by 66.7 percent. And as is clear from Figure 2.5, there was nothing at all extraordinary about a differential of this order. In at least half of the years in the period 1566–96, in fact, rye prices in these villages varied by at least 50 percent. Each village was a spatial isolate, an exchange economy unto itself.

If the spatial dimension of monetary exchange at Ottobeuren resembled nothing so much as a collection of fragments, this was equally true of its temporal dimension. For a society in which exchange was well-nigh universal, the actual rhythm of buying and selling was startlingly discontinuous. Perhaps the best illustration of this pattern is provided by the commercial activities of the monastery itself. As will be seen in chapter 3, the monastery derived a sizeable proportion of its income from the sale of grain. A few of these sales

[155] Alfred Marshall, *Principles of Economics*, 8th edn (London, repr.1946,), p. 324.

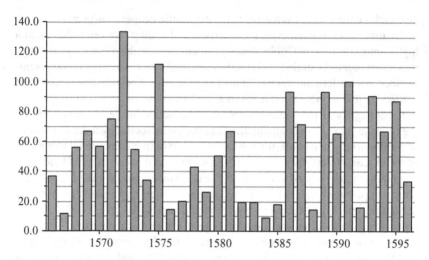

Figure 2.5 Range of variation (percent) in rye prices among four Ottobeuren villages, 1566–96
Sources: StAA, KL Ottobeuren 654, 657, 744a; KA Ottobeuren 189, 240

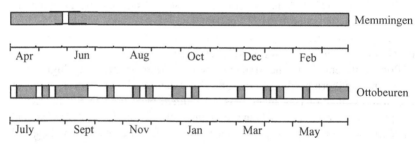

Figure 2.6 Temporal distribution of grain sales at Memmingen, 1488/9 and Ottobeuren, 1527/8.
The shading denotes those weeks on which grain was sold.
Sources: StAA, KL Ottobeuren 541, Heft 1; Kiessling, *Die Stadt und ihr Land,* p. 431

took place in the monastery's house in Memmingen, but most of the grain was offered for sale in the market town of Ottobeuren. The records of the monastery granary do not cover all of the grain sold to the Ottobeuren peasantry, although the granary drew buyers from nearly every hamlet and village in the Abbot's dominions. These records do, however, represent the transactions of a vendor who not only sold more grain than anyone else in the monastery lands, but more importantly always had grain to sell. The monastery milled grain fifty out of fifty-two weeks in the year[156] and regularly had grain stores left over when the harvests recommenced in the fall. Figure 2.6 presents the weekly distribution

[156] See the milling schedule for the years 1549–52 in StAA, KL Ottobeuren 164.

of the monastery's grain sales in the year 1527/8. The sporadic nature of the pattern is arresting, particularly when compared with the smooth continuity of sales in Memmingen.

The phenomenon was to some extent a reflection of the natural rhythms of an agrarian society, where income arrived all in a rush with the fall harvest and then had to be stretched out over the rest of the year. Even those who acquired their subsistence by means of exchange could not escape the influence of the seasons, since the demand for day laborers to help with mowing and threshing always produced a surge of earning opportunities at harvest time.[157] None the less, the ebb and flow of the crop cycle is at best only a partial explanation for the irregular pattern of grain sales. Despite the importance of harvest time day labor, we cannot ignore the leveling introduced into the earning patterns of the rural poor by cow-herding, building maintenance, and other agricultural work unrelated to the harvest, not to mention industrial by-employment such as spinning and weaving. Above all, it must be kept in mind that the same poverty which obliged the majority of the peasantry to earn, rather than harvest, the grain they ate also constrained them from buying an entire year's supply at one fell swoop in the fall. For the land poor, subsistence was necessarily a process of continuous acquisition.[158] That this pattern should have coincided with such irregular purchases of grain is a provocative comment about the relationship between money and exchange.

It turns out, in fact, that the Ottobeuren peasantry disposed of surprisingly little money. In 1529 the monastery drew up a summary of the debts owed to it by its subjects. Given the size of the Abbot's dominions, the monetary sum was quite moderate; some thousand households owed just under 1,900 *gulden*. Total collections, however, amounted to barely a tenth of this sum.[159] Naturally the amortization rate of these debts is not the best indication of the size of peasant cash reserves, and may instead reflect the legendary tightfistedness of the Swabian *Bauer*.[160] After all, a comparable proportion of the peasants' 1529 grain debts also remained unpaid. Be that as it may, the details of peasant indebtedness provide two important indications that money was appreciably scarcer at Ottobeuren than might otherwise be expected.

---

[157] See the discussion in Peter Spufford, *Money and its Use in Medieval Europe* (Cambridge, 1988), pp. 382–7. For an anthropological perspective see Stuart M. Plattner, "Periodic Trade in Developing Areas without Markets" in Carol A. Smith, ed., *Regional Analysis* (2 vols., New York, 1976), Vol. I, pp. 81–5.

[158] The monastery ordinances envision the average purchaser buying only a fourteen-day supply of grain at a time. StAA, KL Ottobeuren 4, Document 289V, ff. 355v–356r [5 Aug. 1601].

[159] StAA, KL Ottobeuren 550 and KL Ottobeuren 541, Heft 2.

[160] A later, but still illustrative example of this trait: in 1601 Balthas and Michael Knaus of Schlegelsberg were fined ten shillings for not paying off a debt of borrowed grain to the monastery "even though, as was later observed, they had the money with them at the time." StAA, KL Ottobeuren 587-II, Heft 21.

First, the very composition of peasant debt is highly suggestive. Why would the peasants be paying debts not only of pounds and *gulden*, but also of rye, oats, and spelt, not to mention iron, wood, and eggs? One possibility is that the debts derived from obligations in kind and were recorded that way to protect their value from inflation. This explanation is clearly inadequate, since the monks were perfectly able to keep track of price changes and convert obligations in kind accordingly. Indeed, both rents and debts of grain were routinely paid in money, and it was standard practice to establish for each accounting year an official cash equivalent for grain obligations known as the *Anschlag*.[161] A more plausible explanation for the only partial monetization of peasant debts is that the economy of the villages was itself only partially monetized.

This explanation is further supported by a second feature of peasant indebtedness, namely that, even when an obligation was incurred in specie, it was frequently repaid in decidedly non-monetary form by rich and poor alike. The reparations taxes imposed by the monastery after the Peasants' War of 1525 provide a perfect illustration of this pattern. Each householder was assessed a sum ranging from three quarters to ten *gulden*, and although most of the payments seem to have been made in cash, a great many of them were not. In the village of Hawangen, Simon Graus paid off some of his assessment by helping to collect the tithe. Hans Baur was credited 25 *kreuzer* for threshing work, Jacob Gaisser the same amount for hunting. Hans Sauter gave up a calf in exchange for a half-*gulden* reduction of his tax bill; the wealthy village miller received two *gulden* for a cow.[162] Other settlements saw arrangements of a different sort. The seven and a half *gulden* charge imposed on rich Ulrich Schlichting of Frechenrieden was paid by a combination of cash, flax, and mowing work. Jerg Lang of Niederrieden settled 45 *kreuzer* of his bill by giving up some of his land.[163] In the hamlets a truly dizzying range of goods was exchanged against the cash obligations, including wood, cattle, lard, coal, cloth, salt, even plums and onions! As in the villages, these in-kind payers included the unambiguously prosperous. Oswald Zettler, the richest man in Guggenberg, paid the first third of his assessment with cash, oats, and cloth.[164]

---

[161] A clear illustration of the flexibility of this system may be found in StAA, KL Ottobeuren 38, an account for various debts since 1604 collected in 1613. For rye, the *Anschlag* was 48 kr. per *viertel* for debts incurred in 1609, 53 kr. for 1610, 56 for 1611, 54 for 1612, and 60 for 1613.

[162] StAA, KL Ottobeuren 541, Heft 2, ff. 17v–18v. A reliable estimate of the overall proportion of the tax paid in kind is not possible. The assessments were supposed to be paid in three installments, but only the first installment has been recorded in any significant number of cases. Even then the entries are not without ambiguity. Where a payment has been recorded without mention of an in-kind exchange, it may seem safe to assume that the assessment was settled in cash. That the scribe should in some cases (e.g. f. 54r) have felt the need to specify 'one *gulden* paid in money' indicates that this may not always have been the case.

[163] Ibid., ff. 32r, 34r.   [164] Ibid., ff. 43r, 46v–61r.

It could of course be argued that the frequency of in-kind payments was in this case the temporary result of post-Peasants' War devastation, but this suspicion is laid to rest by the persistence of the pattern long after 1525. Consider, for example, the following extract from the debt book of 1543 for a wealthy *Hof* tenant[165] from the village of Benningen:

> Jerg Knopff owes 22 fl. *Erdschatz* [; an] old [debt] – to pay four fl. annually paid $2\frac{1}{2}$ fl. by driving to Immenstadt with five horses two days after St. Cecilia's Day[166]

Or this extract from the hamlet of Hof:

> Hans Hildtprandt: new [debt] 19 ß; also old [debt] 6 ß 1 h; also 7 ß Eegart-tithe
> paid 4 ß with eggs Quasimodo Geniti
> paid 3 ß 9 h with eggs on Pentecost
> paid 1 ß with eggs Sunday before St. John's Day also 7 ß cash
> paid 4 *batzen* with a hen on the octave of the Feast of the Twelve Apostles
> paid 7 ß h [cash][167]

A widow[168] from the market town of Ottobeuren:

> Old Barbara Wißmuller: new [debt] £1 5 ß; also old [debt] 17 ß 6 h
> paid 4 ß with spinning five days after Reminiscere
> paid £1 [cash] three days after Oculi
> paid 3 ß with a hen Sunday before St. John's Day
> paid 3 ß 6 h with haymaking before St. John's Day
> paid 5 ß with haymaking . . .[169]

Again from the market town, this time one of the ten wealthiest burghers:[170]

> Petter Stâhele: new [debt] £7 17 ß 9 h; old [debt] 12 ß 4 h; also very old [debt] £1 4 ß 8 h on account of Hans Widenman of Guggenberg
> paid £1 7 ß with 35 lbs. of meat Saturday after St. John's Day,
> also 1 ß 6 h with a liver
> also £1 3 ß 7 h with 32 [lbs.] of meat in the vigil of SS. Peter and Paul's Day
> also 1 ß 6 h with a liver
> also 1 ß 6 h with a liver on the feast of the Visitation of Mary also £3 15 ß with meat, liver and cutlets three days after St. Ulrich's Day . . .[171]

---

[165] Jerg Knopf was the tenant of a huge (83.75 *jauchert*) *Hof* yielding an annual grain rent of 8.5 *malter* in 1544. StAA, KL Ottobeuren 29, f. 35r; KL Ottobeuren 27, f. 49v.

[166] StAA, KL Ottobeuren 409, f. 6r.

[167] Ibid., f. 62r. This man's wealth is impossible to estimate, since the returns from Hof are missing in the 1546 tax register.

[168] Barbara Wißmuller is listed as a widow in the 1548 serfbook. StAA, KL 600, f. 9r. She cannot be identified with certainty in the 1546 tax register, but like most widows she probably was poor.

[169] StAA, KL Ottobeuren 409, f. 89v.

[170] Peter Stehelin's 1546 tax assessment was 1 *gulden*, placing him in the top 7.1 percent of the 141 tax payers (institutions excluded) in the *Markt* Ottobeuren. StAA, KL Ottobeuren 64, ff. 44r–46v.

[171] StAA, KL Ottobeuren 409, f. 90v.

To these examples could be added many others, but the point should by now be clear. Money was a frequent, but nevertheless episodic presence in the economy of the peasantry.

Taxonomically, then, sixteenth-century Ottobeuren proves to be extremely awkward. Too suffused with exchange for a natural or subsistence society, the economy of the peasantry at the same time does not conform to the rules of the neoclassical paradigm. The only way to resolve this paradox, I would argue, is to examine more closely how contemporaries understood exchange. The best place to begin is the Abbot's council room in the early part of the next century.

In the winter of 1622, the Abbot of Ottobeuren convened his advisors for a discussion on markets and prices. The year's harvest had been deficient, and the usual problems of the ensuing grain shortage had been compounded by the currency devaluation then widespread throughout the Holy Roman Empire, resulting in a fearful hyperinflation.[172] The poor of the monastery lands streamed to the Abbot's granary, draining the stocks "and paying with bad little coins, all to the monastery's great disadvantage."[173]

Genuinely concerned to keep the poor supplied with grain, the Abbot was at the same time fearful of antagonizing the peasantry. He asked his advisors to make inquiries in the villages among the mayors and headmen about possible arrangements for grain deliveries. What the Abbot wanted was a way to secure from the hamlets and villages a supply for the market town and the rural poor, but in such a manner "so as to burden them [the peasantry] so lightly that they will have no cause to refuse."[174]

The agreement ultimately reached in December of 1622 contains a series of revealing provisions. It had in November been decided that each village was to be responsible for feeding its own poor. Now the actual distribution process was spelled out in detail. In each village the grain surpluses of the wealthy *Bauern* were to be combined into a common stock. The poor were to be given grain one *viertel* at a time, the total never to exceed the immediate consumption requirements of their households. None of this was without cost. The recipients were expected to pay for their grain: "it shall also be written down which poor in the community do not pay in cash so that their property may be hypothecated to the *Bauern* until payment [of the bill]."[175] The *Markt* Ottobeuren was to be supplied in a similar manner, the villages taking weekly turns selling the townspeople grain.

---

[172] For southwest Germany the best discussion of the hyperinflation remains Gustav Schöttle, "Die große deutsche Geldkrise von 1620–23 und ihr Verlauf in Oberschwaben," *Württembergsiche Vierteljahrshefte für Landesgeschichte* N.F. 30 (1921), pp. 36–57. There is an engrossing discussion of contemporary perceptions of the phenomenon in Fritz Redlich, *Die deutsche Inflation des 17. Jahrhunderts in der zeitgenössischen Literatur: Die Kipper und Wipper. Forschungen zur internationalen Sozial- und Wirtschaftsgeschichte* 6 (Cologne and Vienna, 1972).
[173] StAA, KL Ottobeuren 598, f. 62r [12 Nov. 1622].
[174] Ibid.   [175] Ibid., ff. 66r–v [16 and 19 Dec. 1622].

At first sight this arrangement appears utterly ordinary, even banal. With respect to the stipulated payment pattern, it may be wondered whether the Abbot had any other choice. His worries about unsettling the peasantry and the consultative nature of the agreement suggest that his subjects – or at least the *Bauern* – were in a powerful negotiating position. Still, we would do well to avoid taking for granted the fact that the Abbot's position seems rational to us. As shall be seen, the monastery council room produced other abbatial decisions about prices and markets which are completely out of kilter with the modern understanding of these issues. It would be wrong to gloss over the unhesitating assumption in the 1622 deliberations that the deliveries of grain would have to be balanced by appropriate compensation for the peasantry. The minds which arrived at this arrangement were firmly rooted in a world of exchange; a tribute-like extortion of grain from the peasantry was never even contemplated.

Still more important, though at first sight equally unremarkable, was the compartmentalized approach to the problem. The poor were to stay where they belonged and each village was to assume the care of its own. Poor relief was almost always organized at the level of the parish in early modern Europe. In Germany the Imperial Diet at Lindau had declared in 1497 that each community should be responsible for the care of its own poor, a principle later codified in the Imperial Police Ordinance of 1530.[176] The 1622 arrangement at Ottobeuren nevertheless merits our attention as a particular instance of the general conviction that the social order was best maintained by confining the person and activities of every individual to their natural space. This partitioned conception of creation was a basic legitimating mythos of what I have termed the 'discrete society,' and it powerfully shaped all discussion at Ottobeuren of the norms and nature of exchange.

The Ottobeuren market ordinances are a particularly clear expression of this outlook. Article Three of Abbot Alexander's 1601 promulgation ordains that "in order that all may have access to the same transactions, no one shall buy or sell anything – except for cows, cattle, and swine – until the market has been opened on penalty of the lordship."[177] The prohibition was made still more explicit in the case of linen thread, a prime article of commerce:

Henceforth in the lordship of Ottobeuren, and as far as the laws of its villages, hamlets and other settlements run, at no time either within or without the market town of Ottobeuren shall any sort of thread be bought or sold, except at the customary annual and weekly markets as permitted by the ordinances of the market and after the flag has been raised on penalty for both buyer and seller of one pound *heller* to be paid to the lordship.[178]

---

[176] Robert Jütte, *Poverty and Deviance in Early Modern Europe* (Cambridge, 1994), p. 106.
[177] StAA, KL Ottobeuren 4, Document 289V, f. 352v: "Ottenbeürische Marckhtordnung" [5 Aug. 1601].
[178] Ibid.

Exchange, in short, was only deemed licit when conducted at particular times and particular places.

Even then, the two market ordinances which have survived – one from c. 1550 and another from 1601 – provide only a partial listing of the rules governing the economic life of the peasantry. As is clear from the criminal court papers, still more specific boundaries of acceptable exchange were drawn within the territorial borders of the Ottobeuren lands. The monastery peasants were required, for example, to grind their grain with the miller in their home villages.[179] Above all, it was expected that anyone with goods to buy or sell would go first to a neighbor with the offer. Significantly, this expectation was shared by both overlord and peasant. It is hard to explain the prosecution of Caspar Schütz and Simon Seifridt of Attenhausen for refusing to buy meat from the local butcher in 1598,[180] or of Jacob Mair of Attenhausen for refusing to sell a cow to his neighbor in 1601,[181] unless the neighbors themselves had complained. Trade was thus to be conducted first within the individual settlement, then within the Abbot's dominions, and only thereafter and with permission with an outsider.

Spatio-temporal sequestration of commercial transactions was not, of course, an end in and of itself, but rather a means of ensuring the honesty and fairness of exchange. It was felt, for example, that the quality of merchandise could only be controlled if all transactions took place in public and under official oversight. Justice in exchange concerned not only the integrity of the object transacted, however, but also the nature of the transaction. Justice in transactions, as shall be seen, itself amounted to a particular relation in time and space.

Like most sixteenth- and seventeenth-century European market ordinances, the Ottobeuren regulations reflect a particular concern with two kinds of injustice in exchange. The first was known as *Aufkauf zum Wiederkauf*, or the engrossing of large quantities of goods (grain in particular) for the purpose of export. Unproblematic in times of plenty, grain exports were seen as a serious threat to the poor in years of leaner harvests. Already by the middle of the sixteenth century, the monastery sought to mitigate the export danger by forbidding the peasantry to sell grain of any kind outside the monastery lands without the formal permission of the Abbot or his officials.[182] By 1601 a further restriction, commonly known as the *Einstandrecht*, or parity right, had been introduced.

---

[179] The widow of Bartlome Maÿer of Niederrieden was fined one pound in 1566 for having her grain ground by the miller in Heimertingen. StAA, KL Ottobeuren 587-I, Heft 3 (1566/7).

[180] "At the parish fair, after the *Amman* and the *Vierer* had inspected the wares of the [local] butcher and authorized him to distribute them, Caspar Schütz and Simon Seifridt in violation of the custom of the village bought their meat from the butcher from Riedt in Mindelheim – [fined] 14 shillings." StAA, KL Ottobeuren 587-II, Heft 20 (1598/9).

[181] "Jacob Mair butchered a cow . . . and did not want to give any of it to the neighbors who offered him money for it, but sold all of the meat in Memmingen – [fined] 1 £ heller." StAA, KL Ottobeuren 587-II, Heft 21, "Strafregister 1601/2."

[182] StAA, KL Ottobeuren 4, Document 289X, f. 386v: "Baudingbuch 1551."

Even after the exporter had purchased his grain at the market, if approached by a local who had not yet had a chance to bid for the goods, "before he the buyer has loaded up the grain, the buyer shall sell the other [person] at the [same] price at which he the buyer bought it, as much of the purchased grain as the other [person] requires and requests for the needs of his household for about fourteen days, on penalty of one pound *heller* for any buyer who shall refuse."[183]

The second great villainy envisioned by the market ordinances was *Fürkauf*, or forestalling. The essence of this offense was the buying up of goods (again, usually grain) which would otherwise have been sold at the market before the market had officially been opened. What worried the authorities was that the parasitical forestaller would then go on to extort a higher price from buyers at market day. Forestalling was thus strictly forbidden, particularly in the twenty-four hour period immediately preceding the opening of the market.[184]

The object of the market ordinances was thus to guarantee that the needs of the local community would be met affordably. There was no desire to bar outright either the export of goods or the fluctuation of prices, which were understood to reflect – and properly so – the interplay of supply and demand. It was, however, a firmly held conviction that the ability of the individual settlement and of the monastery lands as a whole to support themselves should not be compromised by the demands of outsiders. As for prices, it was felt that the only fair determination of the balance of supply and demand emerged from the face-to-face encounter of producer and consumer. The attenuation of this encounter through the interposition of a speculating middleman would only deform the relation. Justice in exchange, in other words, was best achieved through temporally instantaneous transactions which gave precedence to the needs of the spatially immediate. These conditions were most likely to be realized, it was felt, when exchange was confined to officially sanctioned times and places.

Even then, the incommensurability of sixteenth- and twenty-first-century exchange is not exhausted by considerations of the formation and meaning of prices. Equally important is the relationship between prices and rural exchange in general. For it is not just that as a quantitative measure, a price quotation is only a crude representation of the balance between resources and requirements. It is also that as signs of one-way monetary transactions, prices stand for only one of the forms of rural exchange.

There is no way precisely to measure the prevalence of barter and other non-monetary forms of exchange in the Ottobeuren rural economy, but we may be sure that they were very common. The most obvious evidence has already been discussed above: the debts owed by the peasantry to the monastery

---

[183] Ibid., Document 289V, ff. 355v–356r [5 Aug. 1601].   [184] Ibid., ff. 354r–355v.

were often recorded not in cash but in kind, and even cash obligations were often repaid in non-monetary forms. Among the peasantry transactions of any kind rarely leave traces in the surviving documentation, but when they were illegal or disputed the particulars may show up in the criminal court papers. These documents provide further evidence of the frequency of barter in the Abbot's dominions. Thus one Steffa Steudlin of Wolfertschwenden was fined £7 in 1577 for engaging in prohibited trade with a vagabond. Steudlin had carried the man out of the monastery lands in his cart in exchange for some coins and a (purloined) bed cloth.[185] Similarly, Enderlin Müller of Dennenberg was sued by his neighbor Jerg Steffa for a debt of borrowed oats in 1574. He defended himself with the argument that he had already repaid his creditor with wood.[186]

In some cases barter arrangements were actually institutionalized in the villages (which is why we know of their existence). In 1545, for example, the village community of Egg drew up a contract with the local blacksmith.[187] Under the terms of the agreement, the smith was required to do all of his work – sheathing cart wheels and sled runners, shoeing horses, etc. – for the villagers without pay and to maintain a grindstone for the use of all. In exchange, all of the *Bauern* were annually obliged to do one day's work for the smith (cutting and delivering wood or ploughing his fields) and nineteen specified *Bauern* were together required to supply him with just under sixteen *malter* of rye each year. Those who required the smith's services had to provide him with the iron themselves. Each time the smith sheathed all of the wheels on a wagon, the owner was to give him a meal. Finally, once a year, on St. Steven's Day (3 August), the smith was entitled to go to the inn and eat and drink as much as he liked at the village community's expense.

Peculiar as this arrangement may seem, it was not at all unusual in a particular series of trades – blacksmiths, millers, bakers, and bathhouse keepers – whose activities were deemed vital to the local community.[188] Those who pursued these trades were accorded special rights known as *Ehehaften*, which required the village community to maintain their workplaces, supply them with food and raw materials, and patronize no other tradesman in exchange for costless or nearly costless provision of the relevant service.

[185] StAA, KL Ottobeuren 587-I, Heft 8 (1577).
[186] Ibid., Heft 6 (1574), Ottobeuren Pfarr und Markt.
[187] Details in Peter Blickle, "Ortsgeschichte von Egg an der Günz," *Memminger Geschichtsblätter* (1971), pp. 5–118, at pp. 63–4.
[188] See for example the contract drawn up between the village community and blacksmith of Ungerhausen on 14 March 1619. The smith was required to maintain a grindstone, to shoe "barefooted" horses even on feast days and to do such other smith work as the peasants required. In exchange the *Bauern* were obliged each year to do one half-day's ploughing for the smith (but were also then entitled to receive a meal from him), and to give him two cart rides, one to the fields and one to the woods. They were also to give him two *viertel* of rye for each horse that he shoed, two-year-old horses excepted. StAA, KL Ottobeuren 907, ff. 236r–v.

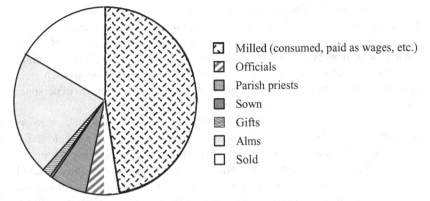

☒ Milled (consumed, paid as wages, etc.)

☑ Officials

▨ Parish priests

▪ Sown

▨ Gifts

☐ Alms

☐ Sold

Figure 2.7 Rye disbursements of the monastery of Ottobeuren, 1586/7
Sources: StAA, KL Ottobeuren 224, Heft 1

Naturally the prevalence of non-monetary exchanges was at least in part the simple result of poverty, but we have already seen that this is a partial explanation at best. Even the wealthiest peasants commonly discharged cash obligations with payments of goods. It turns out, in fact, that the monastery itself was constantly engaged in what can only be described as barter. Almost everyone who worked for the monks, from casual day laborers to contracted artisans to the parish priests and chancellery officials, were paid at least in part in grain.[189] Indeed, it is clear from Figure 2.7 that actual sales of rye for cash represented only a fraction (16.4 percent) of the total volume of rye disbursed by the monastery in 1586. The predominance of moneyless exchanges is the most likely explanation for a curious anomaly mentioned above: the monastery always had grain on hand and its subjects were in constant need of it, yet actual sales from the monastic granary were markedly discontinuous. The evidence presented here suggests that many of these gaps must have been filled by barter. Barter was thus by no means the preserve of the poor and the primitive, but pervaded rural society at all levels of power and affluence. Far from reflecting an inability to function with money, it is argued here, barter was often a positive choice.

Two characteristics of barter made it particularly appealing at sixteenth-century Ottobeuren. First, it represented a hedge against inflation. The crafts-man who was paid in grain had less to fear from fluctuations in food prices, and in times of particular instability we actually find day laborers insisting on payment in grain.[190] Second, barter is a more direct form of exchange. The

---

[189] See the payments in StAA, KL Ottobeuren 541, Heft 1 (1527/8 and 1528/9) and KL Ottobeuren 224, Heft 1 (1586/7).

[190] StAA, KL Ottobeuren 225, f. 33r. "Note that because this year [1621/2] everything [was] very expensive, one had to give each tithe servant two *viertel* of rye."

weaver who sold the fruits of his labor for cash was then obliged to seek out a third party from whom to purchase his sustenance.[191] A simultaneous transfer of cloth for grain or bread unmediated by other transactions with other people quite possibly in other places was more in keeping with the premium placed on spatially compartmentalized and temporally instantaneous exchange. Barter was an efficient vehicle, in other words, for the establishment of personal exchange partnerships and local patron–client relations.[192]

That barter transactions within the Ottobeuren villages often took on a personal character did not preclude the possibility that they also had an exploitative dimension. This was in fact true of all forms of rural exchange. The pronounced disparity between the comfortable *Bauern* and the land-poor *Seldner* ensured that bargaining took place on anything but an even playing field. This did not mean that the *Bauern* sought to drive their poorer neighbors from the village. On the contrary, the mass of the cottagers represented a useful pool from which to hire servants, cowherds, and short-term reapers and threshers at harvest time. It must be emphasized, however, that personal exchanges, whether based on cash sale, barter, or both, very often more closely resembled patron–client relations than the unconstrained haggling of equals.

This ruthless paternalism which characterized so many exchange relations among the peasantry is perhaps most nakedly expressed in a 1607 contract from the hamlet of Eggesried. In that year a certain Jacob Neher acquired from the village community a lot on which to build a house, the lot previously having belonged to one Ulrich Welfle. Neher was not required to pay any money for the lot, but there was a catch:

> The village community grants . . . [the lot] out of grace . . . in such a manner that Neher henceforth shall work for the members of the village community for the appropriate wage. If, however, the said Neher should be parted from his current wife by death, she shall not [re]marry without the [fore]knowledge and assent [*belieben*] of the community. In the event that the said house in the short or long term should be removed, the right to build a[nother] house shall belong to Ulrich Welfle and his heirs; the land [itself] shall belong to the village community . . .[193]

Jacob and his wife had gained a place to build a home in exchange for his labor and her right to remarry. Jacob was to be paid for his work, but he was hardly free to go elsewhere in search of a higher wage. The couple had not gained

---

[191] The inconvenience of having to go outside the village to use money is an important reason for the persistent unwillingness to sell food for cash among the Lhomi of northeastern Nepal. Caroline Humphrey, "Barter and Economic Disintegration," *Man* (N. S.) 20 (1985), pp. 48–72, esp. p. 62, p. 68 n. 7, and p. 70 n. 17.

[192] Cf. R. H. Barnes and Ruth Barnes, "Barter and Money in an Indonesian Village Economy," *Man* (N. S.) 24 (1989), pp. 399–418, esp. p. 412.

[193] StAA, KL Ottobeuren 903, f. 294 [27 Jan. 1607].

permanent title to any land at all; they had in effect become the bond-servants of the Eggesried village community.

Despite the force of an ethos of claustration and the prevalence of non-monetary exchange, the Ottobeuren villages were not completely immune to the lure of the Memmingen market. Illegal sales by the Abbot's subjects outside the monastery lands were rare in the 1540s and still infrequent in the 1580s.[194] Even within the stringent requirements imposed by law and custom, however, trading visits to the city by monastery peasants were frequent enough that urban prices left an unmistakable imprint on their rural counterparts. Still the burghers and city councilors chafed at the norms of exchange at Ottobeuren. The compartmentalization of the monastery villages clashed with their own commercial ambitions, and they therefore undertook to destroy it.

On the face of it, the Memmingen city council shared the same understanding of exchange as the Abbot of Ottobeuren. The laws of the city required that all buying and selling be confined to the municipal marketplace and take place only on officially sanctioned market days. Those who wished to buy up grain for purposes of export were barred from purchasing before two o'clock in the afternoon and were not allowed to buy more than seven *malter* per week. The exporters' activities were further constrained by the parity rights of the citizenry; any burgher had the right to repurchase half of the exporter's acquisitions at the same price the exporter himself had paid. Finally, grain forestalling was if anything more strictly forbidden in the city than it was in the monastery lands. No grain purchased on the Memmingen market could be resold there within six months of the original purchase.[195]

Like the Abbot and his subjects, then, the city council and citizenry of Memmingen strove to secure for themselves a position of precedence in the marketplace. Unlike the monastery villages, however, Memmingen did not have a sufficient food supply of its own. The city thus found itself in the position of seeking privileged access to goods which were produced by the very outsiders whose needs it sought to subordinate to its own. Compounding the dilemma was that no one in Memmingen was content for the urban market to attract only enough grain for the needs of the city itself. Already by the mid-fifteenth century, Memmingen had become a regional marketing center for the trans-shipment of grain from Bavaria and northern Swabia to Switzerland and the Allgäu. As a source of commercial profits on the one hand and export toll revenues on the other, the long-distance grain trade had the active

---

[194] There are only five such offenses among a total of several hundred others recorded in StAA, KL Ottobeuren 587-I, Heft 1 (1546) and 2 (1548). The registers for 1580/1 (Heft 11) and 1582/3 (Heft 12) together record a total of four offenses of this kind.

[195] Kiessling, *Die Stadt und ihr Land*, pp. 448–55.

support of both the wealthier burghers and the city council.[196] Memmingen's appetite for the grain of others and the problems of procurement were thus truly immense.

The solution attempted, as in all early modern German cities,[197] was the imposition of what amounted to a colonial relationship on the surrounding countryside. The weapon of choice was a legal privilege known as the *Bannmeilenrecht*, or ban-mile right,[198] in virtue of which the city unilaterally declared a commercial exclusion zone in a two-mile radius around its walls. Inside the circuit, the peasantry was forbidden to engage in a series of trades deemed important for the employment of the urban citizenry. In addition, the rural inhabitants of the exclusion zone were forbidden to buy or sell any goods in any place other than the Memmingen market. These prohibitions applied not only to those peasants who were the legal subjects of the city, but also to those ruled by other sovereign powers, such as the Abbot of Ottobeuren, the Bishop of Augsburg, or the Fugger dukes.[199]

A variety of means was employed to enforce compliance with the rules of the exclusion zone. Peasants who made purchases elsewhere might be fined, suffer confiscation of their goods, or be banned from the Memmingen market. Those who engaged in prohibited trades were not allowed to sell their wares in the city and might suffer other forms of harassment up to and including imprisonment. The city bakers developed a more insidious mechanism. They loaned out money in neighboring villages and then used the debt to compel the peasants to purchase bread from them alone. Still other burghers resorted to similar means to extract grain at prices disadvantageous to the peasants. The city council disapproved of these tactics but stopped short of forbidding them, preferring that the peasants be exploited by city residents rather than by someone else.[200] The council was also active at higher levels to preserve the integrity of the exclusion zone, lobbying the Emperor himself against the granting of market privileges to potential rivals.

In 1600 the Abbot of Ottobeuren petitioned Emperor Rudolf II for a formal renewal of the market privileges granted to the town of Ottobeuren in 1498. Although it had not objected to the earlier grant, the Memmingen city council now issued a formal protest, complete with a list of reasons for Ottobeuren's unsuitability as a market. The protest was ultimately in vain, and the Ottobeuren

---

[196] Ibid., pp. 459–60.

[197] For a general introduction see Günther Franz, "Die Geschichte des deutschen Landwarenhandels" in Günther Franz et al., eds., *Der deutsche Landwarenhandel* (Hanover, 1960), esp. pp. 17–36.

[198] The coercive character of economic relations between town and country in the Middle Ages has long been recognized by historians. See Winfried Küchler, *Das Bannmeilenrecht*, Marburger Ostforschung, Band 24 (Würzburg, 1964), esp. pp. 20–3.

[199] Kiessling, *Die Stadt und ihr Land*, pp. 448–55, 481–91.

[200] Ibid., also pp. 462, 507–10, 517–18.

privileges were reconfirmed. The details of the effort, however, cast an interesting light on the city's motivations.

Professing concern for the Ottobeuren peasantry, the city council declared that it was "notorious and common knowledge that the subjects of the monastery are endowed and blessed with neither enough cattle, nor grain, nor other victuals or goods to justify the establishment of a single annual market, not to mention two in addition to a weekly market." This claim was transparently specious, since the monastery lands did seem to produce enough surplus for the peasants to visit the Memmingen market. Indeed, the council continued piously, "it would be much more useful to them to patronize the markets of our own and neighboring cities in order that they might . . . at the same time in one trip satisfy their purchasing needs."[201]

The council also alleged that like other rural markets, the town of Ottobeuren was more susceptible to forestalling and other "improper contracts" because it had no market and inspection ordinances, "and is also not equipped with the people to establish ordinances of this sort and administer them in a public place, since it [the town] is not even located on the highway but in fact lies out of the way *in solitudine*." This charge was a bold-faced lie; we have seen above that exchange in the monastery lands was already regulated by ordinance in the middle of the sixteenth century. Ironically, in fact, many of the Ottobeuren regulations were copied directly from Memmingen. For example, Abbot Caspar's 1549 ordinance for innkeepers, butchers, and bakers proclaims that the market overseers "shall together and with each other diligently carry out the inspection of slaughtered and butchered cattle before it [the meat] is distributed, [and] also [the inspection] of the bread as soon as it comes out of the oven, and to the best of their wisdom and knowledge declare its value in accordance with the ordinances in Memmingen . . ."[202]

Ultimately, however, the Memmingen city council revealed the real reason for its opposition to the Ottobeuren market privileges: fear of competition. Market privileges, the council insisted, belonged more properly to the city than to its neighboring villages and hamlets, "so that the trade and industry of the burghers is not drawn out of the city (to the great disadvantage and damage to the same) and into the villages, lest on account of a village a city should be ruined."[203]

The essence of Memmingen's opposition to the Ottobeuren market privileges is thus perfectly clear. The city wanted a maximum number of sellers to confront a minimum number of buyers on the Memmingen market and be unable to go elsewhere in search of a better price. The appeal of the urban market was to be

---

[201] StadtA MM A. Reichsstadt 40/1. *Burgermeister* and *Rat* of Memmingen to Emperor Rudolf II [7 Aug. 1600].

[202] StAA, KL Ottobeuren 4, Document 289X, ff. 395v: "Ordinance and Commandment regarding Innkeepers, Butchers and Bakers proclaimed Anno 1549."

[203] StadtA MM A. Reichsstadt [bisher Stadtarchiv] 40/1.

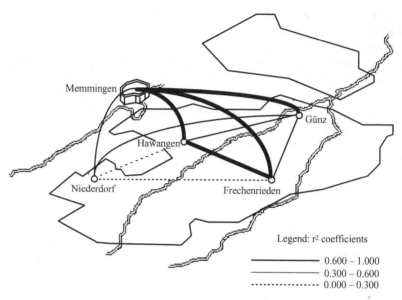

Figure 2.8 Price correlations in the Ottobeuren lands, 1569–96
Sources: See Figures 2.4 and 2.5

further bolstered by discouraging the peasants from producing for themselves those industrial goods they would otherwise have to purchase in the city. The goal, in other words, was an economically undiversified countryside in enforced dependence on the Memmingen market.

The efforts of the merchants and city councilors of Memmingen were not without a certain measure of success. Figure 2.8 demonstrates that in most Ottobeuren villages, rye prices were strongly correlated with Memmingen prices. The city's influence should not be overrated, though. Had the *Bannmeilenrecht* been truly effective, prices would have moved together throughout the exclusion zone, and this was not the case. Although it is clear from Figure 2.8 that the villages were together drawn towards the city, it is equally clear that the pull was not strong enough to draw them closer to each other. The force of the urban market was centripetal without being integrative.

How is Memmingen's failure to break down the boundaries of rural commerce to be explained? We ought to begin by questioning the widespread image of the countryside as the pliant object of bourgeois interests, passively yielding to the solvent force of the urban economy. The evidence of lordly ordinance and peasant custom has shown that both the Abbot of Ottobeuren and his subjects regarded the compartmentalization of exchange as a positive good. Their joint resolve to maintain the economic isolation of the villages was stronger than any pressure the city could exert.

More importantly, the overall objective of this chapter has been to document the deep resonance between this ethos of commercial claustration and peasant constructions of the rural world as a whole. The centrality of honor in the villages, the ferocity with which rural courts punished offenders not known in the community, the preference of personal retribution over official arbitration in disputes – all of these were as closely linked to the special status of face-to-face relations as was the distaste for the shadowy activities of the forestaller. The same force of local solidarity which required that exchange be conducted with neighbors before others was equally at work in the jealous efforts of the Ottobeuren townspeople to bar the villagers from the privileges of the *Bürgerrecht*. The attempts to minimize trading connections across the frontiers of the monastery lands were no more an expression of the strict demarcation of insiders from outsiders than peasant traditions of enmity and feud, or the laws discouraging the immigration, marrying-in, and even sheltering of persons born outside the monastery lands. The insistence on the inviolability of the house and the partibility of the *Hof* reflected an ideal of autonomy whose commercial counterpart was the persistent price discrepancy of fungible goods in neighboring settlements.[204] On both planes, social and commercial, that which is direct, proximate, native, and encapsulated is preferred to that which is mediated, distant, foreign, and permeable. The boundary-building habit of mind is the same.

But it is not enough to refer only to norms and ideals. This reseted economy in which every lordship, village, and household was an island had a material basis as well: partible inheritance. The relationship was not a necessary one, and it would also be wrong to regard the commercial norms discussed above as mere extrusions of land transmission practices. Nevertheless, it must be acknowledged that partible inheritance, by allowing the replacement of one generation by another to be mediated by the redistribution of land, enabled the most fundamental process of rural society to unfold without resort to money.

That coin was extraneous to the social reproduction of the peasantry clarifies a great deal. It accounts for the virtually moneyless character of the rural economy. It helps to explain the minimal success of Memmingen's efforts to colonize its hinterland. But it also highlights an axis of future social change, for partible

---

[204] The persistence of these discrepancies is closely allied to size of the exchange communities in question. Game theoretic modeling of exchanges among small groups of agents, at least some of whom can influence the ratios at which commodities are traded, predicts that "[v]irtually any set of relative prices could emerge. Moreover, there is no reason why different agents should not be able to exchange the same commodities, fetching different exchange ratios with other commodities. In other words, *there is no need for the emergence of prices in the traditional sense*, a unique set of exchange ratios between commodities, prevailing throughout the system." (Luca Anderlini and Hamid Sabourian, "Some Notes on the Economics of Barter, Money and Credit" in Caroline Humphrey and Steven Hugh-Jones, eds., *Barter, Exchange and Value – An Anthropological Approach* (Cambridge, 1992), pp. 75–106, at p. 99. Emphasis mine).

inheritance had other ramifications, above all in the realm of demography. Since a parent could easily create an economic basis for the independence of his children by subdividing the ancestral holding, partibility allowed for the rapid multiplication of new households.[205] In the long run, this population growth put considerable pressure on the productive resources of the countryside, and by extension on traditional customs of inheritance. Any resultant changes in the inner logic of the peasant household would be certain to have repercussions on the myriad boundaries which constituted the late medieval rural world.

[205] Lutz Berkner, "Peasant Household Organization and Demographic Change in Lower Saxony (1689–1766)" in Ronald D. Lee, ed., *Population Patterns in the Past* (New York, 1977), pp. 53–70.

3. A crisis of numbers? (c. 1560–c. 1630)

Anna Langheunz of Reuthen had a problem: her husband, Hans Braun, was a bad householder. It wasn't that he didn't try; Hans was always running off to wheel and deal in other lordships. But horse-trading, his chosen field of endeavor, was a notoriously risky business,[1] and Hans just wasn't good at it. There was also his drinking. Like many peasants, Hans was a bit overfond of the tavern, and any coins gained in his horse-trading were all too often drained away over all too many tankards. By 1555 the situation was critical. Anna and the children were living in destitution, and the Abbot was moved to intervene. Hans was arrested and clapped into prison. The usual drama then ensued. Anna and friends of the family appealed for mercy, Hans promised to reform, and was pardoned and released. Upon release, he solemnly swore not to cause any further trouble, and in particular, "for the rest of my life, neither to live or stay or flee anywhere outside the lands of the monastery of Ottobeuren . . . Also shall and will I completely avoid taverns [both] inside and outside of the lordship, [and I] will give up horse-trading altogether." Four of Hans' friends and neighbors also swore to bring Hans to jail themselves or to pay a fine of 20 *gulden* if he ever broke his oath.[2]

He did. It must at first have seemed like a godsend, the inheritance from relatives in far-away Speyer. Unfortunately, Hans had a falling-out with his co-heirs. The argument degenerated into a fistfight, and in the fall of 1558 Anna's husband was incarcerated again. Released at the intercession of his wife and

---

[1] Because they often sold on credit outside the monastery lands, horse-traders were particularly vulnerable to problems of non-payment. See StAA, KL Ottobeuren 918, f. 69r [14 Oct. 1580], whereby a Hawangen peasant empowers a Memmmingen burgher to collect an unpaid debt of 21.5 fl. for a horse sold to a "foreigner," and KL Ottobeuren 907, f. 211v [24 Dec. 1618], by which three Ottobeuren peasants appoint an emissary to collect an outstanding debt of 36 fl. for horses sold in Bregenz in 1615. Similarly KL Ottobeuren 919, ff. 122r–v and 127v–128r [31 Oct. and 14 Nov. 1680], KL Ottobeuren 921, ff. 177r–v [17 May 1696] and 203v–204r [6 Sep. 1696], KL Ottobeuren 922, f. 43r [9 May 1698]. More generally, see Ludwig Scheller, *Pferdehändler aus dem Allgäu: von der Nordsee bis zum Mittelmeer* (Kempten, 1976).

[2] StAA, KL Ottobeuren 4, Document 2930, ff. 647v–651v [28 Jan. 1555].

an additional fine of 10 *gulden*, Hans again promised to stay out of trouble[3] and again couldn't keep his promise. The old vices of ill-advised trading and mismanagement of the household's resources landed him back in jail in the summer of 1562, and for a third time Anna found herself pleading for her husband's release. In this she succeeded, but by now the Abbot had decided that drastic measures were needed. Hans' *Urfehde* oath spelled out the terms:

> Henceforth, I will under no circumstances engage of my own accord in any trades, sales, or purchases, large or small, unless specially permitted by the *Vogt* and the officially appointed guardians of myself, my wife, and my children. I will also conduct myself humbly, peacefully, and in all moderation [*aller gebür nach*] with my wife, my children, and all others.[4]

The two guardians now assumed fiscal control of the household; Anna's husband had been unmanned. Four years later he left her a widow.[5]

At first sight, the foregoing episode is simply a variation on a theme encountered in the previous chapter, i.e. the vulnerability of peasant women and their children to the managerial incompetence of male householders. But even if Hans Braun cannot be said to have played his cards very well, we must also in all fairness consider the hand he was dealt. Hans and Anna lived in Reuthen, a hamlet previously encountered as an example of the fragmentation of landholding caused by partible inheritance. Hans held one of the two smallest of these fragments. It is not possible to calculate the physical area of his property, but a tithe list from the year 1584 (a year of average harvest quality) indicates that the holding yielded 4.12 *malter* ($\approx$ 9 hectoliters) of grain.[6] Even notwithstanding the tithe obligation, four and one-tenth of a *malter* was only enough to feed two adults and one child for a year. Hans and Anna had seven children, the largest brood in the hamlet. As if these numbers were not bad enough, the later 1550s saw a general deterioration of grain production in Reuthen. The harvest of 1561, the last before Hans' final arrest and declaration of incompetence, was the worst in eighty-five years (see Figure 3.1). The land simply did not yield enough to feed the family. Others may have been shrewder, luckier, or better able to resist the temptation of drink, but it is hard not to sympathize with Hans Braun's desperation, and it is small wonder that he was driven to gamble on the horses.

To shift our discussion from the rules governing peasant society to the resources which sustained (or in Hans and Anna's case failed to sustain) it is to enter the lists of a venerable debate about the basic economic stability of early modern Europe. Thirty years or so ago, a scholarly consensus emerged that something had gone seriously wrong with the economy of Western Europe

---

[3] Ibid., Document 293Q, ff. 656r–659v [20 Oct. 1558].
[4] Ibid., Document 293R, ff. 659v–662r [15 July 1562].
[5] Cf. StAA, KL Ottobeuren 688-I, Heft 1 (f. 19r), Heft 2 (f. 26r), Heft 3 (f. 25v), and Heft 4 (f. 8v).
[6] StAA, KL Ottobeuren 31, f. 68v.

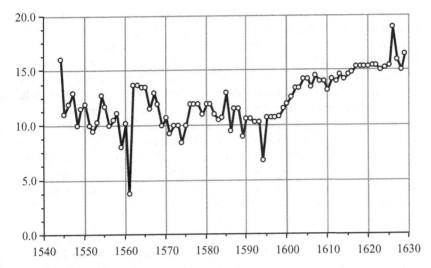

Figure 3.1 Tithe receipts (*malter*) in Reuthen, 1544–1629
Sources: StAA, KL Ottobeuren 34–36, 40

by the beginning of the seventeenth century. Debate persisted on many aspects of this crisis: the role of precious metal imports from the Americas, the repercussions in Eastern Europe and on European trade patterns with the rest of the world. Even the chronology of the economic crisis and its root causes was a matter of considerable controversy. On one issue, however, there was general agreement: whereas the West European economy grew both in size and in sophistication during the sixteenth century, this performance was not sustained in the following century. The forces of growth were stopped short by the structural limitations of early modern society, and most of the continent settled into a hundred years of stagnation if not outright depression. Not until the later eighteenth or even the nineteenth century, it was argued, would the economy transcend the limits of the Middle Ages.[7]

It was admittedly somewhat difficult to make meaningful use of terms like "growth," "stagnation," and "depression" for the pre-industrial and pre-statistical economy of early modern Europe. There were no indices of physical output, of household income, or of any of the other kinds of information economists use to analyze the material well-being of the modern world. In the absence of figures of this sort, historians were forced to resort to proxy measurements. In well-documented regions of the early modern economy, such as the urban sector or international trade, customs or toll records could be used to provide a fairly reliable indication of overall trends. But in the rural sector,

[7] See Introduction, note 2.

where the vast majority of the population lived, where most of the value of the economy was produced, and where any economic crisis of general significance would therefore have had to begin, the statistical picture was (and still is) much bleaker. In general, historians came to rely on two variables to provide an indirect measurement of long-term trends in the rural economy: population and grain prices. The rationale behind the use of these two proxies (aside from the fact that little else is available) was as follows: an expanding economy can feed and employ more people, while higher grain prices reflect greater demand for agricultural products and therefore increased rural incomes. Thus, rising grain prices and above all a growing population were seen as signs of a healthy rural economy whereas the reversal of these two trends was felt to indicate economic depression.[8] There is a great deal of common-sense plausibility to this scenario, which became the standard model for the economies of both medieval and early modern Europe.

For many years, the most popular representation for the early modern economy was a demographically determined model where material well-being is a function of population density. The essence of the model was Thomas Malthus' famous postulate that a growing population tends to outstrip its food supply. On the basis of a series of very influential French studies[9] and buttressed by investigations in other parts of Europe,[10] historians advanced a starkly simple explanation for the apparent economic slowdown at the end of the sixteenth century: the continent – at least, most of it – was overpopulated and had reached a state of permanent near-starvation.

The root cause of the problem, it was argued, was the miserably low level of agricultural productivity. The land had to be worked by hand or with the use of undersized draught animals, and against the vagaries of the weather and the ravages of agricultural pests there was no defense save prayer. Moreover, given the short supply of natural fertilizers and the absence of artificial ones, the peasant was obliged to leave fallow as much as a third of his arable land every

---

[8] The oscillating relation between population, food supply, and grain prices was first proposed by Wilhelm Abel. His landmark 1935 work is available in English as *Agricultural Fluctuations in Europe from the Thirteenth to the Twentieth Centuries*, trans. Olive Ordish (London, 1980).

[9] Fundamental are Fernand Braudel, *The Mediterranean and the Mediterranean World in the Age of Philip II*, trans. Siân Reynolds (2 vols. New York, 1972; orig. pub. 1949); Pierre Goubert, *Beauvais et le Beauvaisis de 1600 à 1730* (Paris, 1960); Emmanuel LeRoy Ladurie, *Les paysans de Languedoc* (Paris, 1966); and Jean Jacquart, *La crise rurale en Île-de-France 1550–1670* (Paris, 1974).

[10] For England see summaries in D. M. Palliser, "Tawney's Century: Brave New World or Malthusian Trap?" *Economic History Review*, 2nd ser., 35 (1982), pp. 339–53 and Roger Schofield, "The Impact of Scarcity and Plenty on Population Change in England, 1541–1871," *Journal of Interdisciplinary History* 14, 2 (1983), pp. 265–91. For Germany see Wilhelm Abel, *Massenarmut und Hungerkrisen im vorindustriellen Europa* (Hamburg, 1974) and David Sabean, "German Agrarian Institutions at the Beginning of the Sixteenth Century: Upper Swabia as an Example" in Janos Bak, ed, *The German Peasant War of 1525* (London, 1976), pp. 76–88.

year or risk exhaustion of the soil. Even then, the seventeenth-century peasant managed to harvest only a risible multiple of the seed sown. As a result, peasant farming produced a decidedly modest food supply capable of feeding only a minimal non-agricultural population in good years and not even the peasants themselves in unhappy ones.[11] As long as agricultural productivity remained stalled at such low levels, so the theory went, there was no way out of the Malthusian impasse.

The technical stagnation of European agriculture was thus held to have created a biological ceiling, beyond which additional mouths simply could not be fed. At the end of the fifteenth and at the beginning of the sixteenth century, this limit was merely a theoretical concern. The population had only recently begun to recover from the demographic disasters of the later Middle Ages, and additions to the ranks of the peasantry were absorbed without difficulty. Abandoned lands were reoccupied, new lands were cleared and put under the plough, the food supply thus kept pace with population increases and the economy as a whole was free to grow and diversify.

By the middle of the sixteenth century these earlier favorable conditions no longer obtained. After a century of demographic growth, the rural world was now full. Significant extension of the arable was no longer possible, with the result that the food supply had effectively been capped. Further population growth was now a positive liability, driving up food prices, eroding the standard of living, and planing away any remaining safety margin for the years of leaner harvests. Obviously, this imbalance between population and food supply could not continue to deteriorate indefinitely. On the demographic model, a breaking point was reached in most of Europe by the middle of the sixteenth century when two mechanisms came into play to force population growth to a halt. Following Malthus, these mechanisms were conventionally referred to as the positive and preventative checks.[12]

The preventative check is most succinctly described as the forestalling of excessive population growth through the control of nuptiality. Effective methods of artificial contraception were not available to early modern Europeans. Accordingly, manipulation of the celibacy rate and the age at first marriage became the contraceptive weapon *par excellence* of the *ancien régime* in Europe. Proponents of the demographic model ground their interpretation in the synchrony between a long-term increase in the cost of living over the period

---

[11] B. H. Slicher van Bath, *The Agrarian History of Western Europe AD 500–1850*, trans. Olive Ordish (London, 1963) has been extremely influential, particularly with respect to yield ratios in arable farming. The concept of productive limits is stressed in Joseph Goy and Emmanuel LeRoy Ladurie, eds. *Les fluctuations du produit de la dîme* (Paris, 1972).

[12] Thomas Malthus, *An Essay on the Principle of Population* (repr. London, 1982). This is a reprint of the seventh (1872) edition of the essay; the positive and preventative checks are outlined in Book I, Chapter 2.

1480–1620 and the simultaneous multiplication of evidence for the preventative check all over Western Europe. The proportion of the population ever marrying declined while those who married did so at later and later ages. Thus, even in the absence of fertility reduction within marriage, the overall fertility rate declined dramatically to the point where an equilibrium of zero population growth was reached.[13]

In spite of these adjustments to fertility, however, the level at which the population stabilized was still dangerously close to the sustainable maximum. This brought in the second of Malthus' mechanisms, the positive check or increased mortality. Malthus himself classed among the various positive checks everything from "unwholesome occupations, exposure to the seasons and bad nursing of children" to "the whole train of common diseases" and epidemics, wars, plague, and famine, including "excesses of all kinds" for good measure. Modern scholars concentrated on a select few of Malthus' causes: plague and above all famine.

Powerful support for the notion that European agriculture was only barely able to meet the needs of the population was provided by the phenomenon of subsistence crises, which multiplied in frequency throughout Europe as the sixteenth century drew to a close. A subsistence crisis is defined by a sudden increase in the price of grain, often to two, three, or even four times the normal level either due to the failure of the harvest or more commonly as a result of consecutive harvest failures. The surge in prices was usually accompanied by a dramatic increase in mortality and by a concomitant collapse in the conception of new infants. All in all, a subsistence crisis could easily scythe away 10 to 20 percent of the population of an affected community while impeding subsequent demographic recovery through its deleterious effects on the birth rate.[14]

It is not hard to see how repeated subsistence crises – and it is still felt that most villages in Europe experienced an ordeal of this sort every twenty to thirty years in the century after 1560 – could result in demographic stagnation if

[13] See the seminal work by John Hajnal, "European Marriage Patterns in Perspective" in D. V. Glass and D. E. J. Eversley, eds, *Population in History: Essays in Historical Demography* (Chicago, 1965), pp. 101–43. For a recent general overview see Michael W. Flinn, *The European Demographic System 1500–1820* (Baltimore, 1981), esp. pp. 19–28.

[14] The pioneering article is Jean Meuvret's "Les crises de subsistance et la démographie de la France de l'Ancien régime," *Population* 1, 4 (1946), pp. 643–50. Pierre Goubert's 1960 study of the Beauvaisis (above, note 9) remains the most famous investigation of susbsistence crises. A recent summary of French research may be found in François Lebrun, "Les crises de démographie en France aux XVIIième et XVIIIième siècles," *Annales: Economies, Sociétés, Civilisations* [hereinafter *Annales E.S.C.*] 35 (1980), pp. 205–33. For England see R. D. Lee, "Short-term Variations: Vital Rates, Prices and Weather" in E. A. Wrigley and R. S. Schofield, *The Population History of England, 1541–1871* (London, 1981), chapter 9, pp. 350–407. For a comparative perspective see Andrew Appleby, "Grain Prices and Subsistence Crises in England and France, 1590–1790," *Journal of Economic History* 39, 4 (1979), pp. 865–87. Rather fewer local investigations have been undertaken in Germany. See, however, Philip L. Kinter, "Die Teuerung von 1570/72 in Memmingen," *Memminger Geschichtsblätter* (1987/ 8), pp. 28–75.

not in outright decline. More fundamentally, it was argued, in the absence of significant technological or institutional change, the chief engine of increased output was the expansion of the labor force. Thus, the stagnation or decline of population, whether occasioned by either or both of Malthus' checks, by its very nature throttled the development of the early modern economy. Indeed, at the peak of enthusiasm for the Malthusian model in the early 1970s, the French historian Emmanuel LeRoy Ladurie went so far as to characterize the entire sweep of the fourteenth through the eighteenth centuries in the following terms:

> For the apparent movement, things had really stayed much the same . . . the active agricultural population whose total dimensions had persistently observed the same norms, was digging away at its plots of land with techniques that had barely changed, obtaining yields that had not significantly improved. Such yields were powerless to prevent some hundreds or thousands of people becoming direct or indirect victims of starvation every thirty years or so.[15]

The "biological ceiling," or "structural constraint," had become the single most significant force in European social history.

In recent years it has become fashionable to attack the Malthusian model. Most objections to the model fall into one of three broad categories. First is a Marxist critique, which argues that the concrete repercussions of the early modern production crisis were decisively determined by class structure. Thus, differently ordered societies saw significantly different outcomes from the same kind of crisis. The second critique comes from the world of cliometrics, and is based on the observation of an imperfect statistical correlation between sudden surges in grain prices and increases in recorded burials. Harvest shocks were indeed associated with increased short-term mortality, but the latter pattern is never explicable completely or even predominantly in terms of the former. The last type of critique is more general, and tends to be voiced in local or regional studies. Here the objection takes the form of a rejection of the conception of peasants as helpless victims, and an emphasis on the variety of economic patterns and the affluence of at least some members of rural society.

To be frank, all of these criticisms fail to blunt the analytic force of the Malthusian model. They quite properly direct attention to the complex reverberations of economic crises. They enrich what had been an unduly stark narrative of the interaction of abstract quantities. But they leave untouched the basic diagnosis that too little food was grown for too many mouths. The reality of *some* kind of structural constraint is nowhere impeached, and the empirical outlines of the Malthusian story – agricultural and demographic expansion in the sixteenth century followed by some hundred years of stagnation – stand uncontroverted.

---

[15] LeRoy Ladurie, "History that Stands Still," p. 21. See also his other articles reprinted in LeRoy Ladurie, *The Territory of the Historian*, trans. Ben and Siân Reynolds (Chicago, 1979).

For all the qualifications of specialized research, the most recent literature surveys continue to narrate the seventeenth century as a cautionary tale of the technological limitations of the early modern period, with real economic transformation postponed until the scientific advances of the Enlightenment.

What can the tribulations of Anna Langheunz contribute to this debate? Anna's subsequent story is one of perseverance in the face of adversity. After the death of her husband, she headed the household for at least eight years. Some of them were good years in which the cows gave her as many as three calves to sell. In other years she had to make do with only one,[16] but she managed to hang on long enough to establish her son Jerg Braun on the farm.[17] Jerg was in turn succeeded by his hard-working son Caspar, who by 1606 was squeezing over 50 percent more grain from the land than his father had managed. By 1620, Anna's grandson owned almost 700 *gulden* worth of property, including 24 *jauchert* of land as well as the unequivocal sign of at least modest comfort: a team of two horses.[18] Heart-warming though all of this may be, it is hard to see that the family had any other choice. Given the straits in which Hans Braun left them in 1566, there was precious little else to do but work harder. Yet for all their work, there were still very definite limits to what could be achieved. Jerg was not the only one of Anna's children to marry, but he was the only one to settle in Reuthen. His brother Johann married a woman from Langenberg in 1574, but the couple seem to have drifted out of the monastery lands shortly thereafter.[19] Even Caspar Braun, for all his land and horses, was up to his neck in debt.[20]

There is thus a sense in which the Brauns of Reuthen both are, and are not, an example of the structural limitations of the early modern economy. On the one hand, Hans Braun does seem to have been caught between an excess of dependants and a shortfall of material resources. On the other hand, his widow, children, and grandchildren did succeed in avoiding the fate of neighbors who simply collapsed under the pressures besetting the hamlet.[21] Then again, the family's long-term survival was but a qualified success, which in any case

---

[16] StAA, KL Ottobeuren 681, Heft 2, f. 6r; KL Ottobeuren 688–I, Heft 5, f. 17v and Heft 6, f. 18v.

[17] StAA, KL Ottobeuren 901, f. 37r [6 July 1583]; KL Ottobeuren 30, ff. 21r–24v; KL Ottobeuren 31, f. 50r; KL Ottobeuren 583, Heft 9 (1593), f. 4r.

[18] StAA, KL Ottobeuren 39, f. 135v; KL Ottobeuren 102, f. 77r.

[19] Ottobeuren Parish Register [hereinafter OttPR], Vol. I, f. 125r [17 Oct. 1574]. Johann is nowhere mentioned in the 1584 rent and tithe roll, the 1586 bond-chicken register, or the notarial protocols for 1580–1 and 1583–4.

[20] StAA, KL Ottobeuren 102, f. 77r.

[21] E.g. the cottager Balthas Herz, who attempted to survive by mortgaging his house and borrowing money from neighbors, but was ultimately driven to crime. On 21 December 1587, he was arrested while attempting to break into and rob the chapel of Our Blessed Lady in Eldern. At first condemned to the gallows, he was ultimately sentenced to be flogged through the streets and then banished from the monastery lands. StAA, KL Ottobeuren 491–I, Heft 3, f. 7v; KL Ottobeuren 918, f. 13v [4 Feb. 1580]; KL Ottobeuren 901, f. 97v [4 Apr. 1584]; KL Ottobeuren 4, Document 292S, ff. 662r–663r [18 Jan. 1588].

extended to only some of its members. All of this warns against the false choice of either completely accepting or utterly rejecting the Malthusian model. It also underscores both the danger of oversimplification and the limitations of a single example. Let us turn, therefore, to a more detailed and more general consideration of the problem of economic resources at Ottobeuren.

Perhaps the most appropriate place to begin is with demography, and it may also be helpful to distinguish between short-term and long-term patterns. The standard investigative model for the short term involves comparison of grain prices and burials in an effort to determine the relation (if any) between the fluctuations of the two. Unfortunately, analysis of this sort for the Ottobeuren lands is handicapped by the scarcity of source material. Although continuous grain price series are available after 1530 from the nearby city of Memmingen,[22] burial records are much harder to come by. Parish registers, the standard source of demographic information, are rare in Catholic Germany before the second half of the seventeenth century (this is only in part due to the destruction of records during the Thirty Years War; it was only in the 1650s that episcopal visitors began to insist that the local priests keep parish registers). For our present purposes, there is only one parish, the double village of Ober- and Unterwesterheim, where the records are complete enough for the period before the Thirty Years War. Nevertheless, the parish register still provides a helpful insight into the eco-demographic world of the Ottobeuren peasantry.

In 1595 one Father Michael Koler was appointed pastor of Ober- and Unterwesterheim. Koler was a diligent man, and for the next thirty years he maintained a detailed register of baptisms, marriages, and burials, a document which is unusually complete in that it also records the deaths of infants (most early modern European burial registers include only those over the age of five or six). Figure 3.2. presents the annual movements of burials over the period 1595–1625, together with the village's tithe receipts and rye prices from Memmingen. At first sight there is no obvious correlation between the two series; at times the relation actually appears to be inverse. Even in the difficult years of 1622–5, when a combination of deficient harvests and currency debasement sent grain prices soaring to stratospheric levels, mortality clearly did not follow suit. Still, it would be misleading to suggest that grain prices had no influence on mortality patterns. Ober- and Unterwesterheim did not constitute a large parish, with a total population of only 340 in 1564.[23] The annual number of burials was small,

---

[22] StadtA MM D Folioband 99, D 102/1a–1h. Memmingen rye prices for the period 1600–99 are available in Thomas Wolf, *Reichsstädte in Kriegszeiten* (Memmingen, 1991). As was seen in chapter 2, the use of urban prices as a proxy for rural prices is not unproblematic, but the Westerheim parish accounts, the only source of price data from the village itself, are missing for the years 1583–1612.

[23] Richard Dertsch, ed. "Das Einwohnerbuch des Ottobeurer Klosterstaats vom Jahre 1564," *Allgäuer Heimatbücher* 50 [*Alte Allgäuer Geschlechter* 34] (1955), pp. III–V.

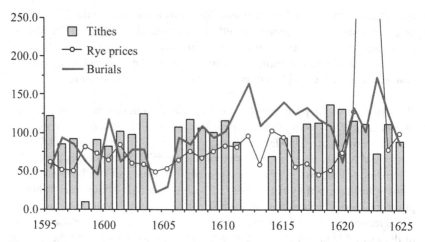

Figure 3.2 Tithes, rye prices, and burials in Westerheim, 1595–1625
Notes: 30 year average = 100. No tithe data are available for 1604–5 and 1612–13
Sources: Westerheim Parish Register; StAMM, D. 19/5, 21, Folioband 1/D452; Wolf, *Reichsstädte in Kriegszeiten*, Table 82, p. 76

usually between seven and fifteen, such that an increase or decrease of two or three produced wide proportionate swings in the total.

Moreover, it has long been known that harvest failures could influence population patterns not only by increasing mortality but also by temporarily depressing natality. Thus, if we examine the overall demographic balance (baptisms minus infant and adult deaths) in the parish in the three decades after 1595, it is striking (and can be no coincidence) that all of the instances of net decrease – 1611–12 and 1623 – were years of bad harvests (see Figure 3.3). But although harvest failures played some role as a check on population in the double village, the more important observation is that this role was very limited. Although the bad harvests of 1611–12 and 1623 coincided with years of net decrease, this was not true of the bad harvests of 1614 and 1625.[24] More fundamentally, it must be emphasized that 90 percent of the time the parish registered a net population increase, and even when this was not the case the deficit was in both cases made up within a year. This was clearly not a demographic regime regulated in any significant way by subsistence crises.

If in the short term rural society at Ottobeuren tended towards population growth, what was the trend in the long term? Here we cannot proceed without

[24] A general idea of harvest quality at Ottobeuren may be gained from the account books of the tithe. StAA, KL Ottobeuren 40, records tithes for the period 1560–1629; receipts plunged dramatically in 1612 and 1623, and substantially in 1614 and 1625. Bad harvests are mentioned in 1611, 1614, and 1624 in the seventeenth-century chronicle of a Memmingen doctor. Christoph Schorer, *Memminger Chronick* (Ulm, 1660; repr. Kempten, 1964), pp. 120–130.

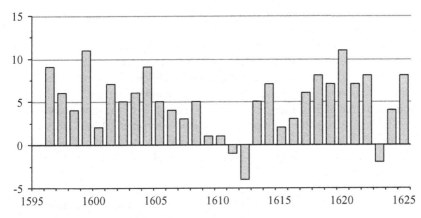

Figure 3.3 Demographic balance in Westerheim, 1595–1625
Source: Westerheim Parish Register

a more detailed discussion of the source material. There are three main kinds of documents which allow us to reconstruct long-term population trends in the period before the Thirty Years War reached the monastery lands in 1632. The first of these are tax records, from which may be extracted the number of households in a given settlement or series of settlements. Tax lists for the entire monastic territory have survived from the years 1525, 1541, 1546, 1620, 1624, and 1627.[25] There is also a shorter list for the *Markt*, or market town, Ottobeuren alone from 1585.[26]

Useful as they are, tax records suffer from a serious weakness in that they list households rather than persons. An estimate of the actual population on the basis of these records thus requires knowledge of an elusive and at times hotly debated quantity, namely the average size of the peasant household. Even then, calculation of long-term population trends from tax records hinges on the assumption that the size of the peasant household remained constant.

Fortunately, a second category of documents is available at Ottobeuren to provide at least a partial solution to these problems. The records in question are known as *Leibeigenbücher*, or "serf books." In consequence of the fragmentation of the different forms of lordship in Swabia, it was often the case that although one authority had an exclusive claim to collect ground rents in a village, the inhabitants themselves "belonged" as serfs to one or even several other authorities. Peasant migration and intermarriage further clouded the picture to the point that sorting out rights of jurisdictional competence or taxation became bewilderingly complicated. In the Ottobeuren lands the peasants belonged to

---

[25] Respectively StAA, KL Ottobeuren 541 (Heft 2), 63, 64, 102, 103, and 104. The first three list only the tax payment, the latter three describe each householder's property in detail.
[26] StAA, KL Ottobeuren 676a.

over twenty different lords, in addition to which slightly less than one fourth of the peasantry was legally free.

In order to remedy this confusion, the monastery periodically drew up a *Leibeigenbuch* to record the specific servile or free status of the inhabitants of its territory. Since members of the same family might have different legal statuses, the process theoretically entailed compiling a list not only of every household, but also of every man, woman, and child in the monastery lands. Serf books are available at Ottobeuren for the years 1486/7, 1548, 1556, 1564, and 1585/6,[27] although only the middle three cover the entire subject population and only the last two are detailed enough for reliable calculations of household size in every village.

Further clarification of demographic trends for the period after 1586 is provided by a third class of records: episcopal visitation reports on the number of communicants in each parish. Under canon law all Catholics having reached the age of majority (usually considered to be twelve) were required to receive communion at least once a year at Easter. In the diocese of Augsburg, where the Ottobeuren lands were located, parish priests were required at intervals of ten or twenty years to submit the number of Easter communicants to the bishop. Four such counts were made between 1593 and 1626, and coverage of the Ottobeuren villages and hamlets is virtually complete.[28]

Like the tax records, the visitation reports have their own particular strengths and weaknesses. It is important to realize that the figures are estimates. The vast majority of the individual parish counts were made in numbers rounded to the nearest multiple of ten; for the pastor of Frechenrieden to have reported 246 communicants in 1620 was exceptional. Despite some degree of imprecision, however, communicant counts have the advantage of being based on a known and fairly constant proportion of the actual population. In addition, village census totals from the 1585/6 serf book can easily be checked against the 1593 communicant counts to allow calculation of the ratio between the two. The problem of potential shifts in the size of the peasant household, which bedevils the use of tax records, thus does not arise with the visitation reports.

In sum, then, the tax records and serf books allow accurate enumeration of the number of households in the period 1525–1620, and permit an estimate of the trend between 1486/7 and 1525. As far as the actual population is concerned, these records furnish a detailed picture of the trend between 1548 and 1585/6. After 1586 reliable if somewhat less precise population figures can be reconstructed on the basis of the communicant counts in the visitation reports. Let us examine these patterns in turn.

---

[27] Respectively StAA, KL Ottobeuren 601-I, 600, 24 (Mü.B), 25 (Mü.B), and 601-II.

[28] The visitation reports are abstracted in Martin Sontheimer, *Die Geistlichkeit des Kapitels Ottobeuren von dessen Ursprung bis zur Säkularisation* (5 vols., Memmingen 1912–20).

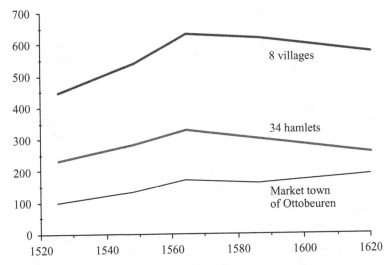

Figure 3.4 Household numbers in selected Ottobeuren settlements, 1525–1620
Sources: StAA KL Ottobeuren 541 (Heft 2), 64, 102, 600, 601-II; Dertsch, "Das Einwohnerbuch des Ottobeurer Klosterstaats 1564"

Figure 3.4 displays the movement of the number of households in forty-three selected settlements representing just over 60 percent of the 1564 population of the monastery lands. In the market town of Ottobeuren, the overall pattern is one of virtually continuous growth. Elsewhere the trend is less straightforward. In the eight villages and thirty-four hamlets the number of households increased steadily from the middle third of the sixteenth century (a pattern which calls into question the widely asserted claim that rural Upper Swabia had reached a point of demographic saturation on the eve of the Peasants' War).[29] After 1564 population growth slowed to a halt and was then reversed, although this did not happen everywhere at the same time. Of the eight villages, two reached the maximum number of households in 1564, five in 1585/6, and one in 1620. In the hamlets the absence of records between 1564 and 1620 prevents specification of the turning point. Whatever the case may be, by 1620 the total number of households had declined by 9.1 percent in the villages and by 21.4 percent in the hamlets since 1564. All of this took place in the context of a tremendous increase in the price of grain, which rose by over 200 percent between the mid-1530s and the late 1580s.[30]

On the face of it, then, the long-term trends seem paradigmatic of a population outgrowing its capacity to feed itself. But before rushing to embrace

[29] E.g. Peter Blickle, *The Revolution of 1525*, trans. Thomas A. Brady Jr. and H. C. Erik Midelfort (Baltimore, 1981), pp. 50–1, 214 n. 52.
[30] StadtA MM D Folioband 99, D 102/1a–1b.

Table 3.1 *Households and communicants in four Ottobeuren villages, 1586–1621*

Settlement	House-holds 1586	Communicants 1593	Communicants/ household 1586/93	House-holds 1621	Communicants 1620	Communicants/ household 1620/1
Frechenrieden	77	160	2.08	69	197	2.86
Hawangen[a]	147	300	2.04	123	400	3.25
Niederrieden	80	180	2.25	74	220	2.97
Sontheim	135	330	2.44	140	400	2.85
Total	439	970	2.21	406	1217	3.00
Index	100	100	100	92.5	125.5	135.7

[a] Includes the adjacent hamlets of Ober- and Untermoosbach
Sources: Sontheimer, *Die Geistlichkeit des Kapitels Ottobeuren*, vols. II–IV; StAA, KL Ottobeuren 102, 601-II

this Malthusian interpretation, there are two important cautions regarding the evidence to keep in mind. As may be expected, the first of these concerns the relationship between the number of households and the actual population. In 1586, the average peasant household contained 4.0 persons,[31] but thereafter it began to grow. At the very least, this increase in household size was enough to stabilize the population at its 1564 peak by the end of the 1620s. It is also entirely possible, however, that the counterbalancing effect was greater still, such that the population continued to grow (albeit at much reduced rates) for another sixty years after the overall number of households peaked in 1564.

The absence of serf books after 1586 makes it difficult precisely to measure the growth in household size, but the episcopal visitations enable a fairly good estimate of the scale of the increase. Taking the 1593 communicant count as a standard of reference, the number of communicants in the monastery lands as a whole had risen 25.5 percent by 1620. As has been seen, the number of households had declined over the same period. Thus the increase in the number of communicants per household was greater still. Table 3.1 illustrates these changes in four of the best documented villages.

There is independent evidence of a considerable increase in household size between the 1580s and 1620s, driven largely by the spread of household service.[32] Nevertheless, the increase detailed in the communicant counts should not be attributed entirely to population growth, for some of it must have been

---

[31] This figure is based on the serf rolls of the villages of Hawangen-Moosbach, Sontheim, Frechenrieden Niederrieden, and Wolfertschwenden. StAA, KL Ottobeuren 601–II, ff. 751–88v, 101r–112v, 116r–121v, 124r–131v and 141r–147v. Household size seems to have remained fairly constant at Ottobeuren since the mid-sixteenth century; between 1546/8 and 1586, the mean number of persons per household rose from 3.91 to 4.23 in Frechenrieden but fell from 3.98 to 3.86 in Hawangen-Moosbach. StAA, KL Ottobeuren 64, ff. 36r–38r and 55v–57r; 600, ff. 127v–152v and 220v–233r.

[32] See below, pp. 225–7.

the result of more widespread compliance with the requirements of canon law. It is quite clear that the proportion of the population receiving communion was substantially higher at Ottobeuren by *c.* 1700 (65–75 percent) than it had been *c.* 1590 (50–60 percent),[33] although it is less certain when this shift took place. Investigations in other parts of Germany suggest that increases in compliance were slight before the second half of the seventeenth century.[34] It must also be pointed out that a dramatic shift in the relatively brief interval 1593–1626 is *a priori* rather implausible.

Be that as it may, it was also the case that important ecclesiastical reforms were introduced at Ottobeuren in precisely this brief interval, reforms which may well have made annual communion somewhat more common among the peasantry. Clerical concubinage, for example, was largely stamped out between 1575 and 1626. By 1626 all of the parish priests had also been trained at universities,[35] and some priests had begun to keep parish registers. The point is not that these reforms would immediately have instilled a deeper piety among the Abbot's subjects, but rather that the growing professionalization of the rural clergy is likely to have enhanced the vigor of pastoral supervision.[36] In this context it does not seem implausible that the proportion of those actually fulfilling the obligation of annual communion should have increased.

But let us return to demography. Table 3.2 presents a summary of the various trends in the nucleated villages of the monastery lands (the data on the hamlets are not complete enough to permit calculations of this sort). Two possible

[33] The 1590 estimate is based on a comparison of the number of communicants reported in the 1593 visitation with the village population recorded in the serf book of 1585/6. Communicants made up 49.1 percent of the population in Frechenrieden, 52.9 percent in Hawangen, 56.3 percent in Niederrieden, and 60.4 percent in Sontheim. The 1700 estimate is taken from the episcopal visitation of 1695, which in several villages lists both the number of communicants and the total number of parishioners. The communicating proportion ranged from 62.1 percent (Egg) and 66.3 percent (Reicholzried) to 70.9 percent (Frechenrieden) and 75.0 percent (Hawangen). StAA, KL Ottobeuren 601-II; Sontheimer, *Geistlichkeit des Kapitels Ottobeuren*, Vols. II–IV.

[34] Marc R. Forster, *The Counter-Reformation in the Villages: Religion and Reform in the Bishopric of Speyer 1564–1720* (Ithaca, 1992), pp. 23, 104–6, 241; Manfred Becker-Huberti, *Die Tridentinische Reform im Bistum Münster unter Fürstbischof Christoph von Galen 1650–1678* (Munster, 1978), pp. 247–8.

[35] In the parishes for which the 1575 visitation survives, seven of twelve priests (58.5 percent) had concubines. By the time of the 1626 visitation, none of the priests had concubines. According to the 1626 visitation, every single parish priest in the monastery lands had had some university training, usually at the Jesuit colleges in Ingolstadt and Dillingen, but also in Munich, Augsburg, Freiburg, and Regensburg. Their fields of study included rhetoric, metaphysics, philosophy, theology, physics, logic, and casuistry. The parish priest in the market town of Ottobeuren had studied theology at the Collegium Germanicum in Rome. Sontheimer, *Geistlichkeit des Kapitels Ottobeuren*, Vols. II–IV.

[36] Thus, for example, in 1606 sixteen men in the village of Günz were fined on the complaint of the pastor that "without any reason [they] never come to church either on Sunday or on other feast days." StAA, KL Ottobeuren 587-II, Heft 26 (1606/7). The miller of Niederdorf was fined one pound in 1594 because "every feast day [he] goes riding off to get his medicines and never goes to church at all." Ibid., Heft 18 (1594/5).

Table 3.2 *Population in five Ottobeuren villages, 1564–1620*

Settlement	1564	1586	1620 Assumption 1	1620 Assumption 2
Hawangen	662	567	560	645
Sontheim	549	546	666	767
Frechenrieden	390	326	344	396
Wolfertschwenden	281	246	262	302
Niederrieden	306	320	349	402
Total	2188	2005	2181	2512
Index [1564 = 100]	100	91.6	99.7	114.8

Sources: StAA, KL Ottobeuren 102, 601-II; Dertsch, "Das Einwohnerbuch des Ottobeurer Klosterstaats 1564"; Sontheimer, *Die Geistlichkeit des Kapitels Ottobeuren*, Vols. II–IV

scenarios have been reconstructed. The first assumes that only half of the increase in the number of communicants per household represented actual population growth; the other half is attributed to more widespread reception of Easter communion by the peasantry. This assumption would imply a mean household size of 4.71 persons in 1620. The second scenario presumes that eucharistic compliance did not change between 1593 and 1620, in which case household size would have averaged 5.42 persons in 1620. On either scenario there was a definite population increase in that interval.

It could of course be argued that none of the foregoing is truly incompatible with a Malthusian interpretation. After all, the population of the Ottobeuren lands did decline between 1564 and 1586, and even if growth resumed after 1593, the rate of increase was much lower than it had been in the first half of the sixteenth century. Moreover, the overall 1620 population was at best 14.8 percent higher and quite probably the same size as it had been in 1564. The last third of the sixteenth century remains a demographic watershed.

These are perfectly legitimate objections, but this only brings us to the second and more important caution about the demographic trend. To interpret a slackening of population growth as an indication of some kind of systemic blockage or breakdown is to presume a rather simplistic relation between economic sophistication and population density. As is clear from Table 3.3, however, the assumption is by no means a safe one. The returns of the 1840 Bavarian state census reveal a population in the former monastery lands only trivially larger than the late sixteenth-century peak. As late as 1890, population was barely 20 percent higher than it had been in 1564 and possibly no higher than it was in 1620. The intent here is not to suggest that the Swabian rural economy was as advanced at the time of the Council of Trent as it would be under Bismarck. Rather, the point is that the relationship between population density and economic development is much less straightforward than has often been assumed. If

Table 3.3 *Population of the lands of the monastery of Ottobeuren, 1564–1890*

Settlement	1564	1793	1840	1890
Attenhausen	355	352	404	453
Benningen	794	471	557	639
Böhen	229	335	369	358
Dietratried	139	129	155	147
Egg an der Günz	384	406	458	593
Frechenrieden	390	414	434	441
Günz	161	189	227	214
Hawangen	662	431	543	615
Niederdorf	191	187	216	282
Niederrieden	359	390	461	551
Schlegelsberg	215	117	227	221
Sontheim	549	549	700	921
Ober- and Unterwesterheim	340	361	485	618
Wolfertschwenden	281	199	312	376
Villages subtotal	5049	4530	5548	6429
Böhen parish	573	374	412	400
Ottobeuren parish	1493	1574	1732	1834
Hamlets subtotal	2066	1948	2144	2234
Markt Ottobeuren	699	1355	1656	1799

Sources: Dertsch, "Das Einwohnerbuch des Ottobeurer Klosterstaats 1564"; Josef Heider, "Grundherrschaft und Landeshoheit der Abtei Ottobeuren: Nachwirkungen im 19. und 20. Jahrhundert," *Studien und Mitteilungen zur Geschichte des Benediktiner-Ordens und seiner Zweige* 73, 2–4 (1962), pp. 63–95, at p. 89 (for 1793); Bayerischen Statistischen Landesamt, ed. "Historisches Gemeindeverzeichnis: Die Einwohnerzahlen der Gemeinde Bayerns in der Zeit von 1840 bis 1952," *Beiträge zur Statistik Bayerns* 192 (Munich, 1953)

the density at which population growth stopped at sixteenth-century Ottobeuren was unsurpassed until far into the industrial age, it behooves us to be cautious about regarding that cessation as a failure.

The ambiguity of the demographic evidence is only part of the problem with a Malthusian vision of rural life at Ottobeuren. For the essence of this vision is not simply that population growth rates vary over time, but rather that the regulatory mechanism of final instance was the size of the food supply. This brings us, at long last, to agricultural technology, customarily regarded as the Achilles heel of the early modern economy.

As was the case in most parts of early modern Europe, the subsistence of the common people of the monastery lands revolved around the production and consumption of grain. The peasants worked the land in the three-course rotation common to much of Europe. One third of the arable land lay fallow each year, and the rest was given over to the production of food grains.[37] Chief amongst

---

[37] See for example StAA, KL Ottobeuren 29. In the section on the village of Egg (ff. 90r–101v) arable land is classed in three categories, (1) sown with rye, (2) sown with oats, and (3) fallow.

these were rye and oats,[38] which were consumed by the peasants in the form of bread and porridge respectively. Spelt and barley were also harvested, but in smaller quantities; the wheat crop was insignificant by comparison.[39]

By all indications, the fields yielded but a grudging multiple of what was sown. Precise figures are hard to come by, but granary accounts from 1623/4 and 1624/5 record the amounts both sown and harvested on the monastery's demesne lands and thus permit the calculation of yield: seed ratios for a variety of grains. Most of the yield ratios are clustered between 4.5 and 5.5:1, scarcely an improvement over medieval yields.[40]

There is of course the question of how reliably we may infer the yields of peasant farming from the harvests on demesne lands. This is an entirely legitimate concern. In the early eighteenth century the Abbot of Ottobeuren felt strongly enough about the greater efficiency of peasant farming that he arranged for his stewards to receive instruction from an elderly villager.[41] The yield ratio figures from the monastery demesne may thus provide a misleading impression of productivity on the peasant holdings. It does not seem likely, however, that the productivity differential was all that great. Although we have no account books kept by peasants, there is a document which sheds at least some light on the matter. In 1637 an unnamed monastic official drew up a list of anticipated tithes on the basis of the peasants' seed corn. From the projected receipts it is easy to see that the scribe assumed that the peasants would harvest only five measures of grain for each measure sown.[42]

The figures from the 1637 account were of course only estimates, but they are unlikely to have been wildly incorrect. This being the case, it does appear that

---

[38] For the consumption of oats in early modern Swabia see Hans Jänichen, *Beiträge zur Wirtschafts-geschichte des schwäbischen Dorfes* (Stuttgart, 1970), pp. 86–9, 99–106.

[39] For the dominance of rye and oats, see the 1586/7 description of the monastery's grain rents in StAA, KL Ottobeuren 224, Heft 1. A later, but more accurate picture may be gained from the 1621/2 breakdown of the monastery's tithe receipts recorded in StAA, KL Ottobeuren 225, ff. 104v–109v. In the villages the tithe was composed above all of rye (42.8% by volume), spelt (26.7%), and oats (22.0%), the remainder consisting of mixed grain (4.0%), barley (3.1%), and wheat (1.4%). In the hamlets the pre-eminent grains were oats (55.7%) and spelt (32.4%), while rye (6.7%), barley (4.5%), and mixed grains (0.7%) were relatively unimportant.

[40] StAA, KL Ottobeuren 226. These accounts from 1622–5 record amounts sown and harvested at five separate demesne farms, although not all farms harvested all grains. Over both years average yields were 5.44:1 for rye and 3.95:1 for oats. Yields for spelt can be calculated only for 1624/5, when the average yield was 5.56:1. For comparison with medieval and other early modern yields see (in addition to the survey by Slicher van Bath) the statistical compilation of Aldo de Maddalena, "Rural Europe 1500–1750" in Carlo M. Cippola, ed, *The Fontana Economic History of Europe*, Vol. II: *The Sixteenth and Seventeenth Centuries* (Glasgow, 1974), pp. 595–622.

[41] Franz Karl Weber, "Wirtschaftsquellen und Wirtschaftsaufbau des Reichsstiftes Ottobeuren im beginnenden 18. Jahrhundert," *Studien und Mitteilungen zur Geschichte des Benediktiner-Ordens und seiner Zweige* 58 (1940), pp. 107–37, at p. 108.

[42] StAA, KL Ottobeuren 202, ff. 91v–98v. The manuscript contains accounts from 1635/6, 1636/7, and 1637/8. The tithe list comes from the last account, and covers all of the hamlets in the parishes of Böhen and Ottobeuren.

the level of agricultural productivity at early modern Ottobeuren was entirely in keeping with the Malthusian scenario. Be that as it may, it is worth asking whether these paltry yield ratios were really as much a sign of backwardness and a hindrance to economic development as they are so often held to have been.

In the first place, it should be kept in mind that advanced techniques for the more intensive use of the soil had been well known at Ottobeuren since the end of the Middle Ages. The alternating use of land as both arable and pasture in a pattern of convertible husbandry and the flooding of pasture land to create water meadows were key technical innovations argued to have revolutionized agricultural productivity in other parts of early modern Europe.[43] Neither technique was ever adopted on a large scale at Ottobeuren, but the fact that both are documented there at least as far back as the fifteenth century[44] indicates that peasant ignorance is not a plausible explanation for low yield ratios. Instead, it may well have been that the expensive techniques associated with intensive grain farming did not make economic sense given the quality of the soil in Upper Swabia. In this regard it warrants mention that with the coming of the railroad and improved marketing opportunities in the late nineteenth century, the response of the Upper Swabian peasantry was a drastic reduction in grain growing in favor of specialization in milk and cheese production.[45]

More to the point, it is not at all clear from the yield ratio figures *alone* that the wider economy was hamstrung by the level of agricultural productivity. Naturally, all things being equal higher yield ratios were preferable to lower ones. All the same, the relationship between the amounts harvested and sown does not tell us how much food was actually available and whether or not that amount was adequate. This may seem like an otiose objection, but it turns out that yield ratios at the levels observed at seventeenth-century Ottobeuren remained the norm in southern Germany as late as the middle of the nineteenth century, which shows just how ambiguous an economic indicator yield ratios can be (see Figure 3.5, which presents rye yield:seed ratios in Bavaria as reported in the agricultural census of 1863). If, then, we are to judge the agricultural viability of early modern rural society, we must turn our attention from productivity to production.

---

[43] For Flanders see Slicher van Bath, *Agrarian History*, pp. 178–9; for England see Eric Kerridge, *The Agricultural Revolution* (London, 1967), pp. 181–221, 251–67.

[44] Hermann Hoffmann, ed. *Die Urkunden des Reichsstiftes Ottobeuren 764–1460*, Schwäbische Forschungsgemeinschaft Reihe 2a, Urkunden und Regesten; Band 13 (Augsburg, 1991), Document no. 154 [10 June 1398] for convertible husbandry and no. 337 [29 May 1449] for water meadows.

[45] Josef Wilhelm Pregler, "Milchwirtschaft und Tierzucht und deren Grundlagen" in Aegidius Kolb, ed., *Landkreis Unterallgäu* (2 vols., Mindelheim, 1987), Vol. I, pp. 470–543. Pregler's calculations show that in the district where the monastery lands were located, the proportion of agricultural land occupied by meadows rose from 37.9 percent in 1830–6 to 43.2 percent in 1893 to 63.2 percent in 1939.

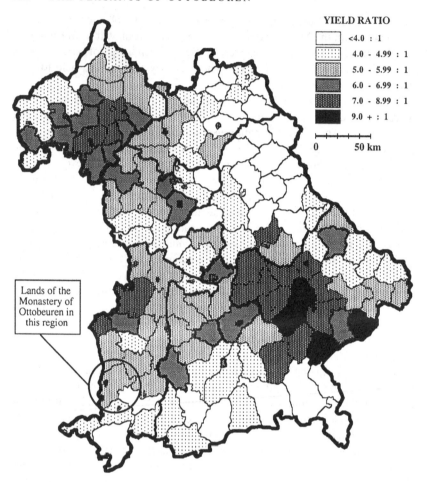

Figure 3.5 Rye yield ratios in Bavaria, 1863
Source: F. von Hermann, "Die Ernten im Königreich Bayern und in einigen anderen Ländern," *Beiträge zur Statistik des Königreichs, Bayern*, Heft 15 (Munich, 1866), pp. 1–21

The clearest obtainable picture of food production at Ottobeuren comes to us from the records of the ecclesiastical tithe.[46] Our dependence on this source imposes several limitations on what we can know. Simply put, the tithe was an imposition which like all impositions the peasantry resented and tried to avoid paying whenever and however possible. Some peasants surreptitiously

---

[46] Briefly: StAA, KA Ottobeuren 245 (1517–41), StAA, KL Ottobeuren 34–6 (1544–96), 40 (1560–1629), 55 (1652–72), 227 (1672–82), 230–2 (1692–1708), and 281–307 (1652–1714). There is considerable overlap in the records after 1652; the monastery's granary prepared several summative accounts on the basis of the threshing registers in StAA, KL Ottobeuren 281–307.

mixed chaff in with their grain payments; others blithely left only every eleventh instead of every tenth sheaf to be collected.[47] Alternatively, a peasant would claim that a particular parcel of arable land was legally exempt from the tithe. There were indeed a few such parcels in every village, but the impression gained from the documents is that the villagers had a more generous conception of the exempt acreage than did the monastic officials. All in all, it is clear that if we simply multiply the monastery's tithe receipts by ten, we will almost certainly not end up with the total volume of grain actually harvested.

But what will we end up with? If honesty compels us to admit the defects and biases of our source, fairness requires us to recognize the direction of these biases. Here there can be only one answer to the question: the records of the tithe, imperfect as they are, enable a minimum estimate of the size of the harvest. In other words, if a given tithe receipt when multiplied by ten yields a figure high enough to meet the needs of the population in question, we can be rather confident that at least enough was harvested to feed the inhabitants of the settlement.

Of course, we still need to know what the minimum volume of grain necessary for subsistence actually was, but here we are on much firmer ground. Grain consumption patterns in early modern Germany have been the subject of intensive investigation. While it cannot be denied that differences of opinion remain, most investigations have concluded that the subsistence minimum per capita grain requirement of the population as a whole (i.e. children and the elderly included; the requirement for working adults alone was a good deal higher than the global average) was approximately three hectoliters of grain per annum.[48] In terms of the measure of capacity at Ottobeuren, this translates into

---

[47] StAA, KL Ottobeuren 587-II, Heft 17 (1593/4): Michael Rauch of Benningen fined three pounds for leaving only the eleventh sheaf of grain. Jacob Heinrich of Hawangen left only the sixteenth sheaf; fined three pounds ten shillings. Balthas Widenmann of Benningen fined one pound because the sheaves he delivered as his tithe were "bound too small compared with the other ones" (which he kept for himself). StAA, KL Ottobeuren 587-II, Heft 20 (1598/9): Mathias Rauch junior of Benningen "left the eleventh sheaf instead of the tenth"; fined four pounds.

[48] I am here relying on the painstaking work of Rainer Beck, *Naturale Ökonomie. Unterfinning: Bäuerliche Wirtschaft in einem oberbayerischen Dorf des frühen 18. Jahrhunderts* (Munich, 1986), esp. pp. 176–89, 232–4. Beck argues quite convincingly that the subsistence minimum for an early modern peasant adult was between 245 and 265 kg of grain per annum. If we assume that this was composed one third of oats and two thirds of rye, we arrive at a volume of 325.8–352.1 liters or 1.49–1.61 Ottobeuren *malter*. Beck calculates that the needs of the village population as a whole (i.e. taking into account the lower consumption requirements of children and the elderly) represented 77 percent of an adult's requirement. This gives us an Ottobeuren equivalent of 1.15–1.24 *malter*. Other important studies are Dietmar Ebeling and Franz Irsigler, *Getreideumsatz, Getreide- und Brotpreise in Köln 1368–1796* (2 vols., Cologne/Vienna, 1976–7), Vol. 1, pp. ix–xii, and Bernd Roeck, *Bäcker, Brot und Getriede in Augsburg* (Sigmaringen, 1987), pp. 73–7, both of which arrive at an estimated per capita requirement of 3 hectoliters, or 1.37 *malter*. I have chosen to err on the side of caution and adopt the figure of 1.5 *malter*.

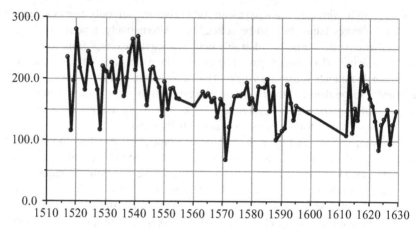

Figure 3.6 Estimated proportion (%) of minimum grain requirement harvested in Hawangen-Moosbach, 1517–1629
Sources: StAA, KA Ottobeuren 245; KL Ottobeuren 34–6, 40, 64, 102, 541 (2), 600, 601-II; Dertsch, "Das Einwohnerbuch des Ottobeurer Klosterstaats 1564"; Sontheimer, *Die Geistlichkeit des Kapitels Ottobeuren,* Vol. II

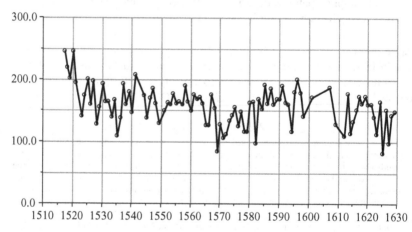

Figure 3.7 Estimated proportion (%) of minimum grain requirement harvested in Frechenrieden, 1517–1629
Sources: As for Figure 3.6

roughly one and a half *malter* of grain. Let us assume, therefore, that the annual subsistence minimum at early modern Ottobeuren was 1.8 *malter* per capita, that is 1.5 *malter* for consumption and 0.3 *malter* for the next year's seed corn given an average yield ratio of about five to one.

Figures 3.6 and 3.7 represent best guess reconstructions of the long-term evolution of the food supply in two Ottobeuren villages, Hawangen-Moosbach and Frechenrieden.[49] Needless to say, these estimates are subject to many qualifications, some of which have been discussed above. All the same, it is also the case that direct attempts to measure the balance between population and food supply in early modern Europe are exceedingly rare. Despite the well-known methodological pitfalls of so doing, most investigations are content to rely on urban grain prices as an indirect indicator. Thus, in light of the near unanimity with which early modern Europe has been pronounced a society ever on the verge of starvation, these two reconstructions offer an important new perspective. It is perfectly clear from Figures 3.6 and 3.7 that there were indeed years when there was truly not enough food to go around at Ottobeuren. At Hawangen-Moosbach the harvest failures of 1571, 1623, and 1627 must have visited enormous suffering upon the village. Frechenrieden saw similar hardship in 1569, 1582, and 1625. The extreme variability of the harvest is equally striking. In 1612 the harvest at Hawangen-Moosbach was more than twice what was needed; the next year there was just barely enough for the villagers to eat. The most important revelation of these two reconstructions, however, is that the third horseman only rarely darkened the village streets. Almost all of the time the harvest was more than large enough to feed the peasantry.

The surprisingly optimistic conclusions of the subsistence reconstructions for these two villages are also valid for the monastery lands as a whole. It is not possible to calculate longitudinal series for each and every settlement, but we are able to draw up a territorial balance sheet for two crucial decades of peak population, the 1560s and the 1620s. Our first balance sheet (see Table 3.4) coincides with the demographic peak of the mid-sixteenth century, after which point the population went into decline or at least stagnation for a generation. But although this pattern has all the hallmarks of a Malthusian inflection point (and has been designated as such for Upper Swabia),[50] it was not the case that the population had outgrown its capacity to feed itself.

Naturally the picture is not unambiguously Panglossian. As is clear from Table 3.4, the food supply in the hamlets was rather less secure than in the nucleated villages. The safety margin in the parish of Ottobeuren was rather exiguous, whereas the parish of Böhen operated in a definite food deficit. The unsatisfactory food output of the hamlets was more than outweighed, however, by the abundant harvests in the nucleated villages. Taken as a whole, the Abbot's subjects produced more than enough grain to feed themselves.

---

[49] In calculating population growth after 1586, I have worked with the first scenario from Table 3.2, i.e. that half of the increase in communicants per household was the result of increased compliance with canon law.

[50] David Warren Sabean, *Power in the Blood: Popular Culture and Village Discourse in Early Modern Germany* (Cambridge, 1984), p. 7

Table 3.4 *Grain supply at Ottobeuren in the 1560s*[a]

Settlement	1564 population	Grain requirement (*malter*)	Mean tithe 1560–9 × 10[b]	+/– (*malter*)	+/– (%)
8 villages	2895	5211.0	9084.79	+3873.79	+74.3
33 hamlets (Ottobeuren parish)	1493	2687.4	3209.03	+521.63	+19.4
16 hamlets (Böhen parish)	533	959.4	783.30	–176.10	–18.4
Total	4921	8857.8	13077.12	+4219.32	+47.6

[a] The villages are Attenhausen, Böhen, Egg, Frechenrieden, Günz, Hawangen-Moosbach, Sontheim, and Unterwolfertschwenden. The hamlets in Ottobeuren parish are Eggisried, Stephansried, Gumpratzried, Dennenberg, Frölins, Wetzlen, Langenberg, Guggenberg, Halbersberg, Betzisried, Hof, Unterhaslach, Oberhaslach, Ölbrechts, Hohenheim, Rempolz, Vogelsang, Oberried, Dasperg, Höhe, Ollarzried, Schoren, Bibelsberg, Bühel, Reuthen, Oberböglins/Scherenberg, Unterböglins, Obermotz, Untermotz, Leupolz, Hössen, Hörlins/Schrallen, and Haitzen. The hamlets in Böhen parish are Karlass, Hüners, Lietzheim/Fricken, Bernhalden, auf dem Berg, Lampolz, the three sub-hamlets of Warlins, Nollen, Theilen, Günzegg, Waldmühle, Osterberg, Wetzlen, and Guntershalden/ Pfaudlins.
[b] The Sontheim tithe is from 1572–8
Sources: StAA, KL Ottobeuren 34–6, 40; KA Ottobeuren 343; Dertsch, "Das Einwohnerbuch des Ottobeurer Klosterstaats 1564"

By the 1620s, as the resurgent rural population regained its mid-sixteenth-century peak, the picture was somewhat different (see Table 3.5). In the nucleated villages the harvest had declined by about 8 percent since the mid-1560s, a phenomenon visible in more detail in the two subsistence series from Hawangen-Moosbach and Frechenrieden. In the hamlets, by contrast, grain production had increased dramatically, by 33.5 percent in Ottobeuren parish and by 47.5 percent in Böhen parish. As a result, subsistence in the monastery lands had become more secure in a double sense. On the one hand, the grain-deficit and near grain-deficit hamlets were now not only self-sufficient, but actually generating surpluses. On the other hand, the surplus in the monastic territory as a whole had risen from 47.6 percent in the 1560s to 57.7 percent in the 1620s. Put differently, far from deteriorating into a Malthusian crisis over the course of the sixteenth century, the relation between population and grain supply at Ottobeuren had actually improved.

Despite the rather surprising results of the foregoing investigation, it is important to keep them in proper perspective. When all is said and done, the fact remains that after several generations of virtually untrammeled expansion, population growth at Ottobeuren slowed down dramatically after the 1560s if it did not come to a complete halt. There is no intent here to deny this fact. Rather, the point is that the conventional interpretation of this pattern is flatly contradicted by the sources. In the first place, it remains an open question whether zero

Table 3.5 *Grain supply at Ottobeuren in the 1620s*

Settlement	1620 population	Grain requirement (*malter*)	Mean tithe 1615–24 × 10[a]	+/− (*malter*)	+/− (%)
8 villages	2948	5306.4	8346.56	+3040.16	+57.3
33 hamlets (Ottobeuren parish)	1352	2433.6	4284.61	+1851.01	+76.1
16 hamlets (Böhen parish)	557	1002.6	1155.09	+152.49	+15.2
Total	4857	8742.6	13786.26	+5043.66	+57.7

[a] The Sontheim tithe is from 1606–8 and 1618–20
Sources: StAA, KL Ottobeuren 40, 102, 601-II; KA Ottobeuren 343; Sontheimer, *Die Geistlichkeit des Kapitels Ottobeuren*, Vols. II–IV

population growth is to be equated with economic stagnation. More fundamentally, whatever we may make of the demographic deceleration in the monastery lands, the phenomenon has to be explained in terms other than a Malthusian ceiling. Famine of biblical proportions was by no means unknown, and hungry winters may have been more common still, but the vast majority of the time the peasants of Ottobeuren did not starve.

True though it may be that the Ottobeuren peasantry harvested more than enough grain to feed itself, it must be conceded that there is an air of irreality about the fact. In a society as stratified as the peasantry by the mid-sixteenth century had become, there was no necessary correspondence between material needs and the ability to meet them. Even before we may address ourselves to this problem, however, another interposes itself. For the wealth so painfully wrung from the soil, the loom, and the marketplace and then piled up in barns and storehouses was never left to the disposal of those who had produced it. A truly bewildering variety of impositions were levied upon the peasantry, and many of their hard-earned gains were siphoned away by the landlord, the church, and the territorial state.

For obvious reasons, then, no discussion of the sixteenth-century rural economy can afford to overlook the extractive relationship between the peasantry and its overlords. This said, the precise historical role to be assigned to this relationship remains a matter of some dispute. Broadly speaking, there are two main approaches to the problem. The first view, an extension of the Malthusian position encountered above, is that the level of prestation was dictated by demography. When population rose, as in the thirteenth or sixteenth century, the economic position of the rural population deteriorated and the demand for land became intense. The peasants could thus be forced to pay higher rents. When, as in the fifteenth or seventeenth century, the population stagnated or declined, the tables were turned. It was now the landlords who were obliged to offer rent reductions in order to attract and retain tenants. Surplus extraction is thus conceived as yet another function of the grand agrarian cycle.[51]

A second view accords more autonomy to the extractive relationship between peasant and overlord, seeing in the process an independent influence if not indeed the root cause of the cycles of expansion, crisis, and contraction in the European economy.[52] On this view the expansion of the rural economy allowed landlords repeatedly to reduce the rate of prestation while still enjoying an increase in overall incomes. The falling rate of levy also encouraged further economic growth. On the other hand, the slowing or cessation of growth reduced the income of the landlords and provoked a response known variously as a rent offensive or a seigneurial reaction. Old impositions were increased and new ones were introduced in a short-sighted attempt to restore the *status quo*. Instead, the outcome was the disruption of rural production, growing resentment among the peasantry, and ultimately a dismal cycle of peasant uprisings, lordly repression, and economic decline.

Perhaps the most helpful summary that can be made of the foregoing dispute is that the two approaches actually have a great deal in common.[53] At issue is the extent to which the burdens imposed on the peasant by his overlord are to be seen as causes or consequences of the fluctuating health of the rural economy as a whole, but it would be misleading to present the matter as an either/or proposition. Adherents of both views are often willing to see seigneurial exactions and overpopulation as co-contributors to the economic malaise held to have beset Europe in the early seventeenth century. Moreover, irrespective of the factor to which primacy is accorded, the predicted sequence of events is virtually identical: a crisis of seigneurial incomes in the fifteenth century, a recovery in the sixteenth, and then a second crisis in the seventeenth century.

It is the obsession with crisis with which I take issue. Whether inspired by Malthus, Marx, or both, almost all contributions to the discussion of landlord–tenant relations in early modern Europe are anchored in the notion of a perpetual susceptibility to crisis. More specifically, the early modern economy is regarded

---

[51] This view is associated with the *Annales* school. See (in addition to the works cited above at note 9) Joseph Goy and Emmanuel LeRoy Ladurie, eds. *Prestations paysannes, dîmes, rente foncière et mouvement de la production agricole à l'époque préindustrielle* (2 vols., Paris, 1982).

[52] This is the approach of most scholars inspired by Marx. Particularly influential has been Guy Bois, *The Crisis of Feudalism: Economy and Society in Eastern Normandy c. 1300–1550* [English translation; translator not cited] (Cambridge, 1984). Peter Kriedte, "Spätmittelalterliche Agrarkrise oder Krise des Feudalismus?" *Geschichte und Gesellschaft* 7 (1981), pp. 42–68 is an extended review of the original 1976 French edition of Bois' book from a German perspective. See also John E. Martin, *Feudalism to Capitalism: Peasant and Landlord in English Agrarian Development* (Atlantic Highlands, NJ, 1983).

[53] An intense debate between Marxist and Malthusian interpretations of the early modern economy was sparked by Robert Brenner, "Agrarian Class Structure and Economic Development in Pre-Industrial Europe," *Past and Present* 70 (1976), pp. 30–75. His original essay, the responses of several critics, and Brenner's 1982 rejoinder are reprinted in T. H. Ashton and C. H. E. Philpin, eds. *The Brenner Debate* (Cambridge, 1985).

as fundamentally self-defeating, since the very process of expansion sowed the seeds of future decline. At least at Ottobeuren, this was not the case. Naturally the interests of the Abbot and his subjects were on several issues decidedly at variance. It also goes without saying that debilitating short-term disasters of various sorts might dramatically shift the power balance between overlord and peasant, and that long-term fluctuations in seigneurial prestations are certainly in evidence. The point here is that for all its inner contradictions, the extractive relationship between the monastery and its subjects did not lurch from crisis to crisis under the of aegis of some self-destructive teleology. When catastrophe did ultimately come it was visited from without; it did not grow up from within.

By comparison with its late medieval counterpart,[54] the early modern German seigneurie has been the subject of little scholarly attention, at least in so far as its economic (as opposed to legal) history is concerned.[55] Thus, although there is considerable evidence that both secular and ecclesiastical lords were experiencing serious financial difficulties in the early fifteenth century, the corresponding picture one hundred years later is frustratingly opaque. Given the widespread opinion that a seigneurial reaction lay behind the events of 1525 this is a particularly frustrating lacuna.[56]

The state of the monastery's finances in the early sixteenth century is recorded in a pair of accounts from the years 1527/8 and 1528/9. The registers were apparently drawn up on the basis of separate accounts maintained by the cellarer, the "Kornmeister," and others, and record receipts and disbursements grouped under various headings. The registers seem largely complete, but it is clear that one important source of income, namely those rents paid in cash, has been left out of the reckoning. Fortunately, a second account book has survived for the years 1536–45. Though less comprehensive than the older pair of registers, the later account does allow us to estimate cash rents for the years 1527/8 and 1528/9,[57] permitting at least an approximation of the overall finances of the monastery (see Table 3.6)

The financial picture revealed by the registers displays a number of interesting features, three of which seem worthy of particular attention. First, despite the common perception that most German landlords were hopelessly insolvent at the time of the Peasants' War, the monastery of Ottobeuren seems to have been in stable financial health. True enough, the account for 1527/8 reveals a steep

---

[54] The literature on the fifteenth and early sixteenth centuries is enormous. A recent collection of investigations may be found in H. Patze, ed. *Die Grundherrschaft im späten Mittelalter* (2 vols., Sigmaringen, 1983).

[55] Important exceptions are Christian Heimpel, *Die Entwicklung der Einnahmen und Ausgaben des Heiliggeistspitals zu Biberach an der Riß von 1500 bis 1630* (Stuttgart, 1966), and Rudolf Schlögl, *Bauern, Krieg und Staat: Oberbayerische Bauernwirtschaft und frühmoderner Staat im 17. Jahrhundert* (Göttingen, 1988).

[56] There is a classic statement in Blickle, *The Revolution of 1525*, pp. 71–3.

[57] Cash rents increased in a slow but steady and linear fashion between 1536 and 1545. I have extrapolated backwards to estimate the receipts for the late 1520s.

Table 3.6 *Income of the monastery of Ottobeuren, 1527/8 and 1528/9*

	1527/8		1528/9	
Source	£ heller	%	£ heller	%
Grain sales	2262.39	45.1	3675.04	54.0
Transfer fees	400.38	8.0	30.10	0.4
Serfdom	122.26	2.4	63.00	0.9
Wood, stone, charcoal, fish, cattle	207.71	4.1	1187.57	17.5
Tolls	79.50	1.6	103.30	1.5
Fines	143.20	2.9	0.00	0.0
Miscellaneous	58.67	1.2	0.00	0.0
Estimated cash rents	1739.26	34.7	1743.85	25.6
Total income	5013.37	100.0	6802.86	100.0
Total expenditures	7763.53		6196.96	
Balance	−2750.16		+605.90	

Sources: StAA, KL Ottobeuren 541, Hefte 1 and 3

deficit of £2750 5 ß, but this was largely due to an extraordinary charge of £1791 16 ß 2 d subsequently added to the account. Moreover, the account for 1528/9 records a healthy surplus of £605 18 ß. In any case, it is hard to imagine how the monastery could have managed so many territorial acquisitions in the sixteenth century – a series of vineyards on the lake of Constance in 1522–34, the village of Rummeltshausen in 1564, the *Maierhof* in Sontheim in 1578, and the village of Ungerhausen in 1593 to name only the most important[58] – had it not been in robust financial shape.

Second, the monies derived from charges associated with serfdom – manumissions, heriots, and *Ungenossame*, or fines for marriages to other lords' serfs – made a derisory proportion of the monastery's income: 2.4 percent in 1527/8 and 0.9 percent in 1528/9. Again, this flies in the face of the often encountered assertion that serfdom was an important financial prop for landlords in the German southwest.[59]

The most striking feature of the Ottobeuren accounts, however, is the fact that so little of the monks' income was originally in the form of cash. The bulk of their receipts – 49.2 percent in 1527/8 and fully 71.5 percent in 1528/9 – came from the sale of agricultural products, chiefly grain.[60] The monastery was thus protected from the ravages of inflation, since the sixteenth-century price revolution which impoverished so many landlords was driven for the most part by increases in the price of grain.

---

[58] Heider, "Grundherrschaft und Landeshoheit," p. 68; Franz Ludwig Baumann, *Geschichte des Allgäus* (4 vols., Kempten, 1883–94; repr. Aalen, 1971–3), Vol. III: 1517–1802, p. 266.

[59] Claudia Ulbricht, *Leibherrschaft am Oberrhein im Spätmittelalter* (Göttingen, 1979), pp. 294–8.

[60] The same has been noted for the lower nobility of the German southwest by Kurt Anderman, "Grundherrschaft des spätmittelalterlichen Niederadels in Südwest-deutschland," *Blätter für Deutsche Landesgeschichte* N. F. 127 (1991), pp. 145–90.

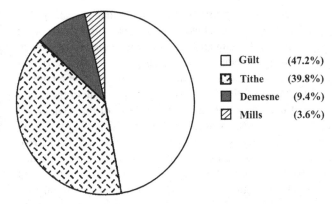

☐	Gült	(47.2%)
▨	Tithe	(39.8%)
■	Demesne	(9.4%)
▨	Mills	(3.6%)

Figure 3.8 Grain revenues of the monastery of Ottobeuren by source, 1536
Source: StAA, KL Ottobeuren 541, Heft 3

What was the source of these grain receipts which formed the bulk of the monastery's revenue? The two older registers are silent on this matter, but clarification may be had from the later account book. As is shown by Figure 3.8, very little of this grain – less than a tenth – was produced on the monastic demesne lands. Instead, like most south German landlords the monks had largely given up direct farming, preferring to rely on rents collected from peasant tenants.[61] The monks were careful, however, never to commute these grain rents into cash payments, and continued to collect them in grain until the Abbot's lordship was dissolved in 1803. Together with the tithe, rye and oat rents known as *Gült* made up almost 90 percent of the monastery's grain revenues in 1536.

Although the monastery derived at least half of its income from the sale of grain, not all of the total grain receipts were actually sold on the market. For although the monks sold some 1,200 *malter* (≈ 2,600 hectoliters) of grain in 1528/9, if the records of the later 1530s are any indication their total receipts must have been at least 3,000 *malter* (≈ 6,500 hectoliters). Three thousand *malter* of grain were enough to feed at least a third of the monastery's subjects for a full year. What kind of a burden did the extraction of so much grain impose on the peasantry?

Ever since David Sabean's pioneering 1972 monograph on the Swabian cloister of Weingarten,[62] there has been considerable interest in attempting to

---

[61] The prominence of rent income from life-term or hereditary tenants is a distinctive feature of the German seigneurie. French and English landlords relied much more heavily on short-term leases. See Eberhard Weiss, "Ergebnisse eines Vergleichs der grundherrschaftlichen Strukturen Deutschlands und Frankreichs vom 13. bis zum Ausgang des 18. Jahrhunderts," *Vierteljahrschrift für Sozial- und Wirtschaftsgeschichte* 57 (1970), pp. 1–14 and J. P. Cooper, "In Search of Agrarian Capitalism" in Aston and Philpin, eds., *The Brenner Debate*, pp. 161–78.

[62] David W. Sabean, *Landbesitz und Gesellschaft am Vorabend des Bauernkriegs: eine Studie der sozialen Verhältnisse im südlichen Oberschwaben in den Jahren von 1525* (Stuttgart, 1972).

measure the economic weight of seigneurialism on the German peasantry. The typical point of departure is an *Urbar*, a land cadastre describing the physical area of the peasant holdings and the annual charges to which they were subject. To the annual charges is usually added the *Erdschatz*, or entry fine, levied at the admission of a new tenant, prorated over the presumed length of tenure. A further 10 percent of the harvest is deducted to cover the payment of the ecclesiastical tithe. The result is a reasonably accurate estimate of the payments a peasant would make to his various overlords each year. Calculating the peasant's income is a less exact proposition. The conventional approach is to arrive at an estimate for grain yields per unit of surface area and then to apply this figure to the arable land described in the cadastre (strictly speaking the yield estimate is applied to only two-thirds of the arable surface area, one third of the land was left fallow each year in the three-field rotation system commonly practiced in the German countryside).

Given the character of the surviving sixteenth-century sources, a comparison of the estimated harvest with the aggregated rents and other charges is as close an estimate of the burden of seigneurialism as is possible. The method employed here is different only in minor detail. This said, it serves no purpose to overlook the limitations of the approach outlined above. In terms of the charges, it should be pointed out that an *Urbar* only lists those charges which were both regular and imposed in right of the lord's jurisdiction over the land and its tenants (a right commonly referred to as *Grundherrschaft*). Charges arising from serfdom (manumissions, heriots, etc.) and those levied only sporadically (e.g. territorial taxes) are perforce left out of the debit side of the equation. These shortcomings are hardly damning, but omissions on the credit side are much more serious. First of all, an *Urbar* only describes land held of the lord. Allodial land, or *freies Eigen* as it was known, made up only a small proportion of the total surface area in most of Upper Swabia,[63] but those freeholds which did exist had a value completely out of proportion to their physical extent. The description in the *Urbar* thus understates the amount of land at the peasant's disposal. More significantly, before the advent of more detailed tax books in the seventeenth century, it is impossible even to estimate any source of income apart from the grain harvest. The produce of the intensely worked gardens escapes our purview, as does the income from animal husbandry. This last lacuna is particularly unfortunate, since investigations of the later seventeenth century have shown that at that time the south German peasantry derived some 30–45 percent of its income from the sale of cattle.[64]

In sum, then, like almost all efforts of historical quantification the attempt to measure the burden of sixteenth-century seigneurialism produces at best a

---

[63] Peter Blickle, "Bäuerliches Eigen im Allgäu," *Zeitschrift für Agrargeschichte und Agrarsoziologie* 17, 1 (1969), pp. 57–78.
[64] Schlögl, *Bauern, Krieg und Staat*, pp. 383–5.

qualified estimate. Nevertheless, the value of these estimates remains considerable. Since the preponderance of the unfathomable elements remains on the credit side of our equation, we can know that our results are in all likelihood a maximum estimate of the proportion of the peasant's income extracted by the landlord.

At Ottobeuren the available records are somewhat different from those normally used for an investigation of seigneurialism. Regrettably, no *Urbar* has survived from the sixteenth century. Instead, we are obliged to fall back on a series of *Gültbücher*, or rent rolls, which list the grain payments due from each of the tenants,[65] but record neither the annual cash rents, the entry fine or *Erdschatz*, nor a description of the dimensions of the holding. It turns out, however, that almost all of this information is available from other sources. The monastery accounts for 1536–45 record the annual cash rents due from most of the villages (although the total is not broken down for each tenant), and a virtually complete record of the entry fines for the period 1530–1603 has been preserved in a pair of *Erdschatzbücher*.[66] An aggregate of the seigneurial charges at the village level may thus be fairly easily put together. Reconstructing the harvest proves to be the easiest gap to fill. It is not possible to estimate each tenant's individual harvest, but with the help of the now familiar tithe records a direct estimate of the grain produced by the village as a whole, allodial lands included, is readily available.

The results of these various calculations are displayed in Table 3.7.[67] The total burden imposed on the peasantry ranged from 22 to 27 percent of the grain harvest. Was this a great deal? A levy between a fifth and a quarter was completely unremarkable by comparison with seigneurial levies elsewhere in southern Germany.[68] The burden was almost certainly resented, but the amount extracted hardly seems confiscatory; it certainly left enough for the village to meet its nutritional needs, not to mention the unknowable quantum of income from other sources. Furthermore, as has already been seen in chapter 1, the

---

[65] StAA, KL Ottobeuren 29–30.   [66] StAA, KL Ottobeuren 26–7.

[67] I have provided estimates only for those settlements in which the monastery was the exclusive landlord. Until 1588 one of the farms in Attenhausen was under the landlordship of the so-called 'lower' hospital in the nearby city of Memmingen. I have taken the rent for this farm from the abstract of the hospital's 1572 rent roll in Hannes Lambacher, *Das Spital der Reichsstadt Memmingen* (Kempten, 1991), pp. 162–8. See also Blickle, *Memmingen*, p. 66.

[68] On the lands of the cloister of Weingarten total prestations represented 28 percent of the harvest of the average farm in 1531. Sabean, *Landbesitz und Gesellschaft*, pp. 62–3. Just south of Ottobeuren in the lordship of Kronburg, seigneurial dues made up 26.9 percent of the entire harvest in 1529–34. Since the more numerous smaller farms bore a heavier proportional burden, the average farm paid 31.5 percent of its harvest. Burkhard Asmuss, "Das Einkommen der Bauern in der Herrschaft Kronburg im frühen 16. Jahrhundert," *Zeitschrift für Bayerische Landesgeschichte* 43, 1 (1980), pp. 45–91. In the north Swabian region of the Hesselberg, Gabler estimates that in 1535 dues consumed 18–26 percent of the harvest on a large farm and 14–16 percent on a small one. A. Gabler, "Die wirtschaftliche Lage des Bauerntums im Hesselberggebiet des 16. Jahrhunderts," *Schwäbische Blätter* 14, 3 (1963), pp. 73–98.

Table 3.7 *Seigneurial dues as a proportion (%) of the harvest[a] at Ottobeuren, 1544*

Settlement	Gült	Cash rent	Tithe	Erdschatz	Total
Attenhausen	10.8	2.4	10.0	0.6	23.8
Böhen	6.7	4.3	10.0	0.5	21.6
Frechenrieden	9.1	3.7	10.0	0.5	23.4
Hawangen-Moosbach	10.0	2.0?	10.0	0.7	22.7?
Niederdorf	14.0	1.9	10.0	0.6	26.5
Hamlets of Ottobeuren parish	4.1	2.0?	10.0	1.0	17.1?

[a] Harvest estimated from the mean tithe, 1540–9
Sources: StAA, KL Ottobeuren 27, 29, 34, 541(Heft 3); KA Ottobeuren 245; Lambacher, *Das Spital der Reichsstadt Memmingen*, pp. 162–8

Table 3.8 *Finances of the monastery of Ottobeuren in* gulden, *1527/8–1620/1*

Year	Income	Expenditure	Nominal balance	Deflated balance
1527/8	2864.73	4436.30	−1571.57	−1571.57
1528/9	3887.30	3541.12	+346.18	+346.18
1619/20	40493.41	28187.15	+12306.26	7180.65
1620/1	43848.46	27137.03	+16711.43	9751.05

Sources: StAA, KL Ottobeuren 541, Hefte 1 and 7; StadtA MM D Folioband 99, D 102/1a–1b; Wolf, *Reichsstädte in Kriegszeiten*, Table 82, p. 276

burden of seigneurialism at Ottobeuren was almost entirely borne by those most able to do so.

But if the evidence of the 1530s and 1540s will not support the notion of an impending crisis, what of the later period? What became of the stable equilibrium of the post-Peasants' War period after several generations of demographic flux and galloping inflation? Here the best place to begin is with an extremely detailed account of the monastery's finances drawn up for the years 1619/20 and 1620/1 (see Table 3.8). When compared with the two older accounts for 1527/8 and 1528/9 it is clear that a number of major changes have taken place. First of all, even after adjusting for the intervening surge in prices, the monastery's revenues have increased more than eight-fold. Still more significantly, whereas in the 1520s the monks were just able to cover their expenses with their income, by the 1620s the monastery was racking up surpluses of 12,000–16,000 *gulden*, a sum greater than their entire revenue in the earlier period. Finally, as is clear from Figure 3.9, the composition of the monastery's income had undergone a dramatic transformation.

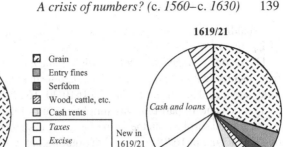

Figure 3.9 Composition of the revenues of the monastery of Ottobeuren, 1527/9 and 1619/21
Sources: StAA, KL Ottobeuren 541, Hefte 1 and 7

Two main tendencies had shaped the new profile of the monastery's income. The first was a gradual accumulation of new sources of revenue. The *Umgeld*, or excise tax on wine, was first instituted in 1564 when Abbot Caspar Kindelmann secured an imperial privilege authorizing him to collect a 1/13 (7.7 percent) levy on all the wine sold throughout the monastery lands. Abbot Caspar was shrewd enough simultaneously to grant a monopoly on wine sales to the innkeepers responsible for the payment of the excise (it had previously been legal for anyone to sell wine out of his house), thereby ensuring their co-operation.[69] In 1601 Abbot Alexander Sauter had the market rights of the *Markt* Ottobeuren reconfirmed by Emperor Rudolf II, and then promptly began collecting a toll on all goods sold in the marketplace.[70] The introduction of annual property taxes cannot be dated precisely, although it seems to have fallen sometime between 1603 and 1619.[71] Whatever the case may be, by the 1620s the monastery had begun compiling massive surveys of every piece of land and head of livestock in its territory. A new survey was completed every three to four years[72] and the

---

[69] Maurus Feyerabend, *Des ehemaligen Reichsstiftes Ottenbeuren, Benediktiner Ordens in Schwaben, sämmtliche Jahrbücher* (4 vols., Ottobeuren, 1813–16), Vol. III, pp. 216–19.

[70] Ibid., pp. 297–8. The tolls are listed in the Market Ordinance of 5 August 1601 copied in StAA, KL Ottobeuren 4, Document 289V, ff. 350v–358v.

[71] During the later sixteenth century, the subjects of the monastery were periodically called upon to pay the so-called 'Turk taxes' to finance the expeditions of the Holy Roman Emperor against the Ottoman Turks. A six-year Turk tax was levied in 1577, and again in 1594. A third Turk tax was levied in 1603, and all small portions of all three tax registers are abstracted in StAA, KL Ottobeuren 4, ff. 62v–77r. In many German territories, these periodic Turk taxes were transmuted into regular taxes paid to the territorial overlord (see Winfried Schulze, *Reich und Türkengefahr im späten 16. Jahrhundert* (Munich, 1978), pp. 278–9, 299–301, 367–8); this may also have happened at Ottobeuren. Whatever the case may have been, the account of 1619/20 records property taxes as a regular impost.

[72] Surveys from 1620/1, 1624, and 1627 are preserved in StAA, KL Ottobeuren 102–4. Post-war records document the existence of a 1630 tax survey, but this manuscript seems to have since been lost.

net wealth of the peasantry (i.e. gross wealth minus debts) was taxed at the rate of 1 percent.[73]

The second change in the composition of the monastery's income was a shift from income in kind to income in cash. Income in kind averaged 62.1 percent of total income in 1527/8 and 1528/9; by 1619/20–1620/1 the proportion had fallen to 32.4 percent. In part this was simply a result of the monastery's prosperity. Accumulated surpluses in the form of loans or cash on hand made up 28 percent of total income in 1620/1. It is worth pointing out, however, that all of the new sources of revenue were collected in cash, and that together the excise and property taxes made up a fifth of the monastery's total revenues.

It goes without saying that the new prestations increased the burden on the peasantry. It is also clear that some of the older obligations became more onerous over the course of the sixteenth century. Chief among these were the entry fines for *Gotteshaus* properties, the level of which quintupled in real terms between 1530 and 1620. On the other hand, although the nominal value of cash rents collected from the peasantry increased by some 94.6 percent between 1544 and 1619, the price increase over the same period was greater still, such that the real value of the cash rents actually declined.[74] As for the grain rents which constituted the core of the monastery's income in the late 1520s, they remained for all intents and purposes unchanged between 1544 and 1621.[75] The tithe remained by definition the same.

The net effect of these various shifts is presented in Table 3.9,[76] and the pattern is fairly surprising. Although the monastery had clearly enriched itself at the expense of the subject population, the burden of seigneurialism had risen only slightly, from 20–25 percent of the harvest in 1544 to 26–30 percent in 1621. It must be said that in so far as the new impositions did not spare the poorer members of the village community in the manner of *Erdschatz* and *Korngült*, the proportional increase in the burden imposed on the poor must have been still greater than is suggested by a comparison of Tables 3.7 and 3.9. Nevertheless, the figure of 26–30 percent applies primarily to the villages; in the hamlets the burden was only a little more than 20 percent. It should also be re-emphasized

---

[73] The rate of taxation is nowhere formally proclaimed; the 1 percent rate emerges from a comparison with the net wealth of the peasantry as surveyed in 1620 and the tax receipts for 1620/1. StAA, KL Ottobeuren 102, KL Ottobeuren 541, Heft 7.

[74] StAA, KL Ottobeuren 541, Hefte 1, 3, and 7; StadtA MM D Folioband 99, D 102/1a–1b; Thomas Wolf, *Reichsstädte in Kriegszeiten*, Table 82, p. 276.

[75] Compare StAA, KL Ottobeuren 29 (1544) with KL Ottobeuren 225, ff. 76r–103v (1621).

[76] Two of the calculations in this table require some explanation. There are no sources recording payments of cash rents or entry fines at the level of the individual settlement during the 1620s; we have only the receipts from the monastery lands as a whole in the accounts of 1619/20 and 1620/1. Cash rents have therefore been estimated by applying the overall rate of increase between 1544 and 1620/1 to the village-level totals previously calculated for 1544. Entry fine figures have been estimated at the village level by assigning a fraction of the total receipts to each settlement on the basis of the number of households reported in the 1620 tax survey.

Table 3.9 *Seigneurial dues as a proportion (%) of the harvest at Ottobeuren, 1621*

Settlement	*Gült*	Cash rent	Tithe	*Erdschatz*	Taxes	Total
Attenhausen	10.8	1.6	10.0	1.2	3.4	27.0
Böhen	6.2	2.7	10.0	2.3	6.6	27.8
Frechenrieden	9.4	2.5	10.0	1.3	3.6	26.8
Hawangen-Moosbach	9.8	2.0?	10.0	1.2	3.4	26.4?
Niederdorf	14.6	1.2	10.0	1.0	4.7	31.5
Hamlets of Ottobeuren parish	2.8	1.5?	10.0	1.0	6.2	21.5?

Sources: StAA, KL Ottobeuren 40, 102, 225, 541, Hefte 3 and 7

that the harvest was by no means the only source of income for the Ottobeuren peasantry.

Furthermore, the "grain equivalent" of seigneurialism should not be seen as a vanished proportion of the harvest. The monastery was happy, indeed eager to resell the grain it collected in rents and tithes.[77] Since most peasants were not self-sufficient in grain, they would have had to purchase or barter for the larger part of their subsistence anyway. Whether acquired from a wealthy neighbor directly, or indirectly when the monks resold that same neighbor's *Korngült*, the grain tasted the same. Finally, it would be misleading in the extreme to depict the influence of the monastery as exclusively baleful. The monks may have collected 2,245 *gulden* in excise taxes from the peasantry in 1620, but they also paid out some 2,351 *gulden* in wages to everyone from carters and masons to seamstresses and common day laborers. The monastery also spent 1,867 *gulden* on victuals (lard, fish, cattle, herbs, etc.),[78] much of which was probably purchased from its own subjects. Thus, if in consequence of the transformation of its finances the monastery had become a heavier if by no means ruinous burden to the peasantry, it had also become a more generous employer and a more lucrative market.

Perhaps the best way to gain an overview of the welter of detail preserved in the account books and rent rolls is to turn to another class of records altogether: the *Baudingbücher*. The *Bauding* was an annual assembly of the village population where the peasants reaffirmed their loyalty to the Abbot. At the same time the peasants' debts to the monastery were entered in a series of volumes known as *Baudinghücher*.[79] These books record debts of all kinds: rent arrears, outstanding *Erdschatz* payments, even cash advances made by the monastery to its subjects.

---

[77] According to the granary accounts, the monastery sold a total of 1,260 *malter* in 1586/7, 2,107 in 1614/15, and 2,219 in 1621/2. StAA, KL Ottobeuren 224, Hefte 1 and 6; KL Ottobeuren 225.
[78] StAA, KL Ottobeuren 541, Heft 7.   [79] StAA, KL Ottobeuren 400–34, 550–77.

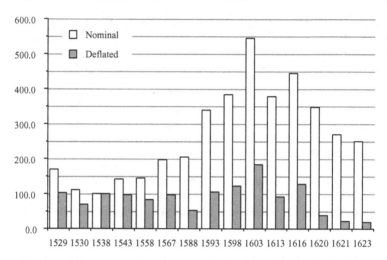

Figure 3.10   Debts of the peasantry to the monastery of Ottobeuren, 1529–1623
Notes: 1538 = 100
Source: StAA, KL Ottobeuren 403, 409, 417, 424, 433, 550, 555, 558, 559, 565, 568, 570, 571;
StadtA MM D Folioband 99, D 102/1a-1b; Wolf, *Reichsstädte in Kriegszeiten*, Table 82, p. 276

That these debts should have existed at all is neither surprising nor in and of itself a sign that the peasantry was overburdened. Since the rural economy was only partially monetized, it was common practice for large cash prestations such as *Erdschatz* to be paid to the monastery in installments over three or four years. And given the extreme variability of the harvest, it often also happened that the payment of rents due in a bad year was postponed in anticipation of a more bountiful harvest in the following year. The absolute level of short-term debt is thus a rather ambiguous piece of information. On the other hand, the long-term movement of debt in the *Baudingbücher* is a valuable indicator of the ability of the Ottobeuren peasantry to support the weight of the Abbot's lordship.

Figure 3.10 summarizes the trend of peasant debt to the monastery in the century after the Peasants' War. As may be expected, the nominal level of debt increased dramatically as a series of new impositions were introduced at the end of the sixteenth century. The *Baudingbücher* do not always itemize the source of every debt, but it is interesting to note that in 1603, fully half of the value of the total debt consisted of outstanding entry fines.[80] This dramatic increase in the nominal level of peasant debt is, however, only part of the story. For although debt increased to 1603, thereafter it fell dramatically, such that peasant indebtedness to the monastery in the 1620s was lower than it had been

[80] StAA, KL Ottobeuren 560.

at any time since the late 1580s. More importantly, the real level of peasant debt followed a decidedly different pattern. After deflating for increases in the price of grain, it turns out that peasant indebtedness remained remarkably stable over time. The surge at the very end of the sixteenth century reveals itself as a short-term aberration; by the early 1620s debt levels were actually lower than they had been a century earlier.

Be that as it may, the burden of lordship was more than mere prestation, and if the monks were collecting only slightly more of the peasant's harvest in the early seventeenth century, they were collecting vastly more information about his or her household in the process. The introduction by 1620 of comprehensive triennial tax surveys has already been noted. During the same period an equally striking intensification of oversight would reinvigorate the institution of serfdom.

Given the virulence of complaint about servile status during the Peasants' War of 1524/5, we might be forgiven the assumption that the decades leading up to the revolt had seen an effort by the Abbots to maximize their claims as *Leibherren*, or bond lords.[81] In fact, the monastery had then taken a rather lackadaisical approach to these rights. The single surviving serf roll from this era (dating to 1486/7) records only serfs of the monastery, excluding both free peasants and the serfs of other lords, while the perquisites of serfdom were collected with similar insouciance. In 1527/8 and 1528/9, for example, an annual average of only four exogamous marriage fees and seven death duties were taken from a subject population of almost 1,200 households.[82]

From the mid-sixteenth century, by contrast, the administrative record becomes much denser. Complete serf rolls listing all of the inhabitants (men, women, and children) of the monastery lands irrespective of legal status were compiled in 1548, 1556, 1564, and 1586. Average annual collections of exogamous marriage fees and death duties accordingly rose to fifteen and seventy-three respectively in 1586/7–1589/90.[83] Pressure was brought to bear on free peasants and serfs of other lords, whether locals[84] or immigrants,[85] to become

---

[81] As seems to have been the case in several other Swabian lordships. For a classic statement of the argument, see Blickle, *Revolution of 1525*, pp. 29–35.

[82] StAA, KL Ottobeuren 541, Heft 1, ff. 9r–v, 56v. The 1525 tax register records a total of 1,155 households. Ibid., Heft 2.

[83] StAA, KL Ottobeuren 583, Hefte 4–7.

[84] Thus the 1586 serf roll notes in the village of Niederrieden that Johann, stepson of Barthlome Maier, "shall give himself [in serfdom] to the monastery if he wishes to live in Niederrieden." Similarly StAA, KL Ottobeuren 918, ff. 42r [20 June 1580] and 69v [15 Dec. 1580], KL Ottobeuren 903, ff. 281r–282r [8 Jan. 1607], KL Ottobeuren 904, f. 77r [1 Nov. 1608] and 210r [11 Aug. 1610]; see Dertsch, "Das Einwohnerbuch des Ottobeurer Klosterstaats 1564," pp. 11, 73, for cases of free Ottobeuren subjects who yielded themselves to gain tenancy of a *Gotteshausrecht* bathhouse and *Erblehen Hof*.

[85] See the case of Conrad Höltzlin of Rummeltshausen, who became a monastery serf the same day he purchased his father-in-law's *Erblehen Hof* in Egg for 2,800 fl. StAA, KL Ottobeuren

Ottobeuren serfs, often as a condition of tenancy. The monks were even willing to negotiate the legal freedom of some of a peasant's children if he "yielded his spouse" (and the remaining children) to the monastery.[86] Finally, between 1564 and 1578 the monks redacted a series of treaties with the Prince-Abbot of Kempten, the Bishop of Augsburg, and the Marshall of Pappenheim, yielding jurisdiction over Ottobeuren serfs outside the Abbot's dominion in exchange for rights over "foreign" serfs within the monastery lands.[87] The end result was the creation of a legally uniform subject population.[88] In the village of Wolfertschwenden, for example, the proportion of householders who were monastery serfs rose from 38.1 percent in 1564 to 73.0 percent in 1586 to 81.8 percent in 1621/2,[89] while in the thirty-three hamlets of Ottobeuren parish, the proportion leaped from 35.2 percent in 1564 to 82.6 percent in 1601/2 to 93.5 percent in 1627/8.[90] So complete had the monastery's servile jurisdiction become that after 1586, the monks ceased to compile elaborate serf rolls of the entire population, and instead contented themselves with simple "bond-chicken registers," which merely listed servile household heads.

Income from serfdom remained a tiny fraction (3.1 percent in 1620)[91] of overall revenues, but information-intensive lordship of this sort was driven by a desire not simply (or even primarily) to increase the monastery's "take" from the peasantry, but more importantly to manage the claims (and exercise the power) of lordship more efficiently. Indeed, contemporary German political tracts[92] ranging from Georg Obrecht's *Policey Ordnung und Constitution* (1608) to Christoph Besold's *De Aerario* (1620) to Kaspar Klock's *Tractatus de Contributionibus* (1634) all enjoined rulers regularly to make detailed surveys of the

901, ff. 7v–8r, 9r [28 Feb. 1583]. For the enserfment of other immigrants, see ibid., ff. 3r [22 Jan. 1583], 7v–8r and 9r [28 Feb. 1583] and 11r [25 Feb. 1583].

[86] This is clear from the marginal notes to the 1564 serf roll. Dertsch, "Das Einwohnerbuch des Ottobeurer Klosterstaats 1564," pp. 39, 45, 56, 60, 64, 68. For the notarized "yielding" of immigrant spouses, see also StAA, KL Ottobeuren 918, ff. 46r [19 July 1580] and 53r [30 Oct. 1580].

[87] Heider, "Grundherrschaft und Landeshoheit," pp. 86–7.

[88] The seminal work on this process is Peter Blickle, "Leibeigenschaft als Instrument der Territorialpolitik im Allgäu" in H. Haushofer and W. A. Boelcke, eds., *Wege und Forschungen der Agrargeschichte: Festschrift zum 65. Geburtstag von Günther Franz* (Frankfurt a.M., 1967), pp. 51–66.

[89] Dertsch, "Das Einwohnerbuch des Ottobeurer Klosterstaats 1564," pp. 86–9; StAA, KL Ottobeuren 601-II, ff. 116r–121v; KL Ottobeuren 491-I, Heft 4, ff. 21v–22r; KL Ottobeuren 102, ff. 162r–175v; KL Ottobeuren 491-II, Heft 26, ff. 9v–10r.

[90] Dertsch, "Das Einwohnerbuch des Ottobeurer Klosterstaats 1564," pp. 11–27; StAA, KL Ottobeuren 688-I, Hefte 7–8; KL Ottobeuren 681, Hefte 1–2; KL Ottobeuren 491-I, Heft 10, ff. 2r–7v; KL Ottobeuren 104, ff. 34r–92r; KL Ottobeuren 491-III, Heft 33, ff. 2r–8r.

[91] StAA, KL Ottobeuren 541, Heft 7.

[92] Most of these works were heavily influenced by the Flemish scholar Justus Lipsius' *Politicorum Libri Sex* (1589), which went through twenty-seven Latin editions by 1650, and was translated into German in 1599 and again in 1618. Gerhard Östreich, *Antiker Geist und moderner Staat bei Justus Lipsius, 1547–1606* (Göttingen, 1989), pp. 116, 138–40, 195–217.

wealth, status, and numbers of their subjects. The 'fiscal census' was promoted as an indispensable tool of good government, guarding against destructive over-taxation of the citizenry, and promoting good will and unity through uniform and equitable imposition.[93] For its part, the Ottobeuren peasantry was rather less enthusiastic. Peasants often claimed to be free in order to escape the fees associated with serfdom,[94] and resentment over the unprecedented increase in jural and fiscal surveillance on several occasions culminated in prosecution and even violence.[95]

Thus far, our investigations of the health of the rural economy at Ottobeuren has produced a set of distressingly incongruous results. There is no gainsaying the unspectacular level of agricultural productivity in this period. That a long wave of population growth came to a decisive halt in the last third of the sixteenth century is similarly undeniable. At the same time, however, it seems clear that the demographic system was not regulated by mortality. There is unequivocal evidence of a substantial and even slowly growing agricultural surplus. Finally, the increase in the monastery's exactions was borne manage-ably (if not cheerfully) by its subjects. It is hard, in other words, to discern the traditional production crisis amidst this evidence, but it is equally hard to avoid the conclusion that *some* kind of structural constraint had come into play.

For a clearer understanding of the nature of this constraint, we need to take a closer look at the process of agricultural production. What we will find is that even if the monastery lands as a whole produced an agricultural surplus, this was not true of the majority of individual households. As was seen in chapter 1, significant social stratification between rich and poor was already obvious by the early sixteenth century. Over the course of the next hundred years, the gap only widened further (see Figure 3.11). Since land and buildings were the most important constituents of taxable wealth, this trend can only have meant that an increasing proportion of the population lacked the productive resources to feed itself directly.

How big was this proportion? Given the documentation at our disposal, the only way to estimate household self-sufficiency is by reconstructing the relation between agricultural production and cultivated area. There are three ways to do

---

[93] Wilhelm Röscher, *Geschichte der National-Oekonomik in Deutschland* (Munich, 1874), pp. 150–8, 194–200, 216.

[94] Appended to the receipt of a 3 fl. death duty from the estate of Johann Hueber of Sontheim is "Nota: claimed to be free." StAA, KL Ottobeuren 583, Heft 5, f. 3v [3 Dec. 1587]. Marginal notes in the 1564 serf roll indicate that a number of peasants rejected the servile status ascribed to them. Dertsch, "Das Einwohnerbuch des Ottobeurer Klosterstaats 1564," pp. 70, 78.

[95] StAA, KL Ottobeuren 587-II, Heft 14 (1586/7): Hans Aÿchele of Böhen "criminally resisted the *Amman* and *Vierer* when taxes were collected." Ibid., Heft 21 (1601/2): Brosi Weckerlin of Benningen did not declare 400 fl. worth of property for taxation "and uttered idle talk about it." Görg Steur of Frechenrieden "when asked to pay his wife's death duty by the *Pittel* did strike him right in the face."

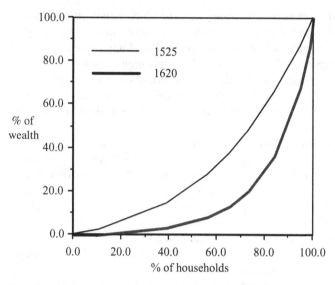

Figure 3.11 Distribution of taxable wealth in nine Ottobeuren villages, 1525 and 1620
Sources: StAA, KL Ottobeuren 102 and 541 (2)

this. As we have seen that agricultural productivity increased only marginally at Ottobeuren between the seventeenth and mid-nineteenth centuries, the easiest method is to adopt the figures reported in the Bavarian agricultural census of 1863.[96] In that year, the rye harvest in the *Bezirksamt* Memmingen (where the former monastery lands were located) was 18.8 hectoliters per hectare. Correcting for the slight increase in yield ratios between 1637 (5.0:1)[97] and 1863 (5.49:1) reduces our estimated early modern rye harvest to 17.13 hl/ha. The 1863 oat harvest was 27.04 hl/ha; there seems to have been no increase in the yield ratio of this grain since the seventeenth-century.

A second approach, based entirely on seventeenth-century figures, is to compare the tithe receipts from each village with the arable surface area reported in a massive 1620 tax survey. The results are summarized in Table 3.10; the average yield from eight villages comes to 2.45 *malter/jauchert* for all grains. After adjusting for harvest composition[98] we arrive at a rye harvest equivalent of 2.89 *malter/jauchert* or 14.92 hl/ha. For oats the corresponding figures are 2.24 *malter/jauchert* and 23.23 hl/ha.

A third estimate comes from a series of documents generated by the monastery's purchase of various properties in Oberwesterheim and Sontheim

---

[96] Von Hermann, *Die Ernten im Königreich Bayern*. Earlier harvest statistics do exist, but they are not available at the district level before 1863.

[97] Taken from StAA, KL Ottobeuren 202, ff. 91v–98v.

[98] Based on the 1621 composition of tithe receipts in StAA, KL Ottobeuren 225, ff. 104v–109v.

Table 3.10 *Estimated yields in eight Ottobeuren villages, c. 1620*

Village	Arable 1620 (*jauchert*)	Mean tithe 1615–24 (*malter*)	Yield (*malter/jauchert*)
Attenhausen	611.50	109.17	2.68
Egg	765.50	135.54	2.66
Frechenrieden	540.00	95.78	2.66
Günz	453.75	73.44	2.43
Hawangen	1185.25	178.97	2.26
Niederdorf	461.62	53.73	1.75
Rummeltshausen	313.00	55.88	2.68
Sontheim	888.00	150.00	2.53
Total	5218.62	852.51	2.45

Sources: StAA, KL Ottobeuren 40, 102; KA Ottobeuren 343, Document no. 5

from the 'Lower' hospital in the city of Memmingen.[99] In 1655 the hospital declared the value of the offering at thirty thousand *gulden*, but the monks were wary of this figure. After consulting with the *Kastenvogt*, or bailiff, of their neighbor the Prince-Abbot of Kempten, the monks decided to conduct their own assessment. Since one of the items under consideration was the right to collect the tithe in Sontheim, the mayors of Sontheim and Westerheim were questioned in the summer of 1663 about the average yield of the tithe in the two villages.

According to the *Amman* of Sontheim,[100] the tithe from a *jauchert* of rye or barley could be as high as twelve *metzen*, but a tithe of eight, nine, or ten *metzen* was the norm. With oats and spelt a larger tithe could be expected: normally nine to ten and exceptionally fourteen *metzen* per *jauchert*. In Westerheim the reported rye yields were virtually identical: the tithe averaged nine or ten *metzen* per *jauchert* with a maximum of twelve. Spelt and oat yields seem to have been higher than in Sontheim, averaging ten to twelve *metzen* per *jauchert*. A rye tithe of nine to ten *metzen* implies of yield of between 2.813 and 3.125 *malter/jauchert* or 14.5–16.1 hl/ha. The equivalents of a ten to eleven *metzen* oat tithe are 1.471 to 1.618 *malter* per *jauchert* and 15.2–16.7 hl/ha.

None of these estimates is definitive on its own, but at least with rye a definite pattern emerges. The yields are clustered around 2.9 *malter* per *jauchert* or 15 hectoliters per hectare, which will be taken here as the average yield. The estimates are less uniform when it comes to oats and spelt. It appears, however, that the 1663 reports for oats and spelt are underestimates, since the *Amman* of Sontheim declared the maximum tithe yield for spelt as fourteen *metzen* per *jauchert* when we know it to have been fifteen in 1655. Furthermore, careful

---

[99] StAA, KA Ottobeuren 343. The *Kastenvogt*'s report (Document no. 3) is dated 1656.
[100] Ibid., Document no. 12 [2 June 1663].

comparison of the Sontheim tithe receipts for the years 1663–70[101] with the arable surface area recorded in a 1669 tax survey[102] produces an estimated average oat harvest of 2.013 *malter* per *jauchert* or 20.84 hl/ha. In light of these discrepancies, we shall assume that the average oat yield was closer to 2.0 *malter* per *jauchert* or 20.7 hectoliters per hectare.

Given these grain yields, how much land did a peasant household need in order to feed itself? Earlier in this chapter, the size of the average household was estimated at 4.71 persons, which in terms of consumption requirements may be likened to a family of two adults and three children. Let us assign our household the now familiar amount of 1.5 *malter* of grain per capita per year. The household must be able to pay the tithe on the harvest, meet its nutritional needs, and still have enough seed corn for the next year. These constraints imply a harvest no smaller than 10.243 *malter*. If it is assumed that the grain crop was equally composed of oats and rye, and that one third of the land had to lie fallow each year, we arrive at a minimum holding size of about 6.5 *jauchert* (= 2.75 hectares)[103] of arable land. Of course, this allows for no servants, no horses or other grain-eating livestock, and no seigneurial obligations beyond the tithe, but for the poor these conditions usually obtained.

The earliest survey of landholding in the entirety of the Abbot's dominions is the tax survey of 1620. This document, a ponderous volume of some 400 folios, allows us to disaggregate the village population into three groups. The first consists of those households holding less than 6.5 *jauchert* of arable land, which households cannot have been self-sufficient in grain. A second group, made up of households holding between 6.5 and 13 *jauchert*, may be considered to have been normally self-sufficient, but not immune to a serious crop failure. Households holding more than 13 *jauchert* would regularly have harvested considerable surpluses. These comfortable households, which actually stood to profit from the high prices associated with bad harvests, make up the third group.

Table 3.11 summarizes the distribution of arable land in the Ottobeuren villages in 1620, broken down into the above three categories. The overwhelming majority of households held less than the minimum 6.5 *jauchert* of land. Since the villages account for some 63.3 percent of the households listed in the 1620 survey, it seems clear that most Ottobeuren peasants did not have enough land to feed themselves, and therefore could survive only by obtaining grain from others.

---

[101] StAA, KL Ottobeuren 55.
[102] StAA, KL Ottobeuren 105, ff. 334r–362v. I have assumed that the proportion of the total arable devoted to oats in 1669 was the same as the proportion given for 1655 in StAA, KA Ottobeuren 343, Document no. 2.
[103] This figure is almost identical with the estimate reached by Rainer Beck (2.70 hectares) of the minimum holding size needed by a family of five in Upper Bavaria in *c.* 1720. Beck, *Naturale Ökonomie*, pp. 176–85.

Table 3.11 *Arable land per household in the Ottobeuren villages, 1620*

Village	Number of households holding		
	<6.5 *jauchert*	6.5–12.99 *jauchert*	13.0+ *jauchert*
Altisried	6	0	7
Attenhausen	58	1	17
Benningen	72	6	25
Dietratried	19	3	8
Egg	74	7	19
Frechenrieden	51	3	15
Günz	20	2	10
Hawangen	93	3	28
Niederdorf	19	2	11
Niederrieden	49	5	18
Oberwesterheim	35	1	13
Rummeltshausen	7	0	9
Schlegelsberg	29	3	11
Sontheim	116	4	20
Ungerhausen	48	3	16
Unterwesterheim	28	1	10
Wolfertschwenden	39	5	12
Total	763	49	249
Percentage	71.9	4.6	23.5

Source: StAA, KL Ottobeuren 102

Crucially, the polarization of landholding was far from new in 1620. In 1571 the fields of Ober- and Unterwesterheim were surveyed and recorded in a *Zehentbeschreibung*, or tithe description. If we combine this evidence with the appropriate section of the 1564 census, the pattern which emerges (see Table 3.12) is hardly different from the one recorded fifty years later. More generally, we have in chapter 1 seen that an extreme disparity in taxable wealth was already evident throughout the monastery lands by the middle of the sixteenth century. That the skew in tax payments was the result of a skew in landholding is certain. But even without the benefit of a sixteenth-century equivalent of the 1620 survey, it is still possible to demonstrate that the divide in the villages between a well-endowed minority and a land-poor majority was a long-standing feature of rural life.

The key to this demonstration is the aforementioned observation that almost all of the arable land in each village was in 1620 monopolized by ten to twelve big *Höfe*. These *Höfe* were held under *Gotteshausrecht* tenure and saddled with grain rents (*Gült*) calibrated to the size of the arable. As is clear from the long-term immobility of the rent assessments, the *Höfe* remained virtually constant in size from the sixteenth through the seventeenth century. Moreover, unlike the elusive mass of freehold fragments, the sprawling *Gotteshausrecht* farms can be

Table 3.12 *Arable land per household in Ober- and Unterwesterheim, 1564/71 and 1620*

	Number of households holding		
Village	<6.5 *jauchert*	6.5–12.99 *jauchert*	13.0+ *jauchert*
Oberwesterheim			
1564/71	39	1	14
1620	35	1	13
Unterwesterheim			
1564/71	23	3	8
1620	28	1	10

Sources: Dertsch, "Das Einwohnerbuch des Ottobeurer Klosterstaats 1564," pp. 65–70; StAA, KL Ottobeuren 102, 744b

Table 3.13 *Distribution of landholding in five Ottobeuren villages, 1544/6*

Village	Households 1546	*Hof* tenants 1544	Average arable per *Hof* household (*jauchert*)	Remaining households	Average arable per *non-Hof* household (*jauchert*)
Attenhausen	63	19	28.8	44	1.50
Frechenrieden	78	18	26.5	60	1.05
Hawangen	133	32	27.5	101	2.14
Oberwesterheim	44	14	26.2	30	3.43
Sontheim	109	25	27.6	84	2.35

Sources: StAA, KL Ottobeuren 29, 64, 102

followed through the rent rolls from tenant to tenant at least as far back as 1544. Thus, if we make the entirely plausible assumption that the total cultivated area was no larger in 1544 than it was in 1620, it is possible to estimate for the earlier date the amounts of land held by the village aristocracy on the one hand and the mass of the poor on the other.

Table 3.13 presents an estimate of the distribution of landholding for five Ottobeuren villages in the middle of the sixteenth century. The holdings of the *Hof* tenants are based on the 1620 area of their *Gotteshausrecht* farms; the rest of the arable has been assigned to the other villagers. These estimates will actually understate the disparity between rich and poor, since the *Hof* tenants almost always held a few untraceable *jauchert* of freehold land as well. Despite this limitation, the thrust of the estimates is clear. Twenty to thirty percent of households in 1544 had enough land to feed at least four families; the rest could not even come close to feeding themselves alone.

There is nothing particularly novel about this conclusion. Similar conditions have been discovered in so many parts of early modern Europe that the land-poor seventeenth-century peasant has become something of a historiographical commonplace. The more important issue, to my mind, is what to make of this fact. The most obvious implication, and the one which has traditionally drawn the most attention, is that most of the peasantry was desperately poor. The scale of rural poverty at Ottobeuren was indeed undeniable. In the village of Sontheim, we know that at least 23.4 percent of households were in receipt of alms in 1626.[104]

The actual living conditions of these paupers were arduous to say the least. Among the alms recipients in Sontheim, for example, was one Anna Wagner, the widow of Narcissus Schmidt. Narcissus and Anna had always been poor.[105] When Narcissus first appears in the monastery's bond-chicken registers in 1595, he was already a member of the village underclass: his two *kreuzer* assessement put him in a category normally reserved for destitute widows.[106] The couple had never had more than a half-house to live in; in 1616 debt forced them to sell off even this and withdraw to a single room.[107] It goes without saying that they now belonged to the poorest of the poor; in 1620 the total value of their worldly possessions was assessed at 25 *gulden*, roughly the equivalent of two milk cows.[108] But even after Narcissus died in 1621,[109] Anna carried on alone. She lived in that small room for at least another fourteen years, her burdens

[104] Household totals and identifications taken from StAA, KL Ottobeuren 104, ff. 309r–337r. The alms list is in StAA, KA Ottobeuren 348.

[105] The couple's parentage is uncertain, but this Anna seems to have been the same woman who is listed as the daughter of the Sontheim baker Michael Wagner in 1585. Michael Wagner was very poor; his bond-chicken assessment was 3 kr. in 1587 and only 2 kr. in 1590. Michael's place in the register's name sequence has been taken by one Jerg Wagner in 1595. This man was almost certainly the same one listed as Michael's second child in 1585; Jerg Wagner is in turn "replaced" by Anna Wagner's husband, Narcissus Schmidt, in the 1602 register. StAA, KL Ottobeuren 601-II, f. 81r; KL Ottobeuren 491-I, Heft 3, f. 28r, Heft 5, f. 17v, Heft 6, f. 20r and Heft 10, f. 22r.

[106] StAA, KL Ottobeuren 491-I, Heft 6, f. 20v. Almost all serfs listed in the bond-chicken registers are assessed either a hen if they were "rich" (i.e. *Bauern*) or 3 kr. if they were "poor" (i.e. *Seldner*). This classification is set out explicitly in the 1622 register (KL Ottobeuren 491-II, Heft 26, f. 1r): "Nota bschaid, firohin sollen die Reichen die hennen geben, die Armen aber, wie von alters hero mit einnemûng d. drei kreitzer für iede hennen, gehalt. werd." Narcissus rose briefly to *Seldner* status in 1602, but is again listed in the widow class in 1613 and 1617. He is inexplicably missing from the register for 1609; his absence from the 1622 register must be due to his death. KL Ottobeuren 491-II, Heft 16, f. 14v and Heft 21, f. 23r.

[107] StAA, KL Ottobeuren 907, f. 14v [14 Oct. 1616]. That the sale was the result of financial pressure is indicated by a clause in the accompanying maintenance agreement stipulating that the buyer assume a number of Narcissus' debts. See also KL Ottobeuren 904, f. 168v [9 Jan. 1610], where Narcissus and Anna borrow 15 fl. from a widow in the village.

[108] StAA, KL Ottobeuren 102, f. 338v.

[109] Narcissus is listed in the 1620 tax survey, but not the 1622 bond-chicken register. The 1623 register lists "the widow of Narciß Schmidt" in Sontheim. StAA, KL Ottobeuren 491-III, Heft 27, f. 21v.

slightly – but only slightly – relieved by the dole of half a dozen *kreuzer* from the parish church.

Hard as it is not to admire the couple's dogged ability to survive, it must be emphasized that they were not exceptional. In 1630 the churchwardens of Sontheim drew up a list of the paupers, including the aforesaid Anna Wagner, who had been granted alms by the parish church. The list contains forty-seven names, thirty-two of which can be linked to a particular household (most of the other fifteen were either adults appearing only under nicknames ['long Michael'] and professions ['the locksmith'], or orphans, who are notoriously difficult to trace). As may be expected in a village where 80 percent of the households did not have enough land to support themselves, these paupers were truly destitute. Most of them had no property deemed worthy of taxation, and they lived in miserable little cottages often crammed with two, three, or even four households. Remarkably, however, of the thirty-two identifiable paupers from the 1630 list, all but two, or 93.8 percent, had been resident in Sontheim for at least ten years.[110] Several had lived there for much longer, persisting in the village for fifteen, twenty, and even thirty-five years.[111]

The point here is not to minimize the hardships of the rural poor, but rather to draw out the implications of their tenacity. That so many could maintain themselves on so little for so long calls into question conventional notions of peasant self-sufficiency. That is to say, it may well be true that 6.5 *jauchert*, or 2.75 hectares of arable land was a minimum requirement *in a context where the peasant household's survival depended on the grain it could produce for itself*. The evidence of the early seventeenth century demonstrates quite clearly, however, that this was not how most Ottobeuren peasants lived.

How they did in fact live is a complex question. It will be discussed in greater detail in the next two chapters, as it cannot be answered merely in terms of the productive activities of individual households, which is our present concern. Preliminary indications, however, may be gleaned from those tiny parts of the property that Narcissus and Anna had carefully reserved for themselves when they gave up their half-house in 1616, "namely the table by the door, the forward room, a little strip in the herb garden, half use-rights to the pear tree, all of the cabbage garden, the rearward half of the beehives and the cow stall and the nearest dungyard next to the threshing-floor."[112]

---

[110] StAA, KA Ottobeuren 348; KL Ottobeuren 102, 104.

[111] A few examples: Enderas Dietrich purchased his house on 13 December 1613 (StAA, KL Ottobeuren 905, f. 135v). Michael Maier purchased his half-house on 20 May 1610 (KL Ottobeuren 904, f. 199v). Johann Hartmann purchased his half-house on 5 December 1605 (KL Ottobeuren 903, f. 199r). On 14 December 1630, it was certified that the widow Maria Schmidt had married Ulrich Albrecht in Sontheim about the year 1595 (KL Ottobeuren 911, f. 97). All of these persons are listed on the Sontheim alms account for 1630.

[112] StAA, KL Ottobeuren 907, f. 14v [14 Oct. 1616].

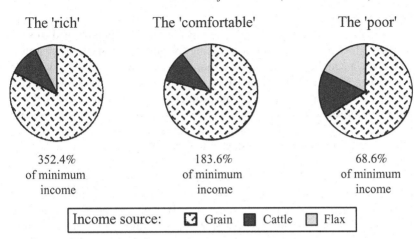

Figure 3.12 Structure of agricultural production in Ottobeuren parish, 1598–1601
Sources: StAA, KL Ottobeuren 102, 164, 681 (1–2), 688-I (7–8); StadtA MM, D. 64/8a

The particular significance of animal husbandry and horticulture to the economy of the poor is more broadly confirmed by the tithe registers of Ottobeuren parish for the years 1598–1601. Two of these registers (for 1600 and 1601) are records of the "greater," or grain tithe. The others (for 1598 and 1599) are records of the "lesser" tithe, which at Ottobeuren was levied on new calves, gardens, and flax-growing. The registers provide detailed information on the activities of 183 households, which have been broken down into three groups: (1) the "poor," who did not produce enough grain to feed an average family; (2) the "comfortable," who harvested between 100 percent and 200 percent of this minimum amount of grain; and (3) the "rich," who produced more than twice as much grain as the minimum family ration. Comparison of greater and lesser tithe data provides an estimate of the relative value of different kinds of production.[113] It also allows us to calculate the relation between total production and the amount of money needed to purchase enough grain to feed an average family for a year (see Figure 3.12).

Why does any of this matter? Because it emphasizes the dependence of the land-poor, who by the later sixteenth century made up the overwhelming majority of the Ottobeuren peasantry, on wider circuits of commerce beyond

[113] For the value of grain, I have used five-year average prices of oats and rye for the years 1598–1602 from the churchwarden's accounts of the nearby village of Sontheim (StadtA MM. D. 64/8a). The price of a calf (3 *gulden*) has been interpolated between the standard 5 *gulden* taxable value of calves in the 1620 tax survey (StAA, KL Ottobeuren 102) and the average price (1 *gulden*) given in the 1549 granary account (KL Ottobeuren 164). The average value of a measure of flax (4.4 *kreuzer*) has been calculated from the lesser tithe register for 1598 (KL Ottobeuren 688-I [7]).

the boundaries of the household. It was a two-fold dependence. Not only were the poor of Ottobeuren parish, to take our present example, obliged to seek at least a third of their income by working for others, but much of what they did produce could not be directly consumed. Calves were much too valuable to be eaten at home; any cottager with even a modicum of sense would take them to market and buy grain with the proceeds. As for flax, it would be dried, spun into thread, and then sold to a weaver. Production within the household necessitated exchange without, and as the example of Anna Wagner and the other Sontheim paupers suggests, even the seemingly destitute could thereby find a way to scrape along.

It must, therefore, have been in the realm of exchange that the Ottobeuren peasantry devised a solution to the problematic mismatch of numbers between those who needed food and those who produced it. This is not at all to say that the mass of the rural poor would not have been helped by higher grain yields or more land; of course they would have. All the same, we would do well to recall the fact that the levels of population density and agricultural productivity "required" for the onset of industrialization in Bavaria in the later nineteenth century were hardly different from the level already "achieved" at Ottobeuren by the end of the sixteenth century. The argument here has been that the immediate constraint on the early modern economy was not so much insufficient production *per se*, as a problem of access to and circulation of the fruits of that production. As it happened, the end of the sixteenth century and especially the beginning of the seventeenth century would indeed see a transformation of rural commerce. Given the almost sacral character of the traditional constraints on exchange, however, any such transformation was bound to be traumatic.

4. Integrity and the market (c. 1560–c. 1630)

The hamlet of Osterberg lay at the southeastern rim of the monastery lands, just short of the border with the Princely Abbacy of Kempten. So close, indeed, was the power of the Prince-Abbot that until 1564, when a treaty between the two monasteries altered their status, every single one of the settlement's fifty-seven inhabitants was a Kempten serf.[1] Founded (like so many of the Ottobeuren hamlets) sometime in the later fifteenth century,[2] Osterberg shared the experience of population growth in the following century, swelling from eight households in 1548 to eleven in 1564 as the children of older residents married and settled down next to their parents.[3] But thereafter the pattern changed, for by 1587 the hamlet had shrunk back to seven households and by 1602 to four.[4] It was not a problem of food supply; despite devastating hailstorms in 1569, 1597, and 1603, Osterberg's average tithe payment rose by some 40 percent between the early 1570s and the early 1620s.[5] Nevertheless, by the late sixteenth century it is possible to document the emigration of the young from every household in the settlement.[6] The age-old rules of family succession had clearly undergone a series of profound changes, and there is no better example of this than the Münch family.

Balthas Münch of Osterberg succeeded his father, Michael, sometime between 1564 and 1583. He worked himself up from fairly modest

---

[1] Dertsch, "Das Einwohnerbuch des Ottobeurer Klosterstaats 1564," pp. 34–5. Blickle, *Memmingen*, pp. 112–13 citing negotiations in StAA, KA Ottobeuren 455 and charter of final agreement dated 14 June 1564 (KU Ottobeuren 1624).

[2] The earliest charter reference appears to be in 1467. StAA, KU Ottobeuren 296.

[3] All but one of the 1548 households are still listed in 1564, and three of the four new ones are clearly headed by either a son or son-in-law of those listed in 1548. Dertsch, "Das Einwohnerbuch des Ottobeurer Klosterstaats 1564," pp. 34–5; StAA, KL Ottobeuren 600, ff. 253r–254r.

[4] StAA, KL Ottobeuren 491-I, Heft 3, f. 23r and ibid., Heft 10, f. 19r.

[5] StAA, KL Ottobeuren 34, ff. 122r–v and KL Ottobeuren 40, ff. 102r–103r.

[6] StAA, KL Ottobeuren 491-I, Heft 3, f. 23r and Heft 4, f. 25v; KL Ottobeuren 583, Heft 1, f. 4r, Heft 5, f. 13v and Heft 7, f. 15r; KL Ottobeuren 901, f. 14r [14 Mar. 1583]; KL Ottobeuren 903, f. 136v [20 Jan. 1605]; KL Ottobeuren 904, f. 189r [17 Mar. 1610]; KL Ottobeuren 905, ff. 42v–43r [24 Dec. 1612].

beginnings,[7] carefully watering his meadows and building wells with his neighbors,[8] and by the early seventeenth century had ascended to a position of considerable prosperity.[9] Gaps in the archival record preclude a complete reconstruction of his land acquisitions, but Balthas clearly operated according to the traditional fissile practices of household formation discussed in chapter 2. Balthas and his mother maintained separate households after the death of Michael Münch,[10] and Balthas' own landholdings were a combination of inheritances from his own parents and other properties picked up during fractioning of other households in the hamlet.[11] Certainly after Balthas' death in 1610,[12] his widow Anna Wagegg expected the traditional pattern to continue. In 1613 she divided the farm into two halves of 33 *jauchert*, and sold one of the halves, along with half of the farmhouse, to her son Jacob Münch for 700 fl. Anna retained for herself "her bedlinens, chest [and] its contents, and the other things in her room." She also stipulated that

> Both parties, buyer and seller, shall farm, use, exploit, enjoy and inhabit the entire property together at common gain and expense . . . and after her death, the other half [of the property] shall descend and pass to the buyer's brother Mathias Münch if he wants or needs it. And the aforesaid married couple [i.e. Jacob and his wife] shall help him [Mathias] to build a [new] house on the house-lot in the upper garden . . . at [either] his marriage or after his mother's death, in which house the said Mathias Münch shall have his undisturbed residence, whereas the buyers [shall have their residence] in the house purchased [here].[13]

It was a perfectly conventional arrangement, and it was never carried out.

In the spring of 1616, with his mother now deceased, Jacob bought out claims of his sister and four brothers (Mathias among them) to the other half of the

---

[7] His 1584 tithe payment put him in the middle of the three categories ("comfortable") worked out from the Ottobeuren large and small tithe registers of 1598–1601. StAA, KL Ottobeuren 31, f. 81r.

[8] StAA, KL Ottobeuren 903, ff. 128v–129r [2 Dec. 1604] and KL Ottobeuren 904, ff. 196v–197r [29 Apr. 1610].

[9] In 1606 Balthas' tithe was 44.25 *viertel* (StAA, KL Ottobeuren 39, f. 151v), an increase of 84.4 percent over 1584 which put him in the "rich" tithepayer category. He also had enough spare cash to be able to loan 80 fl. to one Michael Enderas of Günzegg. KL Ottobeuren 903, ff. 299r–v [1 Mar. 1607].

[10] Balthas and his mother, Appolonia Weinhart, are listed separately in the 1587 bond-chicken register (StAA, KL Ottobeuren 491-I, Heft 3, f. 23r). That the widow Münch retained considerable property after her husband's death is suggested by the hefty 9 fl. death duty collected for her estate on 20 March 1589. KL Ottobeuren 583, Heft 6, f. 7v.

[11] In March of 1583 the *Hof* of Johann Maurus of Osterberg was subdivided and sold off to three separate parties, among them Balthas Münch. StAA, KL Ottobeuren 901, ff. 14v–15r [7 Mar. 1583]. Balthas' relative share of the hamlet's 1584 tithe payment and the amount of property he held at his death indicate that he must have previously acquired the bulk of the land he farmed.

[12] StAA, KL Ottobeuren 491-I, Heft 14, f. 18r; KL Ottobeuren 904, f. 219v [3 Dec. 1610].

[13] StAA, KL Ottobeuren 905, ff. 145r–v and 145v–146r [19 Dec. 1613]. The quoted passage is taken from the latter document.

property for an additional payment of 700 fl.[14] Whatever their mother's wishes had been, the children had apparently decided that it made rather more sense to divide the capital value of the family farm and seek their fortunes elsewhere, than to remain in their natal hamlet and break up the physical asset itself. In fact, the other children had already begun to leave even before the first half of the farm was sold to Jacob, and by 1616 all of the siblings except Mathias had already left the Ottobeuren lands to settle elsewhere in the region.[15] In the end only Jacob remained in Osterberg, struggling to clear the enormous debts he had incurred in taking over the entire property,[16] and aggressively, even illegally, marketing the fruits of his labors to do so.[17]

Though rarely so explicitly documented, this resolve to maintain landholdings intact and the consequent emigration of non-inheriting children had become the norm at Ottobeuren by the close of the sixteenth century. The other hallmarks of Jacob Münch's career – the sale rather than the costless handover of farms and the associated burden of debt – became equally essential features of peasant inheritance, and all together these new practices rewrote the fundamental rules of the rural socio-economic order. This is admittedly a rather drastic claim, and it will be the burden of the present chapter to establish it. It should be emphasized at the outset, however, that the transformation in question is not to be found where it has conventionally been sought, i.e. in the comfortingly quantifiable realms of demography and agricultural technology. Rather, the mutation concerned less tangible dimensions of rural life – in particular an enormous increase in the mediation of social and kin relations by money – and was most strikingly manifest in the inscription of human activity in time and space. By 1620 the discrete village economies of the early sixteenth century had completely collapsed.

The best way to investigate the transformation of peasant inheritance practices is to consider each element of the change in turn, and the logical point of departure is the shift to impartibility. For all its advantages, partible inheritance also presented serious drawbacks, and as the sixteenth century wore on these drawbacks became more acute. The problem was perfectly simple: the long-term growth of population led to pulverization of the landholding and to the impoverishment of the tenant. During the fifteenth century these had not been serious concerns. Then, as noted in chapter 1, the problem had been one of abandoned farms, a shortage of tenants, and a great deal of uncleared land in the southern part of the monastic territory. After a century of land clearance,

---

[14] Ibid., f. 353v [18 Apr. 1616].   [15] Ibid., KL Ottobeuren 904, f. 219v [3 Dec. 1610].
[16] The 1620 tax survey reveals that his gross wealth of 1428 fl. was considerably offset by debts of 848 fl. StAA, KL Ottobeuren 102, f. 128v.
[17] On 17 March 1626 Jacob Münch was fined for hauling grain south to the city of Kempten for sale instead of bringing it to the Ottobeuren market. StAA, KL Ottobeuren 587-III, Heft 33, f. 30v.

population growth, and subdivision of the holdings, however, the situation had changed.

By the middle of the sixteenth century both the Abbot and his subjects had become convinced that there were too many people on the land. This was a fairly common complaint at the time, although historians eager to attribute the Peasants' War of 1525 to overpopulation have tended to backdate the highpoint of these complaints to the beginning of the century. The monastery's view of partibility was perhaps most bluntly expressed by Abbot Caspar in 1551, in reaction to a proposed subdivision in the hamlet of Günzegg:

in truth we have found that these subdivisions, as most of them [the peasants] admit, take place in order that they may establish more inhabitants, co-residents [*Hausgenossen*] and hearths and thus enable their children to set up house near them, whereby their holdings are then overtaxed, overstocked and overpopulated, which would not only result in Our own disadvantage, but also in the certain ruin of the [inhabitants] of Günzegg . . . It would in short come to pass that most [of the inhabitants] for want of land, pasture and wood would ultimately be forced to abandon their holdings or otherwise live in extreme poverty and resort to begging.[18]

The problem was not one of literal, but of relative, overpopulation. As was shown in chapter 3, the Ottobeuren peasantry continued to harvest more than enough grain than was needed to feed itself throughout the sixteenth century. Nevertheless, this did not do away with the fear of population growth. The concern was not so much the long-term danger of chronic starvation but rather the more immediate fear that continued subdivision of the larger holdings would undercut their value and drive their tenants down into poverty. Long before famine could become a reality, the fear of degradation would move both the Abbot and his more prosperous subjects to put a stop to partible inheritance.

The monastery resorted to a variety of means in order to achieve this goal. With *Gotteshausrecht* land, where the Abbot's legal position was the strongest, the simplest device was the refusal to allow any further subdivisions. The suspension of partibility was a gradual process, and initially took the form of making the partitions less even. When Johann Benger died in Dietratried in 1562, his *Hof* was divided between his two sons-in-law, Hans Magg and Jerg Vorster. The *Hof* included 60 *jauchert* of arable land, four gardens measuring 6 *tagwerk*, and another 6 *tagwerk* of meadow.[19] Vorster received only a house, courtyard, and garden as well as the right to collect two measures of wood from the rest of the property. Everything else went to Magg.[20] This pattern of

---

[18] Hans Bergmeier, " 'Wie sie Einödinen gemachet:' Vereinödung im Kempter Raum – ein Beitrag zur Geschichte der ländlichen Neuordnung durch Flurbereinigung," *Berichte aus der Flurbereinigung* 56 (1986), p. 106.

[19] StAA, KL Ottobeuren 27, f. 67v; KL Ottobeuren 102, f. 157r.

[20] StAA, KL Ottobeuren 27, ff. 65v–66r.

sectioning only a small parcel out of a larger holding and leaving the bulk of the *Hof* intact predominates among the subdivisions recorded after mid-century. Thus Clement Schussman's *Hof* in Sontheim was split into two segments upon his death in 1569, one of 30 *jauchert* and one of 9. The 1565 subdivision of Veit Bürklin's *Hof* in Ungerhausen was more uneven still: one 'half' measured 6 *jauchert*, the other measured 50.[21] Eventually, subdivision ceased altogether. After 1571 the *Erdschatz* registers record only a single (uneven) partition of a *Gotteshausrecht* holding.[22]

Refusing requests for further subdivisions was a fairly effective means of maintaining the existing holdings intact, but the monastery was not satisfied to stop there. Scattered evidence indicates that the monks also attempted to reverse some of the more recent subdivisions. In 1543, for example, Martin Zick was admitted to a "half quarter" of a *Gotteshausrecht* holding in Böhen only on condition that he also purchase the *Erblehen* holding which had previously been separated from it.[23] Two years later rather more forceful tactics were employed in the village of Attenhausen. Hans Böglin, the local blacksmith, was a little behind in his rent on half of a large *Hof*[24] which had originally been divided in 1512.[25] The monastery foreclosed on him and transferred the property to a neighbor, who by no coincidence was the imminent heir of the other half. By 1547 the *Hof* was again intact.[26] Böglin resigned himself to the eviction, but his son Hans junior was less accepting of the loss of wealth and status.[27] Leaving the monastery lands, he filed lawsuits with the Bishop of Augsburg and even with the Holy Roman Emperor himself in an attempt to regain the property. Böglin's effort was unsuccessful, but his lawsuits were highly embarrassing to the Abbot. Böglin junior was imprisoned at the earliest opportunity, forced to recant his "calumnies and defamations," and then hastily banished from the monastery lands.[28]

---

[21] Ibid., ff. 142r–v, ff. 35v–36r.   [22] In the village of Niederrieden in 1601. Ibid., f. 219r.

[23] StAA, KL Ottobeuren 27, f. 89v.

[24] StAA, KL Ottobeuren 29, ff. 65r, 160v–161v. Böglin had in the past been something of a troublemaker, becoming embroiled in a feud with the Schick family. KL Ottobeuren 4, ff. 838v–840v, Document 303B [15 Sep. 1526].

[25] StAA, KU Ottobeuren 803–4 [1 Mar. 1512]. Böglin was admitted to the half-*Hof* on 24 February 1528 in exchange for a smaller property he had held since 26 May 1509. He had been the village smith since 21 April 1501 (KU Ottobeuren 640, 757, 1025–6).

[26] StAA, KL Ottobeuren 27, f. 126r.

[27] After losing the half-*Hof* Hans Böglin ranked in the middle (twenty ninth of sixty three) of Attenhausen householders in the 1546 tax roll. Judging by the wealth of those who farmed lands of comparable size, he would have ranked in the top tenth had he retained the property. StAA, KL Ottobeuren 29, ff. 65r–70r and KL Ottobeuren 64, ff. 54v–55v. Note that Böglin remained as the village blacksmith until at least 1546, despite having ceded his rights to the property four years earlier. Cf. KU Ottobeuren 1243 [3 July 1542].

[28] StAA, KL Ottobeuren 4, Document 303F, ff. 847v–851r [18 Mar. 1546]. Neither Böglin is listed in Attenhausen in the 1548 serf roll. KL Ottobeuren 600, ff. 234r–245r.

Although the Böglin affair offered a warning of the likely repercussions of an extensive consolidation campaign, the monastery pressed on. The next showdown of which we have knowledge took place in 1559 with a certain Georg Clostermaier in the village of Egg. Clostermaier had for forty years worked a small *Gotteshausrecht* holding consisting of no more than a house, a garden, and a single *jauchert* of land. Now an old man and no longer capable of farming, he went with his friends to the monastery to request that the property be granted to his son-in-law, Hans Rot. There, Clostermaier later related, he was informed that "it had been found in [record] books that this property had some time ago been subdivided, and [actually] belonged to another holding. When I die, His Grace intends to reunite it with the other [holding]."

The decision struck Clostermaier as unjust in the extreme. The other half of the property was held by the village innkeeper, Georg Vögele, an already prodigiously wealthy man with property worth over three thousand pounds. Clostermaier appealed to the Holy Roman Emperor, Ferdinand I, that the Abbot be instructed to grant the property to his son-in-law "according to the monastery's privileges, which were intended and granted [in order to ensure] that as long as they work and care for it properly, no tenant or tenant's relative shall be evicted from [his] holding with the land [then] granted to others."[29] The Emperor was sympathetic, and asked the Abbot to accede to Clostermaier's request.[30] The Abbot dug in his heels and prepared for a fight.

The battle continued for another thirteen years. When Clostermaier died in 1565, the monastery proceeded with its declared intentions, but Clostermaier's son Georg junior carried on the struggle. A citizen of Munich, he appealed to both the city council[31] and the Duke of Bavaria, charging that "after the death of my dear father the said Abbot has against all Imperial freedoms and commands completely shared out the holding which belongs to the monastery [!] with others: the house to the *Amman* [of Egg] and the land to one Vögele, who is now the innkeeper in Egg; and has driven my sister's children from the land into misery."[32]

The family did have other lands in the village,[33] but Clostermaier sensed the dramatic impact of a tale of dispossession. He hammered on the point in almost

---

[29] StAA, KA Ottobeuren 86: Georg Clostermaier "from Egg in Swabia" to Emperor Ferdinand I [25 Aug. 1559].

[30] Ibid.: undated letter from Emperor Ferdinand I to Abbot Caspar.

[31] Ibid.: undated letter (*c.* March 1566) from Georg Clostermaier junior to the mayor and city council of Munich; also mayor and council of Munich to Abbot Caspar [28 Mar. 1566].

[32] Ibid.: undated letter (*c.* October 1566) from Georg Clostermaier junior to Duke Albrecht of Bavaria.

[33] The 1544 rent roll lists two properties under Clostermaier senior's name; the disputed holding was not only the smaller of the two (1 as against 2.5 *jauchert* of arable land), it was tenurially inferior (*Gotteshausrecht* rather than *Erblehenrecht*). StAA, KL Ottobeuren 29, ff. 94v–95r, 180r. In the 1567 rent roll, the larger property is held by Clostermaier senior's son-in-law Hans Rot, while the smaller one is still in Clostermaier's own name. KL Ottobeuren 30, ff. 106r,

all of his communications, appealing finally to the Holy Roman Emperor that "it is against God and the Imperial and Roman freedoms to drive poor people from their own [land] into misery."[34] The Duke of Bavaria took up the same refrain in a letter to Emperor Maximilian,[35] who in 1566 sternly informed the Abbot that "it is Our gracious [and] solemn command to you that you shall without any further ado render the supplicant satisfaction [*unclaghafft machen*] and conduct yourself in such a manner towards him that he shall have no further cause for complaint . . ."[36]

Abbot Caspar could not ignore a direct imperial rescript, but he was not prepared to concede Clostermaier anything. In a lengthy reply to the Emperor, the Abbot insisted that like all tenants of *Gotteshausrecht* land, Clostermaier senior had been admitted to the property for the term of his life only. Thus, the monastery did in no way deprive the family of anything which had legally belonged to them. Indeed, continued the Abbot indignantly, "I have during the time of my blameless reign and prelature never been truthfully accused of having evicted and driven anyone from his own and from his ancient paternal property into misery."[37] Clostermaier had also helped his father rebuild the house in Egg after a fire, and hoped at least to extract from the monastery his share of the building costs. To this, the Abbot now retorted that the sum in question could not have exceeded 10 *gulden*, that the monastery had in any case provided wood at no cost to the family and therefore owed Clostermaier nothing, and then cheekily offered assistance if Clostermaier wished to reclaim the building costs from his own relatives.[38]

The squabbling between Clostermaier and the Abbot continued for several years, but in the end Clostermaier gained nothing for all of his troubles. By 1572 he was reduced to complaining to the Abbot that he had received no response from the monastery in more than five years.[39] In return he received nothing more than a blunt and disdainful refusal to accede to what the Abbot termed Clostermaier's "utterly insolent, threatening communications and indecent petitions."[40]

On the face of it the monastery emerged triumphant from each of these consolidation drives, but the victory was dearly bought. For what is striking

---

113v. This latter attribution is clearly an error, since by 1567 Clostermaier senior was dead and Clostermaier junior was living in Munich. When the smaller property is next mentioned in the records (1585), it had been merged with the lands of the hated innkeeper. KL Ottobeuren 27, f. 229r.

[34] StAA, KA Ottobeuren 86: undated letter (April–October, 1566) from Georg Clostermaier junior to Emperor Maximillian II.

[35] Ibid.: Duke Albrecht of Bavaria to Emperor Maximilian [9 Oct. 1566].

[36] Ibid.: Emperor Maximillian II to Abbot Caspar [8 Nov. 1566].

[37] Ibid.: undated draft of a response from Abbot Caspar to Emperor Maximillian.

[38] Ibid.   [39] Ibid.: Georg Clostermaier to Abbot Caspar [23 Nov. 1572].

[40] Ibid.: Abbot Caspar to Georg Clostermaier [29 Nov. 1572].

about the two contested consolidations is that in both instances it is obvious the Abbot's case was legally correct. *Gotteshausrecht* holdings, as even Georg Clostermaier junior admitted, were the property of the monastery, and as long as they respected the term of the lease – which they did – the monks had every legal right to dispose of the land as they saw fit. Even so, and as has been seen in chapter 1 in the 1565 exchange between the Abbot and Simon Eck, the monastery's subjects clung to a different conception of property rights. As far as the peasants were concerned, long-standing tenants had a moral right to pass on their holdings to their children independent of legal niceties. In the words of Georg Clostermaier senior, the very purpose of the monastery's imperial privileges was to protect the peasantry against eviction. Crucially, the Holy Roman Emperor himself sympathized with this position, even if he was unwilling to forbid the Abbot outright to consolidate the holding. As stubborn as they were, the monks were ultimately forced to realize that the cost in ill will among the peasantry and embarrassment before the Emperor was too high a price to pay for a modest reduction in the number of tenants.[41]

And so a sort of compromise was reached: no one was to be dispossessed for the sake of consolidation, but at the same time no one was to subdivide his holdings any further. This decision was never formally enunciated, but it was clearly implicit in a striking revision of the rent rolls carried out by the monastery between 1567 and 1584. Between these dates, two recording changes were introduced. First, each tenant's various parcels of *Gotteshausrecht* land, often of different origin, were henceforth to be classed as a single *Hof* with a consolidated rent obligation. In exchange, the *de facto* separation of individual *Höfe* between two tenants was now legally recognized. Each tenant's share was now considered a separate *Hof* unto itself, and the threat that the two halves would be merged was lifted.[42]

For example, according to the 1567 rent roll, Clement Schussman and Matheus Stedelin were the co-tenants of a *Hof* in the village of Sontheim owing an annual grain rent of four *malter*. Each man paid two *malter* in rent. Schussman also held a second *Hof* owing four and three-quarters *malter* of grain.[43] In 1569 Stedelin was formally admitted to 9 *jauchert* of arable and four and

---

[41] Even legally justified foreclosures could generate considerable discontent. After the tenant of the "Ried" mill near the village of Benningen was evicted in 1601/2, three other villagers made "all sorts of inappropriate and unnecessary disputations" about the matter in the Memmingen marketplace. StAA, KL Ottobeuren 587-II, Heft 21. For a similar incident concerning the very same property, see KL Ottobeuren 4, ff. 724v–728r, Document 295G [5 Apr. 1558].

[42] Note that this did not prevent *tenants* from consolidating the land. The rent rolls list seven *Gotteshausrecht* holdings in the hamlet of Knaus in 1544, six in 1567, five in 1584, and three in 1606. All of this was the work of the peasantry: one holding was divided between two others in 1546, and three tenants were "swallowed" by their more successful neighbors between 1583 and 1590. StAA, KL Ottobeuren 27, ff. 171r–175r; KL Ottobeuren 29, ff. 77r–v; KL Ottobeuren 30, ff. 81r–82r; KL Ottobeuren 31, f. 14r and KL Ottobeuren 39, ff. 30r–v.

[43] StAA, KL Ottobeuren 30, ff. 74r, 75v.

a half *tagwerk* of meadow described as "coming out of Schussman's holding." On the same day Schussman's son Johann was admitted to all of his deceased father's lands.[44] Stedelin had thus been awarded his own *Hof*, while Schussman's various properties had been amalgamated. The 1584 rent roll describes the situation in simplified terms: two tenants, each with his own holding, one owing two and the other owing six and three quarters *malter* in grain rent.[45]

A similar process can be traced in the hamlet of Untermoosbach, where the 1544 rent roll lists Barthlome Weissenhorn and Leinhart Burklin as co-tenants of one *Hof*.[46] In 1549 the *Erdschatz* register records the transfer of the property as a single *Hof* from Weissenhorn to Mang Widenmann,[47] but the 1567 rent roll again lists two tenants for the same holding: Widenmann and a certain Peter Steidlin.[48] Shortly thereafter the fiction was given up. When Peter Steidlin died in 1567, the *Erdschatz* register officially records the transfer of his holding to Michael Dodel and at Mang Widenmann's death in 1573 his land was transferred to his son Jerg.[49] The 1584 rent roll concedes the existence of two separate *Höfe*.[50]

On land held under heritable tenure (*Erblehenrecht*), the tenant's property rights were much stronger than on the life-term tenancies. Nevertheless, the partibility of *Erblehenrecht* land was also suspended before the end of the sixteenth century, a cessation occasionally underscored by explicit agreement among family members.[51] Thus, in the parish of Ottobeuren, where almost all of the land was held under *Erblehenrecht*, the number of landholdings in thirty-two hamlets remained remarkably constant after 1584 (see Table 4.1).[52] This is not to say that heritable tenancies were never divided after this date, but seventeenth-century *Hof*-divisions had a very different character (in addition to being far less common) than in the previous century. In the first place, several of the transactions were not true divisions, because they represented either the shedding of previously cobbled-together fragments (rather than the subdivision of an integral *Hof*) or a fiction to preserve the autonomy of retired parents

---

[44] StAA, KL Ottobeuren 27, f. 142r.   [45] StAA, KL Ottobeuren 31, ff. 10r–v.
[46] StAA, KL Ottobeuren 29, f. 31r.   [47] StAA, KL Ottobeuren 27, f. 27r.
[48] StAA, KL Ottobeuren 30, f. 32v.
[49] StAA, KL Ottobeuren 27, ff. 28v [15 Feb. 1567] and 29r [6 Feb. 1573].
[50] StAA, KL Ottobeuren 31, f. 19r.
[51] For example, when Jerg Koler of Eheim sold his house, land, and half of the moveable wealth to his son-in-law, it was agreed that buyer and seller were to work the property together and that after the seller's death "nothing else shall be divided except for the [other] half of the moveables and what they [the seller and his wife] have in their room." StAA, KL Ottobeuren 908, ff. 56r–v and 56v–57r [7 Apr. 1620].
[52] The figures for 1584–1606 are based on the number of tithepayers (i.e. holders of arable land), while the figures for 1620–7 are based on the number of taxpayers who owned land of any kind. The hamlets were grouped into headmanships of four to eight settlements each. Hamlets missing from the 1584 tithe list have not been included.

Table 4.1 *Number of farms in the hamlets of Ottobeuren parish, 1584–1627*

Hauptmannschaft (no. of hamlets)	1584	1600	1606	1620	1627
Dennenberg (5)	26	25	26	27	27
Betzisried (4)	25	25	25	24	24
Halbersberg (3)[a]	33	36	33	39	35
Eheim (5)	25	20	23	22	20
Ollarzried (3)[b]	13	12	12	11	11
Bühel (4)	31	29	30	31	30
Leupolz (8)	28	33	33	33	33
Total (32)	181	180	182	187	180

[a] One hamlet (Oberhaslach) missing data 1584
[b] Two hamlets (Ollarzried and Höhe) missing data 1584
Sources: StAA, KL Ottobeuren 31, 39, 102, 104 and 681, Hefte 3–4

(rather than the apportionment of land between distinct households).[53] More commonly, the later *Hof*-divisions involved either the division of property which already included two separate houses or house-lots [*Hofstätte*], or the hiving off of land to a purchaser or purchasers previously established on the basis of other holdings. The essential point is that in the seventeenth century, the "division" of *Höfe* did not create new households, but instead reapportioned land among a fixed number of propertyholders. This was not a coincidence.

In the middle of the sixteenth century the monastery began to restrict the building of houses by manipulating a legal privilege known as the *Hofstatt-recht*, or "house-lot right." Strictly speaking, houses could only be built on land endowed with *Hofstattrecht*, and each holding was supposed to have only one such plot,[54] but in the fifteenth century these rules were rarely enforced. In chapter 1 we saw how the 1427 *Erblehen* charter in Bernhalden and Kräpflins allowed the tenants to build "as many houses and barns as they desire" on the holding. In a similar vein the 1430 grant of two properties known as Wallris and Lampolz to Hanns Wÿller and his heirs stipulates that "they may also indeed erect more houses on them." Recopying the 1468 charter granting a *Hof* in Guggenberg to Jos Vögelin a later scribe casually noted "there are now two [tenants] on the property and two houses [built] upon it."[55] The monastery might

[53] For example, Johann Maier of Hofs sold "half of his land" to his son Johann junior in the spring of 1620, but the tax survey of the hamlet drawn up eight months later records the son as the owner of the entire property while the father is listed with "a claim of 256 fl. on his son." StAA, KL Ottobeuren 908, ff. 58[a]r–v [12 Apr. 1620] and KL Ottobeuren 102, ff. 52v–53r [16 Dec. 1620].

[54] Karl S. Bader, *Das Mittelalterliche Dorf als Friedens- und Rechts-bereich* (Weimar, 1957), pp. 52–60.

[55] StAA, KL Ottobeuren 18, ff. 254v (1430) and 46v–48r (1468).

also formally create new *Hofstätte*.[56] In 1488, for example, Abbot Nikolaus Röslin granted Martin Schuster a small garden in the village of Hawangen and authorized him to build a house upon it. Still more explicit was the 1541 grant of a garden to Martin Pfaltzer in Benningen. The charter granted him heritable tenure to the property, "also with the special privilege that it henceforth shall have *Hofstattrecht*, and that in and on it the tenant may build and erect a house."[57]

By the time of this last grant, however, the earlier tolerance for new house building was already beginning to ebb. During the 1540s the monastery began to insist that each holding have only one house. In 1549, for example, Benedict Gebelin was granted permission to build a new *Erblehen* house in the hamlet of Hofs only on condition "that in exchange he forthwith demolish his [other] house . . . and [that] its plot henceforth for all time no longer have a house [on it] nor shall any *Hofstattrecht* or privilege be claimed [for it] by anyone."[58] The 1584 *Erdschatz* register entry recording the admission of Balthas Sanz to two *Gotteshausrecht* properties in Wolfertschwenden reflects a similar determination. The first property was a large *Hof* consisting of a house and more than 50 *jauchert* of land. The second, the register continues, was a smaller property "which also has a house and barn next to each other; they shall be demolished and the first house thereby improved [with the rubble]."[59] Still more careful oversight is evident in a 1602 entry from Hawangen. After being admitted to a holding, Michael Heinrich exchanged a small parcel of meadow for a garden next to his house. The scribe was careful to note that on the garden "Hans Roggen's house once stood and it burned down; [the garden] shall henceforth no longer have *Hofstattrecht* and shall remain part of [Michael Heinrich's] *Hof* as a garden."[60]

But although the most explicit evidence for this change is found in the rent rolls and entry fine ledgers of the Abbot, it should not be assumed that he was the only one opposed to the subdivision of *Höfe* and the erection of new houses. In 1557, for example, a certain Blesi Merhardt of Attenhausen was obliged to confess that

---

[56] StAA, KU Ottobeuren 689 [6 May 1504] (the baker Cunrat Mair is granted the right to build a house in Attenhausen and to live there, but Mair is not entitled to wood-rights for building or heating); KU Ottobeuren 903 [23 July 1529] (Hans Martin of Ottobeuren is admitted to a meadow and arable parcel next to the garden of a farm called the "Conenhof," "in which garden Hans Martin has built a house"); KU Ottobeuren 1154 [26 June 1536] (Anthoni Mair of Rempolz is allowed to keep his house on the common in exchange for an annual payment of 6 d.); KU Ottobeuren 1161 [23 Aug. 1536] (Urban Merhart of Attenhausen is granted the right to build a house in the garden of his father Anthoni Merhart in exchange for an annual payment of 4 ß).

[57] StAA, KL Ottobeuren 18, ff. 180v–181r (1488), 186v (1541).

[58] Ibid., f. 78r.   [59] StAA, KL Ottobeuren 27, f. 83r.

[60] Ibid., f. 34v. See also the *c.* 1551 prohibition on the subdivision of houses in KL Ottobeuren 4, Document 289X, ff. 382r–v.

after I had for the third time been forbidden by My Gracious Lord's advisors and also by My Gracious Lord himself to build a new house on a site . . . where in human memory no house [ever] stood, and in opposition to and to the disadvantage of the village community of Attenhausen [I did] of my own authority and with my own hands [durch mich selbs gelegt] enlarge the house and carry out the building . . .⁶¹

Merhardt's acknowledgment that the unauthorized construction was an offense against the village community is an important reminder that the more prosperous of the Abbot's subjects shared their overlord's alarm at the growing numbers in the villages.⁶²

The easiest scapegoats for this worry were the poor. As was the case in most German states, the monastery's response to the complaints of its subjects was a steady stream of repressive legislation. In 1545 the Abbot forbade those of his subjects who were in receipt of alms to go drinking, either publicly or privately.⁶³ A statute of 1561 raised legal barriers to immigrants from outside the monastery lands.⁶⁴ After 1567 the poor at Ottobeuren were obliged to wear special badges if they wished to obtain alms. It is a revealing sign that the stated justification for these ordinances was the burden the poor imposed on the rest of the peasantry. The 1567 ordinance, for example, bemoaned the inefficacy of earlier attempts to control beggars and vagrants, "in consequence whereof those in the towns and on the land who live [literally 'feed themselves'] from heavy sweat and hard work in order to support their wives and children have suffered grievous damages, and who if it [i.e. improvement] is not presently forthcoming must fall into certain collapse and ruin."⁶⁵

---

⁶¹ StAA, KL Ottobeuren 4, Document 303J, ff. 859r–862r [4 Sep. 1557]. Merhardt came from a *Bauer* family that had degenerated to *Seldner* status at the end of the fifteenth century. Blesi's forebear Jerg Merhardt is mentioned as tenant farmer on 24 March 1483. He exchanged his *Hof* for a much smaller property on 4 February 1491 and then gave up the smaller holding on 10 December 1494 (KU Ottobeuren 411, 498–9, 561). In 1525 Blesi is listed as *Seldner* and ranked in the bottom 45 percent of Attenhausen taxpayers (KL Ottobeuren 541, Heft 2, ff. 43v–46r), but he seems to have been able to pull himself up by his bootstraps. On 4 September 1538 Blesi purchased a garden for £93 with the right to build a house there (KU Ottobeuren 1191), and by 1546 his 30 kr. tax payment placed him in the village's upper third (KL Ottobeuren 64, ff. 54v–55v). Merhardt did not, however, ever break into the elite group of nineteen *Hof* tenants who controlled some nine tenths of the land in the village (KL Ottobeuren 29, ff. 65r–70r; KL Ottobeuren 30, ff. 69r–73r).

⁶² Prosecutions for illegal building crop up regularly in the criminal court papers. A few examples: Wolfertschwenden – "Caspar Biller installed two hearths in a half-house without the permission of the authorities – [fined] £1" and "Jacob Steger without permission again set his house on the *Hofstatt* – [fined] £1": StAA, KL Ottobeuren 587-I, Heft 3 (1566/7); Niederrieden – "Hans Raibel did without permission again rebuild his shed on the spot where he put it before – [fined] £1": ibid., Heft 10 (1579/80); Ottobeuren – "Pighead [*sic*! a nickname] installed another hearth in his new house without permission – [fined] 10 ß": KL Ottobeuren 587-II, Heft 26 (1606/7). Given the weakness of the monastery's policing power, these prosecutions were inconceivable without the co-operation of at least some of the villagers.

⁶³ StAA, KL Ottobeuren 4, Document 289E, ff. 300r–304r (1545).

⁶⁴ Ibid., Document 289G [4 Sep. 1561], ff. 308v–311r.

⁶⁵ Ibid., Document 289H, ff. 311r–314v [10 Dec. 1567]; the quotation on f. 312v.

Despite this stigmatization of the poor and of rootless outsiders, both the Abbot and the wealthy *Bauern* were well aware of the fact that the basic problem came from within the solid ranks of the village residents. As Abbot Caspar had noted in 1551, the pressure for subdivision and new house building came from the desire of even wealthy peasants to "enable their children to set up house near them." The most effective way to brake the pulverization of the *Höfe* and the degradation of their tenants was thus to restrict the formation of new households. It is here that the co-operation between the monastery and *Bauern* is most obvious, because village officials – the *Amman* and *Vierer* "in the name of" the entire *Gemeinde* – exercised a great deal of authority over the creation and regulation of new house-lots.[66]

Between 1603 and 1621, at least twenty-nine[67] documentable grants of land for new house-lots were made at Ottobeuren by the monastery (eight), individual peasants (four), and village and hamlet *Gemeinden* (seventeen). The bare statistics suggest an almost charitable program of supporting the establishment of new residents (particularly when one considers that these grants were usually made in exchange for the very modest payment of 10–20 *gulden*, or even at no cost at all), but this impression is quite misleading. It turns out that the overwhelming majority (69.0 percent) of the house-lot 'creations' were made to people already resident in the settlement. In some cases the grant document itself declares that a (larger?) *Hofstatt* is being granted to an existing house;[68] in others earlier documents either record the grantee as an established householder[69] or even indicate that s/he previously owned a residence on the lot in question.[70] In one case the new house-lot was intended to replace an old one the recipient owned elsewhere in the hamlet, on condition "that in exchange

---

[66] For a nice illustration of the respective competencies of overlord and peasant officials see StAA, KU Ottobeuren 1596 [15 June 1562], in which the *Amman* and *Vierer* of Benningen, with the consent of Abbot Caspar, grant Hanns Zuckenrigel genannt Eysenman "at his request a building lot out of the common."

[67] This number omits two house-lot creations in Ungerhausen, which have been excluded from the calculations because the poor quality of the bond-chicken registers for Ungerhausen precludes judgment of whether or not the grants created new households. Since Ungerhausen was only acquired by the monastery from a Memmingen burgher family in 1594, it was not until the 1620s that most of the villagers had become Ottobeuren serfs and therefore appear in the listings.

[68] StAA, KL Ottobeuren 903, f. 156r [3 Mar. 1605] grants Jacob Gering of Niederdorf a *Hofstatt* "on which stands the house he currently inhabits." Similarly KL Ottobeuren 907, f. 60v [14 Mar. 1617] in Günz.

[69] The most useful sources in this regard are the bond-chicken registers for 1586–1613. StAA, KL Ottobeuren 491-I, Hefte 4–15, and 491-II, Heft 16.

[70] StAA, KL Ottobeuren 907, f. 88v [5 June 1617] grants a *Hofstatt* to Johann Scheffler "Schwarz" of Frechenrieden for 20 fl. He had purchased a half-house on the very same lot from his father, Jerg, on 12 March 1609 (KL Ottobeuren 904, f. 118v). Similarly the grant on 31 October 1617 of a house-lot to Caspar Teufel of Niederrieden (KL Ottobeuren 907, ff. 119r–v), who had mortgaged the house on the same *Hofstatt* ten years earlier (KL Ottobeuren 903, f. 283r [8 Jan. 1607]), and the grant dated 15 March 1618 to Johann Neher of Niederrieden, who mortgaged his house on 9 December 1616 (ibid., ff. 31r, 146r).

168   THE PEASANTS OF OTTOBEUREN

he . . . and his heirs shall have no right to build another house on the [old] *Hofstatt* which he held by the upper mill in the field, but shall instead simply let it [i.e. the old house] sink and fall down."[71]

Still more revealing of the spirit governing the granting of house-lots are the restrictions that neighbors and village officials often placed on the grantees The parcel's *Hofstattrecht* might be slated to last only for the lifetime of the current residents,[72] and if one spouse died the survivor might be forbidden to remarry in that house-lot.[73] The grantee might be prohibited from keeping poultry or required to work for the other members of the settlement.[74] Even rich peasants were subject to these constraints. When Jerg Betterich of Günzegg[75] decided to retire in 1609, his first instinct was to acquire a new house-lot so as to be able to live separately from his heir. The headman did sell him a "plot for a *Hofstatt* and for the erection of a house" for 30 fl., but the contract went on to insist that should Betterich and his wife die, "and should the said house be occupied by another resident who or whose heirs should prove objectionable and unsuitable for day labor [*sic*!], the said [resident] shall be obliged to vacate the premises and the sellers [i.e. the headman and his wife] shall be obliged to repay him [i.e. the evicted party] the building costs in addition to the 30 fl."[76] In the end Betterich shelved the plan altogether, choosing instead to live in comfort with his son, to whom he sold the family estate for a total of 1,800 fl.[77] The poor could of course be treated more harshly. In 1603, the very same Jerg Betterich, in his capacity as an official of the Günzegg *Gemeinde*, had granted a new *Hofstatt* to an impoverished long-term resident by the name of Jerg Schiess.[78] The *Gemeinde* reserved the right to revoke the grant at will as well as the right to reclaim the lot if Schiess ever sold the house built on it.[79] In 1614 he did sell the house to his son Michael,[80] and shortly thereafter the *Gemeinde* apparently acted on its powers. By 1620 both father

[71] StAA, KL Ottobeuren 903, f. 170v [2 June 1605].
[72] StAA, KL Ottobeuren 904, f. 180v [1 Mar. 1610].
[73] StAA, KL Ottobeuren 903, ff. 187r [13 Oct. 1605].
[74] Ibid., ff. 209r [15 Feb. 1606] and 294r [27 Jan. 1607].
[75] Family status inferred from StAA, KL Ottobeuren 31, f. 82v, KL Ottobeuren 491-I, Heft 6, f. 19v and Heft 10, f. 19, and KL Ottobeuren 918, f. 64r [11 Nov. 1576].
[76] StAA, KL Ottobeuren 904, f. 151v [21 Oct. 1609].
[77] StAA, KL Ottobeuren 904, f. 160v [4 Dec. 1609]; KL Ottobeuren 907, f. 104v [25 July 1617]; KL Ottobeuren 102, f. 120v.
[78] Jerg Schiess is listed in the hamlet from 1586, and was assessed the *Bauer*'s hen in 1586, 1590, and 1595. By 1602 he had dropped to the *Seldner*'s assessment of 3 *kreuzer*. StAA, KL Ottobeuren 491-I, Heft 4, f. 25v, Heft 5, f. 24r, Heft 6, f. 19v, and Heft 10, f. 19r.
[79] StAA, KL Ottobeuren 903, ff. 39r–v [18 Sep. 1603]. Schiess was allowed to keep one cow on the common meadow, but was obliged to ensure that his chickens caused no damage to his neighbors' grain fields.
[80] StAA, KL Ottobeuren 905, f. 195v [31 July 1614]. The associated *Schuldbrief* (ibid., ff. 195v–196r) displays the typical concerns of the poor, with careful provisions for the harvesting and drying of fruit and for the cultivation of the garden.

and son were utterly destitute, and within two years they had vanished from the hamlet.[81]

By the beginning of the seventeenth century, in other words, peasant society (or at least its wealthier elements) pursued a deliberate policy not just of preserving the integrity of larger agricultural enterprises, but also of controlling the actual number of households in a given settlement. Indeed, the two efforts often went hand in hand. Stephan Geromüller, for example, came into a comfortable holding[82] of about 34 *jauchert* in the hamlet of Ollarzried some time in the early 1590s.[83] Within ten years, however, he began falling into debt[84] and losing land.[85] In 1613 he attempted to sell his remaining property to his wealthier brother Michael,[86] intending to retain only a kettle, a few pans, and some bedlinens, and the right to live out his days in a house he no longer owned.[87] For reasons which were never specified, the sale fell through, and Stephan's land was instead cannibalized by his wealthier neighbors. In keeping with the pattern discussed above, most of the land was divided between two established householders.[88]

Stephan now owned little more than a house,[89] and was reduced to begging his brother Michael and the local headman, Jacob Epplin, to let him sow a little flax seed on their land and to help him cart the dung needed to fertilize his garden.[90] Both men agreed, but now that Stephan was an impoverished cottager, the second house-lot he owned between his two benefactors' own residences was a potential point of entry for another poor household into the hamlet. In exchange for a small payment, Jacob Epplin and Michael Geromüller accordingly obtained from Stephan and his wife the promise "that they and their heirs for all of their lives will neither build nor seek to build any house

---

[81] Neither father nor son owns any property in the 1620 tax survey and they are instead assessed the minimum head tax of 6 *kreuzer* (StAA, KL Ottobeuren 102, f. 123r). Both are listed in the 1617 bond-chicken register, but both are gone in 1622 (KL Ottobeuren 491-II, Heft 21, f. 22r and Heft 26, ff. 22v–23r).

[82] StAA, KL Ottobeuren 681, Heft 3, f. 1v and Heft 4, f. 2r.

[83] StAA, KL Ottobeuren 491-I, Heft 5, f. 2r and Heft 6, f. 4v.

[84] StAA, KL Ottobeuren 903, ff. 36v [29 Aug. 1603] and 220r [14 Feb. 1606]. For the second debt Geromüller was obliged to mortgage "each and every piece of his real and moveable property" and also provide several guarantors. Also KL Ottobeuren 905, f. 213v [26 Oct. 1614].

[85] StAA, KL Ottobeuren 904, f. 15v [22 Dec. 1607].

[86] OttPR, Vol. I, f. 104r. StAA, KL Ottobeuren 102, ff. 85r–v; KL Ottobeuren 583, Heft 6, f. 8r; KL Ottobeuren 681, Heft 3, f. 1v and Heft 4, f. 2r; KL Ottobeuren 688-I, Heft 8, f. 10v.

[87] StAA, KL Ottobeuren 905, f. 84v [10 Ian. 1613]. The entry is crossed out in the MS.

[88] StAA, KL Ottobeuren 905, ff. 254r [22 Mar. 1615], 263r [20 Apr. 1615], and 263v [20 Apr. 1615]. Status of neighbors based on KL Ottobeuren 904, f. 158r [19 Feb. 1610], KL Ottobeuren 905, ff. 42v–43r [24 Dec. 1612], KL Ottobeuren 681, Heft 3, f. 1v and Heft 4, f. 2r, and KL Ottobeuren 102, f. 87v.

[89] StAA, KL Ottobeuren 102, f. 86r

[90] StAA, KL Ottobeuren 905, f. 263v [20 Apr. 1615]. The agreement was to last for three years, and Stephan was to provide the flax seed himself.

on the garden between their houses."[91] Seven years earlier Epplin had himself used his ownership of two houses to separately establish both his son and his stepson in Ollarzried,[92] but that was a different story. The headman owned some 90 *jauchert* of land – 16 *jauchert* of which he had bought up from the unfortunate Stephan Geromüller – which thus allowed for the foundation of two *Bauer* households whose descendants would continue to farm the land into the eighteenth century.[93]

The 'closure' of the village (in the sense of capping the number of house-lots) was a widespread phenomenon in late sixteenth-century Germany,[94] and it was clearly this remorseless social constraint, rather than the biology of plague or starvation, which put a halt to the growth of population at Ottobeuren. The new property regime made life particularly difficult for the rural poor, and to state that they needed a great deal of creativity and determination to survive is merely to assert the obvious. Nevertheless, it is worth inquiring more closely into how they did survive, because even our friend Stephan Geromüller managed to live out all of his days in the hamlet where he was born,[95] dying there in his late sixties in 1629.[96] His 1615 agreement about flax-sowing indicates that he must have earned much of his living by making linen thread, but notarial records from the later 1620s suggest he also followed a deliberate policy of mortgaging his real property in exchange for an income stream.[97] Stephan did end his life in total bankruptcy,[98] but he also died in his own house, which under the circumstances was no mean accomplishment.

If Stephan Geromüller was able to pull himself back from the initial res-ignation to living as his brother's dependant, other Ottobeuren peasants who started with much less proved even more adept at navigating the economy of

[91] Ibid., ff. 353v–354r [18 Apr. 1616].

[92] StAA, KL Ottobeuren 904, ff. 156[a]v [17 Nov. 1609] and 158r [19 Feb. 1610].

[93] StAA, KL Ottobeuren 225, f. 79v; KL Ottobeuren 42, f. 21r; KL Ottobeuren 56, ff. 55v–56r; KL Ottobeuren 109, ff. 547r–v; KL Ottobeuren 202, f. 94v; KL Ottobeuren 921, ff. 313r–v [7 Nov. 1697]; Ottobeuren *Liber Status Animarum* [hereinafter OttLSA] 1681, p. 62.

[94] The closure of villages has been documented all over rural Swabia by Hermann Grees. Grees is not always clear about when this happened; at some points he dates the phenomenon to the fifteenth century (*Ländliche Unterschichten*, pp. 155–6) and others to the sixteenth century (ibid., p. 141). One way or another, most of his *documented* examples come from the later sixteenth century. Thus, for example, the ebbing of household formation in Langenau after *c.* 1580 (ibid., p. 288), the prohibition on new house building in the lands of the city of Ulm in 1590 (ibid., p. 171, n. 27), and the restrictions imposed on the rights of landless indwellers by various lordships in 1559, 1562, 1584, 1588, and 1613 (ibid., pp. 157–8). Other studies documenting the introduction of impartible inheritance in southern Germany during the later sixteenth century include Martha White Paas, *Population Change, Labour Supply and Agriculture in Augsburg 1480–1618* (New York, 1979), esp. pp. 99–100, and Thomas Robisheaux, *Rural Society and the Search for Order in Early Modern Germany* (Cambridge, 1989), esp. pp. 80–3, 127–9.

[95] StAA, KL Ottobeuren 64, ff. 42v–43r; Dertsch, "Das Einwohnerbuch des Ottobeurer Kloster-staats 1564," p. 11.

[96] StAA, KL Ottobeuren 491-III, Heft 34, f. 6r: "Stefan Geromiller – obiit."

[97] StAA, KL Ottobeuren 909, ff. 103v–104r [15 Dec. 1625] and 119v–120r [31 Jan. 1626].

[98] StAA, KL Ottobeuren 104, f. 78v.

the 'closed' village. The best illustration is provided by the village of Böhen, where at least three new house-lots were created between 1606 and 1614. The last of these was granted by the monastery at no cost to Mathias Bauschmid out of land ceded by his stepfather, Ulrich Melder, a wealthy *Hof*-tenant. Mathias wasted no time in building his new home, and then promptly turned around and sold half of the house to one Caspar Rapp for no less than 139 fl. The Abbot was not at all pleased by this manipulation of the rules, and allowed the sale only on condition "that the buyer and seller shall have and use in common only a single oven and hearth in the entire said house. They may and shall, however, divide the *Stube* [i.e. the ground-floor room heated by the hearth] with a partition-wall."[99] The house was accordingly split into halves, and Mathias then used the acquired capital (supplemented by illegal flax trading in the city of Memmingen)[100] to buy various parcels of land in the village.[101] By 1627 he held property worth a total of 230 fl.[102] Mathias Bauschmid's co-resident, Caspar Rapp, was also not deterred by the monastery's effort to keep him in check. He bought a quarter *jauchert* of land in 1618, exchanged it along with 45 fl. for a full *jauchert* in 1624, and then a few weeks later traded his original half-house for a better one five doors down the street.[103]

On the other side of Ulrich Melder's house was another new house-lot, granted by the *Gemeinde* to the recently married[104] Michael Walch in 1610.[105] Walch was even more of an operator than either of the previous *Hofstatt* grantees, and never even lived on the lot for which he had paid a mere 18 *gulden*. Instead, he built a house there, divided it into halves, and then promptly unloaded them. The first half was sold for 58 fl. in February of 1610 and the second was traded ten months later to Jerg Leufel (about whom more presently) in exchange for a half-house and some arable land in the adjacent hamlet of Berg.[106] Michael Walch paid 22 fl. to compensate for his greater gain, but had no intention of settling in the hamlet. Instead, he used the property in Berg as a security to raise capital[107] and then resold it in 1612 for fully 140 fl.[108] All of this time Michael lived in the front half of his widowed stepmother's home, the possession of which he only formalized with a 90 fl. payment in 1613.[109] Despite (or perhaps

---

[99] StAA, KL Ottobeuren 905, ff. 246v–247r [6 Mar. 1615]. For an earlier incident of the same sort, see KU Ottobeuren 1473 [10 June 1555], pursuant to which Hans Reichart of Böhen is granted the right to maintain two hearths in his house, but only for the lifetime of one Michael Riegg and Riegg's wife, Elizapethe Kläss, who presumably shared the house with him.

[100] StAA, KL Ottobeuren 587-II, Heft 28 (1615).

[101] StAA, KL Ottobeuren 909, f. 166v [28 May 1626].   [102] StAA, KL Ottobeuren 104, f. 96v.

[103] StAA, KL Ottobeuren 907, ff. 212v–213r [26 Dec. 1618]; KL Ottobeuren 909, ff. 17r [23 Oct. 1624] and 20v [4 Nov. 1624]; KL Ottobeuren 104, f. 103r.

[104] StAA, KL Ottobeuren 583, Heft 23 (1606/7), f. 4v.

[105] StAA, KL Ottobeuren 904, f. 178v [25 Feb. 1610].

[106] Ibid., ff. 178r [25 Feb. 1610] and 219v [2 Dec. 1610].

[107] Ibid., f. 263r [5 July 1611].   [108] StAA, KL Ottobeuten 905, f. 23v [13 Sep. 1612].

[109] Ibid., ff. 57v–58r [25 Dec. 1612] and 77v–78r [14 June 1613]; KL Ottobeuren 904, f. 210r [11 Aug. 1610]; KL Ottobeuren 583, Heft 27 (1611/12), f. 4r.

because of) this frenetic activity, Michael Walch did not live to enjoy the fruits of his labor, and died in 1615 or 1616.[110] Nevertheless, he succeeded in passing on to his children a much more stable beginning for their own lives[111] than he himself had been given,[112] a position which they consolidated by dabbling in moneylending and illegal cattle trading.[113]

Jerg Leufel of Berg had a more uneven trajectory than the other house-lot recipients discussed thus far. His father, Johann, and stepmother, Anna Beppel,[114] were poor *Seldner*[115] who struggled desperately to establish their son as an independent householder. In 1607 the parents mortgaged "all of their thus far unencumbered property" in order to raise 25 fl.[116] and then two years later secured approval from the *Gemeinde* to purchase from two wealthy neighbors, Michael Bergmann and Jacob Schiess, for 24 fl. a patch of land for a second house-lot.[117] Johann Leufel and his wife were then able to sell their original house and 3 *jauchert* of land to their son Jerg and withdraw to the new house in August of 1609. But if the *Gemeinde* was willing to allow the Leufels the extra house-lot, it clearly wished to avoid sharing resources with another poor household. As the notarial protocol put it, "in consideration for the good deed done to them, namely that they [Bergmann and Schiess] have allowed them to build a house next to their [Bergmann's and Schiess'] fields and live in it," Leufel and his wife had to promise "henceforth in perpetuity to keep no cows, geese or hens, but instead to guard them [Bergmann and Schiess] and their heirs against all future damage and disadvantage."[118] Hamstrung in this way by their neighbors, the parents were forced to rely on credit in order to make ends meet.[119]

Between the enormous sacrifices made by his parents and the handsome dowry brought by his wife, Anna Heuss,[120] one is tempted to say that Jerg Leufel ought to have been more successful. As it happened, he sold off half of his inheritance within six months of receipt, and in December of 1610 traded away the remainder to the canny Michael Walch and relocated to the nearby

[110] StAA, KL Ottobeuren 907, ff. 3r–v [c. 30 July 1616].
[111] Ibid.; KL Ottobeuren 909, ff. 8v–9r [6 Aug. 1624]; KL Ottobeuren 104, f. 101r.
[112] StAA, KL Ottobeuren 491-I, Heft 3, f. 21r, Heft 5, f. 22r, Heft 6, f. 18v, Heft 10, f. 17r, and Heft 14, f. 16r; KL Ottobeuren 491-II, Heft 16, f. 20r.
[113] StAA, KL Ottobeuren 587-III, Heft 33 (1626/7), f. 30v.
[114] StAA, KL Ottobeuren 583, Heft 3 (1585/6), f. 7v and Heft 13 (1596/7), f. 3v.
[115] StAA, KL Ottobeuren 31, f. 85r; KL Ottobeuren 491-I, Heft 4, f. 24v. Dertsch, "Das Einwohner-buch des Ottobeurer Klosterstaats 1564," p. 29.
[116] StAA, KL Ottobeuren 903, f. 326r [28 May 1607].
[117] The neighbors' wealth from StAA, KL Ottobeuren 102, ff. 112v, 143r; KL Ottobeuren 905, f. 109v [20 June 1613]; KL Ottobeuren 907, f. 236v [15 Mar. 1619]; KL Ottobeuren 908, ff. 11v–12r [2 June 1619].
[118] StAA, KL Ottobeuren 904, f. 146r [17 Aug. 1609].
[119] StAA, KL Ottobeuren 904, f. 218r [21 Oct. 1610] and KL Ottobeuren 905, f. 95v [5 Mar. 1613].
[120] StAA, KL Ottobeuren 904, f. 155v [13 Nov. 1609].

village of Böhen.[121] The move to Böhen was a step down, but Jerg Leufel's decline only continued thereafter. By 1620 he had ceased to be an independent householder, probably living with his parents whose debts had now risen to the entire value of their meagre property.[122]

But the story does not end there. Jerg Leufel managed to stage a comeback, marrying a widow in the village of Benningen in 1625[123] and mortgaging his half-house to the local parish church in order to raise cash.[124] Jerg's father, Johann Leufel, proved similarly resilient, lasting long enough on credit for a second son, Jacob, to come of age and borrowing further in order to more than double his gross wealth – including the acquisition of a second house! – by 1627.[125] In 1632, the father passed on the modest family property in Berg to Jacob Leufel,[126] thus finally realizing his ambition to establish two independent Leufel households in the monastery lands.[127]

Despite differences of detail, these various efforts to cope with the closure of the Ottobeuren villages share many common features, the most striking of which is the centrality of land and credit markets in the economies of the *Hofstatt* grantees. Careful examination of the repercussions of impartibility thus brings us to the second main feature of the late sixteenth-century transformation of inheritance practices at Ottobeuren: the transmission of property by sale rather than gift, and the division of the proceeds among the retiring parents and the "yielding" heirs, as they were called. The attendant consequences for the character of family relations will be discussed in the next chapter, but first, given all that has been shown in earlier chapters of the moneyless character of the late medieval peasant economy, the novelty of inheritance by sale deserves a more extended discussion.

The legal foundations of a specifically peasant land market (as opposed to the circulation of rent-yielding properties among lords)[128] at Ottobeuren were

---

[121] Ibid., ff. 162v [7 Jan. 1610], 189r [18 Mar. 1610], and 219v [2 Dec. 1610].

[122] StAA, KL Ottobeuren 102, f. 144v.

[123] Johann Leufel is not listed anywhere in the bond-chicken register for 1624 and first appears in Benningen in a register drawn up on 5 December 1625. StAA, KL Ottobeuren 491-III, Heft 30, f. 14r. That he married (rather than bought) into the village is indicated by the absence of a *Kaufbrief* in the notarial protocols (complete from July 1624 to October 1626) and the fact that he had a new wife by 1631.

[124] StAA, KL Ottobeuren 911, f. 157 [10 May 1631].

[125] StAA, KL Ottobeuren 104, f. 118v;, KL Ottobeuren 909, f. 180r [17 Sep. 1626].

[126] StAA, KL Ottobeuren 911, ff. 256–257 [23 July 1632].

[127] Jacob Leufel seems to have died in the plague of 1635; he is recorded as having borrowed 2 *viertel* of seed grain from the monastery in 1634, but is missing from a list of tithepayers in Berg drawn up in the following year. StAA, KL Ottobeuren 43, f. 86r and KL Ottobeuren 202, f. 97r. Johann probably suffered a similar fate; he is not mentioned after 1631 and his burial is not recorded in the Benningen parish register, which survives from 1637.

[128] There were of course a great many fourteenth-century sales at Ottobeuren of the following form: land held in "tenure of the monastery" (*Lehen des Gotteshaus*) and farmed by an (often named) undertenant is sold by a rent-collecting overtenant to a third party, usually a citizen of

laid in the mid-fifteenth century. From the 1440s onward, *Erblehen* charters issued by the monastery began to certify the tenant's right to sell the land, after it had first been offered to the lord, "to other people, whomsoever he may wish, according to his desire and need . . . entirely unimpeded and unbothered by the lord in any fashion or way."[129] An outgrowth of the overall enhancement of peasant property rights, this right of sale (*Kaufrecht*) had by the 1470s become a virtually universal feature of *Erblehen* charters.[130] This is not to say that peasants never bought or sold land before the later fifteenth century. Occasional sales of freehold properties crop up from fairly early on,[131] although the most common occasion for a freehold's appearance in the documentary record is its surrender to the monastery.[132] Not until the 1490s, however, is the charter evidence dense enough to allow us to speak of an actual market in peasant freehold and *Erblehen* properties, consisting mostly of small-scale transactions of a house or a few acres of land,[133] but also including the occasional *Hof* or mill.[134]

It was not a large market. Even after allowing for the imperfect survival of the archival evidence, a total of twenty charters of sale from the entire Ottobeuren lordship for the decade 1490–9 bespeaks a rather modest traffic. Furthermore, the market seems only rarely to have intruded into the practice of inheritance.[135] Of course, rarely does not mean never, and it should be emphasized that the buyout of other members of the kin group by the heir was not an "invention" of the late sixteenth century.[136] It was, rather, an eminently medieval technique

Memmingen or the Abbot of Ottobeuren himself. See for example StAA, KU Ottobeuren 97 [23 Jan. 1355], 104 [3 Feb. 1359], 107 [6 Dec. 1363], 109 [23 June 1365], and 111 [16 Oct. 1365].

129   *Erblehen* charter (1441) of Conrad Korber of Oberwolfertschwenden copied in StAA, KL Ottobeuren 18, ff. 212v–213r.

130   This chronology is suggested by the 150-odd *Erblehen* charters copied in StAA, KL Ottobeuren 18. Note the absence of any right of sale in *Erblehen* charters from 1413 (f. 200v), 1417 (ff. 105r–v), 1424 (205r–v), 1437 (149r–150r), 1440 (135r–v and 136r–v), 1441 (165r–v), and 1443 (44r–45r), and its presence in charters from 1438 (76v–77v), 1441 (75r–76r), 1454 (199r–200r), 1455 (100v–101r), 1462 (183r–184v), 1463 (159v–160v and 197r–198r), 1464 (214r–215v and 275v–276r), 1466 (221r–222v), 1468 (46v–48r and 49r–50r), and 1470 (130v–132v).

131   For example StAA, KU Ottobeuren 210 [6 June 1416]: an Ollarzried peasant sells his land to another peasant for £48.

132   Records of peasant sales of their land to the monastery include StAA, KU Ottobeuren 117 [27 Jan. 1372], 143 [24 Nov. 1403] (the sale explicitly declared to have been forced by debt), 165 [25 May 1405], and 219/1 [30 July 1420] (the land explicitly described as a freehold).

133   StAA, KU Ottobeuren 501 [25 Feb. 1491], 516 [7 Jan. 1492], 573 [9 Aug. 1495], 587 [30 Nov. 1496], 592 [13 June 1497] and 612 [20 Sep. 1498].

134   StAA, KU Ottobeuren 535 [13 Apr. 1493], 554 [23 May 1494], and 589 [Feb.–Mar. 1497].

135   Cases when a child stayed behind after the family moved out of the territory are naturally exceptions. See, for example, StAA, KU Ottobeuren 583 [6 Sep. 1493].

136   The oldest surviving example is an isolated charter dated 2 March 1450 from the hamlet of Eheim whereby Johann Körricher and his wife sold their inherited share of his father's *Hof* to his brother and brother-in-law (who presumably divided the land) for £60. StAA, Kloster Ottobeuren, Neuburger Urkundensammlung, Ungeordnete Einzelstücke.

relegated to a minor role by the abundance of land and ease of partibility. Thus, for example, when the widow Ursula Winnenberger of Wolfarts divided her late husband's lands in 1504, she did have a charter drawn up and sealed by the monastery to certify the sale of one fourth of the property to her son-in-law Veit Zedtler for £95. Her two sons, Thoma and Vallentein, by contrast, received their shares without any such formality; that the land was transferred to them at all was only later recorded when the brothers traded it to the monastery in exchange for property in the hamlet of Leupolz.[137] Equally noteworthy, especially in light of subsequent developments, is the fact that the few early instances of inheritance by sale were transacted almost exclusively among siblings. The traditional insistence on the nuclear household made it extremely unusual for an heir to buy out a (still living) father or father-in-law. Even the single surviving early sixteenth-century example stipulates that the son was to be admitted to actual tenancy only after his father's death.[138]

As a result of the shift to impartibility, inheritance at Ottobeuren over the course of the later sixteenth century came increasingly to be mediated by cash. It is difficult to get a sense of the absolute number or overall monetary value of such transactions. Because they pertained to agreements between the buyer and seller and did not detail the obligations of tenure, deeds of sale (*Kaufbriefe*) were less assiduously preserved in the monastery's archive than the charters of tenancy (*Lehensreverse*). Since the latter documents do, however, identify those new tenants who purchased the land from the previous one, it is still possible to demonstrate at least the rising relative frequency of inheritance through sale, especially from the 1560s (see Figure 4.1).

At this same time resistance to the extended household also began to ebb, as the pressures that had led to impartibility now began to compel the stacking of multiple generations in the same household. In 1547, for example, Veit Maier senior of Unterwesterheim sold his *Erblehen Hof* and half of his moveable property (i.e. livestock, tools and equipment, and household goods) to his son Enderlin for 420 fl. In a clear sign that he nevertheless intended to continue to work and reside on the farm, the father retained both the other half of the moveables and half-use rights to the land for the term of his life.[139] In his own

---

[137] StAA, KU Ottobeuren 684 [27 Mar. 1504] and KU Ottobeuren 971 [16 June 1524]. Similarly KU Ottobeuren 671 [5 Apr. 1503], which details the history of the *Hof* of Johann Merz of Günz. He was admitted to the property on 18 January 1468 (KU Ottobeuren 303a), on 21 March 1499 (KU Ottobeuren 616a) his two married daughters sold their shares of the property for £60 to his two sons, who had assumed their own shares without any payment, and only in 1503 did one of the brothers sell out his half to the other for £63.

[138] StAA, KU Ottobeuren 920 [26 Nov. 1520]. There is also an example from the village of Egg of a wealthy *Bauer* yielding the *Hof* to his son-in-law in exchange for an annual delivery of grain, pork, and flax, but the charter also requires the new tenant to provide a house for the previous tenant outside of the *Hof*. KU Ottobeuren 973 [16 Aug. 1524].

[139] StAA, KU Ottobeuren 1300 [23 May 1547]. The earliest surviving *Hof* sale of this sort is KU Ottobeuren 1240 [12 Feb. 1542], according to which Johann Biler and his wife, Barbara

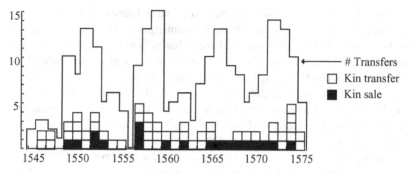

Figure 4.1 Transfer and sale in the Ottobeuren *Lehensreverse* 1545–75
Sources: StAA, KU Ottobeuren 1275–1856

day, Enderlin Maier was still somewhat unusual in buying out his living father, but after 1565 father to son or son-in-law transfers became the most common form of inheritance by sale recorded in the tenancy charters.[140] A similar shift took place on the monastery's big *Gotteshausrecht* farms, where, as has been seen, the formal rule of life-term tenancy only had long since been replaced by a *de facto* heritability of the *Höfe*. More systematic recording of *Gotteshausrecht* transfers allows a clearer chronology of the rise of "retirement" among the *Hof*-tenants; of those *Bauern* who were succeeded by their own kin, the proportion who handed over the land in their own lifetimes rather than remaining in tenancy until death rose from less than a fifth in the 1570s to well over half by the 1610s (see Figure 4.2).

Although inheritance through sale resolved the tension between the demands of impartibility and equity, there remained the question of where the money would come from. If the heir were buying out only a single sibling, it might be possible to scrape together the cash to cover the claim, but as heirs were increasingly called upon to compensate all of their siblings and their parents as well, long-term debt became an additional characteristic fixture of peasant inheritance. As with impartibility and sale, it is both difficult to say exactly when this happened, and equally clear that the last third of the sixteenth century was the decisive interval. The first intimation of a "financing" agreement dates from

Vorger, of Schachen sold half of their land and moveable property to their son-in-law, Jos Epplin, for £380. This case is discussed in more detail above in chapter 2, p. 80. See also KU Ottobeuren 1281 [24 Oct. 1545]: Silvester Geromüller and his wife, Ursula of Waldmühle, sell their *Erblehen* mill and fishpond to their son Steffan for £800. Although here the parents also retained half-use rights to the property for both of their lifetimes, they chose not to work it directly, and instead, in a transaction separate from the sale itself, leased this right to their son for an annual payment of £20.

[140] Although it must be conceded that the numbers involved are not large. Father to son or son-in-law transfers made up three of the ten kin sales recorded 1545–64, and seven of the nine recorded 1565–75. Figure 4.2, by contrast, is based on 261 kin transfers recorded 1560–1621.

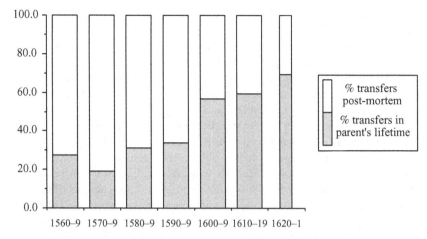

Figure 4.2 Timing of kin transfers of *Gotteshausrecht* land, 1560–1621
Sources: StAA, KL Ottobeuren 27, 903–8

1566, when Jerg Helzlin and his sisters Elisabeth and Catharina bought out their stepfather, Peter Leuprecht, in the hamlet of Hofs. The children agreed on a sale price of £527 10 ß, and after the sisters elected not to assume tenancy (the charter gives no indication of what other plans, if any, they had),[141] Jerg gave his stepfather a cash deposit of £100 and a promise of lifetime maintenance.[142] The implicit and informal debt arrangement seems to have worked well enough for Jerg (he farmed the land for almost thirty years before passing it on to his daughter and son-in-law),[143] but in time inheritance financing became not only more common, but also more formal and more complex, even among Jerg Helzlin's own descendants.[144]

Charter evidence of this new complexity first appears in the 1580s, and takes the form of separate deeds of sale and mortgage among the relations. The arrangements of the Maier family of Unterwesterheim are a good example. In 1584, Catharina Schellang, the widow of Johann Maier, sold her *Erblehen Hof* and half of her moveable property to her son Jerg for the staggering sum of 1,350 fl. Jerg and his wife, Agatha Maier, somehow came up with 550 fl. (much of it came from Agatha's dowry), but drew up a mortgage to acknowledge

---

[141] Although other records indicate that Catharina married one Hans Hemmerle, also of Hofs. StAA, KL Ottobeuren 904, f. 11r [22 Nov. 1607]. A 1565 record of Hemmerle's ownership of horses suggests that he was a comfortable farmer. KL Ottobeuren 688-I, Heft 3, f. 15r.

[142] StAA, KU Ottobeuren, Neuburger Urkundensammlung G171 [21 June 1566]; Dertsch, "Das Einwohnerbuch des Ottobeurer Klosterstaats 1564," p. 19.

[143] StAA, KL Ottobeuren 31, f. 69r; KL Ottobeuren 491-I, Heft 3, f. 4v, Heft 5, f. 6r, and Heft 6, ff. 5r–v; KL Ottobeuren 583, Heft 6, f. 11r; KL Ottobeuren 903, ff. 241r–v [24 June 1606].

[144] StAA, KL Ottobeuren 904, ff. 242r–v and 242v [5 Apr. 1611]; KL Ottobeuren 905, f. 224v [18 Dec. 1614]; KL Ottobeuren 102, f. 54v.

the outstanding debt to Jerg's mother and three other brothers, and stipulating repayment at specific intervals.[145]

Similar debt relations could even be insinuated into the transfer of *Gotteshausrecht* land, which the peasants technically had no legal right to inherit or sell, but whose tenure, the monastery was grudgingly forced to concede, was a genuine and valuable species of property.[146] Thus in 1586, Jerg Weiss of Frechenrieden sold his "moveables" at a hugely inflated price to his stepson Martin Hering as a cover for the transfer of the village tavern and a *Gotteshausrecht Hof* of 29 *jauchert* and 17 *tagwerk*. Martin and his wife, Catharina Dellenmaier, acknowledged a debt of 850 fl., and promised scheduled repayments to their parents and to Martin's sister Anna.[147] Even for an innkeeper with extensive lands, however, 850 *gulden* was an enormous amount of money, and Martin and his wife were soon scrambling to make payments. They borrowed 100 *gulden* from the guardians of a wealthy orphan in 1587 and another hundred from the parish priest in 1588, mortgaging arable, meadow, and garden land outside the *Hof* to do so.[148] It still wasn't enough, and when Martin died in 1592, the guardians of his own orphans were forced to sell the "moveables" at a reduced rate in order to induce Martin's brother Michael Hering to give up his own, larger *Hof* in the nearby village of Attenhausen and come home to salvage the family's fortune.[149]

Unfortunately, Michael's efforts were no more successful than his brother's had been, and he was rapidly overwhelmed. In 1599 he lost the *Hof* and the tavern.[150] Michael did manage to emerge from this debacle with the purchase of a stately and status-preserving house,[151] but the lack of any agricultural land drove him into a debilitating pattern of consumption borrowing, which eventually took its own toll. He was dropped into the *Seldner* class by the

---

[145] StAA, KU Ottobeuren 1975 and 1975/1 [29 June 1584]; KL Ottobeuren 744b.

[146] No acknowledgment was ever formally made, of course, but the concession is already implicit in a number of early sixteenth-century charters. Thus, in 1518 Sebastian Korber was admitted to a small *Gotteshausrecht* property in the village of Benningen which had previously been held by Hans Gütler. There is a separate charter explicitly documenting the sale of the property to Korber and the waiving of any further right to it by Gütler. StAA, KU Ottobeuren 875 and 876 [7 Jan. 1518]; KU Ottobeuren 918 [27 Aug. 1520]; and KL Ottobeuren 29, f. 34v.

[147] The *Kaufbrief* itself has not survived, but the *Schuldbrief* (mortgage) may be found in StAA, KU Ottobeuren 1987 [4 May 1587]. See also KL Ottobeuren 27, ff. 105v–106r [12 July 1566] and 110r [3 Dec. 1587]; KL Ottobeuren 601-II, f. 141r.

[148] StAA, KU Ottobeuren 2000 [16 June 1587] and 2020 [9 Oct. 1588].

[149] StAA, KU Ottobeuren 2072 [20 Jan. 1593]; KL Ottobeuren 27, ff. 131r [13 Feb. 1587], 132v [22 Jan. 1593], and 111v [5 Mar. 1593]. The monastery reduced Michael's entry fine for the Frechenrieden property "since he . . . gave up his *Hof* in Attenhausen and has assumed all of the debts [of his brother]."

[150] StAA, KL Ottobeuren 27, f. 113r [4 Nov. 1599].

[151] StAA, KL Ottobeuren 903, f. 252r [17 Aug. 1606]. Michael was continually listed as a *Bauer* in the bond-chicken registers between 1595 and 1609. KL Ottobeuren 491-I, Heft 6, f. 7r; ibid., Heft 10, f. 9r and Heft 14, f. 8r.

village assessors in 1613, and two years later was forced to move into humbler quarters.[152] His brother's son, whose savior he was to have been, packed up and left the Ottobeuren lands.[153] Michael eventually checked his own slide in 1619 with the purchase of 2 *jauchert* of land, and one year later a tax survey reveals that he now also had a small sum (14 *gulden*) of cash on hand.[154] But even this modest recovery proved ephemeral. Hering was ruined in the hyperinflation of 1623–4, and as an old man in his sixties he was forced on to the roads in search of work. He left Frechenrieden for Austria in 1623 and never returned.[155]

That the purchase and financing of inheritances was a challenging business where a misstep could spell disaster is only the most obvious lesson of the misadventures of the Hering brothers. One wonders how Michael would have fared had he remained on his own lands in Attenhausen, and one presumes that the same thought must also have occurred to him, perhaps in the very tavern that had once been his. Rather more important (if less melodramatic), however, is the observation that the "business" of inheritance, whether successfully or unsuccessfully pursued, was intimately linked with wider markets for land and credit outside the boundaries of the kin group. This mutuality between the commercialization of inheritance and the overall pace of buying and borrowing in rural society deserves particular emphasis, not least because both phenomena intensified decisively at Ottobeuren in the last third of the sixteenth century.

The most straightforward evidence for a surge in the activity of the land market comes from the monastery's receipts of *Vergunstgeld*, a levy on sales of *Erblehen* land fixed at 2.5 percent of the price of the property transacted. Even after adjusting for inflation, these receipts rose almost four-fold between 1528 and 1586 followed by an even sharper six-fold increase between 1586 and 1620.[156] Credit markets followed a similar course, and if the evidence – the account books of rural chapels and parish churches – is indirect, it is no less unequivocal.

---

[152] StAA, KL Ottobeuren 904, ff. 65v [10 July 1608] and 227r [3 Feb. 1611]; KL Ottobeuren 905, ff. 108r [16 June 1613], 280r–v [25 June 1615], and 331v [6 Feb. 1616]; and KL 907, f. 103r [13 July 1617]. That these were consumption loans is suggested by their small size (all under 20 fl.) and the fact that Hering never bought any land with the money; the lack of agricultural land is further underscored by what he mortgaged for these payments: his house (1608, 1616, 1617), his garden (1611), "everything" (1613), but never any land, the preferred security. For Hering's reclassification as a *Seldner* see KL Ottobeuren 491-II, Heft 16, f. 9v and Heft 21, f. 15r.

[153] StAA, KL Ottobeuren 905, ff. 185r, 185v [5 June 1614].

[154] StAA, KL Ottobeuren 908, ff. 20v–21r [21 Aug. 1619]. KL Ottobeuren 102, f. 370r. The tax survey and complete run of notarial protocols for 1603–21 indicate that Michael was landless by 1603, and probably by 1599.

[155] Dertsch, "Das Einwohnerbuch des Ottobeurer Klosterstaats 1564," p. 60. StAA, KL Ottobeuren 491-II, Heft 26, f. 11v and Heft 27, f. 8r–v.

[156] StAA, KL Ottobeuren 541, Hefte 1 and 7; KL Ottobeuren 550; KL Ottobeuren 583, Heft 4a; StadtA MM Folioband 99, D 102/1a–1b.

Since the thirteenth century canon law had permitted a form of agricultural credit known as the *census*. In theory the debtor sold the creditor an annual share (*census*) of the produce from a particular piece of land in exchange for a sum of money twenty times the value of the *census* payment. Thus conceived, the *census* did not contravene the canon law prohibition on loaning money at interest, particularly since the debtor could not be obliged to repay the principal. In practice the *census* was virtually indistinguishable from a loan at 5 percent interest secured by the piece of land in question. The *census* payment was made in cash, not in produce, and if the debtor defaulted on the payments the creditor was entitled to seize the land in compensation.

For parish churches and rural chapels, for urban hospitals and leprosaria, the *census*, or *Zins* in German, was an ideal source of income. The proceeds of rents and tithes could be loaned out to local peasants whose *Zins* payments then constituted a regular stream of cash. In time the *Zins* became so widespread in Germany that it was referred to by Italians as the "German contract."[157] In the Ottobeuren lands, most parish churches had taken on the supplementary role of lending institution no later than the middle of the sixteenth century. Not only does *Zins* income figure in all surviving parish account books from this period, including those of Benningen (1549), Günz (1549), Frechenrieden (1550), Hawangen (1551), Altisried (1553), and Niederdorf (1566),[158] but most of them registered substantial increases in lending during the later sixteenth century.[159] Still more important than the parish churches in terms of scale were two independent chapels: St. Niklas in the market town of Ottobeuren and Our Blessed Lady in Eldern. The account books of St. Niklas survive from 1539 and those of Our Blessed Lady from 1526 (see Figure 4.3), and both pinpoint a prodigious increase in peasant borrowing from the last third of the sixteenth century.

Who were these debtors? The social context of peasant borrowing is illustrated in Figure 4.4, which for the account year 1586/7 plots the wealth of seventy-nine chapel debtors in the hamlets of Ottobeuren and Böhen parish and a further fifty-seven debtors in the market town of Ottobeuren. The overall populations of the hamlets and the market have been divided into five equal quintiles on the basis of a 1584 tithe register and a 1585 tax roll respectively, and the debtors of St. Niklas and Our Blessed Lady have then been apportioned among

---

[157] John Thomas Noonan, *The Scholastic Analysis of Usury* (Cambridge MA, 1957), pp. 230–48.

[158] In addition to the manuscripts cited in note 159, see StAA, KA Ottobeuren 17 and KL Ottobeuren 625-I (Benningen), KL Ottobeuren 657, Hefte 1–2 (Günz), and KL Ottobeuren 619, I–II (Altisried).

[159] Significant increases in total loaned capital included 40.5 percent at the parish church of Niederdorf (1566–99), 211.5 percent at the chapel of St. Marx in Stephansried (1548–92), 340.3 percent at the parish church of Hawangen (1553–97), and 1570.4 percent at the parish church of Frechenrieden (1558–93). StAA, KA Ottobeuren 240, KL Ottobeuren 735, KA Ottobeuren 189, KL Ottobeuren 744a, and KL Ottobeuren 654.

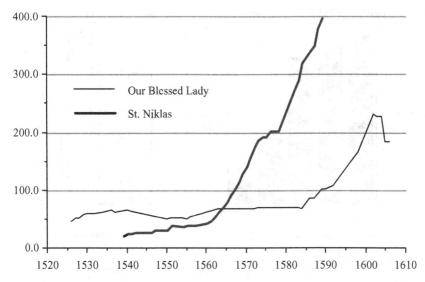

Figure 4.3 Annual interest receipts in *Pfund Heller* of the chapels of St. Niklas and Our Blessed Lady, 1526–1606
Sources: StAA, KL Ottobeuren 636 I-II; KA Ottobeuren 274

these quintiles. A given wealth cohort is thus over- (or under-)represented if it makes up more (or less) than 20 percent of the total number of debtors. The clear implication of this rather tedious exercise is that credit not only underwent a quantitative increase, but was also available to even the poorest elements of rural society.

The richest evidence for a quickening of land and credit markets at Otto-beuren is the appearance of a new kind of register among the masses of records generated by the monastic chancellery: the *Briefprotokolle*, or notarial proto-cols, which survive in fragmentary form from 1579 and more or less contin-uously from 1603.[160] The *Briefprotokolle* were a centralized register – and in this respect they differed from the Mediterranean tradition of private notaries – of notarial acts. Their contents were dominated by the sale of land and the borrowing of money, but also included marriage contracts, acknowledgments of payment, and certificates of apprenticeship, legal freedom, and legitimate birth. Major transactions, such as the leasing of large farms, had of course been recorded by sealed charter since the fifteenth century. But that it was now also deemed necessary to begin systematically registering all but the most minor of peasant financial transactions similarly implies that rather more such transac-tions were taking place.

---

[160] StAA, KL Ottobeuren 918 (*Briefprotokolle* for 1576–80), 901 (1583–4), 903 (1603–7), 904 (1607–12), 905 (1612–16), 907 (1616–19), 908 (1619–21), 909 (1624–6), and 911 (1630–42).

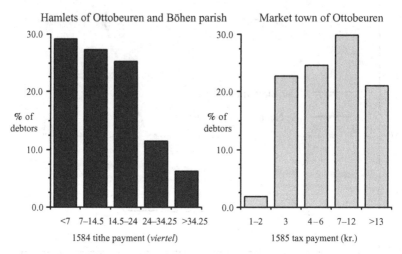

Figure 4.4   Social distribution of the debtors of St. Niklas and Our Blessed Lady, 1586/7
Sources: StAA, KL Ottobeuren 31, 491-I, Heft 4, 636-I, 686a; KA Ottobeuren 274

Crucially, the advent of the notarial protocol at the end of the sixteenth century[161] was a regional phenomenon by no means confined to Ottobeuren. As long ago as 1973, Hans-Martin Maurer drew attention to the fact that monastic lordships all over Upper Swabia began keeping *Briefprotokolle* (also known as *Amtsprotokolle* or *Verhörprotokolle*) after the mid-sixteenth-century. They appear in the monasteries of Weingarten (1551), Rot an der Rot (1553), Ochsenhausen (1554), Buchau (1565), Schussenried (1566), Heggbach (1573), Weißenau (1578), and Marchtal (1598), to name only the earliest.[162] Maurer's investigations were confined to the Württemberg, or western half of Upper

[161] Note that registering the comings and goings of land and money was certainly not a new technology in this period. The Lower Hospital in Memmingen kept records of this sort as early as the 1460s, the Fugger zu Babenhausen kept them for their lands in Biberach-Wellenburg from 1514, and yet it is a rare Swabian territory where protocols appear before 1560. In most they survive only from the seventeenth century. Lambacher, *Spital der Reichsstadt Memmingen*, p. 150; Heribert Sturm, ed. "Staatsarchiv Neuburg an der Donau," *Bayerische Archivinventare*, Heft 1 (Munich, 1952).

[162] Hans-Martin Maurer, "Die Ausbildung der Territorialgewalt oberschwäbischer Klöster vom 14. bis zum 17. Jahrhundert," *Blätter für deutsche Landesgeschichte* N. F. 109 (1973), pp. 151–95, at pp. 179–80. A helpful discussion of the content of these protocols may be found in Walther Vock, "Der Wert der Fürstlich-Kemptischen Hofratsprotokolle für den Heimatforscher," *Schwäbische Blätter* 1, 1 (1950), pp. 3–11. Rudolf Schlögl and his students have recently made extensive use of seventeenth-century Bavarian protocols. See (in addition to Schlögl's *Bauern, Krieg und Staat*) Rudolf Schlögl, "Zwischen Krieg und Krise: Situation und Entwicklung der bayerischen Bauernwirtschaft im 17. Jahrhundert," *Zeitschrift für Agrargeschichte und Agrarsoziologie* 40, 2 (1992), pp. 133–67. Also Elisabeth Schepers, "Bäuerliche Wirtschaften im Dreißigjährigen Krieg: Schrobenhausen zwischen 1600 und 1700," *Materialien zur Geschichte des Bayerischen Schwaben* 16 (1992).

Swabia, but his finding is equally true in the Bavarian, or eastern half of the region. *Amtsprotokolle* show up both in monastic territories, including Roggenburg (1554), Edelstetten (1579), Kaisheim (Tapfheim) (1572), Buxheim (1586), St. Moritz-Augsburg (1590), and Heilig Kreuz-Donauwörth (1599), as well as in secular territories, such as the lands of the Schertel von Binswangen (1575), the von Langenmantel (Ottmarshausen) (1580), the Fugger zu Babenhausen-Boos (Heimertingen) (1590), and the Fugger zu Glött (Oberndorf and Ellgau) (1597).[163]

Maurer saw the appearance of the *Briefprotokolle* as a sign of the growing centralization and sophistication of monastic lordship, and this is certainly an important part of the explanation. As was seen in chapter 3, the collection of ever more extensive and detailed information on the subject population was a hallmark of late sixteenth-century lordship at Ottobeuren and elsewhere. It is not clear, however, that notarial protocols were at all necessary for this intensification of lordship. The increased scrutiny of the legal status of individual peasants was maintained through a series of documents (serf rolls, bond-chicken registers, death duty and exogamous marriage fee accounts, etc.) completely separate from the protocols. And as for the monastery's main sources of revenue, they were already being recorded in their own classes of documents long before the introduction of the protocols in 1579: grain rents in rent rolls (from 1544), entry fines on *Gotteshausrecht* land in so-called *Erdschatz* registers (from 1530), tithe receipts in a series of *Zehentregister* (from 1518), and entry fines from *Freilehen* land in *Lehenbücher* (from 1508).

The very triviality of so many of the recorded transactions further belies the suggestion that the protocols were merely an instrument of centralized lordship. Why should the Abbot care about the sale of six cherry trees (4 *gulden*) or the right to draw water from a well (11 *gulden*)?[164] About the receipts of 20 *gulden* for the purchase of two cows, 9 *gulden* inherited from a deceased brother, or 1.6 *gulden* for the purchase of a horse?[165] When Caspar Dietrich of Hawangen mortgaged his two cows in exchange for 10 *gulden*, when the saddler Michael Lang of Ottobeuren needed a guarantor for a 9 *gulden* loan, when Michael Vetter of Waldmühle borrowed 7 *gulden* from a neighbor's orphans,[166] it is hard to see how it was even worth the monastery's effort to register the loan . . . and yet over

---

[163] Selected from the inventory in Sturm, ed. "Staatsarchiv Neuburg an der Donau." Note that these holdings are now in the Staatsarchiv Augsburg.

[164] Respectively StAA, KL Ottobeuren 905, f. 237r; *Kaufbrief* [5 Feb. 1615] and KL Ottobeuren 904, f. 159v; *Kaufbrief* [28 Nov. 1609]. See also the sale of a well for 8 fl. (KL Ottobeuren 903, f. 249v; *Kaufbrief* [3 Aug. 1606] and the sale for 2 fl. of transit rights through a field over a path measuring six feet wide (KL Ottobeuren 904, f. 143r; *Kaufbrief* [31 July 1609]).

[165] Respectively StAA, KL Ottobeuren 905, f. 159v [11 Feb. 1614], KL Ottobeuren 903, ff. 139r [3 Feb. 1605], and 120[a]v [24 Oct. 1604].

[166] Respectively StAA, KL Ottobeuren 904, ff. 276v [9 Feb. 1612], 237v [20 Mar. 1611], and 72r [11 Sep. 1608]. The 10 *gulden* loan, especially by rural chapels and parish churches, was not at all uncommon in this period. There are more than a dozen such *Zinsbriefe* registered in StAA, KL Ottobeuren 903 alone.

6,300 notarial acts were registered at Ottobeuren between 1603 and 1621 alone. Why bother? Because the peasants who transacted these agreements wanted the additional security.

Of course, in terms of their actual content most protocol entries were no different from the sealed parchment charters which the monastery had been issuing for centuries. With the rapid multiplication of the number of notarial acts, however, the susceptibility of individual charters to loss, destruction, or fraud[167] seems to have been felt more keenly, and as soon as the protocols were established the peasants themselves began bringing in old documents to be copied into the register.[168] Heinrich Moser of Oberwesterheim, for example, purchased his father[169] Jerg's freehold lands for 800 fl. in 1568, but one year later the documents were burned in a fire. Heinrich himself died in 1574, leaving his widow, Catharina Allgäuer,[170] to manage these and other properties until their children came of age.[171] By 1583 an heir was finally ready to marry and take over the reins,[172] but in order to secure the son's claim to the land against any future accidents, all of his father's old transactions were carefully re-entered in the notarial protocol.[173] It was a sensible precaution for a valuable asset; by the time Heinrich's grandchildren sold the property in 1609, it was worth two and a half times what he had originally paid for it.[174]

The protocols had thus become a kind of public necessity at Ottobeuren as rural society grew increasingly dependent on the burgeoning traffic in parcels of land and fistfuls of coins. But if the monastery ultimately became the

---

[167] See the prosecution of the miller Jörg Haberbosch of Frechenrieden for deceiving a scribe into inserting an overly generous demarcation of Haberbosch's recently purchased property into the charter of sale. StAA, KL Ottobeuren 4, Document 301G, ff. 821v–3v [19 Jan. 1532]. The falsification of documents was a very serious offense at Ottobeuren; Niclaus Hackh of Schoren was fined £14 in 1566 for falsely accusing village and monastery officials of so doing. KL Ottobeuren 587-I, Heft 3.

[168] As might be expected, this pattern is most apparent in the earliest protocol volumes. Thus, although StAA, KL Ottobeuren 918 has been labeled "*Briefprotokolle* 1576–80," careful inspection reveals that the volume was drawn up as a running record only in December of 1579. It does contain entries from 1578 (ff. 24r, 64r), 1577 (f. 7r), 1576 (f. 64r), and even 1568 (f. 60r), but these are clearly retroactive additions.

[169] StAA, KL Ottobeuren 600, f. 211v.

[170] Dertsch, "Das Einwohnerbuch des Ottobeurer Klosterstaats 1564," p. 66

[171] Heinrich Moser was also the tenant of a large (69 *jauchert*) *Hof* held in life-term tenancy from the Lower Hospital of Memmingen. This *Hof*, which had been held by members of the Moser family since at least 1490, passed at Heinrich's death to his widow and sometime thereafter to his son Balthas. StAA, KA Ottobeuren 344.

[172] StAA, KL Ottobeuren 491-I, Heft 4, f. 18v; KL Ottobeuren 901, f. 126v [13 Aug. 1584]; KL Ottobeuren 903, f. 256r [17 Sep. 1606].

[173] StAA, KL Ottobeuren 901, ff. 20r–v, 21r, and 21r; three *Kaufbriefe*, dated 6 June 1568, inexplicably corrected to 1572, with the marginal comments "No[ta]: uf Hainrichen Mosern zestöllen, allain anzumelden, das die [alten] brief verbrunen [und] ainen and. n. vörtigt brieve [ist] zuverfertig" and "No[ta]: d. alt brief ist bey 14 Jaren verbrünen und Hainrich Moser vor 9 Jaren gestorben." These entries are preceded and followed by others from March of 1583.

[174] StAA, KL Ottobeuren 904, ff. 150[a]r–v [21 Oct. 1609]; KA Ottobeuren 344; Westerheim Parish Register [hereinafter WestPR], Vol. I, pp. 111, 113, 180.

registrar of all this activity, it did so quite reluctanctly. For all its medieval antecedents, the new economy of the late sixteenth century radically altered the rules of peasant life. Only after trying (and failing) to obstruct this transformation did the Abbot resign himself to it, and nowhere was the reality of and resistance to change more strikingly evidenced than in the area of rural credit.

That the monastery's subjects should borrow money was itself no innovation, and cash-strapped Ottobeuren peasants were resorting to lenders in the nearby city of Memmingen as early as 1369.[175] Indeed, by the time charter evidence of peasant borrowing becomes a little more continuous in the 1490s, the Abbot of Ottobeuren was himself the most frequent source of credit.[176] The characteristic structure of the early modern Swabian borrowing agreement – a cash loan at a fixed interest rate of 5 percent and guaranteed by real estate – was also firmly established by the end of the fifteenth century, if not before. Nevertheless, not only did the number of loans remain fairly small, but as noted above, the creditor was generally prohibited from demanding redemption. Most late medieval lending at Ottobeuren was thus a form of permanent investment; the creditor was primarily concerned with regular interest payments and did not expect repayment of the principal.[177]

Despite these limitations, there remained the danger that a peasant would overburden himself with debt, and if financial embarrassment ballooned into bankruptcy, the turmoil might be considerable. Anthoni Teufel of Unterwesterheim, for example, borrowed 30 *gulden* from a Memmingen convent in 1503 in exchange for an annual delivery of 12 *viertel* of rye.[178] For many years Anthoni's extensive *Erblehen* lands supported this interest payment, but the sale of the property to his son Enderas for 114 *gulden* in 1520 (a sale which, as

---

[175] As part of a lawsuit filed in the aftermath of the Thirty Years War, the city of Memmingen drew up a list of the debts incurred by Ottobeuren peasants to a series of urban charitable foundations. The two oldest dated *Zinsbriefe* were from 1369 and 1468, followed by three in the decade 1490–9, eight in 1500–9, and nine in 1510–19. Thereafter peasant urban borrowing began to decline, with four *Zinsbriefe* in the 1520s, three in each of the 1530s and 1540s, and one in the 1550s. StAA, KL Ottobeuren (Mü.B.) 225 [7 June 1655].

[176] There are nineteen loans by the Abbot to his own peasants between April 1491 and March 1505 in StAA, KU Ottobeuren 507–698. Other lenders included burghers of Memmingen (KU 536 [15 Apr. 1493] and 667 [4 Mar. 1503]), Kempten (KU 505 [13 Apr. 1491]), and Ottobeuren (KU 483 [6 Feb. 1490] and 584 [7 Sep. 1496]), the Ottobeuren parish church (KU 629 [25 June 1500]), the chapel of Our Lady in Eldern (KU 646 [28 May 1501]), and the Memmingen Hospital (KU 623 [17 Dec. 1499]).

[177] In addition to the fact that the peasantry simply didn't have much spare cash, these features of the borrowing agreement help to explain the prominence of charitable and ecclesiastical foundations as lenders to the peasantry. There are no peasant lenders in the chartered *Zinsbriefe* and *Schuldbriefe* for 1490–1505, and the list of creditors who laid claim to the property of the deceased Johann Aberöll of Betzisried in 1496 is exclusively composed of institutional lenders. StAA, KU Ottobeuren 576 [15 Apr. 1496].

[178] StAA, KU Ottobeuren 667 [4 Mar. 1503]. Anthoni Teufel first appears in the archival record as a participant at a court ruling on 22 November 1490. KU Ottobeuren 492.

has been seen, the monastery sought to obstruct)[179] seems to have overtaxed the household. By 1527 Anthoni and Enderas were embroiled in a lawsuit with the convent over non-payment of interest,[180] and by 1528 father and son had been driven into bankruptcy. Enderas took the ensuing losses very hard – the family had formerly belonged to the upper echelon of the village[181] – and his threatening utterances soon landed him in prison. Seeking to minimize the damage, the monastery released him in exchange for the revealing promise that

> for the rest of my life I will say nothing to suggest that I intend to assume, own, or procure those lands which my father and I forfeited in right and law in a public foreclosure, but will completely and utterly cede and renounce them, and will in no way seek to prevent anyone from buying, selling or renting them out. Rather, I shall await payment by the lordship to me or my father if any money is left after the debts have been cleared.[182]

Having descended into a morass of debt, however, Enderas found himself unable to get out. By the next year he was back in prison, charged with trying to sell off his remaining lands while fraudulently concealing the extent to which they were already encumbered. At the pleas of his friends and pregnant wife, "and in recognition of his poverty and misery," Enderas was again released, but by now the authorities had decided that the family was hopeless and banished them all from the Ottobeuren lands.[183]

Enderas Teufel's was a relatively private tragedy, but by mid-century foreclosure proceedings were becoming more publicly disruptive. Debtors summoned before the bankruptcy courts refused to answer questions about their finances, "contemptuously and abusively slandered" the officers of the court, and threatened them with violence.[184] On occasion the anger escalated to a truly dangerous pitch, at least in the nervous eyes of the monastery's officials. Johann Notz of Wolfertschwenden was a locksmith of modest means[185] with a gambling habit. These traits got him into fights (and prison) during his lifetime[186] and left him heavily indebted at its end. When he died in 1568, the village officials

---

[179] StAA, KU Ottobeuren 920 [26 Nov. 1520]. See above, p. 175.

[180] StAA, KU Ottobeuren 1002 [18 Apr. 1527]. Strictly speaking the Teufels' legal quarrel was with the urban charitable foundation which had assumed the convent's property in the wake of the Reformation in Memmingen.

[181] StAA, KL Ottobeuren 541 (3), ff. 23r–24r.

[182] StAA, KL Ottobeuren 4, Document 306B, ff. 1004v–1007r (10 Mar. 1528).

[183] Ibid., Document 306C, ff. 1007r–1010v [5 May 1529].

[184] Ibid., Document 291DD, ff. 523r–525r [4 Sep. 1545]; Document 293A, ff. 606r–610v [9 June 1542]; and Document 293F, ff. 621r–627v [20 May 1549]; quotation from Document 293A.

[185] StAA, KL Ottobeuren 64, ff. 29v–32r.

[186] StAA, KL Ottobeuren 4, Document 298D, ff. 763r–766r [20 Mar. 1549]. Notz was obliged to promise never again to gamble in or even enter a tavern, "unless I should be invited or called by my relations to a wedding, in which case I shall have the right to partake in the wedding meal, but as soon as it [the meal] is finished, I shall return to house arrest and thereafter shall drink no more."

accordingly convened a hearing to liquidate the estate and pay off his creditors, but any hopes of an orderly financial resolution were soon dashed by Notz's son-in-law Michael Beppel. Beppel had inherited a great many of the locksmith's debts, and felt entitled to his father-in-law's tools in compensation. The court demurred, and ordered that the tools be handed over with only a vague promise of some money "if it is possible to sell the tools." Furious, Beppel not only threatened the officers of the court but also garnered enough support from "other malicious subjects" to be charged with inciting a "rebellious uprising."[187]

Michael Beppel was of course clapped into prison at once, and upon release resumed the role of a poor[188] but law-abiding subject (and orderly debtor!),[189] his family quietly fading out of the village over the next thirty years.[190] Nevertheless, successful containment of the outbursts of disgruntled individuals did not mean that the broader dislocation produced by the increase in peasant borrowing could be ignored. However paternalistic it may have been, the monastery's concern for the welfare of its subjects was also genuine, and the Abbot's correction of peasants deemed guilty of "bad householding and the keeping of evil company" or the "excessive and unnecessary waste of the greater part of . . . [their] goods and chattels"[191] should not be written off as a mere preoccupation with rents and incomes. There was, moreover, a further repercussion of peasant indebtedness that proved at least as worrisome to the monastery as the feared ruin of its subjects: the intrusion of the jurisdiction of external authorities at the behest of creditors living outside the Ottobeuren lands. These interventions were inevitable, of course, as credit relations spilled over the traditional boundaries of the medieval economy. As far as the monks were concerned, however, any effort by a "foreign court" to dispose of the property of their peasants was a threat to the monastery's autonomy. To protect both their subjects and their sovereignty, therefore, the monks resolved to seal off their territory from alien sources of credit, and the easiest targets of this effort were the Jews.

Though small in numbers, Jewish communities were widely distributed in early modern rural Swabia.[192] At Ottobeuren Jews were familiar enough figures

---

[187] Ibid., Document 298G, ff. 768v–771r [15 Dec. 1568].

[188] StAA, KL Ottobeuren 491-I, Heft 4, f. 21v.

[189] StAA, KL Ottobeuren 918, f. 3v [8 Jan. 1580]; KA Ottobeuren 274, Hefte 39 (1589/90), 33 (1590/1), and 40 (1590/1).

[190] StAA, KL Ottobeuren 491-I, Heft 6, f. 17v; KL Ottobeuren 491-II, Heft 10, ff. 13v–14r; KL Ottobeuren 583, Heft 14, f. 4v; KL Ottobeuren 601-II, ff. 166v–174v; Dertsch, "Das Einwohnerbuch des Ottobeurer Klosterstaats 1564," p. 86.

[191] Respectively StAA, KL Ottobeuren 4, Document 308Q, ff. 1085r–1086v [8 June 1564) and Document 298F, ff. 767v–768v [22 Feb. 1557].

[192] For a helpful introduction, see two collections edited by Rolf Kießling and Sabine Ullmann, *Judengemeinden in Schwaben im Kontext des Alten Reiches* (Berlin, 1995) and *Landjudentum im deutschen Südwesten waehrend der Fruehen Neuzeit* (Berlin, 1999).

for the monastery's court ordinances to make special provision for Jewish witnesses to swear oaths in Hebrew.[193] And although no Jews lived in the monastery lands proper, they were resident in nearby villages immediately to the north and west, including Amendingen, Schwaighausen, Heimertingen, Lachen, and Zell. The Swabian Jews are most commonly encountered in the monastery lands as small merchants, purchasing cloth and trading in livestock.[194] They were also engaged in moneylending, but their status as legal outsiders – a disability forced upon them by the Abbot's refusal to allow Jews to settle in his dominions – put them at a disadvantage when the recalcitrance or insolvency of a debtor obliged them to resort to legal action to recover their loans.

Ottobeuren courts took their responsibilities fairly seriously and would certainly punish local hotheads for "railing against the Jews,"[195] but they were none the less decidedly unenthusiastic about assisting "foreigners" in collecting debts from Ottobeuren subjects. In the absence of official co-operation, some Jewish moneylenders turned to more creative means of recovering their money. In 1562, for example, Solomon ("Schlauma") the Jew of Amendingen got hold of funds impounded from the indebted brothers Jerg and Mathias Schregle of Eheim (and claimed by their creditors in the city of Memmingen) by plying the *Amman* of Ottobeuren with wine and then befuddling him with "all sorts of unauthorized documents and registers."[196] More commonly, however, Jewish moneylenders appealed for assistance to the higher courts of the Holy Roman Empire, in particular the so-called Swabian Territorial Court "on the Leutkirch heath," which operated out of the cities of Rottweil and Wangen.[197]

The monastery had always frowned upon its subjects borrowing from Jews, but had initially confined itself to sporadic acts of intimidation. Thus, in 1535 the Abbot arrested and imprisoned a certain Simon the Jew of Schweighausen, and pressured from him the revealing pledge henceforth to confine his lawsuits

---

[193] StAA, KL Ottobeuren 4, Document 289X: a 1548 formulary for oaths apparently copied into the "Baudingbuch 1551." The "Jewish oath" is detailed on ff. 405r–408v.

[194] StAA, KL Ottobeuren 587-I, Heft 5 (1569/70); KL Ottobeuren 587-II, Heft 18 (1594/5) and Heft 20 (1598/9).

[195] StAA, KL Ottobeuren 587-II, Heft 12 (1582/3). Martin Maier of Sontheim fined £7 15 ß for this offense; he was extremely poor (KL Ottobeuren 491-I, Heft 3, f. 27v). There were, of course, Jewish hotheads as well; the monastery fined Michael the Jew of Amendingen and the butcher Michael Merckhle of Memmingen a total of £5 5 ß for fisticuffs. KL Ottobeuren 491-II, Heft 13 (1584/5), Ottobeuren Markt and Pfarr.

[196] StAA, KL Ottobeuren 4, ff. 531r–536r, Document 291LL [11 Dec. 1562]. The Schregles were rather a sad case. In the 1540s their father, Jerg, had been one of the largest tithepayers and richest men in the hamlet, but the small tithe registers for 1563–6 suggest that Mathias had no cows and that Jerg had no land at all (KL Ottobeuren 29, f. 130r; KL Ottobeuren 64, f. 39r; KL Ottobeuren 688-I, Hefte 1 (f. 7v), 2 (f. 14r), 3 (f. 13v), and 4 (f. 15r).

[197] StAA, KU Ottobeuren 1049a [6 July 1529]. The Territorial Court in Rottweil orders the *Untervogt* and judges in Ottobeuren to assist "the Jew Lev of Schweighausen" in recovering money from the property of Jerg Keppeler (*sic*) of Reuthen. The 1525 tax register lists Jerg Keppelin as a prosperous *Bauer*. KL Ottobeuren 541, Heft 2, ff. 57v–58v.

against peasants to the courts in whose jurisdiction they resided. Simon was also required to call in his outstanding loans among the Ottobeuren peasantry and never to lend money to them again. As borrowing by the monastery's subjects from Jews only increased, however, it was decided to adopt sterner measures.

In 1545 Abbot Leonhard issued the first of a distasteful series of so-called *Judenordnungen*. "[W]e had hoped," the ordinance laments,

> that daily experience, learning, and knowledge of the Jews' burdensome dealings, whereby those who borrow from them are not only brought to the irrecoverable ruin of their lands and goods, but are also together with their wives and small ungrown children sent and driven into beggary and lamentable destitution . . . all of which is clearly and daily before the eyes, would have brought improvement, and put an end [at least] in part to this ill.

Since, however, the situation was only getting worse, the Abbot commanded all of his subjects who owed money to Jews to clear their debts within a month and never again to borrow from Jews. Henceforth anyone who for any period of time mortgaged any of his property to, or even bought or borrowed anything from, Jews, was together with wife and children to be banished from the monastery lands. Furthermore, the Abbot continued,

> It is no less our earnest order and command, that henceforth any of our *Ammänner* who [personally or] through his subordinates should receive or be shown any summons, mandate, order, ruling, proscription, prohibition or other official document from foreign courts, shall, by the oath of office sworn to us, in no way comply [with the order]. Instead [the *Amman*] shall show and bring forth [the document] . . . to Us or Our chancellery as soon as possible, and irrespective of what any Jew or court emissary should declare or say, he, the *Amman*, shall not promulgate the document . . .[198]

It was a hard decision. "We would much rather feel, notice, and see the obedient and definitive compliance of each and every one of you," the ordinance wistfully concludes, but such was not to be. As was the case in other German territories,[199] the prohibitions on borrowing from Jews would be regularly and vainly reissued by the monastery throughout the later sixteenth century. At Ottobeuren the 1545 *Judenordnung* would be repromulgated in 1572, in 1587, and again in 1596.[200]

---

[198] StAA, KL Ottobeuren 4, Document 289E, ff. 300r–304r.

[199] Financial dealings between Christians and Jews were heavily circumscribed in the cities of Nördlingen (1541), Heilbronn (1543), Leutkirch (1559), Lindau (1559), and Überlingen (1566), and prohibited outright in the cities of Kaufbeuren (1530), Memmingen (1541), Ravensburg (1559), and Reutlingen (1561), in the Duchy of Württemberg (1557), in Pfalz (1581), and in the Markgravate of Baden (1622). Max Neumann, *Geschichte des Wuchers in Deutschland bis zur Begründung der heutigen Zinsgesetze (1654)* (Halle, 1865), pp. 328–43.

[200] StAA, KL Ottobeuren 4, Documents 289M, ff. 323v–327r [20 July 1572], 289O, ff. 331r–334r [18 Apr. 1587], and 289O (*sic*) dated simply "1596," ff. 340v–346r.

These ordinances were enforced with periodic crackdowns, although the monastery usually held back from the draconian penalty of banishment. The most common punishment was a fine of up to 12 pounds and the requirement of an oath of future obedience posted by the offender's relatives. On occasion the monastery sought to pre-empt the problem altogether by exacting a promise not to borrow from Jews as a condition of admission to tenancy.[201] If, on the other hand, illegal borrowing were coupled with other offences, the full force of the law could be ruthlessly applied. When Adam Maier of Rempolz was first arrested in 1549 for mortgaging his property to Jews, a solemn promise to clear his debts and to stay inside the monastery lands was all the authorities demanded. When two years later Adam added theft to the list of his transgressions, he was banished along with his wife and children, having only narrowly escaped the noose.[202] In the same way Steffa Müllegg of Untermotz was banished in 1559 not only for having borrowed money from the Jews but for theft as well.[203]

There is no way of knowing whether the social profile of the borrowers is accurately represented by those who were prosecuted, but it is at least clear that those who borrowed from the Jews came from every stratum of rural society. The convicted included wealthy burghers from the town of Ottobeuren, comfortable *Bauern*, mid-level craftsmen, and poor cottagers from both villages and hamlets.[204] All they had in common was a pressing need for capital. Indeed, at least on some occasions it is clear that Jewish moneylenders were willing to advance funds to peasants who could not obtain (or had already exhausted) any credit among Christians.[205] As Hans Zeller of Mindelheim explained after being arrested in 1558, he had tried to borrow funds in Augsburg and other places in order to build a smithy in the town of Ottobeuren. Even though he had offered to pay as much as 13 percent in interest, no one would lend him the money. He thus had had no other choice but to borrow from Jews.[206]

---

[201] StAA, KU Ottobeuren 1747 [1 Mar. 1571].

[202] StAA, KL Ottobeuren 4, Documents 293F, ff. 621r–627v [20 May 1549] and 293G [10 Oct. 1551].

[203] Ibid., Document 293X, ff. 671r–673v [30 Apr. 1559].

[204] Ibid., Documents 291DD, ff. 523r–525r (*Urfehdebrief* of Peter Stehelin of Ottobeuren [one of the ten wealthiest burghers in the town]) [4 Sep. 1545]; 294F, ff. 693v–699r (*Urfehdebrief* of Michael Vochenzer of Hawangen [45th of 126 householders in the village; tenant of a *Gotteshausrecht* holding] [6 June 1549]; 303F, ff. 847v–851r (*Urfehdebrief* of Hans Böglin junior of Attenhausen [blacksmith; 28th of 63 householders in the village] [18 Mar. 1546] 293D, ff. 599v–602v (*Urfehdebrief* of Jacob Ruoff of Guggenberg [tied for the poorest householder in the hamlet] [21 Aug. 1553]. Identifications and rankings on the basis of KL Ottobeuren 29, 64.

[205] See, for example, StAA, KL Ottobeuren 4, Document 293D, ff. 599v–602v [21 Aug. 1553]. Jacob Ruoff of Guggenberg borrowed money from Jews after his property was already mortgaged to Christians. Ruoff was one of the poorest residents of his hamlet (KL Ottobeuren 64, f. 40v), which may have made it particularly hard for him to borrow. The role of Jews as creditors of last resort is similarly implied in KL Ottobeuren 4, Document 293A, ff. 606r–610v [9 June 1542].

[206] StAA, KL Ottobeuren 2, Document ff 217, 444r–446r [*c.* Dec. 1558].

The surge in peasant indebtedness to Jews was thus a symptom of a society growing ever more needy of money and credit. The Jews were convenient scapegoats for the stresses of a changing economic order, but they were hardly the only ones engaged in the business of lending money. This is perhaps best illustrated by the case of the Ottobeuren peasant Hans Betz, who in May of 1548 was sued in the Imperial Swabian Territorial Court by a certain Moses the Jew of Heimertingen for non-payment of a debt more than two years overdue.[207] Betz had for many years[208] farmed a good-sized *Gotteshausrecht* holding (approximately 13 *jauchert* of arable and 9 *tagwerk* of meadow land)[209] in the village of Attenhausen. Moses' attempt to have this land impounded was ultimately unsuccessful, but his lawsuit touched off a squabbling match for precedence among Betz's other creditors which reveals a pattern of extensive borrowing at several doors. Betz, it turned out, also owed money to one Jacob the Jew of Schweighausen,[210] to the Memmingen burgher Peter Allgewer, to a series of the monastery's subjects including Peter Stehelin of Ottobeuren (himself indebted to Jews),[211] Mathias Zobel of Oberwesterheim,[212] and Hans Maier of Attenhausen, and finally to a pair of impeccably Christian institutions, namely the parish church of Attenhausen and the Abbot of Ottobeuren himself![213]

The Memmingen burgher Peter Allgewer proved a particularly tenacious creditor,[214] maintaining that his loans antedated (and therefore took precedence over) not only the claims of Moses the Jew,[215] but also those of the Abbot of Ottobeuren.[216] Still more outrageously, Allgewer maintained that the

---

[207] StAA, KU Ottobeuren 1283a [8 Dec. 1545]. Moses was authorized to impound Betz's land if the debt was not cleared by 9 March 1546.

[208] StAA, KU Ottobeuren 1028a [24 Feb. 1528].

[209] Betz's farm was absorbed by one Caspar Hegel sometime between 1544 and 1567. The rent rolls suggest that the Betz farm made up about one half of Hegel's total holdings, which were reported as measuring 26 *jauchert* and 18 *tagwerk* in 1587. StAA, KL Ottobeuren 27, f. 131r; KL Ottobeuren 29, f. 68v; KL Ottobeuren 30, ff. 69r–73r.

[210] StAA, KU Ottobeuren 1301a [8 July 1547].

[211] StAA, KL Ottobeuren 4, Document 291DD, ff. 523r–525r [4 Sep. 1545].

[212] StAA, KU Ottobeuren 1267a [25 May 1544].

[213] StAA, KL Ottobeuren (Mü.B.) 197: Jacob Schedler, Gerichtsamman of Memmingen, to Peter Allgewer, Burgher of Memmingen [5 Jan. 1549], which lists all of Betz's creditors.

[214] He was also willing to employ openly illegal methods, sending threatening letters to the Attenhausen blacksmith in 1548 via the thuggish Simon Kopp. In the same year Kopp also attacked Peter Stehelin of Ottobeuren – another of Betz's creditors – with a pig spear, although it remains unclear precisely how all of these events fit together. StAA, KL Ottobeuren 4, Document 303G, ff. 851v–855r [30 July 1549]. See also KL Ottobeuren 587-I, Heft 2, 'Strafregister 1548,' Attenhausen and Ottobeuren Pfarr.

[215] StAA, KL Ottobeuren (Mü.B.) 197: Peter Allgewer of Memmingen to Gori Prew, procurator of the Landgericht in Wangen [30 July 1548].

[216] Ibid.; Peter Allgewer of Memmingen to the Landgericht in Wangen [May 1549]. Allgewer asserted that his claims dated from 1544, whereas the Abbot's claims dated from 1547 at best. This was clearly incorrect; the monastery's debt ledger for 1543 shows Betz with cash debts of a little over £3, only some of which he cleared that year (StAA, KL Ottobeuren 409, f. 29r). More importantly, the 1544 rent roll (KL Ottobeuren 29, ff. 68v, 161r–v) indicates that Betz had arrears of 6.9 *malter*, almost twice his annual rent of 4 *malter*.

subjects of the monastery "have had the following freedom and grace confirmed by five emperors, [namely that] whenever a subject of the monastery is no longer able to farm his *Gotteshausrecht* holding, he may sell his right to [the property] to other people." Abbot Caspar was horrified at the idea that the fate of the monastery's most valuable properties should be left to the vagaries of the open market, and he strenuously insisted to the Swabian Territorial Court that it was

> a praiseworthy tradition, that none of the said *Höfe* or properties can in any other way be held or transferred than [as follows:] if the tenant dies, or is otherwise no longer capable of managing the property, or does not pay the rent, then the land and all of its appurtenances returns freely [i.e. 'to the free disposition of'] the monastery, without interference by anyone else.[217]

The Abbot's argument for the traditional precedence of an overlord's claim did ultimately carry the day,[218] but the Betz incident and others like it[219] only reinforced the monastery's misgivings about its subjects' seemingly insatiable appetite for credit. Moreover, the machinations of Peter Allgewer underscored the fact that lending by Christians – even lending by chapels[220] – could have all of the undesirable consequences that the monastery had blamed on the Jews. What was needed, therefore, was a more generalized approach to the problem of peasant borrowing.

The attempted solution was an abolition of long-term credit. The monastery had neither the ability nor the intention of stamping out borrowing altogether, but hoped to make debt a temporary expedient rather than a permanent fixture of the rural economy. From the 1530s, therefore, the monastery increasingly began to require new debts to be cleared within eight years (see Figure 4.5). This redemption obligation was confined neither to the loans of Jews[221] nor to the loans of foreigners; even peasants who borrowed from their own kin were saddled with the pledge of redemption within eight years.[222]

It proved impossible to stem the tide. After the mid-1550s, the number of *Schuldbriefe* with obligatory eight-year redemptions fell back sharply, not so much because credit itself contracted, but because the monastery finally

---

[217] StAA, KL Ottobeuren (Mü.B.) 197: draft response of Abbot Caspar to the Landgericht in Wangen, undated (but clearly early 1549).

[218] StAA, KU Ottobeuren 1354 [4 Feb. 1550]: ruling by Caspar Klöckhler, Freilandrichter in Ober– und Niederschwaben auf Leutkircher Heide, awarding first priority among all of the creditors of Hans Betz of Attenhausen to the Abbot of Ottobeuren.

[219] For example the lawsuit of Jacob the Jew of Schweighausen against the heirs of Thomas Küefer of Rummeltshausen. StAA, KL Ottobeuren 757, "Schwäbische Landgericht Acta, 1545–63."

[220] See the prosecution of Mathias Rauch of Benningen for impudent utterances when he was supposed to make an interest payment to St. Niklas chapel. StAA, KL Ottobeuren 587-I, Heft 10 (1579/80), Benningen.

[221] StAA, KL Ottobeuren 4, Documents 299F and 299G, ff. 785r–788r and 788r–790v [28 Jan. and 26 Feb. 1555].

[222] StAA, KU Ottobeuren 1193 [17 Oct. 1538] and 1209 [14 July 1539].

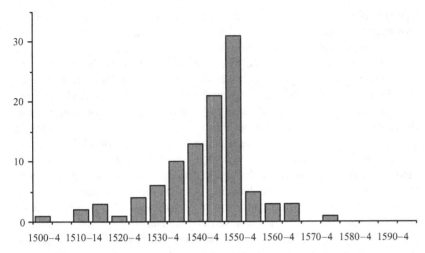

Figure 4.5 Number of *Schuldbriefe* with obligatory eight-year debt clearance, 1500/4–1595/9
Source: StAA, KU Ottobeuren 629–1686

conceded that there was no way to rein in the borrowing of its subjects. On the contrary, in fact, as has been seen from the evidence of church and chapel accounts and the central notarial protocols, the later sixteenth century saw a massive increase in indebtedness at all levels of rural society. From time to time the monastery did require a mandatory redemption period for a debt to a foreign creditor, but even in these cases the obligation was only infrequently imposed. By the early seventeenth century, Ottobeuren peasants were routinely borrowing considerable sums from outside the monastery lands without any contractual bar to a lengthy period of indebtedness. Debts could be legally secured not only against land and houses, but also against moneys owed by third parties to the debtor himself,[223] livestock,[224] or even bed linens.[225] The Abbot's chancellery began registering obligations where now the creditor, and not just the debtor, had the right to demand redemption of the principal, usually at three months' notice. Even the land market was opened up to buyers residing outside the monastery lands. With the single qualification that Ottobeuren subjects have the first option of repurchase, freehold lands could now be sold to the subjects of foreign lords, including dependents of the city of Memmingen and its charitable institutions, of the Bishop of Augsburg, and of the Fugger dukes of Babenhausen.

[223] StAA, KL Ottobeuren, 905, ff. 49v–50r [24 Dec. 1612] and 69r [26 Apr. 1613].
[224] StAA, KL Ottobeuren, 904, f. 276v [9 Feb. 1612]; KL Ottobeuren 905, f. 60r [27 Dec. 1612]. See also ibid., ff. 146r–v [19 Dec. 1613] where the debt is secured against a ropemaker's tools. A great many debts were secured against unitemized "moveables."
[225] StAA, KL Ottobeuren 911, f. 128 [23 Feb. 1631].

The most obvious result of the introduction of impartible inheritance and village closure in the monastery lands was the consolidation of a characteristically south German landholding structure, distinguished by the domination of the landscape by surplus-producing, mid-sized tenant farms (the *Bauernhöfe*), while very large holdings on an English or East Elbian scale remained a rarity. Given the argument in chapter 3 about the scale of the agricultural surplus at Ottobeuren, the long-term economic significance of impartibility should be obvious, and the landholding patterns established by the early seventeenth century would in fact remain in place for some three hundred years.[226] Yet for all the attention garnered by the static question of the scale in which German peasants held their land, rather less effort has been devoted to the implications, and in particular to the market implications, of the dynamics of rural property systems.[227]

The central objective of the present chapter has been to illustrate the intimate connection between the metamorphosis of peasant inheritance practices and the growth of markets for land and credit. It is no easy matter to disentangle the direction of causal influences between these two circuits of exchange. To suggest that the rise of inheritance through sale by itself energized the anemic land and credit markets of the late fifteenth century would be misleading (although it is worth noting that kin transactions made up fully 54.84 percent of the value of all land sales between 1603 and 1621). It would be still less accurate, however, to cast peasant inheritance as a realm resistant to 'the' economy, monetized in the end from the outside by overmighty market forces.[228] Both of these constructions presume a seductive but misleading dichotomy between processes of social reproduction on the one hand, and production and exchange on the other, such that the former set of relations can be thought either to generate or to be colonized by the latter. It makes rather more sense, I would argue, to see each set of relations as constitutive of the other. To put it more concretely, the transformations of the later sixteenth century are best understood as the result of a new style of householding developed in response to a series of demographic and

---

[226] According to the 1620 tax survey, the 11,000 hectares of agricultural land in the lordship of the monastery were distributed thus among the following five size classes: <2 ha (2.5%), 2–5 ha (3.6%), 5–20 ha (34.8%), 20–100 ha (59.1%) (within which 20–50 ha [58.1%] and 50–100 ha [1.0%]), > 100 ha (nil). In 1907, the agricultural land of the *Bezirksamt* Memmmingen was distributed among the same five size classes as follows: 1.1%, 7.5%, 50.9%, 40.1%, 0.4%. StAA, KL Ottobeuren 102; "Die Landwirtschaft in Bayern nach der Betriebszählung vom 12 Juni 1907," *Beiträge zur Statistik des Königreichs Bayern 81* (Munich, 1910), pp. 44–5.

[227] Schlögl, "Zwischen Krieg und Krise," is a useful critique of earlier literature, but tends to see the exactions of the early modern state as the essential impetus for change.

[228] Thus, in Martin Hille's otherwise excellent *Ländliche Gesellschaft in Kriegszeiten: bäuerliche Subsistenz zwischen Fiskus und Feudalherrschaft* (Munich, 1997), we encounter the claim (p. 92) that "the money economy had thus within thirty to forty years [i.e. 1490–1530] conquered even the realm of the rural family," a phenomenon explained by "the rising fiscal demands of the early modern state" (p. 93).

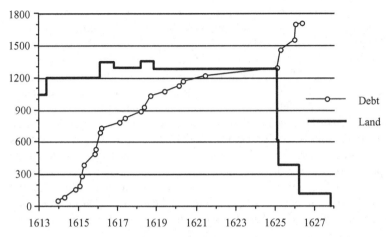

Figure 4.6 The debts and landholdings (fl.) of Johann Teufel, 1613–27
Sources: StAA, KL Ottobeuren 102, 104, 903–9

ecological challenges. This new style was characterized by much more intensive involvement in land and credit markets, but built on institutional foundations – in particular the establishment of stable and transferable peasant property rights – laid in the previous century. The site of the most dramatic and consequential changes was inheritance.

What were the consequences? The question admits of no simple answer, but in light of the monastery's fears of the impoverishment of its subjects, perhaps the logical way to begin an assessment of the spread of market relations is to investigate the stability of the peasant household during the early seventeenth century. It must be said that there were individuals, like Johann Teufel of Egg, who became dependent on credit and ultimately lost the greater part of their property (see Figure 4.6). Even in this case, however, indebtedness had a pattern and an outcome rather different from the scenario envisioned by the monastery. First of all, although Teufel had lost most of his land by the spring of 1625, he did in the following year succeed in establishing his daughter as his heir (albeit in reduced estate),[229] took a second wife in 1639, and survived as a village householder until the 1650s.[230] Second, none of his land was lost to "outsiders," but was instead bought up by other Ottobeuren peasants. Third, and perhaps most striking of all, the overwhelming majority (81.2 percent) of the 1,759 *gulden* he is known to have borrowed between 1613 and 1626 was raised from creditors inside the monastery lands.

---

[229] StAA, KL Ottobeuren 909, f. 145r [16 Mar. 1626].
[230] Egg Parish Register [hereinafter EggPR], Vol. I, p. 118 [25 Apr. 1639]; StAA, KL Ottobeuren 160, ff. 50r–52r; KL Ottobeuren 56, ff. 266v–295v.

The ability of peasant society to generate its own capital ill accords with the customary image of a countryside dominated by urban mercantile interests,[231] but at least in this respect, Johann Teufel's experience was clearly the norm at Ottobeuren. Of 273,681 *gulden* in notarized loans to monastery peasants between 1603 and 1621, the burghers and urban institutions of Memmingen advanced a mere 3.4 percent. The most prominent "foreign" lenders were actually the peasants of neighboring lordships, who advanced 6.5 percent of the funds borrowed in those years. Still larger sums were borrowed from Ottobeuren village churches and chapels (8.1 percent) and the guardians of local widows and orphans (10.8 percent), while kin remained by far the largest single source (47.9 percent) of rural credit. Of course, that most debt was locally incurred was itself no bar to destructive consequences, but it turns out that Johann Teufel's downward spiral into penury was a most unusual pattern. An Ottobeuren peasant was if anything more likely to grow richer, rather than poorer, over the course of a lifetime.

The reconstruction of early seventeenth-century rural social mobility is a complicated process,[232] as marriage registers are unavailable for this period and there is no equivalent to the urban citizenship rolls (*Bürgerbücher*) which document formal entry into social adulthood in German towns.[233] It is possible, on the other hand, to recover from the notarial protocols the acquisition of "household properties" (houses, tenant farms, or at least 5 *jauchert* of land) by almost two hundred new householders[234] in the quinquennium 1603–7 and then track these individuals forward to a 1627 tax survey. Even the very poor are well represented in this sample[235] – 40 percent of the foundations were based on an initial capital of less than 250 fl. – and the results are quite surprising (see Table 4.2). Since I am more concerned with the stability of the household as a social formation than with the biological resilience of its male head, I have defined a household's survival as the persistence of the original male

---

[231] Most recently exemplified in Kiessling, *Die Stadt und ihr Land.*

[232] And therefore rarely undertaken. See, however, Volkmar Weiss, *Bevölkerung und soziale Mobilität: Sachsen 1550–1880* (Berlin, 1993).

[233] The subsequent discussion owes a great deal to Christopher R. Friedrichs' pioneering *Urban Society in an Age of War: Nördlingen 1580–1720* (Princeton, 1979). In order to maintain strict comparability with Friedrichs' urban social mobility calculations, it would have been preferable to track peasants over an interval of twenty-five to twenty-nine (rather than twenty to twenty-four) years. Unfortunately, the Ottobeuren notarial protocols are not complete before 1603, while the 1627 tax survey is the last that survives before the Thirty Years War.

[234] Since most of these householders are not listed in the 1595 bond-chicken register and appear for the first time in 1602 or (more commonly) 1609, documenting the "newness" of these householders is usually fairly straightforward. Where there is any doubt, I have excluded from consideration all cases where the 1620 tax survey reveals significant property holdings whose acquisition cannot be documented in the (complete) notarial protocols for 1603–21.

[235] The 1,676 households described in the 1620 tax survey were distributed as follows by gross wealth: 47.5 percent (<250 fl.), 15.0 percent (250–499 fl.), and 37.5 percent (> 500 fl.). StAA, KL Ottobeuren 102.

Table 4.2 *Social mobility at Ottobeuren, 1603/7–1627*

Fate by 1627	Initial estate value (1603–7)					
	<500 fl. (*Seldner*)		≥500 fl. (*Bauern*)		All householders	
	(no.)	(%)	(no.)	(%)	(no.)	(%)
Untraceable/exit	37	27.0	4	6.7	41	20.8
Loss (>50%)	7	5.1	1	1.7	8	4.1
Stability (±49%)	44	32.1	22	36.7	66	33.5
Gain (+50–99%)	12	8.8	13	21.7	25	12.7
Doubled (+≥100%)	37	27.0	20	33.3	57	28.9
Total	137	100.0	60	100.0	197	100.0

Sources: StAA, KL Ottobeuren 102, 104, 491 I–III, 903–8

householder, his widowed or remarried spouse, or (in a few cases) their heir. On this definition, the overwhelming majority of rural households survived for twenty to twenty-four years, even among the *Seldner*. Most of them managed at least to preserve their property, and significant numbers of *Seldner* (35.8 percent) and *Bauern* (55.0 percent) were able to increase what they owned.[236] The optimistic global calculations of per capita grain production made in chapter 3 thus gain powerful support from the aggregated trajectories of individual households. This was not a society in crisis.

Less obvious, but equally important, is the fact that this impressive stability overlay a turbulent traffic in property at all levels of the peasantry. In 1588 or 1589, for example, a peasant by the name of Cyriacus Schwarz moved to Attenhausen[237] with his wife, Ursula, and his two children, Caspar and Maria. It was a poor family. Already in January of 1604, Cyriacus exchanged his house for shabbier quarters at the other end of the village. Three years later, when Cyriacus regulated the inheritance of his children, Caspar was promised an inheritance of only 10 *gulden*, while his sister was to receive 5 *gulden* and her deceased mother's clothing.[238]

The son, Caspar Schwarz, began his own career in the fall of 1608 with the purchase of a *jauchert* of meadow, followed by the acquisition of a half-house in the following year.[239] With the death of Cyriacus Schwarz (*c.* 1612), the family entered into a flurry of real-estate transactions. Caspar and his widowed

---

[236] Calculated from a comparison of the value of each household's real property in 1627 with the value of the "foundational" property acquired in 1603–7. I have not adjusted these values for inflation because tax assessments were based (and explicitly so) on the original purchase price.

[237] StAA, KL Ottobeuren 491-I, Heft 3, ff. 24r–v and Heft 5, f. 11v.

[238] StAA, KL Ottobeuren 903, ff. 60v, 60v–61r [19 Jan. 1604], and 288v–289v [12 Jan. 1607].

[239] StAA, KL Ottobeuren 904, f. 75r [6 Oct. 1608]; KL Ottobeuren 491-I, Heft 14, f. 19v.

stepmother sold off their interests in Cyriacus' house to Maria Schwarz and her husband in June of 1613.[240] In October and November of 1613, Caspar sold some land to raise money and then traded his own half-house for the back half of a better house in another part of the village. In December he attempted to purchase the more desirable front half of the house, but the deal fell through. In February of 1614 he finally succeeded in exchanging the back for the front half of the house. Over the next few years Caspar continued to speculate in the land market,[241] and by 1620 he owned property worth 190 fl., including a cow and a small flock of sheep.[242] The last reference to Caspar Schwarz is in a debt ledger of 1633;[243] he probably perished in the plague that swept the Ottobeuren lands in 1634–5.

Caspar Schwarz's brief career has at least two noteworthy features. The first is that his determined efforts resulted in very real social mobility. Although he started with next to nothing (a miserable inheritance of 10 *gulden*), all of his moves were to better (half-)houses. He was not, in other words, being pushed around by poverty. Caspar was constantly angling for a better deal. Not only did he end up with the house he wanted and several painfully cobbled-together strips of land, but he had the sense as a smallholder to concentrate on animal husbandry (hence his sheep and purchases of meadowland) rather than arable agriculture. Furthermore, as has been seen, Caspar's social mobility was far from unusual at seventeenth-century Ottobeuren.

The second striking feature of Caspar's life is what may somewhat awkwardly be called the porosity of the space in which he lived. He was constantly shuffling about the village, and spent much of his life in houses shared with other people. Indeed, although his sister, Maria, and her husband established their "own" household by buying out Maria's stepmother, Salome Biller, Salome in fact carved out her own living space within their household by retaining the front room, half of the fruit crop, a specified sector of the garden, and the right to use all of the household tools. The stepmother was also taxed as a separate household in the 1620 tax survey, with a net worth equal to that of her stepdaughter.[244]

None of this spatial porosity was at all unusual. Another village resident, Caspar Maier, lived in four different half-houses between 1613 and 1618.[245] One Mathias Karrer lived in five different houses between 1608 and 1621,

---

[240] StAA, KL Ottobeuren 905, ff. 103r–v (*Kaufbrief* [10 June 1613]).
[241] StAA, KL Ottobeuren 905, ff. 119r–v [11 Oct. 1613], 128r [28 Nov. 1613], 133r (crossed-out) [2 Dec. 1613], 139v [11 Dec. 1613], 162v [19 Feb. 1614], 166r [13 Mar. 1614], 189v [24 June 1614], 189v–190r [24 June 1614], 196v–197r [4 Aug. 1614]; KL Ottobeuren 907, ff. 4v–5r [18 Aug. 1616] and 77r [2 May 1617].
[242] StAA, KL Ottobeuren 102, f. 388r.   [243] StAA, KL Ottobeuren 43, f. 52v.
[244] StAA, KL Ottobeuren 905, ff. 103v–104r [10 June 1613]; KL Ottobeuren 102, f. 392r.
[245] StAA, KL Ottobeuren 905, ff. 141r [14 Dec. 1613], 149v–150r [7 Jan. 1614], 162r–v [19 Feb. 1614], and 162v [19 Feb. 1614].

the last of which he shared with the parents of the previous owner.[246] Still more complicated was the residential history of Jerg Weber, who lived in three different houses between 1612 and 1614. In 1612 Weber bought a house halfway across the village, and then traded it to the man who up to that point had lived in the back half of Weber's own house so that Weber could occupy the entire building. The "satellite" house – into which Weber himself moved two years later – was shared with the widowed mother of the man who had sold the house to Weber in 1612.[247]

Yet the land and credit markets were more than a solvent of the household's traditional boundedness or a vehicle for its residents' accumulative ambitions. They also allowed property to serve as congealed labor, as a reserve of value from which to generate cashflow in times of need. The career of Martin Schmalholz of Hawangen is a typical example of this pattern. In 1613, Martin's father, Johann, decided to retire. He sold his property – a house, a garden, three *jauchert* of arable land and one and a half *tagwerk* of meadow – to Martin for 450 *gulden*. Martin only paid 150 *gulden* at the time; the 300 *gulden* shortfall was bridged by a mortgage to be cleared after Johann's death.[248] When the father died in 1616, the reckoning became due. Johann had meant for Martin's brothers to receive even more than the 300 *gulden* debt: Jerg Schmalhoz junior had been promised 516 *gulden* by his father while Johann Schmalholz junior was to receive 110. Martin cleared the first obligation in October of 1616 and tendered a promissory note for the second in November.[249] Again, what made all of this possible was the ease with which he could borrow: 100 *gulden* from the local village community on 11 February, 50 *gulden* from the guardians of an Ungerhausen orphan two weeks later, another 100 *gulden* from a Hawangen widow in May of 1617 . . . Between 1616 and 1621 Martin borrowed at least 530 *gulden* from various sources all over and even outside the monastery lands.[250] It was a hard life. Martin was always in debt and most of his seven children died in infancy,[251] but he nevertheless managed to stay afloat. The 1627 tax survey finds him in Hawangen clinging doggedly to his house, his snippets of land, and his two cows.[252] He lived on in the village into his fifties, finally

---

[246] StAA, KL Ottobeuren 904, ff. 76r [8 Oct. 1608] and 275v–276r [6 Feb. 1612]; KL Ottobeuren 905, ff. 254r–v [22 Mar. 1615] and 274v–275r [10 June 1615]; KL Ottobeuren 908, ff. 140r–v [2 Apr. 1621].

[247] StAA, KL Ottobeuren 904, f. 72r [11 Sep. 1608]; KL Ottobeuren 905, ff. 21v [13 Sep. 1612], 22r [13 Sep. 1612], 84r [10 Jan. 1613], and 209r–v [16 Oct. 1614].

[248] StAA, KL Ottobeuren 905, ff. 126r–v and 126v–127r [28 Nov. 1613].

[249] StAA, KL Ottobeuren 907, ff. 13v [13 Oct. 1616] and 27r [20 Nov. 1616].

[250] StAA, KL Ottobeuren 905, ff. 334r [11 Feb. 1616] and 335v [26 Feb. 1616]; KL Ottobeuren 907, ff. 78r–v [4 May 1617]; KL Ottobeuren 908, ff. 129r [12 Mar. 1621], 130v [19 Mar. 1621], 150r [7 June 1621], 150r–v [7 June 1621], and 158r [15 June 1621].

[251] Children baptized 1608, 1610, 1612, 1613, 1615, 1615, 1617. HawPR, Vol. I, ff. 6v, 15r, 19v, 22v, 30r, 30v, 36v.

[252] StAA, KL Ottobeuren 104, f. 201r; KL Ottobeuren 908, f. 70v [7 May 1620].

selling off his arable land in 1632, and last appearing in the records in 1634.[253] For Martin Schmalholz and countless other peasants like him, patrimony had become capital.

Equally important, though less obvious, was an intimate link between property holding and the "economy of makeshifts"[254] which characterized the lives of the rural poor. The connection was most apparent when a retiring householder sought to preserve rights which would otherwise be lost by the sale of the home. This was often a matter of access to dedicated workplaces, such as stall space for a cow or goat,[255] a bakeoven to dry fruit,[256] a cellar to store vegetables,[257] or the use of a room for weaving.[258] Yet registered guarantees of a retiring widow's freedom to sell her cow's calves "at her [own] desire and pleasure"[259] or to spin without interference[260] underscore the additional tie between the ownership of property and the autonomy of labor itself, particularly when one considers that this autonomy was on some occasions explicitly abridged by the new owners.[261] Finally, beyond sustaining the capacity to labor, property rights could also be made to compensate for incapacity, a facility best illustrated by the attempts of the poor to cope with illness.

The archival record does not permit a satisfactory social history of infirmity at Ottobeuren, but it is clear that responsibility for direct medical intervention fell to the ubiquitous village bathhouse keeper, who was trained even to treat kidney stones and hernias[262] and who often kept an extensive set of surgical implements.[263] Supported by an annual grain delivery (*Ehehaften*) from the village community, the bathhouse keeper belonged to the richer sector of rural

---

[253] StAA, KL Ottobeuren 911, f. 240 [29 Apr. 1632], KL Ottobeuren 601-II, f. 103r; KL Ottobeuren 43, f. 13v.

[254] A memorable characterization first proposed in Olwen Hufton, *The Poor of Eighteenth-Century France 1750–1789* (Oxford, 1974).

[255] StAA, KL Ottobeuren 907, f. 52v [2 Feb. 1617] and KL Ottobeuren 908, f. 175v [30 July 1621]. See also the reservation of the right to keep two chickens in KL Ottobeuren 904, ff. 44v–45r [1 May 1608].

[256] StAA, KL Ottobeuren 905, ff. 195v–196r [31 July 1614].

[257] StAA, KL Ottobeuren 907, f. 245r [23 Apr. 1619].

[258] StAA, KL Ottobeuren 903, ff. 99r–v [19 June 1604] and KL Ottobeuren 907, f. 68r [6 Apr. 1617].

[259] StAA, KL Ottobeuren 908, ff. 90v–92r [26 June 1620]. This contract also assured use of the cellar as a weaving space to a non-inheriting son.

[260] StAA, KL Ottobeuren 904, ff. 190v–191r [29 Mar. 1610]. Unlike all previous cases cited, this one involved a rich widow, but the same problem would have obtained among the poor.

[261] StAA, KL Ottobeuren 903, ff. 17v–18r [29 Apr. 1603] assures a widowed mother the right to keep a cow but all of its calves belong to her *Seldner* son. KL Ottobeuren 911, ff. 214–217 [18 Dec. 1631] similarly obliges a retiring widow to share half of the proceeds of her spinning with her *Bauer* son and his wife. See also KL Ottobeuren 104, f. 98v.

[262] StAA, KL Ottobeuren 903, ff. 58v [9 Jan. 1604] and 305r [8 Mar. 1607]. The bathhouse keepers trained more apprentices than any other Ottobeuren trade.

[263] Implied by careful provision for the ownership and inheritance of these tools. StAA, KL Ottobeuren 903, ff. 87r–v [8 Apr. 1604].

society.[264] His simpler services like bleeding and cupping seem to have been fairly affordable,[265] but even the repair of a serious foot fracture could cost a half-dozen *gulden* (the price of a calf), while complicated procedures like the treatment of gunshot wounds could at 50 fl. run to the price of a small half-house.[266] Many peasants must therefore have turned to less-established healers, like midwives and cunning-women, or the itinerant barber-surgeons who seem to have been able to remove growths from the neck[267] and on occasion even restore sight to the blind.[268]

That such services were available at all in the seventeenth-century Swabian uplands may seem impressive,[269] but it should be emphasized that physical trauma requiring surgery was normally of less concern than the chronic enfeeblement which accompanied old age.[270] The rich could afford to hire maids to care for them in their dotage,[271] but a poor widow was more likely to fall back on the expedient of selling her home on credit, retaining a right of co-residence, and requiring that "should she become bedridden and unable to earn for herself, she shall be supplied [by the buyers] with food and drink according to her needs and the abilities of the household."[272] Anchored as they were in deeds of sale or mortgage, maintenance agreements of this kind were a robust sort of right, and there is clear evidence of their surviving subsequent resales of the property.[273] They could also be extremely detailed, as in the case of a contract drawn up

---

[264] The 1620 tax survey lists bathhouse keepers in the market town and in fifteen of eighteen villages; all of the village proprietors were taxed (among other property) on *Ehehaften* of 5–26 *malter* valued at 50–300 fl. StAA, KL Ottobeuren 102.

[265] StAA, KL Ottobeuren 919, ff. 80v–82r [11 Sep. 1680] includes a lengthy description of the bathhouse keeper's duties and a fee schedule, e.g. 2 kr. for bleeding, 1 kr. for cupping in the bathhouse, 2 kr. for cupping in the patient's house, and 1 kr. for a shave. A similar (and earlier) description of duties, but without the fee schedule, may be found in KL Ottobeuren 904, f. 252v [5 May 1611].

[266] StAA, KL Ottobeuren 904, f. 218r [22 Oct. 1610] and KL Ottobeuren 905, f. 190v [3 July 1614].

[267] StAA, KL Ottobeuren 918, ff. 11r [14 Jan. 1580] and 39v [12 June 1580].

[268] StAA, KL Ottobeuren 908, f. 100r [8 Aug. 1620].

[269] At one bathhouse keeper for every 105 households, the Ottobeuren lands had a density of medical practitioners equal to that of the urbanized provinces of North Holland; cf. Mary Lindemann, *Medicine and Society in Early Modern Europe* (Cambridge, 1999), p. 197. The quality of this medical care is hard to assess. That traveling healers could do business at all suggests at least some unmet needs, but explicit complaints about the village bathhouse keepers, though not unknown, seem to have been rare. See StAA, KL Ottobeuren 919, ff. 71r–v and 73v–74r [21 and 27 June 1680] for the complaints of the village of Böhen against their bathhouse keeper, who, it was alleged, "must rather poorly understand the execution of his duties, as his incompetence and laziness are often manifest . . . in irreparable harm [to his patients] "

[270] The bond-chicken registers in fact recognized "ill" as a wealth category which exempted the sick from payment. The gravity of this condition is reflected in the disappearance of most of these individuals from the subsequent register.

[271] StAA, KL Ottobeuren 903, ff. 92r–93r [19 May 1604].

[272] StAA, KL Ottobeuren 903, ff. 78v–79r [11 Mar. 1604].

[273] StAA, KL Ottobeuren 904, f. 205r [25 June 1610]. The rights were assured to the retiring widow in an earlier sale of the house, and are here reconfirmed at the transfer to a third party.

between Elisabeth Bergmann of Niederrieden and Martin Pfaudler and his wife, Ursula Mangler. Elisabeth was promised

that for the rest of her days they will supply the fodder and wages [*sic*] for her to maintain a nanny goat in both summer and winter, and that in addition to the mother, she shall have the right to raise one of its young. Item: should she later fall sick and infirm, the married couple and their heirs shall cook for her her food (which she must, however, herself provide) and carry it to her bed, care for her in this her illness according to her needs, [and] clean her bedclothes at appropriate times . . . She shall also always be given the fruit that grows on the wild grape tree in the garden by the house, as well as a basket of pears from the tree by the bakeoven, should it yield any . . . [274]

Of course, to cope with poverty was in no way to alter the fundamental condition, and there is no intention here to deny the deprivation and insecurity which was the lot of so many Ottobeuren peasants. Still less ought we to minimize the significance of informal networks of co-operation and reciprocity in the struggles of the poor to survive.[275] Nevertheless, the very evidence that the Ottobeuren poor lived in squalid half- or even quarter-houses[276] simultaneously documents the character of these residences *as assets*,[277] and the growing ease with which real property could be mortgaged, exchanged, and sold invested the rural underclass with powerful tools for the mitigation of insecurity. Similar consequences flowed from the elaboration of the credit market, and by the early seventeenth century we find even very poor widows and orphans loaning out small sums at interest to generate income streams.[278] Furthermore, self-help and co-operation were themselves often grounded in the manipulation of

For a more elaborate example, see the guarantee of residence and maintenance rights to an Attenhausen widow through three sequential sales of her home in ibid., ff. 253r [5 May 1611] and KL Ottobeuren 905, ff. 21v and 22r [13 Sep. 1612].

[274] StAA, KL Ottobeuren 905, ff. 64r–v [24 Apr. 1613].

[275] These networks are receiving growing attention in a literature previously dominated by the study of institutionalized poor relief. See the essays in Peregrine Horden and Richard Smith, eds., *The Locus of Care: Families, Communities, Institutions and the Provision of Welfare since Antiquity* (London, 1998), esp. Sandra Cavallo, "Family Obligations and Inequalities in Access to Care in Northern Italy, 17th to 18th Centuries" and Martin Dinges, "Self-Help and Reciprocity in Parish Assistance: Bordeaux in the 16th and 17th Centuries." Also Robert Jütte, *Poverty and Deviance in Early Modern Europe* (Cambridge, 1994), pp. 83–99.

[276] For sales of quarter-houses, see StAA, KL Ottobeuren 904, ff. 138v [9 July 1609] and 198v–199r [8 May 1610]; KL Ottobeuren 905, ff. 151r–v [9 Jan. 1614]; KL Ottobeuren 907, ff. 32v–33r [16 Dec. 1616] and 155v [12 Apr. 1618]. For the sale of a one-sixth house see KL Ottobeuren 907, ff. 16r–v [16 Oct. 1616].

[277] For a powerful assertion of this point in an urban context, see Valentin Groebner, *Ökonomie ohne Haus: zum Wirtschaften armer Leute in Nürnberg am Ende des 15. Jahrhunderts* (Göttingen, 1993).

[278] For example Michael Neher of Hawangen, who in the 1602 bond-chicken register was assessed the 2 kr. normally asked only of widows. His house was sold after his death in 1606, and seven years later his orphans loaned out 16 fl. at interest. StAA, KL Ottobeuren 491-I, Heft 10, f. 19v; KL Ottobeuren 903, ff. 205r–v [7 Feb. 1606]; and KL Ottobeuren 905, f. 146r [19 Dec. 1613]. In the same way the orphan Maria Wespach of Niederdorf, whose house was sold

property rights, like the 1611 agreement in which the four orphans of Marx Kopp ceded the use of their half-house in Egg to a married man in exchange for eight years of maintenance.[279] This is more than a matter of emphasizing the agency of the poor (important though that concern may be);[280] we also need to appreciate the effectiveness and institutional foundation of this agency. Three of Marx Kopp's four orphans ultimately settled in their natal village,[281] and his daughter Barbara managed to purchase the half-house in 1618.[282] At the same time, the children's original patron turns out to have been their older half-sister's husband, who used the eight years to borrow funds in half a dozen different villages[283] and double the value of his landholdings.[284] It seems clear, in other words, that all of this buying and borrowing had complex implications for relations among kin, and it is to these kin relations that we now turn.

for 80 fl. by her guardians in 1611, four years later loaned out 22 fl. at interest. KL Ottobeuren 904, ff. 268v–269r [19 Sep. 1611] and KL Ottobeuren 905, f. 259r [6 Apr. 1615]. See also the case of the widow Elisabetha Blank of Benningen, who was assessed the minimum head tax in both 1620 and 1627. She made loans of 50 fl. and 47 fl. shortly after her husband's death in c. 1609, and her daughters loaned out 30 fl. some years later. KL Ottobeuren 491-II, Heft 16, f. 17r; KL Ottobeuren 102, f. 196v; KL Ottobeuren 104, f. 175v; KL Ottobeuren 904, ff. 157v [17 Nov. 1609] and 183v [10 Mar. 1610]; KL Ottobeuren 905, ff. 318r–v [5 Dec. 1615].

279 StAA, KL Ottobeuren 904, ff. 238r–v [23 Mar. 1611]. The use of the half-house and 1.25 *jauchert* of arable land was ceded to one Michael Ruoff, who at the end of the eight years was to be sold the arable for 60 fl.

280 See the insightful remarks in Andreas Maisch, *Notdürftiger Unterhalt und gehörige Schranken: Lebensbedingungen und Lebensstile in württembergischen Dörfern der frühen Neuzeit* (Stuttgart, 1992), pp. 9–13.

281 StAA, KL Ottobeuren 102, ff. 282r, 287r–v, and 289r. Also KL Ottobeuren 907, ff. 110v–111r [2 Oct. 1617] and KL Ottobeuren 908, f. 62v [26 Apr. 1620].

282 StAA, KL Ottobeuren 907, f. 21r [24 Dec. 1618].

283 StAA, KL Ottobeuren 904, f. 275r [27 Jan. 1612]; KL Ottobeuren 905, ff. 159r [7 Feb. 1614], 182r [23 May 1614], 182v [23 May 1614], 229v [17 Jan. 1615], 296v–297r [2 Oct. 1615], 330r–v [4 Feb. 1616], 333v–334r [8 Feb. 1616], and 348r [7 Apr. 1616]; KL Ottobeuren 907, f. 45r [29 Jan. 1617].

284 StAA, KL Ottobeuren 903, f. 228v [28 Apr. 1606]; KL Ottobeuren 904, ff. 19r [3 Jan. 1608], 165r [9 Jan. 1610], 274v [27 Jan. 1612], and 274v–278r [27 Jan. 1612]; KL Ottobeuren 907, ff. 147r–v [15 Mar. 1618], 158r [15 Mar. 1618]; KL Ottobeuren 908, ff. 62v–63r [26 Apr. 1620].

5. Living on borrowed time (c. 1560–c. 1630)

In the midwinter of 1616/17, Barbara Sontheimer of Dietratried married the widower Caspar Herz of Leupolz under less than ideal circumstances.[1] She was not a virgin, he was landless, and no part of the story – including its eventual happy ending – makes sense outside the context of peasant inheritance practices.

Barbara's father, Melchior Sontheimer, had farmed 7 *jauchert* of land in Dietratried since the late 1570s.[2] In the spring of 1614 he decided to retire, and, in keeping with the newer custom of impartibility, sold the entire property to his eldest son, Johann, for 200 *gulden*. Barbara Sontheimer and her sister, Maria, were now expected to leave home to work as servants elsewhere, retaining only the right to convalesce at the house if they came back sick from service. Johann also agreed to later provide meals for a cobbler, tailor, and seamstress to make his sisters' wedding clothes.[3] The arrangement was clearly not to the sisters' liking, and a year later it was amended to allow them to remain at home "if they do not wish to go into service." In that case, however, Barbara and Maria "shall [still] be obliged to feed themselves."[4] Johann was not going to support his sisters, who therefore had only two options: to remain at home and work as unmarried dependants, or to go into service against their will. Maria chose the former,[5] and Barbara the latter, finding work in the village of Unterwesterheim in the home of the *Bauer* Hans Rauch.

In Unterwesterheim Barbara met up with her employer's stepson, Jacob Magg, and by year's end she was carrying his child. Marriage was out of

[1] StAA, KL Ottobeuren 907, ff. 41r–v [27 Jan. 1617].
[2] Dertsch, "Das Einwohnerbuch des Ottobeurer Klosterstaats 1564," p. 83; StAA, KL Ottobeuren 601-II, ff. 133r–136r; KL Ottobeuren 64, ff. 32r–33v.
[3] StAA, KL Ottobeuren 905, ff. 168v–169r [7 Apr. 1614].
[4] Ibid., ff. 249–250r [11 Mar. 1615].
[5] She is listed as an unmarried resident in Johann's household in the 1620 tax survey. Her property was worth 90 fl.; his totalled 350 fl. StAA, KL Ottobeuren 102, f. 157v. After her brother's death Maria married and acquired the property herself for 400 fl. KL Ottobeuren 909, f. 50r [6 Mar. 1625].

the question, as Barbara had no dowry to match the enormous wealth of Jacob's household, and the stepfather was in any case in no hurry to retire and hand over the *Hof*.[6] By the early seventeenth century, however, almost all human obligations at Ottobeuren could be commuted to cash equivalents, and in Barbara Sontheimer's case the cost of "defloration and impregnation" was settled at 115 *gulden* and duly registered in the notarial protocols.[7] Barbara took her money and found herself a husband.

Caspar Herz came from equally straitened circumstances. The second son of a poor *Seldner*,[8] he lost his father while still a boy in 1607, and Caspar's mother spent the last years of her life clinging to the front half of a house, sharing a cow with the other residents but carefully keeping all of its dung for her own garden.[9] The half-house and its few patches of land were no more divisible than Barbara Sontheimer's home, and Caspar therefore ended up with no property at all when his mother sold out to his older brother Martin in 1609. Indeed, Caspar did not even receive a convalescence right in his natal home, because his brother was forced to sell the family's land to a neighbor,[10] in whose house Caspar was granted four weeks to recover from any illness he might contract as a servant.[11] Like his other non-inheriting siblings,[12] Caspar did receive a cash settlement from his brother, and was therefore able to marry one Ursula Diepolder shortly thereafter in about 1614. On the other hand, Caspar's first wife was one among eight heirs in her own family,[13] and it is unclear whether her inheritance was ever collected before she died two years later. One way or another, Caspar's only recorded acquisition was the purchase of six cherry trees for 4 *gulden* in 1615,[14] and it was only the premature death of his brother Martin which made him a householder by default.[15]

Barbara Sontheimer's 115 *gulden* were thus as much of a lifeline for Caspar as the respectability of house and wedlock which he offered her. The couple

---

[6] He had married Jacob Magg's mother, Barbara Weber, on 19 October 1603 after the death of her first husband, Mang Magg, on 26 April 1603. In 1620 Hans Rauch had a gross wealth of 3,862.5 fl. [including 93.25 *jauchert* of land] and retained this property until 1627 at least. His burial is unrecorded, but Barbara Weber died on 3 February 1634. StAA, KL Ottobeuren 102, ff. 307v–308r and KL Ottobeuren 104, ff. 288v–289r. WestPR, Vol. I, pp. 111, 124, and 180.

[7] StAA, KL Ottobeuren 907, f. 12r [29 Sep. 1616].

[8] StAA, KL Ottobeuren 681, Heft 3, f. 19r and Heft 4, f. 19v.

[9] StAA, KL Ottobeuren 39, f. 136v; KL Ottobeuren 904, f. 24r [30 Jan. 1608].

[10] StAA, KL Ottobeuren 904, ff. 116r–v, 138r, 168r, and 181r [7 Mar. 1609, 26 July 1609, 9 Jan. 1610, and 4 Mar. 1610 respectively]. Also ibid., ff. 64r–v [30 June 1608].

[11] Ibid., f. 168r [9 Jan. 1610].

[12] Ibid., f. 168v [9 Jan. 1610]. Also KL Ottobeuren 903, f. 104r [5 Aug. 1604].

[13] StAA, KL Ottobeuren 905, f. 169r [7 Apr. 1614]. Caspar had probably only just married, as he is not listed as a householder in the 1613 and 1614 bond-chicken registers.

[14] Ibid., f. 97v [5 Feb. 1615].

[15] Martin Herz is listed in Leupolz in the 1614 bond-chicken register, but has been replaced by Caspar by 1617. There is no notarial evidence of his relocation within the monastery lands or emigration without. StAA, KL Ottobeuren 491-II, Heft 18, f. 8r and Heft 21, ff. 6v–7r.

went on to modest prosperity, doubling the value of their property between 1620 and 1627,[16] and providing heartwarming evidence (should any more be required) of the Ottobeuren peasantry's ability to exceed its circumstances. Yet the deeper lesson of this rural drama is the degree to which its acts, both the tragic and the triumphant, were shaped by an essential feature of the new system of generational transition which emerged at the end of the sixteenth century: the introduction of unprecedented strictness into kin relations combined with an effort to mitigate that strictness by means of cash payments. The subject of the present chapter, accordingly, is the impact of impartibility, parental retirement, inheritance by sale, and long-term debt on peasant kinship, and in particular on the roles into which individuals were cast by the politics of inheritance.[17]

The notarization of the terms by which one generation replaced another suddenly presents us at the end of the sixteenth century with a much more detailed picture of rural kinship. This suddenness is of course somewhat deceptive, since not everything that was recorded in the protocols was then new. Even in so far as inheritance agreements restated traditional rights and obligations, however, the fact of their commitment to protocol underscores the regulatory problem created by the new customs of impartibility, parental retirement, inheritance by sale, and long-term debt.

The medieval system of social reproduction was predicated on social roles that were both discrete and stable. Children were unambiguous subordinates during their parents' (or at least their fathers') lifetimes, but thereafter became independent householders on the basis of equal shares of inherited land. By 1600 both the discreteness and the stability of these roles were in serious jeopardy. What happened to sibling equality and independence when one child inherited a familiar home and the others had to parlay their cash installments into a life somewhere else? What happened to a parent's authority when in his or her declining years the house and farm were shared with a married adult child? And what happened more generally to the heir when the traditional imperative to marry well acquired a sharper specificity itemized in a deed of sale and bill of mortgage? The short answer is that the appropriate performance of social roles could no longer be guaranteed by simple respect for tradition, and instead came to be shored up by contracts of ever-increasing number and detail. As for the longer answer, we shall have to take a closer look at each of the standard roles in turn.

Let us begin with the "yielding heirs," a role contemporaries used to refer to the siblings of a designated heir, but which may also be extended to include

---

[16] StAA, KL Ottobeuren 102, f. 97v and KL Ottobeuren 104, f. 86r. The increase (from 160 to 380 fl.) was mainly due to moneylending; Caspar Herz had loans of 220 fl. in 1627.

[17] I must here acknowledge a deep debt to Hermann Rebel, *Peasant Classes: The Bureaucratization of Property and Family Relations under Early Habsburg Absolutism, 1511–1636* (Princeton, 1983).

the ungrown children of a remarrying widow or widower, since the new spouse customarily insisted that the land pass to a child of the second marriage. Of these children the first thing to be said is that their mere survival was an accomplishment in itself. The Ottobeuren lands were an area of fearsome infant and child mortality, and the region as a whole would remain so deep into the nineteenth century.[18] In the parish of Westerheim the years 1595–1625 saw 34.8 percent of children die in infancy; in the larger parish of Hawangen the rate in 1607–25 was even higher at 46.1 percent.[19] The frailty of young children clearly weighed on the minds of their parents. Pregnant women did not assume that their children would be born "joyfully into the world,"[20] and even after birth it was not taken for granted that the offspring would outlive their parents.[21] Inheritance and remarriage arrangements often contained complex contingency plans in case several children should die,[22] and the fiscal ramifications to the heir of the sibling's death were detailed with grim precision.[23]

The fact that children were so vulnerable did not, however, diminish their value either to their own families or to society at large. The Ottobeuren courts vigorously punished the negligence of maids towards infants in their care and the

---

[18] See the map of infant mortality rates in 1875–80 in John E. Knodel, *The Decline of Fertility in Germany, 1871–1939* (Princeton, 1974), p. 164. Upper Swabia and Bavaria have infant mortality rates of more than 30 percent, the highest in all of Germany.

[19] WestPR, Vol. I, pp. 1–66; HawPR, Vol. I, ff. 1r–63v. Infant deaths were recorded in the baptismal registers as a black cross next to the child's name. The pastor of Hawangen also subtotaled the figures at the end of each year (e.g. for 1610 on f. 15v: "Hoc Anno baptizati sunt Infantes 29, et ex iis mortui sunt 14"). Only the Westerheim register has a separate burial register, kept for youths and adults only.

[20] StAA, KL Ottobeuren 905, ff. 115–116v (*Heiratsbrief* of Maria Schmidt of Sontheim dated 26 Sep. 1613). Maria had four sons and was pregnant with a fifth child from her deceased husband, Johann Sanz, when she married one Johann Gebelin of Wetzlen. Each of the four 'before-children,' as they were called, was promised 50 fl. and a metal-bound chest. If the unborn child survived, it was also to receive 50 fl. and "if the said Maria Schmidt should bear a daughter from and by her deceased husband, [the daughter] shall inherit her mother's chest and linens, and at her wedding, in addition to the aforesaid *Voraus* of 50 fl., shall be given a dress and coat." Similar contingencies are detailed in KL Ottobeuren 903, ff. 21r–v [23 May 1603] and 98r–99r [19 June 1604], and KL 905, ff. 101v–102r [21 May 1613].

[21] StAA, KL Ottobeuren 904, ff. 224v–225r [10 Jan. 1611].

[22] StAA, KL Ottobeuren 905, ff. 228v–229r: *Heiratsbrief* of Elisabeth Leupold of Egg dated 17 Jan. 1615. Elisabeth had two children from a previous marriage, each of whom was granted a *Voraus* of 100 fl. If either died unmarried, the money was to be inherited by the other, and if both of them died unmarried the money was to be divided between their mother and another relative. Clauses redistributing the portion of a child from the first marriage among his or her siblings should s/he die unmarried are quite common in seventeenth-century *Heiratsbriefe*.

[23] After Stephan Geromüller of Waldmühle bought a house, mill complex, and 11 *beschlagungen* of land from his father, Johann, for 1,200 fl., lifetime residence rights on the property were granted to Stephan's cousin Silvester and his sister Catharina. The mortgage and maintenance agreement also stipulated that "in so far as the aforesaid Catharina should survive fifteen years from the present date and not die beforehand, one half of her property shall be inherited by and belong to the younger married couple [i.e. Stephan and his wife]." StAA, KL Ottobeuren 904, ff. 88v and 88v–88[a]r [2 Jan. 1609].

excessive correction of apprentices.[24] Parents devoted considerable energy to the upbringing of their young, as is clear from the value they placed on schooling. The market town of Ottobeuren had a long history of education for children; a schoolmaster is mentioned there as early as 1495 (and a schoolmistress in 1516).[25] Even in the villages, scattered references in various documents make it clear that schoolmasters were active in at least six rural parishes by the early seventeenth century.[26] And although the position of village schoolmaster was not especially lucrative, the fact that it was in several cases filled by someone from outside the monastery lands suggests that the peasants went to some effort to find the right person to teach their children.[27]

For a few peasant boys, in fact, booklearning did not stop in the village school but was continued at a university.[28] Thus when Ursula Hess of Sontheim remarried in 1620, she promised to provide her son Johann Ruoff with "honorable clothing, food and drink to the best of the household's abilities until he shall begin studies at a university,"[29] while the Ungerhausen innkeeper's

---

[24] "Hans Joder's two maids struck each other and knocked over the young child in the crib so that the child was injured. Fined 13 ß h." StAA, KL Ottobeuren 587-II, Heft 17 (1593/4), Benningen. "Othmar Schütz's wife struck Jerg Fackler's daughter with a stick – [fined] 7 ß." Ibid., Heft 20 (1598/9), Benningen. "Bläsi Aberöll's son struck a boy at the worksite without reason – [fined] 10 ß." KL Ottobeuren 587-I, Heft 3 (1566/7), Egg. "Jerg Neher struck Hans Diepolder's child with a weapon and drew blood – [fined] £1 15 ß." Ibid., Heft 6 (1574), Hawangen. For a later example, see the case of the steward Niclaus Mayer of Wolfarts, who "very wickedly beat" a little boy "because he was pilfering [literally 'went among'] the strawberries in the Meier's cow pasture." The steward was "fined £2 because of this excess of his . . . [and] is to pay 45 kr. to the plaintiff for damages." KL Ottobeuren 919, f. 68v [21 June 1680].

[25] StAA, KU Ottobeuren 568 [15 June 1495] and 848 [5 Jan. 1516]. Christian Rottermelin served as the market town's schoolmaster for over forty years, from before 1564, when he is listed in a serf roll (Dertsch, "Das Einwohnerbuch des Ottobeurer Klosterstaats 1564," p. 3), to his retirement in 1604 (KL Ottobeuren 903, ff. 81v–82r [15 Mar. 1604]). He was eventually succeeded as schoolmaster by Johann Wurm, son of the blacksmith of Unterwesterheim. KL Ottobeuren 907, f. 59v [14 Mar. 1617].

[26] The following schoolmasters can be documented: Johann Maier (1628) in Benningen (KL Ottobeuren 491-III, Heft 33, f. 10r); Martin Schmidt (1620) in Egg (KL Ottobeuren 908, ff. 90r–v); Johann Scheifelin (1625) in Frechenrieden (KL Ottobeuren 491-III, Heft 30, f. 10v); Johann Gärtner (1630) in Hawangen (HawPR, Vol. I, f. 79r); Jacob Maier (1602) in Niederrieden (KL Ottobeuren 491-I, Heft 10, f. 13r); Jerg Baumer (1621) in Sontheim (KL Ottobeuren 102, f. 353r). Fuller documentation for the early eighteenth century confirms that every village had its own school. Weber, "Wirtschaftsquellen" (Teil I), p. 181.

[27] See the immigration records – all from 1619/20 – for the schoolmasters of Benningen (from the lands of the monastery of Rot), Egg (from Schönegg in the lands of the Bishop of Augsburg), and Sontheim (from Mindelheim in the lands of the Duke of Bavaria). StAA, KL Ottobeuren 583, Heft 41, ff. 3r–v.

[28] See for example StAA, KU Ottobeuren 1887 [25 Aug. 1577]. Johann Losherr of Benningen and his wife, Anna Pfeiler, borrow 9 fl. from the Abbot "to support their son Caspar in his studies at [the Jesuit college in] Dillingen." The father was an Ottobeuren serf (Dertsch, "Das Einwohnerbuch des Ottobeurer Klosterstaats 1564," p. 39), but he was not a Hof tenant (KL Ottobeuren 27, ff. 43v–52r and KL Ottobeuren 31, ff. 34r–36v).

[29] StAA, KL Ottobeuren 908, ff. 44r–45v [12 Mar. 1620]. Johann was also promised a cow and 200 fl. in cash, all of which was compensation for not inheriting the enormous Hof (30 jauchert of arable and 42 tagwerk of meadow land) of his father, David Ruoff, which shortly thereafter

son Jerg Schütz was in 1607 promised the cost of his education if he "should subsequently acquire a desire and affection for study."[30] Of course, most of these peasant scholars came from the tenant farming elite, but the children of smallholders did occasionally manage to become clerks[31] or attend university.[32] There was even a small scholarship, endowed by an Ottobeuren parish priest, for the support of a needy pupil studying for holy orders.[33]

As parents came to retire in their own lifetimes, responsibility for the care of younger children devolved increasingly upon the heir. In an effort to ensure the proper care of the "yielding heirs," long lists of their rights were appended to the mortgage (*Schuldbrief*) and maintenance (*Leibgeding*) agreement accompanying the deed of sale (*Kaufbrief*) to the heir. These documents are marked by an often touching solicitude for the dignity and well-being of all of the children, the most striking examples of which are the provisions made for the disabled, who otherwise almost never appear in the historical record.

There is no way of knowing how many people lived with physical and mental handicaps in the Ottobeuren lands. It is difficult even to gain a sense of the nature of the disabilities involved, since the descriptions are rarely more precise than "burdened with constant infirmity," "sick and damaged body," or even "not, indeed, very able."[34] Occasionally we learn a little more, for example that the child was mute or had a seriously injured knee.[35] At any rate, the definitive

---

passed to Ursula's new husband, Johann Heffelin (ibid., f. 74r [12 May 1620]). The marriage thus made Heffelin a very wealthy man; he had a gross wealth of 1,475 fl. in 1620 and 1,818 fl. in 1627. StAA, KL Ottobeuren 102, ff. 337r–v and KL Ottobeuren 104, ff. 324r–v.

30 StAA, KL Ottobeuren 904, ff. 1r–v [2 Sep. 1607].

31 For example Barthlome Hagg of Hawangen, who became a scribe for Marshall Pappenheim (StAA, KL Ottobeuren 903, f. 75v [20 Feb. 1604]). His father, Johann Hagg, was extremely poor, being assessed only 2 kr. in the bond-chicken registers for 1586 and 1590, and having even that sum waived due to poverty in 1587 (KL Ottobeuren 491-I, Hefte 3, f. 13v, 4, f. 15r, and 5, f. 7r).

32 See the remarkable *Schuldbrief* of the smallholder Christian Allgäuer and his wife, Anna Karg, of Bossarts, who in 1612 mortgaged their garden to the Memmingen Spitalmeister for the 100 fl. "which was little by little extended to their son for necessary maintenance during the undertaking of his studies." It was agreed that either the parents would repay the debt in cash or the son would work off the debt for the creditor (StAA, KL Ottobeuren 905, f. 17r [22 Aug. 1612]). The son, Harthaus Allgäuer, eventually finished his studies and became a chaplain and schoolmaster in Memmingen. The modesty of the family's resources may be judged from a *Kaufbrief* of 21 November 1620 (KL Ottobeuren 908, ff. 117r–v), whereby Harthaus and his brother sold off their now deceased parents' estate. The lands measured a mere 3 *beschlagungen* (≈ 9 *jauchert/tagwerk*); in the 1620 tax survey the buyer (one Michael Enderas) had a gross wealth of only 300 fl. (KL Ottobeuren 102, f. 154v).

33 There is a delightful discussion by the Abbot's council about which of four boys recommended by their pastors most deserved (based on financial need, intellectual talents, and progress to date) the scholarship in StAA, KL Ottobeuren (Mü.B.) 64, "Ratsprotokolle 1631–1638," ff. 128v–129v [30 Aug. 1631].

34 StAA, KL Ottobeuren 908, ff. 159r–v [16 June 1621], KL Ottobeuren 905, f. 148v [7 Jan. 1614] and KL Ottobeuren 907, ff. 244v–245r [23 Apr. 1619].

35 StAA, KL Ottobeuren 904, ff. 77r–v [1 Nov. 1608] and KL Ottobeuren 911, pp. 12–13 [9 Apr. 1630].

element seems to have been the judgment that a child would be unable to marry, a misfortune that was enough of a worry that parents included clauses to provide for a currently healthy child "should it *become* so wanting and deficient of body that it should be incapable of going into service or marrying."[36]

Parents sought to protect these children, not least because very little allowance was made for them if they contravened the harsh rules of rural society. Enderas Reubel of Sontheim, for example, was a poor cottager's son.[37] The victim of long-standing rumors that he was a thief and a sodomite, he was arrested in August of 1611 at a parish festival in the nearby village of Attenhausen. Although the court ruled that he was "an unwell, simple-minded person, so much so that he cannot even recite the Lord's Prayer," the young man was condemned to a slow death in the noose. The appeals of the parish clergy and the Sontheim village *Gemeinde* could effect only a commutation to the swifter dispatch of the headsman.[38] But as tragic as his story is, it is worth noting that in his short life – he was only twenty when he was executed – Enderas had also been the beneficiary of two cash payments from the estates of his grandparents, one of them received less than six months before his death.[39] A mental disability was thus no bar to a claim to family property, and it was above all through inheritance that parents sought to secure the future of handicapped children.

The most common approach was to convert the child's share of the inheritance into a lifetime right to be fed, clothed, and sheltered by the heir (or whoever might purchase the property).[40] The contract might even give the disabled child

---

[36] StAA, KL Ottobeuren 908, ff. 162r–163r [28 June 1621]. For a similar clause see ibid., ff. 142v–143r [4 Apr. 1621]. Emphasis mine.

[37] Enderas was the son of Johann Reubel 'Decker' and Anna Briechlin, who were briefly married sometime between 1585 (when he was single) and 1587 (when Johann took a second wife) (StAA, KL Ottobeuren 601-II, ff. 75r–88v and KL Ottobeuren 583, Heft 5, f. 18r). Johann Reubel's 2 kr. assessment in the bond-chicken registers for 1590 and 1595 (KL Ottobeuren 491-I, Heft 5, f. 17v and Heft 6, f. 20r) place him among the poorest of the poor, and although he later rose to the standard 3 kr. *Seldner* assessment (ibid., Heft 10, f. 22r and Heft 14, f. 14v for 1602 and 1609 respectively), the 1620 tax survey shows that his circumstances remained very modest (KL Ottobeuren 102, ff. 343v–344r). Johann "retired" in 1616 and sold half of his heavily mortgaged house and 4 *jauchert/tagwerk* of land to another son, Johann junior. KL Ottobeuren 907, f. 31v (16 Dec. 1616).

[38] StAA, KL Ottobeuren 4, Document 292, ff. 872r–873v [15 Sep. 1611]. The role of rumor is attested by the court's declaration that Enderas "for some time now has been vehemently decried not only for commiting various thefts, but also for staining and polluting himself with the repellent sin of sodomy." The document records no specific charge of which he was convicted.

[39] StAA, KL Ottobeuren 904, ff. 115v–116r [7 Mar. 1609] and 226r [1 Feb. 1611]. The first payment is explicitly described as Enderas' share of his deceased mother's claim to the estate of her father, Jerg Briechlin of Ottobeuren, the monastery's chief teamster.

[40] StAA, KL Ottobeuren 904, ff. 167v–168r [9 Jan. 1610]; KL Ottobeuren 905, ff. 310v–311r [18 Nov. 1615]. For an early example of this custom, see KU Ottobeuren 760 [5 July 1509]. Enderas Fogelin of Sontheim promises the executors of his parents' estate to house and maintain his handicapped sister Appolonia and to give her 3 shillings annual pocket money.

an extra share of the inheritance or the right to claim his/her inheritance in cash and move away if s/he so desired.[41] All in all, these provisions might be quite detailed, as in the case of Maria Karg, a miller's daughter in the market town of Ottobeuren:

Balthas Batzer and his wife Barbara Karg grant their daughter Maria Karg, in consideration of her protracted and also worrisomely incurable bodily infirmity [the following]. First, that for the rest of her days she shall have her meals in the heated room near the door. Second, that she shall live undisturbed in the small room in the garret. Furthermore they grant her a closet in the house and the end-strip in the garden by the house to be used and enjoyed as she wishes. In the same way she shall and may cook on the hearth in the kitchen, and walk to and from the fire without interference by anyone. She shall also not be forced by anyone to do any work beyond that which she does herself of [her own] good and free will.[42]

Equally noteworthy is the frequency with which these contracts cling to the hope of recovery from disability. Thus, for example, the Stephansried *Seldner* Johann Zick was sold the family home for 150 fl. in 1608, but was required to share ownership of the property with his sister "if his sister Catharina should recover the health of her body."[43] In the same way Michael Diepolder of Ollarzried's four brothers were promised 170 fl. when their stepmother, Anna Friesorg, sold the family home in 1606. "In consideration of his bodily infirmity," Michael was instead guaranteed a right to lifetime residence and maintenance on the property, "but in the event that he should later learn a craft, which he is free to do," the protocol carefully stipulated, "he shall be given his share of the aforesaid 170 fl."[44] In wealthier families the sums held in reserve for the disabled might be quite handsome. Sibilla Magg of Dietratried was the daughter of the *Hof*-tenant Johann Magg.[45] In keeping with the standard pattern, Sibilla

---

[41] StAA, KL Ottobeuren 908, ff. 176r–177r [30 July 1621] grants an extra 20 fl. to Christina, the daughter of Caspar Salb of Dennenberg and KL Ottobeuren 904, ff. 130v–131r [19 May 1609] grants Stephan Epplin of Oberried 200 fl., a set of linens, a chest, and a suit of clothes if she decides not to live with the new householders.

[42] StAA, KL Ottobeuren 903, f. 35v [8 Aug. 1603]; KL Ottobeuren 903, f. 35v. Balthas Batzer is identified as the "upper" miller of the market town of Ottobeuren in a *Kaufbrief* dated 13 Apr. 1605 (ibid., f. 161v). He was thus a wealthy man, ranking in the top 10 percent of householders in the market town in the 1585 tax register (cf. KL Ottobeuren 676a).

[43] StAA, KL Ottobeuren 904, ff. 28r–v [20 Feb. 1608]. According to the *Kaufbrief* (f. 28r) the property amounted to no more than a house and 4 *jauchert* of land.

[44] StAA, KL Ottobeuren 903, ff. 242v–243r [3 July 1606]. The grant was connected with the (unregistered) transfer of 8 *beschlagungen* from the widowed stepmother to one Michael Kürchoff, who replaced the boys' father, Johann Diepolder (as is clear from a comparison of the 1601 list of Ollarzried tithe payers [KL Ottobeuren 681, Heft 4, ff. 1v–2r] with a later list from 1606 [KL Ottobeuren 39, ff. 130r–132r]). The size of the property is recorded in KL Ottobeuren 102, ff. 87r–v.

[45] Sibilla's father, Johann Magg, had been admitted to his *Hof* on 31 August 1562; it passed after his death to Sibilla's brother Jerg on 28 March 1600 (KL Ottobeuren 27, ff. 65v, 67v). The

was promised the right to be housed, fed, and clothed in her sister Ursula's house in the neighboring village of Wolfertschwenden. In exchange, Sibilla ceded to Ursula her future inheritance, whose value was projected at 260 fl.,

> unless the aforesaid daughter Sibilla should recover enough in body and mind that she can marry, and should be sufficiently advanced in understanding to do so [auch zu solch. verstandts halber genuegsamblich qualificiert befiende]. In that case the aforesaid couple [i.e. Ursula and her husband] shall without delay return and restore to her her money, that is the 260 fl., for which their lands shall stand security.[46]

As it happened Sibilla never recovered, and at her death less than five years later her inheritance, now totalling 568 fl. 28 kr. 4 h., two cows, and some linens, was divided between her sisters Ursula and Anna.[47] Nevertheless, the arrangements made for her care illustrate how, even in cases of severe disability – and Sibilla seems to have been both physically and mentally handicapped – families refused to give up on their kin.

For all the humanity embodied in these agreements, however, the implication of their preservation in the archival record is quite clear: the care of the disabled cost money, the provision of which could only be guaranteed by contractual obligation. Of course, we cannot know the frequency with which the love of a handicapped sibling or stepchild ran up against harsher fiscal realities, but every now and then a protocol entry adverts to the predicament in which many householders must have been caught. Indications range from the mild aside that "in consideration of her bodily indisposition," a sister will have lifetime residence and maintenance rights, but "that work which is possible for her to accomplish, she shall be obliged to do," to the sharper declaration that a handicapped daughter may live at home "if she should not marry . . . but [in that case] the daughter Maria shall be obliged to come up with [literally 'see to'] her food by herself."[48] But even in the absence of restrictive clauses like these, the support of the disabled was ultimately subject to an unsentimental logic of cost and expense, and in some cases it is possible to reconstruct the operation of this calculus in considerable detail.

Anna Schmalholz and Johann Velk were married in about the year 1590.[49] They lived in the small hamlet of Höhe, where Johann's father, Stephan Velk,

---

Hof included 6 tagwerk of garden, 6 tagwerk of meadow, and 60 jauchert of arable land. In combination with a few smaller parcels purchased in 1615–16 and worth a total of 304 fl. (KL Ottobeuren 905, ff. 236r, 262v, and 327v), the Hof made Jerg Magg a very wealthy man; in 1620 his gross wealth was 1,355 fl. (KL Ottobeuren 102, f. 157r).

[46] StAA, KL Ottobeuren 905, ff. 272v–273r [1 June 1615].

[47] StAA, KL Ottobeuren 908, ff. 39r–v [20 Feb. 1620].

[48] StAA, KL Ottobeuren 905, ff. 310v–311r [18 Nov. 1615] and KL Ottobeuren 903, f. 327r [28 May 1607].

[49] StAA, KL Ottobeuren 911, pp. 50–1 [8 July 1630] records that Jerg Velk of Höhe's parents were married "about 40 years ago."

scraped an existence[50] from a subsistence holding of about 15 *jauchert*. Father and son worked the land together until Johann Velk died in about the year 1603.[51] Anna quickly remarried, to a certain Johann Kessler from the hamlet of Unterhaslach, but died herself shortly thereafter,[52] leaving her blind son Michael and three other children in the care of their stepfather. Johann Kessler came from an even poorer family than the Velks,[53] but his trail in the archival record leaves a powerful impression of a hard-driving and calculating peasant. He quickly bought out old Stephan Velk's half of the land in Höhe, but held on to the property only as long as it took to find a gullible buyer on whom to unload it. In 1611 that victim materialized in the person of a certain Mathias Helzlin, who purchased the land – and along with it the responsibility for the Velk orphans – for the absurdly high price of 700 fl., almost twice what Johann Kessler had paid for it.[54] Kessler at once packed up and moved back to his home in Unterhaslach, and swiftly assembled a holding as large as the one he had just sold, but for half the price.[55] In the years that followed, Kessler made acquisition after acquisition[56] while Helzlin sank deeper into debt.[57] Finally, in 1621 Kessler agreed to resume the responsibility for the care of his stepchildren, but only after extracting another 130 fl. from the unfortunate Mathias Helzlin.[58] By 1627 Mathias Helzlin was on the verge of bankruptcy,

---

[50] Stephan Velk's tithe payments in 1600 and 1601 suggest an annual grain harvest of 6.47 *malter*, not even two-thirds of the minimum requirement for a family of five (and there were at least seven people living on the farm). StAA, KL Ottobeuren 681, Heft 3, f. 2r and Heft 4, f. 2v.

[51] The size of the property and its division between Johann and his father is recorded in StAA, KL Ottobeuren 903, f. 124r [17 Nov. 1604]. Johann Velk first appears as a householder (listed together with his father) in the bond-chicken register for 1595; he is not listed in 1590 (KL 491-I, Heft 5, f. 2r and Heft 6, f. 4v). Johann is still listed in the bond-chicken register for 1602 (KL 491-I, Heft 10, f. 6r), but was deceased by 1604.

[52] These events inferred from StAA, KL Ottobeuren 904, f. 124v [17 Nov. 1604].

[53] Michael Kessler's tithe payments in 1600 and 1601 (StAA, KL Ottobeuren 681, Heft 3, f. 4v and Heft 4, f. 6v) average 3.82 *malter*. He earned almost as much from flax growing and livestock raising (both calves and foals) as he did from grain growing, but his estimated total agricultural income in those years (34.6 fl. per annum) was still less than Stephan Velk's (42.46 fl.).

[54] StAA, KL Ottobeuren 904, f. 124r [6 Feb. 1611]. Johann Kessler's purchase of the second half of the land for 200 fl. is detailed in the 1604 *Kaufbrief*, which also indicates that he acquired the first half when he married Anna Schmalholz.

[55] StAA, KL Ottobeuren 905, ff. 12v–13r: three *Kaufbriefe* dated 9 Aug. 1612 for a house, 4 *beschlagungen* (≈ 12 *jauchert/tagwerk*) of land, a half-*tagwerk* of meadow, and two unmeasured parcels of arable land for a total of 364 fl. Most of this land was purchased from his father, and the rest from two unrelated sellers.

[56] StAA, KL Ottobeuren 907, f. 62r (*Kaufbrief* for 30 fl. worth of arable land dated 20 March 1617); KL Ottobeuren 908, ff. 65r (*Tauschbrief* [i.e. an exchange] of a garden for 2 *tagwerk* of meadow) and 118v (*Kaufbrief* for 1 *beschlagung* [≈ 3 *jauchert/tagwerk*] of land worth 110 fl. dated 23 Nov. 1620).

[57] Michael Helzlin seems to have purchased the land in Höhe without having to borrow, but by 1620 he had debts of 320 fl. StAA, KL Ottobeuren 102, f. 82r.

[58] StAA, KL Ottobeuren 908, ff. 183v–184r [22 Oct. 1621].

while Johann Kessler had achieved the wealth and status of a *Bauer*.[59] As for the Velk orphans, their fate is unknown. One of them, a son Jerg, did manage to complete an apprenticeship as a smith, but he thereupon left the Ottobeuren lands and never returned.[60] Of the other three, blind Michael and his sisters, Ursula and Magdalena, we know even less. How they felt about being shuffled – sold, indeed – from place to place like so many head of cattle can only be guessed at.

The suspicion that an heir's relationship with yielding (or disabled) siblings was marked by a tension between embracing and ridding one's self of the burden of supporting one's kin is further deepened by the workings of rural apprenticeship. Entry into many of the rural crafts (blacksmith, butcher, miller, shoemaker, tailor, etc.) was organized at Ottobeuren through a system of formal instruction. At the age of about fourteen[61] a boy would begin working for a master, and after a two-year term of training and service (three years in especially skilled trades like cabinetmaking)[62] would be issued with a *Lehrbrief*, or certificate of apprenticeship. Over the period 1580–1630 there was a marked tendency for increased elaboration and formalization of both the training process and the crafts as a whole. The three-year term began to be introduced into other apprenticeships like milling and shoemaking,[63] and the masters began to organize into guilds governed, after the model of the village community, by a council of four.[64] The Ottobeuren tailors in particular not only established a guild (*c.* 1601) but also began aggressively prosecuting the performance of tailoring work by non-members of the guild.[65] By the early seventeenth century the *Lehrbrief* itself had become a much more formal document, systematically

---

[59] StAA, KL Ottobeuren 104, ff. 50r (Johann Kessler's gross wealth is 745 fl.) and 82r (Mathias Helzlin has since 1620 lost a garden and an ox, and his debts of 400 fl. equal the entire value of his property). Johann Kessler was assessed a hen (a mark of *Bauer* status) in the bond-chicken register for 1628; as late as 1625 he was still assessed the *Seldner*'s 3 kr. KL Ottobeuren 491-III, Heft 30, f. 4r and Heft 33, f. 4v.

[60] StAA, KL Ottobeuren 911, pp. 50–1 [8 July 1630]. The latter document indicates that Jerg Velk completed his apprenticeship in about 1607.

[61] StAA, KL Ottobeuren 905, ff. 325r–v [29 Jan. 1616] envisions a boy beginning his apprenticeship at this age.

[62] See the cabinetmaker *Lehrbriefe* in StAA, KL Ottobeuren 918, f. 27r [Easter 1580], KL Ottobeuren 901, f. 42v [14 August 1583], KL Ottobeuren 905, ff. 284r–v [4 July 1615], and KL Ottobeuren 907, ff. 209r–210v [17 Dec. 1618].

[63] StAA, KL Ottobeuren 904, f. 100r (miller's *Lehrbrief* [29 Jan. 1609]) and KL Ottobeuren 908, f. 128v (shoemaker's *Lehrbrief* [22 Feb. 1621]).

[64] See StAA, KL Ottobeuren (Mü.B.) 163, "Zunftordnung der Hafner (1623) mit einem Nachtrag de 1644" and KL Ottobeuren (Mü.B.) 164, "Zunftordnung der Metzger (1631)" for the guild ordinances of the potters and butchers respectively. The ordinances often post-date the establishment of the guild itself; thus the earliest surviving ordinance for the baker's guild (KL Ottobeuren [Mü.B.] 172) dates from 1690, while there is an unambiguous reference to the guild in KL Ottobeuren 908, f. 92r [26 June 1620].

[65] StAA, KL Ottobeuren 587-II, Hefte 21–23b (1601/2–1603/4).

listing witnesses and adding lengthy attestations of the apprentice's good and honorable behavior.[66]

As an extension of the conviction that an heir (or stepfather) should support and help the yielding heirs to establish themselves as independent householders in their own right, retirement and remarriage agreements frequently required the heir to pay for the apprenticeship of the younger children.[67] Alternatively, the heir might be required to teach his own craft to a sibling at no cost.[68] Considerable sensitivity was displayed for personal occupational preferences, and explicit guarantees that a yielding heir was to be trained in the craft "which the son would himself most like [to learn]" were quite common.[69] Furthermore, although these rights were enjoyed almost exclusively by male yielding heirs, there are at least a few references to young women being taught to knit.[70]

The learning of a craft was a great help to a yielding heir, since a trained apprentice (i.e. a journeyman) was typically paid 4 to 6 kr. per diem, twice as much as an unskilled worker.[71] It was an added boon if the training fee (*Lehrgeld*) was paid by his relatives, since at around 10 fl., an apprenticeship would otherwise cost at least five months' wages.[72] At the same time, though, a young man who sought to make an actual living as a craftsman faced a series of grave difficulties. In the first place, wage work at early modern Ottobeuren (as in the European countryside as a whole) was extremely seasonal. Even the

[66] Witnesses are listed in less than half of the *Lehrbriefe* from 1580–4, but are invariably listed after 1603. The earlier certificates are often quite informal, sometimes omitting the length of the training period (StAA, KL Ottobeuren 901, f. 122r [16 July 1583]) or merely affirming that the apprentice had worked for the master, rather than certifying that he had been taught a particular trade (ibid., f. 6r [15 Feb. 1583]).

[67] StAA, KL Ottobeuren 903, ff. 104v–105r [11 August 1604]; KL Ottobeuren 905, ff. 260r–v [10 Apr. 1615] and ff. 336r–v [4 March 1616]; KL Ottobeuren 907, ff. 9r [28 August 1616], 70v–71r [20 Apr. 1617], 231r [22 Feb. 1619], and 237r–v [15 March 1619]; KL Ottobeuren 908, ff. 183r–v [21 Oct. 1621].

[68] StAA, KL Ottobeuren 903, ff. 241r–v [24 June 1606]; KL Ottobeuren 907, ff. 41v–42r [27 Jan. 1617]; KL 908, ff. 5r–v [8 May 1619] and 48v–49r [20 March 1620].

[69] StAA, KL Ottobeuren 905, ff. 260r–v [10 Apr. 1615]. Similarly KL Ottobeuren 903, ff. 46r–47r [17 Nov. 1603]; KL Ottobeuren 904, f. 72r [12 May 1613]; KL Ottobeuren 907, ff. 159v–160r [26 Apr. 1618].

[70] StAA, KL Ottobeuren 908, ff. 108r–v [1 Oct. 1620]. Johann Danner of Ottobeuren, in exchange for the interest-free loan of his niece's 20 fl. inheritance, agrees to shelter and feed her and teach her how to reel and knit. Once the young woman left his house he was to repay her the money.

[71] StAA, KL Ottobeuren 607, "Tagwerkerregister 1611–22." Daily wage rates in this ten-year account were as follows: cabinetmakers: 10 kr; other masters (masons, locksmiths, carpenters) and journeymen cabinetmakers: 6.8 kr.; other journeymen: 4–6 kr.; haymowers and common laborers: 3 kr.; grain threshers: 1.7 kr.

[72] The arrangements in the notarial protocols assuring a yielding heir the cost of an apprenticeship invariably fix the sum at 10 fl. At a daily wage of 5 kr. and a six-day work week, this translates into twenty weeks or about five months of work. Note, however, that an apprentice did not earn 5 kr. per diem until the end of his training; there was a hierarchy of wages at the workplace. The monastery's chief tailor, for example, was paid a daily wage of 6.75 kr., his 'first journeyman' received 5.125 kr., the 'second journeyman' 4 kr., and the apprentice [*Lehrjunge*] only 2 kr. StAA, KL Ottobeuren 607, f. 2v.

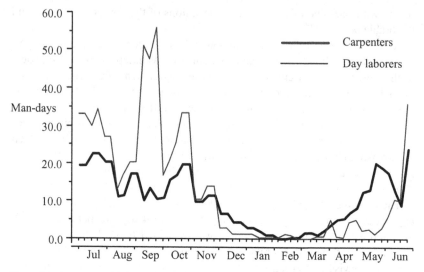

Figure 5.1 Average weekly labor hiring by the monastery of Ottobeuren, 1618–21
Source: StAA, KL Ottobeuren 607

monastery, the largest single employer in the region, had a highly variable need for workers. As is clear from Figure 5.1, a skilled master faced a long lean period in the winter, not to mention the predicament of a common laborer. Far more serious than the seasonality of the demand for labor, however, was a source of instability inherent in the apprenticeship system itself: the Ottobeuren masters trained too many craftsmen for the local economy to absorb.

The problem was commonly acknowledged, but although the guild ordinances attempted to restrict the number of apprentices that any one master could take on,[73] equilibrium was not attained. A newly trained journeyman thus often faced the prospect of permanent rather than simply seasonal under- or unemployment. Since he was not only unmarried but also by contemporary standards a little young to marry, the journeyman could stay on and work a few years for his master,[74] but this merely postponed rather than solved the problem. The only real solution was to leave.

Of the thirty-seven apprentices to whom apprenticeship certificates were issued in the period 1603–21, only eight (21.6 percent) can be shown to have settled in the monastery lands. At least nineteen (51.4 percent) are known to

[73] For the example of the linen-weavers, see StAA, KL Ottobeuren (Mü.B.) 166, "Zunftordnung der Leinenweber," f. 3v: "Item: whenever a master has finished training an apprentice or journeyman, and his [the trainee's] learning years are complete, the same master shall in the following two years thereafter take on no apprentices or journeyman-in-training" (Ordinance of 1641/3, copied into the ordinance of 1670).

[74] StAA, KL Ottobeuren 918, f. 27r [Easter 1580]: a journeyman cabinetmaker worked two years for his master after completing his apprenticeship; KL Ottobeuren 901, f. 42v [14 August 1583]: another journeyman cabinetmaker worked three years.

have emigrated, and the remaining ten (27.0 percent) disappear from the archival record. Travel papers were issued to an additional twenty-nine journeymen for whom no *Lehrbrief* has survived. It must be conceded that the emigration of journeymen was occasionally due to 'pull,' rather than 'push,' since a few very specialized crafts such as bookbinding could be learned only in the cities.[75] All the same, the claim that a journeyman needed to leave "in order to gain more experience"[76] was most often an effort to put a brave face on the harsh reality of an oversupply of craftsmen. Indeed, the pressure to leave home was already apparent at the beginning of the training process; some 40 percent of the early seventeenth-century *Lehrbriefe* were issued to apprentices from outside the Ottobeuren lands.[77]

Emigration was not universal, of course, and journeymen from moneyed families could certainly settle in their home villages, though more on the basis of inherited landed property than of the craft training *per se*,[78] and even then at the potential cost of displacing other siblings.[79] Poorer young craftsmen might bounce from village to village, but with luck could still hope to establish

---

[75] See the temporary passport issued gratis to the journeyman bookbinder Jerg Schmidt of Ottobeuren "at his . . . appeal and explanation that he could otherwise not complete his learning of the the craft . . . but under the condition that once he has presented this [*Freibrief*] to the guild at Augsburg, he shall return it to the monastery here [in Ottobeuren], and if he should later wish to leave the monastery lands [permanently], he must, as is customary, buy his freedom and release himself from serfdom with [the payment of] money." StAA, KL Ottobeuren 905, f. 96v [28 March 1613].

[76] StAA, KL Ottobeuren 908, f. 149v; *Lehrbrief* of the journeyman shoemaker Caspar Uderbold of Ottobeuren dated 7 June 1621. He was the son of the desperately poor Nicolaus Uderbold and Anna Maier, who in 1620 owned only a half-house worth 80 fl. and a cow worth 10 fl. Caspar's parents' situation deteriorated further during the 1620s; by 1627 they had lost the cow and their debts had doubled from 50 to 100 fl. (KL Ottobeuren 102, f. 25v and KL Ottobeuren 104, f. 25r). Caspar's brother Balthas Uderbold did marry in the market town on 21 Nov. 1621 (OttPR, Vol. I, f. 6v), but he disappeared shortly thereafter, and is nowhere listed in the monastery lands in 1627.

[77] StAA, KL Ottobeuren 903–905, 907–908. Of sixty-two *Lehrbriefe* issued in these years, twenty-five or 40.3 percent went to "foreigners." Note also that exactly half of these apprenticeship certificates were issued to men trained as bathhouse-keepers (fifteen), bakers (eight), or brewers (eight), with almost all brewers being also certified as bakers (though not vice versa). The other half of the *Lehrbriefe* were issued to cabinetmakers (four), smiths (four), tailors (four), teamsters (four), coopers (four), millers (two), potters (two), butchers (one), and painters (one). The proportion of "foreign" apprentices – five of sixteen or 31.3 percent – was somewhat lower in the *Lehrbriefe* for 1580–4 recorded in KL Ottobeuren 918 and 901.

[78] For example Adam Scheffler of Frechenrieden, who completed his apprenticeship as a baker in 1612 and two years later succeeded to his father's *Hof* in the village. StAA, KL Ottobeuren 905, ff. 45v [24 Dec. 1612] and 164r–v [23 Feb. 1614]. See also the case of Johann Aichelin of Frechenrieden, who completed an apprenticeship (also as a baker) in 1617 and formed a joint household with his father on a large *Hof* (38 *jauchert/tagwerk*) by 1620. KL Ottobeuren 907, f. 75r [28 Apr. 1617] and KL Ottobeuren 102, f. 362v.

[79] Jerg Mangler of Altisried ceded his *Hof* to his son Caspar a few years after the latter finished his baker's training in 1603. Jerg's daughter Barbara emigrated four months after her brother received his apprenticeship certificate. StAA, KL Ottobeuren 903, ff. 20r [14 May 1603], 33r [20 Sep. 1603], and 327v [28 May 1607]. Caspar is a comfortable farmer in the 1620 tax survey (KL Ottobeuren 102, ff. 373v–374r).

themselves somewhere in the Ottobeuren lordship.[80] Even "foreign" craftsmen occasionally[81] immigrated to the monastery lands, but this was only possible if the craftsman could find an open niche, usually by marrying the daughter (or widow) of a man who had carried on the same trade.[82] This may seem self-evident in the case of crafts like bathhouse-keeping, milling, smithing, or innkeeping (i.e. baking and brewing), which were based on a fixed physical plant and limited to one establishment per village. Even in trades with minimal capital requirements, however, immigrant craftsmen still often married into households where the same craft had previously been practiced.[83]

Failure to find a pre-existing trade niche (or to acquire enough agricultural land to compensate) made it very hard for any craftsman, foreign or native, to

---

[80] The shoemaker Michael Benker of Wolfertschwenden completed his apprenticeship in the village of Böhen (KL Ottobeuren 903, f. 24v [20 June 1603]) and ended up in the market town of Ottobeuren (KL Ottobeuren 102, f. 11r). There is also the case of the baker Jerg Geromüller of Günz, who trained in Altisried (KL Ottobeuren 905, f. 366r [26 May 1616]), and then moved to Ungerhausen for a year. From Ungerhausen he bought a half-house in Hawangen for 140 fl. (KL Ottobeuren 907, f. 114r [18 Oct. 1617]), and then exchanged the half-house and 8 fl. in cash for a full house elsewhere in the village (ibid., ff. 153r–v [21 March 1618]). He is listed in Hawangen in the 1620 tax survey with the house, a cow, and two small meadows worth a total of 157 fl. (KL Ottobeuren 102, f. 224r); by 1627 he had doubled his assets through the acquisition of a *jauchert* of valuable arable land worth 165.5 fl. (KL Ottobeuren 104, f. 181r).

[81] For the years 1603–21 there are only ten such cases listed in StAA, KL Ottobeuren 583, which is rather fewer than the documented outflow in the same period. See above note 77.

[82] A few examples: the miller Melchior Maier immigrated from Immenhof to Niederrieden in 1607/8 (KL Ottobeuren 583, Heft 24, f. 4v); he married Margareta, the daughter of the local miller Michael Bitzer, and bought out his father-in-law for 1,000 fl. (KL Ottobeuren 904, f. 166v [9 Jan. 1610]). The innkeeper Martin Heussler immigrated from Weinried to Unterwesterheim in 1612/13 (KL Ottobeuren 583, Heft 29, f. 3r); he married Catharina Aberöll, the stepdaughter of the local innkeeper Jacob Amman, and bought out his father-in-law for 2,200 fl. (KL Ottobeuren 905, ff. 41v–42r [24 Dec. 1612]). The miller Martin Eggensperger immigrated from Staubers to Ottobeuren in 1614/15 (KL Ottobeuren 583, Heft 32, f. 3v); he married Maria, the daughter of the market town's "upper" miller, Heinrich Staiger, and bought out his father-in-law for 1,000 fl. (KL Ottobeuren 905, ff. 271r–v [12 May 1615]). Note also that not all immigrant craftsmen were truly 'foreigners.' Thus the bathhouse-keeper Jacob Merk, who moved to Egg in 1603/4 (KL Ottobeuren 583, Heft 21, f. 5r), was in fact the son of the local proprietor Jacob Merk senior, from whom he purchased the bathhouse and its associated properties for 975 fl. (KL Ottobeuren 903, f. 87r [8 Apr. 1604]). Jacob junior had presumably worked as a journeyman somewhere outside the monastery lands before returning home.

[83] The weaver Jerg Aichelin immigrated to Wolfertschwenden in 1616/17 (KL Ottobeuren 583, Heft 36, f. 3r). No parish register survives from this period, but careful comparison of the bond-chicken registers indicates that Aichelin replaced another weaver, Melchior German (KL Ottobeuren 491-I, Heft 6 [1595], f. 17v, Heft 10 [1602], f. 13v, and Heft 14 [1609], f. 12r; also KL Ottobeuren 491-II, Heft 16 [1613], f. 23r, and Heft 21 [1617], f. 12v). See also KL Ottobeuren 904, ff. 48v–49r [2 May 1608]. The fact that there is no deed of sale from German to Aichelin suggests that the latter married the former's widow. Similarly the potter Christian Ruoff of Dassberg near Erkheim, who immigrated to the hamlet of Stephansried in 1617/18 (KL Ottobeuren 583, Heft 38, f. 3r) married Anna Gebelin (OttPR, Vol. I, f. 13r [21 May 1617], widow of the potter Jerg Steffa (KL Ottobeuren 905, ff. 277v–278r [23 Jan. 1615]).

survive.[84] The career of the tailor Jacob Merklin of Stocken is a typical example of this difficulty. He arrived in the village of Attenhausen in 1587/8, where he lived until at least 1595 before drifting over to Schlegelsberg by 1602.[85] In 1609 Merklin gave up his modest residence in Schlegelsberg in exchange for still shabbier quarters in Attenhausen, but was nevertheless constrained to borrow further to make ends meet.[86] By 1613 his back was to the wall. The half-house in Attenhausen was sold to a certain Jerg Weber with the understanding that Merklin and his wife could stay on there for two more years, "but at the end of the said two years shall be obliged to clear out without hesitation or protest." Jacob's daughter Anna saw no reason to await the inevitable and left the Ottobeuren lands in the fall of 1614, her travel papers issued "at no cost, in consideration of her poverty." By the time Jerg Weber resold the half-house one month later, Merklin and his wife, Appolonia Schelhorn, had already vanished.[87]

For an heir or stepfather to pay for the apprenticeship of the yielding heirs was thus a deeply ambivalent legacy: an undeniable increase in earning potential which, in all likelihood, could only be realized if the beneficiary went away. An emigrating journeyman did still retain his right to a share of the family estate, and there are notarized aquittances [*Quittungen*] of Ottobeuren craftsmen claiming their inheritances not only from nearby territories like the Princely Abbacy of Kempten or the Bavarian lordship of Mindelheim but also from more distant locales such as Upper Austria.[88] But not everyone managed to collect. Mathias Herz of Leupolz must have been only a boy when his home (a house and 9 *jauchert* of land) was sold to his stepmother in 1603. Along with the other five children, Mathias was promised his share of the 200 fl. sale price,[89] and in 1610, probably about the time he began his apprenticeship to be bathhouse-keeper, his 33 fl. were loaned out at interest by his guardians to a peasant in the

---

[84] See the case of the weaver Johann Bürklin, who was born in Amendingen outside the monastery lands sometime in the 1580s, moved to the Ottobeuren hamlet of Dennenberg – without leaving any traces in the tithe, bond-chicken, or notarial records – and then exited the monastery lands in 1607. StAA, KL Ottobeuren 903, f. 333v [3 July 1607].

[85] StAA, KL Ottobeuren 583, Heft 5, f. 17r; KL Ottobeuren 491-I, Heft 5 (1590), f. 11v, Heft 6 (1595), f. 10r, and Heft 10 (1602), f. 22v.

[86] StAA, KL Ottobeuren 904, ff. 117v [12 March 1609] and 170v–171r [9 Jan. 1610]. Merklin had been living in a half-house in Schlegelsberg; that he was given 77 fl. to accept a different half-house in Attenhausen indicates he was coming down in the world. The amount of the 1610 mortgage – a mere 20 fl. – suggests that it was a consumption loan.

[87] StAA, KL Ottobeuren 905, ff. 84r [10 Jan. 1613], 21v [22 Sep. 1614], and 209r–v [16 Oct. 1614].

[88] Respectively StAA, KL Ottobeuren 905, f. 361v [from Ronsberg, 5 May 1616] and 368r [from Schöneberg, 1 June 1616]; KL Ottobeuren 908, ff. 34r–v [from Mindelheim, 15 Nov. 1619]; KL Ottobeuren 907, f. 97v [from Aug. in Upper Austria, 4 July 1616/19].

[89] StAA, KL Ottobeuren 903, ff. 9r and 9r–v [6 March 1603]. Mathias' father, Jerg Herz, harvested an average of 4.1 *malter* of grain in 1600–1, which put him in the bottom half of those peasants in the parish already classed as "poor." KL Ottobeuren 681, Heft 3, f. 19r and Heft 4, f. 19v.

neighboring hamlet of Schrallen.[90] Unfortunately for Mathias, he either died or lost all contact with his family before he was able collect the money, and in 1619 his inheritance was instead paid to his brother Jerg.[91]

The surviving records do not permit a precise calculation of the wastage rate of these supernumerary journeymen, but there is abundant evidence that a yielding heir who went (or was sent) off to seek his fortune ran a very real risk of never seeing his family again. Sometimes relatives would be able to stay in touch, as in the case of the shoemaker Johann Zech, who died far away from home, but whose brother and sister in Sontheim knew that he had settled in Colmar in the Rhineland, and that he had married and had had a son.[92] But all too often the protocol relates a rather sadder state of affairs, like the 1609 entry about the journeyman Johann Glatz of Niederrieden, who "nine years ago left here to pursue the blacksmith's craft, and from whom thus far nothing at all has been heard, [either about] where he is living [or] whether he is even alive."[93] The Ottobeuren notarial protocols contain several entries like this about relatives missing for eighteen, nineteen, twenty, and even twenty-six years.[94] There was, in fact, a standardized kind of document – the *Schadlosbrief*, or indemnification – to regulate matters in the aftermath of such a disappearance. The *Schadlosbrief* awarded the missing person's inheritance to some other relative, required the recipient to return the legacy should its original beneficiary return, and indemnified the guardians or administrators of the estate from any future claims against themselves.

The disappearance of the aforementioned Johann Glatz may have been at least the indirect consequence of a family disaster. His father, Martin, had been granted the lease of the Niederrieden village smithy in 1573,[95] but none of Martin's children had reached the age of majority (Martin only married in 1578)[96] when both father and mother died between 1588 and 1592.[97] The property thus passed outside the family,[98] and although Martin's son Martin junior did manage in 1599 to establish himself in the hamlet of Ollarzried,[99] the

---

[90] StAA, KL Ottobeuren 904, f. 168v [9 Jan. 1610]. The principal was to be repaid to Mathias on demand at one month's notice. On the same folio there is a second *Schuldbrief* recording the loan of the inheritance of Mathias' brother Jerg.

[91] StAA, KL Ottobeuren 908, f. 4v [8 May 1619]. Mathias is described as a journeyman bathhouse-keeper in the document.

[92] StAA, KL Ottobeuren 901, ff. 50r–v [3 Nov. 1583].

[93] StAA, KL Ottobeuren 904, ff. 136r–v [11 June 1609] and f. 200r [31 May 1610].

[94] Respectively StAA, KL Ottobeuren 907, ff. 38r–v [24 Dec. 1616]; KL Ottobeuren 904, ff. 10v–11r [22 Nov. 1607] and 52v–53r [27 May 1608]; KL Ottobeuren 903, ff. 225r–v [31 March 1606].

[95] StAA, KL Ottobeuren 27, f. 215v [23 Nov. 1573].

[96] StAA, KL Ottobeuren 908, f. 53r [3 Apr. 1620].

[97] Death duties for Martin Glatz senior and his wife, Barbara Guggeisen, were paid on 9 May 1588 and 4 June 1592 respectively. StAA, KL Ottobeuren 583, Heft 5, f. 9v and Heft 8, f. 8r.

[98] StAA, KL Ottobeuren 27, f. 216v [4 June 1592].

[99] StAA, KL Ottobeuren 908, f. 75v [14 May 1620]. Martin Glatz junior is first listed in the hamlet in the 1602 bond-chicken register (KL Ottobeuren 491-I, Heft 10, f. 6r).

other four children[100] were fatally undermined and never managed to establish themselves in the monastery lands. For the most part, however, the phenomenon of the vanishing journeyman was the result of the normal operation of the rules of inheritance. Indeed, not only did it occur in comfortable families,[101] but in some cases it can be shown to have been of positive benefit to the remaining kin, harsh as that may seem.

Martin Koler of Attenhausen was a poor cottager[102] who nevertheless left his children, Jacob, Johann, and Anna, a legacy of 25 fl. each. Jacob was apprenticed to be a shoemaker, and left the monastery lands as a journeyman in about 1595. He never returned, and after sixteen years it was decided that he must have died. His inheritance was divided between the other two children[103] and paid out three years later.[104] Both of them needed the money badly. Anna Koler, who had married a certain Heinrich Blank, was living in a half-house which the couple had been repeatedly mortgaging for consumption loans.[105] Her brother Johann Koler, a tailor by trade, was caught in a similar cycle of debt, and had just been forced to sell off half of his house in order to raise cash.[106] The ten or fifteen *gulden* Jacob's exit afforded his siblings may not seem like a lot of money, but these were precisely the kinds of sums that they had hitherto been forced to borrow. After 1614 both households stabilized, and by 1627 Johann was even able to move back into a full house.[107] We cannot say that Jacob Koler was deliberately sacrificed for the sake of his brother and sister, but the fate he suffered certainly helped to save his siblings from a similar end, and it is hard to believe that this outcome was unforeseen.

---

[100] The 1586 serf roll for Niederrieden lists Martin Glatz senior and his wife, Barbara Guggeisen, with five children: Jerg, Johann, Michael, Martin, and Anna. StAA, KL Ottobeuren 601-II, ff. 124r–131v.

[101] StAA, KL Ottobeuren 903, ff. 236r–v [1 June 1606] declares that the tailor Peter Schneider left home eighteen years ago, but has not been heard from in the last nine years. That Peter's inheritance was fully 250 fl. indicates considerable family wealth. His sister Regina Schneider married Balthas Hagg of Schlegelsberg, who was admitted to a large *Hof* of 38 *jauchert/tagwerk* on 14 February 1603 (KL Ottobeuren 27, f. 157r) and by 1620 had a gross wealth of 500 fl. (KL Ottobeuren 102, ff. 319v–320r).

[102] Martin Koler was a freeman and thus does not appear in the bond-chicken registers. He is listed as a child in Attenhausen in the 1564 serf roll (Dertsch, "Das Einwohnerbuch des Ottobeurer Klosterstaats 1564," p. 80). Since he is not listed as a *Hof* tenant in Attenhausen in the rent rolls for 1567 (StAA, KL Ottobeuren 30, ff. 69r–73r), 1584 (KL Ottobeuren 31, ff. 7v–8r), or 1606 (KL 39, ff. 1r–5v), and since the monastery owned all of the *Höfe* in the village, he must have been a *Seldner*.

[103] StAA, KL Ottobeuren 904, ff. 233r–v [10 March 1611].

[104] StAA, KL Ottobeuren 905, f. 198r [14 Aug. 1614] Heinrich Blank and his wife, Anna Koler, received 14 fl. of Jacob's money. Johann Koler was presumably given the remaining 11 fl.

[105] StAA, KL Ottobeuren 904, ff. 112v [5 March 1609] and 249v [27 Apr. 1611].

[106] StAA, KL Ottobeuren 904, f. 21v [3 Jan. 1608]; KL Ottobeuren 905, ff. 108v (*Kaufbrief* selling the half-house for 60 fl. [20 June 1613]), 152r–v [14 Jan. 1614], and 162r–v [19 Feb. 1614]; KL Ottobeuren 907, f. 51v [1 Feb. 1617]. Johann Koler is described as a tailor in the 1608 *Zinsbrief*.

[107] StAA, KL Ottobeuren 102, ff. 376r and 386v; KL Ottobeuren 104, ff. 338r and 347v. Heinrich Blank and his wife borrowed no more money after 1611. Johann's half-house, assessed at 50 fl. in 1620, had by 1627 been replaced by a full house assessed at 120 fl.

Now, most yielding heirs were neither disabled nor apprenticed and instead hoped to buy or marry on to agricultural land somewhere in the vicinity of their homes. Nevertheless, the support they received in this endeavor from the designated heir was accompanied by similarly grave liabilities.

The support itself was real enough. Tradition strongly favored the equal inheritance of all siblings, and strenuous efforts were also made to ensure parity among "before-children" and "after-children," i.e. children from first and second marriages.[108] And although the land could no longer be divided among the children as a physical asset, its capital value certainly could. As Barbara Weckerlin of Günzegg put it when remarrying in 1610, at her death "the house and land shall be sold to him [i.e. her new husband] at the normal market price [*in ainem landtleüfigen kaufschilling*], and the before- and after-children and he as well shall receive equal shares of the realized sale price and none [of them] is to have any advantage."[109]

The accounting that ensued among family members was often very careful, as is clear from the following example from a craftsman's household, also from 1610:

> Martin Thoma, cabinetmaker of Sontheim, disposes and ordains [as follows], that if, according to the will of the Almighty, he should die before his current wife Elisabeth Schlichting, that . . . at the division of the property he leaves behind, a before- and an after-child, and with them Elisabeth Schlichting, shall [all] inherit equally [literally 'shall be kept equal'], and none is to be treated more favorably than the others. [He] also [ordains] that his daughter Ursula, wife of Johann Lutz of Günz . . . [if she collects] the 20 fl. which he has promised her if he has no children by his current wife, shall stand back at the division [of the property] until the other children as well as his current wife have all received as much . . .[110]

Similar arrangements were made by agriculturalists. When, for example, the smallholder[111] Jerg Steger of Niederrieden remarried in about 1613, his *Heiratsbrief* declared that

> among the aforesaid before-children the son Caspar has received 30 fl. at his marriage, the son Jerg also 30 fl. and then the daughter Margaret 60 fl. as well as a dress and coat, whereas the daughter Cordula is still single and unmarried. It is therefore agreed that at the [final] division [of the property]

---

[108] Clauses explicitly insisting on the equal inheritance of before- and after-children are very common in *Heiratsbriefe*; there are twenty-two such arrangements between June 1612 and April 1616 in StAA, KL Ottobeuren 905 alone.

[109] StAA, KL Ottobeuren 904, ff. 194r–v [20 Apr. 1610]. Similarly KL Ottobeuren 905, ff. 180r–v [15 May 1614].

[110] StAA, KL Ottobeuren 904, ff. 212v–213r [24 Aug. 1610]. Martin had recently purchased a house for 160 fl. KL Ottobeuren 903, f. 204v [7 Feb. 1606].

[111] Jerg Steger's widow has 5.75 *jauchert* of arable land and a gross wealth of 590 fl. in the 1620 tax survey. StAA, KL Ottobeuren 102, f. 240v.

after Jerg Steger's death, the said three married before-children shall stand back until both the daughter Cordula as well as the [new] wife Maria and her five children have all received as much. Only then shall they [i.e. the before-children] claim an equal share of the remaining property.[112]

Among the *Bauern* the amounts of money in question were decidely larger, but the basic principle remained the same. Anthoni Stedelin of Warlins was the headman of his district and owned almost thirty *jauchert* of land. He kept horses, dabbled in moneylending, and had a gross wealth of more than a thousand *gulden*.[113] His children could therefore be promised a cash advance on their inheritance (*Voraus*) of 200 fl., but when Anthoni sold his land in 1621 he and his wife still insisted "that at the [property] division after their deaths, those children who have already received their 200 fl. shall stand back until the others have also been given as much, and then if anything is left, they shall [all] inherit it equally."[114]

Every now and then, it is true, the protocols record what seems to be an example of favoritism towards one child: a daughter who receives a coat when her sister does not,[115] an inheritance advance for a daughter and not for a son,[116] or the grant to a daughter of all of the family's moveable wealth "to which the other four before-children shall have no claim at all."[117] In most of these cases, however, the disparity turns out to be less mean-spirited than it seems. In the first instance the family was so indigent that there was only one coat to be had, in the second other documents confirm that the son received an identical advance from an older brother,[118] and in the third case (again a situation of extreme poverty) the parents had at least sold their half-house to another son.[119] Partiality that was both significant and deliberate – such as the Schlegelsberg widow who insisted that a daughter who had already received a dowry 100 fl. larger than

---

[112] StAA, KL Ottobeuren 905, ff. 63r–v [24 Apr. 1613].

[113] StAA, KL Ottobeuren 102, f. 137r. This 1620 tax declaration disclosed 200 fl. in loans. Two of them are registered in KL Ottobeuren 904, f. 181r [25 Feb. 1610 and 4 March 1610].

[114] StAA, KL Ottobeuren 908, f. 164r–v [30 June 1621]. The *Kaufbrief* itself in the amount of 800 fl. is on ff. 163v–164r. For a similar arrangement see KL Ottobeuren 903, f. 30r [30 June 1603]. The *Amman* of Niederrieden had already given 70 fl. to each of his three "before-children" when he remarried. He declared that his *Hof* was worth 600 fl., and insisted that any 'after-children' also receive 70 fl. each before the property was divided at his death.

[115] StAA, KL Ottobeuren 907, f. 53r–v [20 Feb. 1617].

[116] StAA, KL Ottobeuren 904, ff. 54v–55r [29 May 1608].

[117] StAA, KL Ottobeuren 905, ff. 257r–v [2 Apr. 1615].

[118] StAA, KL Ottobeuren 903, ff. 91r–v [13 May 1604]. For a fuller picture of this family's inheritance arrangements see also ibid., ff. 16v [28 Apr. 1603] and 91r [13 May 1604], and KL Ottobeuren 904, f. 54v [29 May 1608].

[119] In the 1620 tax survey, the father, Johann Gering of Ungerhausen, owns no real property at all and pays only the minimum head tax of 6 kr. StAA, KL Ottobeuren 102, f. 238v. The sale of the half-house to his son Thoma for 95 fl. is in KL Ottobeuren 903, f. 48r [26 Nov. 1603]. A second son had already emigrated by the time of the 1615 *Ausgemacht*. KL Ottobeuren 905, f. 175r [26 Apr. 1614].

that of her sisters was nevertheless to have the same share of the remaining property[120] – did occur, but all in all it was quite rare.[121]

In addition to emphasizing the equality of material inheritance, retirement and remarriage arrangements also attempted to maintain parity in the less tangible dimensions of the lives of the yielding heirs. These contracts thus often stipulated that the younger children were to be raised, fed, and clothed "in keeping with their status [*irem stand gemäss*]."[122] When they married the heir was to ensure that the wedding clothes and the wedding meal of the younger children adhered to a similar standard.[123] Naturally these clauses are most encountered among the transactions of the wealthy, which often more precisely stipulated that the finery of the wedding was to be "as is customary among the *Bauern*."[124] But even craftsmen[125] and smallholders[126] had a sense of their families' social standing, and they wanted it preserved for their yielding heirs as well.

Amid all of this concern for sibling parity, there was also a recognition that genuine equality was not possible under a regime of partible inheritance. A proportional share of a farm's capital value was not truly equivalent to the ownership of the farm itself, encumbered though the property might be. The familiar comfort of a childhood home, the intimate knowledge of the family

---

[120] StAA, KL Ottobeuren 904, ff. 254r–v [9 May 1611]. The favored daughter, Maria Hagg, was not poor; she was married to the Frechenrieden blacksmith Caspar Helzlin, who in 1620 had a gross wealth of 590 fl. (KL Ottobeuren 102, f. 361v). Helzlin had presumably married Maria around the time he was admitted to the smithy on 12 June 1603 (KL Ottobeuren 27, f. 114r).

[121] I have not included under this rubric cases of stepfamilies where division of the same total allocation to children from different marriages produced unequal individual inheritance because of varying family sizes. Thus, for example, StAA, KL Ottobeuren 905, ff. 352v–353r [18 Apr. 1616], where a mother assigns 100 fl. to her children (three) by her first husband and also 100 fl. to her child by her second husband. Cases like these are discussed below on pp. 260–2.

[122] StAA, KL Ottobeuren 904, ff. 1r–v [2 Sep. 1607] and 133r–v [22 May 1609], and KL Ottobeuren 905, ff. 42r–v [24 Dec. 1612].

[123] StAA, KL Ottobeuren 905, ff. 50r–51r [24 Dec. 1612]; KL Ottobeuren 907, f. 44r [28 Jan. 1617]; KL Ottobeuren 908, ff. 87r–v [21 June 1620] and 176r–177r [30 July 1621]. KL Ottobeuren 907, ff. 78v–79r [12 Apr. 1617] explains in more detail that the before-children are "at their weddings to inherit and have things paid for them in keeping with their status *as is the custom of the monastery [lands]*." Emphasis mine.

[124] StAA, KL Ottobeuren 905, ff. 23r [13 Sep. 1612], 27v–28r [14 Oct. 1612], 72v–73r [12 June 1613], 101v–102r [21 May 1613], 115v–116r [26 Sep. 1613], 117r–v [10 Oct. 1613], and 191v–192r [7 July 1614].

[125] StAA, KL Ottobeuren 904, ff. 201v–202r [22 May 1609] declares that the before-children are to receive food and clothing "appropriate to their status." The stepfather was a potter; when he later bought out the before-children, he paid 535 fl. for the house and garden (KL Ottobeuren 907, f. 170v [10 June 1618]). See also his 1620 tax declaration in KL Ottobeuren 102, f. 16r. Similar stipulations in KL Ottobeuren 904, ff. 59v–60r [6 June 1608]. The head of this household in the market town of Ottobeuren (i.e. probably a craftsman) bought his house and garden for 350 fl. on the same day (ibid., f. 59r) and in 1620 (KL Ottobeuren 102, f. 6v) had a gross wealth of 420 fl.

[126] StAA, KL Ottobeuren 907, ff. 162r–v [5 May 1618] declares that the before-son is to receive a wedding garment "appropriate to his status." The household was in 1620 (KL Ottobeuren 102, f. 385v) worth 644 fl. and had 6 *jauchert* of land.

land, the personal connections with neighbors and friends, all of this the yielding heirs lost. Even when the numbers balanced (and as has been seen, considerable effort was expended to ensure that they did), everyone knew that the lot of the yielding heirs was still to be "children who receive no home of their own, but *must* yield" to the designated heir.[127] In fact, a custom of symbolic payments by the heir to another sibling in explicit compensation "for yielding" can be documented at all levels of rural society, with the amount ranging from 5–15 fl. among the mass of the poor, to 10–40 fl. among the comfortable middle peasantry, to 30–90 fl. among the village elites.

Although younger children did not incur the full consequences of the yielding heir's role until they were ready to marry, the logic of impartible inheritance already began to transform their lives at adolescence by obliging them to go into service. The imperative was straightforwardly fiscal. Now that heirs had to realize the capital value of the land in order to pay pensions and inheritances – and all of this in addition to the traditional obligations of rents, tithes, and taxes – the peasant household had to generate a great deal more cash than had previously been necessary. There were a variety of responses to this pressure, but sending unmarried yielding heirs out of the home to support themselves was unquestionably one of the most dramatic.

Agricultural servants were such a prominent feature of the rural economy of the early modern (and modern) German south that it is easy to assume that this had always been the case. It is well known that servanthood became the focus of much more regulatory interest from the early seventeenth century,[128] but it is less well appreciated that this coincided with a significant increase in the actual number of rural servants. As late as 1546, when a tax register was drawn up at Ottobeuren listing both heads of households and the number of their servants, fully 87.2 percent of 1,184 households had no servants at all. And although strictly comparable figures are not available until the early eighteenth century, the inheritance and remarriage agreements preserved in the notarial protocols indicate that an expectation that yielding heirs would begin service "when they can earn their own bread and porridge" had already become much more common by the 1620s (see Figure 5.2). Many yielding heirs did retain the older right to be fed and sheltered at home until they married, but the trend was for the right of residence to be replaced by the right to be fed and sheltered only if s/he came home sick from service. This convalescence right

---

[127] StAA, KL Ottobeuren 905, f. 312v [2 Dec. 1615]. Emphasis mine. Similarly KL Ottobeuren 903, f. 306v [15 March 1607].

[128] The Bavarian territorial ordinances of 1516 and 1555 contain isolated provisions about rural servants, but comprehensive regulation came only with the code of 1616, and ordinances exclusively concerned with servanthood were issued only after 1630. Walter Hartinger, "Bayerisches Dienstbotenleben auf dem Land vom 16. bis 18. Jahrhundert," *Zeitschrift für Bayerische Landesgeschichte* 38, 2 (1975), pp. 598–638, at p. 602.

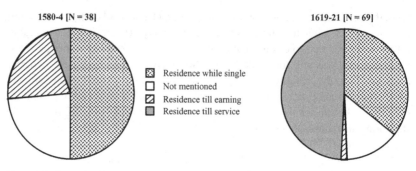

Figure 5.2 Type of residence right granted to yielding heirs, 1580–4 and 1619–21
Sources: StAA, KL Ottobeuren 901, 907–8, 918

was frequently limited to four weeks, and was occasionally accompanied by sanctions if a yielding heir overstayed the allotted time.[129]

The rise of service brought a multiplicity of changes to the rural economy, foremost among which was a rationalization and intensification of agricultural labor. As Lutz Berkner pointed out more than thirty years ago, servanthood allowed labor to be redeployed from households with too many mouths to those with too few hands.[130] Equally importantly, it allowed households mutually to substitute unrelated employees (who could be worked very hard) for resident, rights-bearing unmarried kin (who could not). In this regard it is interesting to note that a few families did experiment with requiring the yielding heirs to work either for their own retired parents[131] or for the designated heir,[132] but such explicit subordination of kin to kin seems in most cases to have been too difficult to manage.[133] It is also worth mentioning that the engagement of servants and

---

[129] For example StAA, KL Ottobeuren 905, ff. 208r–209r [16 Oct. 1614], in which a younger brother and sister have the right "while they are single, if they fall sick, to be given food and drink and shelter by them [i.e. their older brother and widowed mother] for four weeks. If, however, their health does not recover within this time, they shall be obliged to maintain and feed themselves." This was a very wealthy household; the accompanying sale deed (on f. 208r) records the transfer of a house and over 50 *jauchert* of land for 1,000 fl.

[130] Lutz Berkner, "The Stem Family and the Developmental Cycle of the Peasant Household: An 18th Century Austrian Example," *American Historical Review* 77 (1972), pp. 398–412.

[131] StAA, KL Ottobeuren 904, ff. 72r–v [1 Nov. 1608] imposes on the yielding heirs the obligation to work for their parents without pay(!). Similarly KL Ottobeuren 905, ff. 228v–229r [17 Jan. 1615] envisions a possible parental need for the labor of their unmarried children, in which case the children are to receive clothing in addition to the food and shelter which is already their right.

[132] StAA, KL Ottobeuren 907, ff. 84r–v [15 May 1617]. The Ungerhausen miller Johann Heuss owes his three brothers 900 fl. from the sale of the mill. The siblings have the right to be fed, clothed, and sheltered by the designated heir, but when they are old enough they are to work for their brother for food and wages and he is no longer obliged to clothe them.

[133] It was also rare for the designated heir to be granted any formal powers over the marriage choices of his or her siblings. I have found only one such example, a wealthy *Bauer* family where five yielding heirs were promised dowries of 200 fl. "if they behave well, and marry

even of day laborers can be documented not only on large farms presumably in labor deficit, but also in the households of smallholders and craftsmen, who cannot have been short of labor.[134]

If servanthood represented the temporary exile of yielding heirs from their homes, their marriage made that condition permanent. Once again, the logic was brutally simple and flowed from the effort (discussed in chapter 4) to freeze the number of households in a settlement. A constant number of households meant that every married couple could in effect provide a niche for only two of their children: one as the designated heir, and the other as a spouse in another household in exchange for the spot occupied by the spouse of the designated heir. Individual exceptions were always possible, but over rural society as a whole, adult children beyond the first two would have to leave.

The dimensions of the problem are clearest in the twin villages of Ober- and Unterwesterheim, where the survival of the parish register allows a detailed family reconstruction. Both villages maintained impressive stability in numbers. Unterwesterheim had forty households in 1586, thirty-nine in 1620, and thirty-eight in 1627. The 1586 serf roll for Oberwesterheim has not survived, but to the forty-nine households which can be documented in the village in 1595, none had been added by 1620 and only two by 1627.[135] Now, if the number of households in the parish remained unchanged, making a new marriage depended upon finding an open niche. If a married man or woman died, the remarriage of the surviving spouse represented a single opening. If both members of a resident couple died, a niche for two was created. As it happened, between 1596 and 1621, 114 marriages were celebrated in Ober- and Unterwesterheim. Forty-two (36.8 percent) of these involved a remarriage by one spouse and two a remarriage by both. In addition, in four cases the couple disappeared from the parish immediately after the wedding. Thus, in a twenty-five-year period, 176 niches opened in the two villages. At the same time, approximately 242

and come into a household with the [fore]knowledge and consent of the married couple [i.e. the designated heir] . . . but if one or the other [of the yielding heirs] does not behave well, marries by himself and establishes himself badly, to that child no more than 50 *gulden* shall be given . . ." StAA, KL Ottobeuren 905, ff. 5v–6r [9 July 1612].

[134] The engagement of servants and/or day laborers was foreseen in the household of an Ollarzried *Bauer* owning 33 *jauchert* of land, a Hawangen shoemaker with 4.5 *jauchert*, and a Frechenrieden sheriff with no more than a housegarden and a small meadow. StAA, KL Ottobeuren 903, ff. 184r–v [24 Sep. 1605] and 307v [15 Mar. 1607]; KL Ottobeuren 904, f. 96v [23 Jan. 1609]; KL Ottobeuren 102, ff. 85v–86r, 208r, 358r–v.

[135] StAA, KL Ottobeuren 601 II, ff. 137r–140r (Unterwesterheim 1586); KL Ottobeuren 102, ff. 295r–315r (both villages 1620); KL Ottobeuren 104, ff. 274r–294v (both villages 1627). The 1595 figure for Oberwesterheim is derived from the forty-five households listed in the bond-chicken register for that year (KL Ottobeuren 491-I, Heft 6, ff. 10v–11r), supplemented by an additional four households whose existence for that year can be documented from the parish register. Note also that the 1564 serf roll lists fifty-four households in Oberwesterheim. Dertsch, "Das Einwohnerbuch des Ottobeurer Klosterstaats 1564," pp. 65–8.

adolescents reached marriageable age.[136] The implication is obvious: one in four youths was obliged to leave the home village if s/he wanted to marry.

That they did in fact leave the parish is clear from a series of documents known as *Freibriefe*, or charters of freedom. In early modern Swabia, any peasant who wished to immigrate to a new territory was first obliged to prove that s/he was legally free. The requirement was imposed by the peasant's prospective overlord, in order to ward off future claims on the estate of his new subject by the former overlord. Ottobeuren peasants who were already free simply arranged to have their status documented; those who were serfs of the monastery could purchase their freedom for two or three *gulden*. The charges were often waived for the poor, whose lord and neighbors may indeed have been pleased to be rid of them.[137] The acquisition of a *Freibrief* was thus almost invariably a prelude to departure from the Abbot's dominions.

The *Freibriefe* document a regular outflow of the supernumerary young, and permit a fuller picture of the politics of household formation than is possible with the parish register alone. The fate of the children of Pelagius Wurm is an illuminating example of the process. Like his father before him, Pelagius was the village blacksmith in Unterwesterheim. He and his wife, Anna Beir, had at least five children, of whom three survived to adulthood. Their son Michael Wurm left for the nearby village of Egg in 1616.[138] His brother Johann purchased a *Freibrief* in 1617 and then left the monastery lands.[139] Only Maria, the youngest of Pelagius and Maria's children, would settle in Unterwesterheim.

Maria Wurm married in 1620 at the tender age of sixteen. The precocity of her marriage was no doubt a result of her father's death in 1618; Maria's husband, Paul Schweiggart junior, took over the smithy in February of 1621.[140] The Schweiggarts were a much wealthier family than the Wurms, but they too

---

[136] The number of marriageable single people has been estimated as follows: over the twenty-five years between 1 Jan. 1596 and 1 Jan. 1621, the average annual numbers of baptisms, infant deaths, and adolescent/single adult deaths in the parish were 16.8, 5.72, and 1.40 respectively. This implies an average of 9.68 youths reached marriage every year or 242 over the period as a whole.

[137] See for example the *Freibrief* of Jerg Maier of Egg, whose freedom is granted "in consideration of his poverty gratis," but who also "renounces and recuses himself from each and every possession of his father Martin Maier, in particular the half-house and moveables which he [i.e. Martin] now owns and occupies." StAA, KL Ottobeuren 905, f. 36v [21 Dec. 1612]. For a similar incident see the marginal note dated 5 January 1589 in the serf roll of 1564: Christina, daughter of Balthas Möst of Unterwarlins, is not entered on the roll but "has renounced all rights in the Ottobeuren lordship." Dertsch, "Das Einwohnerbuch des Ottobeurer Klosterstaats 1564," p. 33.

[138] He purchased a half-house there for 60 fl. on 22 Nov. 1616 (StAA, KL Ottobeuren 907, f. 28r). Michael is listed in Egg in the 1620 tax survey (KL Ottobeuren 102, f. 293v), and the Egg parish register indicates that he and his wife, Eva Sparer, baptized three children there in 1628, 1630, and 1633. Michael Wurm was buried on 11 July 1633; Eva on 21 May 1634.

[139] StAA, KL Ottobeuren 907, f. 59v [14 March 1617].

[140] StAA KL Ottobeuren 908, ff. 126v–127r [20 Feb. 1621].

were subject to the strictures imposed by the household cap. Paul Schweiggart senior had five other children reach marriageable age. Only two of them settled in the village. Maria Schweiggart managed to bag the village innkeeper after his first wife died in 1623,[141] and Jerg Schweiggart succeeded to his father's lands after Paul senior died in 1624.[142] The rest were forced to leave the Ottobeuren lands: Heinrich in 1617, Johann at the age of twenty-three in 1618, and Barbara at twenty-four in 1625.[143]

The absence of parish registers (especially burial registers) in the rest of the Ottobeuren villages precludes global calculations like the ones made for Westerheim, but notarial records leave little doubt that a similar dynamic prevailed throughout the monastery lands. In the first place, 93.2 percent of the emigrants in the years 1602–21 were single adults. Moreover, in many cases the travel papers of a departing yielding heir can be linked to the deed transferring ownership of the family property to a luckier sibling;[144] on occasion the documents were all drawn up on the very same day.[145] The pattern obtained among both rich and poor,[146] and in some families it is possible to trace a veritable procession of yielding heirs out of the household both before and after the sale of the family home to another sibling.[147] Of course, there was also a substantial inflow of immigrants from other territories who, like the emigrants, were overwhelmingly (91.5 percent for the period 1602–21) composed of single adults. As a whole, however, the balance was clearly negative (see Figure 5.3). For

---

[141] StAA, KL Ottobeuren 909, f. 2v [*c.* 7–9 July 1624].

[142] In 1627 Jerg Schweiggart held all of the lands that his father, Paul, had held in 1620. StAA KL Ottobeuren 102, ff. 303r–v; KL Ottobeuren 104, f. 283v.

[143] Respectively StAA KL Ottobeuren 907, ff. 113v–114r [16 Oct. 1617]; ibid., f. 164r [14 May 1618]; KL Ottobeuren 909, f. 69r [16 June 1625]. Ages calculated from baptismal dates in the Westerheim parish register.

[144] StAA, KL Ottobeuren 903, ff. 151r–v *Freibrief* [9 Feb. 1605] and KL Ottobeuren 905, ff. 348v–349r *Kaufbrief* [16 Apr. 1616]; KL Ottobeuren 903, f. 256r *Freibrief* [17 Sep. 1606] and KL Ottobeuren 904, ff. 150[a]r–v *Kaufbrief* [21 Oct. 1609]; KL Ottobeuren 904, f. 268r *Freibrief* [25 August 1611] and KL Ottobeuren 907, f. 151r *Kaufbrief* [17 March 1618]; KL Ottobeuren 905, ff. 128v–129r *Freibrief* [28 Nov. 1613] and ibid., ff. 71v–72r *Kaufbrief* [14 May 1613]; KL Ottobeuren 905, f. 348r *Freibrief* [28 March 1616] and ibid., ff. 319v–320r *Kaufbrief* [24 Dec. 1615].

[145] StAA, KL Ottobeuren 903, ff. 117v–118r [21 Oct. 1604] for the sale of a house and some land to Jerg Weissenhorn of Niederdorf for 240 fl. Ibid., f. 118v *Freibrief* of his sister Anna Weissenhorn bearing the same date.

[146] StAA, KL Ottobeuren 903, f. 20r: *Freibrief* of Martin Epplin of Ollarzried [9 May 1603] and ibid., ff. 68v–69r: *Kaufbrief* to his brother Jerg of a house and 66 *jauchert* of land for 1,000 fl. [5 Feb. 1604]. KL Ottobeuren 903, f. 60v *Freibrief* of Jerg Schlichting of Hawangen [16 Jan. 1603] and ibid., ff. 118v–119r *Kaufbrief* to his brother Johann of a half-house for 40 fl. [21 Oct. 1604].

[147] StAA, KL Ottobeuren 903, ff. 257v–258r: *Kaufbrief* to Johann Dreier of Rummeltshausen of a house, 7 *jauchert* of arable land, and 2 *tagwerk* of meadow for 230 fl. [2 Oct. 1606]. KL Ottobeuren 903, f. 117r *Freibrief* of his brother Peter [21 Oct. 1604]; ibid., f. 193v: *Freibrief* of his brother Jacob [3 Nov. 1605]; and KL Ottobeuren 904, f. 233v: *Freibrief* of his brother Philip [9 Mar. 1611].

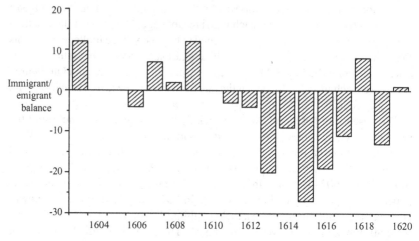

Figure 5.3 Legal migration at Ottobeuren, 1603–20
Note: 1604–5 and 1610 no data
Sources: StAA, KL Ottobeuren 583, 903–8

the years 1603–20, emigrants outnumbered immigrants by 22.4 percent,[148] a relation which seems to have dated back at least to the 1580s.[149]

That so many yielding heirs took the trouble and expense to acquire *Freibriefe* suggests that they had particular destinations in mind. Moreover, as we have seen, it is most unlikely that they were without financial assistance from their relatives. These advantages did not obtain for the least affluent members of the village community, in consequence whereof their migration patterns were less stable. Instead of planned moves to take up fixed residence elsewhere, the poorest emigrants drifted from place to place. This is not to say that they wandered randomly. The Westerheim parish register contains evidence of vagabond families who seem to have traveled on a sort of circuit. Johann Urbich and his wife, Eva Seglere, for example, whom the parish priest described as "vagabundi," baptized children in the parish in 1619 and again in 1625. In May of 1619 Eva also served as godmother for the child of Jacob Sommer and Salome Rembold, another pair of "vagabundi." Jacob and Salome returned to Westerheim

---

[148] Because of missing or incomplete data, the years 1602/3, 1604/5, 1605/6, and 1610/11 have been left out of this calculation, which is based on 304 immigrants (282 single and 22 married) and 372 emigrants (336 single and 36 married).

[149] 'Seems' because the data are neither complete nor strictly comparable. Immigration records for the account years 1586/7, 1587/8, 1588/9, and 1589/90 are preserved in StAA, KL Ottobeuren 583, Hefte 4–7 and average 15.0 entrances per annum. Emigration records for the account years 1579/80, 1580/81, 1582/3, 1583/4, and 1584/5 are preserved in KL Ottobeuren 901 and 918 and average 20.4 exits per annum, although the documentary run is incomplete for every year except 1583/4.

to baptize another child in the winter of 1620.[150] There is no way to estimate the number of these vagrant families, but it is sobering to note that in the quinquennium 1616–20, one in every twelve infants baptized in Westerheim was the child of vagabonds.

The itinerant poor supported themselves with a combination of casual labor, peddling, begging, and pilfering, a pattern which aroused both anger and fear among the sedentary population of the countryside. Repressive edicts aimed at beggars and vagrants multiplied all over Germany during the later sixteenth century, and the Ottobeuren lands were no exception. The monastery issued ordinances against beggars in 1551, 1567, and 1597,[151] all of which were similar in content. "Strangers" were forbidden to beg in the Abbot's dominions. The peasants were on pain of banishment forbidden to offer them shelter at any time, day or night, "but as soon as they set foot in the towns, villages or hamlets, the subjects [of the monastery] shall alert the officials, who shall send them back to the lordships whence they came, and if they refuse and do not instantly wish to comply, they shall be arrested and turned over to us for appropriate punishment."[152] Harsh words were backed by harsh practices. Beggars were regularly driven out of the monastery lands, strangers were arrested on the faintest of suspicions, and woe betide the vagrant convicted of even a slight offense. Martin Hentschen of Reutlingen was arrested in the hamlet of Halbersperg on 27 November 1588 as a "suspicious, irksome person on account of his vagabondlike wanderings." Interrogated and tortured, Hentschen confessed to having broken into the house of the hamlet headman and having stolen a sack, two linen shirts, and some "children's things" [*kinderwerke*]. He was beheaded.[153]

Much of this pattern of suspicion and brutal treatment of wandering strangers has already been elaborated in chapter 2, but the foregoing discussion points to a new feature of vagrancy – that it was often involuntary. Of course, not everyone who tramped the highways was an exile from a village that had decided it was full. Many were demobilized soldiers, some were professional thieves, and others were migrant workers following the harvest. The fact that early modern vagrants were disproportionately male further cautions us against seeing them as representative of the poor as a whole. Be that as it may, still less ought we to accept the sixteenth-century conviction that the vagrant's life was for the most part a choice made by the lazy and the shiftless. An obligation to leave home and seek fortune elsewhere was not just a product of folkloric imagination but a

---

[150] WestPR, Vol. I, pp. 50, 52, 54, 65.

[151] StAA, KL Ottobeuren 4, Documents 289X ff. 397r–398v (1551), 289H ff. 311r–314v (1567), and 289S ff. 346v–347r (1597).

[152] Ibid., Document 289H (1567), f. 313v.

[153] Ibid., Document 292, ff. 586v–588r [25 Feb. 1589].

very real fate which awaited a substantial proportion of peasant youths. Stability in numbers was maintained at Ottobeuren through the expulsion of the young.

The new inheritance customs introduced at least as many complications into the role of the parent as they did to the yielding heir. Retirement in particular was a mixed blessing. It reduced a parent's workload, but at the price of a considerable loss of authority. Independent of any changes in the ownership of property, there were always some grown children who chafed at their subordinate status. In 1569, for example, the brothers Peter and Michael Aberöll of Benningen seem to have sought a degree of symbolic equality with their father, Blesi, by urging him "against filial loyalty and natural justice, and over his paternal refusal" to drink wine with them.

> And when he would not do so, we both not only repeatedly reviled him with offensive and unseemly words but also, in neglect of the honor and loyalty owed [to him] as children, we laid actual hand on him and by criminally and scandalously pushing him back and forth, we forced him to [drink the wine], so that for the protection of his and his wife our stepmother's lives and limbs, he was obliged to call for help from the Benningen village officials and [even from] strangers . . .[154]

Even in the case of post-mortem successions, the potential for conflict was considerable. When Lucas Reinhart of Ungerhausen succeeded to his deceased father's *Hof* in 1541, the monastery thought it prudent to include as a condition of his admission that "he shall together with his mother and those who share his sup and bread contractually bind himself to uphold ancient Christian order."[155] Given the greater authority traditionally claimed by the male parent, the risk of a power struggle between the heir and a retired father can only have been greater.

Johann Vels, for example, was in many respects a good son-in-law. He married Anna, daughter of the potter Jerg Müller, and purchased half of Müller's house in the market town of Ottobeuren for 130 fl. in 1608. The sale of half of the house was in fact a convenient expression for the creation of a joint household, and both men agreed that each would have the right to use the house, cowstall, and barn "according to his will and desire."[156] Vels worked as a shopkeeper, buying goods on credit in the city of Memmingen and reselling them to locals.[157] The business flourished, and by the end of 1612 he had managed to clear all of the money he owed his father-in-law.[158] Jerg Müller was less successful. He

---

[154] StAA, KL Ottobeuren 4, Document 295E ff. 717r–720r [24 Oct. 1569].
[155] StAA KL Ottobeuren 27, f. 35r.
[156] StAA, KL Ottobeuren 904, f. 31v [26 Feb. 1608].
[157] Ibid., f. 134r [4 June 1609]. Johann Vels owes 24 fl. to the burgher and trader Michael Ruprecht of Memmingen for "goods and wares"; he is to repay the sum at the rate of 1 fl. per month and mortgages his half of the house as a security.
[158] StAA, KL Ottobeuren 905, f. 61v [27 Dec. 1612].

had never been enormously wealthy,[159] but after 1610 he became increasingly indebted to wealthier town dwellers, and was forced to turn to his son-in-law for help. Johann Vels assumed Müller's debts, and in exchange was sold the remaining half of the house in 1616.[160] But the price of the son-in-law's help was steeper yet, for Vels was now no longer willing to share living quarters with the old potter. On the same day he gave up the remainder of his home, Jerg Müller agreed to help Vels build on to the house a small room and kitchen with a separate entrance. Here Müller, his wife, and their unmarried daughter, Barbara, were to live, "and all three of them are to have no further business in his Johann Vels' house."[161]

Co-residence, in other words, was an inherently tension-ridden relationship. In extreme cases the house had to be formally demarcated into separate zones; one widow was able to resolve the "misunderstanding and ill-will" with her stepchildren only by designating as her space "the corner with the table in it in the heated room [*Stube*], the rearward sleeping room, the small section [*Gaden*] in the kitchen and the forward places in the cowstall and hayrack," and giving up the rest.[162] Heirs might also be eager to bar a widowed parent from starting another family, and a few contracts explicitly prohibited retiring parents from remarrying if they wished to remain in the house.[163]

Retiring parents therefore deployed a range of strategies in order to preserve their status and autonomy. The most obvious approach was to retire in stages and yield control only gradually. Thus Jerg Betterich of Günzegg sold half of his house and 66 *jauchert* to his son Johann for 500 fl. in 1609, reserving the right to sell the second half "either dearer or cheaper" at a later date. When Johann purchased the second half of the property eight years later, he was obliged to pay fully 1,300 fl. to complete his inheritance.[164] Similar arrangements were equally possible among the poor; after Balthas Lercher of Attenhausen bought half of the family house from his father in 1604, he had to wait a further eleven years

---

[159] His 1585 tax payment ranked him close to the middle (54.1 percent of households paid less than he, 39.6 percent paid more) of the households in the market town. StAA, KL Ottobeuren 676a.

[160] StAA, KL Ottobeuren 904, f. 161r [4 Jan. 1610]: Jerg Müller owes 40 fl. to the innkeeper Johann Albrecht of Ottobeuren. KL Ottobeuren 905, ff. 60v–61r [27 Dec. 1612]: Johann Vels assumes his father-in-law's debt of 35 fl. to Balthas Maier of Ottobeuren. KL Ottobeuren 907, f. 23v [6 Nov. 1616]: Müller sells the second half of the house to Vels for 130 fl. Ibid., f. 24r [6 Nov. 1616]: Vels assumes his father-in-law's debt of 82 fl. to the innkeeper Johann Albrecht of Ottobeuren.

[161] StAA, KL Ottobeuren 907, f. 24r [6 Nov. 1616].

[162] StAA, KL Ottobeuren 904, ff. 48r–v [2 May 1608].

[163] StAA, KL Ottobeuren 905, ff. 193v [31 July 1614; remarriage prohibition for a widowed *Seldner* father], 344v [10 Mar. 1616; for a widowed *Seldner* father], 361r–v [5 May 1616; for both *Bauer* parents], and 366v [27 May 1616; for both *Seldner* parents]. Social status based on the value of the estate sold, respectively 40, 150, 925, and 200 fl.

[164] StAA, KL Ottobeuren 904, f. 160v [4 Dec. 1609] and KL Ottobeuren 907, f. 104v [25 July 1617].

to buy the second half.[165] In some cases retirement was drawn out over several transactions, as in the case of Michael Willer of Böhen, who was admitted to two *Höfe* (one *Gotteshausrecht*, one *Erblehen*) totaling 45 *jauchert* of land in 1591.[166] Nineteen years later Michael sold a half-interest in both properties to his son Michael junior for 550 fl. Six months after that he ceded his interest in the *Erblehen* property for an additional 192 fl., and then at the end of 1612 he gave up his interest in the *Gotteshausrecht* property in exchange for an annual delivery of specified amounts of food and other necessities.[167]

Alternatively, a parent would sell off the entire property while retaining co-ownership with the heir. The 1584 contract drawn up between Jerg Geromüller of Waldmühle and his son Jacob is a typical example of this device. Having conveyed his mill, millworks, lands, and personal property to his son, Jerg then reserved for himself half-usage rights on everything he had sold. Father and son agreed "[t]o work, use and enjoy the property together and also have equal receipts and costs . . . the old one shall not, however, be forced to do any work." Jerg was not with this last clause proposing to sit back and do nothing; he was seeking rather to strike a balance, to maintain his own independence while contributing to the work at the mill complex and acknowledging his son as the legal owner.[168]

Agreements of this sort to establish an equipoise of authority were actually much more common than the practice of selling off the family estate by degrees, and the multi-generational or "stem-family" peasant household must in fact often have functioned as a co-operative venture.[169] Thus when Jacob Thoma of Egg bought the village smithy from his uncle in 1607, both men were content to agree

> that he [i.e. Jacob] shall oversee [the property] with the assistance of a jour-neyman, whom he shall hire at his own cost, but at the same time the said blacksmith Pelagius Thoma shall be obliged to help him with the work in so far as is possible and necessary, and each party shall receive and enjoy half of the yearly receipts and income for as long as Pelagius Thoma shall live.[170]

---

[165] StAA, KL Ottobeuren 903, ff. 61v–62r [16 Jan. 1604; *Kaufbrief* missing] and KL Ottobeuren 905, ff. 284v–285r [10 July 1615].

[166] StAA, KL Ottobeuren 27, ff. 94v–95r [28 Feb. 1591], which mentions both properties.

[167] StAA, KL Ottobeuren 904, ff. 220r–v and 220v [7 Dec. 1610]; ibid., ff. 261v–262r [1 July 1611]; KL Ottobeuren 905, ff. 60r–v [27 Dec. 1612].

[168] StAA KL Ottobeuren 901, ff. 88v–89r [27 Feb. 1584].

[169] For example Balthas Maier of Oberwesterheim, who sold his extensive holdings to his son Mang for 1,100 fl. in 1606. Fourteen years later father and son are still listed as joint-owners of the property. StAA, KL Ottobeuren 903, ff. 260v–261r [24 Oct. 1606] and KL Ottobeuren 102, f. 295v.

[170] StAA, KL Ottobeuren 903, ff. 302v–303r [1 Mar. 1607]. The *Kaufbrief* [ibid., ff. 302r–v] reiterates that Pelagius retains half of the property "together with half of the yearly income."

Nevertheless, the fact that some retiring fathers either explicitly reserved "the authority and command of the household" [*den gewalt und das regiment ÿber die ganze haushaltung*],[171] or prohibited the son who purchased the land from actually using it until after the father died,[172] suggests that alternatives to hierarchy were not always easy to maintain. Several retirement contracts provided for the construction of separate living quarters for a retired parent "if in the future, against all hope, she cannot get along with them [i.e. the heirs]."[173] Indeed, that the documents sometimes contain positively contradictory provisions reveals that some parents were deeply reluctant to share authority with their children.

Johann Lontner and his wife, Anna Gantner, for example, retired in 1606 shortly after borrowing 100 *gulden* against the security of their home in Benningen.[174] Accordingly, when the family home was sold to their sons Johann junior and Michael for 200 fl., the sale deed explicitly stated that "the buyers have reserved for themselves alone the use and enjoyment of the said house and garden for as long as their father is alive, but in return must themselves pay the 5 *gulden* interest [owed from mortgages taken out on the house]."[175] Yet this seemingly definitive transfer of authority did not stop the father not only retaining the right of both parents to live in the house "for the rest of their lives" but also insisting that "it remains otherwise open to him to repurchase the house at the same price and to sell it to someone else as he pleases." And as if to further underscore their sense of who really owned the property, Johann Lontner senior and his wife proceeded to mortgage the house for a third time two weeks after they had sold it to their sons![176] The brothers Michael and Johann junior seem to have found it equally difficult to share the house with each other. In early 1607, an agreement to resolve the "misunderstanding and ill-will" between them split the house into separate sectors, with the older brother, Michael,[177] retaining the forward half of the house and the right to build himself a separate kitchen.[178] The two brothers then maintained separate

---

[171] StAA, KL Ottobeuren 905, ff. 187r–v [12 June 1614]. This contract still insists that the property is to be worked by father and son together "at equal cost."

[172] StAA, KL Ottobeuren 905, ff. 126r–v [28 Nov. 1613].

[173] StAA, KL Ottobeuren 904, ff. 2v–3r [6 Sep. 1607]. Similarly KL Ottobeuren 903, ff. 40r–v [9 Oct. 1603] and 92r–93r [19 May 1604]; KL Ottobeuren 904, f. 69r [2 Aug. 1608]; KL Ottobeuren 908, ff. 40r–v 1 [1 Mar. 1620].

[174] StAA, KL Ottobeuren 903, ff. 42v [24 Oct. 1603] and 122r [4 Nov. 1604]. The parents had lived in the village at least since 1587/8, when Anna shows up as "Johann Lontner's wife" in a list of the Bishop of Augsburg's serfs in Benningen. KL Ottobeuren 583, Heft 5, f. 15v.

[175] StAA, KL Ottobeuren 903, ff. 244v–245r [6 July 1606].

[176] StAA, KL Ottobeuren 903, ff. 245r [6 July 1606] and 246r–v [20 July 1606].

[177] Michael Lontner is already listed as a serf of the Bishop of Augsburg in 1603/4; his brother Johann does not appear in the registers until 1606/7. StAA, KL Ottobeuren 583, Heft 21, f. 2v and Heft 23, f. 2v.

[178] StAA, KL Ottobeuren 903, ff. 291v–292r [27 Jan. 1607].

households[179] until Johann's death in 1625/6.[180] His successor, Balthas Frick (who probably married Johann's widow),[181] seems to have had better relations with Michael Lontner,[182] who died in 1629/30.[183]

Whatever a retiring parent's ambitions of (and misgivings about) governing jointly with the heirs, advancing age made it progessively more difficult for them to meet the strenuous labor demands of a peasant household. As it was difficult to sustain a claim to shared authority without also sharing the work, most parents were sooner or later obliged to withdraw into more definitive retirement. At the same time as they did this, however, parents commonly insisted on notarized guarantees of material comfort, status, and autonomy. The contract in question was usually known as a *Leibgeding*, and took the form of a list of food and other necessities owed, as one couple put it, "because they retained [the right] to use and enjoy half of the property they had [previously] sold, but no longer can work the land due to their age."[184]

Even among less affluent peasants, the *Leibgeding* was a favorite tool for the regulation of generational turnover. The tailor Jerg Hafner of Niederdorf was possessed of only a house and seven small parcels of land totalling four and a quarter *jauchert*.[185] All the same, the contract whereby he sold these holdings to his son Jacob in 1617 was full of detail. Jacob kept all of the property, but his parents retained the right to live in the house while Jacob was to furnish them with food, drink, and firewood. Jacob further agreed annually to provide his parents with 4 *claber* of prepared flax, 1 *viertel* of spelt, 10 pounds of lard, 100 eggs, one quarter of the yield from the fruit trees in the garden, and "every week between St. George's Day [23 April] and Michaelmas [29 September] a *maß* of fresh milk."[186]

When a great deal of property changed hands, the provisions of the *Leibgeding* could be quite extensive. Hans Henckhel was the *Amman* of Niederdorf

[179] In 1620 the brothers are listed separately (and not sequentially) as owners of half-houses; each has a taxable wealth of 130 fl. Michael's occupation is given as a drummer. StAA, KL Ottobeuren 102, ff. 196r and 197v.

[180] StAA, KL Ottobeuren 583, Heft 47, f. 2v. "Johann Lontner – deceased."

[181] Balthas was the son of Valentein Frick (StAA, KL Ottobeuren 909, ff. 90v–91r [16 Oct. 1625]), a poor Benningen cottager with a taxable wealth of only 80 fl. in 1627 (KL Ottobeuren 104, f. 165r). That he assumed the ownership of Johann Lontner's half-house is clear from a comparison of the 1620 and 1627 tax books. Since there is no record of Balthas purchasing the half-house, he probably acquired ownership by marriage.

[182] Judging by the fact that they jointly took out a loan, mortgaging the entire house to the parish church of Benningen for 50 fl. StAA, KL Ottobeuren 911, ff. 45–6 [1 July 1630].

[183] StAA, KL Ottobeuren 583, Heft 52, f. 2v. The scribe has noted "in Benningen both of the Lontners have [now] died." Michael is still listed in the register for the previous year (ibid., Heft 50, f. 2v).

[184] StAA, KL Ottobeuren 904, f. 33r [26 Feb. 1608].

[185] StAA KL Ottobeuren 907, ff. 112v–113r [17 Oct. 1617]. The 1620 tax survey lists the arable as measuring only 3.75 *jauchert*. KL Ottobeuren 102, f. 146v.

[186] StAA KL Ottobeuren 907, f. 113r [7 Oct. 1617].

and a prodigiously wealthy man.[187] When his son Balthas came into his father's lands in the spring of 1632, Hans expected (and exacted) the following: every year 2 *malter* of rye, 1 *malter* of spelt, a sack of oats, 30 pounds of lard, 150 eggs, a quarter of beef, a quarter of pork, every three months 5 *gulden* in cash, a new shirt, as many shoes and as much sweet milk as he required. The son Balthas was also to provide his father with his meals, "and whenever and as often as he wishes shall let him have something special cooked from his stores, whatever he shall desire." Finally, Balthas and his wife were bound

> diligently to care for and look after him in sickness and in health, equally at his every request to provide him with their horses. And if it should come to pass that the said young couple, the purchasers [of the land], should in the annual fulfillment of the said *Leibgeding* or otherwise in any other respect prove negligent, then shall the said *Amman* each time have the power and authority to hire a maid and servant of his own, whose meals shall be provided by the buyer but whose wages shall be paid out of his own [income] . . .[188]

The nervous father went so far as to reserve from the conveyed property a bed for the servant he feared he might someday have to hire.

The extreme specificity of *Leibgeding* clauses among comfortable households leaves little doubt that retired *Bauern* lived well. Their diets included not only large amounts of grain, but also beef and pork,[189] salt,[190] milk,[191] eggs,[192]

---

[187] In 1627 he held 56.5 *jauchert* of arable land, 8 *tagwerk* of meadow, 1 *jauchert* of wood, and 3 *tagwerk* of garden. His gross wealth was 1,769 fl. StAA KL Ottobeuren 104, f. 134v.

[188] StAA KL Ottobeuren 911, f. 250 [28 May 1632].

[189] A very common allocation was "one quarter of beef and one quarter of pork," the cash value of which is given as 4 *gulden* in StAA, KL Ottobeuren 905, ff. 299r–v [5 Oct. 1615]. KL Ottobeuren 903, ff. 265v–266r [15 Nov. 1606] allows a widowed mother 10 *gulden* for meat. As for the physical amount, KL Ottobeuren 903, ff. 126r–127r [26 Nov. 1604] and KL Ottobeuren 905, ff. 156r–v [16 Jan. 1614] both give the annual consumption of a widowed *Bauer* mother as 20 pounds of meat (half beef, half pork) while KL Ottobeuren 904, f. 257r [9 June 1611] gives the annual consumption of two *Bauer* parents as 20 pounds of beef and 10 pounds of pork, and KL Ottobeuren 905, ff. 205v–206r [13 Oct. 1614] allows a widowed mother fully 25 pounds of beef and 12 pounds of pork per annum. On the lower end of the social spectrum, a *Seldner* widow's son agreed to provide her annually with 6 pounds of beef and 4 pounds of pork "when he has meat to butcher and otherwise none." KL Ottobeuren 907, ff. 192v–193r [4 Oct. 1618]. The associated sale deed [ibid., ff. 192r–v] lists the family's property as a house and 3 *jauchert* of arable land worth a total of 230 fl.

[190] StAA, KL Ottobeuren 903, ff. 92r–93r [19 May 1604] and 237v–238r [8 June 1606].

[191] The most common annual allowance was a half-*Maß* of milk per day; for example StAA, KL Ottobeuren 903, f. 2v [22 Feb. 1603] and KL Ottobeuren 904, ff. 10r–v [22 Nov. 1607]. The cash value of this allotment is given as 2 fl. in KL Ottobeuren 905, f. 186r [8 June 1614]. KL Ottobeuren 908, f. 93r [27 June 1620] allows a father a full *Maß* of milk per day "when available."

[192] The most common level of annual egg consumption reported in the *Leibgedinge* was 100 per year, but amounts varied widely, ranging from 30 (StAA, KL Ottobeuren 903, ff. 79v–80r [11 Mar. 1604] and ff. 77v–78r [6 Feb. 1603]) to 50 (ibid., f. 74v [12 Feb. 1604]) to 100 (KL Ottobeuren 905, ff. 12v–13r [9 Aug. 1612]) to 150 (ibid., ff. 134v–135r [3 Dec. 1613]) to 200 (ibid., f. 145r [19 Dec. 1613] and KL Ottobeuren 904, f. 219r [7 Nov. 1610]).

cheese,[193] fruit,[194] peas,[195] root vegetables,[196] and both fresh and pickled cabbage.[197] Parents were commonly given the cost of visiting the bathhouse,[198] and a new pair of shoes whenever needed (sometimes elaborated as both "high and low shoes").[199] The most particular of details were registered in these contracts, whether a father's right to be given a measure of wine every feast day[200] or the heirs' obligation "every time they go to visit the city of Memmingen, they shall always bring him [i.e. the retired father] back one *kreuzer*'s worth of white bread."[201]

Lurking behind the haggling over issues of comfort and taste like the color of a parent's shoes or the right to choose the front as opposed to the back cut of meat[202] was a more fundamental concern for the autonomy of retired parents. Even with food, the physiological act of eating was inseparable from the social act of the meal, and the particular context of a meal was laden with all kinds of status implications. Retired parents were commonly meant to take their meals with the *Hausgebrauch*,[203] that is, with the household servants.[204]

---

[193] StAA, KL Ottobeuren 905, f. 343r [8 Mar. 1616] allows a widowed mother "three cheeses" and "as much milk as she needs" per annum, also 6 *metzen* of green fruit and 5 *viertel* of ripe apples. Cheese is also mentioned in KL Ottobeuren 908, f. 111v [9 Oct. 1620].

[194] StAA, KL Ottobeuren 905, f. 98v [28 Apr. 1613] allows the parents cherries, 1 *viertel* of apples, 1 *viertel* of wild pears [*Holzbirnen*] and 1 *viertel* of domestic pears [*Langbirnen*]. It also fixes their annual salt allotment at three pounds.

[195] StAA, KL Ottobeuren 903, ff. 40r–v [9 Oct. 1603] and 269r–v [19 Nov. 1606].

[196] *Leibgeding* references to the consumption of root vegetables [*Rüben*] include StAA, KL Ottobeuren 903, ff. 158v–159r [7 Mar. 1605]; KL Ottobeuren 904, ff. 89r [2 Jan. 1609], 129[a]v–130r [14 May 1609], and 156[a]v–157v [17 Nov. 1609]; and KL Ottobeuren 905, ff. 11r–12r [7 Aug. 1612].

[197] StAA, KL Ottobeuren 903, ff. 265v–266r [15 Nov. 1606]. Also ibid., ff. 158v–159r [7 Mar. 1605] and KL Ottobeuren 904, f. 189v [29 Mar. 1610].

[198] StAA, KL Ottobeuren 903, ff. 158v–159r [7 Mar. 1605]; KL Ottobeuren 904, f. 220r [7 Dec. 1610]; KL Ottobeuren 905, ff. 322r–323r [7 Jan. 1616].

[199] StAA, KL Ottobeuren 904, f. 184v [10 Mar. 1610]; KL Ottobeuren 905, ff. 11r–12r [7 Aug. 1612]; KL Ottobeuren 908, ff. 90v–92r [26 June 1620].

[200] StAA, KL Ottobeuren 903, ff. 94v–95r [10 June 1604].

[201] StAA, KL Ottobeuren 904, ff. 71v–72r [11 Sep. 1608].

[202] StAA, KL Ottobeuren 908, ff. 5r–v [8 May 1619]: the parents' shoes are to be made with black leather; KL Ottobeuren 903, ff. 92r–93r [19 May 1604]: a mother reserves the right to choose which cut of meat she shall have.

[203] There are nine *Leibgedinge* with this clause between July 1616 and Dec. 1618 in StAA, KL Ottobeuren 907 alone.

[204] That eating with the *Hausgebrauch* meant eating with the servants is indicated by the following passage from the remarriage contract of Anna Steger of Schoren, who married Martin Kustermann after the death of her first husband: "in case Martin Kustermann should subsequently no longer be able or desire to eat daily with the *Hausgebrauch*, or, rather, if the . . . before-child should . . . take over the property [and] no longer wish to have him eat with the household servants [*Hausgesindt*] . . . Martin Kustermann shall in that case, instead of the meals, be annually given one sack of oats, one sack of spelt, two quarters of rye . . ." etc. StAA, KL Ottobeuren 905, ff. 137r–v [9 Dec. 1613]. See also KL Ottobeuren 903, ff. 237v–238r [8 June 1606], where a widowed mother is given the right "in addition to the aforesaid *Leibgeding* to eat with the household servants [*Hausgesindel*] at her pleasure" and KL Ottobeuren 916, f. 13v [12 Feb.

Now, there were a few households where the entire household seem to have eaten together,[205] but for the most part the legal divide between owners and servants was reflected (reinforced, indeed) by their dining apart. For parents to be consigned to the subordinates' table was thus a degradation of enormous symbolic import – even when their actual food was the same as that eaten by their heirs[206] – and some parents explicitly reserved the right to eat alone instead.[207]

Parental concern for the preservation of their status was expressed in a number of other ways, ranging from the ubiquitous general injunction that a parent "shall be forced to do no work other than that which he does of his own free will" to the more specific right of parents to use the horses, with the associated connotations of prestige, or the right "to have something special cooked" should the parent so desire. More strikingly, and in keeping with the traditional categories of order discussed in chapter 2, parental dignity was often framed in terms of control over time and space, for example a father's reservation of specified rooms "such that without his knowledge and consent no one shall have any business in there at all"[208] or a mother's insistence that "if she does not arise at the right time in the morning, she may still make herself some reheated porridge at the [younger] couple's expense."[209]

Of course, for all the guarantees that might be demanded and recorded, a parent's comfort and status was in the end still contingent upon the overall economic health of the household. A stepfather like Ulrich Öxlin of Ölbrechts,

1661], where it was declared at the retirement of an Ungerhausen innkeeper that "Niclaus shall provide his parents with food and drink, not at the servants' [table] but at a special table."
[205] StAA, KL Ottobeuren 908, f. 16r [6 July 1619] has an unusual formulation detailing a father-in-law's right to have his "daily meals with them [i.e. the owners] and the *Hausgebrauch*." See also KL Ottobeuren 904, ff. 261v–262r [1 July 1611], which stipulates that "the old and young married couple shall also eat together."
[206] See for example the *Leibgeding* of Anna Reich of Rempolz, granted by her son Jacob Kustermann in exchange for the sale of half-use rights to his deceased father's *Gotteshausrecht Hof*. Anna was assured the right "to be provided with food and drink from the couple's [i.e. the heirs'] table, as good as they themselves have every day," but the contract also foresaw that this still might not be acceptable, and went on to state that "In so far as she [i.e. Anna] should no longer wish to eat with the *Hausgebrauch*, which she is free to choose, she is to receive a quarter of beef, a quarter of pork, one *malter* of rye, . . ." etc. StAA, KL Ottobeuren 905, ff. 134v–135r [3 Dec. 1613].
[207] StAA, KL Ottobeuren 908, ff. 79v–80r [20 May 1620]. Similarly KL Ottobeuren 907, ff. 2r–3r [14 July 1616].
[208] StAA, KL Ottobeuren 904, f. 95v [23 Jan. 1609]. See also KL Ottobeuren 903, ff. 334–335r [3 Aug. 1607] (an orphaned sister is to be given a room that locks in her brother's house) and KL Ottobeuren 905, f. 72r [17 May 1613] (three yielding siblings are to get a room of their own after their mother dies).
[209] StAA, KL Ottobeuren 905, ff. 156r–v [16 Jan. 1614]. See also ibid., ff. 342r–v [7 March 1616] (a father has the right to have food cooked for him between meals if he likes) and ff. 373v–374r [27 June 1616] (two parents have "the right, as often as they wish, mornings or evenings, if they do not reach the meal [on time], to cook for themselves what they would like [to eat]").

who ran up debts during his own leadership of the household, might find himself obliged to keep working in his retirement.[210] Even an otherwise capable householder like Balthas Dabratshofer of Günzegg might suffer the indignity of being bounced on three-year terms between two daughters eager to keep their expenses to a minimum.[211] It should be emphasized that in each of the foregoing cases, the fiscal health of the household did in time improve. Between 1620 and 1627, Ulrich Öxlin's son-in-law managed to preserve the household's property while halving its debt.[212] Balthas Dabratshofer's two daughters both became significantly wealthier in the generation after the family's 1609 agreement,[213] and Magdalena's husband in particular virtually doubled the value of his property between 1612 and 1617.[214] At the same time, these examples also show that material well-being could not be frozen by parental fiat but instead hung on the managerial diligence and accounting skill of the children.

In light of their ultimate dependency on their heirs, many parents sought to pre-empt future problems by controlling the marriage plans of their children, and in this endeavor they had the firm support of their overlord. In the year 1570 Abbot Caspar promulgated an "Ordinance pertaining to the admission of the monastery's common people to the domestic state." Disorder, the Abbot declared, had become widespread in matters of marriage, and after consultation with the monastery's *Vogt*, servants, and village officials, he had determined to put an end to it. Henceforth,

> none of our [subjects] shall be permitted or allowed to engage and give himself in marriage without the foreknowledge of his father and mother, or if he has neither [without the foreknowledge] of their officially appointed overseer and guardian and of his nearest relatives; and whosoever shall marry otherwise, whether man or woman, he or she shall forthwith be expelled and banished from the monastery's lands and territories . . .[215]

---

[210] StAA, KL Ottobeuren 907, ff. 203v–204r [7 Dec. 1618]. Öxlin borrowed almost 250 fl. in the last four years before he sold the *Hof*. KL Ottobeuren 905, ff. 98v–99r [2 May 1613], 224v [18 Dec. 1614], 238v–239r [12 Feb. 1615], and 334r [8 Feb. 1616], and KL Ottobeuren 907, f. 54v [20 Feb. 1617]. Also ibid., ff. 49v–50r [29 Jan. 1617].

[211] StAA, KL Ottobeuren 904, f. 88[a]v [2 Jan. 1609].

[212] StAA, KL Ottobeuren 102, f. 74r and KL Ottobeuren 104, f. 66r.

[213] Anna Dabratshofer's husband, Jerg Becherer of Osterberg, did borrow another 100 fl. in 1615 (KL Ottobeuren 905, f. 249r [11 Mar. 1615]), but he eventually managed to reduce his total debt from 1,065 fl. in 1620 to 636 fl. in 1627, while increasing the value of his assets from 1,690 to 1,800 fl. [KL Ottobeuren 102, f. 127v and KL Ottobeuren 104, ff. 110r–v].

[214] In those five years, Jerg Welfle of Günzegg purchased a garden worth 200 fl. (StAA, KL Ottobeuren 905, ff. 16r–v [19 Aug. 1612]), a house and 18 *jauchert* worth 200 fl. (ibid., f. 53r [25 Dec. 1612]), and a second garden worth 120 fl. (KL Ottobeuren 907, ff. 91r–v [19 June 1617]). These acquisitions make up 47.2 percent of the 1,990 fl. worth of property he held in 1620 (KL Ottobeuren 102, f. 122v). By 1627 Jerg's gross wealth had increased to 2,307.5 fl., while his debts had fallen from 600 to 200 fl. [KL Ottobeuren 104, f. 106v].

[215] StAA, KL Ottobeuren 4, Document 289K, ff. 317r–320v; the quotation on f. 318v.

The introduction of parochial registration in the parish of Ottobeuren helped to provide the heightened oversight required by the ordinance, and the marriage register (regrettably maintained only in 1570–6 and 1613–25) was filled with cranky annotations that a couple had been clandestinely engaged, or that the new wife of an "ancient" widower was in fact "his very young servant."[216] The 1570 Ordinance was not the first time the monastery had legislated on the subject of marriage among the peasantry, but earlier regulations had been more concerned with limiting the number of guests who could be invited to weddings.[217] Now the object was to grant parents control over the marriages of their children, and it was a power which was embraced with enthusiasm.[218]

Catharina Trunzer of Unterwesterheim was working as a servant in the village of Attenhausen when she fell foul of this power in 1601. She and one Thomas Zuckh of Ungerhausen had been associating with each other "in a forbidden manner," and her father did not approve of him. Jerg Trunzer ordered Catharina to break off the liaison, but Zuckh was not easily dissuaded. It is a measure of Trunzer's patriarchal authority that his unfortunate daughter was reduced to paying her suitor 4 *gulden* "that he should henceforth stay away from her" in a desperate attempt to comply with her father's wishes. This did not prevent the Attenhausen village authorities from fining the couple £3 10 ß.[219] In the end Catharina would have to wait until after her father died in 1603 before she married, and then it was to Jacob Weissenhorn of Niederdorf.[220]

It should not be thought that the promulgation of the marriage ordinances resulted in the unrelieved tyranny of children by their parents. Most parents wished their children to marry happily, and several parents simply refused to comply with the punitive measures of the marriage ordinances. When Lienhardt Hueber of Hof's two daughters both came home pre-maritally pregnant in 1601, the authorities banished them from the monastery lands. Hueber demurred. However much he may have disapproved of his daughters' actions (and despite his poverty),[221] he was not prepared to turn his back on them and instead

---

[216] OttPR, Vol. I, ff. 23r [24 Oct. 1574] (hamlet of Dennenberg) and 41r [28 Nov. 1571] (hamlet of Guggenberg) respectively. See also (ibid., f. 104r) the observation at the marriage of Veit Schmalholz on 2 May 1574 that the groom had already been married twice before.

[217] A section on marriages in the *c.* 1551 collection of ordinances prohibits the invitation of more than forty guests to a wedding. StAA, KL Ottobeuren 4, Document 289X, ff. 381r–v.

[218] Laws increasing the control of parents over the marriages of their children were promulgated all over Germany during the later sixteenth century; there is a good survey in Joel F. Harrington, *Reordering Marriage and Society in Reformation Germany* (Cambridge, 1995). For an excellent analysis of the phenomenon in the county of Hohenlohe see Robisheaux, *Rural Society*, esp. pp. 95–120.

[219] StAA, KL Ottobeuren 587-II, Heft 21 (1601/2).

[220] Catharina's father, Jerg Trunzer, was buried on 26 March 1603; Catharina married on 8 June of the same year. WestPR, Vol. I, pp. 111, 180.

[221] Hueber's 1600 and 1601 tithe payments indicate that he did not harvest enough grain to feed even three adults. StAA, KL Ottobeuren 681, Heft 3, f. 3v and Heft 4, f. 8r. In 1620 his property

sheltered them illegally in his house.[222] Furthermore, there were clearly some cases where parental oversight was warranted. The close supervision Jerg Trunzer exercised over his daughter Catharina ought more properly to have been directed towards his son Martin. The year after his sister's friendship was broken up, Martin Trunzer managed to impregnate one Anna Schuster, who like him was a servant in the house of Michael Lang in Egg.[223] Whereas Catharina settled down in the end to a humble but stable married life in their home village of Unterwesterheim, her brother drifted out of the monastery lands and never returned.[224]

Despite these qualifications, the harshness of the marriage ordinances ought not to be minimized. Some young offenders fled the territory before the ordinance could be applied;[225] others either could or would not leave and thus bore the full force of its provisions. Georg Hummel's stepson, who in 1602 married his pregnant girlfriend "by himself without the knowledge of his parents and the authorities against the promulgated mandate," was fined five pounds.[226] Also premaritally pregnant, the daughter of the wealthy innkeeper of Attenhausen was fined £5 5ß in 1601 for her unauthorized marriage to Jerg Bergmann of Günzegg.[227] The innkeeper's daughter was relatively lucky: her husband had enough money to allow the couple to purchase a house and establish themselves in her home village.[228] Less fortunate was Barbara Besch of Dennenberg. The daughter of a poor cottager,[229] she contracted an unauthorized marriage with a

---

(a house, 12 *jauchert*, a horse, and two cows) was valued at 380 fl. (KL Ottobeuren 102, f. 54v). In 1623, hyperinflation drove him off to Austria in search of work (KL Ottobeuren 491-III, Heft 27, f. 4r). and by 1627 his land had been swallowed by one of his wealthier neighbors (KL Ottobeuren 104, f. 46r).

[222] StAA, KL Ottobeuren 587-II, Heft 21 (1601/2).

[223] Ibid., Heft 22 (1602/3). The child was baptized on 25 Nov. 1603. WestPR, Vol. I, p. 17.

[224] Catharina had five children between 1604 and 1614; she died of dropsy in 1629 (ibid., Vol. I, pp. 17, 20, 26, 29, 36, 122). According to the 1620 tax survey her husband, Jacob Weissenhorn, owned a house, one *jauchert* of arable land, and two cows, with a gross wealth of 230 fl. (StAA, KL Ottobeuren 102, f. 310r). Martin leaves no record in the Westerheim parish register, the bond-chicken registers of 1602–29, the 1620 and 1627 tax surveys of the entire lordship, or the land sales registered between 1603 and 1621.

[225] Thus, for example, the following incidents from the village of Benningen: "Michael Breg of Altisried on the Iller and Barbara Mair of Zell, [also] Michael Enderess of Benningen's serving-man and Michael Rauch of Benningen's maid have committed fornication. [They] have [all] gone away together to Zell. Fined £4." "Johann Schüess' stepdaughter Barbara Höltzlerin has been impregnated by Enderas Hiltprand from the hamlet [of Niederrieden?]. [They] have gone away together to Lachen. Fined 16 ß." StAA, KL Ottobeuren 587-II, Heft 22 (1602/3).

[226] StAA, KL Ottobeuren 587-II, Heft 22 (1602/3), Westerheim. Hans Maugg of Westerheim was fined the same amount for a similar offense.

[227] Ibid., Heft 21 (1601/2).

[228] Jerg Bergmann purchased a house and garden from Anthoni Allgäuer, the miller of Attenhausen, for 250 fl. on 8 Dec. 1605 (StAA, KL Ottobeuren 903, f. 200v). The 1620 tax survey lists Bergmann as a baker in Attenhausen, holding the house, one *jauchert* of arable land, and a cow, with a gross wealth of 360 fl. (KL Ottobeuren 102, f. 388v).

[229] Her father, Hans Besch, did not have enough land to be listed as a tithe payer in the 1584 tithe list (StAA, KL Ottobeuren 31, f. 77r). Her maternal grandfather was the poorest householder in

certain Christof Schmeltzlin of Horgen in 1583. Barbara and her husband were banished from the monastery lands.[230]

Independent of the powers with which they had been endowed by the marriage ordinance, parents exercised still more influence over the marriage choices of their children through simple financial inducement. In 1607, for example, the widow Anna Ruoff of Benningen had an agreement notarized promising her son Jacob Michel that "if and in the event that, as has heretofore been the case, he should carry out and fulfill all filial duties and obligations towards her, and should in the future marry with the foreknowledge of [both] his Lord and mother, then her house, house-lot and garden shall be offered first to him before anyone else for sale at a manageable [*leidenlich*] price."[231] Jacob apparently did not behave to his mother's satisfaction, and the contract's implicit threat was carried out. This was not easy for the widow to do, as she was pinched for funds[232] and the alternative heirship choices were not particularly attractive. Her daughter Barbara lived in another territory and her daughter Anna had lost her virginity to a man who subsequently went back on his promise to marry her.[233] Nevertheless, the daughter Anna did eventually manage to marry a "poor journeyman" and cottager's son[234] from the village of Niederdorf, and this son-in-law, Jerg Hüemer, was the eventual beneficiary of Jacob Michel's disobedience. Unfortunately for the widow, her triumph was fleeting, as her son-in-law (with whom she had equally strained relations)[235] was in 1613 constrained to sell back the house and land in Benningen to Jacob Michel,[236] and then bounced through the village of Niederrieden before settling down in extreme poverty in the village of Egg.[237] Anna Ruoff thus lived to

the hamlet in 1546 (KL Ottobeuren 64, f. 40r), and before him Barbara's great-grandfather had been the poorest man in the hamlet in 1525 (KL Ottobeuren 541, Heft 2, ff. 47r–v). Genealogy from Dertsch, "Das Einwohnerbuch des Ottobeurer Klosterstaats 1564," p. 25.

[230] StAA, KL Ottobeuren 4, Document 311, ff. 1175r–v.

[231] StAA, KL Ottobeuren 903, ff. 313r–v [4 Apr. 1607].

[232] She was shedding land, such as the half-*jauchert* parcel sold for 39 fl. on 23 Dec. 1612. StAA, KL Ottobeuren 905, f. 38r.

[233] This was Anna's claim, at least; the defendant (also from another territory, in this case the village of Boos in the Fugger lordship) denied everything. Archiv des Bistums Augsburg [henceforth ABA], Offizialatsprotokolle [henceforth OPr] 1602–6, p. 529 [10 Dec. 1604]. That Barbara lived in Woringen, in the territory of the free imperial city of Memmingen, is revealed by the *Kaufbrief* of 28 Feb. 1613.

[234] Jerg Hüemer's father, Jerg, is assessed 3 kr. in the bond-chicken register for 1602. StAA, KL Ottobeuren 491-I, Heft 14, f. 14r.

[235] StAA, KL Ottobeuren 903, f. 331r [16 June 1607]. This somewhat cryptic document regulates an unspecified "dispute and misunderstanding" between Anna Ruoff and her son-in-law. The dispute culminated in court action and generated legal expenses of 54 fl. which Hüemer "as a poor journeyman" was unable to pay. Anna Ruoff assumed the costs for the present and Hüemer agreed to reimburse her heirs after her death.

[236] StAA, KL Ottobeuren 905, f. 93v *Kaufbrief* for 674 fl. [28 Feb. 1613].

[237] Ibid., ff. 29r *Kaufbrief* for a half-house in Niederrieden for 120 fl. [20 Oct. 1612] and 69v–70r *Tauschbrief* for a slightly inferior house (Hüemer received 4 fl. in the exchange) in Egg [4 May 1613]. In 1620 Hüemer held property worth only 136 fl. and had debts of 109 fl. KL Ottobeuren 102, ff. 292v–293r.

see[238] her refractory son established in the house she had sought to deny him, but she had managed to make his ascent rather more expensive[239] and time-consuming – Jacob did not marry until 1614/15[240] – than it otherwise would have been.

To play Jacob and Esau with children was, of course, rather rare, and most parents employed less drastic means of shaping their children's decisions. At least as far as the archival record is concerned, the most common device was the parent's power over a child's *Voraus*, an advance on his or her inheritance normally used as the start-up capital for a marriage. The inheritance itself was virtually never revoked, but parents derived considerable leverage from the fact that the timing and size of the advance were of enormous consequence for a child's chances on the marriage market. Thus, a parent might force children to delay marriage by refusing a *Voraus* if they married in his lifetime[241] or insist on the right to determine the size of the younger children's *Voraus* even after yielding ownership of the property to the heir.[242] The receipt of an advance was also often conditional upon appropriate conduct, and a father might promise a son a *Voraus* only "if he marries with the foreknowledge and approval of his father"[243] or further require that the son "also behave obediently and compliantly."[244] Still closer conformity was occasionally demanded, as in the case of Balthas Mehaber of Benningen, who promised one of his daughters a *Voraus* only "if she marries or resides in the monastery [lands] or an immediately adjacent location,"[245] or the widow Barbara Salb of Dennenberg, who pledged 200 fl. to her four nieces and nephews but warned that "if any of the said heirs should claim to be unhappy with his or her portion, he or she shall thereby forfeit it."[246]

In this climate of generalized fiscal pressure on the marriage choices of all children, the process of choosing the heir was informed by a still more

---

[238] She is listed in the 1617 bond-chicken register. StAA, KL Ottobeuren 491-II, Heft 21, f. 19v.

[239] The property was sold for 674 fl. but according to the 1620 tax assessment was worth only 524 fl. The difference is neatly made up by the 150 fl. obligation which Jacob assumed to the three children of his deceased sister Anna Michel. StAA, KL Ottobeuren 102, f. 189v and KL Ottobeuren 903, f. 90r [7 Feb. 1613].

[240] StAA, KL Ottobeuren 583, Heft 32, f. 3r. Jacob is described as unmarried in the 1613 transactions.

[241] StAA, KL Ottobeuren 903, ff. 176v–177r [23 June 1605].

[242] StAA, KL Ottobeuren 905, ff. 208r–209r [16 Oct. 1614].

[243] StAA, KL Ottobeuren 903, ff. 187r–v [17 Oct. 1605]. The promised *Voraus* was 50 fl.; if the son did not comply, he was not to receive anything until after his father's death.

[244] Ibid., ff. 268r–269r [19 Nov. 1606]. The father was the *Amman* of the village of Egg, and the promised *Voraus* was 200 fl.

[245] Ibid., ff. 243v–244r [6 July 1606]. Balthas was not completely heartless, and was fined £1 in 1590/1 for sheltering an unmarried woman in childbed. He was a *Seldner* and in 1620 had 1.5 *jauchert* of arable land and a gross wealth of 400 fl. KL Ottobeuren 587-I, Heft 15; KL Ottobeuren 102, f. 192r.

[246] StAA, KL Ottobeuren 905, ff. 343v–344r [8 Mar. 1616]. In two separate transactions on the same date (ibid., ff. 342v and 343r), Barbara sold her heir a *Hof* of 30 *jauchert* for 750 fl. and was assured very generous maintenance in food, clothing, and other necessities.

explicitly economic calculus. Parents were utterly blunt in their directions that house and land pass to "that before-child who among the others can pay the best [price]."[247] The same logic overrode even the traditional rule that property pass to the second spouse (instead of the before-children) at the death of the head of the household. As Jerg Steger, the sexton of Niederrrieden, put it in 1615, when fixing the value of his house and 2.75 *jauchert* of arable land at 359 fl., the property was to pass at his death to his second wife, Maria Widenmann, "but should the said Maria Widenmann . . . prove unable to buy all of the said land, the said [property] shall pass to the one among his children who can most easily pay the said price . . ."[248]

Now, it was certainly the case that the Ottobeuren peasantry also evinced a bias towards male succession, most clearly illustrated by the fact that compensatory payments to siblings "for yielding" were often made by sisters to brothers, but never vice versa. At the same time, it should be pointed out that this crude patriarchal prejudice was significantly modified by the peasant economy's gender-based division of labor. As is clear from Figure 5.4,[249] daughters inherited almost at parity with sons among the landless and smallholders, where the traditionally female tasks of spinning, gardening, and caring for poultry made up a particularly significant proportion of the household's income. Among the wealthier elements of rural society, by contrast, the economic dominance of plough agriculture[250] (a male preserve) seems to have made parents much less willing to hand over the property to an untested son-in-law, rather than a son who had grown up on and knew the land.

Having come in this way to the heir, that is, to the last of the social roles to be investigated, it goes without saying that the new inheritance practices drastically upped the stakes of marrying well (or not!). Although marriages had always been social statements, they now became even more so, and successful matches were

---

[247] StAA, KL Ottobeuren 904, ff. 18r–v [3 Jan. 1608]. Similarly ibid., ff. 127v–128r [3 Mar. 1609], which ordains that the property shall pass to "the one among the aforesaid sons Hans and Enderlin who is fittest and richest."

[248] StAA, KL Ottobeuren 905, ff. 278v–279r [23 June 1615]. Similarly ibid., ff. 15r–v [10 Aug. 1612], in which the second spouse is a man and the property is valued at 690 fl.

[249] This graph is based on 156 cases of succession where the parents are known to have had both male and female children. In most cases the presence of both daughters and sons was revealed by the deed of sale and mortgage or maintenance agreement, but in several instances it could only be established on the basis of emigration, apprenticeship, or parish records. The number of cases in each category was as follows: 37 (<250 fl.), 38 (250–499 fl.), 52 (500–999 fl.), and 29 (≥1000 fl.).

[250] The four wealth categories used here respectively made up 47.5% (<250 fl.), 15.0% (250–499 fl.), 16.1% (500–999 fl.), and 21.4% (≥1000 fl.) of the 1,676 households described in the 1620 tax survey. Of those in the poorest category, 95.7% had less than 5 *jauchert* of land of any kind and 69.2% had none at all. Of those in the second category, 67.1% had less than 5 *jauchert* but only 19.8% had no land at all. Of those in the third, 79.3% had at least 5 *jauchert* and 68.9% had 10 or more *jauchert*. Of those in the wealthiest category, 95.3% had at least 5 *jauchert* and 90.2% had 10 or more. StAA, KL Ottobeuren 102.

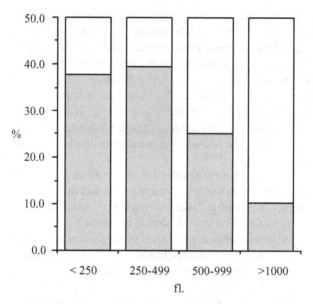

Figure 5.4 Percentage of female heirs by size of estate (fl.), 1603–21
Sources: StAA, KL Ottobeuren 27, 102, 903–8

celebrated with elaborate weddings proclaiming the family's status to the local community. Wedding clothes were deliberately designed to reflect the standing of the couple.[251] Seamstresses, tailors, and shoemakers might be brought in from other settlements to make them,[252] and might work for days[253] in the new couple's village. The wedding meal was equally extravagant, often including delicacies like white bread and wine which otherwise rarely graced a peasant's table.[254] Even though parents or heirs covered most of a wedding's cost, grooms

---

[251] Remarriage and mortgage/maintenance contracts commonly assured the before-children and yielding heirs wedding clothes "in keeping with their status [*irem stand gemäss*]." See for example StAA, KL Ottobeuren 904, ff. 58r–v [2 June 1608]; KL Ottobeuren 905, ff. 50r–51r [24 Dec. 1612]; KL Ottobeuren 907, ff. 162r–v [5 May 1618]; KL Ottobeuren 908, ff. 87r–v [21 June 1620]. Variations on this theme include the promise that the quality of the wedding clothes will be "as is customary among the *Bauern*" (KL Ottobeuren 905, ff. 27v–28r [14 Oct. 1612], 72v–73r [12 June 1613], and 115v–116r [26 Sep. 1613]) and even the assurance that a son and daughter "will at their weddings in all respects [and] as is the custom of the monastery [lands] be fêted and dowered in keeping with their status" (KL Ottobeuren 907, ff. 69r–v [12 Apr. 1617]).

[252] StAA, KL Ottobeuren 903, ff. 197v–198r [17 Nov. 1605]. The heir agrees to provide "shelter and sleeping room" for the craftspeople engaged for his siblings' weddings.

[253] Ibid., f. 42r [24 Oct. 1603] limits the support of wedding craftspeople to "one or two or three days."

[254] That white bread and wine were luxuries is indicated by their exclusion from the wedding costs which heirs were obliged to pay for their siblings. There are eight *Leibgedinge* with this clause between November 1609 and February 1610 in StAA, KL Ottobeuren 904 alone.

might still go into debt to pay for the festivities,[255] but this was clearly a long-term investment in prestige. Decades after a wedding, and without reference to a marriage register, the guests could often recall the date with surprising precision.[256]

Now, not all nuptial plans worked out so well, and although it may seem unfair to analyze an institution through examples of frustrated hope, the evidence in question – disputed engagements brought before the Bishop of Augsburg – reveals a great deal about the complexities (and risks) of peasant marriage-making. In the first place, the depositions underscore the fact that parents had only so much control over their children. Efforts were made to protect children from the wrong sort of company,[257] but liaisons could all too easily be struck up in mills and bathhouses,[258] and especially in the houses of third parties, often outside the Abbot's dominions,[259] an opportunity enormously expanded by the rise of servanthood for single young adults. Even within the the the monastery lands, venues for spouse-hunting abounded, including "dance houses"[260] and parish festivals at which the Abbot himself might pay the players.[261]

---

[255] StAA, KL Ottobeuren 904, f. 88r [18 Dec. 1608]: two brothers mortgage their cattle to cover wedding debts of 26 fl. 21 kr. and 17 fl. 3 kr. respectively.

[256] The certificates of legitimate birth issued to emigrants record the date of their parents' marriage as remembered by witnesses present at the wedding. In Ottobeuren parish, these recollections can sometimes be checked against a fragmentary marriage register. Guests remembered weddings as having taken place "about 33 years ago" (actually 31 years 3 months), "about 32 years ago" (actually 33 years), or "about 32 years ago" (actually 32 years 9 months). StAA, KL Ottobeuren 903, ff. 151r–v [9 Feb. 1605], 180r–v [22 Aug. 1605], and 216r–v [22 Feb. 1606]; and OttPR, Vol. II, ff. 1v [8 Nov. 1573], 47r [7 Sep. 1572], and 133r [17 May 1573]. It is unclear why in these cases no reference was made to the marriage register; explicit citation of parochial records in legitimacy certificates began only in the 1630s. See KL Ottobeuren 911, ff. 117 and 117–18 [11 Feb. 1631].

[257] See StAA, KL Ottobeuren 587-II, Heft 28 (1615), f. 34r: "Caspar Gufer [of Westerheim], with a weapon challenged Georg and Jacob Krumb to come out [of their house and fight him] because they would not let him fornicate with their sister – fined £1."

[258] ABA, OPr 1602–6, pp. 158–9 [22 Apr. 1603]: Anna Kopp and Michael Sauter, both of Egg, were allegedly engaged in the village mill; p. 467 [17 Sep. 1604]: Anna Danner of Wolfertschwenden and Michael Lusch of Gosmashofen were allegedly engaged in the bathhouse in Aptenweiler; pp. 742–3 [9 Dec. 1605]: Magdalena Greuther of Altdorf and Johann King of Ochsenhausen were allegedly engaged in the bathhouse in Sontheim. Note that the claim of a bathhouse engagement was far from preposterous: when Johann Menhelt married Barbara Maÿr in Guggenberg on 26 February 1571, it was recorded in the parish register that the couple had been engaged thirteen days earlier "in the bathhouse in [the market town of] Ottobeuren." OttPR, Vol. II, f. 41r.

[259] ABA, OPr 1598–1602, pp. 27–8 [10 Nov. 1598]: Barbara Koler of Ottobeuren and Ulrich Melder of Eggesried allegedly engaged in the house of Blesÿ Rauch of Neuenried; and pp. 573–4 [22 May 1601]: Marka Weckerlin of Benningen and Ambrosi Binz of Wolfertschwenden allegedly engaged in the house of Jacob Dreier of Hawangen, OPr 1602–6, pp. 460–1 [3 Sep. 1604]: Agatha Sauter of Hawangen and Andreas Scheir of Scheiringen allegedly engaged in the house of Urlich Reischin of Augsburg. See also the examples cited in the previous reference.

[260] StAA, KL Ottobeuren 905, ff. 240r–v [17 Feb. 1615]. The 'Dance House' seems to have been a portable structure, because the contract stipulates that the buyer pay for it to be moved from the hamlet of Vogelsang to the village of Böhen.

[261] Payments of 4–6 kr. each to musicians at the *Bauding*, or annual assembly of the village residents are recorded (oddly enough) in the accounts for the receipt of exogamous marriage fees. StAA,

A second feature of Swabian courtship that emerges from the records of the bishop's marriage tribunal, or *Offizialat*, is that sexual relations commonly began once the parties were engaged: "carnal copulation immediately followed [*copula carnali statim subsecuta*]" in the standard words of the court protocol.[262] As a result, a good many brides were already pregnant on their wedding day. In the parish of Westerheim, for example, of those women whose marriages and first births are recorded between 1595 and 1634, one in five (20.8 percent) bore a child less than seven months after getting married. The custom of pre-marital (though post-sponsal) sex was broadly tolerated, with only the occasional prosecution to keep up appearances.[263] On the other hand, if something went awry in the two to five weeks between engagement and wedding day,[264] the *Offizialat* might be visited by an abandoned (and often pregnant) woman, desperately hoping the ecclesiastical court would enforce the marriage promise she was sure she had been given.

It is important to keep the problem in proper perspective. The twenty-seven disputed engagements from the Ottobeuren lands brought before the Augsburg *Offizialat* in 1598–1606 represented a tiny fraction (perhaps 3–4 percent) of the weddings celebrated in those years.[265] Illegitimacy was also quite rare at Ottobeuren. Only 1.5 percent of children baptized in Westerheim (1595–1634) and 1.4 percent in Hawangen (1607–35) bore the stigma of bastardy (the pastor of Hawangen preferred the gentler annotation "father unknown"). Finally, it is worth pointing out that a non-trivial proportion (30 percent) of Ottobeuren plaintiffs in disputed engagment suits were men. But none of this should minimize the very real straits in which the female plaintiffs found themselves,

KL Ottobeuren 583, Heft 14, f. 5v (two players in Egg in 1598); Heft 15, f. 6r (two players in Egg in 1599); Heft 17, f. 6r (two pipers in Egg in 1601); Heft 20, f. 6v (a trumpeter in Benningen in 1603); Heft 21, f. 6r (three players in Benningen, three players in Westerheim, and a piper in Attenhausen in 1604); and Heft 26, f. 6v (three trumpeters in Ungerhausen in 1610).

[262] ABA, OPr 1598–1602, pp. 27–8 [10 Nov. 1598], 394 [25 Aug. 1600], 573–4 [22 May 1601].

[263] StAA, KL Ottobeuren 587-III, Heft 33 (1626/7), ff. 37v and 38v: Lorenz Geist and Michael Schmidt of Westerheim each fined 4 fl. for "having their weddings too late." Schmidt had been married on 7 Feb. 1625, and his first child was baptized four months later on 12 June 1625. Geist's marriage is not recorded, but his first child was baptized 20 Apr. 1627. According to the 1627 tax survey, Michael Schmidt was a *Seldner*, living in a half-house with one *tagwerk* of meadow and a gross wealth of 315 fl. Lorenz Geist owned no property at all. WestPR, Vol. I, pp. 66, 69, 190; KL Ottobeuren 104, ff. 279v, 294v.

[264] The marriage register of Ottobeuren parish often lists both engagement and wedding dates. For thirty-eight couples married between 1617 and 1625 in the market town of Ottobeuren, the mean interval between engagement and marriage was 24.6 days (median 25). Just over three-quarters of the couples had an engagment period of fourteen to thirty-five days. OttPR, Vol. II, ff. 5r–8r.

[265] The estimate was arrived at as follows: between 1598 and 1606, thirty-four weddings were celebrated in the parish of Westerheim. With seventy-eight households in 1620, the parish represented 4.65 percent of all Ottobeuren households. Assuming the same ratio between weddings and households in the lordship as a whole, the monastery lands would have seen about 730 weddings in the same period.

since it was very difficult for them to prove what canon law required, that is, that particular words had been exchanged between two lovers in the middle of the night. The *Offizialat* protocols suggest that only about one fourth of the male defendents agreed to marry the plaintiff. Another fourth were ordered to acknowledge their paternity and pay the expenses of delivering and rearing the child, but were absolved of any obligation to marry. The remaining half of the men were absolved unconditionally.

How did engagements come into dispute? In some cases it is hard to believe that there was ever any real promise of marriage, and it seems more likely that the lawsuit was an effort to redeem a moment of unguarded passion. Thus, when Magdalena Fuchsschwantz of Frechenrieden alleged that Balthas Fischer of Ottobeuren told her "I want to screw and to shit, and by God I must have you!", or when Barbara Lutz of Attenhausen claimed that Jerg Meschlen said "Let me into your house! If I can't have you my ass will burst!", the modern reader is hard-pressed not to wince at the court clerk's continuation ". . . which words she understood as a marriage proposal."[266]

In other instances, it appears that the groom did intend to marry, but got cold feet at the last minute. Here episcopal pressure could extract a promise to marry,[267] but considerable determination on the woman's part might still be necessary. Catharina Motz, for example, was the daughter of a dirt-poor cottager in the village of Sontheim.[268] In 1599, around the time of her father's death, Catharina became intimate with a certain Johann Miller from the village of Köngetried in the neighboring lordship of Mindelheim. Miller was a smooth-talking fellow who knew how to calm a woman's fears, and whose exhortations were unmarred by the coarser outbursts of many peasant lovers. "If you do my will," he assured Catharina one night in a village which lay between their respective homes, "I would want both you and the child. Have no more fear than you would of the shadows on the wall."[269] But for all his fine words, Johann Miller proved as feckless as so many other young men. When Catharina found herself pregnant in the spring of 1600, Miller didn't want to marry her

---

[266] ABA, OPr 1598–1602, p. 390 [23 Aug. 1600] and OPr 1602–6, p. 420 [14 May 1604] respectively. Although the language of the protocols is Latin (written in an italic hand), the vital importance in canon law of the precise words exchanged caused the "proposals" to be recorded in German (and in a secretary hand). Fuchsschwantz's claim was rejected; the verdict in Lutz's suit is missing.

[267] ABA, OPr 1602–6, pp. 474–5 [24 Sep. 1604]. Anna Maier of Ottobeuren charges Johann Öxlin of Unterhaslach of promising to marry her and of being the father of her child. He agrees to marry and to legitimate the child, Johann, born eight weeks ago "and who is still living," and she accepts his "confession and offer . . . and is prepared to accept him in marriage."

[268] A serf roll of 1585/6 lists Catharina in Sontheim as the daugher of Jerg Motz. StAA, KL Ottobeuren 601-II, ff. 75r–88v. Her father was assessed "0" in the 1590 bond-chicken register and then the widow's 2 kr. in 1595. KL Ottobeuren 491-I, Heft 5, f. 17r and ibid., Heft 6, f. 20v.

[269] ABA, OPr 1598–1602, pp. 394–5 [25 Aug. 1600]. The words were allegedly exchanged on 27 December 1599 at the home of 'Caspar N.' in the village of Erisried.

after all. And when Catharina hauled him before the Bishop of Augsburg, he admitted to having slept with her, but insisted that this had only begun too late in the previous year for him to have been the father of Catharina's child. As Catharina had no proof of Miller's promise, the *Offizialat* absolved him of any obligation to marry, but the court did expect Miller to help pay for the child's upbringing. Catharina herself, on the other hand, was not about to give in just yet, and in September of 1600, now heavily pregnant, she made a second journey to Augsburg, claiming to have witnesses who could attest that Miller had admitted to having made her an offer of marriage. In February, she made a third trip to the *Offizialat* to announce the birth of her child (on 9 November 1600) and again to demand justice. Miller gave up, and agreed to marry Catharina. On 14 February 1601, the engagement was solemnized. The unscrupulous groom again tried to wiggle out of even this public committment, but Catharina again appealed to Augsburg, and the Bishop, his patience now exhausted, flatly ordered Johann Miller to marry Catharina Motz.[270]

There were also more than a few cases of cold-hearted victimization. Michael Lusch of Goßmanshofen freely admitted to the episcopal court that he had asked Anna Danner of Wolfertschwenden, "Do you wish to marry me?" and to having slept with her in January and May of 1604. Lusch pointed out, however, that as he was already engaged to someone else (!), his promise to Anna could not be binding in canon law.[271] Lusch and Danner seem to have been peers, but the classic target for sexual exploitation was a maid.[272] Anna Fehler, who hailed from Dickenreishausen in the territory of the free imperial city of Memmingen, found this out to her cost while working in the home of the *Bauer* Johann Ergart of Niederrieden.[273] In late August of 1604, her employer's son Leonhard

---

[270] ABA, OPr 1602–6, pp, 701–2 [4 Oct. 1605]. It is unclear what happened to the couple thereafter. On 27 June 1606, the Westerheim parish register (Vol. I, p. 21) records the baptism of Jacob, son of Catharina Motz of Sontheim and Jerg (*sic*) Miller of Köngetried. This pregnancy is probably what prompted Catharina's lawsuit in the fall of 1605, but Jacob's designation as illegitimate suggests that Miller still had not married Catharina Motz. Her father, Jerg Motz, is missing from the bond-chicken register for 1602, and seems to have been replaced in Sontheim by a certain Martin Helzlin (StAA, KL Ottobeuren 491-I, Heft 10, f. 22r), who sold half of his house to Catharina's brother (?) Jerg Motz on 16 March 1618 (KL Ottobeuren 907, f. 149v). A mortgage document dated 29 November 1617 suggests that Jerg Motz may have lived in (i.e. rented) the house before he bought it (ibid., f. 123r). In 1620, Jerg Motz held property worth 405 fl., including loans of 200 fl. (!), and had no debts (KL Ottobeuren 102, ff. 356r–v).

[271] ABA, OPr 1602–6, p. 467 [17 Sep. 1604]; Goßmanshofen was part of the Princely Abbacy of Kempten.

[272] See, for example, the following examples from the village of Benningen: "Jerg Knopf called Redbeard, while drunk, made dishonorable demands of his then maid, which [demands] she rejected" and "Thoma Schütz, while drunk, sought to commit adultery with his maid in his barn, such that if his wife had not come there herself and caught them, the deed would have been committed." StAA, KL Ottobeuren 587-II, Heft 21 (1601/2) and Heft 22 (1602/3) respectively.

[273] Johann Ergart is assessed one hen in the bond-chicken registers for 1590, 1595, and 1602. StAA, KL Ottobeuren 491-I, Heft 5, f. 15v, Heft 6, f. 12v, and Heft 10, f. 12v.

"pressed her for sex [*insteterit pro copula*], to which she consented in the hope of marriage," and this continued until early February of 1605 when the maid found herself pregnant. Of course he wouldn't marry her. Indeed he couldn't, Leonhard coolly explained, because he was already promised to marry[274] the daughter of a wealthy Unterwesterheim *Bauer*. The match had been in the works since early 1604[275] and the wedding took place less than three weeks after Leonhard stopped sleeping with his father's maid.[276] Leonhard succeeded to his father-in-law's *Hof*[277] and settled down to a life of wealth and comfort in Unterwesterheim.[278] Anna Fehler could prove nothing, was awarded nothing, and disappeared.

In most cases, however, there is no direct indication from the court protocol as to the cause of a broken engagement, and we are left to surmise that the defendant's initial attraction (if any) waned, and that he or she (or both parties)[279] made other plans. Often this must have been due to the collapse of the marriage's finances. Thus Andreas Scheir of Scheiringen "admits to having promised [marriage], [but] on condition . . . that the plaintiff bring, in addition to her [own] promise, 40 *gulden* in ready money and the [cost of] the wedding feast . . . but as events have made it clear that the plaintiff cannot satisfy the condition, he therefore seeks . . . to be absolved from the plaintiff's petition."[280] In a similar vein, Ambrosi Binz of Wolfertschwenden, the second son of a declining family,[281] agreed – despite having been absolved by the

---

[274] ABA, OPr 1602–6, p. 603 [19 Apr. 1605]. According to Anna Fehler, the liaison began around 24 August 1604 and continued until at least 2 February 1605.

[275] Leonhard's father loaned an older son, Jacob, 100 fl. on 8 January 1604, with the principal to be repaid to Leonhard at his upcoming wedding. StAA, KL Ottobeuren 903, f. 56v. Leonhard was also promised an additional 25 fl. and his father's clothes for "yielding" the family lands in Niederrieden to Jacob. Ibid., ff. 179v–179[a]r [18 August 1605].

[276] WestPR, Vol. I, p. 180 [20 Feb. 1605].

[277] StAA, KL Ottobeuren 903, f. 163r [14 Apr. 1605]. The *Hof* measured 33 *jauchert* of arable land, 15 *tagwerk* of meadow, and 1 *tagwerk* of garden. Leonhard paid 400 fl. to his father-in-law, Jacob Maier, for the rights to the *Hof* and cleared the debt in a little over a month. Ibid., ff. 179[a]r [18 Aug. 1605] and 182v [24 Sep. 1605].

[278] In 1620, Leonhard held the *Hof* and sixteen head of livestock, for a gross wealth of 690 fl. By 1627, he had added a large garden (350 fl.) and had begun lending money (197 fl.) to increase his gross wealth to 1,297 fl. StAA, KL Ottobeuren 102, ff. 309r–v and KL Ottobeuren 104, ff. 289v–290r.

[279] ABA, OPr 1602–6, p. 624 [10 May 1605]. Johann Dodel of Moosbach and Catharina Teufel of Frechenrieden manipulate the rules of the Council of Trent to dissolve their engagement by mutual consent.

[280] Ibid., pp. 460–1 [3 Sep. 1604].

[281] According to the 1586 serf roll, Ambrosi was the son of Johann Binz senior, who was assessed the *Bauer*'s hen in the bond-chicken registers of 1595 and 1602, but whose successor, Johann junior, who married *c.* 1601, was assessed the *Seldner's* 3 kr. from 1609. Johann Binz junior was the beneficiary of a *Hofstatt* grant in 1605, and in 1620 had to his name only a house and cow worth a total of 70 fl. StAA, KL Ottobeuren 601-II, ff. 116r–121r; KL Ottobeuren 491-I, Heft 6, f. 17r, Heft 10, f. 13v, and Heft 14, f. 12r; KL Ottobeuren 903, f. 156r [3 Mar. 1605]; KL Ottobeuren 102, f. 172r.

Offizialat – to marry the rather wealthier[282] Maria Weckerlin of Benningen if she could come up with 135 fl.[283] Some defendants were clearly holding out for a better match. Why should Michael Sauter of Egg marry a poor local girl like Anna Kopp (worth perhaps 30 fl.)[284] when he could attract a mate like Anna Rogg of Hausen, whose 265 fl. dowry[285] alone was worth more than the entire wealth of the Kopp household?[286] And then there were a few defendants who seem to have preferred not to marry at all, like Lucia Farrer of Ottobeuren, who was sued (unsuccessfully) for breach of a marriage promise by Jerg Steffa, another resident of the market town, in January of 1605.[287] Lucia was far from rich: her father worked as the Abbot's messenger[288] and his estate was worth only 208 fl. Nevertheless, after the death of her father Lucia stayed on with her sister Magdalena, who married a poor shoemaker from Altisried.[289] The unmarried life seems to have suited Lucia, and she lived together with her sister's family for at least another fifteen years.[290]

---

[282] Maria Weckerlin seems to have been a relative (a sister?) of Ambrosi Weckerlin, the tenant of a large *Hof* from the Memmingen hospital who married in 1596/7 and who had a gross wealth of 1,030 fl. in 1627. StAA, KL Ottobeuren 583, Heft 13, f. 3v and KL Ottobeuren 104, ff. 164v–165r. Jerg Weckerlin, the only other Benningen Weckerlin in the 1602 bond-chicken register (KL Ottobeuren 491-I, Heft 10, ff. 7v–8v), did not have a daughter named Maria. See KL Ottobeuren 903, ff. 211v–212r [15 Feb. 1606].

[283] ABA, OPr 1598–1602, pp. 573–4 [22 May 1601]. Ambrosi had a house worth 80 fl. and loans of 112 fl. (some of the 135 fl. he was promised?) in the 1620 tax survey. StAA, KL Ottobeuren 102, f. 171r.

[284] Anna seems to have been the daughter of Caspar Kopp. She is listed as an unmarried resident of her brother's house owning property worth 30 fl. and 20 fl. in the tax surveys of 1620 and 1627 respectively. StAA, KL Ottobeuren 102, ff. 287r–v and KL Ottobeuren 104, f. 266r. Anna Kopp's parentage is not entirely certain, as there were six Kopp households in Egg in the 1602 bond-chicken register (KL Ottobeuren 491-I, Heft 10, ff. 15r–v). When all six are traced forward to 1620, however, none has a gross wealth greater than the 210 fl. of Anna's brother Johann. KL Ottobeuren 102, ff. 287r–294r.

[285] StAA, KL Ottobeuren 905, f. 228v receipt of Anna Rogg's dowry [17 Jan. 1615]. Michael Sauter had purchased his parents' *Hof* for 1,000 fl. on 26 November 1613. Ibid., f. 324r.

[286] ABA, OPr 1602–6, pp. 158–9 [22 Apr. 1603]. Sauter was absolved of the charge of "defloratio et impregnatio" after Anna Kopp could not prove any of her allegations. She received no damages.

[287] ABA, OPr 1602–6, p. 537 [14 Jan. 1605]. Steffa could offer no proof of a promise.

[288] Lucia is mentioned in the 1606 remarriage contract of her father, Caspar Farrer, while Caspar's position as court messenger is given in a deed of sale from the following year. StAA, KL Ottobeuren 903, ff. 222r–v [16 Mar. 1606] and 311v [29 Mar. 1607].

[289] On 23 February 1617, Magdalena Farrer married Johann Bürklin of Altisried, who had purchased the Farrer home for 208 fl. one month before. Bürklin was the son of Michael Bürklin of Altisried, who is listed as "poor" in the 1590 bond-chicken register, is assessed 3 kr. in 1595 and 2 kr. 1602, and who seems to have died by 1609. OttPR, Vol. I, f. 4r. StAA, KL Ottobeuren 907, f. 41v [27 Jan. 1617] and KL Ottobeuren 491-I, Heft 5, f. 9v, Heft 6, f. 7v, Heft 10, f. 9v and Heft 14, ff. 8v–9r.

[290] In the 1620 tax survey, Lucia is listed with property worth 50 fl. in the house of her brother-in-law, Johann Bürklin. By the time of the 1627 survey, Lucia, her stepmother Catharina Stedelin, and her brother Michael Farrer are no longer listed. StAA, KL Ottobeuren 102, f. 5r and KL Ottobeuren 104, f. 9r.

Whatever the cause of a disputed engagement, the usual consequence for the plaintiff was deep disappointment. Some men can be shown to have married elsewhere,[291] but the lot of female bastard-bearers, few in number though they may have been, was rather more difficult. A woman could not easily remain in her home village after the shame of an illegitimate birth. Of the eight women who bore bastards in Hawangen between 1607 and 1635, all but one disappeared from the parish thereafter; the lone survivor probably lasted only because she married the child's father a few months later.[292] A wealthy woman who bore a bastard might hold out in her home village at the price of dropping into the underclass. Catharina Schmalholz of Bibelsberg, for example, married a wealthy widower, Jacob Vogele of Unterwesterheim, shortly after the death of Vogele's first wife in 1589.[293] Near the end of Vogele's life, Catharina began an affair with another wealthy *Bauer*,[294] and within five months of her husband's death gave birth to an illegitimate son in 1610. A poorer woman might have been drummed out of the village, but Catharina was entitled to 100 fl. from her deceased husband's estate,[295] and on that basis married a poor cottager from the adjacent village of Oberwesterheim. She lived out the rest of her days in a miserable half-house[296] and died in childbirth in 1616.[297]

---

[291] For example Johann Moser of Oberwesterheim, whose marriage suit against Maria Hiebeler of the same village was dismissed for want of proof. ABA, OPr 1602–6, pp. 692–3 [16 Sep. 1605]. He emigrated one year later, and in 1609, now married to someone else and living outside the Ottobeuren lands, he appeared as party to the sale of his family home to his stepfather for fully 2,000 fl. StAA, KL Ottobeuren 903, f. 256r [17 Sep. 1606] and KL Ottobeuren 904, ff. 150[a]r–v [21 Oct. 1609]. A *Schuldbrief* appended to the deed of sale (ibid., ff. 150[a]v–151r) awards *Voraus* of 250 fl. to each of Johann's three unmarried siblings; he probably received as much himself.

[292] HawPR, Vol. I, ff. 23r, 32v, 36r, 45v, 60v, 67v, 79r, and 81r. The survivor, Anna Dreier, bore a child on 26 December 1626 and married on 11 February 1627.

[293] StAA, KL Ottobeuren 583, Heft 7, f. 1v death duty of 10 fl. collected 16 October 1589. The remarriage is documented in KL Ottobeuren 903, ff. 22r–v [9 June 1603]. Jacob was the son of Ludwig Vogele, who held 36 *jauchert* of arable land according to a 1571 tithe survey. KL Ottobeuren 744b; Dertsch, "Das Einwohnerbuch des Ottobeurer Klosterstaats 1564," p. 68.

[294] Martin Gufer held 39.5 *jauchert* of land and had a gross wealth of 910 fl. in 1620. He and his wife baptized their last child on 21 October 1602 and Martin was buried on 17 January 1622. StAA, KL Ottobeuren 102, f. 297v; WestPR, Vol. I, pp. 14, 118.

[295] StAA, KL Ottobeuren 904, f. 237r: *Quittung* dated 13 March 1611 and paid to David Hagg and his wife, Catharina Schmalholz, by the guardians of Jerg, the eldest son of Catharina's first husband, Jacob Vogele.

[296] David Hagg and four other siblings initially intended to sell the half-house inherited from their parents to a certain Jerg Schneider for 50 fl., but a sale deed for the back half of the house drawn up four years later indicates that David still lived in the front. StAA, KL Ottobeuren 904, f. 212v [23 Aug. 1610] and KL Ottobeuren 905, f. 168r [22 May 1614]. Comparison of the 1613 and 1617 bond-chicken registers (KL Ottobeuren 491-II, Heft 16, ff. 10v–11r and Heft 21, ff. 7v–8r) indicates that David had by the latter date been replaced by his brother Johann, who married on 13 January 1617 (WestPR, Vol. I, p. 186). Johann Hagg's 1620 tax declaration lists the half-house worth 50 fl. as his only property. KL Ottobeuren 102, f. 305r.

[297] Jacob Vogele was buried on 8 December 1609, and Catharina's son by Martin Gufer was christened on 5 May 1610. Her marriage to David Hagg was celebrated on 28 September 1610.

What could a poor woman do? Notarial records indicate that the child support payments ordered by the Bishop of Augsburg were, in fact, often paid,[298] and emigration papers suggest that unmarried mothers could at least make planned moves somewhere else.[299] That a truly enterprising woman could make a life for herself is shown by the career of Anna Weidler, who had been the maid and mistress of the pastor of Reichartsried in the Princely Abbacy of Kempten. Anna left Reichartsried after she bore the priest an illegitimate daughter, Magdalena, but managed to meet up with Caspar Widenmann, a poor and recently widowed *Seldner* in the Ottobeuren hamlet of Ollarzried. She married him in about 1608, and had a document drawn up ensuring Magdalena the same rights as Widenmann's other children.[300] But most women who bore children out of wedlock were fated to a lonely existence. Barbara Maier grew up in the village of Egg in a small half-house, the other half of which belonged to her grandparents.[301] After Barbara became pregnant in 1618 by a certain Johann Doppeler of Klosterbeuren, her father did secure compensation to the amount of 70 fl.,[302] but Barbara never married, and lived on alone in the half-house after her father's death in 1626.[303]

Catharina's only child by David Hagg was baptized on 15 April 1616, and she was herself buried less than two weeks later on 27 April 1616. WestPR, Vol. I, pp. 28, 42, 113, 116, and 184.

[298] Payments for defloration and/or impregnation are recorded in StAA, KL Ottobeuren 901, f. 54r for 13 fl. [6 Dec. 1583], the child now deceased; KL Ottobeuren 903, f. 286r for 30 fl. "whether she is pregnant or not" [12 Jan. 1607]; ibid., f. 298r for 30 fl. [22 Feb. 1607]; KL Ottobeuren 904, f. 224r for 33 fl. [4 Jan. 1611]; KL Ottobeuren 907, f. 12r for 115 fl. [29 Sep. 1616]; ibid., f. 228r for 12 fl. [10 Feb. 1619]; KL Ottobeuren 908, f. 139v for 25 fl. [16 Apr. 1621].

[299] ABA, OPr 1598–1602, p. 390 [23 Aug. 1600] and OPr 1602–6, pp. 460–1 [3 Sep. 1604], 467 [17 Sep. 1604], and 539–40 [14 Jan. 1605]. The plaintiffs in these four cases, all of them women, acquired *Freibriefe* on 14 April 1608, 26 August 1607, 1 July 1611, and 4 February 1608 respectively. StAA, KL Ottobeuren 904, f. 37r; KL Ottobeuren 903, f. 335v; KL Ottobeuren 904, f. 262v; ibid., f. 25r.

[300] StAA, KL Ottobeuren 904, ff. 34v–35r [26 Feb. 1608]. Caspar Widenmann arrived in Ollarzried between 1602 and 1604. In 1620 he owned only a house worth 80 fl. He seems to have left Ollarzried during the hyperinflation of 1623 – he is listed as "gone" in the bond-chicken register for that year – and was replaced by a certain Johann Geromüller, who married Agnes Hiebeler on 28 September 1624. KL Ottobeuren 491-I, Heft 10, ff. 5v–6r and Heft 14, f. 7v. KL Ottobeuren 903, ff. 66v–67r [29 Jan. 1604]; KL Ottobeuren 102, f. 85v; KL Ottobeuren 491-III, Heft 27, f. 5v. and Heft 28, f. 6r; OttPR, Vol. II, f. 104v.

[301] StAA, KL Ottobeuren 907, ff. 206v–207r [9 Dec. 1618]. Martin Maier-Betzhaus and his wife, Christina Ziegler, sell a half-house to their son Johann Maier-Betzhaus for 100 fl. The other half is held by Martin's brother Caspar Maier (the suffix 'Betzhaus' was inconsistently added to the surname). Caspar, Johann, and their father are all listed together in the 1620 tax survey. KL Ottobeuren 102, f. 286v.

[302] StAA, KL Ottobeuren 907, f. 145r [14 Mar. 1618].

[303] Barbara is listed as the "daughter of Caspar Maier" in the 1627 tax survey. By this time her uncle no longer lived in the other half of the house. StAA, KL Ottobeuren 104, ff. 265r–v. Barbara's father was buried on 28 July 1626. EggPR, Vol. I, p. 144.

The lot of illegitimate children was equally difficult. Anna Schweiggart of Hawangen lost her husband, Martin Blender, in 1588 after only five years of marriage.[304] For over twenty years thereafter, she toiled alone[305] to provide a home not only for her son Johann, but also for her niece Magdalena, the bastard daughter of Anna's sister Catharina Schweiggart. When Johann came of age in 1611,[306] he took over the small half-house that remained to the family,[307] and Magdalena Schweiggart's position was now in jeopardy. Her aunt took the trouble to have a contract drawn up assuring her the undisturbed use of "the rearward room and the corner by the door," but the document also envisioned an unhappy end to the arrangement, with the widow promising Magdalena 40 *gulden* "if her son Johann Blender should no longer be willing to tolerate her [i.e. Magdalena] in the said house."[308]

The obvious implication of all of these tragedies is that a marriage had to be planned with enormous care. The challenge was not simply that the heirs to a tradition of an independent house for each married couple now had to share living space with their elders, but also that the lifecourse's temporal sequence had to be co-ordinated across the generations. If an intention to wed was not married to a corresponding intention to retire, there was a price to be paid, a lesson Simon Reichart learned the hard way. Simon's father, Urban Reichart, farmed 3 *jauchert* of arable land in Unterwesterheim, and supplemented this income with his position as the parish sexton.[309] By 1611, now in his later twenties,[310] Simon felt he was ready to marry, a decision whose urgency was enhanced by the pregnancy of his fiancée, Regina Schön.[311] Urban Reichart, on the other hand, was not yet prepared to give up his lands and office, as a result of which Simon ended up in abject poverty and disappeared from the

---

[304] Martin purchased a half-house from his father-in-law, Johann Schweiggart, for 60 fl. in 1583, having already acquired the other half. At the time of the 1586 serf roll Martin Blender and Anna Schweiggart still had no children, and Martin's 1.5 fl. death duty was paid on 27 August 1588. StAA, KL Ottobeuren 901, f. 44v [24 Sep. 1583]; KL Ottobeuren 601-II, f. 101v; KL Ottobeuren 583, Heft 6, f. 1r.

[305] Anna was assessed the widow's 2 kr. in Hawangen in the bond-chicken registers for 1590, 1595, and 1602. StAA, KL Ottobeuren 491-I, Heft 5, f. 7r, Heft 6, f. 8r, and Heft 10, f. 19v.

[306] Johann Blender married Anna Sauter on 28 September 1611. HawPR, Vol. I, f. 5r.

[307] There is no *Kaufbrief*, but Johann Blender replaced his mother as the householder between the 1609 and 1613 bond-chicken registers. StAA, KL Ottobeuren 491-I, Heft 14, f. 24r and KL Ottobeuren 491-II, Heft 16, f. 25r. The family lost the other half of the house some time before 1607, when Jerg Widenmann mortgaged it. KL Ottobeuren 903, f. 324r [17 May 1607].

[308] StAA, KL Ottobeuren 905, f. 282r [3 July 1615]. Magdalena is nowhere explicitly described as illegitimate, but her status is betrayed by the fact that she bore her mother's surname.

[309] The 1613 tithe survey measures Urban's arable land and lists his office. StAA, KL Ottobeuren 744c.

[310] Simon is listed as Urban Reichart's son in the 1586 serf roll. StAA, KL Ottobeuren 601-II, f. 137v.

[311] Simon and Regina were married on 6 February 1611. Their first child Johann was baptized on 1 July 1611. WestPR, Vol. I, pp. 30, 184.

parish by 1627.[312] Simon's sister Ursula Reichart, on the other hand, bided her time for another six years until her father was ready to retire. In July of 1617, she married Johann Sanz, the second son of a comfortable farmer in the hamlet of Leupolz,[313] and in exchange for 250 fl. and half of the future income from the churchwarden's office, Urban Reichart sold his house, land, and office to his son-in-law.[314] Not every contingency could be anticipated, of course, and Ursula's careful plans were ended abruptly when she was struck and killed by lightning in the summer of 1629. All the same, by harmonizing her own plans with those of her father, she had established a stable home for her children,[315] and had succeeded in "buying" a considerable amount of time for herself. Her marriage would have been postponed by eight years had she needed to wait for Urban Reichart's death in 1625.[316]

The well-timed landing of a well-endowed partner was not in itself enough, however, since unlike sales of houses or considerable amounts of land among non-kin, the great majority of inheritances were now tied into complex, long-term debt obligations in order to support retiring parents and yielding siblings (see Table 5.1).[317] A new heir was therefore under intense pressure to produce a steady flow of coin above and beyond the demands of his or her own spouse, children, and overlord. The consequence was the pervasion of family relations by an accounting mentality, in order carefully to supervise sources of revenue and adjudicate competing individual claims thereto. This was more than a matter of squabbling over inheritances, though that certainly did occur.[318] Anticipated

---

[312] Simon Reichart owned no property and paid only the minimum 6 kr. head tax in the 1620 tax survey. He is not listed in the 1627 survey. StAA, KL Ottobeuren 102, f. 31v and KL Ottobeuren 104, f. 290v.

[313] Johann's father, Jerg Sanz, sold his house and 24 *jauchert* of land in Lampolz to another son, Martin, for 400 fl. in 1607. The maintenance agreement awarded Johann a set of bed linens as a *Voraus* plus 10 fl. for yielding. His married sister Anna had already received a dowry of 76 fl. and Johann's ultimate inheritance must have been something similar. StAA, KL Ottobeuren 903, ff. 278v and 278v–279r [4 Jan. 1607].

[314] StAA, KL Ottobeuren 907, ff. 97v and 97v–98r [6 July 1617]. Ursula Reichart and Johann Sanz were married on 16 July 1617. WestPR, Vol. I, p. 187.

[315] Johann Sanz held the house, two cows, 3 *jauchert* of arable land, and 5 *tagwerk* of meadow in 1620. By 1627 he had added two oxen and had reduced his debts from 105 to 70 fl. StAA, KL Ottobeuren 102, f. 310v and KL Ottobeuren 104, f. 290v. Ursula's three surviving children had their cash inheritance of 34 fl. loaned out at interest in 1631. KL Ottobeuren 911, f. 113 [23 Jan. 1631].

[316] Urban Reichart was buried on 19 July 1625 and Ursula Reichart on 24 June 1629. WestPR, Vol. I, pp. 119, 122.

[317] The table analyzes for the period 1603–21 those 914 transactions in the monastery lands involving the minimum of property to form the basis of an independent household, here defined as either (1) a house, or part of a house, or (2) 5 or more *jauchert* of land, or (3) an inflated sale of moveable wealth used to "cover" the conveyance of a legally unsaleable *Gotteshausrecht* farm.

[318] StAA, KL Ottobeuren 905, ff. 41r–v [24 Dec. 1612], according to which Johann Zick of Au in Legau parish acknowledges receipt of his wife's inheritance from Johann Becherer of Ollarzried.

Table 5.1 *The financing of household property sales at Ottobeuren, 1603–21*

	Kin transactions				Non-kin transactions			
	Debt financed		No debt		Debt financed		No debt	
Type of sale	No.	%	No.	%	No.	%	No.	%
House and/or ≥5 *jauchert/tagwerk*	267	64.2	153	35.8	115	26.0	327	74.0
Moveables "cover sale"	39	86.7	6	13.3	3	42.9	4	57.1
Total	306	65.8	159	34.2	118	26.3	331	73.7

Sources: StAA, KL Ottobeuren 903–5, 907–8

revenue from incoming dowries became an integral part of a family's financial planning. As one *Bauer* mother put it when laying down the schedule for her son to repay the 1,000 fl. worth of property she had sold him, the heir was to pay 20 fl. per annum "as soon as he marries (and not before) . . . and in addition, however much he marries [*sic*!] is to be paid [as a lump sum] against the sale price."[319] By the 1620s the remarriages of the widowed and the receipt of the new spouse's inheritance were often registered together,[320] and even among the rural poor, household formation was organized around complex financial interlinkages. Thus Johann Reubel "Decker" of Sontheim, a poor *Seldner* with no more than 3 *jauchert* of land,[321] survived on credit[322] (and textile

Zick also agreed to lay no further claims to Becherer's property, while Becherer agreed to make no demands on an inheritance which Zick expected to receive from his aunt in Woringen. See also ibid., f. 369r [9 June 1616], which certifies the receipt of an inheritance of 130 fl. "pursuant to the resolution issued in the matter, to which the parties, with the foreknowledge of the authorities, have finally agreed."

[319] StAA, KL Ottobeuren 903, ff. 69r–70r [5 Feb. 1604]. For similar arrangements, see KL Ottobeuren 904, ff. 158r–v [19 Feb. 1610] and f. 209r [25 July 1610].

[320] StAA, KL Ottobeuren 909, ff. 67v–68r and 68r–v [27 May 1625]: The widow Ursula Schmidt of Bibelsberg marries Martin Kessler of Ollarzried and Kessler acknowledges receipt of his inheritance of 256 fl. Similarly ibid., ff. 153v–154r and 154r [4 May 1626]: The widower Jerg Rauch of Fricken marries Anna Schiess of Niederdorf, and then acknowledges receipt of her 626 fl. inheritance. Somewhat less chronologically neat is ibid., ff. 98r and 98r–v [2 Dec. 1625]: Jerg Schindelin of Stocken sells his son Balthas a house, a few *jauchert* of land and a wooded parcel for 300 fl. and Balthas Schindelin (a widower) marries Anna Biller of Briechlins. Ibid., ff. 139r–v [10 Mar. 1626]: Balthas Schindelin of Stocken acknowledges receipt of his wife Anna Biller's inheritance of 55 fl.

[321] According to the 1620 tax survey, Johann Reubel "Decker" owned a half-house, two horses, a cow, 1 *jauchert* of arable land, and 1 *tagwerk* of meadow land. His gross wealth of 265 fl. was offset by debts of 200 fl. StAA, KL Ottobeuren 102, ff. 343v–344r. Johann sold his son 0.5 *tagwerk* in 1616.

[322] Johann Reubel's *Schuld-* and *Zinsbriefe* document the borrowing of at least 126 fl. in the decade before his son's marriage. StAA, KL Ottobeuren 903, ff. 105r (30 fl.) [18 Aug. 1604] and 261v

smuggling)[323] while waiting for his own children to grow up. His son Johann junior married a woman from Erkheim in 1612/13, but the father waited until his daughter-in-law's dowry of 104 fl. 6 kr. was safely in hand before selling half of his house and a bit of meadow to his son for 200 fl. in December of 1616.[324]

Financial oversight of this sort can be documented at virtually every nexus of the kin relationship. Parents took care that equal inheritance did not lead to the dispersal of farming equipment (wagons, harnesses, ploughs, harrows, etc.)[325] from the home,[326] and yielding heirs began to demand that their advance portions (*Voraus*) accrue interest not merely once they married, but as soon as they had gone into service and had thus "come out of his [i.e. the heir's] bread and porridge."[327] Johann Thoma of Attenhausen allowed his father to keep the proceeds from the sale of land the two had worked together only on condition "that after his [i.e. the father's] death 14 fl. in cash shall be deducted from the price which his son [shall pay] for the rest of the tools in the smithy."[328] Barthlome Maier of Niederrieden wanted it set down in writing that grain still standing in the fields at his father's death was Barthlome's alone and would not be shared with his siblings.[329] Those who stood surety for the debts of their sons or acted as guarantors for the good behavior of their brothers-in-law began requiring indemnification contracts to protect them against any financial loss,[330] thus completely undermining the system of collective responsibility

(10 fl.) [24 Oct. 1606]; KL Ottobeuren 904, f. 251r (26 fl.) [3 May 1611]; KL Ottobeuren 905, ff. 116v–117r (60 fl.) [26 Sep. 1613].

[323] StAA, KL Ottobeuren 587-III, Heft 30 (1621/2). Reubel claimed to be innocent of the charge, but his plea is scarcely credible given the massive scale of textile smuggling in the village.

[324] StAA, KL Ottobeuren 583, Heft 29, f. 3v; KL Ottobeuren 905, f. 233v [22 Jan. 1615]; KL Ottobeuren 907, f. 31v [16 Dec. 1616].

[325] Farming equipment is not described in much detail in the early seventeenth-century protocols. At the sale of a large *Hof* of 40 *jauchert* of arable land and 27 *tagwerk* of meadow, the moveables are itemized as five cows, four horses, two young cattle, two full linens, two wagons, a plough, and a harrow. StAA, KL Ottobeuren 903, f. 336r [27 Aug. 1607]. The moveables of another peasant who in 1620 farmed 29 *jauchert* of arable land and 11 *tagwerk* of meadow were described as "horses, cows, harnesses and gear, two wagons, a plough and a full set of bed linens." KL Ottobeuren 903, f. 40r [9 Oct. 1603] and KL Ottobeuren 102, f. 182r.

[326] StAA, KL Ottobeuren 903, ff. 278v–279r [4 Jan. 1607]; KL Ottobeuren 904, ff. 158r–v [19 Feb. 1610] and 220v [7 Dec. 1610]; KL 908, ff. 160r–v [16 June 1621].

[327] StAA, KL Ottobeuren 905, f. 149r [7 Jan. 1614]. Similarly ibid., ff. 2v–3v [5 July 1612], 113v–114r [19 Sep. 1613], 210r–v [16 Oct. 1614], and 276v [22 June 1615]; KL Ottobeuren 904, f. 249r [24 Apr. 1611].

[328] StAA, KL Ottobeuren 903, ff. 231r–v [11 May 1606].

[329] StAA, KL Ottobeuren 904, ff. 245v–246r [12 Apr. 1611]. For even more careful hair-splitting, see the retirement agreement of Thoma Graf of Schlegelsberg, pursuant to which his son Johann had no claim to the grain which had already been cut and put in the barn, but a half-share of the grain which had currently been sown in the ground. KL Ottobeuren 903, ff. 77v–78r [6 Feb. 1603].

[330] StAA, KL Ottobeuren 903, f. 56v [8 Jan. 1604] and KL Ottobeuren 905, f. 197r [4 Aug. 1614].

which underlay the *Urfehde*. Indeed, the *Urfehde* itself went out of favor during the 1580s, and by the early seventeenth century the criminal pardon issued against the pledge of the convict's friends and relatives had become a rarity.[331]

Whether or not there were any adverse effects of all this accounting among kin is hard to say, since there was some variety of practice. Many parents, for example, paid their children wages for household help,[332] but a few refused to do so.[333] There are also cases where fiscal hair-splitting does seem to have coincided with destructive family relations. Thus we find Johann Rapp of Böhen certifying final receipt of his wife's inheritance of 295 fl. on the same day he was party to an accord resolving the "ill-will and disunity" between himself and his father-in-law, Jerg Kürchoff of Waldmühle, ill-will which had culminated in Rapp chopping off one of Kürchoff's fingers.[334] Rapp had previously borrowed money from his father-in-law and would later find himself mortgaging his property to Kürchoff for (among other things) the flour that he had received from his wife's family.[335] But what may seem to be a man's ruthless exploitation of his son-in-law looks rather different against the backdrop of Johann Rapp's other activities – he was a wastrel[336] who in twelve years reduced himself from *Hof*-tenancy to bankruptcy[337] – and Jerg Kürchoff is

---

[331] *Urfehde* charters are reasonably continuous at Ottobeuren up to 1588, but thereafter there are only two examples for the rest of the seventeenth century. StAA, KU Ottobeuren 3245 [20 June 1588]; Neuburger Urkundensamm G167 [18 Sep. 1606]; KU Ottobeuren 2656 [26 Nov. 1643].

[332] StAA, KL Ottobeuren 901, f. 28r [9 May 1583]: Johann Stedelin of Untermotz certifies that he owes his emigrating son 30 fl. in earned wages; KL Ottobeuren 903, ff. 304r–v [8 Mar. 1607]: Johann Ergart of Niederrieden owes his son Leonhard 18 fl. in earned wages.

[333] StAA, KL Ottobeuren 907, ff. 28v–29r [22 Nov. 1616]: Melchior Vogt of Egg requires his son Hans to provide him with wood when the father can no longer do so himself "and to do and carry out for him what he otherwise needs without pay."

[334] StAA, KL Ottobeuren 904, ff. 146[b]v and 146[b]v–147r [10 Sep. 1609].

[335] StAA, KL Ottobeuren 903, ff. 249v–250r (70 fl.) [3 Aug. 1606] and KL Ottobeuren 905, ff. 369v–370r (152 fl.) [10 June 1616] respectively.

[336] Johann Rapp managed to amass debts of almost 900 fl. between 1603 and 1616. In addition to the debts of 70 fl. (1606) and 152 fl. (1616) accrued to his father-in-law, the protocols record the following debts: StAA, KL Ottobeuren 903, ff. 21v–22r (50 fl.) [5 June 1603], 47v (100 fl.) [20 Nov. 1603], 72v (100 fl.) [12 Feb. 1604], 259r (30 fl.) [2 Oct. 1606], and 308v (100 fl.) [15 Mar. 1607]; KL Ottobeuren 904, ff. 237r (20 fl.) [16 Mar. 1611] and 263v (50 fl.) [9 July 1611]; KL Ottobeuren 905, ff. 279v (80 fl.) [28 Aug. 1615] and 279v (100 fl.) [28 Aug. 1615]; KL Ottobeuren 907, f. 18r (20 fl.) [17 Oct. 1616]. That this was not productive investment is indicated by Johann Rapp's loss of all of his lands between 1605 and 1617.

[337] Johann Rapp was admitted to a large Böhen *Hof* on 6 Mar. 1603 after briefly working a different *Hof* between 1593 and 1597. StAA, KL Ottobeuren 27, ff. 95r–v, 97r. As late as 1608 he held property worth more than 1,400 fl., but had sold off all of his land by 1617. KL Ottobeuren 903, ff. 148v [7 Feb. 1605] and 249v [3 Aug. 1606]; KL Ottobeuren 904, ff. 54r [29 May 1608], 55v [20 June 1608], and 149v [8 Oct. 1609]; KL Ottobeuren 905, f. 72v [2 June 1613]; KL Ottobeuren 907, ff. 67v–68r [6 Apr. 1617]. At the time of the 1620 tax survey he held only a house (worth 150 fl.) which was completely mortgaged, and paid the minimum head-tax of 6 kr. KL Ottobeuren 102, f. 118v.

Table 5.2 *The decline of common-property remarriage at Ottobeuren, 1580–1620*

Period	Remarriage contracts (No.)	Property merger clause (%)
1580–4	26	88.5
1603–5	36	66.7
1606–10	75	10.7
1611–15	70	2.9
1616–20	62	6.5

Note: Data are not available for the years 1585–1602
Sources: StAA, KL Ottobeuren 901, 903–5, 907–8, 918

more fairly understood as a businessman trying to minimize his losses on a bad investment.[338]

This hard-nosed fiscal realism was particularly evident in remarriages, where the death of the head of the household could generate rivalry for control of the property between the survivor and his or her stepchildren. During the sixteenth century, a person who married a widow or widower could expect that the property of each spouse would be joined seamlessly, such that

whatever each of the current spouses brings together, or acquire together in the course of the marriage, shall be and remain a common, merged [*eingeworfen*] property, and after the death of one [spouse] nothing shall be apportioned out [on the basis of pre-marital holdings], and the surviving spouse together with the before- and after-children (if there should be any) shall [all] be equal in the division of the inheritance.[339]

But once the farm (or the house, or even the half-house) became a capital asset which had to be transferred by sale, headship of the family was increasingly conferred on the basis of command of funds, rather than by mere seniority. There could no longer be any guarantee that the indivisibility of the marital fund would survive the death of the senior spouse, and during the first generation of the seventeenth century, the clause merging the property of the two spouses practically vanished from remarriage contracts (see Table 5.2).

---

[338] Jerg Kürchoff was the miller of Waldmühle and in 1620 had 24 *jauchert* of land and a gross wealth of 1,625 fl. He was also a moneylender of reasonable significance, and reported outstanding loans of 425 fl. in that year. All of this money was loaned out to local peasants; in addition to the loans of 70 fl. and 152 fl. to Johann Rapp in 1606 and 1616, the notarial protocols document at least four other loans for a total of 450 fl. StAA, KL Ottobeuren 102, f. 126r; KL Ottobeuren 905, f. 225r (40 fl.) [5 Jan. 1615]; KL Ottobeuren 907, f. 173r (42 fl.) [20 Apr. 1617]; ibid., ff. 168v–169r (100 fl.) [1 June 1618]; KL Ottobeuren 908, f. 96r (46 fl.) [24 July 1620].

[339] StAA, KL Ottobeuren 904, ff. 59v–60r [6 June 1608]. This contract admittedly comes from the seventeenth century, but has been chosen for the explicitness of its language.

Incoming spouses became correspondingly cautious about the future of any capital they brought into an existing marriage, and began making provision for the reversion [*Rückfall*] of dowries to their relatives should they die without offspring to inherit the investment.[340]

It must be said that the decline of what may be called common-property remarriage did not impair the new spouse's right of first purchase of the property (and consequent right to remarry *in situ*) on the death of the remarried spouse.[341] On the other hand, the formal right of pre-emptive purchase was of little value to a survivor who could not raise the money,[342] and the amount of equity an incoming spouse acquired in a marriage began to be counted rather more carefully. Thus, by the early seventeenth century we begin to see the blunt declaration that a second wife is entitled to purchase the estate precisely because she brought a dowry of 130 fl. to the marriage,[343] or conversely that in the event of the death of a householder worth almost 1,000 fl.,[344] his second wife, who brought only bed linens, a cow, and 30 fl. to the household,

> shall in her widowhood have her house and home there but [literally 'and'] shall own only what she brought in [to the marriage] . . . and if she should later change her [marital] status and marry someone else, she shall then be obliged to leave the house in exchange for compensation from whoever shall purchase the property [at a price] set by the judgment of honorable people,

[340] There is only a single example of this kind of reversion in the sixteenth-century remarriage contracts (StAA, KL Ottobeuren 901, ff. 83v–85r [20 Feb. 1584]), but more than thirty in the contracts for the early seventeenth century.

[341] The frequency with which this right was assured was quite stable. The quinquennial figures are 61.5% (1580–4), 50.0% (1603–5), 53.3% (1606–10), 57.1% (1611–15), and 51.6% (1616–20).

[342] See for example the case of Agatha Vogler of Woringen, who immigrated to the Ottobeuren village of Böhen and married the widower Jerg Walch in 1610. She was granted the right to purchase his house at his death, but was in fact unable to do so when her husband died two years later. She sold the rearward half of the house at the end of 1612, retaining the right for herself and two daughters to live there for eight years, and sold the forward half of the house to a stepson six months later. StAA, KL Ottobeuren 904, f. 210r [11 Aug. 1610]; KL Ottobeuren 905, ff. 57v–58r [25 Dec. 1612] and 77v–78r [14 June 1613]. Similarly, the 1605 contract between the widow Maria Helzlin of Sontheim and her second husband, Michael Zwirgel, gave him the house at her death, and only 5 fl. to each of his four stepchildren. As it happened, one half of the house was sold to one of Maria's "before-sons" in 1610 and the other half was sold outside the family in 1619. KL Ottobeuren 903, ff. 143v–144r [19 Feb. 1605]; KL Ottobeuren 904, ff. 181v–182r [4 Mar. 1610]; KL Ottobeuren 907, f. 245r [23 Apr. 1619].

[343] StAA, KL Ottobeuren 903, ff. 177v–178r: *Heiratsbrief* of Jerg Egg of Unterwesterheim and Ursula Schneider of Sontheim dated 3 Aug. 1605. Subsequent sale deeds imply that the husband's estate was worth about 553.5 fl. at the time of the marriage. Note also that in this particular case, the second wife, Ursula Schneider (died 28 July 1611), actually predeceased her husband, Jerg Egg (died 7 Apr. 1615), giving him time to marry a third wife, Anna Hüemer (18 Sep. 1611), who with her own second husband purchased the property from Jerg Egg's children. KL Ottobeuren 904, f. 123r [2 Apr. 1609] and KL Ottobeuren 905, ff. 266v–267r [30 Apr. 1615]. WestPR, Vol. I, pp. 114–16, 180–6.

[344] In 1620 Jerg Schneider of Hessen held 45 *jauchert* of land and had a gross wealth of 955 fl. StAA, KL Ottobeuren 102, f. 104v.

but [literally 'and'] nothing more shall be paid out to her than what she [now] brings her current husband.[345]

All of this seems rather heartless, of course, a severity most poignantly personified by the spectacle of a widowed immigrant trudging back out of the monastery lands on the death of her spouse.[346] But capital had indeed become an inescapable requirement for the foundation of a new household, and in its absence even the ownership of a house might not suffice. Thus, the weaver Jerg Beck lived over fifty years in the village of Oberwesterheim together with his wife, Eva Doppeler, and their children,[347] but never managed to acquire any land.[348] On his death in 1607, the family house passed to a son, Johann Beck, but Johann was unable to attract a spouse and died unmarried in his forties in the spring of 1615.[349] The house then passed to an unmarried sister, Anna, also in her forties, who worked (probably as a servant) in the neighboring village of Günz. Anna seems not to have had the wherewithal to assume the property, and therefore sold it outside the family for the lump sum of 100 fl. plus an annual payment of 10 fl. for the next seventeen years. She reserved for herself only a single room in the house, with the added understanding that she come up with her meals by herself.[350]

Of course, not every member of the rural poor resigned him or herself to a lifetime of celibacy, but family stability was hard to maintain without financial resources of some kind. Johann Schuster's kin, for example, had lived in Oberwesterheim since the 1520s.[351] Some of his ancestors had been reasonably prosperous, but Johann himself was left with little more than a half-house when

---

[345] StAA, KL Ottobeuren 904, ff. 278r–v [16 Feb. 1612].

[346] StAA, KL Ottobeuren 904, f. 160r: *Freibrief* of Anna Müller of Herbishofen [2 Dec. 1609]. Anna had immigrated to the Ottobeuren lands and married the tailor Caspar Kopp of Egg after his first wife died in 1586/7. Kopp himself died in about the year 1608; his property was assumed by his son-in-law Johann Gross, who had married a daughter, Maria Kopp, in 1602. KL Ottobeuren 583, Heft 4, f. 2v and Heft 4b, f. 6r. KL Ottobeuren 491-I, Heft 10, f. 15v and Heft 14, f. 11r.

[347] Both parents died in their bed on 25 January 1607. The parish priest recorded the longevity of their marriage in the burial register. Note also that the parents and their children, Johann, Barbara, Elisabeth, and Anna, are all recorded in the village in the 1564 serf roll. WestPR, Vol. I, p. 112. Dertsch, "Das Einwohnerbuch des Ottobeurer Klosterstaats 1564," p. 67.

[348] Jerg Beck had no arable land in the 1571 tithe survey and his son Johann had none in 1613. Jerg did acquire 1 *tagwerk* of meadow in 1604, but the property was purchased on credit and was resold shortly after his death. StAA, KL Ottobeuren 744b; KL Ottobeuren 903, f. 131v [13 Dec. 1604]; KL Ottobeuren 904, f. 19v [3 Jan. 1608].

[349] WestPR, Vol. I, p. 116 [7 Apr. 1615]. Johann Beck was also a weaver.

[350] StAA, KL Ottobeuren 905, ff. 338r and 338r–v [6 Mar. 1616]. A second unmarried sister, Barbara Beck, was a co-seller of the house.

[351] Three male Schusters (one of them a *Bauer*) are listed in the 1525 tax register, two males and a widow in a 1546 tax register, and then only Johann's father (also named Johann) in the 1548 serf roll. StAA, KL Ottobeuren 541, Heft 2, ff. 21r–22v; KL Ottobeuren 64, ff. 8r–10v; KL Ottobeuren 601-II, ff. 208r–215r.

he married some time in the late 1570s.[352] At his death in 1622, the property finally passed to his son from a second marriage,[353] but this meant that Johann's two daughters from the first marriage had grown to adulthood with virtually nothing to marry on, and it cost them dear. Anna Schuster had an illegitimate child in 1603 while working as a servant in another village,[354] and shortly thereafter married a Bavarian vagabond and left Westerheim to live on the roads. She did, however, maintain contact with her parents, and spent three months in their house with her husband and child in the summer of 1605.[355] Anna's sister, Barbara Schuster, formed a liaison with another vagabond, and had at least three children by him between 1618 and 1624.[356]

The simplest way to sum up the discussion in the chapter thus far is to observe that the new inheritance practices of the late sixteenth and early seventeenth centuries profoundly complicated kin roles at Ottobeuren. Traditional relations of both equality (among siblings) and inequality (of children *vis-à-vis* their parents) became much more difficult to maintain as yielding heirs were farmed out as servants and then ejected from the home and as parents came to retire and live in households headed by their heirs. The boundaries of household and family had ceased to coincide, and the resulting tensions are amply documented by the growing use of notarized instruments to order and apportion the rights and claims of the different members of the kin group. Equally important, however, is the spirit in which this ordering and apportioning was conducted, and here it is impossible to avoid the conclusion that by 1600, householding at Ottobeuren was characterized by a constant preoccupation with questions of cost, investment, and yield.

It may seem unnecessary to insist on (perhaps to belabor) this latter point, but the time-honored contrary view, according to which the logic of the peasant family economy is diametrically opposed to the logic of a capitalist economy, remains extremely tenacious.[357] I do not mean to suggest that the Abbot's

---

[352] In the 1620 tax survey he held only the half-house (worth 35 fl.) and a cow (10 fl.). StAA, KL Ottobeuren 102, f. 301r. He held no arable land in the 1613 tithe survey, just as his widowed mother, Katharina Belm, had held no land in a 1571 survey. The notarial protocols for 1603–21 contain no evidence of any other property. KL Ottobeuren 744b; Dertsch, "Das Einwohnerbuch des Ottobeurer Klosterstaats 1564," p. 66.

[353] Johann Schuster's first wife, Agatha Bozer, was buried on 23 June 1598, and he remarried seven weeks later on 10 August. He was buried on 21 December 1622 and his son Johann (christened 18 April 1601) married on 9 February 1625. WestPR, Vol. I, pp. 12, 110, 118, 178, 190. See also StAA, KL Ottobeuren 491-II, Heft 26, f. 18v and KL Ottobeuren 491-III, Heft 30, f. 16v.

[354] StAA, KL Ottobeuren 587-II, Heft 22 (1602/3). The child was baptized in Westerheim on 25 November 1603. WestPR, Vol. I, p. 17.

[355] StAA, KL Ottobeuren 587-II, Heft 25 (1604/5), Westerheim.

[356] WestPR, Vol. I, pp. 47 [14 Mar. 1618], 59 [23 Dec. 1622], and 64 [4 Aug. 1624]. Barbara's husband, Michael Scheffler, was described as a "vagabundus" at the 1618 christening.

[357] See, for example, Jean-Michel Boehler, *Une société rurale en milieu rhenan: la paysannerie de la plaine d'Alsace, 1648–1789* (Strasbourg, 1995).

tenant farms were run no differently from an Antwerp trading concern or a Manchester cotton mill. At the same time it is immeasurably farther off the mark to view the Ottobeuren household as an organic unity where, in Weber's famous characterization, the members worked to the best of their ability, consumed on the basis of their needs, and no accounts were kept among kin.[358] Not only was the household internally stratified between active and retired owners on the one hand and unrelated workers (i.e. household servants) on the other, but it is clear that accounts were indeed kept, even among kin.[359]

More importantly, it is simply wrong to suggest that the German peasant was unconcerned with accumulation or profit *because* s/he sought to preserve the security of the kin group.[360] If the foregoing analysis of household formation has shown anything, it is that the individual householder had to produce a surplus (and a cash surplus at that) precisely in order to support relatives outside the nuclear family, and, in the case of yielding heirs, outside the physical boundaries of the household itself. In fact, the collective right to family property was itself routinely framed in terms of the "common profit and loss" that retiring parent and newly married heir would achieve or incur together,[361] and if this construction was most commonly employed by *Bauer* families, it did also figure in the arrangements of smallholders[362] and poor

---

[358] Max Weber, *Wirtschaft und Gesellschaft: Grundriss der verstehenden Soziologie*, 4th edn (Tübingen, 1956), Vol. I, Part 2, Chapter 3, §1, p. 214.

[359] The actual form in which accounts were kept is somewhat less clear. Stray references in the notarial protocols indicate that some peasants kept their own ledgers (for example the hard-driving Johann Vels, encountered above on pp. 232–3, acknowledged a debt of 480 fl. to his widowed sister-in-law "for the purchase of wares and two account books," StAA, KL Ottobeuren 908, ff. 60r–v [14 Apr. 1620]), but the one account book of an Ottobeuren innkeeper that has survived (KL Ottobeuren 677, "Schulden der Handwerker 1632/3") is concerned with the business debts of local craftsmen. The occasional sale deed appends a list of how much money each sibling has so far received from the parents (e.g. KL Ottobeuren 905, ff. 279v–280r [25 June 1615]), but the most common accounting device seems to have been to use the verso of the actual mortgage document to keep track of the heir's payments to parents and siblings. This arrangement is prescribed in several *Schuldbriefe* and *Leibgedinge*, including KL Ottobeuren 903, ff. 199v [5 Dec. 1605] and 245r [6 July 1606]; KL Ottobeuren 904, ff. 36v [14 Apr. 1608], 41r–v [3 Mar. 1605], 223r–v [30 Dec. 1610], and 257r [9 June 1611]; KL Ottobeuren 905, ff. 214v [26 Oct. 1614] and 322r–323r [7 Jan. 1616].

[360] Hille, *Landliche Gesellschaft in Kriegszeiten*, pp. 17–18.

[361] This phrase shows up in many *Leibgedinge*: StAA, KL Ottobeuren 904, ff. 158r–v [19 Feb. 1610], 213v [26 Aug. 1610], 220v [7 Dec. 1610], 223r–v [30 Dec. 1610], and 261v–262r [1 July 1611]; KL Ottobeuren 905, ff. 145v–146r [19 Dec. 1613], 214v [26 Oct. 1614], 245r–246r [2 Mar. 1615], 269r–v [10 May 1615], 322r–323r [7 Jan. 1616], 361r–v [5 May 1616], and 374v [27 June 1616]; KL Ottobeuren 907, ff. 50r–v [29 Jan. 1617], 135v–136r [30 Jan. 1618], 207v–208r [14 Dec. 1618], and 244v–245r [23 Apr. 1619]; KL Ottobeuren 908, ff. 51r–v [31 Mar. 1620], 98r [27 July 1620], 131r–v [19 Mar. 1621], 142v–143r [4 Apr. 1621], and 160r–v [16 June 1621].

[362] StAA, KL Ottobeuren 908, ff. 113r–v [22 Oct. 1620]. The household in question held 3.5 *jauchert* of arable land, 0.5 *tagwerk* of meadow, and 2.0 *tagwerk* of garden and had a gross wealth of only 210 fl. in the 1620 tax survey. KL Ottobeuren 102, f. 313v.

craftsmen.[363] The economics of kinship drove Ottobeuren households to operate much more like businesses.

Did they succeed? It is not hard to find examples of peasants who produced prodigious sums of money. We may be unimpressed to encounter a *Bauer* from Günz who bought his father's *Hof* for 1,300 fl. in 1615 and cleared the entire sum by 1626,[364] or an Unterwesterheim innkeeper who reduced an enormous debt to his father-in-law by 1,100 fl. in four years.[365] Even among the rural poor, however, proportionately similar accomplishments can easily be documented. Thus, for example, the Frechenrieden shoemaker Johann Biller, who purchased his father's house and 2 *tagwerk* of meadow for 250 fl. in 1612 and scraped the entire sum together by 1616.[366] Still more spectacular was the career of the Benningen *Seldner* Michael Merz, who became a householder in 1607 with a 100 fl. payment towards the house and 5.4 *jauchert* of his father-in-law.[367] Merz paid off the remaining 300 fl. on the sale by 1616,[368] and then proceeded to buy parcel after parcel until he owned over a thousand *gulden* worth of property by 1620.[369]

Anecdotal evidence will carry us only so far, of course, but it is possible to get a broader sense of the cash "output" of Ottobeuren households by tracking

---

[363] StAA, KL Ottobeuren 904, f. 86r [11 Dec. 1608]. Father and son agreed at the sale of the house in the market town of Ottobeuren that "they shall buy, butcher and sell cattle at common profit and loss as long as [the father] can manage on account of his age." In 1620 the son had a gross wealth of 215 fl. and his widowed mother paid the 6 kr. minimum head tax. KL Ottobeuren 102, f. 13v.

[364] StAA, KL Ottobeuren 905, ff. 244v–245r, 245r–246r, and 246r: *Kaufbrief* and *Leibgeding* [5 Mar. 1615] and *Bestandbrief* [2 Mar. 1615]. KL Ottobeuren 909, f. 136v: *Quittung* [7 Mar. 1626]. The peasant in question, Johann Moser, held a *Gotteshausrecht Hof* of 42 *jauchert* of arable, 26 *tagwerk* of meadow, and 1 *tagwerk* of garden land plus 7.25 *jauchert* of freehold arable land. In 1620 and 1627 he had a gross wealth of 1,985 fl. and 1,675 fl. respectively. KL Ottobeuren 102, ff. 258r–v and KL Ottobeuren 104, ff. 236r–v.

[365] StAA, KL Ottobeuren 905, ff. 41v–42r [24 Dec. 1612] and 358v–359r [28 Apr. 1616]. The son-in-law, Martin Heussler, held a *Gotteshausrecht Hof* measuring 36 *jauchert* of arable, 28 *tagwerk* of meadow, and 1 *tagwerk* of garden land and had a gross wealth of 1,025 fl. in 1620. KL Ottobeuren 102, ff. 306r–v. There is an even more spectacular case of the *Bauer* Jerg Maier of Egg, who cleared a debt of 1,515 fl. in three years, but much of this sum must have been brought in as a dowry. KL Ottobeuren 903, f. 314r [4 Apr. 1607] and KL Ottobeuren 904, f. 196r [29 Apr. 1610]. Maier's gross wealth was 675 fl. in 1620; his *Gotteshausrecht Hof* included 33 *jauchert* of arable and 15 *tagwerk* of meadow land. KL Ottobeuren 102, f. 280r.

[366] StAA, KL Ottobeuren 905, ff. 18v–19r [27 Aug. 1612]; ibid., f. 366r [20 May 1616]. In 1620 Johann held only a house (190 fl.), a small parcel of land (25 fl.), and a single cow (10 fl.) for a total gross wealth of 225 fl. KL Ottobeuren 102, f. 370v.

[367] StAA, KL Ottobeuren 904, ff. 2r–v [6 Sep. 1607].

[368] StAA, KL Ottobeuren 905, f. 329r [2 Feb. 1616].

[369] Merz's other land purchases are preserved in the notarial protocols: ibid., f. 214r: 115 fl. for 1.5 *jauchert* [26 Oct. 1614]; f. 277v: 60 fl. for 0.5 *jauchert* [23 June 1615]; f. 336r: 112 fl. for 0.75 *jauchert* [4 Mar. 1616]; KL Ottobeuren 908, f. 65r: 100 fl. for 0.75 *jauchert* [27 Apr. 1620]. The 1620 tax survey lists him with a house, 7.5 *jauchert* [sic] of arable land, moveables, a horse, two cows, and two oxen for a total of 1,015 fl. His 1627 assessment was virtually unchanged. StAA, KL Ottobeuren 102, f. 195v and KL Ottobeuren 104, f. 175r.

Table 5.3 *Mean inheritances (fl.) at Ottobeuren, 1580–92 and 1610–19*

	1580–92		1610–19 (nominal)		1610–19 (deflated)
Class	No.	fl.	No.	fl.	fl.
Bauer	41	104.9	82	203.3	182.0
Seldner	20	14.5	30	80.3	71.9

Sources: StAA KL Ottobeuren 102, 491 I–III, 583, 901, 905, 907–8, 918

the amount of money peasants received as inheritances. This is trickier than it seems, because the sums promised at the time the family holdings were sold to the heir may not always have been paid in the end. The conventional way of mitigating this problem is to measure advances rather than inheritances *per se* on the theory that the former were more likely to be paid than the latter. At Ottobeuren, however, the practice of notarizing the full receipt of inheritances provides a much firmer basis for calculation, and the results (see Table 5.3) are striking. Even after adjusting for inflation, the average *Bauer*'s inheritance went up by almost three quarters, while the average *Seldner*'s inheritance quintupled.

Where did all of this money come from? The data analyzed in chapter 3 provide little support for the idea of an increase in agricultural productivity, and the extreme seasonality of the demand for unskilled labor makes supplemental wage work an equally unlikely candidate. Some of the funds must have been borrowed, and the 1620 tax survey indicates that the declared debts of Ottobeuren households averaged 30–40 percent of their gross wealth.[370] But the bulk of the cash came from two other key sources: the fabrication of textiles and an intensified commercialization of peasant production in general. Seventeenth-century Ottobeuren thus represents a classic example of what economists call 'Smithian growth,' the enormous potential of specialization and gains from trade in a heretofore compartmentalized economy.[371]

Textile production, in particular the production of linens and fustians (flax–cotton mixes known as *Barchent*), had a long history in Upper Swabia, and

---

[370] The proportion varied inversely with gross wealth. The average debt load by wealth class was: 41.2% (<250 fl.), 39.4% (250–499 fl.), 34.9% (500–749 fl.), 32.5% (750–999 fl.), and 28.7% (≥1000 fl.). The number of households in each class was 600, 252, 160, 110, and 358 respectively. Note that these figures do not include the 196 households with a gross wealth of zero who therefore could not borrow. StAA, KL Ottobeuren 102.

[371] The distinction between 'Smithian' (commercially driven) and 'Schumpeterian' (technologically driven) growth is stressed in Joel Mokyr, *The Lever of Riches: Technological Creativity and Economic Progress* (New York, 1990). See also Morgan Kelly, "The Dynamics of Smithian Growth," *Quarterly Journal of Economics* 112 (1997), pp. 939–64.

weaving in the monastery lands is already documented in a charter of 1410.[372] The market town of Ottobeuren had a bleaching works no later than 1549,[373] and a dyer by the name of Jacob Fischer is listed there in 1564.[374] At least until the early seventeenth century, however, the weaving and processing of cloth remained a minor activity in the Ottobeuren lands due to the vehement opposition of the weavers' guild in the neighboring city of Memmingen. Fearful of being undercut by cheaper country labor, the Memmingen weavers sought to prevent their rural competitors from selling cloth in the city, the region's most important market. After an unsuccessful effort in 1467, the guild secured from the city council a partial ban on rural weavers in 1482 and a total ban in 1489.[375] The spinning of linen thread, on the other hand, was an activity that the guild was happy to leave to the peasantry.[376] In fact, as a central European textile boom boosted their ranks from 124 in *c.* 1420 to 256 in 1530 to 403 by 1625,[377] the Memmingen weavers found themselves desperately short of raw material. A 1532 effort with several other Upper Swabian cities to control the thread supply by a collective ban on engrossing soon proved ineffective, and by 1554 the weavers were petitioning the city council to allow the import of cheaper spinnings from the surrounding rural districts.[378]

Flax had long been grown in the Ottobeuren lands, but the combination of rising urban demand (and therefore higher prices)[379] for linen thread and the new cash needs of peasant households resulted in a significant expansion of cultivation. Flax received no special mention in the 1546 small tithe register of Ottobeuren parish, but had become a separate category of its own by 1563.[380] The Abbot's market ordinance of 1601 had an entire section devoted to the buying and selling of linen thread (the only product to receive this kind of attention),[381] and early seventeenth-century maintenance agreements routinely

---

[372] Kiessling, *Die Stadt und ihr Land*, p. 482.

[373] StAA, KU Ottobeuren 1225 [8 Apr. 1549]. Also KL Ottobeuren 27, f. 11r [23 Feb. 1577].

[374] Dertsch, "Das Einwohnerbuch des Ottobeurer Klosterstaats 1564," p. 5. Fischer's son Balthas ranked among the wealthiest 5 percent of the market town's households in the 1585 tax register and is listed as a weaver in the 1620 tax survey. StAA, KL Ottobeuren 676a and KL Ottobeuren 102, f. 9r.

[375] See the extensive discussion in Kiessling, *Die Stadt und ihr Land*, pp. 481–91.

[376] Thomas Max Safley, "Production, Transaction and Proletarianization: The Textile Industry in Upper Swabia, 1580–1660" in Thomas Max Safley and Leonard N. Rosenband, eds., *The Workplace before the Factory: Artisans and Proletarians, 1500–1800* (Ithaca, 1993), pp. 118–45, at pp. 121–2.

[377] Kiessling, *Die Stadt und ihr Land*, p. 481; Wolf, *Reichsstädte in Kriegszeiten*, p. 195.

[378] Kiessling, *Die Stadt und ihr Land*, pp. 491–8.

[379] In Augsburg the price of flax increased 230 percent between 1550–4 and 1615–19. Claus-Peter Clasen, *Die Augsburger Weber: Leistungen und Krisen des Textilgewerbes um 1600* (Augsburg, 1981), p. 355.

[380] Compare StAA, KL Ottobeuren 681, Heft 1 and KL Ottobeuren 688-I, Heft 1.

[381] StAA, KL Ottobeuren 4, ff. 350v–358v Document 289V [5 Aug. 1601]. The "Ordinance of the Weavers and of Those who buy and sell Thread" is on ff. 353r–354r.

required the heir to sow flax seed for the retired parents or share his or her own flax harvest with them.[382] The flax alone might bring a household 5–10 fl. per annum,[383] and the spun thread perhaps 30 percent more. By 1620 the Abbot was reporting to the Augsburg city council that he could not forbid the spinning of lower-grade linen threads (as the Augsburg weavers' guild had demanded) because too many of his subjects were dependent on this activity for their survival.[384]

The expansion of textile work represented a number of changes in the rural economy. Flax was a labor-intensive crop both to grow and to process,[385] and almost all of the work (weeding and manuring the land, bundling, soaking, drying, beating and combing the plants) had to be done with simple hand tools.[386] The surge in flax and thread production thus entailed a reorganization and intensification of labor – especially female labor. There was also some technical innovation, specifically the development (c. 1580) of a method of spinning finer (and therefore more) thread from a measure of flax.[387] The most profound change, however, was a much tighter articulation of peasant households with market networks. Some of this was legal, for example the arrival in 1626 of an Augsburg textile factor to engage the Abbot's subjects in silk spinning for export,[388] and much of it was illegal, evidenced by the prosecution of over 300 Ottobeuren peasants for textile smuggling between 1615 and 1627.[389]

[382] There are twenty-eight such *Leibgedinge* between August 1612 and April 1616 in StAA, KL Ottobeuren 905 alone.

[383] The estimates made in chapter 3 (see above pp. 152–4) suggest that the annual value of the raw flax harvested in the hamlets of Ottobeuren parish in 1598–1601 averaged 5.3 fl. for "poor" households, 8.4 fl. for "comfortable" households, and 10.7 fl. for "rich" households. Note, however, that rather more flax was grown in the nucleated villages (where the bulk of the population lived) than in the hamlets.

[384] Clasen, *Die Augsburgher Weber*, pp. 357–9, 173. The relative values of raw and spun flax are based on the comparable ratios for cotton, as reported in Augsburg in 1587–8.

[385] For an overview of the many steps in early modern flax preparation, see Beck, *Naturale Ökonomie*, pp. 111–14. Most Ottobeuren maintenance agreements state only that the parents are to receive "prepared" flax, but a few (e.g. StAA, KL Ottobeuren 903, ff. 61v–62r [16 Jan. 1604] and KL Ottobeuren 905, f. 57r [7 July 1614]) contain the more precise requirement that the flax be delivered beaten and combed.

[386] The pressing of flax seeds for oil, on the other hand, was done in a mill. StAA, KL Ottobeuren 905, ff. 76r–v [12 June 1613].

[387] Clasen, *Die Augsburger Weber*, p. 156. Some of the earliest reports about the new thread (called *Faden*, to distinguish it from the older, thicker *Garn*) came from the city of Memmingen. It was also reported that a peasant could earn 20 percent more from a pound of flax by spinning *Faden* rather than *Garn*.

[388] StAA, KL Ottobeuren 909, f. 178v [28 Aug. 1626]. The factor, a certain "Signor Marco Antonio Bethega," was an agent of the Augsburg merchant Cosimo Sini. Bethega paid 200 fl. for a three-year lease on a house in the market town of Ottobeuren. Since the 1580s there had been complaints in Augsburg about urban merchants who had raw silk spun in rural villages and then exported the thread to Italy. Clasen, *Die Augsburger Weber*, pp. 327–32.

[389] StAA, KL Ottobeuren 587-II, Heft 28 (1615) and KL Ottobeuren 587-III, Heft 29 (1618–20), 30 (1621/2), 31 (1623–5), 32 (1624), and 33 (1626/7). Thread smuggling outweighed cloth smuggling by twenty to one.

The commercialization of the peasant economy was a general phenomenon that went far beyond the production of textiles. By the early seventeenth century there is abundant notarial evidence of a lively, credit-based trade within the monastery lands in grain[390] and livestock,[391] The Abbot's subjects also sold salt,[392] livestock,[393] and wood[394] as far north as Ulm and as far south as the lake of Constance, and imported wine,[395] iron,[396] flax oil,[397] and fustian cloth[398] from a variety of "foreign" urban merchants. The temporal dimension of rural exchange underwent the same kind of distension as its spatial counterpart, as buying and selling became much more continuous throughout the year. Figure 5.5 presents the weekly distribution of rye sales from the monastery's granary. Between 1527/8 and 1586/7 there was little meaningful change, with sales taking place during only sixteen and seventeen weeks of the year respectively. Thereafter, on the other hand, the sporadicity waned as a growing proportion of the monastery's grain disbursements were disposed of by sale. By 1610/11, twenty-four weeks of the year saw rye sales, and by 1621/2 the number had risen to thirty-seven.

Finally, and as may be expected, the changing structure of rural exchange went hand in hand with an increase in the monetization of the peasant economy. During the last third of the sixteenth century, there was a dramatic falling off in the hoarding of coins in the southwest German countryside,[399] a pattern which

---

[390] StAA, KL Ottobeuren 903, ff. 86v [3 Apr. 1604] and 286v [12 Jan. 1607]; KL Ottobeuren 907, ff. 23v [5 Nov. 1616], 46v [29 Jan. 1617], and 242r [15 Mar. 1619].

[391] For cattle: StAA, KL Ottobeuren 904, f. 147r [17 Sep. 1609]. For horses: KL Ottobeuren 903, ff. 36v [29 Aug. 1603] and 120[a]v [24 Oct. 1604]; KL Ottobeuren 904, f. 228r [7 Feb. 1611]; KL Ottobeuren 907, f. 229r [20 Feb. 1619]; KL Ottobeuren 909, f. 161r [16 May 1626].

[392] StAA, KL Ottobeuren 908, f. 71r [7 May 1620].

[393] StAA, KL Ottobeuren 904, f. 26v [5 Feb. 1608] for sixteen head of cattle exported to the Grafschaft Fluchenstain; KL Ottobeuren 905, f. 159v [11 Feb. 1614] for two head of cattle exported to Schwarzenberg. See also KL Ottobeuren 907, f. 211v [24 Dec. 1618], by which three Ottobeuren peasants appoint an emissary to collect an outstanding debt of 36 fl. for horses sold in Bregenz in 1615.

[394] StAA, KL Ottobeuren 905, ff. 119v–129r [11 Oct. 1613]. Jacob Rauch of Wolfertschwenden agrees to sell and deliver the wood on his land to "the city of Ulm" for 330 fl. See also KL Ottobeuren 904, ff. 81v–82r [13 Nov. 1608]. The monastery of Ottobeuren sells standing wood at Obermotzen to a consortium of five peasants (presumably for resale) for 550 fl.

[395] StAA, KL Ottobeuren 903, ff. 137v [29 Jan. 1605], 165v [18 Apr. 1605], 179r [9 May 1605], and 179r–v [2 May 1605]; KL Ottobeuren 904, f. 202v [20 June 1608]; KL Ottobeuren 905, ff. 141r–v [15 Dec. 1613], 141v–143r [15 Dec. 1613], 274r [4 June 1615], and 358v–359r [28 Apr. 1616]; KL Ottobeuren 907, f. 63v [5 Apr. 1617]; KL Ottobeuren 911, ff. 65–66 [26 Aug. 1630] and 184 [25 Oct. 1630], all owed to various merchants in Memmingen.

[396] StAA, KL Ottobeuren 904, f. 61r [7 June 1608] and KL Ottobeuren 908, f. 20r [21 Aug. 1619] were owed to an iron-trader in Memmingen.

[397] StAA, KL Ottobeuren 905, ff. 31v–32r [12 Nov. 1612] owed to a merchant in Rettenbach.

[398] StAA, KL Ottobeuren 904, f. 207r [5 July 1610] owed to a merchant in Kaufbeuren.

[399] Joachim Schüttenhelm, *Der Geldumlauf im südwestdeutschen Raum vom Riedlinger Münzvertrag 1423 bis zur ersten Kipperzeit 1618* Veröffentlichungen der Kommission für geschichtliche Landeskunde in Baden-Württemberg, Band 108 (Stuttgart, 1987), p. 515.

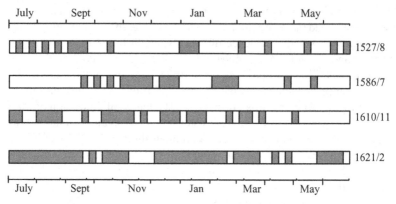

Figure 5.5 Temporal distribution of rye sales at Ottobeuren, 1527/8–1622. The shading denotes those weeks when sales ocurred.
Sources: StAA, KL Ottobeuren 224 (Hefte 1 and 4), 225, 541 (Heft 1)

has also been documented in Franconia[400] and on the German Baltic coast.[401] At Ottobeuren itself, the recording of in-kind peasant debts to the monastery was suspended at some point between 1579 and 1585, and thereafter all obligations were converted into money sums.[402]

The monks were keenly aware of all this commercial quickening. In 1600 they (successfully) petitioned the Holy Roman Emperor to renew the old Ottobeuren market privilege of 1498, explaining that the market had in past years been moribund but was now seeing much more activity.[403] Having secured the privilege for one weekly and two annual markets, Abbot Alexander went on in 1601 to promulgate an ordinance restating the traditional circumscription of peasant commerce to the official times and location of the Ottobeuren marketplace.[404] And when the city of Memmingen tried to stifle the Ottobeuren market by preventing its citizens from buying grain there, the Abbot retaliated in 1604 by forbidding his own subjects to frequent the market of his urban rivals.[405] But

[400] H. Eichhorn, Der Strukturwandel im Geldumlauf Frankens zwischen 1437 und 1610 Vierteljahrschrift für Sozial- und Wirtschaftsgeschichte, Beiheft 58 (Wiesbaden, 1973).

[401] Michael North, Geldumlauf und Wirtschaftskonjunktur im südlichen Ostseeraum an der Wende zur Neuzeit (1440–1570), Kieler Historischer Studien 35 (Sigmaringen, 1990), pp. 105–37.

[402] Compare StAA, KL Ottobeuren 426, 430, 552–5.

[403] StadtA MM A 40/1. Abbot Alexander to Kaiser Rudolf II [31 May 1600] (copy) requesting renewal of the market privilege of 10 July 1498. The Abbot claimed that the inactivity of the sixteenth century was an artificial consequence of the Peasants' War of 1525 and other subsequent conflicts. This view was predictably rejected by the Memmingen city council, which countered that Ottobeuren's 1498 privilege had instead "through negligence and disuse now been doubly lost and extinguished." Ibid., Bürgermeister and Rat of Memmingen to Kaiser Rudolf II [7 Aug. 1600].

[404] StAA, KL Ottobeuren 4, Document 289V, ff. 350v–358v [5 Aug. 1601].

[405] StadtA MM A 40/1. Bürgermeister and Rat of Memmingen to Abbot Alexander of Ottobeuren [11/21 Sep. 1601], where the former disingenuously deny the Abbot's charge of "impeding free

a great deal had changed in the century between the 1498 grant and its renewal in 1600, and the monastery quickly learned that the compartmentalization of its villages could no longer be maintained by mere fiat. The city of Memmingen was active in defense of its interests, and the council quickly secured an imperial mandate quashing Abbot Alexander's 1604 prohibition.[406] Even among the monastery's own subjects there was grumbling about the market ordinance, and the headman of Halbersberg was fined a stiff £1 15 ß because he "spoke scornfully about the establishment of the weekly market before many people, and in addition wagered 10 fl. that the market here would come to nothing."[407] Far more serious than any explicit resistance, however, was simple non-compliance, whether in the form of smuggling, engrossing, or forestalling. Even before the events of 1601–4, in fact, the traditional economic norms had already begun to crumble as exchange was constituted in an ever larger and more continuous envelope of time and space.

The first intimation of a fraying of the traditional exchange boundaries was the appearance of wandering Savoyard peddlers in the middle of the sixteenth century. The Savoyards avoided official marketplaces, preferring to hawk their wares from door to door in the villages. Their activities soon cut into the profits of local merchants, and the ensuing complaints led to typical repressive legislation. In 1551 the Abbot of Ottobeuren prohibited all peddling by the Savoyards outside of official marketplaces, but this does not seem to have made much of a difference.[408]

Although they occasioned a considerable amount of protest throughout southern Germany, the activities of the Savoyards remained at the level of an external irritant. As itinerant peddlers they were confined to dealing in small quantities; it is telling that they seem to have caused the greatest disruption in the spice trade.[409] After about 1590, however, a surge in trading violations by the peasants

---

trade" while insisting on their traditional right to impose a year-long ban from the Memmingen market on anyone who purchased grain within two miles of the city. Abbot Alexander's retaliatory ordinance is preserved in StAA, KL Ottobeuren 4, Document 289W, ff. 358v–360v [20 Nov. 1604].

[406] StadtA MM A 40/1 Kaiser Rudolf II to Abbot Alexander of Ottobeuren [27 Nov. 1604].

[407] StAA, KL Ottobeuren 587-II, Heft 21 (1602/2). The headman in question, a certain Jacob Zick, had been admitted to a middling *Hof* in the hamlet in 1576 and farmed it until his death in 1608. KL Ottobeuren 27, f. 10r [9 Mar. 1576]; KL Ottobeuren 904, f. 43r [19 Apr. 1608]. Zick is not named in the *Strafregister*; identification from KL Ottobeuren 491-I, Heft 6, f. 2r and Heft 14, f. 5v.

[408] StAA, KL Ottobeuren 4, Document 289X, ff. 397r–398v. The ordinance represented the promulgation of a resolution adopted by the Swabian Circle of the Holy Roman Empire on 31 May 1551.

[409] The 1551 Ottobeuren ordinance describes the peddlers specifically as "Italians and Savoyards who peddle saffron and other spices." Ibid. In Memmingen the loudest complaints about the Savoyards were heard from the mercers' guild, which in 1555 and 1557 objected to their peddling "not only of spices, but also of all sorts of pennyworths such as belts, knives and the like." Kiessling, *Die Stadt und ihr Land*, p. 479.

themselves reflected a more fundamental change in the inner workings of the rural economy. The early seventeenth century saw the final collapse of the commercial isolation of the monastery villages. Decade by decade, ever greater numbers of the Abbot's subjects defied the ban on unauthorized trade outside his dominions and ventured out to sell their goods on the urban market (see Figure 5.6). Memmingen was the most common destination, but this was more a reflection of the city's proximity than the strength of its *Bannmeilenrecht*. Not only did Ottobeuren peasants also frequently travel to Kempten, Babenhausen, Leutkirch, Lindau, and Mindelheim, and on occasion as far as Augsburg, but it is clear from the constant hand-wringing in the city council over engrossing and forestalling[410] that the Memmingen exclusion zone had already become a dead letter by the last quarter of the sixteenth century.

The distress over mass violation of commercial law and custom was equally acute in the monastery. By 1616 the Abbot had in desperation taken to stationing a sheriff on the main road to Memmingen in order to intercept the flow of goods to the city.[411] It availed him little. In 1621 the Abbot renewed a pair of traditional ordinances, the first prohibiting the sale of goods outside the monastery lands before the Abbot's subjects had bought all that they wanted, and the second capping the prices of lard and tallow. "It has, however, been found," the monastery council minutes report, "that on the day of the promulgation, in violation [of the ordinance] many [peasants] took back the lard and tallow which they had brought to market and refused to sell at the official price and then on the next market [day] almost none of the said [goods] were brought to market."[412]

Frustrated by the futility of traditional measures and concerned lest the law be flouted with impunity, the Abbot in November convened his advisors for advice on how best to punish those who had withdrawn their goods from the market. The more important question, however, was how henceforth to ensure that the market was adequately supplied with goods. Should the ordinances be reconfirmed, tacitly allowed to lapse, or formally repealed? Most of the Abbot's advisors were of one mind. The prior recommended that the ordinance be reconfirmed and that those who violated it be punished. A more specific proposal was advanced by the cellarer, kitchenmaster, and chancellor. These three wanted those who sold goods outside the monastery lands to be fined and have their goods confiscated. They further suggested that those who reported such infractions be rewarded with a share of the fine. The only dissonant note in this chorus of dirigisme was sounded by the subprior. Unlike everyone else, he did not think that the subjects of the monastery should be compelled to sell

---

[410] Ibid., pp. 448–55.
[411] StadtA MM, A 40/2. Letter by the *Bürgermeister* and *Rat* of Memmingen protesting such practices to the Abbot of Ottobeuren [21 June/1 July 1616].
[412] StAA, KL Ottobeuren 598, f. 32r [29 Nov. 1621].

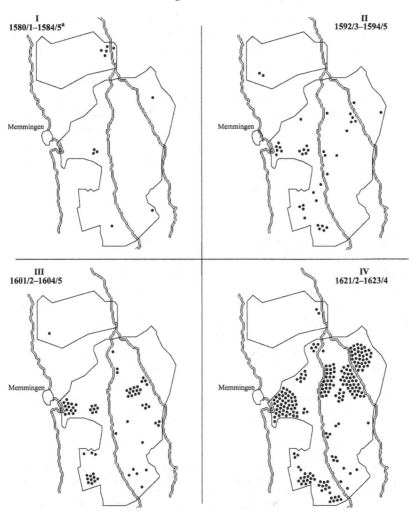

Figure 5.6 Illegal exchanges outside of official marketplaces, 1580–1624. (Each illegal exchange is represented by a dot in the offender's home village.)
[a] 1581/2 and 1583/4 no data
Sources: StAA KL Ottobeuren 587- I, II, III

their goods at fixed prices. Instead, he argued, "if each were allowed to sell at as high a price as could be obtained in other places, there would be sufficient goods at the [Ottobeuren] market."[413]

The ensuing debate continued for another four days, and in the end the subprior was forced to back down. Already at the end of the first day he had

[413] Ibid.

retreated to the position that the peasants could be required to offer their goods for sale at the local market, but that the prices themselves should be allowed to fluctuate freely. By the third day he had conceded that moral theologians did allow the regulation of prices in the interest of justice, but insisted that by a "just price" they meant a commonly available price;[414] atypicality rather than magnitude was the mark of an unjust price. This argument prompted inquiries by the Abbot among the local peasantry and neighboring lords, and on 3 December the Abbot announced a decision. The traditional market regulations were not only morally acceptable, they were positively advisable, and similar restrictions were in use in many neighboring territories. The Ottobeuren market ordinances were to be enforced; the most the Abbot would concede was a slight increase in the official price ceilings.[415]

There is no small irony in an overlord's defense of what historians have come to call the "moral economy" while so many of his subjects were bent on maximizing their gains from trade, but that was indeed the situation. The rejection of the old rules went so far that village mayors and sheriffs and even parish priests were implicated in illegal exchanges.[416] Determined smugglers made payoffs to potential whistle-blowers[417] and intercepted and bought out law-abiding peasants on their way to the official market.[418] The prosecution in 1618/19 of Michael Fries in the market town of Ottobeuren "because he assured the Memmingen weavers that he would inform them when they could buy up thread [*Faden*]"[419] further suggests the existence of *ad hoc* compacts intended to evade the marketing restrictions of both lordships.[420]

---

[414] The subprior was quite correct; this position had been taken by scholastic theologians as far back as the thirteenth century. Odd Langholm, *Economics in the Medieval Schools: Wealth, Exchange, Value, Money and Usury According to the Paris Theological Tradition 1200–1350* (Leiden/New York/Cologne, 1992), pp. 580–3. See also Raymond de Roover, "The Concept of the Just Price: Theory and Economic Policy," *Journal of Economic History* 18 (1958), pp. 418–34, at pp. 420–1.

[415] StAA, KL Ottobeuren 598, ff. 32r–35r [1–3 Dec. 1621]. The Abbot seems to have drawn particular encouragement from the fact that similar ordinances had been enacted by the Bishop of Augsburg for the market town of Sonthofen.

[416] The mayors [*Ammänner*] of Benningen, Egg, Niederdorf, and Wolfertschwenden were all fined for illegal grain sales between 1618 and 1627. In 1621 Hans Sporredle engrossed 3 *malter* of grain from the local pastor. In 1626/7 two Attenhausen peasants were charged with selling thread and cloth in Memmingen: "they deny it and the sheriff [*Büttel*] knows nothing about it" (no fine). StAA, KL Ottobeuren 587-III, Hefte 29 (1618–20), 30 (1621/2), 31 (1623–5), 32 (1624), and 33 (1626/7).

[417] StAA, KL Ottobeuren 587-III, Heft 31 [12 Dec. 1623]: Johann Aichelin of Warlins sold a cow outside the lordship and later gave a calf to his neighbor Martin Stehelin "so that he not betray [him]."

[418] Ibid., [13 Dec. 1623]: Hans Epplin, miller of Niederdorf, engrossed eight and fourteen pounds of lard from his neighbors Hans Braun and Jacob Kless respectively "as they were going to the market."

[419] StAA, KL Ottobeuren 587-III, Heft 29 (1618–20), f. 2r.

[420] The following incident from the village of Ungerhausen may indicate a similar kind of collusion: "Barthle Schweitzer, sexton, did on a Sunday fetch a weaver from Memmingen, who on the

It would be misleading to reduce the hemorrhage of exchange outside traditional boundaries to a mere desire for windfall profits. The steep rise in smuggling and related commercial offenses did, of course, represent an effort to capitalize on the short-range price differentials common to the sixteenth-century countryside. In fact, the search for better prices also led to high-level protests against the privileges of the tailors' guild[421] and to the widespread engagement of female seamstresses to do tailors' work at lower cost.[422] At the same time, liquidity was often more important to the Abbot's subjects than a higher return *per se*. The primary objection to the requirement that cattle be offered first to the butchers of the market town was that payment was too long in coming, as a result of which peasants preferred to sell to urban merchants,[423] even if this meant accepting a lower price.[424]

More fundamentally, the present and previous chapters make it clear that the growing disregard for traditional market norms received enormous impetus from the rise of "cash-intensive" inheritance practices at the end of the sixteenth century.[425] Thus, when Melchior Weissenhorn of Niederrieden found himself 350 fl. short of the 982 fl. he had agreed to pay for his father's *Gotteshausrecht* holding,[426] the solution to the pressure of debt was obvious. In 1620 he was fined for illegal grain sales in Memmingen and for illicit visits to the market in Babenhausen. Continued illegal grain sales in Memmingen resulted in additional fines in 1624 and 1626; by 1627 he had branched out to illicit traffic in

same day set up a loom in the sexton's house – [fined] 7 ß. Zacharias Kharter did shelter the weaver's servant and his cousin, who had been proscribed by the city of Memmingen – fined £1." StAA, KL Ottobeuren 587-II, Heft 25 (1604/5).

[421] In Niederrieden, "The *Amman* had it made known on several occasions that he and other officials of the monastery had completely overthrown the privilege which His Grace [i.e. the Abbot] gave the tailors and [their] guild, and would uphold their [own] position against the tailors without regard for it [i.e. the privilege]." The *Amman* of Günz imposed a tax on the village *Gemeinde* to raise money to contest the guild privilege, while the headman of Eheim approved and praised the decision of two other residents of the hamlet to engage a "foreign" tailor. StAA, KL Ottobeuren 587-II, Heft 22 (1602/3).

[422] There were thirty-five prosecutions for offenses of this sort in 1601/2 and 1603/4 (the register for 1602/3 is incomplete). StAA, KL Ottobeuren 587-II, Hefte 21–23b.

[423] There is an extensive discussion of the cattle smuggling problem in the minutes of the Abbot's council from 19 December 1628. The peasants asked for the right to have a lien automatically placed on the property of a butcher who did not pay within two weeks, rather than having to initiate formal court proceedings. The Abbot was reluctant to concede this, but was in the end persuaded by his advisors to assent. StAA, KL Ottobeuren 598, ff. 299r–301r.

[424] "Hans Sendler refused to sell cattle to Gerhard Schell at the parish festival for 35 fl., but [instead] sold it to someone from Memmingen for 34 fl. and kept the [cattle] for him until Martinmas – fined 10 ß." StAA, KL Ottobeuren 587-II, Heft 28 (1615), f. 20r (Hawangen). Sendler was a rich man with a gross wealth of 1,015 fl. in 1620. KL Ottobeuren 102, ff. 203v–204r.

[425] The prosecutions detailed in this paragraph are found in StAA KL Ottobeuren 587-II, Heft 28 (1615) and KL Ottobeuren 587-III, Hefte 29 (1618–20), 30 (1621/22), 31 (1622–25), 32 (1624), and 33 (1626/7).

[426] StAA, KL Ottobeuren 903, ff. 40v–41r [9 Oct. 1603]; KL Ottobeuren 904, f. 184v [15 Mar. 1610]. The tenancy transfer record has not survived, but Jacob's *Hof* in 1584 (KL Ottobeuren 31, f. 24v) was held by Melchior in 1606 (KL Ottobeuren 39, f. 91v).

cattle. A similar solution was hit upon by Hans Sporredle of Westerheim. In 1613 he bought a small house in the village for 190 *gulden*,[427] but was forced to borrow 50 *gulden* of the purchase price from the parish church of Ungerhausen at 5 percent interest per annum.[428] The criminal court papers leave little doubt as to how Hans obtained the money for his payments: in 1615 he was fined for selling thread in Memmingen, in 1621 the offense was the secret sale of grain to another villager and to the parish priest (!), in 1627 it was the unauthorized sale of a calf and a cow.

Peasant concern for a steady cashflow highlights a major shift in the rural economy towards economic specializaton and consequent dependence on trade. As it happens, the best evidence for the economic specialization of the Ottobeuren peasantry is the prosecution records for smuggling, engrossing, and forestalling, of which there are almost 800 for the years 1615–27. By the early seventeenth century, the monastery's "punishment registers" almost invariably recorded the type of product the offender had sold. As might be expected, the variety was dizzying, and included not only grain, straw, cattle, thread, and cloth, but also flax, dung, eggs, chickens, milk, dried fruit, shoes, window-frames, and even pastry ("Öppfel Schnitz"). Nevertheless, if products are counted by frequency of (illegal) sale and mapped by point of origin, a clear pattern of regional specialization emerges (see Figure 5.7).[429] The riverine villages of the north and northeast (Westerheim, Günz, Attenhausen, Sontheim, and Schlegelsberg) made up a textile production zone, the lower-lying villages of the northwest (Egg and Niederrieden) a grain zone, and a somewhat less coherent cattle zone was formed by the less densely populated hamlets of the southeast (Böhen and Ottobeuren parish) and the villages of Hawangen and especially Ungerhausen.

Specialization spread all the way down the social ladder. Although grain smugglers were (predictably) drawn from the ranks of the prosperous *Bauern*, the production and smuggling of textiles took place at all levels of rural society.[430] In the village of Sontheim, for example, no fewer than twenty-eight households – more than one fourth of the entire village – had members fined between 1621 and 1623 for currency speculation and unauthorized trading both inside and outside of the monastery lands in Memmingen, Mindelheim, and

---

[427] StAA, KL Ottobeuren 905, ff. 89v–90r [7 Feb. 1613].

[428] Ibid., f. 90r [7 Feb. 1613].

[429] I have included only those settlements where there were at least fifteen prosecutions in the period 1615–27, and have counted only prosecutions for the *sale* of an identifiable product, as it would in this context be misleading to count products engrossed by a middleman. The figure is based on a total of 682 prosecutions.

[430] Whereas almost two thirds of 177 identifiable grain smugglers had a gross wealth of at least 1,000 fl. in 1620, the wealth distribution of 261 identifiable textile smugglers was as follows: 57.5% (<250 fl.); 14.6% (250–499 fl.); 14.9% (500–999 fl.); 13.0% (>1000 fl.). The poorer ranks of the peasantry were thus if anything overrepresented in this latter group; see above note 250.

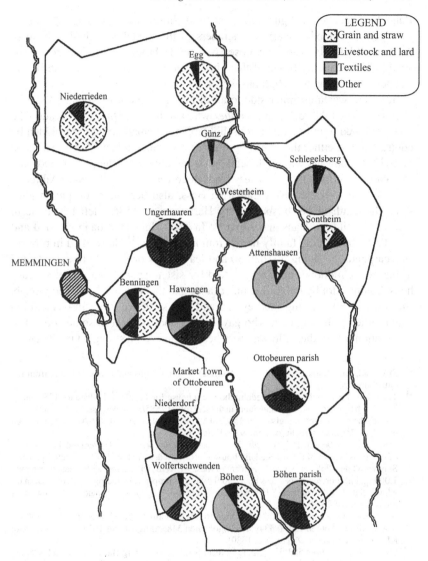

Figure 5.7 The products of illegal trade at Ottobeuren, 1615–27
Source: StAA, KL Ottobeuren 587-II

Babenhausen, and this figure represents only those who were caught.[431] These smugglers included at least six members of the Stedelin kindred, a band of brothers of humble origin[432] whose 1627 tax declarations reveal a prosperous smallholder economy (none of them had even 6 *jauchert* of arable land) with considerable assets in cash, loans, or "in trade."[433]

But there was a grimmer side to all of this. Next door to Michael Stedelin lived old Ulrich Albrecht, an ex-*Bauer* who had lost his *Hof* in 1598, and who now crammed with two other householders into a small cottage, forbidden by contract to use either the threshing floor or even the kitchen.[434] Albrecht died in 1627, leaving his widow dependent on the charity of the parish, and on a son who himself left the monastery lands three years later.[435] Next to Albrecht, in another half-house, lived Catharina Hess, also dependent on parish alms since the death of her husband, Jerg Hartmann, in 1586/7 left her alone to feed their children, Hans and Anna.[436] In 1602 Hans Hartmann married and in 1605 he bought the family home from his mother.[437] He worked in poverty as a carpenter,[438] dying in 1629/30 and leaving his orphans to live, as he had in his own childhood, on alms.[439] And his sister Anna? Shut out of an easy householding slot by impartible inheritance and the logic of the closed village, she fell in with a young journeyman and was soon pregnant. In desperation Anna turned to her mother, who gave her an abortifacient in some soup. The preparation failed, the child was born healthy, and Anna strangled it. Catharina

---

[431] StAA, KL Ottobeuren 587-III, Heft 30 (1621/2). Identifications and household total from KL Ottobeuren 102.

[432] The original patriarch, Johann Stedelin, bought a house for 122 fl. on 13 January 1584 and is listed with three sons and two daughters in the serf roll of 1585/6. He was assessed the *Seldner*'s 3 kr. in the bond-chicken register for 1587. StAA, KL Ottobeuren 901, f. 67v; KL Ottobeuren 601 II, ff. 75r–88v; KL Ottobeuren 491-I, Heft 3, f. 28v.

[433] StAA, KL Ottobeuren 104, ff. 309r–337r. Assets of this form, which averaged 14.6 percent of the gross wealth of the six Stedelin households, were declared by 41 of 140 (29.3 percent) Sontheim householders. Some 40 percent of these 41 were rich *Bauern* with assets worth over 1,000 fl., but fourteen owned less than 500 fl. worth of property, including one Urban Gerhart, who declared 30 fl. "in trade," but owned only a house, 3.5 *jauchert* of land, and a cow, for a gross wealth of 235 fl.

[434] StAA, KL Ottobeuren 905, f. 307r [13 Nov. 1615]; KL Ottobeuren 27, f. 148r [4 May 1598].

[435] StAA, KL Ottobeuren 104, f. 334v; KA Ottobeuren 348, Alms lists for 1626, 1628, and 1630; KL Ottobeuren 911, f. 97 [14 Dec. 1630].

[436] StAA, KL Ottobeuren 583, Heft 4b, f. 1v records the death of Jerg Hartmann and adds "nota: the widow is in receipt of alms." Hans and Anna are listed as Jerg and Catharina's children in the 1585/6 serf roll. KL Ottobeuren 601 II, ff. 75r–88v.

[437] StAA, KL Ottobeuren 583, Heft 20, f. 4r; KL Ottobeuren 903, f. 199r [5 Dec. 1605]. Mother and son are listed together in the 1609 bond-chicken register. KL Ottobeuren 491-I, Heft 14, f. 15r.

[438] KL Ottobeuren 102, f. 339r and KL Ottobeuren 104, f. 326v. In 1620 Hans Hartmann owned only a half-house, half a *jauchert* of land, and a cow; by 1627 the cow was gone. On assets of 105 fl. (1627) he had debts of 70 fl., 40 fl. of which was borrowed from the local parish church on 1 April 1614. KL Ottobeuren 905, ff. 168r–v.

[439] StAA, KL Ottobeuren 491-III, Heft 34, f. 18v; KA Ottobeuren 348.

then hid the body in a cowstall, but it was soon discovered, and both women were tried for infanticide. Found guilty, the aged grandmother had her ears cut off and was whipped out of the monastery lands. The young mother was beheaded.[440]

The point here is not simply that triumph and tragedy lived cheek by jowl, but that both were outcomes of the same process. In so far as the transformation of rural society can be expressed as the advent of a new style of householding, these developments must be derived in the first instance from the interests of household heads themselves. However general the exacting and often unforgiving fiscal discipline of this era may have been, it was still predicated on a hierarchy of authority and asymmetry of benefit. This is not to say that householders abandoned their kin; this chapter has offered ample evidence of the effort expended to care equally for all. Be that as it may, the stability of the vast majority of new households was inextricably linked with the preponderance of the unmarried in the emigrant population. Stepchildren and yielding heirs were all too often, in Hermann Rebel's words, the necessary victims of the household's survival strategy[441] and they knew it.

In the long run, the course adopted at Ottobeuren was probably the best that could have been done within the limits of the possible. In the medium run, the early seventeenth-century economy did bear heavily on the weaker members of rural society, but to acknowledge the reality of the burden does not require us to label the situation a 'crisis.' The truly unprecedented suffering which the entire peasantry would shortly undergo was visited on them completely from the outside.

---

[440] StAA, KL Ottobeuren 4, ff. 972r–975r Document 292 [1611]. For an excellent discussion of the prosecution of infanticide at this time, including materials from the city of Memmingen, see Ulinka Rublack, *The Crimes of Women in Early Modern Germany* (Oxford, 1999), pp. 163–96.
[441] Rebel, *Peasant Classes*, p. 284.

6. *To empty and to refill (c. 1630–c. 1720)*

Father Stephan Mayer's luck ran out on 1 April 1634, when seven Swedish cavalrymen rode into his parish of Unteregg. For two years the mercenary armies of the Swedish crown and the German emperor had waged a see-saw struggle for control of Upper Swabia, but thus far Mayer had managed to stay out of harm's way. Six times he had already fled the village,[1] which lay just to the east of his birthplace in the Ottobeuren lands,[2] and would be acquired by the monastery in 1749. This time the soldiers caught him.

"Stop, you damn thief!" the first rider barked. "Come here! Run!" The priest complied. "It is just that we are so afraid of you sirs," he explained meekly. And with good reason: the soldier promptly pulled out a pistol and bluntly announced, "Today is the day of death. You must die." The trooper was soon joined by one of his comrades, and after taking Mayer's purse the soldiers hauled the priest into the village center and attempted to find out who he was. At first they thought he was the innkeeper, which Mayer denied. The soldiers then asked some bystanders to identify the prisoner, but the peasants lied and said they didn't know him. The priest was caught in a terrifying dilemma. If he didn't hand over at least some valuables to his captors, they were likely to kill him, but if he revealed his true identity, he was even less likely to survive. Thinking quickly, Father Mayer claimed to be the sexton's brother-in-law and offered that he had a few *gulden* stashed in the sacristy. The soldiers laid eager hands on both the money and the church's monstrance, and proceeded to ask

---

[1] Father Mayer's ten flights from the parish between June 1632 and August 1634 are detailed in Unteregg Parish Register [hereinafter UEPR], Vol. I, ff. 133r–134r. From 1 April 1634 to 31 January 1635 he was unable to live in the vicarage "due to riders and pestilence . . . I lived here and there, spent some time in the brewhouse [and also] during the cold winter lived with the sexton in the shed attached to his house." Ibid., f. 131r.

[2] Stephan was the son of Johann Mayer, who was born in 1574 in the Ottobeuren village of Frechenrieden and was admitted to a small *Hof* there on 4 December 1600. Stephan's father had a gross wealth of 800 fl. in 1620, and by 1627 held the position of village *Amman*. UEPR, Vol. I, f. 196v. StAA, KL Ottobeuren 27, f. 113v; KL Ottobeuren 102, ff. 365r–v; KL Ottobeuren 104, f. 363v.

Mayer at knifepoint about the whereabouts of the parish priest. "We have a very timorous priest," Mayer responded. "He has fled to Landsberg." "Damn thief," came the reply, "I can tell that you have more money. You must give us more, or I'll fill you with an entire bucket of water."

The threat of water torture made it clear to the priest that the soldiers were not going to let him off easily.

In God's name only, I thought, I will have to chance it. I let the rider get a little ahead [of me] . . . [Then] I turned around and ran for my life (even if it were to cost me my life). Through the courtyard of Hais's house, between the church wall and the smith's house, and past the sexton's house I ran, the horseman all the while behind me, dagger in hand and shouting "Hey! Damn thief! Stop!" I was trying to get to the woods, but when I reached the sexton's house and looked around in fear and terror, there was another rider at the clearing, who headed after me. I turned around, and ran back to the sexton's house, [but] was out of breath. I could only duck into the latrine and drop in. I covered myself as best I could with rushes and excrement. A third soldier joined the other two. The one on horseback said that I was in the house in front of the latrine. Another said he thought he saw something, and meant to run me through with his blade. But God was merciful. The soldier kicked in the kitchen door [and went into the house].

Lying in the muck, Father Mayer promised God and the Virgin Mary to go to confession and say three masses for the Virgin "at the next opportunity." He managed to get out of the latrine and into the forest, where he hid in a treetop until the soldiers rode off. It had been a very narrow escape, and the priest accounted himself fortunate.[3] But the worst was yet to come.

Both Swedish and imperial troops were given to plunder, and at least in the beginning, Father Mayer was able to remain philosophical about the constant looting. In July of 1633, for example, he had two cows driven off by the Swedes and taken to Ulm. Two months later he somehow managed to recognize and repurchase one of the animals on the market in Mindelheim, only to have the beast stolen by imperial troops four days later. "So it goes in wartime," the priest drily remarked. Mayer even kept up his sense of humor; when soldiers stole the very shoes and stockings off his feet on 22 September 1633, he concluded his account with the observation "and thus they made a Franciscan [a discalced order] out of a parish priest."[4] By the summer of 1634, however, Mayer's (somewhat jumbled) journal entries make it clear that the depredations of the soldiery were taking a serious toll on the rural economy:

Anno 1634. On 4 June a cavalryman beat a horse to death with a hammer because it could go no further. [The animal] was butchered and eaten by my parishioners . . .

---

[3] This remarkable account is preserved in UEPR, Vol. I, ff. 128v–131r.   [4] Ibid., f. 308v.

On the feast of St. Bartholomew [24 August] there were no animals left in the village except for a few goats. [Myself] I still had a dog, and a couple of cats which no one had been able to catch. Otherwise they too would have been eaten.

Anno 1634. On 2 June my parishioner Jacob Schelhorn begged me for the love of God to give him my big dog, so that for once he could have enough to eat. I could not deny him this.[5]

To the spoliation of the parish's livestock, the autumn then added both a drought and the plague. The fields could not be sown, and Father Mayer's parishioners began to die.

"One gobbled and ate what little there was," he noted. Groats, mill-tailings, grass, the flesh of cats and dogs, "in a word, such things as heretofore [even] the pigs didn't eat." The villagers began to look a sickly yellow-white; "yea, the hunger could be seen pressing out from their eyes."[6] At Christmastime there was nothing to bake with save herbs and beans, and by January of 1635 the peasants were eating horsehide, twigs, and rats. Father Mayer's burial register speaks for itself:

Jacob Rauch of Bittnaw in the month of January Anno 1635 ate mice. Indeed, he said, he only wished he could and would get enough of them. O hunger! O misery! . . .

Goodwife Anna Foller from Unteregg, having confessed and received the sacrament of the Holy Eucharist died of hunger 23 February [1635] together with two [of her] children. O God, the darkness is indeed so vast, and daily grows only larger . . .

Barbara Schorer of Unteregg, having confessed and received the Holy Eucharist died of hunger 6 May [1635] aged about 20 . . .

[undated] Goodwife Barbara Hildbränd of Hochholtz died of hunger. This woman ate a great many mice, and as she said to her father (I heard this from her father's mouth), "Father, you would not believe what good soup can be made from mice."[7]

In the end, the priest claimed, even the ultimate taboo was broken:

Anno 1635. In Boos one mother ate her own child. Another [woman] with two children was forcibly driven off by her parish priest; otherwise she would have butchered and eaten her own flesh and blood. In the said village, a[nother] woman tried to cut up and eat her deceased husband. O Misery! O Hunger![8]

---

[5] Ibid., ff. 190v–191r, 313v. The unfortunate man died of plague five months later on 29 November 1634.

[6] Ibid., f. 309r.   [7] Ibid., ff. 193r–195v.

[8] Ibid., f. 131v. There were several reports of starvation-induced cannibalism during the Thirty Years War (e.g. C. V. Wedgwood, *The Thirty Years' War* [Garden City, NY, 1961], p. 400), but

On 15 December 1634, Father Mayer counted 70 households and 112 persons left in the village. Over the course of the following year he performed over two hundred funerals. By 1639 he had buried both of his parents, his brother-in-law, and his beloved sister Catharina. Of Catharina's five young children there remained only two, "on whom I must take pity and feed, in so far as is in my power." Finally, on 23 May 1645, after twenty years' service to the parish, Father Mayer went on to his own reward.[9] It seems a wonder that anyone was left to bury him.

The agonies of the Swabian peasantry during the Thirty Years War (1618–48) could by themselves fill an entire book, for the parish of Unteregg was unusual only in the record, not the magnitude of its suffering. But the interest here in the staggering death toll of the 1630s is the perspective such a cataclysm offers on the inverse phenomenon, that is to say on the addition of so many mouths to rural society during the population boom of the sixteenth century. For all the discussion of inheritance and commerce, money and credit, the interpretation thus far advanced of the sixteenth and seventeenth centuries at Ottobeuren remains anchored in demography. Naturally other influences were at work in the growing sophistication of the peasant economy, in particular an integration with the urban market network that had been growing ever tighter since the fifteenth century at least. Nevertheless, pride of place among efficient causes still goes to the (perceived) overpopulation of the monastery lands, which brought an end to the subdivision of landholdings and led to the closure of the village communities. The subsequent effort to capitalize the now-impartible family farm in order to provide for an heir's siblings and parents then dramatically accelerated the proliferation and monetization of rural exchange networks.

Yet demography was only part of the story. Commodification of the land and its fruits was no mechanical reflex to an objective level of population density, but a conscious adaptation to pressure on the self-imposed boundaries of the rural community. Crucially, the same institutional matrix – property rights, kinship dynamics, lordship and town–country relations – through which this adaptation was effected proved rather more lasting than the ecological pressure itself. As a result, although the highly commercialized Upper Swabian countryside

Mayer's is one of the few contemporary accounts that has plausibility. The village of Boos, it should be pointed out, was not part of his parish, but belonged to the nearby lordship of the Fugger zu Babenhausen on the northern border of the Ottobeuren lands. On the other hand, it is clear from Mayer's description of his flights from Unteregg that he spent much of 1633–5 traveling throughout the wider region (he records stays in Mindelheim, Landsberg, Kaufbeuren, Ronsberg, Obergünzburg, and Ottobeuren), and there is good reason to believe he would have had reliable knowledge of events in Boos. One way or another, Mayer's account left a deep impression on human memory in the region. His manuscript is cited in the early nineteenth-century chronicle of the Ottobeuren monk Maurus Feyerabend (*Ottenbeuren Jahrbücher* III, p. 424) and the details were again reprinted in the Swabian journals *Schwäbische Postbote* (1880) and *Deutsche Gaue* (1910). See also Benigna von Krusenstjern, *Selbstzeugnisse der Zeit des Dreißigjährigen Krieges* (Berlin, 1997), pp. 161–2.

[9] UEPR, Vol. I, ff. 1r, 32r–38v, 185r–198r, 307r–308r, 316r–v.

was depopulated by the Thirty Years War on a scale without precedent (with the possible exception of the Black Death of 1349), there was no relapse into the older habits of compartmentalization and barter. When the demographic *primum mobile* reversed course at Ottobeuren, it did not pull the peasant economy back with it.

The Thirty Years War was a long time in coming to Ottobeuren.[10] Through the 1620s the monastery lands enjoyed a period of relative peace, marred only by forced war levies known as the "Contribution" and the occasional spectacle and inconvenience of armies passing through on their way to wreak havoc elsewhere.[11] As a punishment for having joined the anti-Habsburg Leipzig Bund, the nearby city of Memmingen was occupied by two companies of imperial musketeers in October of 1631, but the garrison was soon withdrawn. It was only in the spring of the following year that a permanent military presence was established in the region. Having defeated the imperial army on the Danube at Rain, Swedish troops moved up the valley of the river Lech, and then struck west to occupy Memmingen on 16 April 1632.

Their imperialist opponents retained bases at Lindau on Lake Constance, in the Vorarlberg and in the Tyrol, and a three-year see-saw struggle for control of Upper Swabia ensued. The imperialist general Aldringer recaptured Memmingen in January of 1633; the two regiments he left behind were then overwhelmed by the Swedes in April of 1634. The tables were turned again in November after Spanish and Bavarian forces destroyed the main Swedish field army across the Danube at the battle of Nördlingen. The Swedes were driven out of Upper Swabia, the Memmingen garrison holding out until 24 June 1635.

The years after 1635 were calmer.[12] The problems associated with war taxation and armies in transit remained, but the only actual fighting in the area of the monastery lands was confined to a single peculiar incident in 1647. In March the Duke of Bavaria signed a truce with the Swedes and turned over the city of Memmingen to them. Six months later the Duke changed his mind and again cast in his lot with the Habsburg emperor. Bavarian and imperial forces encircled Memmingen, battered it with artillery fire for nine weeks, and forced the Swedish garrison to surrender on 23 November. The signing of the Peace of Westphalia found Memmingen still in imperial hands; the occupying

---

[10] Unless otherwise indicated, the narrative of the war years at Ottobeuren is based on Baumann, *Allgäu*, Vol. III, pp. 166–208.

[11] In 1628, the bond-chicken payments from the village of Niederrieden were confiscated by unnamed cavalrymen. A similar incident was reported from Westerheim in 1631. StAA, KL Ottobeuren 491-III, Heft 33; KL Ottobeuren 583, Heft 54, ff. 4v–5r.

[12] This is not to say that they were peaceful. Jacob Dodel of Frechenrieden was murdered in the woods near Moosbach by a group of imperial and Bavarian cavalrymen on 14 January 1644. On 1 December 1647 Jacob Zettler of Eggisried was found lying in the road, murdered by unidentified soldiers. HawPR, Vol. I (Burials), pp. 2, 4.

force remained in the city until it was formally demobilized on 25 September 1649.[13]

Although most of the destruction was concentrated in a seemingly brief spasm of three years, the war was an unmitigated catastrophe for the monastery lands. No front lines demarcated opposing zones of control in the 1630s. The rival armies based themselves in widely separated fortified cities and then disputed the intervening countryside by raiding. Small bands of mercenary soldiers roamed the rural areas, occasionally clashing with enemy patrols, but more often plundering the hapless peasantry.[14] Periodically a major offensive would be undertaken to reduce an enemy strongpoint, and successful campaigns were typically celebrated by subjecting the newly conquered territory to an orgy of violence.

On 3 June 1632 King Gustavus Adolphus of Sweden arrived in recently occupied Memmingen at the head of 12,000 men. The troops were charged with clearing the countryside south to the Alps of imperial outposts, a task which they accomplished with singular dispatch. They also butchered eight peasants in and around the Ottobeuren village of Egg[15] and then disemboweled and tortured to death the parish priest in the neighboring village of Niederrieden.[16] When, two summers later, Memmingen again fell to the Swedes, the atrocities were repeated. Soldiers murdered twelve-year-old Felix Schweiggart in Unterwesterheim and Michael Dreier in the village of Günz.[17] Wealthy Hans Gebelin of Sontheim arranged for his stepson Michael Sanz to flee to Rufen in the Bavarian lordship of Mindelheim; Gebelin stayed behind and was shot by Swedish troops.[18] And then there is the following entry in the Westerheim parish register:

---

[13] See the diary of a member of the imperialist garrison of Memmingen in 1647–9. Jan Peters, ed. *Ein Söldnerleben im Dreißigjährigen Krieg* (Berlin, 1993). The only comment the author makes about the countryside (p. 186) is that "it is a fair and fertile land for grain-growing ... it has nice trout in its waters."

[14] All of these activities are nicely illustrated by the adventures of the imperialist musketeer Christoff Riendlich, who became separated from his companions when their regiment retreated from Memmingen in April of 1634. Riendlich took shelter near the village of Volkratshofen, but was promptly betrayed by a local peasant to a Swedish cavalry patrol, which confiscated Riendlich's horse and coat and left him to flee into the woods ("otherwise they would have shot him"). The musketeer next met up with a local teamster, who "was obliged to reach an accommodation with him regarding his possessions, and had to pay him 22 *Reichsthaler*." His fortunes restored, Riendlich then rejoined his unit in the city of Lindau. StAA, KA Ottobeuren 469, Letter of Lieutenant Johann Tibali in Lindau [27 Sep. 1634].

[15] EggPR, Vol. I, pp. 155–6. Eight deaths explicitly attributed to the *persecutione suedinis* between 6 June and 4 August 1632.

[16] Sontheimer, *Die Geistlichkeit des Kapitels Ottobeuren*, Vol. II, p. 293.

[17] WestPR, Vol. I, p. 124 [17 July 1634].

[18] StAA KL Ottobeuren 43, f. 60v [9 Mar. 1634]. Gebelin had married Michael's mother, widow of the *Hof* tenant Johann Sanz, and had a gross wealth of 1,175 fl. in 1627. StAA, KL Ottobeuren 905, ff. 115v–116r [26 Sep. 1613]; KL Ottobeuren 104, ff. 312v–313r.

July 6 [1634] my stepfather Jerg Lutzenberger was stripped by soldiers in the woods [and] in an inhuman and worse than barbarous manner was tortured in his secret parts and shockingly tormented, on 9 July he was [attacked] by a group of three [soldiers] in the mill in Westerheim, two stabbed him in the hands and one in the back; he died shortly thereafter.[19]

The mercenaries employed by the imperialists were no better behaved. Indeed, the bloodiest massacre in the region followed the sack of the city of Kempten by imperialist forces in January of 1633. In popular memory, however, the sufferings of 1632–5 would always be recalled as the "Swedish war." It was the Swedes, Father Stephan Mayer declared, who had bored through the miller's leg and roasted his wife in her own oven. It was the Swedes who had whipped five- and six-year-old children with sticks and dragged them around on ropes like dogs. And for all the ghastliness he had himself experienced, the priest's only comment on the crushing Swedish defeat at the battle of Nördlingen (6 September 1634) was "I wish that I had been there, too."[20] One way or another, the peasants continued to recount the massacres and desecrations of those unhappy years long after the guns had fallen silent and the wounds had scarred over. For some survivors the burden lay heavier than mere memory. Anna Hurter was raped by the soldiers in 1633. So shattering was the experience, the pastor of Hawangen noted at her death in 1657, "that for twenty-four years she had not one sane hour until suddenly she expired of the enduring malady."[21]

Repellant as their direct brutality was, the soldiers caused even greater loss of life by crippling the rural economy. Seventeenth-century armies of occupation fed themselves by extortion. The garrison commander simply decided how much food, money, and clothing his troops required and then commanded the local authorities to provide the same. In theory this was an orderly process. On 17 April 1632, for example, the monastery signed an accord with the victorious Swedish commander agreeing to make a weekly delivery of grain to the Memmingen garrison. "It did not, however, stop there," the monks noted, and the soldiers soon began asking for more. Now they required venison, fish, poultry, hay, wine, beer, "and vast sums of money." By the end of the year the troops had extorted over 16,000 *gulden* – more than half of the monastery's entire annual revenue.[22]

The Swedish occupation of 1634 was less ceremonious still. On 24 April the monastery lands were handed over as spoils of war to the Swedish Colonel

[19] WestPR, Vol. I, p. 125 [9 July 1634].
[20] UEPR, Vol. I, ff. 135r, 191v, 314r. These particular atrocities took place in July of 1635 in Unteregg and Frechenrieden respectively. The Swedish garrison of Memmingen had capitulated a few weeks earlier, but Mayer reports that the troops were not actually withdrawn until 3 August.
[21] HawPR, Vol. I (Burials), p. 9 [7 Apr. 1657].
[22] StAA, KL Ottobeuren (Mü.B.) 158b, ff. 46r–v; KL Ottobeuren 541, Heft 7.

Melchior Wurmbrand. The conquerors appointed an ersatz chancellor to administer their ill-gotten gains, stationed forty musketeers in the monastery complex, and began issuing demands. The peasants were ordered every month to deliver two to three hundred *malter* of grain and 115 *gulden* to the Swedish base at Kempten, plus additional deliveries to the Memmingen garrison. "You shall know," the Memmingen commandant advised on 16 August, "that in case of refusal I shall begin by burning down a [single] village, and will thus continue until the entire lordship of Ottobeuren has been burned to the ground."[23] Soldiers were then sent to monitor the threshing barns; the grain was impounded and carted off.

Organized confiscations were supplemented with randomized pillage. At least nine Ottobeuren villages were looted between May of 1634 and June of 1635. A single raid ended with sixty wagon-loads of booty hauled off from Günz and Rummeltshausen. Peasant livestock was unsafe either in the fields or on the village streets. A survey made in 1636 counted only 133 horses and 181 head of cattle in the monastery lands;[24] in 1620 the herds had numbered 2,094 and 6,607, respectively.[25] Battered again and again in this way, the economy collapsed. The peasants gave up tilling the fields and many took flight.

By the fall of 1634 the parish register in the village of Egg began recording deaths from starvation. In neighboring Westerheim food shortages were so acute that hunger claimed the lives of even the wealthy.[26] The depth of suffering may be judged from a report written to the exiled Abbot on 8 February 1635 by Father Jeremias Mayer, one of the last priests in the monastery lands who had not yet fled, succumbed, or been murdered:

> In our region most of the mills have been destroyed; hunger has reached the most extreme degree. Horseflesh, skinned cats and flayed dogs are now the customary delicacies of the pallid burghers; necessity also forces them not only to eat mice of all kinds, but also the moss from old trees, nettles, and grass like beasts, and other indigestible or utterly repulsive things. When recently Colonel von Wolkenstein's shabby and mangy donkey dropped, people pounced upon the carcass and eagerly wolfed it down.[27]

Finally, in June this apocalyptic visitation was completed with the arrival of the plague.

Along with virtually every other public function, record keeping broke down at Ottobeuren by the end of 1635, making it difficult to trace a complete picture of the mortality which followed this onslaught of hunger and sickness. For

---

[23] Feyerabend, *Ottenbeuren Jahrbücher*, Vol. III, pp. 410–15; the quoted passage p. 415.
[24] Ibid., pp. 414–23, 429.   [25] StAA KL Ottobeuren 102.
[26] Maria Magg and her two sons, Michael and Jerg, died of starvation on 19 and 28 June 1635 (WestPR, Vol. I, p. 110). Maria was the wife of a *Hof* tenant worth 1,255 *gulden* in 1620. StAA KL Ottobeuren 102, ff. 306v–307r; KL Ottobeuren 907, f. 206r [8 Dec. 1618].
[27] Feyerabend, *Ottenbeuren Jahrbücher*, Vol. III, p. 424.

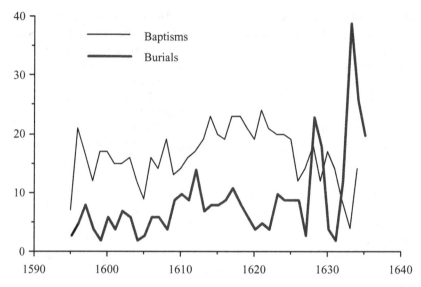

Figure 6.1 Baptisms and adult burials in Westerheim, 1595–1635
Source: Westerheim parish registers

two parishes, however, enough documentation has survived to allow at least a glimpse of the cost in lives of these two scourges, which far outweighed the killings directly committed by the soldiers. In now familiar Ober- and Unter-westerheim, a burial register was kept between 1595 and 1635. Since infant deaths were not recorded after 1625, Figure 6.1 is confined to a presentation of adult mortality in order to maintain consistency throughout the forty-year period. The graph illustrating both the impact of an earlier epidemic in 1628 and the still greater mortality six years later thus necessarily understates the overall toll. The parish registers in Egg (see Figure 6.2) begin only in 1617, but they cover a substantially larger parish and more importantly were maintained for longer. Whereas the Westerheim burial register breaks off in August of 1635 and thereby omits much of the most acute mortality during the fall and early winter of that year, the Egg register continues until 1640, by which point the worst of the dying had passed.

The scale of German population losses during the Thirty Years War has long been a matter of considerable controversy.[28] The Ottobeuren lands will not stand for all of Germany, but they do represent an extensive territory where solid documentation of truly grievous losses has survived. The evidence comes

---

[28] For recent surveys see John Theibault, "The Demography of the Thirty Years' War Revisited: Günther Franz and his Critics," *German History* 15, 1 (1997), pp. 1–21; Manfred Vasold, "Die deutschen Bevölkerungsverluste während des Dreißigjährigen Krieges," *Zeitschrift für Bayerische Landesgeschichte* 56 (1993), pp. 147–60.

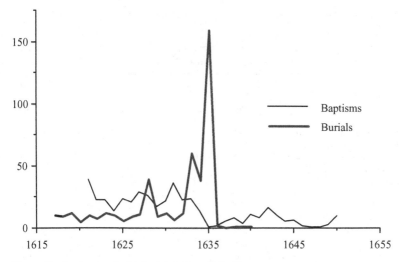

Figure 6.2 Baptisms and adult burials in Egg, 1617–50
Source: Egg parish registers

from the diocesan visitations of the Bishop of Augsburg, which record the number of communicants in every parish both before and after the war. As is clear from Table 6.1, the population seems to have fallen to a fifth of its former size.

Now, it must be said that much of this decline (as is often pointed out by critics of the catastrophic interpretation of the war) was less the result of death than of the mass flight of the peasantry. Indeed, a pathway for distress migration had already been established during the hyperinflation of 1622–3, when the combination of a harvest failure and currency debasement led to a sudden quadrupling of the price of grain.[29] During those years, the Ottobeuren poor left their villages in large numbers, heading for Austria or occasionally for Bohemia in search of work.[30] Some of the men came back richer, others returned to a still deeper poverty than that which they had fled, and most were never heard from again. Taken as a whole, however, the early 1620s provided a valuable learning experience for the Ottobeuren peasantry, and when the full horrors of war engulfed their homes ten years later they were able to organize an even more widescale migration.

Due to gaps in the archival record, the details of the later flight are fairly sketchy, but it is clear from depositions taken after the war that many of the

---

[29] Wolf, *Reichsstädte in Kriegszeiten*, p. 276.
[30] The clearest evidence of this pattern comes from the bond-chicken registers of 1623 and 1624, where the scribe has noted "in Austria," "in Bohemia," or simply "away" next to the names of almost fifty householders. StAA, KL Ottobeuren 491-III, Hefte 27 and 28.

Table 6.1 *Number of communicants in the Ottobeuren monastery lands, 1593–1707*

Parish	1593	1626	1636/42	1659	1675	1707
Attenhausen	170	250	*50*	110	120	200
Benningen	280	300	*60*	200	240	250
Böhen*ᵃ*	400	535	140	250	340	450
Egg	390	500	50	150	350	500
Frechenrieden	160	282	*60*	140	200	250
Günz	150	203	*40*	97	*190*	224
Hawangen	300	422	100	250	*325*	380
Niederrieden	180	230	*50*	132	180	300
Ottobeuren*ᵃ*	1200	1630	*335*	600	1300	1600
Sontheim	330	450	*90*	*205*	250	300
Ungerhausen	*160*	219	50	102	*130*	150
Westerheim	200	310	68	150	239	242
Wolfertschwenden	250	300	*60*	180	180	314
Total	4170	5631	*1153*	2566	4044	5160
Index (1626 = 100)	74.1	100	*20.5*	45.6	71.8	91.6

Notes: Figures in italics are estimates.
ᵃ Includes the hamlets in the vicinity.
Source: Sontheimer, *Die Geistlichkeit des Kapitels Ottobeuren*, Vols. II–IV

villagers packed up their families and again fled to the comparative safety of Habsburg Austria. Hans Zettler was living with his wife, Barbara, and two daughters in the village of Egg in the early 1630s; "thereafter because of the lamentable irruption of the war along with many others [he] left from here to Austria . . . but then after nine years together with his wife and children again returned to the lordship of Ottobeuren."[31] Travel was organized enough that at least some of the Abbot's subjects remained together in exile. While in Austria, for example, the orphaned Magdalena Winkler of Oberwesterheim met and married Jacob Maier from the town of Ottobeuren. The couple returned with several children to the monastery lands in 1637 or 1638.[32] The scale of the exodus is impossible to measure, but it must have been considerable, for by January of 1635 the Swedish occupiers had prohibited all further emigration.[33] And as soon as the Swedes themselves had gone, many of the peasants returned to their homes.

---

[31] Hans married Barbara Notz on 18 May 1624; the couple baptized daughters on 29 November 1625 and 20 January 1627 (EggPR, Vol. I, pp. 25–6, 31–2, 98). Also StAA, KL Ottobeuren 917, ff. 65r–66r [21 Feb. 1665].

[32] Magdalena Winkler was baptized on 21 September 1602; her mother and father were buried on 21 January 1628 and sometime between September and December 1629, respectively (WestPR, Vol. I, pp. 14, 120, 122). The details of her flight to Austria are contained in StAA, KL Ottobeuren 917-II, ff. 1r–2r [26 Jan. 1665].

[33] Feyerabend, *Ottenbeuren Jahrbücher*, Vol. III, p. 425.

Table 6.2 *Decline in population, tithes, and grain rents at Ottobeuren,*
1625–50

Settlement	Households			Average tithes (*malter*)			Grain rents (*malter*)		
	1627	1649	% decrease	1625–9	1649–50	% decrease	1631	1648	% decrease
Attenhausen	72	27	62.5	96.3	41.0	57.4	116.4	32.6	72.0
Böhen	55	15	72.7	45.7	27.5	39.8	24.9	7.7	69.1
Frechenrieden	88	34	61.4	78.8	35.9	54.4	88.2	30.1	65.9
Hawangen	124	51	58.9	155.2	119.1	23.3	175.7	71.2	59.5
Niederdorf	31	16	48.4	48.2	25.0	48.1	77.5	27.6	64.4
Ungerhausen	68	23	66.2	108.8	36.2	66.7	165.9	29.2	82.4
Total	438	166	62.1	533.0	284.7	46.6	648.6	198.4	69.5

Sources: StAA, KL Ottobeuren 40, 42, 47, 104, 160, 199

But even if many of the gaps recorded in 1642 would subsequently be filled
by returning refugees, the losses cannot *all* be explained away in this fashion.
A decade after the last of the soldiers had gone, the visitation of 1659 shows
that 54.4 percent of the pre-war population was still missing. Most of these
unfortunates must have perished. It was not until the eighteenth century that the
population of the monastery lands returned to the size it had been on the eve of
the Thirty Years War; as late as the 1707 visitation the losses had still not been
made good.

Despite the enormity of destruction during the 1630s, the process of recovery
began almost as soon as the Swedes had left. After the battle of Nördlingen,
Colonel Wurmbrand had the singular misfortune to fall into the hands of the
imperialists' dreaded Croatian cavalry. The Croats mockingly led him around
as the "Abbot of Ottobeuren" and after tiring of the game, the monastery chroniclers report with positive glee, cleaved his skull in two.[34] Freed from the burden
of military occupation, the Abbot returned from exile in Salzburg in the fall of
1635 with seed corn for the peasants. In 1636, a scribe noted hopefully in the
granary accounts that "this year in a few villages the subjects began to till
anew."[35] By 1643 the monastery's chancellery had returned to full-scale operation, drawing up rent rolls, compiling accounts, levying taxes, and maintaining
the notarial protocols.

Yet the obliteration of more than half of the Ottobeuren peasantry had consequences for the rural economy which the monks could not ignore. Agricultural
production had plummeted dramatically, dragging down with it the revenues of
the landlord. Table 6.2 compares average tithe receipts in 1625–9 with the collections in the same villages in 1649–50. The fall-off was considerable, on the
order of 47 percent. The monastery's grain rents suffered even more severely;

[34] Ibid., Vol. III, pp. 416–17.   [35] StAA, KL Ottobeuren 202, f. 103r.

between the last year of peace (1631) and the end of the war in 1648, the monks were obliged to pare back their *Korngült* takings by 70 percent.

The semblance of a restored equilibrium between population, production, and rent is quite deceiving, however, as the peasants were weighed down by an additional set of impositions collected without regard for their ability to pay: war taxes. After the end of the Swedish occupation, fighting continued in other theatres for another fourteen years, and the Duke of Bavaria expected Ottobeuren to help fund it. The monks struggled desperately to ward off these charges, alternately protesting and pleading with the court in Munich that their subjects simply could not afford the never-ending stream of quarterings and exactions, but almost invariably in vain.[36] Indeed, even after the Peace of Westphalia ended the Thirty Years War in 1648, Sweden's demand that its enormous military complement be paid off by the devastated German territories loaded yet another burden on to the backs of the Abbot's subjects. The extensive documentation which survives from this parting insult offers revealing insights into the politics and social impact of seventeenth-century war finance.

In January of 1649, the Holy Roman Empire's Swabian Circle, an association of the states of southwestern Germany, was assigned the responsibility of paying a three-month interim subvention to nine Swedish garrisons and the fourteen field regiments of General Robert Douglas, a Scottish soldier of fortune in the service of the Swedish crown. Of this enormous bill of some 460,000 *gulden* (to which would later be added an additional million *gulden* to complete the actual demobilization), over 12,000 fell to the Bishop of Augsburg. Although Ottobeuren was traditionally exempt from the fiscal obligations of the Swabian Circle, the episcopal vice-chancellor promptly reassigned some of Augsburg's cost to the monastery, even though the Imperial Chamber Court had in 1626 affirmed Ottobeuren's complete autonomy from the Bishop. Abbot Maurus objected vigorously, but was bluntly informed that if the money was not forthcoming, the troops would come and collect it themselves. "Under these conditions, and since force had the better part of justice," the cellarer and chancellor were dispatched to Augsburg, "and since there was no choice," they acceded to make a monthly payment of 500 fl. and support a company of Douglas' dragoons.[37]

In February of 1649, a second Swedish company arrived and in October came a third. Each time the monastery appealed to all sides for relief, but the harsh reality was that every authority was endeavoring to fob off the troops on someone else. And so,

> Since [even] after protracted altercations, no help was forthcoming on the part of the bishopric, and [since] there were no means to protect ourselves

---

[36] The surviving correspondence from 1639–48 is preserved in StAA, KL Ottobeuren (Mü.B.) 158b, ff. 49v–177r.

[37] Ibid., ff. 178r–181r; the quoted passages on f. 180v.

from force, since the soldiers encamped around Ottobeuren demanded to be paid from here, we were in the end obliged to submit to these outrages, and indeed above all so that the threat of violence might be averted.[38]

One company (roughly one hundred strong) was quartered in the market town of Ottobeuren; the other troops seem to have been lodged in the villages. The soldiers ate, drank, fraternized with the local women,[39] and over nine and a half months squeezed some 5,300 *gulden* from the peasantry, a tax rate equal to the monastery's pre-war tax burden, but taken from a population less than half the size.[40] By the spring of 1650, monthly war tax collections had fallen by almost two thirds over the previous year. The economy had been bled dry.

Even after the soldiers had left for good, the system of wartime taxation bequeathed a poisonous legacy to the monks' effort to re-establish the edifice of their original lordship. Forced by the incessant demands of the soldiers into a rapid solution to the administrative chaos of the 1630s, monastery officials had been unable to carry out the kinds of careful tax surveys which had previously been the norm. During the 1620s the chancellery had drawn up a detailed valuation of the assets of each household every three years.[41] These surveys evaluated real property on the basis of measured area, land use, and tenurial status, in addition to listing the livestock and deducting the debts of each taxpayer. There was no time for these niceties with the troops banging on the door for money. Debts and landholdings were therefore ignored altogether. War taxes were instead collected in the form of a flat payment of 15 *kreuzer* from each house, with the remainder (and overwhelming brunt) of the imposition falling on more easily enumerable horses and cattle.[42] Since land rather than livestock was the real foundation of a peasant's wealth, a disproportionate burden was thereby imposed on the rural poor. A few modifications were made when peace returned, but this crude and regressive system of assessment remained intact in its essentials well into the 1660s.[43]

The infelicities of taxation were compounded by the monastery's hastiness in restoring its claims as a landlord. By 1657 rents had been raised to their pre-war levels,[44] and the total arrears of the subject population had correspondingly swelled to fully two and a half times what they had been in 1628.[45] And although

---

[38] Ibid., ff. 181r–187r; the quoted passage on f. 187r.

[39] See the birth of a daughter to Veronica Kimerlin of Hawangen and Leonhardt Spiegelberger of Lindau 'quartered [here] from the Regiment Jourdan.' HawPR, Vol. I, f. 101r [31 Oct. 1649].

[40] StAA, KL Ottobeuren 160, ff. 95r–102r and 127r; KL Ottobeuren 541, Heft 7.

[41] Tax surveys from 1620/1, 1624, and 1627 are preserved in StAA, KL Ottobeuren 102–4. Post-war records document the existence of a 1630 tax survey, but this manuscript seems to have since been lost.

[42] Assessment schedule in StAA, KL Ottobeuren 160, f. 95r.

[43] The registers for 1660 and 1667 do tax land via an assessment for "seed," but the bulk of taxation continued to be collected from livestock. StAA, KL Ottobeuren 106, 107.

[44] This is clear from a comparison of StAA, KL Ottobeuren 42 and KL Ottobeuren 56.

[45] StAA, KL Ottobeuren 573 and KL Ottobeuren 387.

grain production seems to have returned to pre-war levels by the early 1670s, the renewed squeeze of the landlord was nevertheless too tight. After a short run of bountiful collections, the monastery's annual tax receipts fell by almost half between 1665 and 1671.[46] It became obvious to the monks not only that they had overburdened their subjects, but also that they had done so out of a profound ignorance of the economic reality in the villages.

There must have been at least some temptation to wipe the slate clean and redraw the map altogether, but this option was never given serious consideration. Over time, the myriad units of peasant property – house-lots, gardens, tenant farms, freestanding parcels of arable and meadow, etc. – had accrued identities of their own that the monks were loath to extinguish. This was not a matter of some sacral inviolability of the physical plot itself. Even before the war, the monastery was perfectly willing to countenance the conversion of meadowland to arable,[47] the exchange of tenurial status among comparably sized pieces of land,[48] and the extinction[49] and (less commonly) the creation of house-lots. Rather more important was each property's individual history as a means of income, object of inheritance, security for debt, or (not least of all) source of rent. Even if so many of the original owners or debtors or creditors themselves had died, as far as the monastery was concerned, the rights and obligations anchored in these properties had not. The monks therefore resolved to unravel and adjudicate the tangled skein of claims and counterclaims, and by choosing (by no means disinterestedly) to respect pre-war property rights, they contributed powerfully to the preservation of the pre-war structure of rural society.

Essential to the success of the monastery's project was the collection of more and better information about the peasantry. This was, of course, a stock recommendation of later seventeenth-century German cameralist literature,[50] but

---

[46] StAA, KL Ottobeuren 337–8.

[47] StAA, KL Ottobeuren 903, ff. 334r–v [24 July 1607]; KL Ottobeuren 904, ff. 207v–208r [21 July 1610].

[48] There are eight such exchanges between June 1619 and November 1620 in StAA, KL Ottobeuren 908 alone. The most common arrangement was the exchange of a freehold and a *Herrengut* arable parcel and transfer of tenurial status between the parcels, occasionally accompanied by a change in land use.

[49] StAA, KL Ottobeuren 904, f. 117r [9 Mar. 1609]. By the first contract Jerg Knaus of Ottobeuren purchased a house-lot from Balthas Negelin for 19 fl.; by the second Negelin foreswore for himself and his heirs any future claim of *Hofstattrecht* in the parcel, now converted to a garden.

[50] In 1656, for example, von Seckendorf advised princes to compile "Land-Charta," "Special-Tabellen" for each district totaling the number of hearths, mills, and breweries, censuses of the population by occupational category, and tax registers evaluating property and applying proportional taxes. The 1665 "Additiones" to this influential book append recommendations on resurveying land and renovating rent rolls. Veit Ludwig von Seckendorf, *Teutscher Fürsten-Staat*, 3rd edn (1665), 1.II–IV, 3.III.§8.3; reprint (Glashütten im Taunus, 1976), Vol. I, pp. 40–55, 495–500. For general overviews see Michael Stolleis, *Pecunia nervus rerum: zur Staatsfinanzierung in der frühen Neuzeit* (Frankfurt, 1983) and Wolfgang Weber, *Prudentia gubernatoria: Studien zur Herrschaftslehre in der deutschen politischen Wissenschaft des 17. Jahrhunderts* (Tübingen, 1992).

the campaign to heighten scrutiny of the economic activities of the Ottobeuren peasantry is for that reason no less impressive. In 1669 the monks commissioned a new tax survey which not only returned to the pre-war pattern of measuring land and deducting debt from taxable wealth, but also reconstructed the genealogy of each household's property on the basis of systematic comparison with a 1630 tax survey.[51] The new assessment brought significant relief to the hard-pressed peasantry. In the village of Böhen, for example, the average household's tax bill was reduced by 20 percent between 1667 and 1674, with the wealthier half of the village seeing a 10 percent reduction and the poorer half a 30 percent reduction.[52] All of this was followed up by a painfully detailed resurvey of every single piece of land in the Abbot's dominions. Completion of this new cadastre consumed four and a half years (from December 1679 to June 1684) and some 1,390 *gulden* in payments to the surveyors, but in the end the monks possessed a survey and valuation of almost 28,000 *jauchert* (i.e. almost 12,000 hectares) of land measured down to 1/520th of a *jauchert*.[53]

The cadastre was only the beginning. Where they had previously only kept track of the nominal grain rent owed by each holding and the monastery's total receipts, the monks now also began recording annual grain rent payments farm by farm,[54] keeping a separate set of books on grain rent arrears,[55] a third on annual tax payments household by household,[56] and a fourth on tax and other monetary arrears.[57] They followed alcohol sales in village taverns,[58] and in Ottobeuren parish went so far as to record the seed corn sown and subsequent tithe paid by each and every household.[59]

Hand-in-hand with the drive to take the measure of the land and its fruits went an effort to resolve the problem of peasant debt. Though dominated by the concerns of lordly rent and tax collection, the debt problem had a much broader public dimension. The Swedish invasion of 1632 and ensuing famine and plague had drastically disrupted the flow of interest payments from peasant borrowers on whom ecclesiastical and charitable foundations as well as orphans, wards, and widows had come to depend.[60] Thus, in December of 1643, when the monastery settled the estate of the Hawangen *Bauer* Jerg Heuss (died *c*. 1635), the Abbot's own claims made up only a third of the total outstanding debt of 682 fl. 53 kr. Heuss' other creditors included the chapel of Our Blessed Lady in Eldern, two charitable foundations in the city of Memmingen, the Hawangen

---

[51] StAA, KL Ottobeuren 105.
[52] StAA, KL Ottobeuren 107, ff. 61v–65v and KL Ottobeuren 68, ff. 70r–71r.
[53] Final reckoning in StAA, KL Ottobeuren 344.
[54] StAA, KL Ottobeuren 48–52.   [55] StAA, KL Ottobeuren 54, 239–47.
[56] StAA, KL Ottobeuren 65–99.   [57] StAA, KL Ottobeuren 388–99.
[58] StAA, KL Ottobeuren 486–90.   [59] StAA, KL Ottobeuren 682–5.
[60] Illustrative examples are StAA, KL Ottobeuren (Mü.B) 225, "Gandtgericht über Niclaß Grotz und Ursula Albrechtin beede Ehegemächten seel. zu Ottenbeuren" [21 July 1636] and "Michael Nehers zu Underwolfarthschwenden Schuldt beschreibung" [25 Aug. 1642].

miller (who had sold Heuss a horse and a load of lumber for 35 fl.), the *Bauer* Hans Weissenhorn (who was owed 38 fl. from money borrowed to build a house), another villager, Hans Sendler (whose orphaned brother's guardians had loaned Heuss 50 fl.),[61] and Heuss' brother-in-law Hans Schütz, who for the past eight years had been responsible for the care of Heuss' orphaned son.[62]

The chapels and foundations were not about to collapse for lack of repayment, but Heuss' neighbors were in rather more pressing need. Some of them ultimately suffered a great deal, for although Heuss had once been a *Hof* tenant with more than a thousand *gulden* of property to his name,[63] by 1643 his estate consisted of no more than a garden and a few patches of land worth less than a tenth of this sum. As a result, most of those clamoring for payment went away empty-handed. Heuss' son soon disappeared from the parish, and Hans Sendler – the man whose wife had lost her mind to rape trauma in 1633 – saw the modicum of prosperity he had acquired in the immediate aftermath of the war[64] slowly slip from his fingers. Sendler lost his farm in 1659,[65] died a cottager in 1670,[66] and left a son to toil in poverty[67] and three grandchildren to struggle in squalor and infamy on the social fringe of a village where the family had lived for two hundred years.[68]

---

[61] StAA, KL Ottobeuren 911, f. 268 [3 Nov. 1632].

[62] StAA, KL Ottobeuren (Mü.B) 225, "Jörgen Heiß Maÿrs zu Hawangen Schuldtbeschreibung und abhandlung" [18 Dec. 1643]. Schütz was seeking payment for only six of the eight years. The boy in question was almost certainly Jerg Heuss, who was christened on 10 December 1630 and confirmed on 7 May 1640. HawPR, Vol. I, ff. 55r, 82r.

[63] He had been admitted to his father's *Hof* on 5 October 1615 and in 1627 declared assets of 1,190 fl. StAA, KL Ottobeuren 905, f. 299v and KL Ottobeuren 104, f. 194v.

[64] Johann Sendler had married on 6 July 1625 and in 1627 held a house, 3 *jauchert* of arable land, 1.5 *tagwerk* of meadow, and two cows for a total gross wealth of 570 fl. HawPR, Vol. I, f. 19v; StAA, KL Ottobeuren 104, f. 180r. He became tenant of a small (29.25 *jauchert*) *Gotteshausrecht* holding in 1637. KL Ottobeuren 202, ff. 65r–67r, 103r–v; cf. also the Hawangen sections of KL Ottobeuren 435 (unfoliated), KL Ottobeuren 338 [3 Mar. 1672], and KL Ottobeuren 109, f. 158v.

[65] StAA, KL Ottobeuren 335 [18 Sep. 1659].

[66] His burial was unrecorded, but he is listed in the 1669 tax survey (now holding only 4.75 *jauchert* of arable land) and his widow remarried on 22 January 1671. StAA, KL Ottobeuren 105, ff. 165r–188r. HawPR Vol. I, f. 43v and Vol. II, f. 1v.

[67] Johann's son, Johann Sendler junior, was the poorest householder in the village in the 1674 tax register. In 1689 he held only a house and garden and neither land nor livestock. He died on 13 June 1691. StAA, KL Ottobeuren 68, ff. 20r–23r; KL Ottobeuren 109, f. 170v. HawPR, Vol. I, ff. 44r, 94r and Vol. II, p. 19.

[68] Johann Sendler junior had three children. Anna (bapt. 6 May 1666) was impregnated in 1696 by a young man from Gottenau while working as a servant in Memmingen. The couple were subjected to public humiliation and banished from the monastery lands, but before leaving did baptize a second child in Hawangen on 22 July 1699. Sabina (bapt. 23 June 1671) also became pre-maritally pregnant by one Karl Gantner ("he owns nothing at all, [and] she very little," the protocol drily remarks) in 1700, and was similarly humiliated and banished, but the couple married (19 February 1700) and managed to stay on as propertyless lodgers with her brother. Gantner found work as the village cowherd, but the couple's situation was always precarious – at the baptisms of their children the parents are routinely described as '[resident] for the time

It is difficult to get a sense of the average creditor's chances of repayment under these circumstances. Perhaps the clearest available picture of the complexities of process and the vagaries of outcome comes from a lawsuit filed against sixty different Ottobeuren peasants in 1655. The plaintiffs were a series of Memmingen charitable foundations (*Pflegschaften*), which were in a somewhat stronger position than a typical small-scale claimant (the loans in question averaged 28 fl.), as they had the support of the city government behind them. The monastery was also willing to help, at least in principle.[69] The peasants themselves, however, were rather less co-operative. There was already a public debate in Germany over the morality of demanding interest payments missed during the war,[70] and the investigators dispatched to track down those on whom the obligations had descended encountered a great deal of evasion.

In the village of Hawangen, for example, Hans Schweickhart did remember that as a small boy, he used to take his father's interest payment from a parcel of arable to the house of Hanns Wiest, who was responsible for the other half of the loan, originally made by the Memmingen leprosarium in 1468. Schweickhart added, however, that his father had owned two different arable parcels, one of which was later sold to a certain Jacob Zick, later passing to one Melchior Schütz, and it was this latter parcel, Schweickhart confidently assured the investigators, rather than any land which he now owned, which was the security for the loan in question. In the hamlet of Hüners, where the same leprosarium had made another loan in 1510, the local headman, Michael Algeyer, was similarly unhelpful. The security in question had belonged to his brother, not himself. The brother had left for Italy some twenty years ago and never returned, and if Michael himself would admit to having used some of the meadow for haymaking, he nevertheless refused to pay anything, emphasizing that he had at his own expense maintained the property's farmhouse, which otherwise would long since have gone to ruin. In several cases, the mortgaged houses and fields had been abandoned, and now lay in ruins or were covered with

being in Hawangen' – and they both died young on 12 and 24 April 1710. The youngest child, Johann (bapt. 6 July 1674), was apprenticed as a mason. He married in 1701 and again on 14 May 1714. According to a 1708 tax register, he owned only a house, but no land or livestock. StAA, KL Ottobeuren 921, ff. 201v–202r [16 Aug. 1696]. KL Ottobeuren 922, ff. 3v–4r [9 Jan. 1698] and 190r–v [14 Jan. 1700]. KL Ottobeuren 146, f. 81v. Hawangen Baptismal Register [hereinafter HawBaR], Vol. I, f. 121v and Vol. II, ff. 3v, 5v, 29r, 31v, 34r, 36r, 40v, 127r. Hawangen Burial Register [hereinafter HawBuR], Vol. II, p. 42. Hawangen Marriage Register [hereinafter HawMR], Vol. II, ff. 7v, 13r. The Sendlers are listed continuously in Hawangen at least as far back as the tax register of 1525.

[69] In some cases the monastery was clearly obstructionist. See, for example, StAA, KL Ottobeuren (Mü.B.) 225, Administrators of the Große Spende to the mayor and council of Memmingen, undated (c. 28 Nov. 1657).

[70] For example, Kaspar Manz, *Zinss Scharmützel, das ist, Ein gefährlicher doch täglicher stritt zwischen den Glaubigern und Schuldtnern: ob man bey disen laidigen Kriegszeiten . . . schuldig sey die Zinss zubezahlen oder nit?* (Augsburg, 1645).

weeds. In others it turned out that the properties had already been foreclosed and sold off at auction, and no representative of the *Pflegschaften* had attended the proceedings. Finally, many peasants simply insisted that they knew nothing about either the debtors or the properties under investigation.[71]

Even when information was reasonably complete, however, it might still be the case that there just wasn't enough capital value to cover all of the claims. "So it happens," the Abbot explained to the *Pflegschaften* administrators, "that both the monastery as well as the other creditors have to suffer losses, because property has fallen [in value], and it is not possible to realize enough [from foreclosure sales] to pay off all of the debts."[72] Thus in the hamlet of Hofs, investigators traced the property of three pre-war debtors to Caspar Beir and Mathias Rauch. Beir was the son of a poor cottager from Ungerhausen,[73] who had moved to Hofs in 1646 and purchased two properties for a total of 168 fl. in a foreclosure auction three years later. Claims against the bankrupt estates by the Abbot alone had exceeded 200 fl., and the result noted on the protocol was blunt: "The monastery lost a great deal here; Memmingen will not be paid."[74] Mathias Rauch's story was essentially the same. He and his wife had moved to the hamlet from the village of Sontheim[75] in the hope of making a better life for themselves. On 14 November 1641, they had offered 112 fl. for a foreclosed holding of 18 *jauchert* of land, against whose previous (and now deceased) owner the monastery's claims exceeded 300 fl. The monastery had had to write off almost 200 fl. in debt; regarding the Memmingen chapel's demand of 57 fl. the court scribe tersely noted, "I do not see a solution."[76] Beir and Rauch were absolved of any responsibility to the *Pflegschaften*. In the end, the Memmingen foundations seem to have recovered money from only about 40 percent of their outstanding loans (see Figure 6.3).

---

[71] StAA, KL Ottobeuren (Mü.B.) 225, Protocol [7 June 1655] and "Auff Memingische Schuldford. Anwort" [28 Nov. 1657].

[72] Ibid., Abbot Peter of Ottobeuren to the "Lords in Memmingen" (draft) [10 Aug. 1657]. The Abbot rejected out of hand the suggestion that he assume responsibility for these debts, which were the personal obligations of the peasants. The Memmingen authorities, he shrewdly pointed out, would not accept that the debts of their own subjects to the monastery be repaid from the revenues or properties of the city.

[73] According to OttLSA 1687, p. 52 (Household No. 245) Caspar was born in Ungerhausen in 1616. The only Beir in that village in the tax survey of 1620 was one Hans Beir, who owned a house, two cows, and 3 *jauchert* of *Herrengut* land to which he had been admitted on 14 December 1617. His gross wealth was 210 fl. and his debts totaled 50 fl. StAA, KL Ottobeuren 102, f. 237r and KL Ottobeuren 907, f. 128v.

[74] StAA, KL Ottobeuren (Mü.B) 225, untitled register [20 Dec. 1656] and undated revision of the same give the sale date as 6 April 1649. An earlier protocol of 7 June 1655 notes (f. 5v) that the previous owner's estate was settled on 6 April 1644, "but no one from Memmingen showed up." See also the relevant sections of KL Ottobeuren 435.

[75] See the sale (1641) of the half-house the couple had inherited from her father in StAA, KL Ottobeuren 911, f. 394.

[76] StAA, KL Ottobeuren (Mü.B) 225, untitled register [20 Dec. 1656] and revised copy of the same (undated).

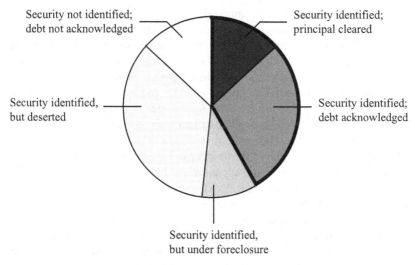

Security not identified;
debt not acknowledged

Security identified;
principal cleared

Security identified,
but deserted

Security identified;
debt acknowledged

Security identified,
but under foreclosure

Figure 6.3 Outcome of 60 *Pflegschaften* debt cases, 1657
Source: StAA, KL Ottobeuren (Mü.B.) 225

For all the complaints of the Memmingen administrators, it must be emphasized that the widespread disappointment of creditors by no means implied a
mass amnesty for debtors. Even with the write-off of a great many peasant
debts, the rural population was now so reduced in numbers that there were
enough surviving pre-war obligations to burden the vast majority of the survivors. Caspar Beir and Mathias Rauch of Hofs did both go on to prosper,[77]
but their obligations to the monastery from their holdings remained in force
for the rest of their lives.[78] Furthermore, the monastery's enormously enhanced
powers to collect and analyze information now made it much more difficult for
a peasant to hide.

For its part, the monastery was forced to confront the same awkward fact
that it had presented to the Memmingen foundations: despite the legality of
the outstanding claims, the accumulated debts simply exceeded the value of
the peasantry's property. By law the monastery could of course foreclose on
an insolvent debtor and have his property sold. This was unlikely to yield a
satsifactory result, however, since the price of land had fallen drastically in the

[77] In 1674 Caspar Beir was the third and Mathias Rauch the fifth richest of thirty-three households
in the *Hauptmannschaft*. Rauch sold his lands for 820 fl. to his son Michael on 18 August 1678;
Michael held 28 *jauchert* of land and had a gross wealth of 731 fl. in 1689. Beir sold his property
to his son Jerg for 500 fl. on 10 June 1683. In 1689 Jerg Beir owned property worth 1,238 fl.,
including 44 *jauchert* of land, and had no debts at all. StAA, KL Ottobeuren 68, ff. 56r–57v; KL
Ottobeuren 341 (Vergunstgeld); KL Ottobeuren 920, ff. 160r–v; KL Ottobeuren 109, ff. 517r–v,
519r.
[78] StAA, KL Ottobeuren 56, ff. 44v–46v.

wake of the war. In the end, the monks decided that the most fruitful course of action was to leave the sitting tenant in place and negotiate. Debtor and creditor agreed that a certain portion of the debt would be written off, and that the rest would be repaid on a more lenient schedule. Only in hopeless cases would resort be had to foreclosure, and even then the negotiating process was not so much avoided as relocated. The properties were sold at public auctions, where both buyer and seller had to be careful not to offer or to ask either too much or too little. In other words, the debt problem ultimately committed both ruler and ruled not merely to a systematic restatement of property rights but also to a thoroughgoing negotiation of the productive limits of the rural economy.[79]

The resultant challenge to the appraisal and business skills of the peasants and their overlord is perhaps best illustrated by the fate of the inn in the village of Böhen. The property had been inherited in 1626 by a certain Mathias Hafenmaier,[80] who was ruined by the war.[81] After 1632 he became unable to pay his obligations, which included debts to the monastery, to religious foundations, and to other peasants who had advanced him both money and victuals. Although his creditors were willing to be patient, Hafenmaier's indebtedness drove him to despondency,[82] and in September of 1637 he surrendered the inn and its lands to the monastery with the request that they be sold off. A *Gantgericht*, or bankruptcy court, was accordingly convened, and on 23 September 1637, Hafenmaier's debts were officially totaled at 1,726 *gulden* 25 *kreuzer* 1 *heller*, almost two thirds of which was owed to the monastery. Due to wartime instability, however, it proved impossible to find a buyer, and at Hafenmaier's death in 1650,[83] the deserted inn and its lands remained in a sort of legal limbo, exploited on short-term leases by various tenants, but deteriorating all the while.

In July of 1663, the monastery decided to bring an end to the problem, and placed the property, valued at 1,200 *gulden*, on the auction block. It drew a single bid of 500 *gulden* from a brewmaster's servant. One week later a second appeal for bids was made, and 510 *gulden* were offered by the widow Anna

---

[79] This latter element corresponds to the shift David Sabean has described in the tenor of German lordship from the problem of upholding the state's rights of access to peasant property to the problem of raising levels of production and expropriation. David Warren Sabean, *Power in the Blood: Popular Culture and Village Discourse in Early Modern Germany* (Cambridge, 1984), pp. 202–3.

[80] StAA, KL Ottobeuren 909, ff. 138r–139r [10 Mar. 1626]. In 1627 Mathias Hafenmaier declared assets worth 2,920 fl. but debts of 2,114 fl. KL Ottobeuren 104, ff. 102r–v.

[81] The documents for what follows are bundled in StAA, KA Ottobeuren 42.

[82] Judging by the following passage from the bankruptcy court protocol: "The creditors are of one mind that they do not wish to evict the couple, or [even] desire this bankruptcy trial, but would rather wait for their payment, when and as soon under the current times and circumstances it shall be possible. Hafenmaier again requests that the bankruptcy trial continue, because he does not believe that he shall otherwise come away from [his debts]." Ibid. [23 Sep. 1637].

[83] On 7 August 1650 Hafenmaier's widow agreed to pay the Abbot 200 *gulden* as her share of the debts on the inn. Ibid., Extract from the *Verhörprotokolle* [4 and 7 Aug. 1650].

Maria Hipp, whose husband Martin Breg had previously leased the inn for a few years.[84] On 12 August the final auction was held. The brewmaster's servant raised his offer to 520, but was promptly outbid by the Memmingen butcher Michael Klaiber, who in the name of the widow Hipp's daughter Maria Bräg offered 700 *gulden*. No one else entered a bid, but either in order to overawe potential competitors or to appease the monastery, Klaiber proceeded to bid 720 and then 725 *gulden*. The offer was accepted.[85]

The sale of the inn to Maria Bräg must be seen as both a compromise and a calculated risk on all sides. The purchase price still fell far short of the monastery's outstanding claim of 1,100 *gulden* from 1637, but after watching the property lie abandoned for twenty-six years the monks had decided that it was time to cut their losses. The best prospect for the recovery of their claim lay with the success of a new tenant, and to that end the Abbot was prepared not only to waive the entry fine and reduce the rent, but also to pour more than 500 *gulden* into rebuilding the premises.[86] Maria Bräg, for her part, paid only 150 of the 725 *gulden* purchase price,[87] but hoped that with the help of her fiancé, Georg Rauch, the inn could be run profitably enough to clear the rest of the debt. The butcher Klaiber was much more than a disinterested representative; he went on to invest a loan of several hundred *gulden* (at 5 percent interest per annum, naturally) in the couple's future.[88] The new innkeeper's family had a similar stake in the success of the enterprise. Georg Rauch's stepfather loaned him over 400 *gulden* to rebuild the inn and to purchase livestock and supplies.[89]

Heavy the disappointment must have been when the new innkeeper of Böhen turned out to be a wastrel. After his wife's initial contribution of 150 *gulden*, Rauch made no further payments against the purchase price, and within a year he was behind in his rent. Over the next five years he borrowed still more from family, friends, and overlord while his taxes and interest obligations remained unpaid. Finally, in the winter of 1668 the scoundrel simply ran off, leaving his wife to face the anger of their creditors by herself.[90]

On 28 January 1669 the inn and its lands were again placed upon the auction block. Offers began at 500 *gulden*, and then rapidly jumped to 600, to 820,

---

[84] Breg is recorded as having made excise payments for alcohol sold at the inn in 1656 and 1657. StAA, KL Ottobeuren 486. See also KL Ottobeuren 916, f. 29r [24 Mar. 1661], where Breg is described as the Böhen innkeeper. Note also that the 1657 rent roll still lists Mathias Hafenmaier as the legal owner of the inn. KL Ottobeuren 56, ff. 153r, 154r–158r, 161r, 162v.

[85] StAA, KA Ottobeuren 42, three separate "Auction Reports."

[86] Ibid., "Account for the building of the inn in Böhen" [3 May 1663].

[87] Ibid., Extract from the *Verhörprotokolle* [16 Aug. 1663].

[88] Detailed in the document cited below at note 90. The account cited above at note 86 reveals that Klaiber also sold the couple two horses for the exorbitant prices of 30 and 40 *gulden*.

[89] Ibid., "Account of Hans Betschin *Maier* of Benningen regarding the inn in Böhen" [30 Apr. 1666].

[90] Ibid., "Jerg Rauch innkeeper of Böhen's debts to the Cellary" [30 Nov. 1668] and "Debts of the young innkeeperess in Böhen" [7 Dec. 1668].

to 950, and then finally to 1,000 *gulden*. But despite the appearances of enthusiasm, the bids were advanced with careful reservations. Peter Riegg of Böhen,
for example, made his last offer of 950 *gulden* on condition that he be allowed to
pursue the brewing of beer and the distilling of spirits, two particularly lucrative
trades. Were this not permitted, he cautioned, he reduced his bid to 660 *gulden*.
On 20 February the final session of the bankruptcy court was convened. Having
recently decided not to grant brewing and distilling privileges, the monastery
further reminded the court of its outstanding claim of 575 *gulden* in unpaid
debts. The effect was startling – every single offer was withdrawn. Some bid-
ders cited the refusal of the two privileges. Peter Riegg declared that "since
he has [now] taken notice of the debt burden, and has seen that it is a barren,
skimpy property, he completely recuses himself from [the auction] and has no
further intention of buying, because he does not believe that he could manage
it successfully." The perplexed officials asked what now to do, but in the words
of the protocol "the assembled creditors can suggest no other course of action,
only that the matter would have to depend upon a future buyer, when one should
present himself."[91]

Several weeks passed and still the property remained unsold. Finally it was
resolved to grasp the nettle. The Abbot accepted an offer by Peter Riegg to
lease – but not to purchase – the inn and its lands on a year to year basis for
an annual rent of 25 *gulden*.[92] Enraged creditors demanded that the monastery
compensate them for their losses, but they were bluntly turned away. Everyone
had lost money, the Abbot calmly explained, including himself. If the creditors
could find a buyer who would offer better terms, the Abbot would be happy to
co-operate. "Otherwise the negotiations over the property cannot be extended
any longer, since the interim tenant (who as such has no security of tenure) will
not dedicate his labor and effort to the clearing of the still overgrown parcels
and to the renewal of the cruelly impoverished and barren fields, but will only
exploit and further strip it bare."[93]

Shrewd Peter Riegg eventually did buy the Böhen inn in 1671 for 500
gulden[94] – less than half of what the monastery and the other creditors had
vainly insisted it was worth. Excise records (see Figure 6.4)[95] indicate that
he promptly shifted the inn's alcohol business from wine to more profitable

---

[91] Ibid., three separate "Auction Reports," *Gantgerichtprotcoll* [20 Feb. 1669].

[92] Ibid., extract from the *Verhörprotokolle* [9 Mar. 1669].

[93] Ibid., draft of a response by Abbot Peter to the Memmingen city council [24 Oct. 1670].

[94] StAA, KL Ottobeuren 338 (Vergunstgeld) [15 Jan. 1671].

[95] Figure 6.4 gives only an approximate idea of the inn's sale of alcohol (itself only a part of the inn's
business) because whereas the wine excise was collected in proportion to the volume and value
of the product sold, the excise on hard liquor was usually collected as a flat payment for each
quarter in which spirits were sold. As was customary throughout the monastery lands, the Böhen
inn was also attached to a large agricultural holding. Thus Hans Graf was far from unsuccessful;
in 1689 he owned over 2,000 fl. worth of property and in 1704 was easily the richest man in the
village. StAA, KL Ottobeuren 95, ff. 36r–v; KL Ottobeuren 109, ff. 357r–358r.

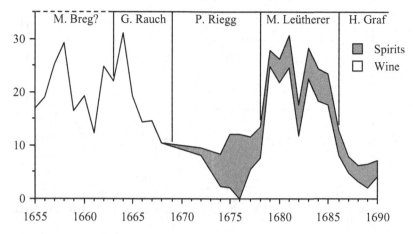

Figure 6.4 Alcohol excise receipts (fl.) of the Böhen inn, 1655–90
Sources: StAA, KL Ottobeuren 486–9

distilled spirits, and the next proprietor[96] was able to restore the tavern to a level of activity it had not seen in a generation. In 1687 the inn sold on the open market for 900 *gulden*,[97] almost doubling in value in sixteen years.

Though rarely so drawn out and dramatic, similar episodes were played out in almost every household in the village. In 1672 the monastery began an effort to achieve a comprehensive resolution of the debt problem. Over the next two years officials pored through the old accounts, totaled the arrears, and then traveled from settlement to settlement, negotiating manageable compromises with the peasants.[98] The result of this process in the village of Böhen is illustrated in Figure 6.5.

Three observations are in order here. First, there was hardly a household in the village which did not owe money to the monastery, and in several cases the debts amounted to half of the value of the household's property. Many of the arrears dated back to the 1640s and 1650s, often having been incurred and remaining unpaid by the previous tenant. Second, although the amounts forgiven usually represented only a small proportion of the total debt, most households in the village had at least some of their debt written off altogether.[99] Finally, Figure 6.5 gives an overly severe impression of the debt retirement process,

---

[96] It is not clear precisely when Michael Leütherer took over the inn; he paid the second half of his entry fine for the property on 25 April 1678; the accounts for the three previous years are defective. StAA, KL Ottobeuren 341 (Erdschatz); KL Ottobeuren 920, f. 322v [27 Feb. 1687].
[97] Ibid., ff. 347r–v [5 Dec. 1687].   [98] Details in StAA, KL Ottobeuren 548.
[99] Other arrangements were also negotiated. In 1673 the Abbot promised special consideration to Hans Dentzel of Benningen if the repayment schedule proved too difficult. In 1680 Dentzel complained that this was indeed the case and was granted a rent reduction for his mill until the debts were cleared. StAA. KL Ottobeuren 548, f. 5v [5 Dec. 1673] and KL Ottobeuren 919, ff. 128v–129r [21 Nov. 1680].

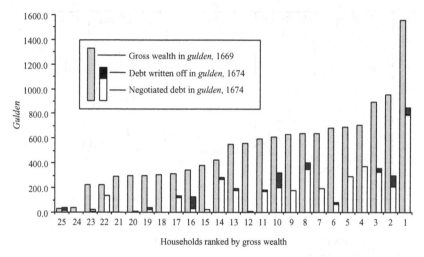

Figure 6.5 The burden of "old debts" in the village of Böhen, 1669–74
Sources: StAA KL Ottobeuren 56, 57 105, 548

because it does not show how the payments were spread out over time. The chronological dimension is better expressed in Figure 6.6, which plots repayments of 'old debts,' as the negotiated arrears were called, for the monastery lands as a whole. The negotiations of 1672–4 were followed by a second round in 1679,[100] and as is obvious, final repayment of these debts dragged on into the next century.

Given the provenance of the archival record, it is perhaps inevitable that the monastery should play such a prominent part in any account of the resurrection of the pre-war property regime at Ottobeuren. Yet as should by now be clear, for all their ledgers and registers, surveyors and court officials, the monks were in the end still forced to harmonize their pretensions with the tempo and cadences of peasant production. If, therefore, the later seventeenth-century social settlement represented the joint (if not necessarily the co-operative) effort of both overlord and subject, it behooves us to take a closer look at the internal dynamic of the villages. The most logical place to begin is the household.

Given the doubling of the rural population between *c.* 1660 and *c.* 1710 (see Table 6.1), we might be forgiven the expectation that rural society after the Peace of Westphalia should operate after the pattern of the boom decades of the early sixteenth century. It did not. Superficial similarities aside, household formation at post-war Ottobeuren was a profoundly altered process from what it had been one hundred years earlier. The most obvious difference was one of size. During the mid-sixteenth century the average size of the peasant household

[100] Details in StAA, KL Ottobeuren 549, which is a survey similar to the one from 1672–4.

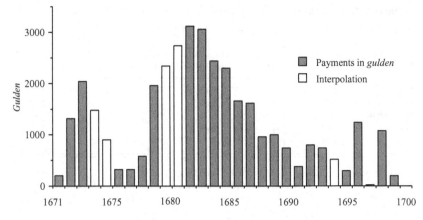

Figure 6.6   Repayment of "old debts" by the peasants of Ottobeuren, 1671–1700
Sources: StAA KL Ottobeuren 338–58

was 3.8 persons. By the early seventeenth century the household had grown to
an average size of 4.7 persons. This increase was an obvious consequence of
the changes discussed in the previous chapter, i.e., the imposition of a limit on
the number of households and the associated co-residence of retired parents and
married heirs in a single household. But since the household cap was a response
to what was seen as the overpopulation of the villages, the household should
have contracted in size with the precipitous decline of population density after
the Thirty Years War. In fact the reverse occurred. The late seventeenth-century
peasant household was not only larger than it had been in the mid-sixteenth
century, it even exceeded the size reached on the eve of the war.

Clear evidence for the increase in household size is contained in the diocesan
visitation of 1695. In three parishes the priest reported both the number of
communicants and the total parish population. These figures can be compared
with the number of households recorded in a tax register of the same year to
produce the figures in Table 6.3. For purposes of comparison, household size
in these same villages during the mid-sixteenth century has been estimated
on the basis of the 1548 serf book and 1546 tax register. Note that despite a
40 percent decrease in the overall number of households, the numbers within
the average household had increased by more than half.

What lay behind this considerable increase in the size of the rural household?
The best evidence for the explanation comes from Hawangen, where in 1707
the parish priest drew up a "Description of all of the Parishioners" for the entire
village.[101] In conjunction with a tax register from 1708,[102] the "Description"
allows a more precise description of household composition than is possible

---

[101] HawPR, Vol. II, ff. 124r–127v.   [102] StAA, KL Ottobeuren 99, ff. 12v–14v.

Table 6.3 *Household size in three Ottobeuren villages, 1546/8 and 1695*

Village	Population 1548	No. of households 1546	Household size 1546/8	Population 1695	No. of households 1695	Household size 1695
Egg	263	77	3.42	340	61	5.57
Frechenrieden	305	78	3.91	275	49	5.61
Hawangen[a]	548	136	4.03	400	60	6.67
Total	1116	291	3.84	1015	170	5.97
Index	*100*	*100*	*100*	*90.9*	*58.4*	*155.5*

Note: [a] Including the adjacent hamlets of Ober- and Untermoosbach
Sources: StAA, KL Ottobeuren 64, 88, 600; Sontheimer, *Die Geistlichkeit des Kapitels Ottobeuren*, Vols. II and IV

from the visitation reports alone. What it shows is that the explanation which most readily comes to mind – an increase in the birth rate – was not the cause. The number of children per *household* was indeed higher in 1707/8 (2.65) than in 1546/8 (2.17). The comparison is misleading, however, since by 1707/8 almost half (43.8 percent) of the households in Hawangen contained other residents, including retired parents, married and unmarried siblings, and poor villagers without homes of their own known as "indwellers," in addition to the householder's spouse and children. As a result, the number of children per *family*, here defined as a married couple or a widowed parent of ungrown children, had actually remained unchanged since 1546/8 (see Table 6.4).

Much more than any changes in the size of the householder's nuclear family, then, it was the presence of these "others" which made for the larger household of the late seventeenth and early eighteenth century. But the presence of related and unrelated co-residents is only part of the explanation, for a second important change had occurred in the composition of the peasant household since the 1540s: a huge increase in the number of servants. Whereas in the mid-sixteenth century servants had been an insignificant presence in Hawangen, by 1707 one in seven villagers was a servant (see Table 6.4).

The Hawangen servants ranged from 14 to 34 years of age, but almost all of them were between 18 and 30, with a mean age of 21.5 for men and 23.8 for women. They were, in other words, for the most part young people who were old enough to marry, but had not yet done so. Why weren't they married? This seems like a pointless question and yet it is worth recalling the conclusion of the previous chapter that in the early seventeenth century, the possibility of marriage depended upon the availability of an open "niche" among the fixed number of households in the village. This restriction was imposed on the grounds that the countryside was overpopulated and could not support any additional

Table 6.4 *Household composition in Hawangen, 1546/8 and 1707/8*

	1546/8^a		1707/8	
		Index		Index
Number of households	133	*100*	73	*54.9*
Population	529	*100*	435	*82.2*
Household size	3.98	*100*	5.96	*149.7*
Number of children	288	*100*	188	*65.3*
Number of families	126	*100*	83	*65.9*
Children per family	2.29	*100*	2.27	*99.1*
Families per household	0.95	*100*	1.14	*120.0*
Number of servants	7	*100*	64	*914.3*
Servants per household	0.05	*100*	0.88	*1760.0*
Servants as % of population	1.32	*100*	14.71	*1114.4*

Note: ^{a} Includes the hamlet of Obermoosbach, which had been absorbed into the village by 1707
Sources: StAA, KL Ottobeuren 64, 99, 600; Hawangen parish register, Vols. I–II

households. In the wake of the destruction of half the population of the monastery lands, these restrictions should have been eased. As late as 1708, the number of households in the monastery lands was barely two thirds what it had been before the war.[103] Nevertheless, the Ottobeuren youth were not marrying any younger.

The Hawangen parish register only begins in 1607 and therefore does not allow us to make reliable comparisons, but in nearby Westerheim it is possible to compute age at first marriage both before and after the great depopulation of the 1630s (see Table 6.5). The results are quite surprising. During the 1690s women married on average one full year and men almost three and a half years later than had been customary in the 1620s.

These marriages were also celebrated in an atmosphere of unprecedented strictness. Despite illegitimacy ratios even lower than the ones obtaining before the war,[104] the punishment of extramarital pregnancy was much more ferocious during the later seventeenth century. Even when the couple agreed to marry, they were often subjected to public humiliation and then summarily

---

[103] The 1620 tax survey lists 1,114 households in the villages and 359 in the hamlets. The 1708 tax register, by contrast, records only 750 households in the villages (67.3 percent of 1620 total) and 242 in the hamlets (67.3 percent). The market town of Ottobeuren recovered much more quickly. With 170 households in 1708, it was 90.9 percent of its 1620 size of 187 households. StAA, KL Ottobeuren 99, 102.

[104] In Westerheim the proportion of children declared born out of wedlock dropped from 1.5% (1595–1634) to 0.5% (1646–1710); in Hawangen the proportion fell from 1.4% (1607–35) to 1.1% (1636–1710), the latter figure including two cases where the parents were already married at the time of the baptism!

Table 6.5 *Median age at first marriage in Westerheim, 1620–30 and 1690–9*

	Men (no.)	Age	Women (no.)	Age
1620–30	14	24.5	17	24.4
1690–9	16	27.9	12	25.4

Source: Westerheim parish register

banished from the monastery lands.[105] Of course, to a great extent the crackdown reflected the intensified moral stringency characteristic of the south German Baroque,[106] for in this period we also find the monastery removing its own officials for gross public behavior[107] as well as enthusiastically punishing the peasantry for "excessive" dancing and card-playing.[108] On the other hand, it is equally clear that the moral standards for household formation were closely linked to a fiscal litmus test. Manifest sinners in line for large inheritances were routinely allowed to buy their way out of punishment,[109] while newly engaged couples with poor economic prospects – even those innocent of pre-marital sexual dalliances – were often bluntly instructed to "seek their fortunes elsewhere."[110]

Many peasant elders undoubtedly shared the monastery's opprobrium of sexual non-conformity, and consigned fornicating children to expulsion by refusing to provide funds for commutation.[111] At the same time, however, the disruption of carefully planned heirship strategies was at least as objectionable a feature

---

[105] There are eighteen such cases between June 1695 and September 1699 in StAA, KL Ottobeuren 921–2.

[106] There is a huge literature on this subject. See most recently Marc R. Forster, *Catholic Revival in the Age of the Baroque: Religious Identity in Southwest Germany, 1550–1750* (Cambridge, 2001).

[107] StAA, KL Ottobeuren 921, ff. 82r [28 July 1695], 212r [4 Oct. 1696], 303v–305r [16 Oct. 1697] and 306r [24 Oct. 1697].

[108] Ibid., ff. 291r [5 Sep. 1697] and 292r [5 Sep. 1697]; KL Ottobeuren 922, ff. 34v [25 Apr. 1698], 38r [30 Apr. 1698], 97v [8 Jan. 1699], and 143v [21 May 1699].

[109] StAA, KL Ottobeuren 921, ff. 98r [6 Oct. 1695], 153r [13 Mar. 1696], 154r [15 Mar. 1696], 218r [25 Oct. 1696], 245r–v [7 Mar. 1697], and 298r [4 Oct. 1697]; KL Ottobeuren 922, ff. 23r–v [6 Mar. 1698], 25v–26r [13 Mar. 1698], 34r [17 Apr. 1698], and 135v [7 May 1699].

[110] StAA, KL Ottobeuren 921, f. 316v [14 Nov. 1697]. For other cases, see ibid., ff. 97v–98r [3 Oct. 1695], 124v–125r [19 Jan. 1696], 222r [2 Nov. 1696], 223v [8 Nov. 1696], 238v–239r [24 Jan. 1697], and 247v–248r [22 Mar. 1697]; KL Ottobeuren 922, ff. 88v [13 Nov. 1698], 98v [8 Jan. 1699], and 112r–v [5 Feb. 1699].

[111] Thus Maria Zettler of Günz was humiliated and banished with her husband for pre-marital fornication after it was determined that "neither of them has any property." Maria was the daughter of a wealthy *Hof* tenant who could easily have bought out her punishment. StAA, KL Ottobeuren 922, ff. 164r–v [6 Aug. 1699]; KL Ottobeuren 86, f. 17r.

of "shotgun" marriages as the moral infraction itself. Thus the blacksmith of Günz, a certain Wolf Dietrich Hagg, appeared before the Abbot in December of 1682 with a revealing complaint. In January his son Jacob had been "obliged" to marry the already pregnant Barbara Pfeiler of Sontheim

because he could not deny that he had sinned with her on a single occasion. Subsequently, however, the timing of the birth did not match, as eight weeks were missing from the completion of nine months. It now transpires from the confessions of his son's wife and of Lucas Dümeler the miller of Günz that he Dümeler is the father of the child, and did suborn Pfeiler to cite his son Jacob Hagg [instead]. The miller did thereby cause him great damage, since he [Jacob] would otherwise have made a good marriage and had a chance to gain a smithy and moreover [now] must support the child at [his own] cost.

The angry smith demanded monetary compensation for his son's loss of opportunity.[112]

It is difficult to identify an ecological source for this heightened anxiety about the viability of new households, since the peasantry was no poorer in the 1690s than it had been before the war. On the contrary, the 1689 tax survey indicates that the villagers of the monastery lands, among them the residents of Ober- and Unterwesterheim, were much more plentifully supplied with land than they had been in the 1620s (see Table 6.6). In fact, the 1689 survey also reveals that almost half[113] of all peasant households now held enough land to support themselves, a situation not seen since the 1520s at the latest.

As if this were not enough, it is clear from the monastery's tithe registers that both the hamlets and in particular the nucleated villages were at this time virtually swimming in grain. Idiosyncrasies of the granary's accounting practices make it difficult to construct estimates for both types of settlements during the same time period,[114] but it is possible to estimate the size of the harvest in the hamlets over the decade 1689–98 and in the villages over the decade 1681–90. In the former settlements the records suggest an average harvest two thirds larger than the amount needed to feed the resident population. In the latter, the average harvest was fully two and a half times the size of the subsistence

---

[112] StAA, KL Ottobeuren 919, ff. 364r–365v [4 Dec. 1682]. The monastery was unsympathetic. It was prepared to fine the miller 75 *gulden* for adultery (he had impregnated Barbara while his wife was lying sick in bed), and to order him to pay 100 *gulden* to support the child, but was unwilling to award any damages to the blacksmith.

[113] Since households were 27.7 percent larger in the 1680s than in the 1620s, the minimum farm size for self-sufficiency was now closer to 8.3 *jauchert* than the 6.5 *jauchert* calculated in chapter 3. I have retained the older size categories for purposes of comparability. The 44.2 percent of the 1689 households holding more than 13 *jauchert* were certainly self-sufficient.

[114] The granary accounts often lump tithe and grain rent payments from the hamlets together. The two can only be separated for the period 1689–98. I have retained the village tithe receipts from the 1680s since the 1690s were a decade of unusually bad harvests, and are not representative of the later seventeenth century as a whole.

Table 6.6 *Arable land per household in the Ottobeuren villages, 1689*

| Village | Number of households holding | | | Total households 1689 | Total households 1620 | 1689 as a % of 1620 |
	<6.5 jauchert	6.5–12.99 jauchert	13.0+ jauchert			
Altisried	3	0	6	9	13	69.2
Attenhausen	20	7	17	44	76	57.9
Benningen	22	2	27	51	103	49.5
Dietratried	10	0	9	19	30	63.3
Egg	41	2	20	63	100	63.0
Frechenrieden	31	1	18	50	69	72.5
Günz	9	5	11	25	32	78.1
Hawangen	28	4	29	61	124	49.2
Niederdorf	10	2	11	23	32	71.9
Niederrieden	21	2	20	43	72	59.7
Oberwesterheim	12	3	14	29	49	59.2
Rummeltshausen	3	2	9	14	16	87.5
Schlegelsberg	6	3	12	21	43	48.8
Sontheim	36	5	23	64	140	45.7
Ungerhausen	12	4	19	35	67	52.2
Unterwesterheim	11	1	9	21	39	53.8
Wolfertschwenden	15	5	14	34	56	60.7
Total 1689	290	48	268	606	1061	57.2
Total 1620	763	49	249	1061		
% of 1689 total	47.9	7.9	44.2			
% of 1620 total	71.9	4.6	23.5			

Sources: StAA, KL Ottobeuren 102, 109

minimum. In all, the harvest was more than twice as large as necessary (see Table 6.7).[115]

The late seventeenth century at Ottobeuren thus presents us with a startling paradox. On the one hand the composition of the peasant household, with its multiplicity of unmarried servants, co-resident adult kin, and poor "indwellers," suggests an effort to control the process of household formation akin to the restrictions in place around the year 1600. Indeed, the increase in marriage ages since the 1620s and the harsher punishment of pre-marital and extra-marital pregnancy give the impression that the post-war restrictions had if anything become even more stringent. On the other hand it has been seen that in terms of the traditional Malthusian parameters – the amount of arable land per household and the size of the grain harvest – there was more "room" for the creation of

---

[115] I have assumed a mean household size of 5.97 persons in the villages, an estimate taken from Table 6.3. Since the 1793 census indicates that mean household size in the villages was still 5.97, I have here used the 1793 figure for mean household size in the hamlets (6.65). See Heider, "Grundherrschaft und Landeshoheit," pp. 88–9.

Table 6.7 *Food supply at Ottobeuren in the 1680s and 1690s*

Settlement type	1689 population[a]	Grain requirement (*malter*)	Mean tithe 1681–90 × 10[a]	+/− (*malter*)	+/− (%)
10 nucleated villages	2346	4222.8	10731.5	+6508.7	+154.1
50 hamlets	1470	2646.0	4487.9	+1841.9	+69.6
Total	3816	6868.8	15219.4	+8350.6	+121.6

Note: [a] Estimates for the hamlets are based on the number of households recorded in 1695 and average tithe receipts from the period 1689–98 (overall surplus: +47.6% 1560s; +57.7% 1620s; +121.6% 1680s)

Sources: StAA, KL, Ottobeuren 88, 109, 227, 282–3; Sontheimer, *Die Geistlichkeit des Kapitels Ottobeuren*, Vols. II and IV; Heider, "Grundherrschaft und Landeshoheit," pp. 88–9

new households than had been the case since the beginning of the sixteenth century.

It should be emphasized that the paradox pertains not so much to the level of *population* as it does to the number of *households*. As was shown above, the 1707 diocesan visitation suggests the overall number of persons in the monastery lands was only slightly lower than it had been in the 1620s. At the same time, the monastery's 1708 tax register records a household total not even two thirds the number recorded in 1620. Thus, the issue is not so much the simple size of rural population as its social arrangement in households. What needs to be explained is not the failure of population to recover, for it did so fairly rapidly. The crucial question is why, despite an abundance of land and grain, did the peasantry remain clustered in an arrangement whose original justification had been the shortage of these very resources?

Having belabored a distinction between households and families, it seems appropriate to express more explicitly the essence of the difference. When the scribes and officials of the monastery recorded peasant households in their various registers, they did so for the purpose of taxation. The household, in other words, was conceived above all as a property-holding unit. The family, by contrast, was a genealogical concept referring to the conjugal unit and its immediate offspring (the term *Familie*, or "family" was never actually used at early modern Ottobeuren, but it is clear from the listing of the peasantry in the serf books in units composed only of parents and their children that a functional equivalent of the concept did exist).[116] If, therefore, we wish to explain the paradoxical

---

[116] The vocabulary of household and family in early modern Germany is expertly analyzed in David Sabean, *Property, Production and Family in Neckarhausen 1700–1870* (Cambridge, 1990), pp. 88–123.

character of the rural *household* at the end of the seventeenth century, we must turn our attention from demographic variables to property relations.

What we find is that the landholding structure of the early seventeenth century proved extremely resilient to the effects of wartime depopulation. As has been shown in chapter 3, on the eve of the Thirty Years War the Ottobeuren rural settlement was characterized by the monopolization of most of the arable land by the *Bauern*, the tenants of the large *Gotteshausrecht* farms. The devastations of the 1630s, one might expect, would break the grip of this village elite, carving an empty space where youths and immigrants could establish themselves with relative ease, and thereby prizing apart the pre-war lock imposed on the formation of new households. Such was not the case. Any gaps opened by plague or famine in the ranks of the *Bauern* were filled with remarkable speed.

Let us take as an example the village of Hawangen, a large settlement with twenty-eight large *Gotteshausrecht* farms in 1621. The decade between 1621 and 1631 nicely illustrates the power of the *Hof* tenants: every single holding either remained in the hands of the original tenant, or was passed to a direct heir. Shortly thereafter the village population was decimated by the war. By 1636 the pastor reported a communicant count not even one fourth of the pre-war level. The fate of the *Höfe* was strikingly different. No later than 1637, 67.9 percent of these large farms had been reoccupied, in most cases by the original tenants. By 1648 all of the *Höfe* were again in the hands of a reconstituted peasant aristocracy, at least half of whom had been resident in the village before the war. Over the next fifty years, only twice (in 1682 and 1696) did a *Hof* slip to a tenant who was neither a blood nor a married relation of the 1648 village elite. Even then, in both cases the outsider came from a *Bauer* family resident elsewhere in the lordship. The repopulation of the village had only just begun, and already access to the choicest properties had effectively been closed off.[117]

How was this possible? The problem is perhaps most strikingly posed by the experience of the village of Egg, where an intact burial register permits a fuller accounting of the trauma of war. Ninety-nine householders were listed in the village in 1627, to which may be added a further eighty-five spouses identifiable from parish and notarial registers. Of these 184 persons, no fewer than 119 (64.7 percent) had been buried by 1638. Of the rest, 4 (2.1 percent) are known to have left the parish in 1628, 44 (23.9 percent) are unaccounted for, and only 17 (9.2 percent) can be shown to have survived into the 1640s. Just as in Hawangen, however, all eighteen tenant farms in Egg were reoccupied no later than 1644. Although only one of these householders, a certain Jacob

---

[117] Tenurial patterns reconstructed from StAA, KL Ottobeuren 225, ff. 81v–83v; KL Ottobeuren 42, ff. 2v–4r; KL Ottobeuren 202, ff. 103r–v; KL Ottobeuren 47, ff. 1r–4r; KL Ottobeuren 56, ff. 84r–104v; KL Ottobeuren 106, ff. 30r–36r; KL Ottobeuren 105, ff. 165r–188r; KL Ottobeuren 57, ff. 85v–106r; KL Ottobeuren 109, ff. 144r–173v, KL Ottobeuren 92, ff. 18v–22r; KL Ottobeuren 919–922; and the Hawangen Parish Register.

Stigler, had remained on his farm for the entirety of the war, at least ten others had either inherited the property or married the widow of a previous tenant. A further four had made modest initial marriages into the village between 1625 and 1630, and then moved into an open slot after the onset of the war; the origins of the remaining three are untraceable.[118]

The durability of the pre-war rural elite was thus in part a function of the deep human resources of the *Bauer* household, which retained the ability to reconstitute itself from its members even in the face of savage loss of life. Similarly remarkable resilience can also be documented among the *Seldner*. Jerg Sauter came from a wealthy family, but since he neither inherited the *Hof* (which went to his brother Michael) nor emigrated (like his brother Martin), he was constrained to a life of poverty, toiling as a carpenter in a home he built on a charity house-lot granted out in 1611.[119] Jerg and his wife, Christina Ruoff, had at least four offspring, all of whom were orphaned after their father expired in 1633 and their mother starved to death in January of 1635. It is unclear how many of the children survived, but at least one son, Mathias, did so, married about the year 1649, had children, and worked – also as a carpenter – in the house where he was born until he died at the age of 74 in 1696.[120]

As always, however, demography is only part of the story. Tenurial persistence was often predicated upon a strategy of chain remarriage, so that the continuity of occupation was qualified by an absence of any blood relation between those who worked the land when the war began, and those who filled their shoes at its end. Martin Vetter, for example, grew up in a poor family in the village of Niederrieden, and moved to Egg with his wife and children in 1588 or 1589. He gained the post of village sheriff, improved his wealth by dabbling in land and credit markets, and by 1611 was ready to retire. He sold his own house to a son-in-law, Johann Sauter, the sheriff's service house to a son, Lorenz, and then somehow wheedled from the monastery a third house-lot, where he settled with his newly married second wife, Margareta Kerl. When Martin Vetter died in 1626, Margareta married Jerg Kellenmaier from the neighboring parish of Reichau in the Fugger lordship of Babenhausen. After Margareta died of plague in August of 1635, Kellenmaier took to wife a certain Anna Bitzer. Anna Bitzer,

---

[118] Reconstruction based on StAA, KL Ottobeuren 42, ff. 9v–10v; KL Ottobeuren 47, ff. 17v–19r; KL Ottobeuren 56, ff. 266v–295v; KL Ottobeuren 102, ff. 272r–294v; KL Ottobeuren 104, ff. 250r–273v; KL Ottobeuren 105, ff. 204r–222v; KL Ottobeuren 106, ff. 72r–77v; KL Ottobeuren 160, ff. 50r–52r; KL Ottobeuren 225, ff. 102r–103v; KL Ottobeuren 435 [unfoliated]; KL Ottobeuren 903–911 and the Egg Parish Register, Vol. I.

[119] StAA, KL Ottobeuren 904, f. 234v [10 Mar. 1611]; KL Ottobeuren 905, ff. 123r [26 Nov. 1613], and 320v [31 Dec. 1615]; KL Ottobeuren 907, ff. 229v–230r; and 230r [both 22 Feb. 1619]; KL Ottobeuren 102, ff. 289r, 292v; KL Ottobeuren 104, ff. 267v, 270r–v.

[120] StAA, KL Ottobeuren 160, ff. 50r–52v; KL Ottobeuren 106, ff. 72r–77v; KL Ottobeuren 105, ff. 219r–v; KL Ottobeuren 109, ff. 74r–v; KL Ottobeuren 921, ff. 164r–v [12 Apr. 1696]; Egg Parish Register, Vol. I, pp. 12–14 [24 Feb. 1622], 31–2 [23 Mar. 1627], 41–2 [22 Oct. 1629], 55–6 [18 Sep. 1632], 124–5 [9 July 1650], 159 [11 Apr. 1633], and 168 [18 Jan. 1635].

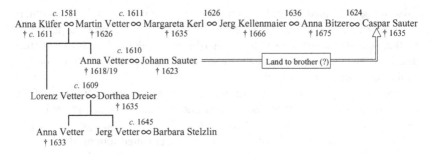

Figure 6.7 The Vetter/Sauter families in Egg during the Thirty Years War
Note: † denotes date of death.
Sources: Egg parish register, Vols. I–II; StAA, KL Ottobeuren 56, 102, 104–6, 160, 435, 904–12

it turns out, was the widow of Caspar Sauter, who had come into the land of his kinsman Johann Sauter after the latter (once Martin Vetter's son-in-law) died in 1623 (see Figure 6.7). Anna also brought with her the *Hof* of one Michael Sauter, the same one whose brother died a poor carpenter in 1633, and who himself had died six weeks earlier. The holdings of three Vetter and Sauter households were in this way combined and preserved by Jerg Kellenmaier and Anna Bitzer, who were completely unrelated to those who had held the land before 1624.

Similar (if less spectacular) examples of this pattern could easily be multiplied, but the point should already be clear: despite the ravages of plague, famine, and war, the land was continuously able to recruit its own labor. To be sure, there was an enormous differential in drawing power between a sprawling *Hof* and a single cottage. Chain remarriage was commonest on the larger holdings (note the rather simpler reproduction pattern in the almost landless household of Lorenz Vetter), whereas as late as 1669 at least a dozen cottage lots in the village remained deserted. It mattered little. The eighteen tenant farmers in place by 1644 controlled some 80 percent of the land in the village. It would be the nineteenth century before Egg had as many householders as had lived there in the 1620s, but the pre-war pattern was already entrenched. The frailty of the individual members of rural society was more than made up for by the robustness of the institutions – marriage, inheritance, and property holding – which informed it.

Having re-established themselves in control of the villages, the *Hof* tenants then moved to consolidate their power. They had no intention of allowing immigrants or other interlopers to encroach upon their position of privilege and therefore turned to the monastery for help. What the *Bauer* wanted, and what the monastery began in the 1650s to issue, was formal certification of title to his various properties. The document typically opens with a declaration that the petitioner had acquired various lands through inheritance and purchase, but that because of the war some acquisitions were never formally registered and the documents recording the others had been lost or destroyed. Accordingly, "in order to forestall future doubt, dispute, and division" the petitioner requests that his holdings be itemized in detail and that he be confirmed in their possession.[121]

These "Universal Ratifications," as the charters came to be titled, tell a fascinating story of tenacity and calculation. The 1659 confirmation issued to Hans Memeler of Sontheim, for example, shows him beginning his rise with the purchase of a house, 3 *jauchert* of cropland, and 6.5 *tagwerk* of meadow from his mother and father in 1613. Three more parcels were added in 1626, and then a sizeable chunk was inherited from his parents in 1634. Memeler stayed on in Sontheim through the war years, carefully buying up the parcels adjoining his lands in foreclosure sales and from the estates of the deceased. In 1620 his wealth had placed him in the uppermost fifth in the village; forty years later he was unmoved from this rank.[122]

If the peasants refused to give up anything to outsiders without payment, they were equally unyielding when it came to their own children. All Ottobeuren landowners, whether old or new, rich or poor, continued to require that even "inherited" land be purchased by the heir according to the terms of a notarized contract. This continuity of practice between pre- and post-war landholders was surely not unrelated to the partial continuity of identity between the two groups, but it is the practice which merits particular attention. For it is this power of those who controlled the land to dictate the conditions of its transmission that explains the extended peasant household of the late seventeenth century.

As was the case in the early seventeenth century, after the Thirty Years War the Ottobeuren peasants preferred to convey land to their heirs in their own lifetimes (see Figure 6.8). They continued to "retire" on their farms supported by a maintenance agreement with the heir,[123] and it is not hard to see how this system of property devolution implied at least the temporary co-residence of parents and adult children. Sometimes this extended household phase lasted for decades. The widow Barbara Hiltprand of Hawangen relinquished her house, lands, and all of her property to her daughter Ursula for 320 *gulden* on 9 October 1681. Ten *gulden* were deducted for Ursula's inheritance, fifty were to be paid in cash, and the rest in annual installments of ten *gulden*. The mother was to

---

[121] StAA, KL Ottobeuren 917-II, ff. 5r–v [22 Feb. 1663], 37v–38v [4 May 1663], 39r–40v [7 May 1665], and 96v–98r [7 June 1663].

[122] StAA, KL Ottobeuren 912-II, ff. 1r–4v [2 Jan. 1659]. Also KL Ottobeuren 102, ff. 347r–v [1620] and KL Ottobeuren 106, f. 47v [1660].

[123] See for example the retirement contract of Christian Vögelin of Attenhausen, whose son Michael agreed to pay 700 fl for Christian's lands, and annually to provide him with 3 *malter* of rye and spelt, 20 pounds of lard, one quarter of the flax crop, and one quarter of the meat butchered on the *Hof*. Michael assumed all of his father's debts, and agreed to pay 100 fl. to his brother Georg and 150 fl., a cow, and set of linens to his sister Maria at their marriages. StAA, KL Ottobeuren 919, ff. 189r–190v [23 May 1681].

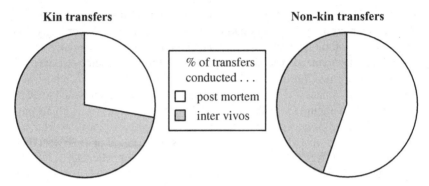

Figure 6.8 Timing of the transfer of *Gotteshausrecht* land at Ottobeuren, 1656–90
Sources: StAA, KLs Ottobeuren 335–50

be maintained in the house and receive eight pounds of lard per annum. Thus envisioned the repayment would have taken twenty-six years, and twenty-six years later the Hawangen "Description of all the Parishioners" records the widow Barbara still living in the house along with her daughter, her daughter's children, and second husband.[124]

Property relations also contributed to the growth in the servant population. As was the case before the war, if inheritances had to be paid for, it behooved a prospective heir to begin earning as soon as possible. Service typically began for Ottobeuren youth at the age of fourteen or fifteen, and although their wages were paid only partly in cash, delaying marriage for a lengthy stretch could enable the accumulation of a sizeable nest egg. When Catharina Geiger of Niederdorf announced her intention to marry Michael Endar of Feldkirch, she was able to report that in twelve years of service in nearby Memmingen, Endar had managed to put aside 150 *gulden*. This was enough for the couple to buy a house, a cow, and a *jauchert* of freehold arable.[125]

A servant's savings more commonly totaled about 50 *gulden*, far from enough to establish a youth as a full-fledged *Bauer*.[126] The vast majority of inheritances at late seventeenth-century Ottobeuren were therefore financed at least in part by debt, so that most heirs were under the same pressure to generate money as their pre-war counterparts (see Table 6.8).[127] This financial pressure brings us,

---

[124] Ibid., ff. 244v–245r; HawPR, Vol. II, f. 125v.

[125] StAA, KL Ottobeuren 919, f. 155v [30 Jan. 1681]. Michael Endar's house, cow, and 1.2 *jauchert* of arable land were valuated at 100 *gulden* in the 1689 tax survey. KL Ottobeuren 109, f. 340r.

[126] According to the protocol entries from the 1690s, the average (mean) servant's accumulated savings at marriage were 45.8 fl. with a median of 50 fl. StAA, KL Ottobeuren 921–2.

[127] Consideration of a longer time span is prevented by a quirk in the records. By the later seventeenth century the monastery was maintaining two series of protocols, the so-called *Verhörprotokolle*, which record all transactions of the Abbot's court, and the *Briefprotokolle*, which record only notarial matters. StAA, KL Ottobeuren 919 contains the *Verhörprotokolle*

Table 6.8 *Financing of household property sales at Ottobeuren, 1680–2*

	Kin transfer		Non-kin transfer	
Type of sale	Debt financed	No debt	Debt financed	No debt
Number	49	2	26	7
%	96.1	3.9	78.8	21.2

Note: Household property is defined as a house and/or at least 5 *jauchert* of arable land or 5 *tagwerk* of meadow
Source: StAA, KL Ottobeuren 919

however, to a second and more important connection between property relations and servanthood: the unwillingness of heavily burdened heirs to support their unmarried brothers and sisters.

Servanthood in the monastery lands was primarily a duty required by those who controlled property from those who did not, and only secondarily the voluntary state of an heir expectant. Upon the death of Balthas Maier of Frechenrieden, his widow and four of his children sold their interests in his lands to the eldest son, Peter, for 614 *gulden* on 29 January 1682. The widow received a comfortable *Leibgeding*, or maintenance agreement, and each heir (the widow included) was to receive an inheritance portion of exactly 46 *gulden* 39 *kreuzer* 5 *heller*. One sister was already married, but as for the rest the protocol firmly states that "the groom [Peter married the same day] shall raise two of the three aforesaid still ungrown children until they can earn their own keep; thereafter they may work for appropriate wages either for him or elsewhere. Jacob Dodel shall raise the third." Idle siblings Peter would not tolerate.[128]

Peter Maier was in this respect an utterly typical *Bauer* of his day. Land sales at Ottobeuren regularly stipulated that the heir was only obliged to support non-inheriting siblings "until they could earn their own sup and bread."[129] Often the siblings had already departed by the time the heir succeeded to the land, in which case the contract might state that the heir shall only be required to house and feed them if they fall sick, and even then for no more than three or four weeks.[130] Exceptions to the pattern certainly existed. The blacksmith Martin

for 1680–2, while KL Ottobeuren 920 contains the *Briefprotokolle* for 1680–9. Unfortunately, a comparison of the two volumes reveals that although KL Ottobeuren 920 covers a longer period of time, it does so at too high a price: the credit arrangements associated with each land sale have been omitted from the entries in the interest of brevity. We are thus obliged to fall back on KL Ottobeuren 919, which covers fewer years but in greater (and essential) detail.
[128] StAA, KL Ottobeuren 919, ff. 280r–282r [29 Jan. 1682].
[129] Ibid., ff. 359v–361r [9 Nov. 1682].
[130] Ibid., ff. 313r–314r [15 May 1682] and 250v–251r [23 Oct. 1681].

Vetter, for example, inserted the following clauses into the sale of his smithy in
the market town of Ottobeuren to his son Michael in 1681:

> The seller hereby grants each of his five dear children and among them also
> the said buyer his son Michael a marriage portion of 50 *gulden*. It is also
> agreed that the buyer shall provide a home for his single siblings as long
> as they remain unmarried. The [daughter] Anna, however, who is somewhat
> simple-minded and therefore presumably will not marry, he [Michael] shall
> care for for the rest of her life. In recognition of this, however, the 50 *gulden*
> granted to Anna shall remain in his hands.[131]

Most of the time, however, the arrangements were less generous, and this applies
not only to relations between inheriting and non-inheriting children, but also to
the relation of children to their parents.

The remarriage of a widowed parent was a classic occasion for the enuncia-
tion of a hard line. The baker Georg Hermann of Sontheim had seven children
with his wife Anna Stedler. After Anna died in 1680, Georg married a certain Barbara Keidler, who brought with her a dowry of 115 *gulden*. The new
couple then decided that "since after Hermann's death it will not be possible
to raise and support all of the children in this home, the said [children] shall
[now] be put into service as soon as they can earn their own sup and bread
or assume service. That which remains from their wages after they have been
honorably clothed shall be handed over and given to Hermann."[132] Though not
a rich man, Hermann was hardly poor. His wealth placed him in the uppermost
40 percent in the village, and he also kept several horses, a characteristic emblem
of comfort among the peasantry. After the 1680 marriage his fortunes only
improved: during the early 1680s the protocols show him paying off old debts
and acquiring new lands.[133] Upon his death in 1686, his widow remarried and
maintained her former position in the village,[134] an outcome Hermann could
easily have foreseen. But like every other Ottobeuren householder, Hermann
still had payments to make, and thus he insisted that his children begin working
as soon as possible.

Hermann was not alone in this view. Hans Unger of Benningen purchased the
family house, lands, and weaving equipment from his five stepchildren when
their mother died in 1682. He also took a new wife. Unger pledged to pay out the
200 *gulden* purchase price in annual installments of 10 *gulden*, but demanded
that the children leave home to take up service, agreeing only that "with respect

---

[131] Ibid., f. 146r [9 Jan. 1681].   [132] Ibid., ff. 100r–v [12 Sep. 1680].

[133] StAA, KL Ottobeuren 920, ff. 99r [5 Mar. 1682] and 129r [29 Oct. 1682].

[134] Ibid., ff. 286v–287v [22 Apr. 1686]. Georg Maierrog, engaged to marry Hermann's widow,
Barbara Keidler, is admitted to the former lands of Georg Hermann. In the 1689 tax survey
Maierrog's gross wealth was given as 719 *gulden*; the village median was 466 *gulden*. StAA,
KL Ottobeuren 109, ff. 194r–v.

to the clothing of the said five children, the stepfather shall at the demand of necessity have the available old clothes altered for them at his own expense."[135] It should be pointed out that Unger was one of the poorer householders in the village and also that his marriage to the stepchildren's mother had lasted less than a year,[136] but similar outcomes can be documented where neither of these conditions obtained. On 22 October 1682 Georg Schalck of Gumpratsried reported that his son Georg junior sought to marry Magdalena Hiemer of Ollarzried. "To be sure," the protocol states, "she brings him [Georg junior] no more than 25 *gulden*, but since she is suitable to Schalk senior to manage the household, he wishes to engage his son as a servant and Hiemer instead of a maid."[137] The monastery consented to the arrangement, but warned that if Georg junior proved incapable (i.e. insufficiently wealthy) to take over the family farm, it would at his father's death be given to someone else. What is striking about this episode is that Georg Schalk senior was a very wealthy man. His *Hof* measured more than 34 *jauchert* of arable and 20 *tagwerk* of meadow. There was no question that it lay in his power to guarantee his son the admission to the land, and almost exactly one year later Georg junior would in fact become the tenant of the *Hof*.[138] Still this did not absolve the son of the obligation at least temporarily to become a servant in his very own home.

Retired parents were themselves subject to the same fiscal discipline. The parent was contractually entitled to the same standard of living as before, but in practice often depended for food and other necessities on a child saddled with many other obligations. The difficulty was compounded by the ambiguity of authority in the household, the parent having ceded legal title to the property but remaining a creditor of the heir. It is not hard to see how this situation was ripe for conflict, and many parents inserted clauses into their retirement contracts specifically requiring the heir to pay the rent so as to allow the parent to live elsewhere "if in the future she cannot get along with her son or daughter-in-law."[139]

Sometimes the records allow us to follow the budgetary problems in revealing detail. Hans Grauss sold his sprawling farm in Betzisried and all of his livestock and moveables to his son Georg for 1,400 *gulden* on 1 February 1680. Two hundred *gulden* were deducted for Georg's own marriage portion, and he was further to give each of his three sisters 200 *gulden* at their marriages, also to be deducted from the purchase price. For the remaining 600 *gulden* Georg paid 50 in cash up front, and agreed thereafter to pay 25 *gulden* each year at Candlemas. The father reserved for himself and his wife the lifetime use of a parcel of

[135] StAA, KL Ottobeuren 919, ff. 302v–303r [16 Apr. 1682].
[136] StAA, KL Ottobeuren 109, f. 20r. Unger's gross wealth was only 340 *gulden*. KL Ottobeuren 919, ff. 230v–231r [11 Sep. 1681] first reports Unger's marriage.
[137] Ibid., ff. 350v–351r.
[138] StAA, KL Ottobeuren 344 (Erdschatz) [7 Oct. 1683]; cf. KL Ottobeuren 109, f. 488v.
[139] StAA, KL Ottobeuren 919, f. 173v [27 Mar. 1681].

arable, all of the fruit in the garden, and unrestricted access to the pantry. It was a perfectly standard arrangement, and it rapidly degenerated into strife.[140]

In September of 1680 Georg and his father amended the contract. Henceforth Hans was to receive 1 *malter* of grain, 15 pounds of lard, one tenth of the fruit crop, and 50 eggs per year. Between Michaelmas and St. George's day he was also to be given one tankard of milk per day. In exchange Georg and his wife gained the right to lock his father out of the pantry.[141] Still the son worried that his obligations were too many, and in February of 1681 Georg and his father decided to resolve the problem at the expense of family members weaker than themselves – the sisters. The original contract had already obliged the sisters to leave home upon attainment of fifteen years of age, and although Georg was to house and feed them if they came home sick from service, the young women were required to pay for their own medicine. The new agreement now stipulated that

> Since with such large marriage portions the debts [on the farm] might remain unpaid, or at least the father might suffer from want, it is held for best that for now and until it shall be seen what remains after the debts have been paid, that the said Georg Grauss shall not give his siblings any more than 150 *gulden*; the remaining 50 *gulden* shall remain *in suspenso*.[142]

Whatever the merits of his original worries, the tight-fisted and calculating son went on to prosper. By 1689 he had a net worth of over 1,600 *gulden*.[143]

The pervasion of peasant life by financial calculation is still more obvious at the occasion of marriage. The young were under considerable pressure to conform their nuptial aspirations to the exigencies of succession. Marriage and inheritance were regularly arranged together, and disclosure of the size and payment schedule of the incoming dowry was a standard feature of contracts for the sale of the family home.[144] The contribution of a prospective spouse was thus an essential component in the underwriting of inheritance.[145] Indeed, the lot of heirship among the children in a family might well turn on the issue of which child made the "best" marriage. Felix Keller of Ottobeuren learned

---

[140] Ibid., ff. 9v–10r; KL Ottobeuren 920, f. 15r [1 Feb. 1680].

[141] StAA, KL Ottobeuren 919 ff. 101v–102r [12 Sep. 1680].

[142] Ibid., f. 164v [25 Feb. 1681].   [143] StAA, KL Ottobeuren 109, f. 527v.

[144] In January of 1681, for example, Michael Vetter of Ottobeuren both purchased a smithy from his father for 400 *gulden* and married Euphemia Endres, the daughter of a local tanner. Two related installment patterns were set out in the protocol: having paid 50 *gulden* up front, Michael was to pay off the remaining 350 *gulden* of the purchase price at the rate of 13 *gulden* per annum while his parents were alive and 25 *gulden* per annum following their decease. At the same time Euphemia's father bound himself to pay half of her 100 *gulden* dowry right away, followed by two payments of 25 *gulden* over the next two years. StAA, KL Ottobeuren 919, ff. 146r–v [9 Jan. 1681].

[145] See the purchase by Balthas Aleze from his stepchildren of a huge farm in Leupolz for 1,602.5 *gulden* [16 Oct. 1681]. The protocol explicitly states that the "mode of paying [*modus solvendi*] can only be determined at Aleze's imminent marriage." Ibid., ff. 248v–249v.

this the hard way. In July of 1681 Felix prepared to succeed to a mill which had once been held by his father, Mathias, and thereafter by his stepfather, Georg Dreier. Felix agreed to pay an entry fine (*Erdschatz*) of 75 *gulden*, and to give marriage portions of 115, 110, and 100 *gulden* to his siblings Hans Georg, Ursula, and Maria, respectively. These commitments were backed by his promise of marriage from Anna Brack, the daughter of the local baker, and the dowry of 150 *gulden* which her father had promised her. Somehow – the details have not been recorded – the engagement collapsed. Anna Brack withdrew her promise of engagement and along with it her dowry, and Felix was forced to give up the mill. It passed instead to his brother, Hans Georg, who in a crowning irony went on to marry Anna's sister Barbara, the protocol carefully noting that "she brings him exactly the same dowry her father promised his other daughter Anna Brack last week."[146]

Given the importance attached to making a good marriage, it is perhaps to be expected that differences of opinion often led to strife. When Maria Brüzger of Frechenrieden announced her intention to marry one Hans Georg Rock, her father, Hans, took intense exception to her choice. The reason was obvious: the Brüzgers were one of the wealthiest families in the village while Rock came from the ranks of the village poor; the protocol skeptically noted that "Rock has supposedly deposited 100 *gulden* of earned wages with his mother." Maria's father could not prevent the marriage itself, but he could – and did – withhold any promise of inheritance from his daughter, "until they [the couple] shall have the prospect of establishing themselves honorably." Rock's 100 *gulden* probably never existed; the court ordered his mother to come forward and certify the sum but she never did so. Hans Brüzger's refusal thus made it virtually impossible for the young couple to acquire the material basis for a household. Whatever he hoped to achieve, the father's decision brought only grief, for Maria was already pregnant. When the child was born "too early," Maria and her husband did not have the money to pay off the punishments of the law, and the court therefore pronounced upon them a sentence of banishment.[147] The unfortunate couple did ultimately manage to return to the village. They remained, however, among the humblest of the village households,[148] while Maria's brother went on to gain his father's lands and comfort,[149] and presumably his approval as well.

Unremarkable as it may seem, the father's objection merits closer attention. It was not that Rock was a bad man; he was simply not rich enough. The inadequacy was less a qualitative defect than a quantitative shortfall – the

---

[146] Ibid., ff. 221r–222r [24 July 1681] and 223v [31 July 1681].

[147] Ibid., ff. 259r [6 Nov. 1681] and 337r [20 Aug. 1682].

[148] The 1689 tax survey puts Rock's gross wealth at only 128 *gulden*, ranking him forty-fourth out of fifty in the village. StAA, KL Ottobeuren 109, f. 297v.

[149] "Adam previously Hans Brüzger" was the fourth richest of fifty householders in the village in 1689, with a gross wealth of 1158.5 *gulden*. Ibid., f. 281r.

unguaranteed sum of 100 *gulden*. I emphasize the point because it is striking how many late seventeenth-century squabbles over marriage and inheritance revolved around the adequacy or fairness of specific sums of money. Thus Thomas Bock of Frechenrieden was the object of a complaint by his son-in-law who "feels most disadvantaged with respect to his wife's inheritance of 130 *gulden* and further maintains that her inheritance should come to a great deal more, since the value of Bock's property runs to 1,800 *gulden*."[150] In a similar vein the potter Georg Claus of the market town of Ottobeuren became embroiled in a bitter dispute with his stepchildren over the value of his house (and therefore over the size of their inheritances). The children felt that the house had a value of 300 *gulden* while Claus insisted that it was worth much less. In the end a compromise was reached – the valuation was set at 200 but the children were required to leave the house.[151]

It goes without saying that the foregoing pattern of rural social reproduction was itself hardly new. Lifetime devolution of property, retirement and co-residence by parents, debt financing of purchased inheritances, the expectation of servanthood for unmarried youths, all of these customs have previously been documented for the early seventeenth century. What is both new and significant in the post-war period is the absence of the ecological pressures which helped to give rise to these practices in the first place. Of course, reference may always be had to "accumulated cultural capital" and "downward stickiness" to explain the apparent irreversibility of social change. Rather than appeal to such nebulous notions of historical inertia, however, we ought more properly to focus our attention on the persistence in rural society of particular mechanisms of power. For as has been seen, it was the insistence of those who owned the land and the prodding of those who taxed it which ensured that the self-perpetuation of the peasantry remained inextricably bound up with the obligation to produce money.

Indeed, whereas rural property relations were clearly modified under demographic pressure during the later sixteenth century, one hundred years later the causal influence seems to have tilted in the opposite direction. Despite the devastations of the war years, the unsentimental rules of property management imposed very real limits on new household formation. The experience of the later seventeenth century at Ottobeuren does not, in other words, indicate the operation of a homeostatic system in which population of its own accord tended toward some 'natural' density. And in order to illustrate this claim, we need to take a closer look at the actual process of the repopulation of the countryside.

During the 1650s and 1660s, Upper Swabia was traversed by throngs of travelers, not a few of whom would have liked to settle there. In those years the

---

[150] StAA, KL Ottobeuren 919, ff. 247v–248r [16 Oct. 1681].
[151] Ibid., ff. 151r–v [23 Jan. 1681] and 153r–154r [30 Jan. 1681].

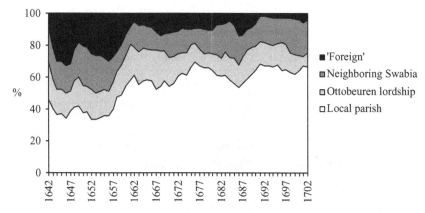

Figure 6.9 Origins of marriage partners in four Ottobeuren parishes, 1642–1702 (five-year moving average)
Sources: Parish registers of Benningen, Hawangen, Ungerhausen, and Westerheim

monastery's account ledgers record grants of alms to literally thousands of travelers. Some of these were established persons from elsewhere, like "Monsieur Robert de Villa, French Nobleman from Dauphiné."[152] A few, such as "crazy Barbara from Äderlass," who was given 30 *kreuzer* at regular intervals in 1664 and 1665, were local unfortunates for whom the almoner appears to have had a soft spot.[153] But most of the recipients appear only briefly before disappearing without a trace. They came from all over Germany and indeed from all over Europe (although what some of them, like "Nicholas Harp from London in England with four children," were doing in Upper Swabia is anyone's guess).[154] Traveling players, demobilized soldiers, widows, orphans, and vagrants, they wandered without homes of their own, and often yearned to find them in the still half-empty villages of the Ottobeuren lands.

It is difficult to ascertain the overall impact of post-war immigration in the monastery lands, but the most reliable picture comes from marriage registers, which generally record the provenance of spouses. These registers survive in most Ottobeuren parishes from the 1660s, and in four (Hawangen, Benningen, Westerheim, and Ungerhausen) from the 1640s. Figure 6.9 accordingly plots

---

[152] StAA, KL Ottobeuren 335 (Almosen) (1660/1).

[153] StAA, KL Ottobeuren 337 (Almosen) (1664/5 and 1665/6).

[154] StAA, KL Ottobeuren 335 (Almosen). Harp and the children received 12 kr. on 5 December 1659. On 10 April 1660 a Simon Harp "from London in England" received 6 kr., and on 30 Mar. 1661 "Niclas Harp soldier" received 6 kr.. The Harps leave no other trace in the Ottobeuren records. The almoner's accounts also contain several references to one Raymond O'Dea, who as a "noble Irish lord . . . plundered and driven into exile by the English heretics" received 15 kr. on 19 June 1658. O'Dea seems to have stayed in Swabia for quite some time; he received alms at Ottobeuren in 1660, 1664, and 1666, the last time as an "Irish pilgrim." KL Ottobeuren 335, 337.

Table 6.9 *Immigration and settlement rates in Benningen, 1640–99*

Home	No. married	% of total	No. settled	% of total	Settlement rate (%)
Benningen	184	45.5	151	59.2	82.1
Ottobeuren lordship	54	13.4	47	18.4	87.0
Neighboring Swabia	94	23.3	40	15.7	42.6
"Foreign"	72	17.8	17	6.7	23.6
Total	404	100.0	255	100.0	63.1

Sources: StAA, KL Ottobeuren 72, 92, 106–9, 914, 919–22; Benningen parish register

the origins of marriage partners in these four parishes between the later stages of the Thirty Years War and the beginning of the eighteenth century, with particular attention to the relative prominence of partners from just outside the monastery lands ("neighboring Swabia") and partners from still further afield ("foreign"), such as Bavaria, the Rhineland, and especially Switzerland and the Tyrol.

For much of the 1640s and 1650s, non-Ottobeuren spouses made up at least 40 percent of the partners married in these four parishes. And yet the most striking feature of this immigration wave is its brevity: by the 1660s the "foreigners" made up less than a fifth of marriage partners and by the 1690s less than a tenth. Furthermore, to marry in a parish did not necessarily mean to settle there, and not everyone's chances were equal. Table 6.9 analyzes the outcome of 202 marriages in the village of Benningen, which had the highest overall proportion of "foreign" partners among the four parishes with the oldest extant marriage registers. Immigrants made up fully 40 percent of those married in Benningen during the later seventeenth century, but they were much less likely to settle (here defined as a documented stay beyond the marriage date) in the village than monastery peasants.

The reasons for this disparity are fairly straightforward. Settlement in a village was predicated on securing an open niche in the form of a house or (ideally) a tenant farm. Securing the niche depended in turn not only on one's own resources, but in most cases also on a marriage alliance with a family already resident in the village. A would-be immigrant thus had to keep a close eye on opportunities as they opened and closed, and jump at just the right moment. This was a manageable challenge for those from the immediately surrounding area, but was much more difficult for the long-distance migrants from the Alpine zone.

Barthlome Thuener, for example, was a blacksmith from Mais, near Meran in the Tyrol. He arrived in the monastery lands in 1656, and worked for two years in the village of Hawangen until the death of the village sexton afforded him an opening. Barthlome proposed to the sexton's widow, promising to bring her his 800 *gulden* inheritance, and in August of 1659 hastened off with the

Abbot's blessing to collect the money.[155] He wasn't fast enough. The widow, Elisabetha Willer, did wait at least nine months for him, but when the Hawangen innkeeper's wife passed away the following spring, Elisabetha was quickly able to choose between the blacksmith's as yet unfulfilled promise and the innkeeper's rather more tangible wealth. She married the innkeeper within two months of his having been widowed, and Barthlome never made a home in the village.[156]

The point is not to minimize the significance of immigration – as late as 1699 one third of Benningen households had at least one immigrant spouse – but rather to emphasize the degree to which it was shaped by forces other than demography. These imperatives are nicely summed up in the travel papers issued in 1656 to one Jacob Ackermann, who had arrived from Gossau near St. Gallen in Switzerland:

> Jacob Ackerman . . . who has already put in two years of honorable service with . . . Georg Herger, headman of [the hamlet] Dennenberg, intends, *if his father will consent and if he should come by the means to gain admission to a holding*, to marry the daughter of the said Georg Herger, and then [hopes] graciously to be accepted by the said honorable monastery [of Ottobeuren] as a subject. Therefore, and in order not only that no one shall doubt him of this [intention], but also that he may forthwith receive official documentation of his legitimate birth and also of what [size inheritance] is due to him by law . . . the present attestation . . . has been prepared for him.[157]

Thus even in the years immediately following the end of the war, household formation remained subject to important constraints. Parental consent still had to be obtained and access to capital was still a necessity.[158] In Jacob's case we do not know which (if either) element was ultimately lacking, but either way he never gained the farm in Dennenberg and never settled in the monastery lands.[159]

Other newcomers were more fortunate. Maria Hohenneger from Hattingen in the Tyrol married Hans Heffelin, a comfortable farmer in the village of Schlegelsberg.[160] Her Tyrolese countryman Jacob Underlochner from Kanur

---

[155] StAA, KL Ottobeuren 912-II, ff. 36v–37r [9 Aug. 1659]. The sexton, Johann Hüemer, had died of dropsy on 17 September 1658. HawMR, Vol. I, f. 42r, HawBuR, Vol. I, ff. 12–14.

[156] Catharina Frei, wife of Johann Heinrich, innkeeper, was buried on 6 May 1660. Heinrich married Elisabetha Willer on 2 July; in that year he ranked sixth in taxable wealth of the fifty-one households in the village. StAA, KL Ottobeuren 106, ff. 30r–36r.

[157] StAA, KL Ottobeuren 914, ff. 408r–v [7 Sep. 1656].

[158] As was noted in Ingomar Bog, *Die bäuerliche Wirtschaft im Zeitalter des Dreissigjährigen Krieges* (1952), pp. 56–7.

[159] Ackerman is not listed in Dennenberg in the 1660 tax survey, at which point Georg Herger was still the headman of the hamlet (StAA, KL Ottobeuren 106, f. 20v). The 1669 survey also contains no trace of Ackerman in Dennenberg. KL Ottobeuren 105, ff. 32r–34v.

[160] StAA, KL Ottobeuren 914, ff. 433v–434r [17 Feb. 1657]. The size of Heffelin's landholdings is unclear, but in 1660 he owned three horses, a filly, three cows, and an ox, a herd betokening a certain prosperity. KL Ottobeuren 106, f. 52r.

succeeded in marrying the widow of a wealthy innkeeper in the market town of Ottobeuren.[161] What made for the better luck of these two, there is every reason to believe, was the money they obtained from home. Maria was bequeathed 144 *gulden* by her mother, while Underlochner's inheritance came to fully 500 *gulden*.

The monastery was also prepared to intervene directly if an immigrant's dream seemed to lack a fiscal foundation. Although moneyed outsiders were warmly received as late as the 1690s,[162] overt resistance to the immigration of the poor crops up as early as 1661, when the monastery acceded to the proposed marriage of Maria Rot of Sontheim with the penniless Michael Ratgeber from the Tyrolese district of Stain, but refused to accept Ratgeber as a subject "because there are still several native sons [*Underthans Khinder*] available."[163] The Abbot's refusal (no doubt in response to complaints by local families) effectively scuttled the engagement, and three years later Maria left the monastery lands to marry elsewhere.[164]

Unsurprisingly, therefore, the notarial records of the 1650s are packed with the passports of peasants heading off to collect inheritances or other sources of capital from "foreign" lands (usually Switzerland and the Tyrol).[165] Most of these travelers were immigrants now settled (or hoping to settle) in the monastery lands, but we also encounter former Ottobeuren subjects recovering funds from Swabia in order to establish themselves somewhere else.[166] Even when the sums in question were quite small, transfer mechanisms existed to enable the exchange of claims and obligations across considerable distances.[167]

---

[161] StAA, KL Ottobeuren 912, ff. 34r–v [13 July 1662]. Underlochner had died by the time of the 1669 tax survey, which lists his widow in Ottobeuren with a gross wealth of 885 *gulden* (KL Ottobeuren 105, ff. 26r–v). Underlochner is last mentioned in Ottobeuren in KL Ottobeuren 917-II, f. 3r [8 Jan. 1665].

[162] Thus Juliana Köglin from Unterreitnau near Lindau, who brought a dowry of 150 fl. to her marriage with Romanus Sommerdorfer of Ottobeuren, was accepted as a subject "gratis," i.e. without paying the normal exogamous marriage fee. StAA, KL 921, ff. 165v–166r [3 May 1696].

[163] StAA, KL Ottobeuren 916, f. 3v [3 Feb. 1661]. Maria's father was himself among the poorest 15 percent of Sontheim householders. KL Ottobeuren 106, ff. 83r–89v.

[164] StAA, KL Ottobeuren 917, ff. 55v–56r [2 May 1664].

[165] StAA, KL Ottobeuren 912, ff. 4r–v [26 Sep 1659], 28v–29r [29 Oct 1661]; KL Ottobeuren 912-II, ff. 31r–v [26 June 1659], 59v–60r [6 Mar. 1660], 72v [7 May 1660], 90v–91r [14 Oct. 1660]; KL Ottobeuren 914, ff. 347r [24 Oct. 1655], 363r [14 Jan. 1656], 366r [14 Feb. 1656]; KL Ottobeuren 915, ff. 27v [29 Mar 1658], 28r–v [6 Apr. 1658], 28v–29r [22 Mar. 1658], 30v–31r [9 May 1658], 51r [5 Nov. 1658], 54v–55r [24 Sep. 1658].

[166] StAA, KL Ottobeuren 912-II, ff. 24r–25r [27 June 1659]. Hanns Luntelin, formerly of Benningen, now in Gilch (Tyrol), recovers 48 fl. pursuant to an agreement originally dated 20 June 1626.

[167] See the case of Jerg Hueber, formerly of Günz and now the village judge of Harmsdorf in Lower Austria, who inherited 2 *jauchert* of land from his father, Conrad Hueber. The property was sold for 32 fl. to the Günz resident Caspar Rogg, who himself had two claims totaling 15 fl. from two other locations in Austria. Rogg transferred his claims to the 15 fl. to Hueber, to be deducted from the 32 fl. purchase price. StAA, KL Ottobeuren 914, ff. 436v–437v [6 Apr. 1657].

In some cases the evidence permits us to trace in considerable detail the importance of inheritance for immigrants. Hans Paul, a saddlemaker by trade, hailed from Bäslin in Bavaria. He first shows up in the village of Hawangen in 1653, at the time of his marriage to another immigrant, Rosina Sailer from Innsbruck in the Tyrol.[168] Hans seems to have started with almost nothing. During the 1650s we see him painfully acquiring a scrap of meadow here and there,[169] but the tax survey of 1660 still places him in the poorest fifth in the village, owning no cropland at all and only a single cow.[170] Then came a windfall. In 1663 news arrived from Innsbruck that Rosina's father had died, leaving her an inheritance.[171] The following spring Hans trudged back over the Alps to claim the money, and when he returned was finally able to buy some arable land, 3 *jauchert* of freehold for 156 *gulden*.[172] The first windfall was then followed by a second. In May of 1665 Hans received word of a further Austrian inheritance, this time of 200 *gulden*. Again he was able to buy land, three more *jauchert* over the next year and a half. By now he was a man of some means; witnesses attested that his property was worth more than 1,000 *gulden*.[173] Hard work of their own was no doubt an essential part of the couple's success, but the infusion of funds from Rosina's family was clearly of decisive importance.[174]

Without capital, on the other hand, an immigrant's opportunities were severely limited. The Steinhauser family arrived from Weingarten in Württemberg in 1656.[175] Desperately poor, the family split up, with two sons going into service in Hawangen, while the rest huddled in the village of Unger-hausen.[176] They were unlucky. In 1659 the father, Jerg Steinhauser, died "after a long and protracted illness," followed by a twelve-year old son, Balthas, five months later.[177] Left utterly destitute, the mother, Salome Reich, fell to begging, and died shortly thereafter in the winter of 1661, leaving her children nothing more in the world than a chest, a few skirts and shawls, and two hats.[178] By now Salome's children all had families of their own, but poverty had made them unattractive to the better-settled peasantry, and most of them were married to

---

[168] HawPR, Vol. I, f. 39r.

[169] StAA, KL Ottobeuren 912-II, ff. 30v–51r [11 Mar. 1658]; KL Ottobeuren 912, f. 3v [26 Mar. 1659].

[170] StAA, KL Ottobeuren 106, f. 33r.

[171] StAA, KL Ottobeuren 917, ff. 29v–30r [8 May 1663], and 54r–55v [19 Apr. 1664].

[172] StAA, KL Ottobeuren 917-II, ff. 10r–v [30 Apr. 1665].

[173] Ibid., ff. 14r–v [6 May 1665], 20v–21r [22 Oct. 1665], and 80v [29 Oct. 1665].

[174] We know little of the later years of Hans' life. Rosina died in 1669 (HawPR, Vol. II, p. 1 undated; before April 30), whereupon Hans and the two surviving children (the couple had six children, four of whom died young) left the monastery lands. StAA, KL Ottobeuren 338 (Freigelt) [31 Oct. 1669].

[175] StAA, KL Ottobeuren 917, ff. 42r–v [24 Jan. 1664].

[176] StAA, KL Ottobeuren 335 (Strafen) [9 Jan. 1659].

[177] UngPR, Vol. I, pp. 181–2 [3 Nov. 1659, and 11 Apr. 1660].

[178] HawPR, Vol. I, p. 15 [9 Feb. 1661]; KL Ottobeuren 916, f. 18r [3 Mar. 1661].

other outsiders: Martin to a woman from Rosshaupten in the Alpine foothills and Anna to a shepherd from Pfaulen in the lands of the monastery of Ellwangen. Even Johann Steinhauser, who wed the daughter of the Hawangen sheriff, had only joined himself to the poorest household in the village.[179]

The Steinhausers therefore remained on the periphery of rural society. Despite having seven children, Anna and her husband never had a home of their own, and had to live as lodgers in other people's houses.[180] After Anna died in 1664, her husband was unable to remarry, and spent the next twenty-seven years as a widower, dying penniless in 1691.[181] Anna's brother Martin Steinhauser floated back and forth between Hawangen and Westerheim, working variously as a laborer and cowherd. By 1664 he was ready to give up and return to his wife's natal village, but somehow his hopes (and fortunes) revived, and in 1669 he managed to buy a house in Hawangen and formally become an Ottobeuren subject. It was not to be. One year later Martin sold off the house and vanished from the monastery lands.[182] Only Johann Steinhauser, alone among his kin, managed to survive. Perhaps as a result of his precarious toehold among the village establishment, he was after the death of his first wife (1663)[183] able to marry the non-inheriting daughter of a modest *Bauer* family,[184] and assume the tenancy of a small abandoned holding in the hamlet of Betzisried (1668). Buttressed by his in-laws – he seems, in fact, to have begun as their tenant[185] – Johann kept hold of the farm, and it passed at his death to a daughter in 1690.[186]

A temporary stay sustained by menial work rapidly became the lot of many poorer migrants. Thus Christina Gätschin of Grutz in the Tyrol worked two

---

[179] His father–in–law, Jerg Bapelaw, owned nothing more than a house in 1660, while Johann Steinhauser's property amounted to a single cow. StAA, KL Ottobeuren 106, f. 35r.

[180] StAA, KL Ottobeuren 68, f. 18v. This 1674 listing as a lodger is the husband, Jerg Handschuh's only mention in the tax rolls; he does not appear in the rolls for 1660–7 or 1679–89.

[181] UngPR, Vol. I, pp. 186, 212 [6 Dec. 1664 and 19 Nov. 1691]. All but one of the couple's children (born 1655–64) died young. Ibid., pp. 19, 22, 24, 26, 31, 35, 183, 185, 187.

[182] StAA, KL Ottobeuren 338 (Ungenossame) [11 Apr. 1669] and (Vergunstgeld) [11 Apr. 1669 and 11 Sep. 1670]. Martin and his wife had a son in Hawangen in 1659 and four children in Westerheim in 1663–8. HawPR, Vol. I, f. 112r; WestPR, Vol. I, pp. 128, 132, 136, 140.

[183] HawPR, Vol. I, p. 19 [4 Apr. 1663].

[184] Kin relations detailed in OttLSA 1687, pp. 44 and 49; Households nos. 199 and 231. For the transfer of the *Hof* in Halbersberg to Johann's brother-in-law Johann Schmalholz junior, see StAA, KL Ottobeuren 337 (Erdschatz) [10 Feb. 1667]. KL Ottobeuren 917-II, f. 88r [10 Feb. 1667] gives the area as 15 *jauchert* of arable and 14 *tagwerk* of meadow.

[185] Johann's brother-in-law is listed as the owner of the property in the 1669 tax survey. Tithe registers suggest a more complicated situation: the tithe was paid by Johann Steinhauser in 1668 (it was not farmed before this date), by his brother-in-law in 1669–71, by his mother-in-law in 1672–3, and by Johann again from 1674. From 1674, Johann Steinhauser is also listed as the owner of the property, which measured 6.2 *jauchert* of arable and 6.8 *tagwerk* of meadow. StAA, KL Ottobeuren 68, f. 56v; Ottobeuren 105, f. 59v; KL Ottobeuren 109, f. 529v; KL Ottobeuren 683.

[186] StAA, KL Ottobeuren 351 (Vergunstgeld) [11 Aug. 1690].

and a half years for the monks as a scullery maid before leaving in 1662 to marry and settle in nearby Buxheim.[187] The rural clergy quickly picked up on the instability of these newcomers, and began noting in their baptismal registers when parents were considered to be residing merely *"pro tempore"* in the parish.[188] Many migrants resigned themselves to the difficulties of permanent settlement, evidenced by the phenomenon of married men leaving wives and children behind and coming to Ottobeuren to labor for a few months or even a few years before returning to their families in the Tyrol.[189] Still others degenerated into a state of permanent itinerancy, drifting from one village to another with entire families in tow.[190] The dry language of the notarial protocol rarely enables us to fathom the adversity of this existence, but of the adversity itself there can be no doubt.

Maria Specht was from Lindenberg in the Austrian lordship of Bregenz. She flits into view as "a wandering female person" when she was sued for defamation by the innkeeper of Oberwesterheim in the winter of 1681. Maria's own account is worth quoting at length:

> In the fall of 1680 she spent the night in Oberwesterheim, at which time nothing happened between her and the innkeeper except that he kissed her. Three weeks later (that is, about two weeks before Christmas), she again sought shelter for the night in the Oberwesterheim inn, where there were also staying an unknown man, an Italian, whose trade or profession she does not know, and [also] a brewmaster's servant. And when it was time to go to sleep, she too asked to rent a room, but was turned down by the innkeeper, who declared that there were no rooms available, unless she wanted to sleep with the Italian and the servant. This she declined. Later on, after both the guests and the servants had gone to bed, the innkeeper approached her by candlelight [as she lay] in a cot [by the fire?], and attempted to induce her into dishonor. She told him that he should go to his wife, at which he left and pretended to go to his room and do so, but then came right back and harassed her into dishonor [*zû unehrlichem werckh angestrengt*] and impregnated her. Thereafter she had two weeks' threshing work for the innkeeper in Mindelheim, but otherwise

---

[187] StAA, KL Ottobeuren 912, ff. 32v–33r, *Schein* [1 July 1662].

[188] See for example OttPR, Vol. IV (Stephansried), ff. 11v, 14r–v, and 18v–19r for baptisms in 1668–72 of children by foreign parents "pro tempore" or "aliquamdiu . . . moratus" in the parish.

[189] StAA, KL Ottobeuren 912-II, ff. 41r–v [30 Aug. 1659] for two Tyrolese who had been working as laborers in the village of Egg since Lent and were now going back to Riez in the lordship of Petersberg. Also ibid., f. 103r [27 Sep. 1661] for another Tyrolese returning to Selrain (Achambs district) who had worked for a year and a half in the market town of Ottobeuren.

[190] StAA, KL Ottobeuren 912-II, f. 6r [13 Mar. 1659]: Christian Ziegler from Württemberg, after working ten years in the village of Böhen and five in the village of Wolfertschwenden, now moves on with his wife and children to Ittelsburg in the lordship of Rottenstein. Similarly ibid., ff. 13r–v [28 Jan. 1660]: Wolfgang Geromüller from Eppenkirch in the Bishopric of Salzburg leaves the monastery lands with his family after working four years in Ungerhausen.

supported herself by begging here and there for alms, until finally in August of this year, in Brünnenweiler in the lordship of Biberach near Riedlingen she took shelter with a peasant named Hanns, at whose [house] after six weeks she gave birth to a child, who was baptized with the help of [i.e. under godparentage by] the beadle and pastor's housekeeper. One week after the birth, she moved on.

Maria's effort to gain compensation from the wealthy innkeeper yielded only a counter-suit. Her admission that she had that same winter also slept with a soldier and a teamster branded her a "lewd and vexatious" person, and destroyed what little credibility she might otherwise have had before the court. The innkeeper was absolved of any responsibility, and Maria was expelled from the monastery lands.[191] Yet this brief and tragic appearance in the documentary record also provides a rare glimpse of the grinding toil and indignity that was the lot of so many migrants. Homeless and kinless, Maria spent her days criss-crossing the Swabian countryside, surviving on appeals to the passing compassion, short-term labor needs, and clandestine lusts of those more powerful than herself. The nameless Italian boasted that he had "used her improperly" for nothing more than a pair of stockings.

Now, to underscore the perils of the rootless life is at the same time to qualify the strictures of its settled counterpart. There is no gainsaying the severity of the requirements at post-war Ottobeuren for household formation, whether by locals or by foreigners. Neither ought we to minimize the unrelenting family pressure – reinforced by much closer seigneurial oversight – to manage a new household as efficiently as possible. Equally worthy of emphasis, however, is the extraordinary stability of the society founded on these rules of fiscal discipline (see Table 6.10). Of the households established in the quinquennium 1680–4, for example, the overwhelming majority (85.7 percent) survived a full generation, and even among the poor, some three quarters of households managed to preserve or even increase their wealth.

Furthermore, social stability in no way entailed economic stagnation. If in the later seventeenth century the individual peasant household was in every sense characterized by a more measured existence, the rural economy as a whole underwent significant expansion and diversification. Nowhere was this more obvious than in the vigor of exchange. During the Thirty Years War organized commerce had been so disrupted that the Ottobeuren market was closed,[192] and even after the market had been reopened, as late as the 1650s we still see

---

[191] StAA, KL Ottobeuren 919, ff. 256v–258v [4 and 6 Nov. 1681] (the quoted passage on 257r–v).

[192] On 14 January 1637 the Abbot asked his advisors whether the Ottobeuren market ought to be reopened; the chancellor advised that without a permanent peace settlement there was no hope that a reopened market would draw much trade. StAA, KL Ottobeuren (Mü.B.) 64, ff. 327v–331v.

Table 6.10 *Social mobility at Ottobeuren, 1680/4–1704*

	Initial estate value (1684)					
	<500 fl.		>500 fl.		All householders	
Fate by 1704	No.	%	No.	%	No.	%
Untraceable/exit	19	21.3	11	9.1	30	14.3
Loss (≥50%)	4	4.5	2	1.7	6	2.9
Stability (±49%)	42	47.2	101	83.5	143	68.1
Gain (+50–99%)	7	7.9	7	5.8	14	6.7
Doubled (≥100%)	17	19.1	0	0.0	17	8.1
Total	89	100.0	121	100.0	210	100.0

Sources: StAA, KL Ottobeuren 72, 78, 86, 92, 95, 109, 919–22

the peasants bartering their livestock and labor for grain and even for land.[193] But although the density of rural population long remained below pre-war levels, the official markets recovered with remarkable speed. Toll receipts at the Ottobeuren market returned to pre-war levels by the mid-1680s and soared far above them by the 1710s (see Figure 6.10).

The surviving documentation allows only an imperfect reconstruction of what was actually traded on the Ottobeuren market. The cellarer's accounts for the year 1698 do provide a breakdown of toll receipts by the kind of good exchanged, but since the rate at which the different goods were taxed is unclear, the information in Figure 6.11 must remain only an approximate guide. Spirits, for example, certainly did not make up 38.9 percent of the value of rural exchange. On the other hand, the very presence in the official market tolls of *Brantwein*, as it was called, reflects a significant liberalization and diversification of the rural economy since the early seventeenth century.

An outright prohibition on distilling had been appended to the 1596 'Judenordnung,' and there were several prosecutions for the offense in the years that followed.[194] After the war, by contrast, these fears gave way to fiscal realism, and the monastery resolved to tax an industry grown too lucrative to prohibit (for that matter it had also authorized the activities of Jewish horsetraders by

---

[193] E.g. on 4 April 1650 Jerg Rauch of Sontheim made up half of the purchase price of 2 *malter* of spelt with salt and a cart-trip to Lake Constance (StAA, KL Ottobeuren 199); on 27 August 1654 Georg Sommer of Eggisried bought 0.75 *jauchert* of land in exchange for a horse and 8 *gulden* (KL Ottobeuren 914, ff. 339r–340r); on 12 September 1659 Jerg Leichtle, the innkeeper of Sontheim, bartered a gelding and a filly to the monastery for 14.7 *malter* of oats (KL Ottobeuren 205).

[194] StAA, KL Ottobeuren 4, Document 289O, ff. 340v–346r. There are twenty prosecutions for distilling in KL Ottobeuren 587-II, Hefte 21–5 (1601/2–1604/5).

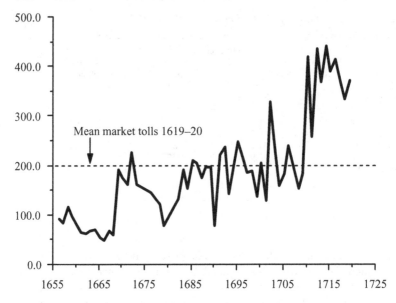

Figure 6.10 Market tolls (fl.) at Ottobeuren, 1656–1719
Sources: StAA, KL Ottobeuren 335–75, 541 (7)

1692[195]). Distilling equipment was openly listed in post-mortem inventories as early as 1661,[196] and an excise on spirits was first paid in the market town of Ottobeuren in 1667. By 1674 this excise was being collected from three settlements and by 1680 from ten.[197] By the end of the century peasants took it for granted that spirits would be served at weddings,[198] and at least one old innkeeper expected a weekly half-tankard when he retired in 1698.[199] The monks did a heady business selling distilling licenses,[200] pausing only to prohibit the serving of spirits at mass time.[201] By 1696 the innkeepers of the market

[195] StAA, KL Ottobeuren 352. Receipts from these traders were by 1699 formalized as the "Jewish toll"; cf. KL Ottobeuren 357. See also the case of the Jewish horsetrader Nazareth Bopffinger, who felt confident enough to sue (successfully) the Hawangen blacksmith in the Abbot's own court for selling Nazareth a sickly horse. KL Ottobeuren 919, ff. 295r–296v [17 Mar. 1682].
[196] StAA, KL Ottobeuren 916, ff. 13r–14r [12 Feb. 1661].
[197] StAA, KL Ottobeuren 486–8.
[198] StAA, KL Ottobeuren 919, ff. 107v–109r [26 Sep. 1680]. See also KL Ottobeuren 921, ff. 191r–v [5 July 1696].
[199] StAA, KL Ottobeuren 922, ff. 43r–45r [9 May 1698].
[200] StAA, KL Ottobeuren 921, ff. 122r [16 Dec. 1695], 224r [8 Nov. 1696], 287r [22 Aug. 1697], 302r [10 Oct. 1697], 309v [31 Oct. 1697], 310v [31 Oct. 1697], and 313v [7 Nov. 1697]. The customary rate was 10 fl. for an annual license.
[201] Ibid., f. 115r [24 Nov. 1695].

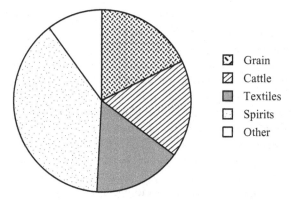

Figure 6.11 Composition of market tolls at Ottobeuren, 1698
Source: StAA, KL Ottobeuren 356

town were complaining that a plethora of peasant distillers was now retailing the product directly and cutting into the receipts of the inns.[202]

Further evidence of the expansion of rural industries in the monastery lands is provided by the multiplication of craft guilds. Peasant guilds had been few in number in the first half of the century; we have the ordinances of only two, the guilds of the Potters (1623) and the Butchers (1631). After the Thirty Years War, by contrast, rural guilds sprang up in virtually every conceivable trade, including those of the Teamsters, Blacksmiths, and Locksmiths (1668), Tailors (1672), Shoemakers and Tanners (1675), Bathhouse-keepers and Barber-surgeons (1685), Cabinetmakers, Glassmakers, Coopers, Painters, Gunsmiths, Cutlers, and Ropemakers (1689), Bakers (1690), Beerbrewers (1695), Millers (1698), Carpenters (1700), and Masons (1700).[203] To be sure, all of these trades had already been practiced for centuries, but their organization into guilds suggests an enhanced importance of rural industries, and a greater ability to compete openly (and effectively) with their urban counterparts.[204]

Linen weaving was the most significant of these industries. Of secondary importance to spinning in the early seventeenth century, weaving rose to prominence even before the end of the Thirty Years War. The earliest reference to a weavers' guild at Ottobeuren dates from 1625, and the first guild ordinance was

---

[202] Ibid., ff. 162v–164r [12 Apr. 1696]. The monastery condemned this practice, and forbade all *unlicensed* distilling, but in the end decided only to ban retailing by the glass, allowing the bakers to continue to sell spirits by the tankard or cask. Ibid., ff. 320v–321r [12 Dec. 1697].
[203] StAA (Mü.B.), KL Ottobeuren 163–76.
[204] For the decline of urban industrial production in Memmingen – especially linen weaving – in the face of rural competition, see Rita Huber-Sperl, *Memmingen zwischen Zunfthandwerk und Unternehmertum: ein Beitrag zur reichsstädtischen Gewerbegeschichte, 1648 bis 1802* (Memmingen, 1995).

promulgated in 1643.[205] Apprentices continued to be trained throughout the war years, even though their certificates could not be registered because of administrative chaos.[206] With the coming of peace, weaving continued to expand. Apprentices were drawn from as far away as Switzerland and the Tyrol, and revised guild ordinances were issued in 1670, 1687, and 1744.[207]

Guilds are often regarded as encumbrances on the industries they regulated,[208] and the Ottobeuren linen weavers certainly imposed severe restrictions on their members. An aspiring master had to be legitimately born. He had to serve a three-year apprenticeship, and was thereafter required to work two years for a master and complete a masterpiece before he could be admitted as a master himself. After training an apprentice, a master could not take on another for the next two years.[209] A master was also forbidden to operate more than two looms.[210] The monastery drew the line at wage fixing, and in 1661 censured a certain Caspar Maier of Ottobeuren for declaring that any weaver who accepted payment below 4 1/2 kr. per ell was a "bungler." Nevertheless, the fact that the monks had to publicly affirm a master's right to accept a wage as low as 2 1/2 kr. without being subject to denunciation[211] is itself powerful testimony of the anticompetitive ethos of the weavers' guild.

Unfortunately for its members, however, the guild never established a monopoly on linen production. The guild's own ordinances affirmed the right of both single and married women to weave the cheaper grades of cloth,[212] and it seems clear that the guild looms larger in the archival record than its actual economic clout would warrant. It is not possible to reconstruct the overall volume of cloth woven in the Ottobeuren lands, but the monastery purchased large

---

[205] StAA, KL Ottobeuren 909, ff. 43v–44r [20 Feb. 1625]. The oldest surviving guild ordinance (1670) refers to an initial charter of 1643. KL Ottobeuren (Mü.B.) 166.

[206] Thus the *Lehrbrief* of Johann Jerg Breth from the Muntafun valley in the Grisons (Switzerland), who was apprenticed to Michael Depperich of Hawangen in 1643, notes "whereas after the end of the three years [of apprenticeship], lamentable warfare recommenced and there was no one at home, he therefore is now [formally] released from his indenture." StAA, KL Ottobeuren 915, f. 47r [15 Nov. 1658].

[207] StAA, KL Ottobeuren 915, ff. 45v–46r [24 Sep. 1658]; KL Ottobeuren 912, ff. 23v–24r [11 July 1660]; KL Ottobeuren (Mü.B.) 166. Minor amendments were added to the last ordinance in 1771 and 1780.

[208] Sheilagh Ogilvie, *State Corporatism and Proto-Industry: The Württemberg Black Forest, 1580–1797* (Cambridge, 1997) offers both a painstaking study of another Swabian district and a thorough review of the literature. For a region still closer to the Ottobeuren lands, see also Anke Sczesny, *Zwischen Kontinuität und Wandel: Ländliches Gewerbe und ländliche Gesellschaft im Ostschwaben des 17. und 18. Jahrhunderts* (Tübingen, 2002).

[209] StAA, KL Ottobeuren (Mü.B.) 166, ff. 2v–3v; regulations of 1643 reproduced in the ordinance of 1670 (§7–11). An amendment of 1671 required that the masterpiece be completed before marriage. Ibid., f. 6r (§22).

[210] StAA, KL Ottobeuren 916-II, ff. 24r and 51r [23 Mar. and 13 July 1662].

[211] StAA, KL Ottobeuren 916, ff. 16v and 43r–v [3 Mar. and 12 May 1661].

[212] StAA, KL Ottobeuren (Mü.B.) 166, ff. 3v–4r (§12). Masters' widows were also allowed to engage journeymen.

amounts of linen from the peasantry every year, and the surviving accounts tell an interesting story. Over the years 1687–93, for example, the monks bought some 2,200 fl. worth of linen from their subjects in just under two hundred individual transactions. Barely a fifth of the total (20.7 percent) was paid out to known members of the weavers' guild. The bulk of the sales (63.6 percent) were made by *Hof* tenants or identifiable members of other trades. The rest was divided between *Seldner* who may or may not have been guild members (7.9 percent) and sellers of indeterminate social status, most of them widows (7.8 percent).[213] Later recensions of the guild ordinances clearly reflect the pressures of competition. In 1687 the guild endeavored to establish its own control over growing disputes between weavers and merchant contractors over the time taken to complete work, but later evidence suggests a lack of success. Still more revealing was the forlorn attempt in 1744 to ensure that a master was paid at least 2 1/2 kr. per ell, a rate rejected by an earlier generation as a bungler's wage.[214] For all the proud claims of the guild, therefore, linen weaving at Ottobeuren was in practice open to almost anyone, and this was even truer of newer textile industries like stocking-knitting, which was apparently never organized into a guild[215] and which by the later eighteenth century was approaching weaving in importance.[216]

Market tolls and incorporated guilds belong to the domain of licit exchange. As was demonstrated in chapter 5, however, illicit exchange also represented an important and growing sector in the rural economy. Even before the last soldiers were mustered out of the countryside, the Ottobeuren peasants had returned to their old tricks of buying and selling outside of officially sanctioned markets. In 1649 Abbot Maurus again felt obliged to enjoin the peasantry "henceforth diligently to patronize . . . the weekly market in Ottobeuren with all [of your] saleable goods, and also outside of it neither to buy nor to sell the slightest thing, whether in cities, villages, houses, or places [either] inside or outside of the lordship."[217] Throughout the eighteenth century the monastery would continue to inveigh against the illicit trading of its subjects,[218] to send spies to

---

[213] Linen purchases in StAA, KL Ottobeuren 348–52. Identifications supplemented on the basis of KL Ottobeuren 78, 86, 109, 919–22 and OttLSA 1687.

[214] StAA, KL Ottobeuren (Mü.B.) 166, ff. 8r and 14r. See also KL Ottobeuren 944, ff. 184r–185r [12 Feb. 1778], where a merchant sues a weaver in the Abbot's court over the time taken to weave cloth.

[215] StAA, KL Ottobeuren 922, ff. 31v–32r and 37v–38r [10 Apr. and 28 Apr. 1698] detail the problems of one Simon Wagner, who had difficulty being accepted as a stocking-knitter in Neuburg an der Kammel because his master was not in a stocking-knitters' guild,

[216] In the village of Wolfertschwenden, 34 percent of all householders were identified as textile producers in 1782, a majority of them stocking-knitters. In the lordship as a whole, however, weaving still predominated by a margin of roughly two to one. StAA, KL Ottobeuren 529.

[217] StadtA MM A. 40/3 "Dekret des Abts zu Ottobeuren" [6 Aug. 1649].

[218] StAA, KA Ottobeuren 646, Printed Ottobeuren Market Ordinance 1770.

monitor their activities,[219] and to fine those whom it caught,[220] but the effort was of little avail. The medieval boundaries of exchange had collapsed for good, and there was nothing the Abbot could do to rebuild them.

It must be said that the papers of the criminal court record fewer marketing offenses in the second half of the seventeenth century than they do in the first half, but this in no way indicates a greater degree of compliance. On the contrary, it reflects the resignation of the monastery's officials in the face of a mass of violations they simply could not contain. In 1679 and 1680, the sheriffs of the monastery lands submitted a series of brief reports on the commercial activity of the subject population. The tone of these reports is almost everywhere the same:[221]

> Hawangen (1679): "Of the eggs, lard, spinning, and other goods, [only] the smallest part is sold on the market here; it is all sold in Memmingen instead."

> Günz (1679): "The subjects here in violation of all orders sell the greatest part of their grain as well as their lard, eggs, spinning, and the like in other places. The Rummeltshausers do the same."

> Wolfertschwenden (1679): "The sheriff reports that no grain from the valley is brought to Ottobeuren, but it is all taken elsewhere and sold. Other goods are taken to Memmingen and other places, and in the entire valley no one is innocent of this."

> Frechenrieden and Altisried (1679): "Except for grain nothing at all is brought to the market here, for it is all sold outside [the market] and to roving traders."

> Schlegelsberg (1679): "Nothing is brought to the market from here; with regards to grain it is also doubtful that everything is brought [to Ottobeuren]."

> Sontheim (1680): "The market is not patronized from Sontheim, but [rather] the greatest part, if indeed not everything, is bought up by roving traders."

> Niederrieden (1680): "Grain and other [goods] are all sold on the Memmingen market."

---

[219] StadtA MM, A. 40/5 Draft of a letter from the mayor and council of Memmingen to the Abbot of Ottobeuren protesting spying by the Abbot's sheriff at the Memmingen market [7 June 1702]; "Aussag von Martin Längerer Weber" detailing continued harassment of Ottobeuren peasants at the Memmingen market by the Abbot's sheriffs [2 Apr. 1715].

[220] See for example the fines of ten peasants in Unterwesterheim and Egg for unauthorized selling of grain outside of the monastery lands in StAA, KL Ottobeuren 356 (1698/9).

[221] StAA, KL Ottobeuren 587-III, Hefte 38 (1678/9) and 39 (1678–82).

All in all, the conclusion is unavoidable that the attempt to confine rural exchange to the times and place of the official marketplace in Ottobeuren had proved an utter failure. The Abbot can hardly have been pleased to receive these reports, and in 1689 we actually find the monastery fining not only its subjects for selling grain in Memmingen on a feast day, but its own officials as well for failing to report the infraction.[222] At times the Abbots themselves seem to have wearied of the hopeless task; by 1702 dispensations from the obligation to trade at Ottobeuren had been issued to several villages "for whom on account of their location the patronage of our weekly market here is somewhat inconvenient."[223]

Indeed, for all their public fulminations, the monks had in fact come to a much closer accommodation with the unbounded rural economy than such grudging concessions would suggest, and this is particularly apparent with regard to the grain trade. In the early seventeenth century, sales from the monastery's granary tended to wax and wane to the rhythm of grain prices (see Figure 6.12). Most transactions involved small volumes, and no individual buyer purchased any significant proportion of the total. By the eve of the Thirty Years War this pattern had begun to change, as the granary's business came to be dominated by large volume buyers who were clearly intending to resell the grain for profit elsewhere. The monastery had become a business partner to the very middlemen it excoriated in its ordinances.

The dominant buyer at the monastery granary in the 1640s and 1650s was a man by the name of Jerg Graf. Born about the year 1584 in the village of Böhen, he got his start in 1614 when a poor widow moved off to a different settlement, and sold him the half-house where she had left behind three of her four orphaned children.[224] Graf did move into better quarters four years later, but his initial foray into the land market was a disappointment, and in 1620 the house remained his only property.[225] Shortly thereafter, however, Jerg Graf found his true calling as a smuggler. In 1623 and again in 1624 he was arrested for illegal trips to the Memmingen market.[226] Fortified by the infusion of his wife's small inheritance in 1625, Graf then became active as a middleman, buying up grain in his home parish and carting it south for sale in the lands of the Prince-Abbot of Kempten. It was a lucrative business, and by 1627 he had added to his house a small herd of four cattle as well as – and rather more

---

[222] StAA, KL Ottobeuren 599, ff. 20r–v [18 Apr. 1689].

[223] StadtA MM, A. 40/5 Abbot of Ottobeuren to the mayor and council of Memmingen [19 Sep. 1702].

[224] StAA, KL Ottobeuren 915, ff. 33r–v [25 June 1658] (where he gave his age as 74); KL Ottobeuren 905, ff. 138r–v [9 Dec. 1613]; ibid., ff. 164r–165r [24 Feb. 1614]; KL Ottobeuren 491-II, Heft 16, f. 20v and Heft 17, f. 25v, KL Ottobeuren 102, f. 386r.

[225] He purchased a half-*jauchert* but was forced to resell it five months later. StAA, KL Ottobeuren 907, ff. 42r, 95v [27 Jan. and 28 June 1617], and 169v–170r [9 June 1618]; KL Ottobeuren 102, f. 117r.

[226] StAA, KL Ottobeuren 587-II, Hefte 31 (1623–5) and 32 (1624).

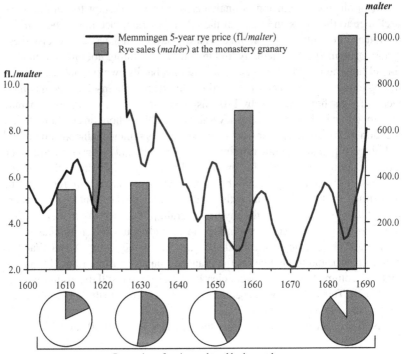

Proportion of grain purchased by largest buyer

Figure 6.12 Evolution of the Ottobeuren grain market, 1610–84
Sources: StAA, KL Ottobeuren 198, 203, 204–5, 208, 224–5

significantly – assets of 300 fl. in cash and loans.[227] Much of this liquid capital was reinvested in the legal grain trade, and in 1632 he made purchases worth more than a thousand *gulden* at the monastery's granary alone.[228]

It was a stunning achievement for a mere *Seldner*, but Graf did not remain in that status for much longer. By 1636 he had parlayed his profits from trade into the tenancy of a large *Hof*, and at the war's end he was the richest man in the village.[229] Graf remained an active grain merchant well into his seventies, ranging as far north as Ulm, and retiring from trading only at the end of 1659.[230] Even thereafter, however, he continued to ruffle feathers by buying

---

[227] StAA, KL Ottobeuren 909, f. 70r [18 June 1625]; KL Ottobeuren 587-III, Heft 33 (1626), f. 31r and Heft 34 (1627), f. 41r; KL Ottobeuren 104, f. 101v.

[228] StAA, KL Ottobeuren 198.

[229] StAA, KL Ottobeuren 43, ff. 74r–79r; KL Ottobeuren 160, ff. 64r–65r; KL Ottobeuren 202, f. 81r.

[230] StAA, KL Ottobeuren 335 (Strafen) [19 Apr. 1657]. Graf made a total of 141 purchases at the monastery granary in 1657/8, 45 in 1658/9, and 8 in 1659/60. KL Ottobeuren 205.

up discounted obligations (the peasantry seems to have recognized the need to discount pre-war debts more quickly than their overlords) and then pressing the original debtors for repayment in full.[231] Jerg Graf died in 1663 or 1664 at the age of about eighty; his lands passed to his son Hans[232] who became village *Amman* in 1682, acquired the Böhen inn in 1687, and by the early eighteenth century was one of the wealthiest men in the entire lordship.[233]

Jerg Graf's departure from the grain trade changed only the players at the table; the rules of the game remained the same. In fact, the granary's business became even more concentrated (see Figure 6.12) as it fell into the hands of a series of peasant syndicates based in the bread-poor uplands of the Princely Abbacy of Kempten.[234] These syndicates were close-knit groups of two to three buyers, united by bonds of kinship and godparentage. They witnessed each other's weddings and notarial transactions,[235] and passed on their "places" in the team to their children. Thus, when Jacob Schmidt of Haslach died in December of 1671, his place as a buyer was taken by his son Michael. In the same way Jacob's old partner Johann Ohneberg of Osterwald was replaced (*c.* 1690) by his sedulous son Jerg, who was so busy trading grain that he didn't marry until the age of forty-eight in 1705.[236]

None of these peasants – and that they were peasants warrants emphasis; urban buyers only rarely appear in the Ottobeuren granary accounts – was unusually rich, even by rural standards. They were neither millers nor innkeepers, but

---

[231] StAA, KL Ottobeuren 916, ff. 47r–v [27 May 1661].

[232] Jerg Graf was still alive in 1662, but by 1665 his (unmarried) son Hans already owned the house. StAA, KL Ottobeuren 916-II, f. 53r [31 Aug. 166]; KL Ottobeuren 917-II, ff. 6v and 85r [5 Mar. 1665 and 13 Jan. 1667]. See also KL Ottobeuren 56, f. 155r and KL Ottobeuren 57, ff. 156v–157r.

[233] Hans Graf succeeded in office one Johann Schmidt, who died *c.* 29 October 1682. StAA, KL Ottobeuren 68, f. 70v; KL Ottobeuren 78, f. 69v; KL Ottobeuren 919, ff. 354r–355r. See also KL Ottobeuren 920, ff. 347r–v [5 Dec. 1687] and KL Ottobeuren 95. In 1704 Hans Graf ranked seventeenth of just under 1,200 households in the monastery lands.

[234] The so-called Montgelas statistics of 1811 indicate that arable agriculture in the former Kempten lordship was still heavily weighted towards oats and barley, as opposed to the bread grains rye and spelt. Christoph Borcherdt, "Die Agrarlandschaft des Regierungsbezirks Schwaben zu Beginn des 19. Jahrhunderts," *Schwäbische Blätter* 8, 2 (1957), pp. 33–43.

[235] Johann Ohneberg "Kisele" witnessed the 1680 retirement agreement of Johann Ohneberg "Schwarz," in addition to serving in 1670 as godfather for "Schwarz's" grandson Martin. Martin Ohneberg was in turn a witness at the 1705 wedding of Jerg Ohneberg, son of Johann Ohneberg "Kisele." Ulrich Epp witnessed the 1663 wedding of Jacob Ohneberg, son of Johann "Schwarz," and Jacob took Ulrich's daughter Barbara as his second wife in 1668. One of the Johann Ohnebergs probably served as godfather to eight of the thirteen children of Michael Schmidt of Haslach; the godfather's surname is given as "Bonenberg" in the parish register between 1668 and 1690, but there is no Johann Bonenberg listed in the parish in the tax registers of 1667 or 1687. Probstried Parish Register [herein after ProbPR], Vol. I, pp. 37, 209, 228, 384, and Vol. II, pp. 322; StAA, KL Kempten 34, ff. 94r–v [7 Aug. 1680]; KL Kempten (Neuburger Abgabe [henceforth NA]) 1641, ff. 4r–10v and KL Kempten (NA) 1680, ff. 19r–4v.

[236] ProbPR, Vol. I, pp. 101, 348; StAA, KL Ottobeuren 207–8; KL Ottobeuren 259; KL Kempten 564, pp. 142–3 [30 Jan. 1705].

solid members of the *Bauer* class.[237] The cousins Johann and Jacob Ohneberg, for example, who bought over 6,000 fl. worth of Ottobeuren grain in 1684/5, held properties measuring only 33.2 and 45.9 *jauchert* respectively.[238] The traders were also survivors. All of the original members of the Kempten syndicate, referred to in the Ottobeuren accounts of the early 1660s as the "three ordinary grain buyers," had been in place before the Thirty Years War,[239] and the Ohneberg family in particular can be documented on the self-same *Hof* at least as far back as 1623.[240]

These peasant middlemen traded on a smaller scale than urban grain merchants like the notorious Hans Mochel of Memmingen, who sold Swabian grain to the textile-producing regions of eastern Switzerland.[241] Where Mochel and his kind operated on the order of several hundred *malter* per transaction, their rural counterparts rarely bought more than thirty *malter* at once, and more commonly ten to twenty. Yet the peasant buyers made up for their smaller individual purchases with a ceaseless, antlike activity, returning week after week to the monastery for yet another cartload of grain. There could be no stopping, even for death. In 1669, for example, Ulrich Epp of Buchen came to Ottobeuren to buy grain on 14 February, on 14 March, on 11 April, and again on 2 May. Ulrich was buried on 30 May 1669 . . . and on 6 June his widow was back at the granary to buy 6 *malter* of rye.[242] Equally relentless was the Ohneberg family, which dominated the granary's business in the 1680s and 1690s. Jacob and Jerg Ohneberg made no fewer than 280 individual purchases in the year 1684/5, and when Jacob died in May of 1691, his widow, Barbara Epp, stepped into his shoes until their unmarried son Martin was ready to assume responsibility for buying the following February. All of these small transactions added up. In 1684/5 the Ohnebergs purchased (and resold, most likely for the Swiss market) over fifteen hundred *malter* of grain – a year's supply for a thousand people.[243]

---

[237] This emerges clearly from the Prince Abbacy's tax registers. See for example the 1667 register in StAA, KL Kempten (NA) 1641, ff. 4r–10v.

[238] StAA, KL Ottobeuren 208; KL Kempten (NA) 147, pp. 440–50. Johann Ohneberg sold this land to his son for 900 fl. KL Kempten 34, ff. 94r–v [7 Aug. 1680].

[239] The 1640 listing of householders drawn up by Prince-Abbot Romanus Giel separately registers long-term residents and recent immigrants; Ulrich Epp of Buchen, Jacob Schmidt of Haslach, and Hans Ohneberg of Osterwald, all in the parish of Probstried, are named in the former category. Alfred Weitnauer, "Die Bevölkerung des Stifts Kempten vom Jahre 1640," *Allgäuer Heimatbücher* 14 [*Alte Allgäuer Geschlechter* 9] (1939), pp. 38–9. See also StAA, KL Ottobeuren 205.

[240] StAA, KL Kempten 19, ff. 198v–199r [21 June 1623]. This is clearly the same property as the one held by Johann Ohneberg in the 1687 land survey.

[241] Mochel was in the 1660s repeatedly cited by the Memmingen authorities for engrossing in particular and for ruthless business tactics in general. His career is discussed in Wolf, *Reichsstädte in Kriegszeiten*, pp. 178–80.

[242] StAA, KL Ottobeuren 207; ProbPR, Vol. I, p. 346.

[243] StAA, KL Ottobeuren 208 and 259; ProbPR, Vol. II, p. 224.

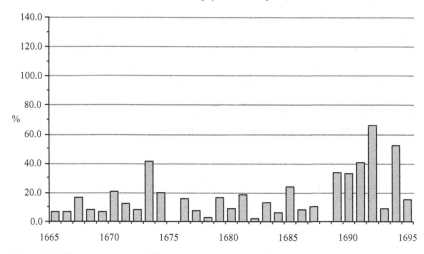

Figure 6.13 Range of variation (%) in rye prices among four Ottobeuren villages, 1665–95
Sources: StAA, KL Ottobeuren 602-I, 625, 654, 666

With the collapse of grain prices in the aftermath of the Thirty Years War, opportunities for arbitrage grew correspondingly tighter. As has been seen, however, it was precisely in these years that the market underwent its decisive transformation. Swollen by a flow of activity both inside and outside the bounds of the law, the rural exchange network grew to a new level of efficiency and a new scale of operations. The repercussions were momentous. In the highly industrialized sector of eastern Switzerland, whose textile producers had become dependent on Swabian grain, the consequence was a population boom.[244] For the Ottobeuren villages themselves, integration into the larger regional market was equally dramatic. Whereas in the later sixteenth century neighboring villages were regularly separated by extreme price differentials of up to 100 percent, a century later this was no longer the case (see Figure 6.13; compare with Figure 2.5)

The very language of money was absorbed into daily usage in the monastery lands, and tardy debtors of the 1680s were constantly claiming to be able to cover a debt with a horse, a load of wax, and so on, but referring to their present inability to "turn it into money" [*versilbern, zu geld machen*].[245] At times one is even tempted to wonder whether the newer system of exchange,

[244] Frank Göttmann, "Aspekte der Tragfähigkeit in der Ostschweiz um 1700" in Joachim Jahn and Wolfgang Hartung, eds., *Gewerbe und Handel vor der Industrialisierung: Regionale und überregionale Verflechtungen im 17. und 18. Jahrhundert* (Sigmaringendorf, 1991), pp. 152–82. See also Göttmann's seminal *Getreidemarkt am Bodensee: Raum, Wirtschaft, Politik, Gesellschaft (1650–1810)* (St. Katharinen, 1991).
[245] StAA, KL Ottobeuren 919, ff. 161r–v and 172r–v [13 Feb. and 27 Mar. 1681].

having broken through the barriers of an older, compartmentalized, and often barter-based pattern, in the end finished by erecting barriers of its own. On 10 February 1680 we find Christian Möst of Hof complaining that he had not received a considerable portion of the grain, lard, and eggs which according to his maintenance agreement were owed to him by his son-in-law. The son-in-law, Mathias Karrer, a comfortable *Bauer*, did not deny the charge. His excuse, however, was not so much poverty as the revealing claim "that it is not possible for him to deliver the said owed grain *in natura*."[246]

---

[246] Ibid., f. 20v. Mathias Karrer had 15.75 *jauchert* of land and a gross wealth of 793 *gulden* in 1689. KL Ottobeuren 109, f. 519v. See also KL Ottobeuren 919, ff. 30v–31r [11 Mar. 1680], where Jerg Schweiggart of Hawangen is ordered to deliver to his mother an outstanding maintenance payment "*in natura*."

Conclusion

In June of 1542, old Benedict Seitz of Betzisried[1] bought a horse from a neighbor, Jörg Stroglin. The deal was formalized with the traditional cup of wine, but does not seem to have rested on an explicit price. When the transaction became the subject of a dispute in the following year, one witness to the sale testified that he could not remember the price, while another declared that buyer and seller "had agreed to nothing more than that Bene should work for Jörg two days a week . . . and that he [Benedict] should pay him [the remainder of] whatever was not worked off by Martinmas [11 November]." Benedict's wage rate was no more clearly stipulated than the price of the horse; the witnesses (a total of five were deposed) added only that Jörg agreed to notify Benedict every Sunday which days of the week he would be needed, "so that he could [also] work in other places."[2]

In March of 1698, another Ottobeuren peasant became embroiled in a similar dispute. Jerg Stich of Böhen complained to the court of the Kempten district of Falken that he had been swindled in a horse trade the previous month by one Franz Meÿr of Dietmannsried. Meÿr had taken advantage of his "drunken imprudence," Stich claimed, to take Stich's horse, worth 25 fl. at least, in exchange for 2 1/2 fl. in cash and a nag worth no more than 10 fl. The defendant took exception to this characterization of the exchange. Stich had been "somewhat inebriated," Meÿr conceded, but not so much so that he did not know what he was doing. Stich had been sober enough to reject one of Meÿr's coins as containing too much copper, and the "nag" had been acquired just the previous year for 25 *gulden*.

Furthermore, he had offered his [own] horse on the market in the same way as the plaintiff . . . and when the 2 1/2 fl. lay before him on the table, [the plaintiff] still had the choice to keep his own horse or to make this trade, and

---

[1] Benedict's home is not given in the 1543 court protocol, but he is listed in Betzisried in the 1525 tax register. His age may be inferred from the fact that his daughter Magdalena was married with two children by 1548. StAA, KL Ottobeuren 541, Heft 3, f. 50r; KL Ottobeuren 600, ff. 44v–47r.

[2] The (incomplete) record of the dispute is in StAA, KL Ottobeuren 900, ff. 51r–52r [5 Dec. 1543].

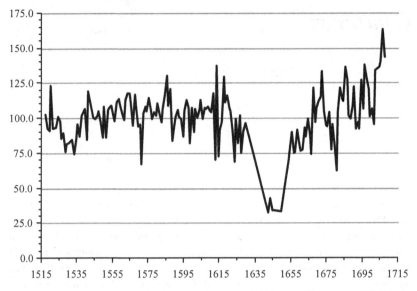

Figure 7.1 Tithe receipts in nine Ottobeuren villages, 1517–1707 (overall average = 100.0)
Sources: StAA, KL Ottobeuren 245 and KA Ottobeuren 34–36, 40, 55, 227, 230–232, and 281–307

since he made the latter choice, he [the defendant] does not believe that he owes him [the plaintiff] any further answer or explanation.

Meÿer demanded 10 *gulden* in compensation to take his horse back; the court moderated the sum to six.[3]

A great deal had changed in Upper Swabia in the century and a half between two horse sales gone bad. Most obviously, Benedict Seitz's world of barter and stable customary value had given way to Franz Meÿr's marketplace where peasants monitored the integrity of currency and a transaction was legitimated by the free choice of rational agents. But how ought we more broadly to characterize the development of rural society between the late fifteenth and early eighteenth centuries?

The logical place to start is with material well-being, and in particular, given its centrality to the economy of early modern Europe, with arable agriculture. Ottobeuren yields per unit area were perfectly respectable by wider European standards,[4] but the long-term trend in grain production was marked by only modest increases. As is clear from Figure 7.1, which presents the aggregated

---

[3] StAA, KL Kempten 563, "Protokolle der Pflege Falken 1696–1702," ff. 213–215 [5 Mar. 1698]; the long quotation on ff. 214–215.

[4] Ottobeuren yields for rye (15.0 hl/ha or 16.7 bushels per acre) and oats (20.7 hl/ha or 23.0 bushels per acre) were in fact fully in line with English yields during the seventeenth century, but did not keep pace during the eighteenth and nineteenth centuries. See the summary figures in M. J. Daunton, *Progress and Poverty: An Economic and Social History of Britain 1700–1850* (Oxford, 1995), p. 32.

Table 7.1 *Number of cows in nine Ottobeuren villages, 1620–1892*

Village	1620	1660	1689	1740	1782	1892
Altisried	44	23	32	41	48	[a]
Attenhausen	135	88	134	164	180	357
Egg	211	115	184	261	253	518
Frechenrieden	148	84	146	171	201	550
Günz	107	69	102	112	121	300
Hawangen	248	141	173	258	237	569
Niederdorf	76	54	85	90	124	322
Rummeltshausen	59	16	50	60	55	[a]
Ungerhausen	123	69	103	174	173	313
Total	1151	659	1009	1331	1392	2929
Index	100.0	57.3	87.7	115.6	120.9	254.5

Note: [a]1892 figures for Altisried and Rummeltshausen included with Frechenrieden and Günz respectively
Sources: StAA, KL Ottobeuren 102, 106, 109, 521, 529; Ergebnisse der Viehzählung im Königreiche Bayern

tithe receipts of nine Ottobeuren villages (Altisried, Attenhausen, Egg, Frechenrieden, Günz, Hawangen, Niederdorf, Rummeltshausen, and Ungerhausen), radical changes in output must have post-dated the period under consideration.[5] In the same way, the eighteenth century did see movement towards the intensive pastoral economy which characterizes the contemporary Allgäu, but the shift was only fully elaborated during the nineteenth century (see Table 7.1).

Does this mean that nothing had really changed between 1480 and 1720? Hardly. If we turn our attention to the inner workings of the productive unit, an unmistakable metamorphosis becomes obvious. In the first place, tax surveys reveal that the peasant household had begun accumulating a great deal more moveable wealth, here defined as personal effects, tools and equipment, excluding livestock (see Table 7.2), a trend further reflected in the (new) concern of later seventeenth-century notarial records to itemize the moveables transferred to the heir at inheritance. Second, the gradually expanding productive activities of the household grew strikingly less dependent on external sources of credit. By the end of the seventeenth century, the Ottobeuren land market had returned to pre-war levels of activity, but the peasantry was now able to sustain this volume of purchase and sale without any significant need to borrow cash

---

[5] There are few studies of German tithe series, making it difficult to assess the typicality of Ottobeuren trends, but a similar picture of long-term stability (based on much larger samples) emerges in Béatrice Veyrassat-Herren, "Dîmes alsaciennes," in Goy and Ladurie, eds., *Fluctuations du produit de la dîme*, pp. 83–102 and Walter Bauernfeind, *Materielle Grundstrukturen im Spätmittelalter und der Frühen Neuzeit: Preisentwicklung und Agrarkonjunktur am Nürnberger Getreidemarkt von 1339 bis 1670* (Nuremberg, 1993).

Table 7.2 *Mean moveable wealth and debts per household in nine Ottobeuren villages, 1620 and 1689*

	Moveable wealth (fl.)		Debts (fl.)	
Settlement	1620	1689	1620	1689
Altisried	8.1	30.0	182.2	32.7
Attenhausen	5.0	31.6	118.2	22.9
Egg	4.3	33.2	188.9	4.4
Frechenrieden	5.8	34.0	153.9	17.3
Günz	10.3	43.2	102.0	7.6
Hawangen	5.2	37.3	178.9	35.9
Niederdorf	6.1	35.2	128.6	13.7
Rummeltshausen	10.6	35.7	187.4	55.2
Ungerhausen	8.4	36.1	86.7	56.7
All nine villages	6.1	35.1	149.4	24.3
Index	100.0	575.4	100.0	16.3

Sources: StAA, KL Ottobeuren 102, 109

(see Table 7.3).[6] In the same way, the late sixteenth-century lending boom by chapels and parish churches was only faintly echoed in the generations after the Thirty Years War (see Figure 7.2). What had changed, in other words, was not so much the level, as the commercialization and social organization of peasant production.

Regarding the former trend, there is no need to repeat here the evidence of the last two chapters for a tremendous deepening of market relations in the monastery lands over the course of the seventeenth century, although it is worth adding that similar tendencies have been documented (with some variation in chronology) all over early modern Germany.[7] Of course, the Upper Swabian countryside had a history of exchange with local urban economies going back to the fourteenth century at least,[8] but we may meaningfully distinguish the

[6] 'Cash borrowing' is here defined to exclude (1) unpaid portions of a sale price still owed by the buyer to the seller and (2) inheritances owed to yielding heirs, both of which were regularly notarized as debts. According to tax surveys of 1620 and 1689, the annual volume of sales in 1603–7, 1630–2, and 1695–8 represented 2.42%, 2.37% and 3.51% of the value of all real property in the lordship respectively.

[7] For helpful surveys, see Heide Wunder, "Agriculture and Agrarian Society" in Sheilagh Ogilvie, ed., *Germany: A New Social and Economic History*, Vol. II: *1630–1800* (1996), pp. 63–99 and Werner Trossbach, *Bauern 1648–1806* (Munich,1993), pp. 64–70. Trossbach maintains that in most of Germany the commercialization of the rural economy came only in the eighteenth century, and even then hesitantly.

[8] Hektor Ammann, "Die Anfänge der Leinenindustrie des Bodenseegebiets," *Alemannisches Jahrbuch* (1953), pp. 251–313; Bernhard Kirchgässner, "Der Verlag im Spannungsfeld von Stadt und Umland," in Erich Maschke and Jürgen Sydow, eds., *Stadt und Umland* (Stuttgurt, 1974), pp. 72–128; Hans Conrad Peyer, *Leinwandgewerbe und Fernhandel der Stadt St. Gallen von den Anfängen bis 1520*, (2 vols., St. Gallen, 1959–60). I owe these references to Tom Scott.

Table 7.3 *Annual volume of property sales and cash borrowing at Ottobeuren, 1580–1698*

Years	Property sales (fl.)	Index	Deflated[a] sales (fl.)	Index	Cash loans (fl.)	As a % of land sales
1580–4	11,241.2	100.0	11,241.2	100.0	2,174.4	19.3
1603–7	18,196.0	161.9	15,582.8	138.6	5,286.7	29.1
1630–2	17,810.1	158.4	14,147.4	125.9	7,683.6	43.1
1663–7	6,385.3	56.8	6,425.1	57.2	1,298.5	20.3
1695–8	20,466.5	182.1	17,161.2	152.7	421.9	2.1

Note: [a] By the price of rye at Memmingen
Sources: StAA, KL Ottobeuren 102, 104, 109, 900, 903, 911, 917, 918, 921–2

Figure 7.2 Outstanding loans of the Sontheim parish church in gulden, 1585–1711
Sources: StadtA MM D. 64/8a; StAA, KA Ottobeuren 348 and KL Ottobeuren 702

late medieval pattern of occasional marketing of textiles and other artisanal products as a supplement to a rural household's income from the early modern phenomenon of market participation as a necessary part of the self-perpetuation of the rural household.[9] Not only was there no necessary progression from the former to the latter form of exchange,[10] but the balance of power between town and country had also shifted rather dramatically in the process.

[9] This corresponds to de Vries' influential distinction between subsistence and specializing peasant economies Ian de Vries, *The Dutch Rural Economy in the Golden Age, 1500–1700* (New Haven, 1974), pp. 4–11.

[10] As is clear from the example of the Upper Rhineland. Tom Scott, *Regional Identity and Economic Change: The Upper Rhine, 1450–1600* (Oxford, 1997), pp. 301–10.

By the later seventeenth century Memmingen had declined from a center of international commerce to a regional distribution center,[11] and had abandoned the effort to impose commercial hegemony over its hinterland. Growing interdependence with the surrounding countryside had also taught the city council a degree of humility, and the 1600 dismissal of the Ottobeuren peasantry as bumpkins "with neither enough cattle, grain, nor other victuals or goods to justify the establishment of a single annual market" was by 1702 replaced with the concession that Memmingen and the monastery lands "are bound together, such that the one always has need of the other, and in such a manner that each party must always uphold and maintain the motto, 'the one hand washes the other.' "[12]

To maintain that market participation had by 1700 (indeed by 1600) become a necessity for the peasantry brings us to the second, and more fundamental trend, i.e. the emergence of new social relations of production over the course of the sixteenth and seventeenth centuries. Did this represent some kind of transition to capitalism? Given the ahistorical rigidity of classic Marxist terms of analysis, and the uniquely convoluted nature of the associated literature,[13] speculation of this sort is currently (and understandably) rather out of fashion. Yet to discard these old red questions altogether too often results in either a historiography of endless qualification concluding merely that a received model of social history is "not as [insert modifier] as has heretofore been thought," or in a preoccupation with seemingly uncomplicated quantitative metrics which conceal as much as they reveal. Thus, for example, a peasantry's balance of subsistence to commodity production is a datum of uncontested importance, but the ratio itself tells us very little about the deeper nature of market participation. As has been clear for a long time to those who work in development economics, both extensive commodity production and significant wage work by peasants are as compatible with regimes of debt bondage and caste oppression as they are with full-blown capitalism.[14] To analyze economic production without reference to social reproduction is therefore to overlook the heart of the story.

---

[11] A transformation admirably analyzed in Huber-Sperl, *Memmingen zwischen Zunfthandwerk und Unternehmertum.*

[12] StadtA MM A. Reichsstadt 40/1, Bürgermeister and Rat of Memmingen to Emperor Rudolf II [7 Aug. 1600] and 40/5, Bürgermeister and Rat of Memmingen to Abbot Gordian Scherrich [30 June 1702].

[13] Michael Kearney, *Reconceptualizing the Peasantry* (Boulder, CO, 1996) is a useful survey. For an overview more sympathetic to the Marxist perspective, see Henry Bernstein and Terence J. Byers, "From Peasant Studies to Agrarian Change," *Journal of Agrarian Change* 1, 1 (2001), pp. 1–56.

[14] There is a huge literature on this subject. For introductions to the discussion on Latin America and South Asia, see respectively Harold Wolpe, ed., *The Articulation of Modes of Production: Essays from Economy and Society* (London, 1980) and Amit Bhaduri, *The Economic Structure of Backward Agriculture* (London, 1983).

Questions about the emergence of capitalism tend to turn on definitions,[15] and it should be stressed at the outset that Marx's own claim that household agrarian enterprise is by definition non-capitalist[16] is no longer credible.[17] Indeed, even scholars working within the Marxist tradition have come to recognize that rural households whose access to land, labor, and capital is mediated through direct, reciprocal, or usurious ties to other households or classes belong to a different order from those which mobilize these resources in monetized markets.[18] The latter pattern (often referred to as "simple commodity production") is conceded a close affinity, if not full identification, with capitalism, and is a fair (if incomplete) description of the seventeenth-century Ottobeuren household's practices of commodified inheritance and preference for the engagement of unrelated servant labor over the assistance of co-resident kin.

It may, of course, be objected that a putative inner transformation of peasant society hardly deserves the name if unaccompanied by traditional features of economic development such as the spread of industry and technical change, but the criticism would be misplaced. As has been seen, Ottobeuren agriculture fed the precocious industrialization of Switzerland, a connection masked by a persistent tendency to frame early modern economic regions in terms of nineteenth-century national borders. Technological innovation in the Upper Swabian rural economy, it must be said, did come only later, but it was never predicated on an English system of large farms worked with a mass of landless wage labor. As late as the Bavarian census of 1907, despite the extensive mechanization of agriculture, holdings of over 100 hectares and day labor were insignificant in the former Ottobeuren lands, making up 0.4 percent and 8.7 percent of the agricultural area and labor supply respectively.[19] Indeed, the composition of the labor supply in this region in 1907, when family labor respectively made

[15] Rodney Hilton, "Capitalism – What's in a Name?" *Past and Present* 1 (February) (1952), pp. 32–43 remains a valuable introduction.

[16] This was the definition advanced by Robert Brenner in his famous article "Agrarian Class Structure and Economic Development in Pre-Industrial Europe," *Past and Present* 70 (1976), pp. 30–75. Brenner was willing to acknowledge alternatives to the English model, but insisted that even these forms were "based on large-scale owner-cultivators also generally using wage labor."

[17] Robert C. Allen, *Enclosure and the Yeoman: The Agricultural Development of the South Midlands, 1450–1850* (Oxford, 1992) and Hoffman, *Growth in a Traditional Society* have been very influential.

[18] The work of Harriet Friedmann has been particularly influential in this regard. See her "Simple Commodity Production and Wage Labour on the American Plains," *Journal of Peasant Studies* 6, 1 (1978), pp. 71–100 and "Household Production and the National Economy: Concepts for the Analysis of Agrarian Formations," *Journal of Peasant Studies* 7, 2 (1980), pp. 158–84.

[19] *Die Landwirtschaft in Bayern nach der Betriebszählung vom 12 Juni 1907* (Munich, 1910), pp. 44–5, 68, 222–3. The data refer to the district (*Bezirksamt*) of Memmingen. By this date mowing and threshing machines had come into use on the overwhelming majority (58.5 percent and 90.5 percent respectively) of farms of between 20 and 100 hectares, which made up 60.4 percent of all enterprises and 91.0 percent of the agricultural area.

up 53.0 percent and 80.7 percent of the personnel on farms larger and smaller than 20 hectares, is strikingly similar to the composition suggested by the Hawangen *Liber Status Animarum* of 1707.[20] The Upper Swabian pattern of medium-sized family farms, purchased inheritance, "slot-system marriage," and life-cycle servanthood for the young persisted not in spite of, but rather in support of economic development,[21] and when transplanted to the American Midwest not only proved economically viable, but actually tended to displace the "English" pattern of large-scale entrepreneurial farming.[22] Despite its contemporary reputation as a bastion of traditionalism and backwardness, the nineteenth-century Allgäu in fact not only boasted one of the highest standards of living in all Bavaria,[23] but also produced one of Catholic Germany's few "rural bourgeoisies," composed of progressive farmers dedicated to liberal politics and discussing the novels of Dickens in their beloved subalpine fastness.[24]

None of this should be taken to deny that there were other paths to economic development in the early modern countryside. If the dynamic potential of inheritance by leveraged purchase has been discovered as far away as the Paris Basin,[25] a connection between an intensive agricultural revolution and partible inheritance can be documented as close as neighboring Württemberg.[26] Still less do I mean to underplay the dramatic changes wrought by the surge in agricultural (and industrial) productivity across the European continent over the

---

[20] On farms measuring more and less than 20 hectares, household servants respectively made up 35.6 percent and 11.5 percent of the agricultural labor force in 1907. Comparison of the Hawangen *Liber Status Animarum* of 1707 with a tax survey of 1708 suggests that the balance between family labor (defined as kin aged 14–60) and servant labor was 58.8 percent/41.2 percent among the *Hof* tenants and 81.8 percent/18.2 percent among the other villagers. Ibid.; StAA, KL Ottobeuren 146, ff. 72r–87r; Haw PR, Vol. II, ff. 124r–127v.

[21] For a similar (and broader) argument, see Josef Ehmer, *Heiratsverhalten, Sozialstruktur, ökonomischer Wandel: England und Mitteleuropa in der Formationsperiode des Kapitalismus* (Göttingen, 1991), pp. 111–14, 231–5. During the late nineteenth century, household servants made up a higher proportion of agricultural labor in Bavaria and Upper Swabia than anywhere else in Germany.

[22] Sonya Salamon, *Prairie Patrimony: Family, Farming and Community in the Midwest* (Chapel Hill, NC, 1992) contrasts "German yeoman" and "Yankee entrepreneur" farming patterns in Illinois. The former is characterized by the synchronization of parental retirement with the marriage of a privileged heir, who was often obliged to buy out his siblings. Farms are smaller, and rarely make use of hired labor. In the "Yankee" pattern parents retire later and without reference to their children's marriage plans. Inheritance is more egalitarian, with a tendency to sell the land outside the family rather than burden a single heir with financial obligatons to siblings. Farms are larger, have high rates of absentee ownership, and often make use of hired labor.

[23] Jörg Baten, *Ernährung und wirtschaftliche Entwicklung in Bayern, 1730–1880* (Stuttgart, 1999), pp. 116–29, 140–50, 183–94.

[24] Oded Heilbronner, "In Search of the Catholic (Rural) Bourgeoisie: The Peculiarities of the South German Bürgertum," *Central European History* 29, 2 (1996), pp. 175–200.

[25] Jean-Marc Moriceau, *Les fermiers de l'Île-de-France: L'ascension d'un patronat agricole, XVe–XVIIIe siècle* (Paris, 1994), pp. 106–18, 156–76, 475–514.

[26] Sabean, *Property, Production and Family in Neckarhausen*, pp. 147–62, 247–320.

course of the nineteenth century. Nevertheless, the historian has to transcend the assumption that the provisioning of food and the formation of households are integral and self-evidently operating mechanisms best described by summary statistics (yield ratios, grain prices, population densities, mortality rates, etc.), rather than complex social processes which can only be understood if their workings are reconstructed in detail and located in the appropriate context.

By the 1720s, the peasants of Ottobeuren were still a society where land was the primary source of wealth. They still worked under primitive technical conditions, and still paid the same rents to the same landlord. The *Seldner* continued to worry about sudden increases in grain prices, and poverty continued to force even married men to leave their families and serve as mercenaries all over Europe, from the Netherlands[27] to Greece.[28] At the same time, however, a series of radical changes over the preceding one hundred and forty years had remade the basic structures and generative processes of rural life. Formerly the village had been made up of smaller, nuclear households definitively split off from an ancestral home. Now it consisted of larger, extended, and less discrete households where the householder only gradually became independent from retired co-resident parents. Kin relations had come to be mediated by transfers of cash and credit, and the face-to-face, episodic, and predominantly local community of exchange had been supplanted by an impersonal, continuous, and supra-regional marketing network. The Ottobeuren peasantry now lived their lives in a different kind of time and a different kind of space, and for that reason in a different kind of world.

Did this make them a different kind of people? Perhaps the question ought not to be posed in this way, for to do so erects a problematic dichotomy between an abstract society and the atomized individual. Accustomed though we are to thinking of social change molding the individual consciousness like clay on the potter's wheel, the fact remains that social change has only a virtual existence, instantiated in the actions of those very individuals it is held to shape.[29] Without seeking to deny this causal conundrum, however, we can still enforce

---

[27] StAA, KL Ottobeuren 901, f. 119v [8 July 1584], recording the death of Ludwig Stehelin of Ottobeuren with the Hohenems regiment of the Spanish Army of Flanders at the siege of Maastricht (March–June 1579). See also ibid., ff. 86v–87r [26 Feb. 1584], KL Ottobeuren 903, ff. 209r [15 Feb. 1606], KL Ottobeuren 904, ff. 105v–106r [6 Feb. 1609], and KL Ottobeuren 601-II, f. 117r for the case of the second son of a Wolfertschwenden shoemaker, who in 1591 left to fight with the Habsburg forces against the Ottman Turks in Hungary and was never heard from again.

[28] StAA, KL Ottobeuren 922, ff. 10r–11r [23 Jan. 1698] and 172v–173r [19 Oct. 1699] records the fate of the *Seldner* Johann Sinnacher of Hawangen, who enlisted with the Venetian army which invaded the Morea in 1694 and never returned. His impoverished wife was forced to sell off half of their house and land to a stranger in order to survive.

[29] Lyndal Roper, *Oedipus and the Devil: Witchcraft, Sexuality, and Religion in Early Modern Europe* (London, 1994), especially chapters 1 and 10, is a ground-breaking engagement with these questions.

an observational distinction between the impersonal trend and the personal experience thereof. And with regard to the latter dimension, the 'long seventeenth century' at Ottobeuren clearly made the individual peasant experience more individual. This was partly a matter of loosening ties to the larger corporate entities (in particular the village and the lordship) in relation to which a peasant's identity had traditionally been defined.[30] Within the household, by contrast, the issue is both more complicated and more interesting. Although individual examples of the pursuit of narrow self-interests at the expense of the kindred are not hard to find, it would be wrong to suggest that this had become a general trend. On the other hand, that the well-being of the household had itself come to be framed in terms of justly balancing the claims of its constituent individuals was a development of enormous import. To conceive of the whole not as an organic unity, but as an aggregate of heterogeneous and potentially antagonistic interests needing active management and formal certification to maintain harmony was to accord the individual identity a prominence which it otherwise would not have had.

Some of the most interesting evidence of the consequences of this process pertains to children. By the eighteenth century, parental concern for the personal salvation of their children was moving Ottobeuren parents to take stillborn infants 40 kilometers north to the Premonstratensian monastery of Ursberg and have them baptized before the "wonder-working crucifix" there.[31] Still more suggestive is a striking shift in children's naming patterns, especially for girls (see Table 7.4).[32] During the sixteenth and early seventeenth century the stock of children's Christian names was rather small, with a large majority of girls receiving one of the three most popular names (Anna, Barbara, or Maria). By the beginning of the eighteenth century, girls' naming patterns had changed in two ways.[33] First of all, the three most popular names (Maria, Ursula, and Anna

---

[30] On this theme, see in particular Natalie Z. Davis, "Boundaries and the Sense of Self in Sixteenth Century France" in Thomas C. Heller, Morton Sosna, and David E. Wellbery, eds., *Reconstructing Individualism: Autonomy, Individuality and the Self in Western Thought* (Stanford, CA, 1986) pp. 53–63.

[31] Episcopal authorities were already seeking to suppress this practice by 1740, which did not prevent the pastor of Ungerhausen (after being assured "that many such children had recently been taken there") from inscribing attestations of two such Ursberg baptisms from 1755 and 1756 in the parish register. On 15 April 1780 the Bishop of Augsburg again ordered these "translations" denounced from every church in the diocese, but the language of the decree makes it clear that his orders were widely disregarded. Ungerhausen Parish Register [hereinafter UngPR], Vol. III, pp. 139–41.

[32] Table 7.4 is based on the names of 1,103 girls in Hawangen, Ober– and Unterwesterheim, taken from the serf rolls for the sixteenth century and from the parish registers thereafter. This has the effect of understating the degree of change, for whereas the serf rolls list the names of surviving children (who were unlikely to share the same name), the parish register data are skewed by the "recycling" of names when parents reapplied a name to a second child after an earlier one died in infancy.

[33] Boys' names also changed in both of these ways, but much less dramatically. The reason for the disparity remains obscure.

Table 7.4 *Girls' names in three Ottobeuren villages, 1564–1710*

Year	Different names per 100 girls	Index	% of girls with top 3 names
1564	0.076	100.0	58.0
1586	0.099	130.3	62.3
1610–19	0.065	85.5	72.3
1640–49	0.130	171.1	75.0
1670–79	0.172	226.3	64.8
1710–09	0.281	369.7	38.8

Sources: Dertsch, "Das Einwohnerbuch des Ottobeuren Klosterstaats"; StAA, KL Ottobeuren 601-II; Hawangen and Westerheim parish registers

Maria) were now given to less than a third of girls. Second, the simple number of names in use had more than doubled, as the older Germanic "Walpurga" and "Kunigunda" were now supplemented by both Mediterranean imports like "Anastasia," "Cecilia," "Jacobina," and "Rosalia," and double names like "Anna Maria" and "Maria Theresa." A girl went to school,[34] had rights of inheritance, and apparently now also needed a name of her own.

It may of course be objected that baptismal patterns reflect religious (rather than socio-economic) change, in particular the intensified spirituality of the Counter-Reformation, a movement commonly characterized as an effort to shift religious life from a collective to an individualistic footing.[35] And although a lack of source material for the Ottobeuren parishes (most lamentably the loss of the episcopal visitation records to bombing in 1944) has precluded a fuller investigation of rural religious life, the modes of orthodoxy typical of the Counter-Reformation – the professionalization of the rural clergy, increased compliance with the eucharistic obligation, a sterner attitude to lapses in moral and especially sexual conduct, etc. – have already been documented in the monastery lands during the seventeenth century. As for specifically peasant initiatives, there is also evidence of the formation of village confraternities,[36]

---

[34] Despite the conviction of many scholars that girls were not schooled in Catholic Germany (e.g. R. Po-Chia Hsia, *Social Discipline in the Reformation: Central Europe 1550–1750* [London, 1989], pp. 115–16), there is explicit evidence at Ottobeuren that they were. StAA, KL Ottobeuren 921, ff. 253r–254r [18 Apr. 1697].

[35] This thesis is most notably associated with John Bossy, *Christianity in the West, 1400–1700* (Oxford, 1985). A connection between an individualization and a feminization of Catholic piety is argued for Germany in particular in Rudolf Schlögl, *Glaube und Religion in der Säkularisierung: Die katholische Stadt – Köln, Aachen, Münster – 1700–1840* (Munich, 1995), pp. 250–2.

[36] Although no statutes or membership lists have survived, notarial records document a Confraternity of St. Bartholemew in the village of Egg by the early seventeenth century. StAA, KL Ottobeuren 905, f. 229v [17 Jan. 1615]; KL Ottobeuren 907, ff. 197r–v [4 Nov. 1618] and 212r [24 Dec. 1618].

the acquisition of devotional art,[37] the growing popularity of pilgrimages,[38] the spread of specifically Catholic testamentary legacies,[39] and even the foundation of a female religious congregation by one Maria Mayr, a "pious virgin" of Westerheim, in 1681.[40] Yet for all this there is no need to choose between worldly and otherworldly impulses, since both were at work and the two are in any case not so easily separable. As was seen in the last chapter, the later seventeenth-century repression of extramarital sexuality also had an unmistakably secular logic, while the purchase of art has to be seen in the context of a broader increase in consumerism among the peasantry. Even Maria Mayr had a kind of civil exceptionality as an independent property holder for many years before her spiritual exceptionality attracted any public attention.[41]

To be sure, Maria Mayr's legal status as an unmarried female taxpayer was as unusual as her athletic piety. The vast majority of Ottobeuren women elected to marry, and thereby – at least with respect to the formal ownership of property – to vanish into households headed by their husbands. Nevertheless, this very fact only enhances the significance of the rising prominence of married women in the public record, and makes the housewife the most compelling (though certainly not the only)[42] exemplar of the general process of social individuation which had emerged by the end of the seventeenth century. My intention is neither to suggest that married women attained a status of equality with their spouses, nor to deny that women had always exercised informal influence over their husbands. But for married women to lend money by themselves,[43] for men to cite in court their wives' objections and claims to the household's community of goods as a reason to renege on a business transaction,[44] for women in their own persons to sue their husbands for mismanagement of family

---

[37] StAA, KL Ottobeuren 911, p. 108 [9 Jan. 1631].

[38] For the request for travel papers by four residents of the market town in order to go on a Marian pilgrimage to Sulgen in Switzerland, see StAA, KL Ottobeuren 917-II, ff. 111r–112r [29 July 1666].

[39] StAA, KL Ottobeuren 921, ff. 107r–v [27 Oct. 1695] and KL Ottobeuren 922, ff. 157r–v [16 July 1699].

[40] Feyerabend, *Ottenbeuren Jahrbücher*, Vol. III, pp. 532–3, 542–3. By 1685 the congregation had grown so large that a new building was needed.

[41] Maria Mayr "still unmarried" was taxed 1 fl. 46 kr. in 1674, a payment which would have put her in the *Seldner* class, although she was in fact the daughter of the *Bauer* and *Amman* Melchior Mayr (died *c.* 23 October 1670), who had been succeeded by his son Hans on 8 January 1671. In 1679 Maria was still taxed on property in Oberwesterheim, but with the annotation that she now lived in the hamlet of Wald, where she would found her congregation two years later. StAA, KL Ottobeuren 68, f. 25r; KL Ottobeuren 72; KL Ottobeuren 338.

[42] For court rulings that the obligation for debt was individual, and did not pass to a man's father or brother, see StAA, KL Ottobeuren 922, ff. 75r–76r [18 Sep. 1698] and 78v–79v [9 Oct. 1698].

[43] StAA, KL Ottobeuren 919, ff. 161r–v [13 Feb. 1681] and 225v–226r [14 Aug. 1681]. See also ibid., ff. 186v–187r [16 May 1681] where a married woman is sued in her own right for debt, and offers two cows, a pig, and a plot of land to cover the obligation of 77 fl.

[44] StAA, KL Ottobeuren 921, ff. 188v–189r [22 June 1696]. Similarly KL Ottobeuren 922, ff. 122r–v and 124r–125r [12 Mar. and 2 Apr. 1699].

property,[45] all of this suggests the mutation of a woman's property rights into a legal personhood which was no longer completely absorbed by her spouse.[46]

Indeed, if the elaboration and public registration of these rights helped to preserve a woman's individuality while she was joined to her husband in marriage, they served an even more vital preservative role should she decide to seek a separation from him. Cases of this sort were quite rare, and even then were less common than the effort to annul a marriage due to male impotency ("utterly inept and incapable of carnal copulation," as Ursula Aberöll of Benningen denounced her husband, Johann Binz, in 1606).[47] Furthermore, even when separations were granted, the land tenure system remained biased against women, above all by reserving *Hof* tenancy to men. In March of 1646, for example, the Hawangen widow Anna Heinrich entered into a marriage agreement with a Bavarian immigrant by the name of Leonhard Opser. Shortly thereafter Anna began to worry that Opser would mistreat her,[48] and at the last minute petitioned the Bishop of Augsburg to suspend the engagement. She was released from her obligation,[49] but Opser had already been admitted to Anna's first husband's stately *Hof*,[50] and not only retained it but promptly took a new wife, while Anna plummeted into the ranks of the *Seldner* and never remarried.[51] But this was not the end of Anna Heinrich. She retained a few patches of freehold arable and garden land,[52] and on this basis managed to sustain herself and her young son Georg for some twenty years[53] until Georg married a *Bauer* daughter and gained tenancy of his own *Hof* in 1666.[54]

---

[45] StAA, KL Ottobeuren 916, ff. 12v [12 Feb. 1661]. The husband was ordered henceforth to observe greater "order and proportion" in his affairs.

[46] For an analogous argument in a contemporary context, see Bina Agarwal, *A Field of One's Own: Gender and Land Rights in South Asia* (Cambridge, 1994).

[47] ABA, OPr 1602–6, pp. 760–1 [3 Feb. 1606]. Binz had other failings as well; the previous year he was fined by the Ottobeuren courts because he "did often and senselessly beat his wife most terribly and blaspheme incessantly." StAA, KL Ottobeuren 587-II, Heft 25 (1604/5).

[48] HawPR, Vol. I, f. 37v [27 May 1646]. The parish priest explicitly recorded that the engagement was suspended due to "the great fear by the bride of being mistreated in marriage."

[49] ABA, OPr 1646–7, pp. 90–1 [3 July 1646]. Anna claimed that the engagement "was contracted for the sake of a sick child, who [since] has died." The child in question was her son Hans, who died at the age of nine months on 7 April 1646. Anna's decision to focus on the conditional nature of the marriage promise rather than her fears of abuse was in all likelihood a legal stratagem to facilitate the engagement's rescission.

[50] StAA, KL Ottobeuren 435 lists Anna's first husband, Hans Dreier, as the tenant in 1641–4, Anna herself as the (temporary) tenant in 1645, and Opser from 1646.

[51] HawPR, Vol. I, f. 37v [13 Aug. 1646]. StAA, KL Ottobeuren 47, f. 2v lists Opser as a *Hof* tenant in 1648, while KL Ottobeuren 106, ff. 30r–36r ranks Anna as the eighth poorest of fifty-three Hawangen households in 1660.

[52] Anna is listed as a tenant in rent rolls of 1648 and 1657; the properties were held by her son Georg Dreier in 1670. StAA, KL Ottobeuren 47, f. 2v; KL Ottobeuren 56, f. 99v; KL Ottobeuren 57, f. 101r.

[53] Anna Heinrich's burial went unrecorded, but she is mentioned as still owning arable land in a notarial protocol of 22 October 1665. StAA, KL Ottobeuren 917-II, ff. 20v–21r.

[54] HawPR, Vol. I, f. 46r [6 June 1666]; StAA, KL Ottobeuren 337 (Erdschatz) [20 May 1666].

Although unusual, Anna Heinrich's experience was hardly unique. After only six months of marriage, Sebastian Hueber of Benningen decided that he had enough of the "quarrels and fights" with his wife, Anna Rogg,[55] and abandoned her about the year 1597.[56] Having then roamed the countryside, striking up a two-year liaison with a certain Catharina Pfeiffer and begetting her with a child, Hueber was shocked to learn that his lawful wife, Anna, would not have him back. Instead she demanded from the episcopal court "to be separated [from him] of bed and board, *together with the award of her dowry and wedding gifts, and those things which come [to her] in her name.*"[57] The Bishop complied, Sebastian disappeared, and Anna settled down in Benningen as a householder in her own right. She does seem, in fact, to have been a truculent soul – in her husband's absence she was prosecuted for slandering a neighbor, scraping muck out of the common pond "against the custom of the village," letting her dogs run loose, and refusing to fence in her garden[58] – and any sympathy she garnered from Sebastian's misdeeds may well have dissipated in 1604 with the revelation of her own sexual relationship with a young servant from Dickerlishausen.[59] Nevertheless, Anna Rogg knew what her rights were, and whatever her neighbors thought of her, she remained in the village for another ten years.[60]

A still more explicit example comes to us from the end of the seventeenth century in the household of the Ottobeuren innkeeper Gabriel Schorer, one of the wealthiest men in the monastery lands.[61] After sixteen years of marriage,[62] Schorer and his wife, Anna Pfanner, were separated of bed and board by the Augsburg *Offizialat* in 1697. A dispute soon erupted over the division of

[55] Anna's surname is given as 'Hueber' (the same as her husband's) in the protocols of the *Offizialat*, but close comparison with the Ottobeuren bond-chicken registers suggests that this is an error, and that she was the daughter of Jerg Rogg. StAA, KL Ottobeuren 491-II, Heft 6 (1595), f. 16r and Heft 10 (1602), f. 8r.

[56] The fee for this exogamous marriage is recorded in StAA, KL Ottobeuren 583, Heft 13 (1596/7), f. 2r; Sebastian Hueber claimed in mid-1601 to have been married "six years ago."

[57] ABA, OPr 1598–1602, pp. 591–3 [19 June 1601]. Sebastian had protested that his behavior was "not a legitimate cause to end cohabitation" and asked the court to force Anna to take him back. Emphasis mine.

[58] StAA, KL Ottobeuren 587-II, Heft 19 (1597/8), Heft 20 (1598/9), Heft 21 (1601/2), and Heft 22 (1602/3).

[59] StAA, KL Ottobeuren 587-II, Heft 25 (1604/5). The court record also notes that Anna's husband "went away from here three or four years ago, and no one knows whether he is dead or alive."

[60] Anna is listed (as "Besti Huebers widow") in the bond-chicken registers for both 1609 and 1613. StAA, KL Ottobeuren 491-I, Heft 14, f. 23r and KL Ottobeuren 491-II, Heft 16, f. 17r. There is some evidence to suggest that she died *c.* 1614, and passed her property to another female household composed of her stepmother and stepsisters. KL Ottobeuren 491-II, Heft 21 (1617), f. 19r; KL Ottobeuren 904, ff. 157v [17 Nov. 1609] and 183v [10 Mar. 1610]; KL Ottobeuren 905, ff. 318r–v [5 Dec. 1615].

[61] Schorer's 1693 tax payment of 15 fl. 2 kr. made him one of the three richest householders (i.e. the top 0.3 percent) in the Ottobeuren lands. StAA, KL Ottobeuren 86, f. 84v.

[62] The couple were married 13 January 1681. Ottobeuren LSA 1687, p. 20 [HH no. 105].

the property, with the innkeeper insisting that he was owed 750 *gulden* which he had brought into the marriage. Anna argued that Schorer (her second husband) had brought her no more than 600 *gulden*, while he declared that he "would rather take nothing at all than anything less than seven hundred and fifty." In the end, the dispute was fairly simply resolved. At Anna Pfanner's request the notarial protocol drawn up at the time of the marriage was consulted, and her assessment of Gabriel's contribution was confirmed.[63] Schorer was forced to accept the smaller sum,[64] and stormed out of the monastery lands. He would return to Anna's house two years later to denounce her as a witch and a whore who was keeping his property, but it availed him little. Anna had already sold the inn, brewery, and the rest of her holdings to a daughter, Catharina Knaus, and a son-in-law, Jacob Gell, for no less than 3,635 fl. 46 kr. Gell replied to Schorer in kind, excoriating him for not having slept with his wife for an entire year before the separation, and adding the insulting insinuation that "nobody really knew what he [i.e. Schorer] did in the bedroom." Now truly outraged, Schorer tried to sue the son-in-law for slander, but the monastery rejected the charge and sternly warned Schorer that any further outbursts would result in his own prosecution.[65]

Anna Pfanner had won. She lived out the rest of her days on a handsome maintenance allowance, including the highly symbolic right to be given a new pair of pants [*Bantopfel*] whenever she needed one. When she died in 1726 at the ripe old age of 87, the admiring parish priest noted that she had fully 109 grandchildren and great-grandchildren.[66] A great deal more evidence has survived about Anna's life than about the lives of her medieval forebears, but this thickening of the documentary record must never be taken for granted, and its causes should be made explicit. As is true for Upper Swabia as a whole, the surge in archival holdings from early modern Ottobeuren was primarily driven by an effort to record the rental, taxation, encumbrance, and transfer of peasant property. It was an equivocal process, reflecting not only closer surveillance and systematization of imposition by the overlord, but also the corresponding solidification of the peasant's right to hold, convey, and inherit. The recoverability of this tale of a marriage gone sour thus depends on that process of jural devolution which in the fifteenth century codified the property rights of peasant patriarchs, but thereafter gradually formalized the legal claims of the household's subordinate members, thereby ensuring that unlike her namesake with which this study began, Anna Pfanner was fully visible in the midst of her own history.

---

[63] The original protocol is StAA, KL Ottobeuren 919, ff. 134v–135r [19 Dec. 1680].
[64] StAA, KL Ottobeuren 921, ff. 255r–256v [19 Apr. 1697].
[65] StAA, KL Ottobeuren 922, ff. 127v–128v [9 Apr. 1699] and 160r–162v [4 Aug. 1699].
[66] OttPR, Vol. III, p. 666 [24 Mar. 1726].

Bibliography

ARCHIVAL SOURCES

Staatsarchiv Augsburg [StAA]

I Kloster Ottobeuren

A Urkunden [KU Ottobeuren]

KU 97 [23 Jan. 1355]–KU 2656 [26 Nov. 1643]

B Akten [KA Ottobeuren]

KA 17, Heiligenrechnungen zu Benningen 1549–60
KA 42, Besitzverhältniße, Schuldenwesen und Vergantungen zu Böhen 1522–1679
KA 44, Schuldverschreibungen zu Böhen 1623–1744
KA 86, Besitz- und Bestandverhältnisse zu Egg 1566–1622
KA 189, Heiligenrechnungen zu Hawangen 1551–95
KA 192, Öde und vergantete Güter zu Hawangen 1653–63
KA 240, Heiligenrechnungen zu Niederdorf 1566–1608
KA 245, Zehenten des Klosters 1517–41
KA 344, Höfe und deren Verkauf zu Sontheim 1572–1663
KA 348, Kirchenrechnungen zu Sontheim 1602–33
KA 390, Verzeichnis leibeigener Klosteruntertanen 1680–1702
KA 469, Sammelakt Militaria 1547–1805
KA 477, Sammelakt Unzucht 1581–1802
KA 482, Schuldenwesen des Klosters 1600–1790
KA 490, Gastwirte-, Krämer- und Tuchhandlerrechnungen 1610–1762
KA 597, Konferenzprotokoll wegen des Landbettels 1730
KA 646, Marktordnung 1770

C Literalien [KL Ottobeuren]

KL 1–7, "Rotuli Probationum" [cartulary 769–1616]
KL 16–21, Lehenbücher 1547/83, 1550, 1600/12, 1656/72, 1676/1710
KL 23, Lehenbuchauszüge 1680
KL 24, Auszug des Überschusses u. Abgangs an Äckern und Mädern aller Dörfer 1680

KL 26–7, Erdschatzbücher 1532–81, 1576–1603
KL 28–47, Gült und Zehentregister 1544–1648
KL 48–52, 61, Gültlieferungsregister 1652–86, 1730
KL 53–4, Gült-Ausstände Register 1529–1692
KL 55, Summarischer Register aller Einnahmen an Gülten, Zehenten etc. 1652–72
KL 56–8, Gültbücher 1657, 1670, 1689
KL 62, Gültbuch 1788/9
KL 63–99, Steuerregister 1541, 1546, 1652, 1657, 1666, 1674–1708
KL 102–4, Steuerbücher 1620, 1624, 1627
KL 105, Steuerbuch 1669
KL 106–8, Steuerbelegungen 1660, 1667, 1684
KL 109, Steuerbuch 1689
KL 110–15, Steuerbücher 1767–96
KL 116–33, Kriegssteueranlagen 1675–1702
KL 134–57, Kriegssteuerbücher 1674–1747
KL 159, Reisgeldregister 1526, 1532
KL 159a, Musterungsregister 1610–19
KL 163–99, Kornregister 1525, 1549–1613, 1620, 1624–7, 1632, 1635, 1642, 1650
KL 204–23, 228–9, Kornkastenregister 1652–1718, 1778–80, 1786
KL 224–6, Kornrechnungen 1586–1625
KL 227, Jahresrechnungen des Kornkastenamts, 1672–82
KL 230–4, Monats- und Jahresrechnungen des Kornkastenamts, 1692–1708, 1793–6
KL 235–6, Restantenregister des Kornkastenamts 1703–22, 1794
KL 237–47, Schuldbücher des Kornkastenamts 1540, 1617, 1657–94
KL 265–78, Samhaberregister 1533, 1564–1627, 1653–92
KL 279, Hausgetreidebuch 1584–95,
KL 280, Zehentkornverzeichnis 1606
KL 281–307, Druschregister 1652–1714
KL 331–4, Großkellereiregister 1547, 1645–51
KL 335–82, Großkellereibücher 1656–1720, 1751–72, 1795–6
KL 385–7, Großkellerei Restantenregister 1641–66
KL 400–81, Baudingbücher 1527–78, 1593, 1598, 1641–1707, 1753, 1757, 1778
KL 486–90, Umgeldregister des Markts Ottobeuren und der Dörfer, 1655–98
KL 491-I, Leib- und Gülthennenbücher 1552–1612
KL 491-II, Leib- und Gülthennenbücher 1613–22
KL 491-III, Leib- und Gülthennenbücher 1623–39
KL 493, Handwerkerrechnungen 1534–8, 1576–1602, 1619–21
KL 494–5, Küchenregister und -rechungen, 1564–1619, 1652, 1668–78
KL 513–29, Viehstandsbeschreibungen 1707–79
KL 541, Generalrechnungen 1527–1621
KL 542–3, Generalrechnungen 1638–95, 1704
KL 547–9, Schulden der Dörfer, 1655–79
KL 550–82a, Allgemeine Schuldbücher 1529, 1552, 1579–1632, 1688–1712, 1792–1802
KL 583, Verhörgefälle 1581–1632
KL 584–6, Verhörgefälle 1676–8, 1684–95
KL 587-I, Straf- und Frevelregister 1546–92/3
KL 587-II, Straf- und Frevelregister 1593–1615
KL 587-III, Straf- und Frevelregister 1618–82
KL 596, Waisenrechnung 1609

KL 598–9, Ratsprotokolle 1619–29, 1686–99
KL 600, Leibeigenbuch 1548
KL 601 I–II, Leibeigenbücher 1486/7, 1585/6
KL 607, Tagwerkerregister 1611–22
KL 625-I, Heiligenrechnungen der Pfarr Benningen 1639–1714
KL 636 I–II, Eldern Rechnungen 1526–1678
KL 637–40, Eldern Rechnungen 1678–93
KL 642, Kirchenrechnungen 1611–28
KL 654, Rechnungen der Pfarrkirchenpflege zu Frechenrieden 1549–1714
KL 657, Heiligen Rechnungen zu Günz 1549–1600
KL 662-I, Heiligenrechnungen zu Hawangen 1642–1713
KL 666-I, Heiligenrechnungen der Pfarr Niederdorf, 1641–1714
KL 676a, Steuerregister der Markt Ottobeuren 1585
KL 677, Schulden der Handwerker 1632/3
KL 680, Rechnungen der Sonder Siechenpflege (Ottobeuren) 1634–1713
KL 681, Zehenteinnahmen der Pfarrei Ottobeuren 1546–1601
KL 682–3, Gült- und Zehentbeschreibung der Pfarrei Ottobeuren 1653–78
KL 684–5, Zehentbeschreibung der Pfarrei Ottobeuren 1652–86
KL 688-I, Rechnungen der Pfarrei Ottobeuren 1563–1606
KL 688-II, Rechnungen der Pfarrei Ottobeuren 1615–95
KL 689-II, Rechnungen der Pfarrei Ottobeuren 1652–1712
KL 692, Zinsregister der Cüsterei St. Alexander in Ottobeuren 1618–25
KL 701, Einkommen der Pfarrei Sontheim 1527–36
KL 702, Heiligenrechnungen der Pfarrei Sontheim 1637–1713
KL 735, Rechnungen der St. Marx Capelle – Stephansried 1531–92
KL 741, Westerheim Kirchenpflegerechnungen 1575–1629, 1682–1796
KL 744a, Heiligenrechnungen zu Hawangen 1563–94
KL 744b, Zehent- und Ackerbeschreibungen zu Westerheim 1545–1756
KL 744c, Zehentverzeichnis zu Westerheim 1613
KL 757, Schwäbische Landgericht Acta 1545–63
KL 900–22, Amtsprotokolle 1541–58, 1576–80, 1583–4, 1603–21, 1624–6, 1630–67, 1680–9, 1695–1701 [incl. two volumes for 1624–35 and 1650–65 from the Herrschaft Stein]

D Literalien, Ehemaliger Münchner Bestand [KL Ottobeuren (Mü.B.)]

KL 8 (Mü.B), "Chronologia Ottoburana" of Gallus Sandholzer (*c.* 1600)
KL 24 (Mü.B), Leibeigenbuch 1556
KL 25 (Mü.B), Leibeigenbuch 1564
KL 64 (Mü.B), Ratsprotokolle 1631–8
KL 158b (Mü.B), Exemptio Ottoburana, Tomus IV (1631–56)
KL 163–79 (Mü.B), Zunftordnungen, 1623–1762
KL 197 (Mü.B), Akt aus einem Konkursverfahren gegen Hans Betz, 1548–9
KL 221 (Mü.B), Akt über Schuldsachen des Balthasar Maÿer in der Waldmühle, 1628–39
KL 225 (Mü.B), Akt über Vergantungen und Schuldenwesen verschiedener Ottobeurischen Untertanen gegenüber einer Reihe von Pflegschaften in Memmingen, 1636–57
KL 231 (Mü.B), Verzeichnis von an Ottobeuren heimgefallenen Äcker zu Hawangen, 1662

E Neuburger Urkundensammlung

G 162, 167, 171, 175, 176, 179, 182, 183, 185
Ungeordnete Einzelstücke

II Fürststift Kempten

A Literalien [KL Kempten]

KL 15–19, Landammanamtsprotokolle 1599–1626
KL 27, 30, Landammanamtsprotokolle 1655–60, 1663–5
KL 34–5, Landammanamtsprotokolle 1680–4
KL 241, 250–2, Kaufbücher 1616–32, 1650–61
KL 563–4, Protokolle der Pflege Falken 1696–1713

B Literalien, Neuburger Abgabe [KL Kempten (NA)]

KL (NA) 147, Feld- und Grundbeschreibung der Pfarrei Probstried 1687
KL (NA) 1637–9, Steuerregister der Pflegen Sulz- und Wolkenberg, auch Falken 1645, 1658
KL (NA) 1640–3, Steuerregister der Landvogtei disseits der Iller, 1661, 1667, 1670, 1678–82
KL (NA) 1680, Steuerregister der Pflege Falken 1687
KL (NA) 1684, Steuerregister der Pflege Falken 1709
KL (NA) 1765, Lehenbuch 1616–31
KL (NA) 1772, Lehenbuch 1639–73

Stadtarchiv Memmingen [StadtA MM]

A. Reichsstadt [bisher Stadtarchiv]
Akten 40/1–40/5, Stift Ottobeuren 1600–1732
D. Stiftungen [bisher StiAM]
Akten 64/8a, Sontheimer Heiligenrechnungen 1585–1662
Band 99, Rechnungen des Unterhospitals 1530–99
Band 102/1a–1b, Summarischer Geldrechnungen des Unterhospitals

Archiv des Bistums Augsburg [ABA]

Offizialatsprotokolle 1598–1602, 1602–6, 1625–8, 1646–7

Family History Library, Salt Lake City, Utah

microfilm copies of:
Benningen Parish Register (1632–1712)
Egg Parish Register [EggPR] (1616–50, 1667–95)
Frechenrieden Parish Register (1655–1734)
Hawangen Parish Register [HawPR] (1607–1725) (incl. *Liber Status Animarum* [1707])
Ottobeuren Parish Register [OttPR] (1570–1626, 1686–1729) (including separate register for Stephansried [1663–1760] and *Liber Status Animarum* [1687])
Probstried Parish Register [ProbPR] (1645–1737)
Ungerhausen Parish Register (1648–1751)

Unteregg Parish Register (1625–45)
Westerheim Parish Register [WestPR] (1595–1759)

PUBLISHED PRIMARY SOURCES

Baumann, Franz Ludwig, ed. *Akten zur Geschichte des deutschen Bauernkriegs aus Oberschwaben* (Freiburg im Breisgan, 1877).
    ed. *Quellen zur Geschichte des Bauernkriegs in Oberschwaben* (Tübingen, 1876).
Bosl, Karl, ed. *Dokumente zur Geschichte von Staat und Gesellschaft in Bayern.* Abteilung II: *Franken und Schwaben vom Frühmittelalter bis 1800*, Vol. IV: *Schwaben von 1268 bis 1803*, edited by Peter Blickle and Renate Blickle (Munich, 1979).
Dertsch, Richard, ed. "Das Einwohnerbuch des Ottobeurer Klosterstaats vom Jahre 1564," *Allgäuer Heimatbücher* 50 [*Alte Allgäuer Geschlechter* 34] (1955).
Ellenbog, Nikolaus. *Briefwechsel*, edited by Andreas Bigelmair and Friedrich Zoepfl, *Corpus Catholicorum* 19/21 (Münster im Westfalen, 1938).
Feyerabend, Maurus. *Des ehemaligen Reichsstiftes Ottenbeuren, Benediktiner Ordens in Schwaben, sämmtliche Jahrbücher* (4 vols., Ottobeuren, 1813–16).
Hoffmann, Hermann, ed. *Die Urkunden des Reichsstiftes Ottobeuren 764–1460*, Schwäbische Forschungsgemeinschaft Reihe 2a, Urkunden und Regesten; Band 13 (Augsburg, 1991).
Manz, Kaspar, *Zinss Scharmützel, das ist, Ein gefährlicher doch täglicher striff zwischen den Glaubigern und Schuldtnern: ob man bey disen laidigen Kriegszeiten . . . schuldig sey die Zinss zubezahlen oder nit?* (Augsburg, 1645).
Peters, Jan, ed. *Ein Söldnerleben im Dreißigjährigen Krieg* (Berlin, 1993).
Schorer, Christoph. *Memminger Chronick* (Ulm, 1660; repr. Kempten, 1964).
Vogt, Wilhelm, ed. "Die Correspondenz des schwäbischen Bundeshauptmannes Ulrich Artzt von Augsburg aus den Jahren 1524–1527," *Zeitschrift des Historischen Vereins für Schwaben und Neuburg* 6 (1879), 281–404; 7 (1880), 233–380; 9 (1882), 1–62; 10 (1883), 1–298.
von Seckendorf, Veit Ludwig. *Teutscher Fürsten-Staat*, 3rd edn (1665; repr. Glashütten im Taunus, 1976), Vol. I.
Weitnauer, Alfred. "Die Bevölkerung des Stifts Kempten vom Jahre 1640," *Allgäuer Heimatbücher* 14 [*Alte Allgäuer Geschlechter* 9] (1939).

SECONDARY SOURCES

Abel, Wilhelm. *Agricultural Fluctuations in Europe from the Thirteenth to the Twentieth Centuries*, trans. Olive Ordish (London, 1980).
    Massenarmut und Hungerkrisen im vorindustriellen Europa (Hamburg, 1974).
Agarwal, Bina. *A Field of One's Own: Gender and Land Rights in South Asia* (Cambridge, 1994).
Allen, Robert C. *Enclosure and the Yeoman: The Agricultural Development of the South Midlands, 1450–1850* (Oxford, 1992).
Ammann, Hektor. "Die Anfänge der Leinenindustrie des Bodenseegebiets," *Alemannisches Jahrbuch* (1953), 251–313.
Anderlini, Luca and Sabourian, Hamid. "Some Notes on the Economics of Barter, Money and Credit" in Caroline Humphrey and Steven Hugh-Jones, eds., *Barter, Exchange and Value – An Anthropological Approach* (Cambridge, 1992), 75–106.

Anderman, Kurt. "Grundherrschaft des spätmittelalterlichen Niederadels in Südwestdeutschland," *Blätter für Deutsche Landesgeschichte* N.F. 127 (1991), 145–90.

Appleby, Andrew. "Grain Prices and Subsistence Crises in England and France, 1590–1790," *Journal of Economic History* 39, 4 (1979), 865–87.

Ashton, Trevor, ed. *Crisis in Europe 1560–1660* (London, 1965).

Asmuss, Burkhard. "Das Einkommen der Bauern in der Herrschaft Kronburg im frühen 16. Jahrhundert," *Zeitschrift für Bayerische Landesgeschichte* 43, 1 (1980), 45–91.

Aston, T. H. and Philpin, C. H. E., eds. *The Brenner Debate* (Cambridge, 1985).

Bader, Karl S. *Das Mittelalterliche Dorf als Friedens- und Rechts-bereich* (Weimar, 1957).

Bader, Karl Siegfried. *Rechtsformen und Schichten der Liegenschaftsnutzung im mittelalterlichen Dorf* (Vienna, Cologne, and Graz, 1973).

Bairoch, Paul. *Economics and World History: Myths and Paradoxes* (New York, 1993).

Barnes, R. H. and Barnes, Ruth. "Barter and Money in an Indonesian Village Economy," *Man* (N.S.) 24 (1989), 399–418.

Baten, Jörg. *Ernährung und wirtschaftliche Entwicklung in Bayern, 1730–1880* (Stuttgart, 1999).

Bauernfeind, Walter. *Materielle Grundstrukturen im Spatmittelalter und der Frühen Neuzeit: Preisentwicklung und Agrarkonjunktur am Nürnberger Getreidemarkt von 1339 bis 1670* (Nuremberg, 1993).

Baumann, Franz Ludwig. *Geschichte des Allgäus* (4 vols., Kempten, 1883–94; repr. Aalen, 1971–3).

Beck, Rainer. *Naturale Ökonomie. Unterfinning: Bäuerliche Wirtschaft in einem oberbayerischen Dorf des frühen 18. Jahrhunderts* (Munich, 1986).

Unterfinning: ländliche Welt vor Anbruch der Moderne (Munich, 1993).

Becker-Huberti, Manfred. *Die Tridentinische Reform im Bistum Münster unter Fürstbischof Christoph von Galen 1650–1678* (Munster, 1978).

Behringer, Wolfgang. *Witchcraft Persecutions in Bavaria: Popular Magic, Religious Zealotry and Reason of State in Early Modern Europe*, trans. J. C. Grayson and David Lederer (Cambridge, 1997).

Bergmeier, Hans. " 'Wie sie Einödinen gemachet:' Vereinödung im Kempter Raum – ein Beitrag zur Geschichte der ländlichen Neuordnung durch Flurbereinigung," *Berichte aus der Flurbereinigung* 56 (1986).

Berkner, Lutz. "Peasant Household Organization and Demographic Change in Lower Saxony (1689–1766)" in Ronald D. Lee, ed., *Population Patterns in the Past* (New York, 1977), 53–70.

"The Stem Family and the Developmental Cycle of the Peasant Household: An 18th Century Austrian Example," *American Historical Review* 77 (1972), 398–412.

Bernstein, Henry and Byers, Terence J. "From Peasant Studies to Agrarian Change," *Journal of Agrarian Change* 1, 1 (2001), 1–56.

Bhaduri, Amit. *The Economic Structure of Backward Agriculture* (London, 1983).

Blickle, Peter. "Bäuerliches Eigen im Allgäu," *Zeitschrift für Agrargeschichte und Agrarsoziologie* 17, 1 (1969), 57–78.

"Leibherrschaft als Instrument der Territorialpolitik im Allgäu: Grundlagen der Landeshoheit der Klöster Kempten und Ottobeuren" in Heinz Haushofer and Willi A. Boelcke, eds., *Wege und Forschungen der Agrargeschichte: Festschrift zum 65 Geburtstag von Günther Franz* (Frankfurt a.M., 1967), 51–66.

Blickle, Peter. *Memmingen: Historischer Atlas von Bayern*. Teil Schwaben Vol. IV (Munich, 1967).

"Ortsgeschichte von Egg an der Günz," *Memminger Geschichtsblätter* (1971), 5–118.

The Revolution of 1525, trans. Thomas A. Brady Jr. and H. C. Erik Midelfort (Baltimore, 1981).

Boehler, Jean-Michel. *Une société rurale en milieu rhenan: la paysannerie de la plaine d'Alsace, 1648–1789* (Strasbourg, 1995).

Bog, Ingomar. *Die bäuerliche Wirtschaft im Zeitalter des Dreissigjährigen Krieges* (1952).

Bois, Guy. *The Crisis of Feudalism: Economy and Society in Eastern Normandy c. 1300–1550* [English translation; translator not cited] (Cambridge, 1984).

Boockmann, Andrea. "Urfehde und ewige Gefangenschaft im mittelalterlichen Göttingen," *Studien zur Geschichte der Stadt Göttingen* Band 13 (Göttingen, 1980).

Borcherdt, Christoph. "Die Agrarlandschaft des Regierungsbezirks Schwaben zu Beginn des 19. Jahrhunderts," *Schwäbische Blätter* 8, 2 (1957), 33–43.

Bossy, John. *Christianity in the West, 1400–1700* (Oxford, 1985).

Bouwsma, William J. "The Renaissance and the Drama of Western History," *American Historical Review* 84, 1 (1979), 1–15.

Braudel, Fernand. *The Mediterranean and the Mediterranean World in the Age of Philip II*, trans. by Siân Reynolds (2 vols., New York, 1972: orig. pub. 1949).

Brenner, Robert. "Agrarian Class Structure and Economic Development in Pre-Industrial Europe," *Past and Present* 70 (1976), 30–75.

Burke, Peter. *The French Historical Revolution: The Annales School, 1929–89* (Stanford, CA, 1990).

Campbell, Bruce M. S. and Overton, Mark. "A New Perspective on Medieval and Early Modern Agriculture: Six Centuries of Norfolk Farming *c*.1250–*c*.1850," *Past and Present* 141 (1993), 38–105.

Carrard, Philippe. *Poetics of the New History: French Historical Discourse from Braudel to Chartier* (Baltimore, 1992).

Clark, George Norman. *Early Modern Europe from about 1450 to about 1720* (London, 1957).

Clasen, Claus-Peter. *Die Augsburger Weber: Leistungen und Krisen des Textilgewerbes um 1600* (Augsburg, 1981).

Cooper, J. P. "In Search of Agrarian Capitalism" in Aston and Philpin, eds., *The Brenner Debate*, 161–78.

Crafts, N. F. R. "British Economic Growth, 1700–1831: A Review of the Evidence," *Economic History Review* 36, 2 (1983), 177–99.

"Macroinventions, economic growth, and 'industrial revolution' in Britain and France," *Economic History Review* 48, 3 (1995), 591–8.

Daunton, M. J. *Progress and Poverty: An Economic and Social History of Britain 1700–1850* (Oxford, 1995).

Davis, Natalie Z. "Boundaries and the Sense of Self in Sixteenth Century France" in Thomas C. Heller, Morton Sosna, and David E. Wellbery, eds., *Reconstructing Individualism: Autonomy, Individuality and the Self in Western Thought* (Stanford, CA, 1986), 53–63.

de Maddalena, Aldo. "Rural Europe 1500–1750" in Carlo M. Cippola, ed., *The Fontana Economic History of Europe*, Vol. II: *The Sixteenth and Seventeenth Centuries* (Glasgow, 1974), 595–622.

de Roover, Raymond. "The Concept of the Just Price: Theory and Economic Policy," *Journal of Economic History* 18, 4 (1958), 418–34.

de Vries, Jan "Between Purchasing Power and the World of Goods: Understanding the Household Economy in Early Modern Europe" in John Brewer and Roy Porter, eds., *Consumption and the World of Goods* (London, 1993), pp. 85–132.

The Dutch Rural Economy in the Golden Age, 1500–1700 (New Haven, 1974).

The Economy of Europe in an Age of Crisis 1600–1750 (Cambridge, 1976).

"The Industrial Revolution and the Industrious Revolution," *Journal of Economic History* 54, 2 (1994), 249–70.

Die Landwirtschaft in Bayern nach der Betriebszählung vom 12 Juni 1907, Beiträge zur Statistik des Königreichs Bayern 81 (Munich, 1910).

Duchesne, Ricardo. "Between Sinocentrism and Eurocentrism: Debating Andre Gunder Frank's *Re-Orient: Global Economy in the Asian Age,*" *Science and Society* 65, 4 (Winter) (2001–2), 428–63.

DuPlessis, Robert S. *Transitions to Capitalism in Early Modern Europe* (Cambridge, 1997).

Ebeling, Dietmar and Irsigler, Franz. *Getreideumsatz, Getreide- und Brotpreise in Köln 1368–1796* (2 vols., Cologne and Vienna, 1976–7).

Ehmer, Josef. *Heiratsverhalten, Sozialstruktur, ökonomischer Wandel: England und Mitteleuropa in der Formationsperiode des Kapitalismus* (Göttingen, 1991).

Eichhorn, H. *Der Strukturwandel im Geldumlauf Frankens zwischen 1437 und 1610*, Vierteljahrschrift für Sozial- und Wirtschaftsgeschichte, Beiheft 58 (Wiesbaden, 1973).

Eirich, Raimund. *Memmingens Wirtschaft und Patriziat von 1347 bis 1551* (Weissenhorn, 1971).

Epstein, Stephan. *Freedom and Growth: The Rise of States and Markets in Europe, 1300–1750* (London, 2000).

Flinn, Michael W. *The European Demographic System 1500–1820* (Baltimore, 1981).

Forster, Marc R. *Catholic Revival in the Age of the Baroque: Religious Identity in Southwest Germany, 1550–1750* (Cambridge, 2001).

The Counter-Reformation in the Villages: Religion and Reform in the Bishopric of Speyer 1564–1720 (Ithaca, 1992).

Franz, Günther. "Die Geschichte des deutschen Landwarenhandels" in Günther Franz, Wilhelm Abel, and Gisbert Cascorb, eds., *Der deutsche Landwarenhandel* (Hanover, 1960), pp. 13–110.

Friedmann, Harriet. "Household Production and the National Economy: Concepts for the Analysis of Agrarian Formations," *Journal of Peasant Studies* 7, 2 (1980), 158–84.

"Simple Commodity Production and Wage Labour on the American Plains," *Journal of Peasant Studies* 6, 1 (1978), 71–100.

Friedrichs, Christopher R. *Urban Society in an Age of War: Nördlingen 1580–1720* (Princeton, 1979).

Gabler, A. "Die wirtschaftliche Lage des Bauerntums im Hesselberggebiet des 16. Jahrhunderts," *Schwäbische Blätter* 14, 3 (1963), 73–98.

Garlepp, Hans-Hermann. *Der Bauernkrieg von 1525 um Biberach a.d. Riß* (Frankfurt a.M., 1987).

Giddens, Anthony. *Central Problems in Social Theory: Action, Structure and Contradiction in Social Analysis* (Berkeley, CA, 1979).

The Constitution of Society: Outline of the Theory of Structuration (Cambridge, 1984).

A Contemporary Critique of Historical Materialism, Vol. I: *Power, Property and the State* (Berkeley, CA, 1981).

Göttmann, Frank. 'Aspekte der Tragfähigkeit in der Ostschweiz um 1700' in Joachim Jahn and Wolfgang Hartung, eds., *Gewerbe und Handel vor der Industrialisierung: Regionale und überregionale Verflechtungen im 17. und 18. Jahrhundert* (Sigmaringendorf, 1991), 152–82.

Getreidemarkt am Bodensee: Raum, Wirtschaft, Politik, Gesellschaft (1650–1810) (St. Katharinen, 1991).

Goubert, Pierre. *Beauvais et le Beauvaisis de 1600 à 1730* (Paris, 1960).

Goy, Joseph and LeRoy Ladurie, Emmanuel, eds. *Les fluctuations du produit de la dîme* (Paris, 1972).

eds. *Prestations paysannes, dîmes, rente foncière et mouvement de la production agricole à l'époque préindustrielle* (2 vols., Paris, 1982).

Grees, Hermann. *Ländliche Unterschichten und ländliche Siedlung in Ostschwaben*, Tübinger Geographische Studien, Heft 58 [Sonderband 8] (Tübingen, 1975).

Groebner, Valentin. *Ökonomie ohne Haus: zum Wirtschaften armer Leute in Nürnberg am Ende des 15. Jahrhunderts* (Göttingen, 1993).

Hajnal, John. "European Marriage Patterns in Perspective" in D. V. Glass and D. E. J. Eversley, eds., *Population in History: Essays in Historical Demography* (Chicago, 1965), 101–43.

Harrington, Joel F. *Reordering Marriage and Society in Reformation Germany* (Cambridge, 1995).

Hartinger, Walter. "Bayerisches Dienstbotenleben auf dem Land vom 16. bis 18. Jahrhundert," *Zeitschrift für Bayerische Landesgeschichte* 38, 2 (1975), 598–638.

Heider, Josef. "Grundherrschaft und Landeshoheit der Abtei Ottobeuren: Nachwirkungen im 19. und 20. Jahrhundert," *Studien und Mitteilungen zur Geschichte des Benediktiner-Ordens und seiner Zweige* 73, 2–4 (1962), 63–95.

Heidrich, Hermann. "Grenzübergänge. Das Haus in der Volkskultur der frühen Neuzeit" in Richard van Dülmen, ed., *Kultur der einfachen Leute: Bayerisches Volksleben vom 16. bis zum 19. Jahrhundert* (Munich, 1983), 17–41.

Heilbronner, Oded. "In Search of the Catholic (Rural) Bourgeoisie: The Peculiarities of the South German Bürgertum," *Central European History* 29, 2 (1996), 175–200.

Heimpel, Christian. *Die Entwicklung der Einnahmen und Ausgaben des Heiliggeistspitals zu Biberach an der Riß von 1500 bis 1630* (Stuttgart, 1966).

Heimrath, Ralf. "Ortsnamen und Siedlungsgeschichte seit dem 6. Jahrhundert" in Aegidius Kolb, ed., *Landkreis Unterallgäu* (2 vols., Mindelheim, 1987), Vol. I, 72–84.

Hille, Martin. *Ländliche Gesellschaft in Kriegszeiten: bäuerliche Subsistenz zwischen Fiskus und Feudalherrschaft* (Munich, 1997).

Hilton, Rodney. "Capitalism – What's in a Name?" *Past and Present* 1 (February) (1952), 32–43.

Hobsbawm, Eric. "The General Crisis of the European Economy in the Seventeenth Century," *Past and Present* 5 (1954), 33–56 and 6 (1954), 44–65.

Hoffman, Philip T. *Growth in a Traditional Society: The French Countryside, 1450–1815* (Princeton, 1996).

Holenstein, André. *Bauern zwischen Bauernkrieg und Dreißigjährigem Krieg* (Munich, 1996).

Holton, R. J. *The Transition from Feudalism to Capitalism* (Basingstoke, 1985).

Horden, Peregrine and Smith, Richard, eds. *The Locus of Care: Families, Communities, Institutions and the Provision of Welfare since Antiquity* (London, 1998).

Hsia, R. Po-Chia. *Social Discipline in the Reformation: Central Europe 1550–1750* (London, 1989).

Huang, Philip C. C. *The Peasant Economy and Social Change in North China* (Stanford, CA, 1985).

Huber-Sperl, Rita. *Memmingen zwischen Zunfthandwerk und Unternehmertum: ein Beitrag zur reichsstädtischen Gewerbegeschichte, 1648 bis 1802* (Memmingen, 1995).

Hufton, Olwen. *The Poor of Eighteenth-Century France 1750–1789* (Oxford, 1974).

Humphrey, Caroline. "Barter and Economic Disintegration," *Man* (N.S.) 20 (1985), 48–72.

Jacquart, Jean. *La crise rurale en Île-de-France 1550–1670* (Paris, 1974).

Jänichen, Hans. *Beiträge zur Wirtschaftsgeschichte des schwäbischen Dorfes* (Stuttgart, 1970).

Jütte, Robert. *Poverty and Deviance in Early Modern Europe* (Cambridge, 1994).

Kearney, Michael. *Reconceptualizing the Peasantry* (Boulder, CO, 1996).

Kelly, Morgan. "The Dynamics of Smithian Growth," *Quarterly Journal of Economics* 112 (1997), 939–64.

Kern, Stephen. *The Culture of Time and Space 1880–1918* (Cambridge, MA, 1983).

Kerridge, Eric. *The Agricultural Revolution* (London, 1967).

Kiesewetter, Hubert. "Zur Dynamik der regionalen Industrialisierung in Deutschland im 19. Jahrhundert: Lehren für die Europäische Union?" *Jahrbuch für Wirtschaftsgeschichte* 1 (1992), 79–112.

Kießling, Rolf and Ullmann, Sabine, eds. *Judengemeinden in Schwaben im Kontext des Alten Reiches* (Berlin, 1995).

eds. *Landjudentum im deutschen Südwesten während der Frühen Neuzeit* (Berlin, 1999).

Kiessling, Rolf. *Die Stadt und ihr Land – Umlandpolitik, Bürgerbesitz und Wirtschaftsgefüge in Ostschwaben vom 14. bis ins 16. Jahrhundert* (Cologne and Vienna, 1989).

Kinter, Philip L. "Die Teuerung von 1570/72 in Memmingen," *Memminger Geschichtsblätter* (1987/8), 28–75.

Kirchgässner, Bernhard. "Der Verlag im Spannungsfeld von Stadt und Umland" in Erich Maschke and Jürgen Sydow, eds., *Stadt und Umland* (Stuttgart, 1974), 72–128.

Kirchner, Gero. "Probleme der spätmittelalterlichen Klostergrundherrschaft in Bayern: Landflucht und bäuerliches Erbrecht," *Zeitschrift für Bayerische Landesgeschichte* 19, 1 (1956), 1–94.

Knodel, John E. *The Decline of Fertility in Germany, 1871–1939* (Princeton, 1974).

Kramer, Karl Sigismund. *Bauern und Bürger im nachmittelalterlichen Unterfranken; eine Volkskunde auf Grund archivalischer Quellen* (Würzburg, Schöningh, 1957).

Kriedte, Peter. *Peasants, Landlords and Merchant Capitalists*, trans. V. R. Berghahn (Cambridge, 1983).

"Spätmittelalterliche Agrarkrise oder Krise des Feudalismus?" *Geschichte und Gesellschaft* 7 (1981), 42–68.

Küchler, Winfried. *Das Bannmeilenrecht*, Marburger Ostforschung, Band 24 (Würzburg, 1964).

Lambacher, Hannes. *Das Spital der Reichsstadt Memmingen* (Kempten, 1991).

Landes, David S. "Some Further Thoughts on Accident in History: A Reply to Professor Crafts," *Economic History Review* 48, 3 (1995), 599–601.

Langholm, Odd. *Economics in the Medieval Schools: Wealth, Exchange, Value, Money and Usury According to the Paris Theological Tradition 1200–1350* (Leiden and New York, 1992).

Lebrun, François. "Les crises de démographie en France aux XVIIième et XVIIIième siècles," *Annales E.S.C.* 35 (1980), 205–33.

Lee, R. D. "Short-term Variations: Vital Rates, Prices and Weather" in E. A. Wrigley and R. S. Schofield, *The Population History of England, 1541–1871* (London, 1981), pp. 356–406.

Lefebvre, Henri. *The Production of Space*, trans. Donald Nicholson-Smith (Oxford, 1991).

LeRoy Ladurie, Emmanuel. *The Mind and Method of the Historian*, trans. Siân and Ben Reynolds (Chicago, 1981).

Les paysans de Languedoc (Paris, 1966).

The Territory of the Historian, trans. Ben and Siân Reynolds (Chicago, 1979).

Liebhart, Wilhelm. "Zur spätmittelalterlichen landesherrlichen Marktgründungspolitik in Ober- und Niederbayern" in Pankraz Fried, ed., *Bayerische Landesgeschichte an der Universität Augsburg 1975–1977* (Sigmaringen, 1979), 151–2.

Lindemann, Mary. *Medicine and Society in Early Modern Europe* (Cambridge, 1999).

Lochbrunner, Wilhelm. "1550–1880: Ländliche Neuordnung durch Vereinödung," *Berichte aus der Flurbereinigung* 51 (1984).

Maddison, Angus. *Chinese Economic Performance in the Long Run* (Paris, 1998).

Dynamic Forces in Capitalist Development: A Long-Run Comparative View (Oxford, 1991).

The World Economy: A Millennial Perspective (Paris, 2001).

Maisch, Andreas. *Notdürftiger Unterhalt und gehörige Schranken: Lebensbedingungen und Lebensstile in württembergischen Dörfern der frühen Neuzeit* (Stuttgart, 1992).

Malthus, Thomas. *An Essay on the Principle of Population*, 7th edn (London, repr. 1982).

Marshall, Alfred. *Principles of Economics*, 8th edn (repr. London, 1946).

Martin, John E. *Feudalism to Capitalism: Peasant and Landlord in English Agrarian Development* (Atlantic Highlands, NJ, 1983).

Maurer, Hans-Martin. "Die Ausbildung der Territorialgewalt oberschwäbischer Klöster vom 14. bis zum 17. Jahrhundert," *Blätter für deutsche Landesgeschichte* N.F. 109 (1973), 151–95.

Maurer, Roman. "Entwicklung und Funktionswandel der Märkte in Altbayern seit 1800," *Miscellanea Bavarica Monacensia* 30 (1971).

Medick, Hans. *Weben und Überleben in Laichingen 1650–1900: Lokalgeschichte als Allgemeine Geschichte* (Göttingen, 1996).

Meuvret, Jean. "Les crises de subsistance et la démographie de la France de l'Ancien régime," *Population* 1, 4 (1946), 643–50.

Mokyr, Joel. *The Lever of Riches: Technological Creativity and Economic Progress* (New York, 1990).

Moriceau, Jean-Marc. *Les fermiers de l'Île-de-France: L'ascension d'un patronat agricole, XVe–XVIIIe siècle* (Paris, 1994).

Morineau, Michel. *Les faux-semblants d'un démarrage économique: agriculture et démographie en France au XVIIIe siècle* (Paris, 1971).

Musgrave, Peter. *The Early Modern European Economy* (Basingstoke, 1999).

Neumann, Max. *Geschichte des Wuchers in Deutschland bis zur Begründung der heutigen Zinsgesetze (1654)* (Halle, 1865).

Noonan, John Thomas. *The Scholastic Analysis of Usury* (Cambridge, MA, 1957).

North, Douglass C. *Institutions, Institutional Change and Economic Performance* (Cambridge, 1990).

Structure and Change in Economic History (New York, 1981).

North, Michael. *Geldumlauf und Wirtschaftskonjunktur im südlichen Ostseeraum an der Wende zur Neuzeit (1440–1570)*, Kieler Historischer Studien 35 (Sigmaringen, 1990).

O'Brien, Patrick K. "European Economic Development: The Contribution of the Periphery," *Economic History Review* 35, 1 (1982).

"The Foundations of European Industrialization: From the Perspective of the World," *Journal of Historical Sociology* 4, 3 (1991), 288–316.

"Path Dependency, or Why Britain Became an Industrialized and Urbanized Economy Long Before France," *Economic History Review* 49, 2 (1996), 213–49.

O'Brien, Patrick K. and de la Escosura, Leandro Prados. "Agricultural Productivity and European Industrialization, 1890–1980," *Economic History Review* 45, 3 (1992), 514–36.

Ogilvie, Sheilagh C. "Germany and the Seventeenth Century Crisis," *Historical Journal* 35, 2 (1992), 417–41.

State Corporatism and Proto-Industry: The Württemberg Black Forest, 1580–1797 (Cambridge, 1997).

Östreich, Gerhard. *Antiker Geist und moderner Staat bei Justus Lipsius, 1547–1606* (Göttingen, 1989).

Overton, Mark. *Agricultural Revolution in England: The Transformation of the Agrarian Economy 1500–1850* (Cambridge, 1996).

Paas, Martha White. *Population Change, Labour Supply and Agriculture in Augsburg 1480–1618* (New York, 1979).

Palliser, D. M. "Tawney's Century: Brave New World or Malthusian Trap?" *Economic History Review*, 2nd ser., 35 (1982), 339–53.

Parker, Geoffrey and Smith, L. M., eds. *The General Crisis of the Seventeenth Century* (London, 1978).

Patze, H., ed. *Die Grundherrschaft im späten Mittelalter* (2 vols., Sigmaringen, 1983).

Peyer, Hans Conrad. *Leinwandgewerbe und Fernhandel der Stadt St. Gallen von den Anfängen bis 1520* (2 vols., St. Gallen, 1959–60).

Plattner, Stuart M. "Periodic Trade in Developing Areas without Markets" in Carol A. Smith, ed., *Regional Analysis* (2 vols., New York, 1976), Vol. I, 81–5.

Pomeranz, Kenneth. *The Great Divergence: Europe, China, and the Making of the Modern World Economy* (Princeton, 2000).

Poos, L. R. *A Rural Society after the Black Death: Essex, 1350–1525* (Cambridge, 1991).

Pregler, Josef Wilhelm. "Milchwirtschaft und Tierzucht und deren Grundlagen" in Aegidius Kolb, ed., *Landkreis Unterallgäu* (2 vols., Mindelheim, 1987), Vol. I, 470–543.

Rebel, Hermann. *Peasant Classes: The Bureaucratization of Property and Family Relations under Early Habsburg Absolutism, 1511–1636* (Princeton, 1983).

Redlich, Fritz. *Die deutsche Inflation des 17. Jahrhunderts in der zeitgenössischen Literatur: Die Kipper und Wipper. Forschungen zur internationalen Sozial- und Wirtschaftsgeschichte* 6 (Cologne and Vienna, 1972).

Robisheaux, Thomas. *Rural Society and the Search for Order in Early Modern Germany* (Cambridge, 1989).

Roeck, Bernd. *Bäcker, Brot und Getreide in Augsburg* (Sigmaringen, 1987).

Roper, Lyndal. *The Holy Household: Women and Morals in Reformation Augsburg* (Oxford, 1989).

Oedipus and the Devil: Witchcraft, Sexuality, and Religion in Early Modern Europe (London, 1994).

Röscher, Wilhelm. *Geschichte der National-Oekonomik in Deutschland* (Munich, 1874).

Rösener, Werner. "Grundherrschaft des Hochadels in Südwestdeutschland im Spätmittelalter" in Hans Patz, ed., *Die Grundherrschaft im späten Mittelalter* (2 vols., Sigmaringen, 1983), Vol. II, 87–176.

Grundherrschaft im Wandel: Untersuchungen zur Entwicklung geistlicher Grundherrschaften im südwestdeutschen Raum vom 9. bis 14. Jahrhundert (Göttingen, 1991).

Rublack, Ulinka. *The Crimes of Women in Early Modern Germany* (Oxford, 1999).

Sabean, David. "German Agrarian Institutions at the Beginning of the Sixteenth Century: Upper Swabia as an Example" in Janos Bak, ed., *The German Peasant War of 1525* (London, 1976), 76–88.

Sabean, David Warren. *Kinship in Neckarhausen, 1700–1870* (Cambridge, 1998).

Landbesitz und Gesellschaft am Vorabend des Bauernkriegs: eine Studie der sozialen Verhältnisse im südlichen Oberschwaben in den Jahren vor 1525 (Stuttgart, 1972).

Power in the Blood: Popular Culture and Village Discourse in Early Modern Germany (Cambridge, 1984).

Property, Production, and Family in Neckarhausen, 1700–1870 (Cambridge, 1990).

Sabean, David Warren and Medick, Hans, eds. *Interest and Emotion: Essays on the Study of Family and Kinship* (Cambridge, 1984).

Safley, Thomas Max. "Production, Transaction and Proletarianization: The Textile Industry in Upper Swabia, 1580–1660" in Thomas Max Safley and Leonard N. Rosenband, eds., *The Workplace before the Factory: Artisans and Proletarians, 1500–1800* (Ithaca, 1993), 118–45.

Salamon, Sonya. *Prairie Patrimony: Family, Farming and Community in the Midwest* (Chapel Hill, NC, 1992).

Scheller, Ludwig. *Pferdehändler aus dem Allgäu: von der Nordsee bis zum Mittelmeer* (Kempten, 1976).

Schepers, Elisabeth. "Bäuerliche Wirtschaften im Dreißigjährigen Krieg: Schrobenhausen zwischen 1600 und 1700," *Materialien zur Geschichte des Bayerischen Schwaben* 16 (1992).

Schivelbusch, Wolfgang. *The Railway Journey: The Industrialization of Time and Space in the 19th Century* (Berkeley, CA, 1986).

Schlögl, Rudolf. *Bauern, Krieg und Staat: Oberbayerische Bauernwirtschaft und frühmoderner Staat im 17. Jahrhundert* (Göttingen, 1988).

Glaube und Religion in der Säkularisierung: Die katholische Stadt – Köln, Aachen, Münster – 1700–1840 (Munich, 1995).

"Zwischen Krieg und Krise: Situation und Entwicklung der bayerischen Bauernwirtschaft im 17. Jahrhundert," *Zeitschrift für Agrargeschichte und Agrarsoziologie* 40, 2 (1992), 133–67.

Schlumbohm, Jürgen. *Lebensläufe, Familien, Höfe: die Bauern und Heuerleute des Osnabrückischen Kirchspiels Belm in proto-industrieller Zeit, 1650–1860* (Göttingen, 1994).

Schofield, Roger. "The Impact of Scarcity and Plenty on Population Change in England, 1541–1871," *Journal of Interdisciplinary History* 14, 2 (1983), 265–91.

Schöttle, Gustav. "Die große deutsche Geldkrise von 1620–23 und ihr Verlauf in Oberschwaben," *Württembergsiche Vierteljahrshefte für Landesgeschichte* N.F. 30 (1921), 36–57.

Schulze, Winfried. *Reich und Türkengefahr im späten 16. Jahrhundert* (Munich, 1978).

Schüttenhelm, Joachim. *Der Geldumlauf im südwestdeutschen Raum vom Riedlinger Münzvertrag 1423 bis zur ersten Kipperzeit 1618*, Veröffentlichungen der Kommission für geschichtliche Landeskunde in Baden-Württemberg, Band 108 (Stuttgart, 1987).

Schwarzmaier, Hans-Martin. *Königtum, Adel und Klöster im Gebiet zwischen oberer Iller und Lech* (Augsburg, 1961).

Scott, Tom. "Economic Conflict and Co-operation on the Upper Rhine 1450–1600" in E. J. Kouri and Tom Scott, eds., *Politics and Society in Reformation Europe* (New York, 1987), 210–31.

Regional Identity and Economic Change: The Upper Rhine, 1450–1600 (Oxford, 1997).

Sczesny, Anke. *Zwischen Kontinuität und Wandel: Ländliches Gewerbe und ländliche Gesellschaft im Ostschwaben des 17. und 18. Jahrhunderts* (Tübingen, 2002).

Sea, Thomas F. "The Economic Impact of the German Peasants' War: The Question of Reparations," *Sixteenth Century Journal* 8, 3 (1977), 75–97.

"Schwäbischer Bund und Bauernkrieg: Bestrafung und Pazifikation" in Hans-Ulrich Wehler, ed., *Der Deutsche Bauernkrieg 1524–1526* (Göttingen, 1975), 129–67.

Slicher van Bath, B. H. *The Agrarian History of Western Europe AD 500–1850*, trans. Olive Ordish (London, 1963).

Sontheimer, Martin. *Die Geistlichkeit des Kapitels Ottobeuren von dessen Ursprung bis zur Säkularisation* (5 vols., Memmingen, 1912–20).

Spindler, Max. *Bayerischer Geschichtsatlas* (Munich, 1969).

Spufford, Peter. *Money and its Use in Medieval Europe* (Cambridge, 1988).

Sreenivasan, Govind P. "The Social Origins of the Peasants' War of 1525 in Upper Swabia," *Past and Present* 171 (2001), 30–65.

Statistisches Jahrbuch für das Königreich Bayern, Band 12 (Munich, 1913).

Steinwascher, G. "Die Osnabrücker Urfehdeurkunden," *Osnabrücker Mitteilungen* 89 (1983), 25–59.

Stolleis, Michael. *Pecunia nervus rerum: zur Staatsfinanzierung in der frühen Neuzeit* (Frankfurt a.M., 1983).

Sturm, Heribert, ed. "Staatsarchiv Neuburg an der Donau," *Bayerische Archivinventare*, Heft 1 (Munich, 1952).

Sweezy, Paul, Dobb, Maurice, Takahashi, Kohachiro, et al. *The Transition from Feudalism to Capitalism* (London, 1978).

Theibault, John. "The Demography of the Thirty Years' War Revisited: Günther Franz and his Critics," *German History* 15, 1 (1997), 1–21.

German Villages in Crisis: Rural Life in Hesse-Kassel and the Thirty Years' War, 1580–1720 (Atlantic Highlands, NJ, 1995).

Thompson, E. P. "Time, Work-Discipline, and Industrial Capitalism," *Past and Present*, 38 (1967), 56–97.

Thompson, I. A. A. and Casalilla, Bartolomé Yun, eds., *The Castilian Crisis of the Seventeenth Century: New Perspectives on the Economic and Social History of Seventeenth-Century Spain* (Cambridge, 1994).

Tilly, Richard. "German Industrialization and Gerschenkronian Backwardness," *Rivista di Storia Economica* 6, 2 (1989), 139–64.

Trossbach, Werner. *Bauern 1648–1806* (Munich, 1993).

Tuck, Richard. *Natural Rights Theories: Their Origin and Development* (Cambridge, 1979).

Ulbricht, Claudia. *Leibherrschaft am Oberrhein im Spätmittelalter* (Göttingen, 1979).

van Zanden, Jan Luiten. "Early Modern Economic Growth: A Survey of the European Economy, 1500–1800" in Maarten Prak, ed., *Early Modern Capitalism: Economic and Social Change in Europe, 1500–1800* (London, 2001), 69–87.

Vardi, Liana. *The Land and the Loom: Peasants and Profit in Northern France, 1680–1800* (Durham, 1993).

Vasold, Manfred. "Die deutschen Bevölkerungsverluste während des Dreißigjährigen Krieges," *Zeitschrift für Bayerische Landesgeschichte* 56 (1993), 147–60.

Veyrassat-Herren, Béatrice. "Dîmes alsaciennes" in Goy and Ladurie, eds., *Fluctuations du produit de la dîme* (Paris, 1972), 83–102.

Vock, Walther. "Der Wert der Fürstlich-Kemptischen Hofratsprotokolle für den Heimat-forscher," *Schwäbische Blätter* 1, 1 (1950), 3–11.

von Hermann, F. "Die Ernten im Königreich Bayern und in einigen anderen Ländern," *Beiträge zur Statistik des Königreichs Bayern* 15 (Munich, 1866), 1–21.

von Krusenstjern, Benigna. *Selbstzeugnisse der Zeit des Dreißigjährigen Krieges* (Berlin, 1997).

Walker, Mack. *German Home Towns: Community, State and General Estate 1648–1871* (Ithaca and London, 1971).

Wallerstein, Immanuel. *The Modern World-System*, Vol. I: *Capitalist Agriculture and the Origins of the European World-Economy in the Sixteenth Century* (SanDiego, 1974) and Vol. II: *Mercantilism and the Consolidation of the European World-Economy 1600–1750* (New York, 1980).

Ward, A. W., Prothero, G. W., and Leathes, Stanley, eds. *The Cambridge Modern History*, Vol. II: *The Reformation* (Cambridge, 1903).

Weber, Franz Karl. "Wirtschaftsquellen und Wirtschaftsaufbau des Reichsstiftes Ottobeuren im beginnenden 18. Jahrhundert," *Studien und Mitteilungen zur Geschichte des Benediktiner-Ordens und seiner Zweige* 57 (1939), 171–208 and 58 (1940), 107–37.

Weber, Max. *Wirtschaft und Gesellschaft: Grundriss der verstehenden Soziologie*, 4th edn (Tübingen, 1956).

Weber, Wolfgang. *Prudentia gubernatoria: Studien zur Herrschaftslehre in der deutschen politischen Wissenschaft des 17. Jahrhunderts* (Tübingen, 1992).

Wedgwood, C. V. *The Thirty Years' War* (Garden City, NY, 1961; orig. pub. 1938).

Weir, David R. "Life under Pressure: France and England 1670–1870," *Journal of Economic History* 44, 1 (1984), 27–48.

Weiss, Eberhard. "Ergebnisse eines Vergleichs der grundherrschaftlichen Strukturen Deutschlands und Frankreichs vom 13. bis zum Ausgang des 18. Jahrhunderts," *Vierteljahrschrift für Sozial- und Wirtschaftsgeschichte* 57 (1970), 1–14.

Weiss, Volkmar. *Bevölkerung und soziale Mobilität: Sachsen 1550–1880* (Berlin, 1993).

Weitnauer, Alfred. *Allgäuer Chronik* (4 vols., Kempten, 1969–84).

Wiedmann, Theodor. *Dr Johann Eck, Professor der Theologie an der Universität Ingolstadt* (Regensburg, 1865).

Williamson, Jeffrey G. "Why Was British Growth So Slow During the Industrial Revolution?" *Journal of Economic History* 44, 3 (1984), 687–712.

Wilson, Geoff A. and Wilson, Olivia J. *German Agriculture in Transition: Society, Politics and Environment in a Changing Europe* (Basingstoke, 2001).

Wolf, Thomas. *Reichsstädte in Kriegszeiten* (Memmingen, 1991).

Wolpe, Harold, ed. *The Articulation of Modes of Production: Essays from Economy and Society* (London, 1980).

Wong, Roy Bin. *China Transformed: Historical Change and the Limits of European Experience* (Ithaca, 1997).

Wunder, Heide. "Agriculture and Agrarian Society" in Sheilagh Ogilvie, ed., *Germany: A New Social and Economic History*, Vol. II: *1630–1800* (1996), 63–99.

Ziegelbauer, Max. *Johannes Eck: Mann der Kirche im Zeitalter der Glaubensspaltung* (St. Ottilien, 1987).

Zoepfl, Friedrich. "Der Humanist Nikolaus Ellenbog zur Frage der bäuerlichen Leibeigenschaft," *Historisches Jahrbuch* 58, 1/2 (1938), 129–35.

Index of places

Some of the villages and hamlets bore shifting names; these are indicated

I OTTOBEUREN

Villages

Altisried 22, 26, 41, 180, 252, 336, 345
Attenhausen 37, 52, 57, 64, 77, 83, 85,
 96, 159, 165–6, 178–9, 191, 197–9,
 210, 219, 221, 233, 241, 242, 249,
 258, 276, 345
Benningen 20, 33, 59, 60, 65, 69, 72, 84, 93,
 165, 173, 180, 232, 235, 243, 244, 252, 265,
 318, 323, 324–5, 355, 356
Böhen 20, 25, 26, 33, 46, 59, 60, 63, 72, 81,
 83, 130, 159, 171–3, 234, 259, 276, 295,
 298–302, 303, 337–9
Dietratried 20, 22, 83, 84, 158, 204, 211
Egg a. d. Günz 9–11, 14, 22, 24, 26, 47, 53,
 60, 62, 63, 72, 98, 160, 161, 195, 203,
 228–30, 231, 234, 242, 243, 252, 254, 276,
 287, 288, 290, 312–14, 345
Erkheim 32, 258
Frechenrieden 22, 26, 34, 41, 77, 89, 92, 118,
 129, 130, 178–9, 180, 249, 265, 317, 321,
 322, 336, 345
Günz 17, 22, 33, 70, 89, 180, 262, 265, 276,
 285, 287, 309, 336, 345
Hawangen 33, 59, 60, 72, 83, 84, 89, 92,
 128–9, 130, 165, 180, 183, 199, 207, 248,
 253, 255, 276, 286, 295, 297, 305–7, 312,
 316, 323, 324–5, 327–8, 334–6, 345, 350,
 355
Niederdorf [= Unterwolfertschwenden] 20,
 31, 58, 89, 180, 236, 241, 243, 316, 345
Niederrieden 22, 25, 34, 59, 66, 77, 78, 92,
 220, 222, 243, 245, 250, 258, 275, 276, 285,
 313, 336

Oberwesterheim 60, 69, 77, 83, 115–16,
 146–7, 149, 184, 191, 207, 227, 228–30,
 231, 248, 253, 262, 276, 287, 288, 290, 307,
 309, 323, 328, 329, 354
Ottobeuren (market town) see General index
Rummeltshausen 17, 134, 287, 336, 345
Schlegelsberg 83, 219, 223, 276, 325,
 336
Sontheim 33, 34, 36, 37, 39, 40, 41, 51,
 53, 59, 63–4, 66, 72, 77, 83, 84, 134, 147–8,
 151–2, 154, 159, 162, 208, 210, 220, 222,
 249, 257, 276–9, 285, 298–302, 309, 315,
 318, 326, 336
Ungerhausen 159, 208, 232, 241, 276, 323,
 327, 345
Unterwesterheim 13, 115–16, 149, 175, 177,
 185, 204, 227, 228, 241, 242, 251, 253, 255,
 265, 285–6, 288, 309
Unterwolfertschwenden see Niederdorf
Wolfertschwenden 18, 20, 55, 98, 144, 165,
 186, 250, 251, 336

Hamlets

Berg 20, 171–2, 173
Betzisried 69, 319, 328, 343
Bibelsberg 20, 81, 253
Bossarts 20
Briechlins [= Untermotz] 190
Dassberg 20
Dennenberg 98, 242, 244, 315–25
Eggesried 100–1
Eheim [= Höhenheim] 81, 188
Eldern 180, 295

373

II OUTSIDE OTTOBEUREN

General index

accounting
  account books 124
  among kin 256, 320–2
  regarding care of siblings 212–14
  to ensure equal inheritance 222–3
  profit–loss calculations 264–5
adultery *see* sexuality: illicit
agriculture *see* grain production
alcohol
  consumption 232, 238, 246, 269, 331–3, 343
    forbidden to the poor (1545) 166
  distilling 302–3, 331–3
  drunkenness 55, 57, 107, 108, 343
  excise tax (*Umgeld*) upon 138–40, 141
Allgäu 7–8, 28, 101, 345, 350
animal husbandry *see* livestock
Annales school 5, 6
  and agrarian class relations 131–3
  immobilist model 2, 5, 113
apprenticeship *see also* crafts; guilds 181–2, 183, 205, 208, 214–15
  female 215
  oversupply of 216–19; and emigration 216–21
  wages 215
Augsburg, Bishop of 14, 36, 102, 144, 159, 193
  consistory (marriage court) 56, 60, 247–50, 355–6
  relations with the monastery 16–17, 19, 21, 35, 61–2, 292
  visitations of 118, 120, 289, 291, 305, 311, 353

banishment *see* space
bankruptcy and foreclosure 11, 80, 159, 185–7, 213, 259, 298, 299–303, 315

Bannmeilenrecht see Memmingen
barter 97–100, 101
  institutionalization of 98
  by monastery 99
  payment of debts in kind 91–4, 97–8, 99
  seventeenth-century decline of 284, 342, 348
  in wartime 331
  see also money, paucity of
bastardy *see* illegitimacy
Bauern (large peasants, yeoman farmers, *Hof* tenants) 48, 50, 93, 98
  diet of 237–8
  employment of servants 227
  leadership prominence in Peasants' War 40, 41
  opposition to population growth 165–6, 167, 169–70
  proprotional share of rural population (early sixteenth century) 43, 46, 47–8
  relations with *Seldner* 45–6, 100
    forced labor 168
    labor exchanges 48–50
    poor relief 94
  and smuggling 276
  virtual monopoly of arable land 149–50
  after 1648 312, 314
Bavaria, Duke of
  Albrecht V (1550–79) 160
  Maximilian I (1598–1651) 284, 292
begging *see* vagrants and beggars
Berkner, Lutz 226
bleaching *see* textiles
bond-chicken registers (*Leibhennenbücher*)
  assessment scale 151 (and note) 183
  as a replacement for serf rolls 144
boundaries, commercial 6–7, 52, 85–6, 89–91, 95, 99–100, 101, 104
  collapse of 157, 187, 271–4, 284, 335–7

Past and Present Publications

General Editors: LYNDAL ROPER, *University of Oxford*, and
CHRIS WICKHAM, *University of Birmingham*

Family and Inheritance: Rural Society in Western Europe 1200–1800, edited by Jack Goody, Joan
Thirsk and E. P. Thompson*

French Society and the Revolution, edited by Douglas Johnson

Peasants, Knights and Heretics: Studies in Medieval English Social History, edited by R. H. Hilton*

Towns in Societies: Essays in Economic History and Historical Sociology, edited by Philip Abrams
and E. A. Wrigley*

Desolation of a City: Coventry and the Urban Crisis of the Late Middle Ages, Charles Phythian-
Adams*

Puritanism and Theatre: Thomas Middleton and Opposition Drama under the Early Stuarts, Margot
Heinemann*

Lords and Peasants in a Changing Society: The Estates of the Bishopric of Worcester 680–1450,
Christopher Dyer

*Life, Marriage and Death in a Medieval Parish: Economy, Society and Demography in Halesowen
1270–1400*, Ziv Razi

Biology, Medicine and Society 1740–1940, edited by Charles Webster*

The Invention of Tradition, edited by Eric Hobsbawm and Terence Ranger*

Industrialization before Industrialization: Rural Industry and the Genesis of Capitalism, Peter
Kriedte, Hans Medick and Jürgen Schlumbohm*

*The Republic in the Village: The People of the Var from the French Revolution to the Second
Republic*, Maurice Agulhon†

Social Relations and Ideas: Essays in Honour of R. H. Hilton, edited by T. H. Aston, P. R. Coss,
Christopher Dyer and Joan Thirsk

A Medieval Society: The West Midlands at the End of the Thirteenth Century, R. H. Hilton

Winstanley: 'The Law of Freedom' and Other Writings, edited by Christopher Hill

Crime in Seventeenth-Century England: A Country Study, J. A. Sharpe†

The Crisis of Feudalism: Economy and Society in Eastern Normandy, c. 1300–1500, Guy Bois†

The Development of the Family and Marriage in Europe, Jack Goody*

Disputes and Settlements: Law and Human Relations in the West, edited by John Bossy*

Rebellion, Popular Protest and the Social Order in Early Modern England, edited by Paul Slack

Studies on Byzantine Literature of the Eleventh and Twelfth Centuries, Alexander Kazhdan in
collaboration with Simon Franklin†

The English Rising of 1381, edited by R. H. Hilton and T. H. Aston*

Praise and Paradox: Merchants and Craftsmen in Elizabethan Popular Literature, Laura Caroline
Stevenson*

*The Brenner Debate: Agrarian Class Structure and Economic Development in Pre-Industrial
Europe*, edited by T. H. Aston and C. H. E. Philpin*

Eternal Victor: Triumphant Rulership in Late Antiquity, Byzantium, and the Early Medieval West,
Michael McCormick†*

East-Central Europe in Transition: From the Fourteenth to the Seventeenth Century, edited by
Antoni Mączak. Henryk Samsonowicz and Peter Burke*

Small Books and Pleasant Histories: Popular Fiction and its Readership in Seventeenth-Century England, Margaret Spufford*

Society, Politics and Culture: Studies in Early Modern England, Mervyn James*

Horses, Oxen and Technological Innovation: The Use of Draught Animals in English Farming 1066–1500, John Langon*

Nationalism and Popular Protest in Ireland, edited by C. H. E. Philpin*

Rituals of Royalty: Power and Ceremonial in Traditional Societies, edited by David Cannadine and Simon Price*

The Margins of Society in Late Medieval Paris, Bronislaw Geremek†

Landlords, Peasants and Politics in Medieval England, edited by T. H. Aston

Geography, Technology and War: Studies in the Maritime History of the Mediterranean, 649–1571, John H. Pryor*

Church Courts, Sex and Marriage in England, 1570–1640, Martin Ingram*

Searches for an Imaginary Kingdom: The Legend of the Kingdom of Prester John, L. N. Gumilev

Crowds and History: Mass Phenomena in English Towns, 1790–1835, Mark Harrison*

Concepts of Cleanliness: Changing Attitudes in France since the Middle Ages, Georges Vigarello†

The First Modern Society: Essays in English History in Honour of Lawrence Stone, edited by A. L. Beier, David Cannadine and James M. Rosenheim

The Europe of the Devout: The Catholic Reformation and the Formation of a New Society, Louis Châtellér†

English Rural Society, 1500–1800: Essays in Honour of Joan Thirsk, edited by John Chartres and David Hey

From Slavery to Feudalism in South-Western Europe, Pierre Bonnassie†

Lordship, Knighthood and Locality: A Study in English Society c. 1180–c. 1280, P. R. Coss*

English and French Towns in Feudal Society: A Comparative Study, R. H. Hilton*

An Island for Itself: Economic Development and Social Change in Late Medieval Sicily, Stephan R. Epstein*

Epidemics and Ideas: Essays on the Historical Perception of Pestilence, edited by Terence Ranger and Paul Slack*

The Political Economy of Shopkeeping in Milan, 1886–1922, Jonathan Morris*

After Chartism: Class and Nation in English Radical Politics, 1848–1874, Margot C. Finn*

Commoners: Common Right, Enclosure and Social Change in England, 1700–1820, J. M. Neeson

Land and Popular Politics in Ireland: County Mayo from the Plantation to the Land War, Donald E. Jordan Jr.*

The Castilian Crisis of the Seventeenth Century: New Perspectives on the Economic and Social History of Seventeenth Century Spain, I. A. A. Thompson and Bartolomé Yun Casalilla

The Culture of Clothing: Dress and Fashion in the Ancien Régime, Daniel Roche*

The Sense of the People: Politics, Culture and Imperialism in England, 1715–1785, Kathleen Wilson*

God Speed the Plough: The Representation of Agrarian England, 1500–1660, Andrew McRae*

Witchcraft in Early Modern Europe: Studies in Culture and Belief, edited by Jonathan Barry, Marianne Hester and Gareth Roberts*

Fair Shares for All: Jacobin Egalitarianism in Practice, Jean-Pierre Gross*

The Wild and the Sown: Botany and Agriculture in Western Europe, 1350–1850, Mauro Ambrosoli

Witchcraft Persecutions in Bavaria: Popular Magic, Religious Zealotry and Reason of State in Early Modern Europe, Wolfgang Behringer*

Understanding Popular Violence in the English Revolution: The Colchester Plunderers, John Walter

The Moral World of the Law, edited by Peter Coss

Travel and Ethnology in the Renaissance: South India through European Eyes, 1250–1625, Joan-Pau Rubiés*

Holy Rulers and Blessed Princesses: Dynastic Cults in Central Medieval Europe, Gábor Klaniczay
Rebellion, Community and Custom in Early Modern Germany, Norbert Schindler
Gender in Early Modern German History, edited by Ulinka Rublack
Fashioning Adultery: Gender, Sex and Civility in England, 1660–1740, David M. Turner
Emperor and Priest: The Imperial Office in Byzantium, Gilbert Dagron
The Origins of the English Gentry, Peter Coss
A Contested Nation: History, Memory and Nationalism in Switzerland, 1760–1890, Oliver Zimmer
Rethinking the Age of Reform: Britain 1780–1850, edited by Arthur Burns and Joanna Innes
The Peasants of Ottobeuren: A Rural Society in Early Modern Europe, Govind P. Sreenivasan

* Also published in paperback
† Co-published with the Maison des Sciences de L'Homme, Paris